Tom + Kr

Stud

CW00631868

25th ANNIVERSARY EDITION
New Zealand

Wines

2017

Michael Cooper's Buyer's Guide

upstart press

To Linda

My name goes on the cover, but for the past 25 years, two people have been deeply immersed in this book. Linda, my wife, unpacks all the cartons, sorts out the thousands of reviews that pile up each year, and by taking care of the countless other background jobs, frees me up to focus on the fun tasks, such as tasting. So this is my personal toast, to Linda.

— Michael Cooper

A catalogue record for this book is available from the National Library of New Zealand

ISBN 978-1-927262-66-5

An Upstart Press Book
Published in 2016 by Upstart Press Ltd
Level 4, 15 Huron Street, Takapuna
Auckland, New Zealand

Text © Michael Cooper 2016
The moral rights of the author have been asserted.
Design and format © Upstart Press Ltd 2016

All rights reserved. No part of this publication may be reproduced or transmitted in any form or by any means, electronic or mechanical, including photocopying, recording, or any information storage and retrieval system, without permission in writing from the publisher.

Designed by www.cvdgraphics.nz
Printed by Opus Group Pty Ltd

Front cover photograph: Aronui vineyard, Moutere Hills

Reviews of the latest editions

'A remarkable book . . . I don't believe there is a better one, certainly in Australasia and possibly even in the world, of tasting notes for the latest vintages . . . Arguably the best buyer's guide on the planet.' – Leighton Smith, *Newstalk ZB*

'I must say that I agree with much of Michael's ratings and assessments, but I find that I'm just a little more generous in my scores. This is because Michael has the consumer's view foremost . . .' – *Raymond Chan Wine Reviews*

'A "must-have" for all lovers of New Zealand wine.' – Bob Campbell, *The Real Review*

Michael Cooper is New Zealand's most acclaimed wine writer, with 41 books and several major literary awards to his credit, including the Montana Medal for the supreme work of non-fiction at the 2003 Montana New Zealand Book Awards for his magnum opus, *Wine Atlas of New Zealand*. In the 2004 New Year Honours, Michael was appointed an Officer of the New Zealand Order of Merit for services to wine writing.

Author of the country's biggest-selling wine book, the annual *New Zealand Wines: Michael Cooper's Buyer's Guide*, now in its 25th edition, he was awarded the Sir George Fistonich Medal in recognition of services to New Zealand wine in 2009. The award is made each year at the country's largest wine competition, the New Zealand International Wine Show, to a 'living legend' of New Zealand wine. The weekly wine columnist for the *New Zealand Listener*, he is also New Zealand editor of Australia's *Winestate* magazine and chairman of its New Zealand tasting panel.

In 1977 he obtained a Master of Arts degree from the University of Auckland with a thesis entitled 'The Wine Lobby: Pressure Group Politics and the New Zealand Wine Industry'. He was marketing manager for Babich Wines from 1980 to 1990, and since 1991 has been a full-time wine writer.

Cooper's other major works include *100 Must-Try New Zealand Wines* (2011); the much-extended second edition of *Wine Atlas of New Zealand* (2008); *Classic Wines of New Zealand* (second edition 2005); *The Wines and Vineyards of New Zealand* (published in five editions from 1984 to 1996); and *Pocket Guide to Wines of New Zealand* (second edition 2000). He is the New Zealand consultant for Hugh Johnson's annual, best-selling *Pocket Wine Book* and the acclaimed *World Atlas of Wine*.

Michael's comprehensive, frequently updated website, *MichaelCooper.co.nz*, was launched in 2011.

Contents

The Winemaking Regions of New Zealand	6	25 Not-to-be-missed New Zealand Wines	19
Preface	7	Classic Wines of New Zealand	24
Vintage Charts 2007–2016	9	Cellar Sense	30
2016 Vintage Report	10	Cellaring Guidelines	31
Best Buys of the Year	16	How to Use this Book	32

White Wines   35

Albariño	35	Muscat	149
Arneis	39	Pinot Blanc	150
Branded and Other White Wines	41	Pinot Gris	152
Breidecker	46	Riesling	201
Chardonnay	47	Roussanne	233
Chenin Blanc	124	Sauvignon Blanc	234
Fiano	128	Sauvignon Gris	293
Flora	129	Sémillon	294
Gewürztraminer	130	Verdelho	296
Grüner Veltliner	145	Vermentino	297
Marsanne	148	Viognier	298

Sweet White Wines   305

Sparkling Wines   318

Rosé Wines   332

Red Wines   349

Barbera	349	Montepulciano	422
Branded and Other Red Wines	350	Nebbiolo	425
Cabernet Franc	370	Petit Verdot	426
Cabernet Sauvignon and		Pinot Noir	427
Cabernet-predominant blends	373	Pinotage	536
Carménère	384	Sangiovese	537
Chambourcin	385	St Laurent	538
Dolcetto	386	Syrah	539
Gamay Noir	387	Tannat	574
Grenache	388	Tempranillo	575
Lagrein	389	Touriga Nacional	578
Malbec	390	Zinfandel	579
Marzemino	394	Zweigelt	580
Merlot	395		

Index of Wine Brands   581

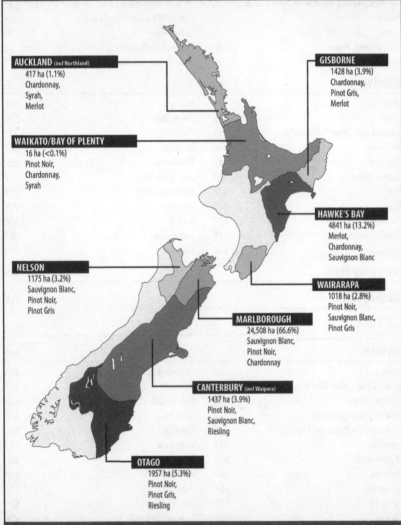

The Winemaking Regions of New Zealand

Area in producing vines 2017 (percentage of national producing vineyard area)

AUCKLAND (incl Northland)
417 ha (1.1%)
Chardonnay,
Syrah,
Merlot

WAIKATO/BAY OF PLENTY
16 ha (<0.1%)
Pinot Noir,
Chardonnay,
Syrah

NELSON
1175 ha (3.2%)
Sauvignon Blanc,
Pinot Noir,
Pinot Gris

GISBORNE
1428 ha (3.9%)
Chardonnay,
Pinot Gris,
Merlot

HAWKE'S BAY
4841 ha (13.2%)
Merlot,
Chardonnay,
Sauvignon Blanc

WAIRARAPA
1018 ha (2.8%)
Pinot Noir,
Sauvignon Blanc,
Pinot Gris

MARLBOROUGH
24,508 ha (66.6%)
Sauvignon Blanc,
Pinot Noir,
Chardonnay

CANTERBURY (incl Waipara)
1437 ha (3.9%)
Pinot Noir,
Sauvignon Blanc,
Riesling

OTAGO
1957 ha (5.3%)
Pinot Noir,
Pinot Gris,
Riesling

These figures (rounded to the closest percentages) are from New Zealand Winegrowers'
Vineyard Register Report 2015–2018. During the period 2015 to 2018, the total area of producing
vines was predicted to expand from 35,463 to 37,542 hectares – a rise of 6 per cent.

Preface

If you line them up side by side, they fill an entire shelf on many bookcases. The *Buyer's Guide* was first published in 1992. This hardy annual is now three times thicker than 25 years ago, and the number of wines reviewed has soared from 800 to around 3000.

A browse through that slender first volume also reveals how far the sorts of wines we drink has changed. Back then, the section devoted to Cabernet Sauvignon-based reds was three times longer than Pinot Noir. You'll search in vain for any Viogniers, Albariños, Grüner Veltliners or Malbecs – and about 25 other single-variety styles featured in this year's edition.

Published recently, New Zealand Winegrowers *Vineyard Register Report 2015–2018* confirms what you probably already knew. The majority of today's wine industry can be summed up in five words – Sauvignon Blanc, Pinot Noir, Marlborough.

So dominant is Marlborough, it is the country's most heavily planted region for varieties that it is not even commonly associated with – Chardonnay (just ahead of Hawke's Bay); Gewürztraminer (well ahead of Gisborne); and – surprise! – Pinot Noir (well ahead of Central Otago).

But what's hot, in terms of less established grape varieties? Albariño and Grüner Veltliner are both expanding, in terms of their area of bearing vines. Riesling, Cabernet Sauvignon, Cabernet Franc and Malbec are stagnant, and Sémillon, Gewürztraminer and Viognier are declining.

New Zealand wine is now sold in nearly 100 countries. The value of wine exports reached $1.54 billion in 2015 – a steep climb from just $34.7 million in 1992. Philip Gregan, CEO of New Zealand Winegrowers, believes that 'at its core, the growth reflects the reputation New Zealand wine has in global markets. That reputation for quality was built in markets such as the UK and Australia. It's there now in markets such as the US and Canada, and we're seeing it in markets like China and the rest of Asia, so we have really strong demand around the world . . .'

America's growing appetite for Marlborough Sauvignon Blanc is crucial. Kim Crawford, Oyster Bay, Nobilo and Matua are becoming familiar brands to countless American wine lovers. Kim Crawford, the most popular New Zealand label in the US, and Nobilo (the third-biggest seller) are both controlled by Constellation Brands, a publicly traded drinks company, based in New York. Constellation NZ ships much of its production to the US, but smaller, 'boutique' producers are more likely to focus on Australia.

Sauvignon Blanc dominates our production, but if you are keen to plunge deeply into New Zealand wine, you can explore white and red wines made from about 45 different grape varieties. The latest arrivals are Lagrein and Touriga Nacional.

Grown in north-east Italy, Lagrein yields deeply coloured reds with plum/cherry flavours, firm and strong. First out of the blocks in New Zealand is Stanley Estates Awatere Valley Marlborough Lagrein 2014, an easy-drinking, medium to full-bodied red, vibrantly fruity, berryish and slightly spicy, with a hint of cherries and a smooth finish.

Touriga Nacional is the most prized blending variety in the traditional ports of the Douro Valley of Portugal. From base wines back to 2004, matured in oak barrels for two to nine years, Trinity Hill Gimblett Gravels Touriga is a 'port style' blend, dark, robust, concentrated, sweet and delicious.

And just when you thought New Zealand wines were all handled in tanks or barrels, the amphora is back. Heron's Flight, at Matakana, north of Auckland, has released New Zealand's first red wine to be fermented and matured in a clay pot, just like the ancient Greeks and Romans did. Made from Sangiovese – the great grape of Chianti – the strikingly packaged Heron's Flight Amphora 2015 is dark and powerful, with lovely harmony and richness.

There's even new life in old – very old – wineries. Invivo, one of New Zealand's fastest-growing producers, recently shifted into the historic Viticultural Research Station at Te Kauwhata, in the Waikato.

The rambling, white-walled winery, built in 1902, has ancient casks and a three-storey-high copper pot-still. Working on a three-level, gravity-feed system, with the crusher at the top and the barrels at the bottom, it is protected by the Historic Places Trust.

Launched from the 2008 vintage, Invivo is majority-owned by winemaker Rob Cameron and marketer Tim Lightbourne. The sixth-largest shareholder is British TV presenter Graham Norton.

Invivo has taken a 10-year lease on the old winery. The installation of new tanks will boost the winery's annual production capacity from 20,000 cases to over 100,000 cases.

For many of the country's winegrowers, things are looking good.

— *Michael Cooper*

Vintage Charts 2007–2016

WHITES	Auckland	Gisborne	Hawke's Bay	Wairarapa	Nelson	Marlborough	Canterbury	Otago
2016	3	4	4	5	3	4–5	5–6	5
2015	5	5	5	5	4	6	6	4
2014	6	6	5–6	5–6	5–6	5	3–5	5
2013	7	7	7	6	5	6–7	6–7	5–6
2012	3–4	2	3–4	3–4	4	4–5	4–5	4–6
2011	3	3	4	4	4	4	4	3
2010	7	6–7	7	6	7	7	6	6
2009	4	6–7	4	5	6	5	6	3–5
2008	5–6	3–4	3–5	5–7	4	2–5	3–6	5–6
2007	6	7	6	4–5	5	5–6	5–6	4–6

REDS	Auckland	Gisborne	Hawke's Bay	Wairarapa	Nelson	Marlborough	Canterbury	Otago
2016	3	4	4	5	3	5	5–6	5
2015	4	4	4	5	4	5	6	4
2014	5–6	5–6	5–6	5–6	5–6	5	3–5	5
2013	6–7	7	6–7	6	6	6–7	6–7	5–6
2012	3–5	2	3	3–4	4	4–5	4–5	4–6
2011	2	2	3–4	4	3	4	4	3
2010	7	6	6	5	6	6–7	5	5–6
2009	5	6–7	6	5	6	6	6	3–5
2008	5–7	3–4	3–5	5–7	4	2–5	3–6	5–6
2007	3–5	7	6	4–5	5	4–6	5–6	4–6

7 = Outstanding   6 = Excellent   5 = Above average   4 = Average   3 = Below average   2 = Poor   1 = Bad

2016 Vintage Report

The shelves are packed with infant wine. Vintage 2016 yielded a huge crop – 34 per cent bigger than 2015.

The season took most winegrowers by surprise. Meteorologists forecast a drought-stricken summer, similar to 1997–1998, when the El Niño weather phenomenon brought months of low rainfall and constant, strong south-westerly winds, turning much of the land into a tinderbox. Hawke's Bay's 1998 red wines were deliciously dark and bold.

Instead, this summer brought a flow of warm, humid tropical air masses from the north-east. Changeable, chaotic weather in December was followed by a wet January and a warm, sunny, moist February. The warm air flows from the tropics persisted into autumn, bringing abundant rainfall to many regions in late March.

The first four months of 2016 were all warmer than usual, according to NIWA, and January–April 2016 was the equal second-warmest January–April on record (equalled by 1998 and exceeded only by 1938). The good news is that April – the key harvest period – enjoyed settled weather, 'with warm temperatures, low rainfall and high sunshine hours characterising the month for many parts of the country'.

In Marlborough – which has two-thirds of the country's total vineyard area – spring and early summer were sunny and dry. Craggy Range noted that 'warm rain events in January during the berry expansion period saw sudden berry swell, resulting in the largest berry weights on record for Marlborough Sauvignon Blanc at harvest time'.

During February, the weather in Marlborough proved warm, very sunny and dry. Thousands of tonnes of grapes were dropped from the vines, as viticulturists – keen to avoid a repeat of the glut-induced discounting that followed previous huge harvests – grappled with heavy crop loads.

At Allan Scott, the harvest was double the size of 2015, but a warm, sunny March, followed by a very sunny, dry and warm April, helped to ripen the region's heavy bunches. Te Whare Ra predicted Marlborough's top 2016 wines 'will be equal to some of the best we've ever had'.

In Hawke's Bay, the second-largest region (with 13 per cent of the national vineyard), a cool, wet spring was followed by a hot, dry summer. 'It was like changing jerseys at halftime,' says Barry Riwai, winemaker at Alpha Domus.

In March, Alpha Domus dropped 'a lot on the ground – a third to a half'. Sacred Hill picked 'great' Chardonnay, but intense humidity in late March adversely affected thinner-skinned red varieties, especially Merlot.

Winegrowers in Otago (the third-largest region, with 5 per cent of plantings) enthused about a notably dry season, which yielded small, flavour-packed berries. Grasshopper Rock, at Alexandra, reported quality 'up with the very best vintages'.

The bumper 2016 harvest underlined the extent to which the New Zealand wine industry still depends heavily on a single variety. Sauvignon Blanc accounted for over

72 per cent of the vintage – dwarfing Pinot Noir (8.5 per cent), Chardonnay (6.9 per cent) and Pinot Gris (5.9 per cent).

Marlborough has a glowing international reputation for Sauvignon Blanc, but the classic grape also dominated the crop this year in several regions normally associated with other varieties – Hawke's Bay (where the Sauvignon Blanc crop was well ahead of Merlot and Chardonnay); Wairarapa (where Sauvignon Blanc outstripped Pinot Noir); Nelson (where Sauvignon Blanc was over half the total harvest); and Canterbury (where the tonnage of Sauvignon Blanc was almost double that of Riesling or Pinot Noir).

Auckland

'We had more rain this summer than ever before,' noted David Hoskins, of Heron's Flight, at Matakana. 'An incredible amount. In February, I actually thought that we were heading for our first complete washout.'

That's what happened at one large vineyard in West Auckland, where nothing was picked. However, the grapes at Heron's Flight withstood the disease pressure and benefitted from 'a beautiful Indian summer'. Sangiovese, the main variety, was harvested on 6 May in 'near-perfect condition'.

At 1267 tonnes, the 2016 Auckland crop was 54 per cent bigger than in 2015, but still only 0.3 per cent of the national harvest. Chardonnay was the major variety (30 per cent of the crop), followed by Pinot Gris (17 per cent), Merlot (11 per cent), Syrah (9 per cent) and Malbec (6 per cent).

After the wet end to summer, March and April proved drier than usual. Villa Maria reported 'an exceptional Chardonnay vintage, perhaps the best for the Ihumatao vineyard [Mangere] since 2010'. But on Waiheke Island, a visiting winemaker noted 'a lot of powdery mildew pressure over the early summer and then rain just before harvest, causing botrytis/sour rot/split skin'.

Goldie Estate, also on Waiheke, had a 'bizarre' season, with record temperatures recorded for January–March, coupled with 'an unusual amount' of rain. Chardonnay, harvested with lower than usual sugar and acid levels, has produced 'elegant, fruit-forward and beautifully balanced' wine. However, subsequent bad weather triggered a 'scramble' to pick the remaining crop.

In Northland, one key producer reported that 'constant rain meant many of the reds didn't get picked. Chardonnay topped the bill and some of the coastal blocks shone, but it was generally disappointing.'

Gisborne

Gisborne growers predicted full-flavoured wines with moderate alcohol levels, after picking 15,944 tonnes of grapes – 8 per cent less than in 2015 and just 3.7 per cent of the national harvest. Chardonnay (49 per cent) and Pinot Gris (29 per cent) dominated the region's crop, followed distantly by Sauvignon Blanc (5 per cent), Pinot Noir (4 per cent) and Muscat (4 per cent).

'The first half of the growing season was cool and wet,' reported Plant & Food

Research. Summer brought 'a couple of humid spells,' Gisborne Winegrowers observed, 'but they had little impact.'

Some grape varieties were picked nearly two weeks later than in 2015. Millton Vineyards described 2016 as 'an excellent growing season, but not especially good for ripening fruit'. Millton reported 'very good flavours in the wines, with moderate alcohols and lower than normal acidity'.

Villa Maria also noted that most varieties were picked 'at lower sugars than normal [hence with less potential alcohol in the wines], but with good flavours'. The highlight was Chardonnay, together with 'very solid' Gewürztraminer, Pinot Gris and Albariño.

Hawke's Bay

Spring — especially in September — was cool and wet, according to Plant & Food Research, and followed by a hot, dry summer. At 42,958 tonnes, the crop in Hawke's Bay was 19 per cent larger than in 2015, accounting for 10.2 per cent of the national harvest. Sauvignon Blanc was the principal variety (28 per cent), followed by Chardonnay (21 per cent), Merlot (19 per cent), Pinot Gris (12 per cent) and Pinot Noir (7 per cent).

In mid-November, Trinity Hill noted that 'El Nino still seems some way off. ... The potential crop looks very solid to the point that crop modification may be needed, provided flowering is good.'

Summer opened with a cool but dry December. In January, Craggy Range reported 'rapid growth conditions, with a record 13 days reaching over 30°C'. February proved dry and hot: 'the heat in February pushed physiological ripeness along,' declared Villa Maria, 'although the lower sugars were a theme.'

On 23 March, Te Mata reported a rushed start to the harvest, 'with whites all ripening at the same time'. According to Craggy Range, in late March 'an intense 10-day humid period . . . saw the thinner-skinned red varieties (primarily Merlot) impacted by the onset of botrytis slipskin'. Merlot needed a 'very selective' harvesting, but the winery picked 'excellent quality Syrah and Cabernets' in the middle of a dry April.

Sacred Hill reported Chardonnay was 'likely to be great to spectacular'. Villa Maria also enthused about an 'exceptional' Chardonnay vintage.

'The 2016 wines are delicious,' declared Trinity Hill. 'The Chardonnays are as good as anything back to 2010.' However, the humid, often moist conditions in the second half of the season 'placed pressure on Hawke's Bay reds,' admitted Villa Maria. 'There will be no shortage of quality for the commercial and mid-tier wines, and small volumes of Reserve wines may be possible.'

Babich agreed. 'Chardonnay off the Irongate vineyard looks outstanding. . . . The reds are at this stage showing promise, elegant and approachable.' Ash Ridge, based in the Bridge Pa Triangle, summed up 2016 as 'a good, solid vintage, but not as consistently great as 2013–2015'.

Wairarapa

At the end of a season described by Ata Rangi as 'very dry' and by Craggy Range as 'almost perfect', Wairarapa growers picked 5049 tonnes of grapes – 42 per cent more than in 2015, but just 1.2 per cent of the national crop. The Sauvignon Blanc harvest (47 per cent) was even larger than Pinot Noir (41 per cent), with both varieties far ahead of Pinot Gris (4 per cent), Chardonnay (4 per cent) and Riesling (2 per cent).

Spring was settled and less windy than usual. 'Moderate crops were set and then able to ripen evenly and slowly,' enthused Ata Rangi. Summer ended with the hottest February since 1998, bringing 'the wonderful advantage of early seed-ripening, allowing us to pick at lower brix [sugar levels]'.

April was cool but with low rainfall, rounding out a dry growing season with fractionally above-average warmth. 'The white wines . . . don't reach the aromatic high points of 2014,' observed Craggy Range, 'but with the fruit in immaculate condition we have wines with beautiful weight, texture and length. The young Pinot Noirs show lovely purity, with moderate alcohol and fine-grained tannins.'

Palliser Estate also praised the vintage as 'excellent'. Ata Rangi reported 'the wines are looking bright and fine, without the excessive alcohol which can result from an extended warm season'.

Nelson

After a 'tricky' growing season, according to Nelson Winegrowers, the region harvested 10,028 tonnes of grapes, 48 per cent above 2015, but just 2.3 per cent of the national crop. Sauvignon Blanc dominated production (58 per cent), far ahead of Pinot Gris (13 per cent) and Pinot Noir (13 per cent).

A cold, dry spring 'had us scratching our heads, wondering when the heat would come,' reported Neudorf. At Greenhough, 'these cool, dry conditions slowed early-season growth'.

Summer, however, proved warm and wet. 'The heat and rain came just after Christmas and flipped the season on its head,' says Neudorf. 'Rapid vine growth and high disease pressure kept us running all through January and February.'

Heavy rains in February were followed by an unusually wet March, with more than double the normal rainfall. Just prior to the harvest, 'torrential rain and strong winds hit the region,' according to Nelson Winegrowers, flooding some vineyards on the Waimea Plains.

April, however, brought settled weather, with below-average rainfall. Overall, the season was 'challenging,' conceded Nelson Winegrowers. 'One moment too dry, the next too wet. Add into that hail, frost, flooding and disease pressures . . .'

Neudorf reported its wines are 'ripe, with lower alcohols and elegance'. Greenhough noted that 'sugars tended to stall and generally remained quite low, while acids were beautifully ripe . . . [It was] a year for lower alcohols in wines which promise lovely aromatics, elegance . . .'

Marlborough

'Lovely warm weather through April ensured a large crop was safely harvested,' declared Fromm at the end of a bumper season. At 323,290 tonnes, Marlborough's grape crop was a whopping 39 per cent bigger than 2015, accounting for nearly 77 per cent of the national harvest. Sauvignon Blanc, the overwhelmingly predominant variety (86 per cent), was trailed by Pinot Noir (6 per cent), Chardonnay (3 per cent), Pinot Gris (3 per cent) and Riesling (1 per cent).

In spring, a cool September with average rainfall was followed by warm, very dry weather in October and November. November frosts at Framingham reduced yields, but Craggy Range reported that relatively mild conditions during spring meant 'berry numbers were moderate but bunch numbers high . . .'.

In early summer, 'dry, sunny weather during December meant flowering was very good,' according to Lawson's Dry Hills. 'Post-flowering, we got the first hit of rain that we needed,' reported Cloudy Bay. 'It was a drought-breaker and helped fill berries out.'

'Warm rain events in January during the berry expansion period saw sudden berry swell,' reported Craggy Range, 'resulting in the largest berry weights on record for Marlborough Sauvignon Blanc at harvest time.' A prominent producer calculated that one of its most fertile sites, in the lower Wairau Valley, had the potential to yield 30 tonnes of Sauvignon Blanc grapes per hectare – far above the regional average of 12 tonnes per hectare.

'With predictions that yields were 20 per cent above average, machine and hand-thinning became the mantra for many growers,' reported *New Zealand Winegrower*. But a pair of 'substantial' rain events in late March/early April 'had a big, positive impact on berry size,' according to Fromm. Seresin noted that 2016 was 'a tough year for mildew and botrytis in Marlborough'.

After 'record-breaking warm temperatures' in February – according to Villa Maria – and a warm March, flavours advanced early, says Nautilus. 'We picked at around one brix lower than normal, which is no bad thing. . . . We have some stunning Pinot Noir and Chardonnay this year and Pinot Gris also looks particularly strong.'

In mid-autumn, April was very sunny, dry and warm, according to Plant & Food Research. Framingham noted that, overall, 2016 was the warmest growing season in Marlborough since 1998.

'Sauvignon Blanc will be a highlight,' declared Villa Maria, 'but there will also be some excellent Pinot Noir, Pinot Gris and to a lesser extent Chardonnay.' Babich described its Sauvignon Blanc as 'the most tropical we have seen in some years'. Fromm was 'especially excited' about its Syrah and Malbec.

Canterbury

'If the rest of New Zealand had half the vintage we had, 2016 will surely go down as one of the crackers of the last 20 years,' enthused Pegasus Bay. The region's growers harvested 12,170 tonnes of grapes (up 144 per cent in Waipara, compared to 2015), accounting for 2.8 per cent of the national crop. Sauvignon Blanc was the major variety (39 per cent), ahead of Riesling (21 per cent), Pinot Noir (19 per cent), Pinot Gris (15 per cent) and Chardonnay (4 per cent).

'We had a warm spring,' reported Pegasus Bay, resulting in 'a good flowering and a large potential crop setting on the vines.' October and November were both warmer and drier than average, although Torlesse, at Waipara, was hit by a 'surprisingly bad' frost on 6 November.

Summer was 'long and hot,' according to Pegasus Bay. Despite much crop-thinning, the winery still ended up with a bigger crop than it intended, 'due to unprecedentedly large bunches'.

Autumn was 'long and dry', with April rainfall well below average. Villa Maria reported 'an excellent harvest with clean fruit, good yields and flavours'. Pegasus Bay enthused about picking all varieties 'in perfect condition . . .'.

Otago

It was 'a vintage vintage, if that makes any sense,' enthused Felton Road. 'Sugars stayed pleasingly low . . . and cool temperatures kept everything fresh.' The region's winegrowers harvested 9177 tonnes of grapes, up 3 per cent on 2015 and accounting for 2.1 per cent of the national grape harvest. Pinot Noir dominated the crop (76 per cent), far ahead of Pinot Gris (12 per cent), Riesling (4 per cent), Sauvignon Blanc (4 per cent) and Chardonnay (3 per cent).

In spring, a cool, very dry September led into a warm, dry October and warm, dry but frosty November. Grasshopper Rock saw no need 'to reduce crop levels, as the cool spring has done this naturally, at least in Alexandra'.

Summer opened with a warm, very dry December, according to Plant & Food Research, and in February the rainfall was well below normal. By the end of February, Prophet's Rock, in the Cromwell Basin, reported 'summer has been great. We're locked into a reasonably early harvest.'

According to Grasshopper Rock, 2016 was a 'two act vintage'. After a cold, dry start to the season, January was 'the interlude', followed by a 'hotter than average' February–April.

Central Otago Winegrowers estimated the region received only half its usual rain during the season, giving 'very small berries packed into tight bunches'. In mid-April, Two Paddocks noted 'great colour and concentrated flavours', but Grasshopper Rock reported 'periods of warm, damp weather and poor canopy management' had 'resulted in botrytis stories circulating'.

One well-respected producer noted the 2016 vintage was 'quite early. We are very happy with everything and I believe across the region people are saying it has been another solid year.' Loveblock reported a 'solid, interesting' vintage at Bendigo. 'Quality was up with the very best vintages,' declared Grasshopper Rock.

Best Buys of the Year

Best White Wine Buy of the Year

Villa Maria Cellar Selection Marlborough Sauvignon Blanc 2016
★★★★★, $20.00 (down to $15)

This classy wine has pretty much everything you could hope for in a Marlborough Sauvignon Blanc, for $20 or less . . . often a lot less.

Positioned above the popular, lower-priced Private Bin wines and below the relatively rare, more expensive Reserve and Single Vineyard ranges, Villa Maria's Cellar Selection wines frequently offer a magical combination of high quality and affordable price. They are made in sufficient volumes to be sold nationwide in supermarkets, and when on special can deliver simply unbeatable value.

Already awarded a gold medal at the New Zealand International Wine Show 2016, this is a five-star Sauvignon Blanc at a three-star price. Notably weighty, with concentrated, vibrant tropical-fruit flavours (Villa Maria says 'melon and ruby grapefruit'), deliciously deep, dry and zingy, it's a bargain at its recommended retail price of $20, but if you buy it when on promotion, you'll be able to snap it up for around $15.

Soon after the warmest grape-growing season in Marlborough since 1998 (when camels were allegedly spotted on the horizon), Villa Maria said that 'Sauvignon Blanc will be a highlight'. The grapes for the 2016 Cellar Selection Sauvignon Blanc were grown in the Wairau Valley and Awatere Valley sub-regions, which offer a diversity of soil types, local climates and flavour profiles.

Nick Picone, appointed chief winemaker for Villa Maria in 2015, spent four years living and working for the company in Marlborough. Sauvignon Blanc accounts for 70 per cent of Villa Maria's total production, and Picone is optimistic about the variety's future. He believes the demand will soon exceed supply, 'which should trigger higher prices, allowing winemakers to work harder on high-end, textural wines with aging potential'.

The 2016 Cellar Selection Marlborough Sauvignon Blanc had a long, cool fermentation with cultured yeasts in stainless steel tanks, to retain its highly distinctive, intense regional and varietal characteristics. Maturing the wine on its yeast lees, prior to bottling, also helped to build up its palate structure and weight.

A compelling wine in its infancy, with notable body, freshness and concentration, Villa Maria Cellar Selection Marlborough Sauvignon Blanc 2016 is a bargain-priced partner for poultry, salads and seafood.

Best Red Wine Buy of the Year

Church Road Hawke's Bay Syrah 2014
★★★★☆, $20 (down to $17)

If you haven't yet discovered the delights of Syrah grown in New Zealand, you are not alone. Many of us are confused because Syrah, the classic red-wine variety of the Rhône Valley, in France, has long been labelled under a different name in Australia – Shiraz. But this sturdy, richly flavoured, bargain-priced 2014 red from Church Road, in Hawke's Bay, is not to be missed.

Chris Scott has headed the winemaking team at the historic Church Road winery for 11 years, producing some of the country's greatest Chardonnays and red blends of Merlot and Cabernet Sauvignon. In recent years, Syrah has also captured his intense interest. Scott describes this highly affordable red as 'a superb Syrah, displaying rich berry fruit, spice and liquorice notes accompanied by a full and supple palate'.

Why is it so moderately priced? 'Syrah is still a relatively hard sell,' he acknowledges. 'It's a new varietal name to most consumers.' But Scott believes Syrah is producing the region's most distinctive reds. 'Hawke's Bay's top Bordeaux-style reds [from Merlot and Cabernet Sauvignon] will stand up in any international comparison and they can be hard to tell apart. But in an international line-up of Syrahs, the Hawke's Bay wines leap out, with an aromatic intensity.'

A 'serious' but highly approachable red, Church Road Hawke's Bay Syrah 2014 is dark, with a very fragrant, spicy bouquet. Mouthfilling and sweet-fruited, with an array of blackcurrant, plum, spice and nut flavours, hints of black pepper and liquorice, and excellent concentration and complexity, it's well worth cellaring, but gentle tannins also give it lots of drink-young appeal.

After an unusually warm, dry growing season, 2014 is widely viewed as an extremely strong vintage in Hawke's Bay, especially for reds. Grown in the Bridge Pa Triangle (77 per cent) and the Gimblett Gravels (23 per cent), the wine was matured for the unusually long period of 20 months in French and Hungarian oak barriques (25 per cent new), and bottled unfiltered.

When entered in *Winestate* magazine's annual regional tasting of Hawke's Bay wines, this classy red scored a ****1/2 rating, ahead of many wines asking twice, or even triple, the price. At $20 (down to $16.99 at some retailers) it's a steal.

Church Road suggests this sturdy, flavour-packed red will drink well for at least another three years, especially with meat, game or robust vegetarian dishes with earthy, savoury elements such as mushrooms and eggplant.

Other shortlisted wines

Whites
Boundary Vineyards Tuki Tuki Road Hawke's Bay Chardonnay 2015 ★★★★ $20
Brancott Estate Marlborough Sauvignon Blanc 2016 ★★★★ $17
Opawa Marlborough Sauvignon Blanc 2016 ★★★★☆ $20
Peter Yealands Marlborough Sauvignon Blanc 2016 ★★★☆ $15
Peter Yealands Reserve Awatere Valley Marlborough Sauvignon Blanc 2016 ★★★★ $18
Rapaura Springs Marlborough Sauvignon Blanc 2016 ★★★☆ $14
Villa Maria Cellar Selection Marlborough Chardonnay 2015 ★★★★☆ $20
Villa Maria Private Bin Marlborough Sauvignon Blanc 2016 ★★★★ $17

Reds
Church Road McDonald Series Hawke's Bay Cabernet Sauvignon 2014 ★★★★★ $27
Church Road McDonald Series Hawke's Bay Syrah 2014 ★★★★★ $27
TK [Te Kairanga] Martinborough Pinot Noir 2015 ★★★★☆ $25
Vidal Reserve Gimblett Gravels Merlot/Cabernet Sauvignon 2014 ★★★★☆ $20
Villa Maria Cellar Selection Hawke's Bay Merlot/Cabernet Sauvignon 2014 ★★★★ $20
Villa Maria Cellar Selection Hawke's Bay Syrah 2014 ★★★★★ $26

25 Not-to-be-missed New Zealand Wines

To help celebrate the milestone 25th edition of the *Buyer's Guide*, here are 25 labels that all lovers of New Zealand wine should taste from time to time. Regardless of whether your interest is in the country's greatest wines, or those that offer the greatest value, the 25 featured here all make a huge contribution.

Don't treat this list too seriously, but simply as a starting point for discussion. I could easily compile a second list of 25 completely different, highly important wines, and other critics would come up with yet another selection. (The wines have been listed alphabetically, so don't read anything into their order.)

Akarua Rua Central Otago Pinot Noir

As an introduction to the drink-young charm of Central Otago's reds, this is hard to beat. Packed with vibrant, plummy, spicy flavour, smooth and lingering, it can be remarkably good for a third-tier label, and irresistible value.

Ata Rangi Martinborough Pinot Noir

This benchmark Pinot Noir is the region's greatest, with a superb string of vintages back to 1984: Rich, complex and age-worthy, it's produced in reasonable volumes, but is still a magical mix of power and finesse.

Bilancia La Collina Syrah

This is arguably New Zealand's greatest Syrah, although less hyped than others. From a stunning terraced vineyard, la collina (Italian for 'the hill') on the north and north-west flanks of Roys Hill, overlooking the Gimblett Gravels, it is a majestic Hawke's Bay red, dark, beautifully fragrant and weighty, with dense plum, spice, nut and slight liquorice flavours, complex and built for the long haul.

Brancott Estate Marlborough Sauvignon Blanc

This huge-selling wine is 'the original Marlborough Sauvignon Blanc,' says its producer, Pernod Ricard NZ, because it is descended directly from the pioneering label, Montana Marlborough Sauvignon Blanc, launched in 1979. The Brancott Estate brand replaced Montana in the company's export markets several years ago, due to its obvious unsuitability for the full-of-potential US market. Invitingly aromatic, with penetrating melon, lime and green-capsicum flavours, it's typically an intensely varietal wine with lots of youthful impact.

Church Road Hawke's Bay Chardonnay

This is the best-value Chardonnay on the market, especially on special – as it often is – at under $15. Since the first vintage in 1990, it has evolved from an emphasis on fresh fruit flavours seasoned with obvious toasty oak to a more subtle and harmonious style, fleshy and rounded, with citrusy, peachy, slightly buttery and mealy flavours, showing very good depth and complexity.

Church Road Hawke's Bay Merlot/Cabernet/Malbec

If there is a better value, claret-style red made in New Zealand than this reliable performer, I haven't tasted it. From one vintage to the next, this Merlot-based, barrel-matured blend is sturdy and full-flavoured, offering unusual richness and complexity for a wine often on special at under $15. (And don't miss its big brother, the powerful, deliciously rich and smooth Church Road McDonald Series Merlot, a classy, refined, five-star wine at a four-star price.)

Clos de Ste Anne Chardonnay Naboth's Vineyard

From mature vines on a steep, north-east-facing hill at Manutuke, with a commanding view over the Poverty Bay flats to the coast, this is a powerful, exceptionally rich, multi-faceted wine with tight, citrusy, minerally flavours. A wine of great personality, it typically drinks superbly at three to five years old, but matures very gracefully for a decade, becoming softer, more toasty and honeyed with age.

Cloudy Bay Sauvignon Blanc

On sale around the world, New Zealand's most internationally acclaimed wine is produced in greater volumes than the total output of many of this country's middle-sized wineries. Cloudy Bay, established in Marlborough in 1985, is now part of the Louis Vuitton Moët-Hennessy luxury goods empire. A refined, weighty wine with deep, ripely herbaceous flavours, it's a more subtle and sophisticated, less aggressive style than most of its competitors, showing impressive complexity, texture and length. For downright drinkability, it's hard to beat.

Craggy Range Le Sol

Le Sol is an exceptional Syrah. A compelling Gimblett Gravels, Hawke's Bay red, launched from the 2001 vintage, it was soon after described by the Hawke's Bay winery as 'a cross-dresser between the lushness and ripeness of Australia, and the poise, balance and elegance of the northern Rhone'. Dense but not tough, with concentrated plum and black-pepper flavours, it impresses with its plushness, complexity and lovely fragrance.

Dry River Martinborough Pinot Gris

For many years after its debut in 1986, this famous, small-volume wine towered above New Zealand's other Pinot Gris, by virtue of its exceptional body, richness and longevity. A seductively scented, sturdy wine that overflows with peachy, spicy flavour, gently sweet and smooth, it is typically delicious in its youth and develops great subtlety and richness with maturity, drinking superbly at five years old.

Esk Valley The Terraces

Grown on steep, north-facing terraces at Bay View, this excitingly bold, dark Hawke's Bay red is muscular, with bottomless depth of firm, blackcurrant-like, plummy, distinctly spicy flavour. Based principally on Malbec and Merlot, and matured for at least 18 months in all-new French oak barriques, it is not produced in lesser vintages or entered in competitions. One of the most expensive wines from the Villa Maria group, it is 'a symbol of what we can do'.

Felton Road Bannockburn Central Otago Pinot Noir

Since the debut 1997 vintage, Felton Road has taken the international wine world by storm. Deliciously perfumed and supple, with a strong surge of ripe plum, spice and nut flavours, this estate-grown red, blended from three sites at Bannockburn, is a major flagship for the region.

Kumeu River Estate Chardonnay

It would be hard to exaggerate the importance of this famous wine. After the first vintage in 1985, it played a pivotal role in the renaissance of winemaking in the Auckland region, stirred the interest of many other New Zealand winemakers in the traditional white-wine production methods of Burgundy, and played a key role in alerting the American market to the white-wine revolution Down Under. Citrusy, mealy and slightly biscuity, with good acid spine, it is typically savoury and seamless, and a delight to drink at three to five years old.

Nautilus Cuvée Marlborough

Refined and intense, this highly acclaimed, non-vintage sparkling is a Pinot Noir-dominant style, with reserve wines from previous vintages, held in old oak casks, included in the blend. Disgorged after a minimum of three years on its yeast lees, it is one of New Zealand's most Champagne-like sparklings, finely scented, crisp and vivacious, with notable complexity and harmony.

Neudorf Moutere Chardonnay

The undisputed heavyweight of Nelson wines and arguably the finest Chardonnay to flow from the South Island, Neudorf Moutere Chardonnay ranks among New Zealand's greatest wines of all. Weighty and rich, but not overblown, it is tightly structured, with searching, citrusy, mealy, minerally flavours that need about four years to reveal their full glory.

Oyster Bay Marlborough Sauvignon Blanc

Jim Delegat, the driving force behind this hugely popular (think 20 million bottles per year) wine, believes 'Oyster Bay is an aspirer's brand and it appeals to those kinds of people who can afford to have wine as an everyday affordable luxury'. Ranked consistently among the top-selling, mid-priced Sauvignon Blancs in New Zealand, Australia, the UK and the US, it is full-bodied and dry, with strong, vibrant tropical-fruit and herbaceous aromas and flavours, crisp and punchy.

Pegasus Bay Riesling

Waipara's cold nights are a critical factor in the arresting quality of this Riesling. Low night temperatures extend the ripening period, enhancing flavour development, while preserving the grapes' natural acidity. A regional classic, garden-fresh, scented and zingy in its youth, it is a gently sweet, appetisingly crisp style, shot through with citrusy, limey flavours. It breaks into full stride at about three years old, acquiring luscious toast, honey and marmalade characters, and matures well for up to a decade.

Sacred Hill Riflemans Chardonnay

On a spectacular inland, elevated site in the Dartmoor Valley, overlooking white papa rock cliffs carved by the Tutaekuri River, the cool Riflemans Terrace vineyard is planted wholly in Chardonnay. This Hawke's Bay regional classic combines great power and elegance, with citrusy, mealy, minerally flavours, tightly structured, poised and intense, and a resounding finish.

Saint Clair Wairau Reserve Marlborough Sauvignon Blanc

From Marlborough's largest family-owned producer, this is an exciting mouthful, winner of countless gold medals and trophies since the first 2001 vintage. A high-impact style with a soaring bouquet, it overflows with pure, ripely herbaceous flavours, but is also smooth and user-friendly. Enjoy it in its exuberant youth, while it is pungent and zingy.

Seresin Marlborough Sauvignon Blanc

Given its certified organic status, wide international distribution and consistently top-flight quality, this is one of the region's most important wines. A sophisticated dry wine, full of individuality and interest, it is subtle and deeply satisfying, with indigenous yeasts, barrel fermentation and lees-aging adding richness and complexity, without swamping its pure, penetrating fruit flavours.

Stonyridge Larose

Dark and perfumed, with smashing fruit flavours of blackcurrants, plums and spices, Larose is a magnificently concentrated, claret-style red from Waiheke Island. Launched from the 1985 vintage, it is now one of the most celebrated, expensive wines in the land (although much cheaper if you buy on an *en primeur* basis). It matures superbly for a decade and longer, acquiring great overall complexity and harmony.

Te Mata Coleraine

With a string of notably elegant, rich and complex wines since its memorable 1982 debut, this blend of Cabernet Sauvignon, Merlot and Cabernet Franc has carved out a reputation second to none among Hawke's Bay reds. Pronounced Cole-raine (rather than Coler-aine), in most vintages it shows the depth and subtlety of a top Bordeaux, and flourishes in the cellar for 10 to 20 years.

Villa Maria Cellar Selection Hawke's Bay Syrah

Villa Maria's middle-tier Cellar Selection wines (positioned above Private Bin and below the Reserve and Single Vineyard ranges) typically offer wonderful value. This is a perfect introduction to the Hawke's Bay region's hottest red-wine variety. Densely coloured, floral and highly concentrated, it is weighty, with deep, ripe blackcurrant, plum and black-pepper flavours, finely balanced tannins, real power through the palate and a long, spicy finish.

Villa Maria Private Bin Marlborough Sauvignon Blanc

While attending the giant Frankfurt Book Fair in 2012, I spotted an extremely familiar label in several wine stores and restaurants. Sold in over 50 countries, this huge seller accounts for much of the production of New Zealand's largest, completely family-owned winery. Buoyantly fruity, ripely herbaceous and punchy, it offers consistently good quality, and terrific value when on special at around $12.

Yealands Estate Single Vineyard Awatere Valley Marlborough Grüner Veltliner

Here's a taste of the future! Rare in New Zealand, but spreading steadily, Grüner Veltliner (often called 'Grü-Vee') is Austria's favourite white-wine variety. It was first produced here in 2008 and most of the vines are now in Marlborough, where Yealands is proving just how good the wine can be – fragrant, fleshy and finely textured, with strong, peachy, slightly spicy flavours, dry and delicious.

Classic Wines of New Zealand

A bumper crop of six new Super Classics, 17 Classics and 33 Potential Classics are the features of this year's closely revised list of New Zealand wine classics.

What is a New Zealand wine classic? It is a wine that in quality terms consistently ranks in the very forefront of its class. To qualify for selection, each label must have achieved an outstanding level of quality for at least three vintages; there are no flashes in the pan here.

By identifying New Zealand wine classics, my aim is to transcend the inconsistencies of individual vintages and wine competition results, and highlight consistency of excellence. When introducing the elite category of Super Classics, I restricted entry to wines which have achieved brilliance in at least five vintages (compared to three for Classic status). The Super Classics are all highly prestigious wines, with a proven ability to mature well (even the Sauvignon Blancs, compared to other examples of the variety).

The Potential Classics are the pool from which future Classics will emerge. These are wines of outstanding quality which look likely, if their current standards are maintained or improved, to qualify after another vintage or two for elevation to Classic status. All the additions and elevations on this year's list are identified by an asterisk.

Super Classics

Branded and Other White Wines
Cloudy Bay Te Koko, ***Dog Point Vineyard Section 94

Chardonnay
Ata Rangi Craighall; Church Road Grand Reserve Hawke's Bay; Clearview Reserve Hawke's Bay; Clos de Ste Anne Naboth's Vineyard; ***Dry River Martinborough; Fromm Clayvin Vineyard Marlborough; Kumeu River Estate; ***Kumeu River Hunting Hill; Kumeu River Mate's Vineyard Kumeu; Neudorf Moutere; Sacred Hill Riflemans; Te Mata Elston; Villa Maria Reserve Barrique Fermented Gisborne; ***Villa Maria Single Vineyard Keltern Hawke's Bay

Gewürztraminer
Johanneshof Cellars Marlborough; Lawson's Dry Hills Marlborough

Pinot Gris
Dry River Martinborough

Riesling
Dry River Craighall Vineyard Martinborough; Felton Road Bannockburn Central Otago; Pegasus Bay

Sauvignon Blanc
Cloudy Bay; Palliser Estate Martinborough; Saint Clair Wairau Reserve Marlborough; Seresin Marlborough

*** New Super Classic

Sweet Whites
Villa Maria Reserve Marlborough
Noble Riesling Botrytis Selection

Bottle-fermented Sparklings
Deutz Marlborough Cuvée Blanc de
Blancs; Nautilus Cuvée Marlborough

Branded and Other Red Wines
Craggy Range Le Sol; Esk Valley
Heipipi The Terraces; Stonyridge
Larose; Te Mata Coleraine

Cabernet Sauvignon-predominant Reds
***Church Road Tom Cabernet
Sauvignon/Merlot

Merlot
Esk Valley Winemakers Reserve
Merlot-predominant blend; Villa
Maria Reserve Gimblett Gravels
Hawke's Bay

Pinot Noir
Ata Rangi; Dry River Martinborough;
Felton Road Block 3 Central Otago;
Felton Road Block 5; Fromm Clayvin
Vineyard Marlborough; Neudorf
Moutere; Pegasus Bay Prima Donna;
Pegasus Bay Waipara Valley; Villa
Maria Reserve Marlborough

Syrah
***Passage Rock Reserve Waiheke
Island; Te Mata Estate Bullnose;
Trinity Hill Homage Hawke's Bay

Classics   🍇🍇

Chardonnay
Babich Irongate; **Church Road Tom;
Cloudy Bay; Dog Point Vineyard;
Esk Valley Winemakers Reserve;
**Felton Road Block 2 Central Otago;
**Greenhough Hope Vineyard;
Martinborough Vineyard; Pegasus
Bay; Seresin Reserve; Te Whau
Vineyard Waiheke Island; Villa Maria
Reserve Marlborough

Chenin Blanc
Millton Te Arai Vineyard

Gewürztraminer
**Dry River Lovat Vineyard;
Framingham Marlborough; **Pegasus
Bay; Vinoptima Ormond Reserve

Pinot Gris
Greystone Waipara Valley; Neudorf
Moutere; Villa Maria Single Vineyard
Seddon Marlborough

Riesling
*Carrick Bannockburn; Neudorf
Moutere; Rippon Mature Vine; Valli
Old Vine Central Otago

Sauvignon Blanc
Brancott Estate Letter Series 'B'
Brancott Marlborough; Clos
Henri Marlborough; **Greywacke
Marlborough Wild; Lawson's Dry
Hills Marlborough; Staete Landt
Annabel Marlborough; Te Mata Cape
Crest; Villa Maria Reserve Clifford
Bay; Villa Maria Reserve Wairau
Valley

Viognier

Clos de Ste Anne Les Arbres; **Te Mata Estate Zara

Sweet Whites

**Framingham F-Series Riesling Trockenbeerenauslese; Framingham Noble Riesling; **Pegasus Bay Encore Noble Riesling

Bottle-fermented Sparklings

Deutz Marlborough Prestige Cuvée; Quartz Reef Méthode Traditionnelle [Vintage]

Branded and Other Red Wines

**Alpha Domus AD The Aviator; Babich The Patriarch; **Craggy Range Aroha; Craggy Range Sophia; Craggy Range The Quarry; Destiny Bay Magna Praemia; **Destiny Bay Mystae; Newton Forrest Estate Cornerstone; Puriri Hills Reserve; Sacred Hill Brokenstone; Sacred Hill Helmsman; Te Whau The Point

Cabernet Sauvignon-predominant Reds

**Babich Irongate Gimblett Gravels Hawke's Bay Cabernet/Merlot/Franc; Brookfields Reserve Vintage ['Gold Label'] Cabernet/Merlot; Te Mata Awatea Cabernets/Merlot; Villa Maria Reserve Gimblett Gravels Hawke's Bay Cabernet Sauvignon/Merlot

Pinot Noir

Akarua Bannockburn Central Otago; Bannock Brae Central Otago; Carrick Bannockburn Central Otago; Dog Point Vineyard Marlborough; Escarpment Kupe by Escarpment; Felton Road Bannockburn Central Otago; Felton Road Cornish Point Central Otago; Fromm Fromm Vineyard; **Gibbston Valley Le Maitre Central Otago; Gibbston Valley Reserve Central Otago; **Grasshopper Rock Earnscleugh Vineyard Central Otago; Greenhough Hope Vineyard Nelson; Mt Difficulty Single Vineyard Target Gully; Palliser Estate Martinborough; Pisa Range Estate Black Poplar Block; Quartz Reef Bendigo Estate; Quartz Reef Central Otago Single Vineyard; Rippon Tinker's Field Mature Vine; Valli Bannockburn Vineyard Central Otago; Villa Maria Single Vineyard Seddon Marlborough; Villa Maria Single Vineyard Southern Clays Marlborough

Syrah

Bilancia La Collina; **Esk Valley Winemakers Reserve Gimblett Gravels Hawke's Bay; Mills Reef Trust Vineyard Elspeth Gimblett Gravels Hawke's Bay; Sacred Hill Deerstalkers Hawke's Bay; **Stonecroft Gimblett Gravels Hawke's Bay Reserve; Stonyridge Pilgrim Waiheke Island Syrah/Mourvedre/Viognier/Grenache; Villa Maria Reserve Gimblett Gravels Hawke's Bay

Potential Classics

Branded and Other White Wines
Seresin Chiaroscuro

Arneis
Clevedon Hills

Chardonnay
*Auntsfield Single Vineyard Southern Valleys Marlborough; Greystone Erin's Reserve Waipara Valley; *Greywacke Marlborough; Kumeu River Coddington; Mahi Twin Valleys Marlborough; Mission Jewelstone Hawke's Bay; *Nautilus Marlborough; Pyramid Valley Vineyards Field of Fire; Pyramid Valley Vineyards Lion's Tooth; Spy Valley Envoy Johnson Vineyard Marlborough; Trinity Hill Gimblett Gravels Hawke's Bay [Black Label]; *Vidal Legacy Hawke's Bay; *Villa Maria Reserve Hawke's Bay; *Villa Maria Single Vineyard Taylors Pass

Chenin Blanc

*Clos de Ste Anne La Bas

Gewürztraminer
Greystone Waipara Valley; *Lawson's Dry Hills The Pioneer Marlborough; Seifried Winemaker's Collection Nelson; Spy Valley Envoy Johnson Vineyard Marlborough; *Stonecroft Old Vine; Villa Maria Single Vineyard Ihumatao

Pinot Gris
Blackenbrook Nelson; *Church Road McDonald Series Hawke's Bay; Greywacke Marlborough; *Misha's Vineyard Dress Circle Central Otago; Seresin Marlborough

*New Potential Classic

Riesling
Carrick Josephine Central Otago; *Felton Road Dry; Framingham Classic Marlborough; Framingham F-Series Old Vine Marlborough; Greystone Waipara Valley; Greywacke Marlborough; Misha's Vineyard Limelight; Misha's Vineyard Lyric; Muddy Water James Hardwick Waipara; Saint Clair Pioneer Block 9 Big John

Rosé
Terra Sancta Bannockburn Central Otago Pinot Noir

Sauvignon Blanc
*Auntsfield Single Vineyard Southern Valleys Marlborough; *Church Road Grand Reserve Barrel Fermented Hawke's Bay; *Churton Marlborough; *Clos Marguerite Marlborough; *Dog Point Vineyard Marlborough; Giesen Marlborough The August; *Greywacke Marlborough; *Hans Herzog Marlborough Barrel Fermented Sur Lie; Jackson Estate Grey Ghost Barrique Wairau Valley Marlborough; Jackson Estate Stich Marlborough; Pegasus Bay Sauvignon/Sémillon; Seresin Marama; *Villa Maria Single Vineyard Graham Marlborough; Villa Maria Single Vineyard Taylors Pass Marlborough

Sweet White Wines
Alpha Domus AD Noble Selection; *Felton Road Block 1 Central Otago Riesling; Framingham F-Series Gewürztraminer VT; *Framingham F Series Riesling Auslese; Framingham Select Marlborough Riesling; Pegasus Bay Aria Late Picked Riesling

Branded and Other Red Wines

Alluviale; Clearview Old Olive Block; Clearview The Basket Press; *Destiny Bay Destinae; Gillman; Messenger; Obsidian Reserve The Obsidian; Puriri Hills Pope; Trinity Hill Gimblett Gravels The Gimblett

Cabernet Sauvignon-predominant Reds

*Church Road McDonald Series Hawke's Bay Cabernet Sauvignon; Mills Reef Elspeth Gimblett Gravels Hawke's Bay Cabernet Sauvignon; Mills Reef Elspeth Gimblett Gravels Hawke's Bay Cabernet/Merlot; *Vidal Legacy Gimblett Gravels Hawke's Bay Cabernet Sauvignon/Merlot

Malbec

Stonyridge Luna Negra Waiheke Island Hillside

Merlot

*Church Road McDonald Series Hawke's Bay; Hans Herzog Spirit of Marlborough Merlot/Cabernet

Montepulciano

Hans Herzog Marlborough; Obsidian Waiheke Island

Pinot Noir

Amisfield Central Otago; Bald Hills Bannockburn Single Vineyard Central Otago; Burn Cottage Central Otago; Craggy Range Te Muna Road Vineyard Martinborough; Doctors Flat Central Otago; Escarpment Kiwa by Escarpment Martinborough; Escarpment Martinborough; Escarpment Te Rehua by Escarpment Martinborough; *Felton Road Calvert Central Otago; *Gibbston Valley China Terrace Bendigo Central Otago; Gibbston Valley School House Central Otago; Hans Herzog Marlborough; Julicher Martinborough; *Lowburn Ferry The Ferrymans Reserve; Mondillo Central Otago; Mt Difficulty Single Vineyard Pipeclay Terrace Bannockburn; Muddy Water Slowhand Waipara; Nautilus Four Barriques Marlborough; Peregrine Central Otago; Rockburn Central Otago; Tatty Bogler Otago; Valli Gibbston Vineyard Otago; Villa Maria Single Vineyard Taylors Pass Marlborough; Wooing Tree Central Otago

Syrah

Church Road Grand Reserve Hawke's Bay; *Church Road McDonald Series Hawke's Bay; Clos de Ste Anne The Crucible; Craggy Range Gimblett Gravels Vineyard Hawke's Bay; *Man O' War Waiheke Island Dreadnought; *Mission Huchet Gimblett Gravels; *Mudbrick Vineyard Reserve; Passage Rock; Trinity Hill Gimblett Gravels; Vidal Legacy Gimblett Gravels Hawke's Bay; Villa Maria Cellar Selection Hawke's Bay

The following wines are not at the very forefront in quality terms, yet have been produced for many vintages, are extremely widely available and typically deliver good to excellent quality and value. They are all benchmark wines of their type – a sort of Everyman's classic.

Chardonnay
Church Road Hawke's Bay; Stoneleigh Marlborough

Gewürztraminer
Seifried Nelson

Pinot Gris
Waimea Nelson

Riesling
Hunter's Marlborough; Lawson's Dry Hills Marlborough; Seifried Nelson; Waimea Classic Nelson

Sauvignon Blanc
Brancott Estate Marlborough; Oyster Bay Marlborough; Saint Clair Marlborough; Stoneleigh Marlborough; Tohu Marlborough; Villa Maria Private Bin Marlborough

Sparkling
Lindauer Brut; Lindauer Special Reserve; Soljans Fusion Sparkling Muscat

Merlot
Church Road Hawke's Bay Merlot/Cabernet/Malbec; Te Mata Estate Vineyards Merlot/Cabernets

Pinot Noir
Akarua Rua Central Otago; Pencarrow Martinborough; Villa Maria Private Bin Marlborough

Cellar Sense

Moana Park, a Hawke's Bay producer, in 2015 launched a Sauvignon Blanc on 1 April that had been picked in early March. When sent a press release about this, some wine writers suspected an April Fool's Day prank.

Sauvignon Blanc, which accounts for about two-thirds of New Zealand wine, is not usually seen as a variety that needs time to develop. Only a decade ago, Marlborough winemakers often stated that the region's Sauvignon Blanc 'should be picked, pressed and pissed by Christmas'. Today, most Sauvignon Blancs develop soundly for a couple of years, but the popularity of New Zealand Pinot Noir has done far more to persuade consumers around the world that this country's wine can mature gracefully – as it must, if New Zealand is to be accepted as a serious wine producer.

'To gain true international recognition, an industry has to be capable of making wines that improve with age – that's the ultimate quality factor,' stresses John Buck, co-founder of Te Mata Estate, acclaimed for its long-lived Hawke's Bay Cabernet/Merlots. 'People need to be able to put wine into their cellars with confidence and know that when they pull them out they will be a damn sight better than when they put them in.'

But do all winemakers share that view? Geoff Kelly, a Wellington-based critic, believes too much emphasis is placed on young wines in New Zealand, partly because many wine judges are winemakers. 'Generalising, winemakers ... speak most highly of fresh and fruity smells and flavours in wine. How else can they sell their young wines? Consequently, it is quite rare to find New Zealand winemakers who really enjoy old wines or attend tastings of them.'

To celebrate a 20th anniversary, two years ago I opened Te Mata Coleraine 1994. From a good but not great year for reds in Hawke's Bay, I was taken aback by how well it had matured and how much pleasure it offered. Tasted in August 2016, Grasshopper Rock Central Otago Pinot Noir 2006 (the first vintage of this trophy-winning, single-vineyard Alexandra red) is still full of life – deliciously rich, complex, savoury and smooth.

Today, most wine in New Zealand is consumed on the day it is bought and just 1 per cent is cellared for more than a year. Fortunately, some wine producers are doing the job for us. At Mazuran's Vineyards, in Henderson, West Auckland, you can still purchase their 1942 Vintage Madeira Port, 1943 Royal Vintage Port and vintage 'ports' from every year since – a great gift for special birthdays.

But if you are keen to build up a cellar of distinguished Chardonnays, Rieslings, Pinot Noirs or Cabernet/Merlots, how do you decide what to buy? Confidence comes from 'vertical' tastings, where several vintages of a wine are tasted side by side. Vertical tastings, staged more and more frequently in New Zealand, let you assess the overall quality of a wine, the evolution of its style, the impact of vintage variation and its maturation potential.

To sum up, I suggest drinking most New Zealand Sauvignon Blancs at six months to two years old. Screwcaps preserve the wines' freshness markedly better than corks did. Most fine-quality Chardonnays are at their best at two to five years old; top Rieslings at three to seven years old.

Pinot Noirs, Merlots and Syrahs typically drink well for up to five years; outstanding examples can flourish for much longer. New Zealand's top Cabernet/ Merlot blends from Hawke's Bay and Waiheke Island are still the safest bet for long-term cellaring over decades.

Cellaring Guidelines

Grape variety	Best age to open
White	
Sauvignon Blanc	
(non-wooded)	6–24 months
(wooded)	1–3 years
Arneis	1–3 years
Albariño	1–4 years
Gewürztraminer	1–4 years
Grüner Veltliner	1–4 years
Viognier	1–4 years
Pinot Gris	1–4 years
Sémillon	1–4 years
Chenin Blanc	2–5 years
Chardonnay	2–5 years
Riesling	2–7+ years
Red	
Pinotage	1–3 years
Malbec	1–5 years
Cabernet Franc	2–5 years
Merlot	2–5+ years
Pinot Noir	2–5+ years
Syrah	2–5+ years
Tempranillo	2–5+ years
Cabernet Sauvignon	3–7+ years
Cabernet/Merlot	3–7+ years
Other	
Sweet whites	2–5 years
Bottle-fermented sparklings	
(vintage-dated)	3–5+ years

How to Use this Book

It is essential to read this brief section to understand how the book works. Feel free to skip any of the other preliminary pages, but not these.

The majority of wines have been listed in the book according to their principal grape variety, as shown on the front label. Lawson's Dry Hills Marlborough Sauvignon Blanc, for instance, can be located simply by turning to the Sauvignon Blanc section. Wines with front labels that do not refer clearly to a grape variety or blend of grapes, such as Cloudy Bay Te Koko, can be found in the Branded and Other Wines sections for white and red wines.

Most entries are firstly identified by their producer's name. Wines not usually called by their producer's name, such as Kim Crawford Marlborough Sauvignon Blanc (from Constellation New Zealand), or Triplebank Awatere Valley Marlborough Pinot Noir (from Pernod Ricard NZ), are listed under their most common name.

The star ratings for quality reflect my own opinions, formed where possible by tasting a wine over several vintages, and often a particular vintage several times. *The star ratings are therefore a guide to each wine's overall standard in recent vintages*, rather than simply the quality of the latest release. However, to enhance the usefulness of the book, in the body of the text I have also given a *quality rating for the latest vintage of each wine*; sometimes for more than one vintage. (Since April 2010 wineries have been able to buy stickers to attach to their bottles, based on these ratings.)

I hope the star ratings give interesting food for thought and succeed in introducing you to a galaxy of little-known but worthwhile wines. It pays to remember, however, that wine-tasting is a business fraught with subjectivity. You should always treat the views expressed in these pages for what they are – one person's opinion. The quality ratings are:

★★★★★	Outstanding quality (gold medal standard)
★★★★☆	Excellent quality, verging on outstanding
★★★★	Excellent quality (silver medal standard)
★★★☆	Very good quality
★★★	Good quality (bronze medal standard)
★★☆	Average quality
★★	Plain
★	Poor
No star	To be avoided

These quality ratings are based on comparative assessments of New Zealand wines against one another. A five-star Merlot/Cabernet Sauvignon, for instance, is an outstanding-quality red judged by the standards of other Merlot/Cabernet Sauvignon blends made in New Zealand. It is not judged by the standards of overseas reds of a similar style (for instance Bordeaux), because the book is focused solely on New Zealand wines and their relative merits. (Some familiar New Zealand wine brands in recent years have included varying proportions of overseas wine. To be featured in this book, they must still include at least some New Zealand wine in the blend.)

Where brackets enclose the star rating on the right-hand side of the page, for example (★★★), this indicates the assessment is only tentative, because I have tasted very few vintages of the wine. A dash is used in the relatively few cases where a wine's quality has oscillated over and above normal vintage variations (for example ★–★★★).

Super Classic wines, Classic wines and Potential Classic wines (see page 24) are highlighted in the text by the following symbols:

Super Classic   Classic   Potential Classic

Each wine has also been given a dryness-sweetness, price and value-for-money rating. The precise levels of sweetness indicated by the four ratings are:

DRY	Less than 5 grams/litre of residual sugar
MED/DRY	5–14 grams/litre of residual sugar
MED	15–49 grams/litre of residual sugar
SW	50 and over grams/litre of residual sugar

Less than 5 grams of residual sugar per litre is virtually imperceptible to most palates – the wine tastes fully dry. With between 5 and 14 grams, a wine has a hint of sweetness, although a high level of acidity (as in Rieslings or even Marlborough Sauvignon Blancs, which often have 4 to 6 grams per litre of residual sugar) reduces the perception of sweetness. Where a wine harbours over 15 grams, the sweetness is clearly in evidence.

At above 50 grams per litre, most wines are unabashedly sweet, although high levels of acidity can still disguise the degree of sweetness. Most wines that harbour more than 50 grams per litre of sugar are packaged in half bottles, made to be served with dessert, and can be located in the Sweet White Wines section. However, a growing number of low-alcohol, sweet but not super-sweet, mouth-wateringly crisp Rieslings, not designed as dessert wines and usually packaged in 750-ml bottles, can also be found in the Riesling section.

Prices shown are based on the average price in a supermarket or wine shop (as indicated by the producer), except where most of the wine is sold directly to consumers from the winery, either over the vineyard counter or via mail order or the Internet.

The art of wine buying involves more than discovering top-quality wines. The real challenge – and the greatest satisfaction – lies in identifying wines at varying quality levels that deliver outstanding value for money. The symbols I have used are self-explanatory:

–V	=	Below average value
AV	=	Average value
V+	=	Above average value

The ratings discussed thus far are all my own. Many of the wine producers themselves, however, have also contributed individual vintage ratings of their own top wines over the past decade and the 'When to drink' recommendations. (The symbol **WR** indicates Winemaker's Rating, and the symbol **NM** alongside a vintage means the wine was not made that year.) Only the producers have such detailed knowledge of the relative quality of all their recent vintages (although in some cases, when the information was not forthcoming, I have rated a vintage myself). The key point you must note is that *each producer has rated each vintage of each wine against his or her highest quality aspirations for that particular label, not against any absolute standard.* Thus, a 7 out of 7 score merely indicates that the producer considers that particular vintage to be an outstanding example of that particular wine; not that it is the best-quality wine he or she makes.

The 'When to drink' (Drink) recommendations (which I find myself referring to constantly) are largely self-explanatory. The P symbol for PEAKED means that a particular vintage is already at, or has passed, its peak; no further benefits are expected from aging.

Here is an example of how the ratings work:

Ata Rangi Pinot Noir   ★★★★★

One of the greatest of all New Zealand wines, this Martinborough red is powerfully built and concentrated, yet seductively fragrant and supple. 'Intense, opulent fruit with power beneath' is founder Clive Paton's goal. 'Complexity comes with time.' The grapes are drawn from numerous sites, including the estate vineyard, planted in 1980, and the vines, up to 36 years old, have a very low average yield of 4.5 tonnes of grapes per hectare. The wine is fermented with indigenous yeasts and maturation is for 11 months in French oak barriques (35 per cent new in 2014). From an early-ripening season, the 2014 vintage (★★★★★) is deeply coloured and mouthfilling, with very generous, youthful cherry, plum and spice flavours. Concentrated, vibrant and savoury, with notable complexity and the structure to mature well, it's a very harmonious red, already highly approachable, but likely to be at its best 2020+.

Vintage	14	13	12	11	10	09	08
WR	07	07	07	07	07	07	07
Drink	16-26	16-25	16-24	16-23	16-22	16-21	16-20

DRY $75 AV

❤❤❤

The winemaker's own ratings indicate that the 2014 vintage is of excellent quality for the label, and is recommended for drinking between 2016 and 2026.

Describes 'Classic' status, ranging from ❤❤❤ for Super Classic, ❤❤ for Classic to ❤ for Potential Classic. This is a wine that in quality terms ranks in the forefront of its class.

Dryness-sweetness rating, price and value for money. This wine is dry in style (below 5 grams/litre of residual sugar). At $75 it is average value for money.

Quality rating, ranging from ★★★★★ for outstanding to no star (−), to be avoided. This is generally a wine of outstanding quality.

White Wines

Albariño

Coopers Creek's 2011 bottling was the first true example of Albariño from New Zealand or Australia. Called Albariño in Spain and Alvarinho in Portugal, this fashionable variety produces light, crisp wines described by Riversun Nurseries at Gisborne as possessing 'distinctive aromatic, peachy characteristics, similar to Viognier'. With its loose clusters, thick skins and good resistance to rain, Albariño could thrive in this country's wetter regions. New Zealand's 30 hectares of bearing Albariño vines in 2017 are mostly in Gisborne (12 hectares), Hawke's Bay (7 hectares) and Marlborough (4 hectares), but there are also pockets in Nelson and Auckland.

Aronui Single Vineyard Nelson Albariño ★★★★

The impressive 2015 vintage (★★★★☆) was estate-grown and hand-picked at Upper Moutere. Aromatic and full-bodied, it is a strongly varietal wine, with good vigour and intensity of peach, grapefruit and spice flavours, dryish (7 grams/litre of residual sugar), crisp, finely balanced and long. It's already drinking well.

MED/DRY $25 AV

Astrolabe Vineyards Sleepers Vineyard Marlborough Albariño (★★★☆)

Grown at Kekerengu, the refreshing 2014 vintage (★★★☆) was hand-picked and mostly handled in tanks, with a small percentage of barrel aging. Made in a bone-dry style, it is a freshly scented, medium-bodied wine with lively, citrusy, peachy, slightly limey flavours, showing a touch of complexity, and good balance and depth.

DRY $25 –V

Babich Family Estates Headwaters Marlborough Albariño (★★★☆)

The 2015 vintage (★★★☆) was estate-grown and hand-picked from first-crop vines in an organically certified vineyard. Light lemon/green, it is an attractively scented, medium-bodied wine with very good depth of vigorous, citrusy, peachy, slightly spicy flavours, a gentle splash of sweetness (8 grams/litre of residual sugar) and firm acid spine. A promising debut.

MED/DRY $27 –V

Coopers Creek Select Vineyards Bell-Ringer Gisborne Albariño ★★★★

The 2015 vintage (★★★★) was hand-harvested in the Bell Vineyard and tank-fermented. Freshly aromatic, it is mouthfilling, with good intensity of vibrant, lemony, peachy flavours, appetising acidity and a dry (4 grams/litre of residual sugar), finely balanced finish.

Vintage	15	14	13	12	11
WR	7	7	7	4	4
Drink	16-17	16-17	P	P	P

DRY $25 AV

Doubtless Albariño (★★★)

Grown at Doubtless Bay, in Northland, the steely 2015 vintage (★★★) was fermented in old oak casks. Light lemon/green, it is medium to full-bodied, with good depth of lively, citrusy flavours, mouth-watering acidity and a dry finish. Good food wine.

Vintage	15
WR	5
Drink	16-20

DRY $22 –V

Hihi Gisborne Albariño   ★★★☆

The 2015 vintage (★★★☆) was estate-grown at Ormond. Made in an easy-drinking style, it is mouthfilling, with ripe, peachy flavours, showing good vigour, a distinct splash of sweetness (14 grams/litre of residual sugar), and a crisp, smooth finish.

MED/DRY $20 AV

Left Field Gisborne Albariño   (★★★★★)

From Te Awa, based in Hawke's Bay, the 2015 vintage (★★★★★) was made from grapes hand-picked in Gisborne and handled without oak. Packed with flavour, it's a mouthfilling, strongly varietal wine. It has strong peach, pear and spice flavours, with slightly leesy, salty notes adding interest, and a crisp, dryish (5 grams/litre of residual sugar), lasting finish. Worth discovering.

MED/DRY $25 V+

Mahurangi River Winery Matakana Albariño   ★★★★

Grown at Matakana, north of Auckland, the 2015 vintage (★★★★) was fermented in a mix of tanks (80 per cent) and barrels (20 per cent). Pale lemon/green, it is mouthfilling, with generous, citrusy, slightly spicy flavours, complexity from the delicate oak seasoning, appetising acidity and a fresh, finely poised finish. Best drinking 2017+.

Vintage	15	14
WR	6	7
Drink	16-18	16-17

DRY $29 –V

Matawhero Church House Gisborne Albariño   ★★★★

The 2014 vintage (★★★★) is from young, second-crop vines in the Tietjen Vineyard. Pale yellow, it is full-bodied and fleshy, with strong, ripe, peachy flavours, a sliver of sweetness (6 grams/litre of residual sugar), and lively, well-balanced acidity. Ready.

Vintage	14	13
WR	6	6
Drink	16-17	P

MED/DRY $28 –V

Matua Single Vineyard Hawke's Bay Albariño   ★★★★★

Consistently impressive since the debut 2013 vintage (★★★★★). Full of personality, the 2015 vintage (★★★★★) is richly scented and mouthfilling, with a strong surge of vibrant, peachy, spicy, slightly limey flavours, mouth-watering acidity and a dry (3 grams/litre of residual sugar), lingering finish.

DRY $35 AV

Nautilus Marlborough Albariño   ★★★★

Delicious from the start, the aromatic 2016 vintage (★★★★☆) is a single-vineyard wine, handled without oak. Bright, light lemon/green, it is mouthfilling, sweet-fruited and dry (4 grams/litre of residual sugar), with strong, peachy, slightly spicy flavours, a slightly salty streak and good complexity.

DRY $29 –V

Neudorf Moutere Albariño   (★★★★★)

The 2015 vintage (★★★★★) is an exciting debut. Estate-grown, it was hand-picked at over 23 brix in Rosie's Block Vineyard and fermented with indigenous yeasts in tanks (81 per cent) and old oak puncheons (19 per cent). Mouthfilling and dry (4.5 grams/litre of residual sugar), it has excellent vigour and intensity of fresh, ripe, citrusy, peachy, spicy flavours, a slightly salty streak running through, a touch of complexity, and a tangy, lasting finish. Finely balanced and full of personality, it's delicious from the start.

Vintage	15
WR	7
Drink	16-17

 DRY $33 AV

Ransom Matakana Albariño   ★★★★

The 2015 vintage (★★★☆) is mouthfilling, crisp and dry, with vibrant, citrusy, slightly spicy flavours that linger well. A very refreshing, appetising summer wine.

 DRY $26 –V

Redmetal Vineyards Block Five Hawke's Bay Albariño   (★★★★)

The debut 2016 vintage (★★★★) was grown in the Bridge Pa Triangle and handled without oak. Bright, light lemon/green, it is already enjoyable, with ripe, peachy, spicy flavours, showing good vigour and concentration, and a dry (3 grams/litre of residual sugar), well-rounded finish.

 DRY $23 AV

Rod McDonald One Off Gisborne Albariño   ★★★☆

The 2015 vintage (★★★☆) was hand-picked and tank-fermented with indigenous yeasts. Light lemon/green, it is vibrantly fruity, with good varietal character, a slightly salty streak and citrusy, appley flavours that linger well.

DRY $28 –V

Sileni Estate Selection Advocate Hawke's Bay Albariño   (★★★★☆)

The 2015 vintage (★★★★☆) is an excellent debut. Hand-picked in the Bridge Pa Triangle, tank-fermented and lees-aged, it is aromatic and full-bodied, with strong, vibrant, peachy, slightly spicy flavours, a slightly minerally streak, and very good drive, depth and personality. It's already delicious.

Vintage	15
WR	6
Drink	16-21

 DRY $25 V+

Spade Oak Vineyard Heart of Gold Gisborne Albariño   ★★★☆

The youthful 2015 vintage (★★★☆) was hand-picked and made in a dryish style (5 grams/litre of residual sugar). Medium-bodied, it is fresh and vibrantly fruity, with ripe, peachy flavours, a slightly salty note, balanced acidity and very good depth.

 MED/DRY $23 –V

Villa Maria Cellar Selection Gisborne Albariño   ★★★★☆

The 2015 vintage (★★★★☆) is a delicious wine, hand-picked and mostly handled in tanks; a small percentage of the blend was fermented with indigenous yeasts in oak. Bright, light lemon/green, it is full-bodied and dry (3.8 grams/litre of residual sugar), with strong, ripe, peachy, spicy flavours, crisp and lively, a touch of complexity, and a lasting finish. Full of personality, it's a drink-now or cellaring proposition.

DRY $26 AV

Waimea Nelson Albariño   ★★★

Grown at Hope, the 2015 vintage (★★★☆) is aromatic and steely, with strong, lemony, peachy, slightly spicy flavours and a crunchy, dry (4 grams/litre of residual sugar) finish. A slightly austere wine (with 'outlandish acidity', according to the winery), it's worth cellaring.

DRY $23 –V

Wairau River Marlborough Albariño   ★★★★

This single-vineyard wine is estate-grown on the north side of the Wairau Valley. The 2016 vintage (★★★★) is aromatic, crisp and dryish (7 grams/litre of residual sugar), with strong grapefruit and green-apple flavours, lively, refreshing and lingering. Best drinking mid-2017+.

Vintage	16	15
WR	6	6
Drink	16-18	16-17

MED/DRY $20 V+

Arneis

Still fairly rare here, with 33 hectares of bearing vines in 2017, Arneis is one of the most distinctive emerging varieties. Pronounced 'Are-nay-iss', it is a traditional grape of Piedmont, in north-west Italy, where it yields soft, early-maturing wines with slightly herbaceous aromas and almond flavours. The word 'Arneis' means 'little rascal', which reflects its tricky character in the vineyard; a vigorous variety, it needs careful tending. First planted in New Zealand in 1998 at the Clevedon Hills vineyard in South Auckland, its potential is now being explored by numerous producers. Coopers Creek released the country's first varietal Arneis from the 2006 vintage. Most of the bearing vines in 2017 are in Gisborne (16 hectares), Hawke's Bay (13 hectares) and Marlborough (4 hectares).

Clevedon Hills Arneis ★★★★★

Estate-grown in South Auckland, the 2013 vintage (★★★★★) is the best since the similarly outstanding 2010 (★★★★★). Highly scented, it is mouthfilling, fleshy and dry, with lovely mouthfeel and depth of citrus-fruit, peach, lychee and spice flavours, deliciously poised and long. What else can you ask from Arneis? A worthy follow-up, the bright, light lemon/green 2014 vintage (★★★★☆) is weighty (14 per cent alcohol) and dry. Still youthful, it is sweet-fruited, with ripe lychee, pear and slight spice flavours that build to a strong, finely textured finish.

DRY $27 V+

Coopers Creek SV Gisborne Arneis The Little Rascal ★★★★☆

Top years are richly scented, with substantial alcohol and strong, slightly spicy and herbal flavours. Hand-picked in the Bell Vineyard and tank-fermented, the 2014 vintage (★★★★☆) is fragrant, full-bodied and dry, with concentrated, ripe tropical-fruit flavours, finely balanced and lingering.

Vintage	14	13	12	11	10
WR	7	7	NM	5	7
Drink	16-18	16-18	NM	P	P

DRY $25 V+

Hans Herzog Marlborough Arneis ★★★★

Organically certified, the 2014 vintage (★★★★) was matured on its yeast lees for 10 months in French oak puncheons. It's a mouthfilling, 'serious' wine, with strong, ripe citrus-fruit and pineapple flavours, balanced acidity, a gentle oak influence and a bone-dry finish. Best drinking mid-2016+.

Vintage	14	13
WR	7	7
Drink	16-19	16-18

DRY $39 –V

Villa Maria Cellar Selection Hawke's Bay Arneis ★★★★

The 2015 vintage (★★★★☆) is a powerful, youthful wine, lemon-scented, with substantial body (14.5 per cent alcohol) and a strong surge of peachy, citrusy, slightly spicy flavours, showing a touch of complexity (5 per cent barrel-fermented). Vibrantly fruity, with fresh acidity and a dry finish (2.7 grams/litre of residual sugar), it's a distinctive wine, well worth cellaring.

Vintage	15	14	13
WR	7	6	7
Drink	16-19	16-18	P

 DRY $20 V+

Villa Maria Single Vineyard Ohiti Gravels Hawke's Bay Arneis ★★★★

The 2014 vintage (★★★★) was fermented in tanks (85 per cent) and seasoned oak puncheons (15 per cent). Attractively scented, it's a medium-bodied, strongly varietal wine with vibrant pear and slight lime flavours, crisp, finely balanced and lingering.

Vintage	14	13
WR	6	7
Drink	16-18	P

DRY $28 –V

Branded and Other White Wines

Cloudy Bay Te Koko, Dog Point Vineyard Section 94 – in this section you'll find all the white wines that don't feature varietal names. Lower-priced branded white wines can give winemakers an outlet for grapes like Chenin Blanc, Sémillon and Riesling that otherwise can be hard to sell. They can also be an outlet for coarser, less delicate juice ('pressings'). Some of the branded whites are quaffers, but others are highly distinguished.

Aurum Central Otago Amber Wine (★★★★★)

Looking for something completely different, made by ancient techniques? The 2014 vintage (★★★★★) is an amber-hued Pinot Gris, estate-grown, made with indigenous yeast fermentation and prolonged skin maceration, barrique-aged for over a year, and bottled unfined and unfiltered. Mouthfilling, it shows good complexity, with strong apricot and spice flavours, a touch of tannin, and a dry, structured finish. Certified organic.

DRY $45 AV

Bellbird Spring Home Block White ★★★★

Showing greater complexity than most aromatic whites, the 2013 vintage (★★★★☆) is a single-vineyard, Waipara blend of Pinot Gris, Riesling, Muscat and Gewürztraminer, hand-picked and fermented and lees-aged for five months in old oak barrels. Pale gold, it is full-bodied, with a strong surge of peachy, slightly spicy and gingery flavours, a splash of sweetness (20 grams/litre of residual sugar), and excellent complexity and richness. A medium style in the traditional Alsace mould, it's full of personality. Ready. The 2015 vintage (★★★☆) was barrel-aged for five months and made in a medium style. Pale yellow, it is medium-bodied, with peachy, slightly spicy flavours, gentle sweetness, fresh acidity, a touch of complexity, and a smooth finish.

MED $32 –V

Bellbird Spring Sous Voile (★★★★★)

The non-vintage wine (★★★★★) released in 2015 is unique for New Zealand, but echoes wines from Jura, France, and amontillado sherry. Made in a deliberately 'oxidative' style from Waipara Pinot Gris, it was fermented dry and matured for four years in old oak barriques under a layer of yeast ('sous voile' means 'under veil'). Light gold, it is an unfortified wine (although harbouring 15.5 per cent alcohol), with substantial body and strong, dry, peachy, yeasty, nutty flavours. Well worth discovering.

DRY $40 (500 ML) AV

Brennan Trio (★★★)

The 2014 vintage (★★★), grown at Gibbston, in Central Otago, is a medium style, based on Riesling (67 per cent), blended with Muscat (28 per cent) and Gewürztraminer (5 per cent). Pale, with a slightly spicy perfume, it has fresh, lemony, appley, slightly spicy flavours and a crisp, gently sweet (22 grams/litre of residual sugar) finish.

MED $31 –V

Cloudy Bay Te Koko ★★★★★

Te Koko o Kupe ('The Oyster Dredge of Kupe') is the original name for Cloudy Bay; it is also the name of the Marlborough winery's intriguing oak-aged Sauvignon Blanc. The 2012 vintage (★★★★☆), grown in the Wairau Valley and fermented with indigenous yeasts in French oak barrels (only 8 per cent new, to ensure a subtle oak influence), was matured in wood on its yeast lees until October 2013, and part of the blend went through a softening malolactic fermentation. Bright, light yellow/green, it is mouthfilling, with generous tropical-fruit and herbaceous flavours, slightly nutty and long. Weighty and complex, with good richness and harmony, it is a slightly 'greener' wine than usual, reflecting the cool growing season. Te Koko lies well outside the mainstream regional style of Sauvignon Blanc, but it is well worth discovering.

Vintage	12	11	10
WR	6	7	7
Drink	16-18	16-18	16-17

DRY $51 AV

Craggy Range Te Muna Four ★★★★

The 2014 vintage (★★★★) is a Martinborough 'field blend' (hand-harvested together) of a quartet of Alsatian varieties – Riesling, Pinot Gris, Gewürztraminer and Pinot Blanc. Fermented with indigenous yeasts and matured for six months in seasoned French oak barriques, it's a medium-bodied, tightly structured wine, scented and vibrantly fruity, with concentrated, citrusy, peachy, spicy flavours, a real sense of drive through the palate, and a long, dry (2.4 grams/litre of residual sugar) finish. Best drinking 2017+.

DRY $43 –V

Dog Point Vineyard Section 94 ★★★★★

Looking for 'texture, rather than rich aromatics', Dog Point fermented and lees-aged its 2014 vintage (★★★★★) Sauvignon Blanc for 18 months in seasoned French oak casks. Hand-harvested in the Dog Point Vineyard (for which 'Section 94' was the original survey title), at the confluence of the Brancott and Omaka valleys, and fermented with indigenous yeasts, it has an invitingly fragrant, complex bouquet. Light lemon/green, it is a very non-herbaceous style, mouthfilling and fleshy, with vibrant, ripe tropical-fruit flavours, slightly toasty notes adding complexity, fresh, appetising but moderate acidity (the lowest to date for this wine), and a bone-dry, harmonious finish. Best drinking mid-2017+.

Vintage	14	13	12	11	10	09	08
WR	7	7	5	7	7	5	6
Drink	16-23	16-22	16-19	16-21	16-19	16-17	16-17

DRY $38 AV

Expatrius Waiheke Island Advenus ★★★★☆

This sturdy blend of Sauvignon Blanc (principally) and Viognier is fermented in tanks and new oak barrels. The 2014 vintage (★★★★☆), 25 per cent barrel-fermented, is ripely fragrant, weighty and rounded, in a sweet-fruited style with concentrated, peachy, spicy flavours, fresh and lively, a subtle seasoning of oak, and an off-dry finish. Showing excellent personality and harmony, it should be at its best now to 2017.

MED/DRY $48 –V

Greylands Ridge Central Otago Blanc de Noir

The 2014 vintage (★★★☆) is a single-vineyard white wine, made from Pinot Noir and partly French oak-aged. Mouthfilling, it has good depth of citrusy, slightly spicy and nutty flavours, a touch of complexity and a slightly creamy finish.

MED/DRY $20 –V

Hans Herzog Marlborough Mistral   ★★★★★

The delicious 2013 vintage (★★★★★) is a blend of traditional Rhône Valley grape varieties – Viognier (mostly), Marsanne and Roussanne. Fermented with indigenous yeasts and matured for 18 months in French oak puncheons, it is powerful, fleshy and dry, with highly concentrated, ripe stone-fruit flavours to the fore, finely integrated oak, and a very harmonious, slightly buttery, lasting finish. Certified organic.

Vintage	13	12
WR	7	7
Drink	16-23	16-22

DRY $53 AV

Hunky Dory The Tangle   ★★★

From Huia, the 2014 vintage (★★★☆) is an attractive Marlborough blend of Pinot Gris (55 per cent), Gewürztraminer (35 per cent) and Riesling (10 per cent). Freshly scented, it is mouthfilling, with good depth of peach, pear, lychee and spice flavours and a dry (3.5 grams/ litre of residual sugar) finish. Enjoyable from the start, it's an ideal 'all-purpose' wine. Certified organic.

Vintage	14
WR	6
Drink	16-18

DRY $18 AV

Kaimira Estate Nelson Hui Katoa   (★★★★)

Certified organic, the pale lemon/green 2015 vintage (★★★★) is a 'white aromatic blend'. The bouquet is floral; the palate is mouthfilling, with generous, youthful flavours of peaches, lychees, pears and spices, fresh and dryish (5 grams/litre of residual sugar). Best drinking mid-2017+.

MED/DRY $25 AV

Kaipara Estate Nine Lakes   ★★★☆

Estate-grown on the South Head peninsula of the Kaipara Harbour, this is a barrel-aged, Chardonnay-based wine, with smaller portions of such varieties as Pinot Gris, Arneis and Viognier. The 2014 vintage (★★★☆) is a light gold, mouthfilling, slightly toasty wine with strong, peachy, slightly honeyed flavours, a touch of sweetness (5 grams/litre of residual sugar) and lots of drink-young appeal.

MED/DRY $36 –V

Man O' War Gravestone ★★★★

The 2013 vintage (★★★★☆) is an age-worthy blend of Sauvignon Blanc (70 per cent) and Sémillon (30 per cent), grown at the eastern end of Waiheke Island and partly barrel-fermented. Mouthfilling, with ripely herbaceous flavours, a hint of toasty oak, and excellent concentration, drive and complexity, it should be at its best during 2017.

DRY $33 –V

Peter Yealands Marlborough PGR (★★★)

The 2015 vintage (★★★) is an 'aromatic blend' of Pinot Gris, Gewürztraminer and Riesling. Lemon-scented, it is medium-bodied, with vibrant, citrusy, slightly peachy and spicy flavours, a sliver of sweetness (7 grams/litre of residual sugar), balanced acidity, and an easy-drinking appeal.

Vintage	15
WR	7
Drink	16-18

MED/DRY $16 V+

Quest Farm Alpino Central Otago Vin Gris ★★★☆

Made entirely from Pinot Noir, the 2014 vintage (★★★☆) is a pale pink, fully dry wine with vibrant strawberry, peach and spice flavours, mouthfilling, crisp and lively. Still fresh and lively, it's ready to roll.

DRY $21 AV

Ransom Matakana Compleat Pig (★★★★)

The very distinctive 2015 vintage (★★★★) is an 'orange' wine, made from Pinot Gris grapes left on their skins for a week, then drained to seasoned oak barrels for the rest of the fermentation (with indigenous yeasts) and several months of lees-aging. Pale orange, it is mouthfilling, with strong, peachy, spicy flavours, dry, lively and lingering. It's already drinking well.

DRY $27 –V

Richmond Plains Nelson Blanc de Noir ★★★☆

Certified organic, the fruity 2016 vintage (★★★☆) is a faintly pink wine, made from hand-picked Pinot Noir. Freshly aromatic, it's a very easy-drinking style, with good depth of vibrant, peachy, slightly spicy flavours and a smooth (9.5 grams/litre of residual sugar) finish. A summertime charmer.

MED/DRY $23 AV

Seresin Chiaroscuro ★★★★★

This certified-organic wine is a full-bodied blend of Chardonnay (for 'structure'), Pinot Gris (for 'texture') and Riesling (for 'fruity acidity'). Estate-grown in Marlborough, hand-picked and fermented with indigenous yeasts in old oak puncheons, the 2012 vintage (★★★★☆) is mouthfilling and vibrantly fruity, with strong, peachy, citrusy, slightly spicy and buttery flavours, woven with fresh acidity, good complexity and a long, tight finish. A wine of strong personality, it's ready to roll.

Vintage	12	11	10
WR	6	7	7
Drink	16-18	16-18	16-17

DRY $65 AV

Sileni Estate Selection Hawke's Bay Alba   (★★★★)

The debut 2015 vintage (★★★★) is an unusual blend of hand-picked Chardonnay, Muscat, Pinot Gris, Sauvignon Blanc and Viognier, hand-picked – mostly at Mangatahi and Te Awanga – and barrel-aged for five months. Weighty and dry (3 grams/litre of residual sugar), it's a fruit-driven style, with very fresh, citrusy, appley, slightly spicy flavours, showing good intensity and vigour. Still youthful, it should be at its best mid-2017+.

Vintage	15
WR	7
Drink	16-25

DRY $33 –V

Supernatural, The   (★★★★)

The distinctive 2014 vintage (★★★★), promoted as an 'old style wine from the New World', is an estate-grown, Hawke's Bay Sauvignon Blanc, closed with a crown seal, rather than a screwcap or cork. A powerful, mouthfilling, dry wine with lively, ripe flavours, it is fleshy, with concentrated melon, lime, peach and herb flavours, showing good complexity. (From Millar Road.)

DRY $28 –V

Terra Sancta Mysterious Diggings Mysterious White   ★★★☆

The 2014 vintage (★★★☆) is a blend of Muscat, Gewürztraminer, Pinot Gris and Riesling, estate-grown and co-harvested at Bannockburn, in Central Otago, and partly (10 per cent) fermented in old oak puncheons. It is mouthfilling, vibrantly fruity and dry (4.7 grams/litre of residual sugar), with youthful citrus-fruit, pear, lychee and spice flavours, showing a touch of complexity. Best drinking 2017.

DRY $25 –V

Wooing Tree Blondie   ★★★☆

This 'blanc de noir' – a white (or rather faintly pink) Central Otago wine – is estate-grown at Cromwell. It is made from hand-picked Pinot Noir grapes; the juice is held briefly in contact with the skins and then fermented in tanks. The 2015 vintage (★★★☆) is a pale pink, mouthfilling, smooth wine with lively peach, strawberry and spice flavours, vague sweetness, balanced acidity, and lots of drink-young appeal. The 2016 vintage (★★★☆) is pale, with the merest hint of pink. Still very youthful, it is fresh and smooth (5.2 grams/litre of residual sugar), with good body and depth of delicate, peachy, spicy flavours.

MED/DRY $28 –V

Yealands Estate Single Vineyard Awatere Valley Marlborough PGR   ★★★★

The 2015 vintage (★★★★) is a blend of Pinot Gris, Gewürztraminer and Riesling, estate-grown at Seaview, in the lower Awatere Valley. Scented and mouthfilling, it is a vibrantly fruity, off-dry wine (5.5 grams/litre of residual sugar), with generous, citrusy, peachy flavours, spicy notes, and excellent delicacy and length.

Vintage	15	14
WR	7	7
Drink	16-18	16-18

MED/DRY $23 AV

Breidecker

A nondescript crossing of Müller-Thurgau and the white hybrid Seibel 7053, Breidecker is rarely seen in New Zealand. There were 32 hectares of bearing vines recorded in 2003, but only 0.6 hectares in 2016 (in Otago and Marlborough). Its early-ripening ability is an advantage in cooler regions, but Breidecker typically yields light, fresh quaffing wines, best drunk young.

Hunter's Marlborough Breidecker   ★★★

A drink-young charmer, 'for those who are new to wine'. Grown in the Wairau Valley, this wine is typically floral, light and lively, with a splash of sweetness, fresh acidity and ripe, citrusy, slightly peachy and spicy flavours.

MED/DRY $18 AV

Chardonnay

Do you drink Chardonnay? Sauvignon Blanc is our biggest-selling white-wine variety by far, and Pinot Gris is riding high, but neither of these popular grapes produces New Zealand's greatest dry whites. Chardonnay wears that crown. It's less fashionable than 20 or 30 years ago, but Chardonnay is our most prestigious white-wine variety. No other dry whites can command such lofty prices; many New Zealand Chardonnays are on the shelves at $50 or more. And although it has lost ground to Sauvignon Blanc and Pinot Gris, Chardonnay is still a big seller. Winegrowers are currently reporting a surge in sales, suggesting that Chardonnay is coming back into fashion. However, New Zealand Chardonnay has yet to make the huge international impact of our Sauvignon Blanc. Our top Chardonnays are classy, but so are those from a host of other countries in the Old and New Worlds. In 2015, Chardonnay accounted for 2.5 per cent by volume of New Zealand's wine exports (far behind Sauvignon Blanc, with over 86 per cent). There's an enormous range to choose from. Most wineries – especially in the North Island and upper South Island – make at least one Chardonnay; many produce several and the big wineries produce dozens. The hallmark of New Zealand Chardonnays is their delicious varietal intensity – the leading labels show notably concentrated aromas and flavours, threaded with fresh, appetising acidity.

The price of New Zealand Chardonnay ranges from under $10 to over $100. The quality differences are equally wide, although not always in relation to their prices. Lower-priced wines are typically fermented in stainless steel tanks and bottled young with little or no oak influence; these wines rely on fresh, lemony, uncluttered fruit flavours for their appeal. Chardonnays labelled as 'unoaked' were briefly popular a few years ago, as winemakers with an eye on overseas markets worked hard to showcase New Zealand's fresh, vibrant fruit characters. But without oak flavours to add richness and complexity, Chardonnay handled entirely in stainless steel tanks can be plain – even boring. The key to the style is to use well-ripened, intensely flavoured grapes.

Mid-price wines may be fermented in tanks and matured in oak casks, which adds to their complexity and richness, or fermented and/or matured in a mix of tanks and barrels (or handled entirely in tanks, with oak chips or staves suspended in the wine). The top labels are fully fermented and matured in oak barrels (normally French barriques, with varying proportions of new casks); there may also be extended aging on (and regular stirring of) yeast lees and varying proportions of a secondary, softening malolactic fermentation (sometimes referred to in the tasting notes as 'malo'). The best of these display the arresting subtlety and depth of flavour for which Chardonnay is so highly prized.

Chardonnay plantings have been far outstripped in recent years by Sauvignon Blanc, as wine producers respond to overseas demand, and in 2017 will constitute 8.9 per cent of the bearing vineyard. The variety is spread throughout the wine regions, particularly Marlborough (where 34 per cent of the vines are concentrated), Hawke's Bay (32 per cent) and Gisborne (22 per cent). Gisborne is renowned for its softly mouthfilling, ripe, peachy Chardonnays, which offer very seductive drinking in their youth; Hawke's Bay yields sturdy wines with rich grapefruit-like flavours, power and longevity; and Marlborough's Chardonnays are slightly leaner in a cool-climate, appetisingly crisp style.

Chardonnay has often been dubbed 'the red-wine drinker's white wine'. Chardonnays are usually (although not always, especially cheap models) fully dry, as are all reds with any aspirations to quality. Chardonnay's typically mouthfilling body and multi-faceted flavours are another obvious red-wine parallel.

Broaching a top New Zealand Chardonnay at less than two years old can be unrewarding – the finest of the 2014s will offer excellent drinking during 2017–2018. If you must drink Chardonnay when it is only a year old, it makes sense to buy one of the cheaper, less complex wines specifically designed to be enjoyable in their youth.

Aitken's Folly Riverbank Road The Reserved Barrel
Wanaka Central Otago Chardonnay (★★★★)

Well worth cellaring, the 2014 vintage (★★★★) was estate-grown, barrel-fermented and oak-aged for 18 months (compared to 10 months for the 'standard' wine). Pale straw, it is mouthfilling, with strong, citrusy, slightly peachy flavours, firm acid spine, and a long, steely, slightly toasty finish. Best drinking 2018+.

DRY $35 –V

Aitken's Folly Riverbank Road Wanaka Central Otago Chardonnay (★★★★)

The 2014 vintage (★★★★) is the only wine in the country based solely on Chardonnay clone 548. Estate-grown, it was fermented in French oak barriques (30 per cent new), given a full, softening malolactic fermentation, and barrel-aged for 10 months. Lemon-scented, it is a distinctly cool-climate, tightly structured style, with very good vigour and intensity of citrusy, slightly buttery flavours, showing good complexity. Still developing, it should be at its best mid-2017+.

DRY $28 AV

Akarua Central Otago Chardonnay ★★★★

The estate-grown 2014 vintage (★★★★) was hand-harvested at Bannockburn and fermented and matured in French oak barrels (10 per cent new). Mouthfilling, it is creamy and biscuity, with youthful, grapefruit-like flavours to the fore, fresh acidity, a hint of spice, and good complexity and length. Subtle and finely poised, it should be at its best 2017+.

Vintage	14	13	12
WR	6	6	6
Drink	16-21	16-20	16-19

DRY $29 AV

Ake Ake Northland Chardonnay (★★★☆)

The 2014 vintage (★★★☆) was fermented and matured for eight months, with weekly lees-stirring, in French and American oak casks (new and seasoned). It has a nutty bouquet, leading into a mouthfilling, dry wine with strong, ripe, peachy, toasty flavours, balanced acidity, and a slightly buttery finish. Best drinking mid-2016+.

DRY $25 –V

Alexandra Wine Company Feraud's Central Otago Chardonnay ★★★☆

The 2014 vintage (★★★☆) was hand-picked and matured in French oak casks (35 per cent new). A mouthfilling, ripe wine with good depth of citrusy, peachy, toasty flavours, it shows considerable complexity, with a smooth, slightly buttery finish.

DRY $22 AV

Allan Scott Generations Marlborough Chardonnay (★★★★)

The debut 2015 vintage (★★★★) is an upfront style, estate-grown in the Wallops Vineyard and matured for 16 months in French oak puncheons (80 per cent new). Light lemon/green, it has a creamy bouquet, leading into a mouthfilling, sweet-fruited, slightly buttery, smoothly textured wine, with ripe, peachy, toasty flavours, showing very good depth and complexity.

DRY $31 –V

Alpha Domus AD Hawke's Bay Chardonnay ★★★★☆

The 2014 vintage (★★★★☆), estate-grown and hand-harvested in the Bridge Pa Triangle, was fermented and matured for a year in French oak casks (60 per cent new). Pale yellow, it is powerful and fleshy, with ripe grapefruit and stone-fruit flavours, woven with fresh acidity, mealy and creamy notes adding complexity, and excellent depth and harmony. Best drinking 2017+.

 DRY $38 –V

Alpha Domus First Solo Hawke's Bay Chardonnay ★★★★

The generous 2014 vintage (★★★★) was estate-grown in the Bridge Pa Triangle and French oak-fermented (25 per cent new.) Fleshy and sweet-fruited, it is slightly toasty and creamy, with strong, ripe, citrusy, peachy flavours and a well-rounded finish.

Vintage	14	13	12	11
WR	7	7	6	5
Drink	16-18	16-17	P	P

 DRY $26 AV

Alpha Domus The Pilot Hawke's Bay Chardonnay (★★★)

The 2014 vintage (★★★) was estate-grown in the Bridge Pa Triangle, partly hand-harvested and made with 'subtle' oak characters. Fresh and lively, it's a mouthfilling, fruit-driven style with ripe, citrusy, slightly buttery flavours, enjoyable young.

 DRY $22 –V

Anchorage Family Estate Nelson Chardonnay ★★☆

The 2014 vintage (★★☆) is a medium-bodied wine, made in a vibrant, 'fruit-driven' style with crisp, lemony, slightly buttery flavours.

DRY $19 –V

Anchorage Family Estate Reserve Nelson Chardonnay ★★★☆

Made in an upfront style, the good-value 2014 vintage (★★★☆) is a single-vineyard wine, barrel-fermented. Pale straw, it is mouthfilling, with strong, peachy, slightly toasty flavours and a creamy-smooth finish. Drink now to 2017.

 DRY $18 V+

Ant Moore Signature Series Marlborough Chardonnay (★★★☆)

The powerful, fleshy 2013 vintage (★★★☆) is a pale gold, moderately complex style with creamy and buttery notes, a slightly oily texture and some richness.

 DRY $27 –V

Archangel Central Otago Chardonnay ★★★☆

The 2014 vintage (★★★☆) has a creamy, biscuity bouquet. The palate shows good depth of peachy, citrusy, slightly spicy flavours, with nutty notes and considerable complexity. Best drinking 2017+.

Vintage	14	13
WR	7	6
Drink	16-20	16-18

 DRY $26 –V

Aronui Single Vineyard Nelson Chardonnay   ★★★★

The creamy-textured 2014 vintage (★★★★) was hand-picked and French oak-fermented. Mouthfilling, it shows good complexity, with youthful, ripe, peachy, slightly toasty flavours, balanced acidity and excellent depth and harmony. (From Kono, also owner of the Tohu brand.)

DRY $25 AV

Ash Ridge Estate Hawke's Bay Chardonnay   ★★★★

Priced sharply, the 2015 vintage (★★★☆) was estate-grown in the Bridge Pa Triangle, fully barrel-fermented, and 50 per cent of the blend went through a secondary malolactic fermentation. Enjoyable from the start, it is medium to full-bodied, with ripe, peachy, slightly toasty flavours, showing considerable complexity, and good depth. Best drinking mid-2017+.

DRY $20 V+

Ash Ridge Vintners Reserve Chardonnay   (★★★★☆)

Estate-grown in the Bridge Pa Triangle, the 2014 vintage (★★★★☆) has a stronger seasoning of new oak than its lower-priced stablemate under the 'Estate' label. A mouthfilling, rich wine with the power to age, it has generous, ripe stone-fruit flavours, good complexity and a finely textured finish. Open 2017+.

DRY $35 –V

Ashwell Martinborough Chardonnay   ★★★★

Barrique-fermented, the 2015 vintage (★★★★) has a fragrant, nutty bouquet. Mouthfilling and sweet-fruited, it has generous, ripe, peachy flavours, showing good freshness and complexity. Enjoyable young, it is well worth cellaring; best drinking mid-2017+.

Vintage	15
WR	5
Drink	16-20

DRY $28 AV

Ashwood Estate Gisborne Chardonnay   ★★★★

The impressive 2013 vintage (★★★★☆) is a single-vineyard wine, hand-picked at Hexton and fermented in French oak casks (30 per cent new). The bouquet is fragrant and complex; the palate is mouthfilling, with ripe stone-fruit flavours and buttery, toasty notes adding complexity. Powerful, weighty and concentrated, it should reward cellaring.

DRY $29 AV

Askerne Hawke's Bay Chardonnay   ★★★

Fleshy and high-flavoured, the 2014 vintage (★★★★) was estate-grown, hand-picked and matured for nine months in seasoned French and Hungarian oak barrels. Mouthfilling and sweet-fruited, it has generous stone-fruit flavours, oak complexity and a well-rounded finish. The 2015 vintage (★★☆), fully barrel-fermented, is a solid, slightly honeyed wine.

DRY $22 –V

Askerne Reserve Hawke's Bay Chardonnay ★★★★☆

The 2014 vintage (★★★★) is a classic regional style. Hand-picked and barrel-fermented (45 per cent new oak), it is fleshy and sweet-fruited, with generous, peachy flavours, finely integrated oak adding complexity, and a well-rounded finish. Retasted in mid-2016, it's maturing well.

DRY $30 AV

Astrolabe Province Marlborough Chardonnay ★★★☆

The 2014 vintage (★★★★) was hand-harvested in the Wairau Valley and Southern Valleys, and fermented and matured for 10 months in French oak barriques and puncheons. Mouthfilling and creamy-textured, it has strong, peachy, slightly buttery and nutty flavours, gentle acidity, and good complexity and harmony.

DRY $24 AV

Ata Rangi Craighall Martinborough Chardonnay ★★★★★

This memorable Martinborough wine has notable richness, complexity and downright drinkability. From a company-owned block of low-yielding Mendoza-clone vines in the Craighall Vineyard, planted in 1983, it is hand-picked, whole-bunch pressed and fermented with indigenous yeasts in French oak barriques (typically 25 per cent new). Light lemon/green, the graceful 2015 vintage (★★★★★) is mouthfilling, sweet-fruited and vibrantly fruity, with concentrated, very youthful, grapefruit and peach flavours, mealy and biscuity notes adding complexity, and a fragrant, slightly smoky bouquet. It should be long-lived; open 2018 onwards.

Vintage	14	13	12	11	10
WR	7	7	6	7	7
Drink	16-22	16-21	16-19	16-19	16-18

DRY $38 AV

Ata Rangi Petrie Wairarapa Chardonnay ★★★★☆

This single-vineyard wine is grown at East Taratahi, south of Masterton, in the Wairarapa. Based on mature vines (over 20 years old), it is hand-picked and fermented and lees-aged in French oak casks. Lemon-hued, the youthful 2015 vintage (★★★★☆) is mouthfilling, with strong, vibrant grapefruit and peach flavours, biscuity and buttery notes adding complexity, fresh acidity and a finely poised finish. Best drinking mid-2017+.

DRY $28 V+

Ataahua Waipara Chardonnay ★★★★

The 2015 vintage (★★★★☆) is fragrant, with a slightly buttery bouquet. A high-flavoured, sweet-fruited wine, it was barrel-fermented and given a full, softening malolactic fermentation. Mouthfilling, with generous, peachy, slightly spicy and mealy flavours, a hint of butterscotch and good complexity, it is well worth cellaring, but already delicious.

DRY $30 –V

Auntsfield Cob Cottage Southern Valleys Marlborough Chardonnay   ★★★★★

This single 'block' – rather than just single 'vineyard' – wine is estate-grown on the south side of the Wairau Valley. The 2014 vintage (★★★★★) is powerful, weighty and sweet-fruited. Matured for 10 months in French oak casks (35 per cent new), it is light lemon/green, with highly concentrated, ripe stone-fruit flavours, youthful, complex and lasting. Best drinking 2018+.

Vintage	14
WR	6
Drink	16-24

DRY $49 AV

Auntsfield Single Vineyard Southern Valleys Marlborough Chardonnay   ★★★★★

This consistently rewarding wine is estate-grown on the south side of the Wairau Valley, hand-picked and fermented and matured in French oak barrels (18 per cent new in 2014). The 2014 vintage (★★★★☆) is light lemon/green, with a slightly creamy bouquet. Mouthfilling, it is tightly structured, with strong, peachy, slightly appley and smoky flavours, woven with fresh acidity, well-integrated oak adding complexity, and a lingering finish.

Vintage	14	13	12	11	10
WR	7	7	6	7	6
Drink	16-20	16-20	16-19	16-18	16-17

DRY $33 AV

Aurum Central Otago Chardonnay   ★★★★

Already drinking well, the 2014 vintage (★★★★) is a creamy-textured wine, fermented with indigenous yeasts and barrel-aged for 16 months (20 per cent new). It has strong, citrusy, appley, slightly peachy flavours, showing good complexity, balanced acidity, and a rounded, lingering finish.

DRY $45 –V

Awatere River by Louis Vavasour Marlborough Chardonnay   (★★★★)

The 2014 vintage (★★★★) is a mouthfilling, high-flavoured wine, fermented and matured in French oak casks (25 per cent new). Drinking well young, but worth cellaring, it has good concentration of fresh, peachy, toasty flavours, a hint of butterscotch, and firm acid spine.

DRY $32 –V

Babich Family Estates Gimblett Gravels Chardonnay   ★★★☆

Fermented in tanks and casks, this is designed as an elegant, fruit-driven style with some complexity. The 2013 vintage (★★★★) is a stylish, full-bodied wine with a citrusy, savoury bouquet. Weighty, with vibrant, grapefruit-like flavours, gently seasoned with toasty oak, it shows excellent vigour, intensity and complexity.

Vintage	13	12	11
WR	7	5	6
Drink	16-17	P	P

DRY $25 –V

Babich Family Estates Headwaters Organic Marlborough Chardonnay ★★★★

The 2015 vintage (★★★★☆), certified organic, has an invitingly fragrant, slightly creamy and nutty bouquet. A youthful, fleshy wine, it has generous, ripe, peachy, citrusy and slightly spicy flavours, showing good complexity, a minerally streak, and excellent vigour, depth and harmony. Best drinking 2018+.

 DRY $27 AV

Babich Hawke's Bay Chardonnay ★★★☆

The 2015 vintage (★★★) is an unoaked style. Grown at Fernhill and in the Gimblett Gravels, it is mouthfilling, fleshy and slightly creamy-textured, with generous, ripe stone-fruit flavours, showing very good balance and depth. Drink now or cellar.

 DRY $22 AV

Babich Irongate Chardonnay ★★★★★

Babich's flagship Chardonnay. A stylish wine, Irongate was traditionally markedly leaner and tighter than other top Hawke's Bay Chardonnays, while performing well in the cellar, but the latest releases have more drink-young appeal. It is based on hand-picked fruit from the shingly Irongate Vineyard in Gimblett Road, fully barrel-fermented (about 20 per cent new), and lees-matured for up to 10 months. Malolactic fermentation was very rare up to the 2002, but has since exerted a growing influence. The 2014 vintage (★★★★☆) is still very youthful. Fleshy and rounded, it has strong, ripe, peachy, slightly mealy and toasty flavours, subtle, finely textured and very harmonious, with a long finish. Open 2017+.

Vintage	14	13	12	11
WR	6	7	4	6
Drink	16-25	16-25	16-18	16-20

 DRY $37 AV

Beach House Hawke's Bay Chardonnay ★★★★

The attractive 2013 vintage (★★★★) is a regional blend. Barrel-fermented, it has strong, crisp, grapefruit-like flavours to the fore and a subtle oak seasoning. An elegant, vibrantly fruity wine, it's a drink-now or cellaring proposition.

 DRY $25 AV

Beach House Levels Hawke's Bay Chardonnay (★★★★☆)

The tightly structured 2013 vintage (★★★★☆) is a single-vineyard wine, grown at Te Awanga and barrel-fermented. It has fresh, rich grapefruit and stone-fruit flavours, showing excellent depth, delicacy and complexity. Best drinking 2016 onwards.

 DRY $35 –V

Beach House Track Gimblett Gravels Chardonnay (★★★★★)

The 2013 vintage (★★★★★) was estate-grown and hand-picked in Mere Road, and matured for 10 months in two French oak puncheons and a new French oak barrique. A classy, vibrantly fruity and finely poised wine, likely to be long-lived, it has concentrated, peachy, citrusy flavours, balanced toasty oak, and excellent structure and length. Best drinking 2016 onwards.

DRY $35 AV

Bell Bird Bay Reserve Hawke's Bay Chardonnay   (★★★)

The easy-drinking 2014 vintage (★★★) was grown in the Bridge Pa Triangle and matured on its yeast lees for 10 months, with some use of French oak. Light lemon/green, it is mouthfilling and sweet-fruited, with fresh, ripe, peachy flavours to the fore, buttery notes and a smooth finish. (From Alpha Domus.)

DRY $23 –V

Bent Duck Bay of Islands Chardonnay   ★★★☆

The 2014 vintage (★★★☆) of this Northland wine was barrel-fermented and oak-aged for nine months. Made in an upfront style, it is weighty and fleshy, with generous, ripe stone-fruit flavours, a toasty oak influence and a slightly creamy finish. (From Byrne Wines.)

DRY $25 –V

Bilancia Hawke's Bay Chardonnay   ★★★★★

The 2014 vintage (★★★★★) was fermented and matured in French oak puncheons. Highly fragrant, it is mouthfilling and creamy-textured, with concentrated, ripe stone-fruit flavours, gently enriched with biscuity oak, excellent complexity, balanced acidity and a well-rounded, persistent finish. Best drinking 2017+.

Vintage	14	13
WR	6	7
Drink	16-20	16-18

DRY $35 AV

Bishop's Head Waipara Valley Chardonnay   (★★★★)

The 2014 vintage (★★★★) is an elegant, tightly structured wine. Hand-picked, fermented with indigenous yeasts in French oak barrels (30 per cent new) and lees-aged for 11 months, it is medium to full-bodied, with vibrant, citrusy, slightly buttery flavours, good acid spine, and mealy, biscuity notes adding complexity. Drink now or cellar.

DRY $30 –V

Black Barn Barrel Fermented Chardonnay   ★★★★☆

Grown on the Havelock North hills, hand-picked and barrel-fermented, this is typically a classy wine, in a classic regional style. The refined 2013 vintage (★★★★☆) is weighty and rich, with concentrated, ripe stone-fruit flavours, buttery, mealy and toasty notes adding complexity, and a rounded finish.

DRY $35 –V

Black Barn Reserve Hawke's Bay Chardonnay   ★★★★☆

Estate-grown and hand-picked at Havelock North, the 2013 vintage (★★★★) was fermented with indigenous yeasts and barrel-aged for nine months. It's a vibrant, citrusy, oak-influenced wine with good concentration and complexity, and a rich, rounded finish.

DRY $50 –V

Black Cottage Reserve Marlborough Chardonnay   (★★★☆)

Offffering good value, the 2014 vintage (★★★☆) is a single-vineyard wine, hand-picked and fermented and matured for 11 months in French oak barrels. Full-bodied, it has very good depth of peachy, citrusy, slightly mealy and buttery flavours, showing considerable complexity, and a rounded finish.

 DRY $18 V+

Black Estate Home Chardonnay   ★★★★☆

The impressive 2015 vintage (★★★★★) was grown in the Home Vineyard at Omihi, in Waipara, planted in 1994. Hand-picked, fermented with indigenous yeasts in French oak barrels of varying sizes (15 per cent new), and given a full, softening malolactic fermentation, it is fragrant, fresh and finely balanced, with strong drink-young appeal. Vibrantly fruity, with concentrated, peachy, citrusy flavours, a subtle seasoning of toasty oak, a hint of butterscotch, appetising acidity and a lingering finish, it's a very 'complete' wine, already delicious. Best drinking 2018+.

 DRY $42 –V

Black Estate Netherwood Waipara Valley Chardonnay   ★★★★☆

The 2015 vintage (★★★★★) was grown on a south-facing block in the Netherwood Vineyard at Omihi, planted in 1986 and now owned by Black Estate. A rare wine (49 cases only), it was hand-picked, fermented with indigenous yeasts in old French oak casks, given a full, softening malolactic fermentation, and bottled unfined and unfiltered. A highly distinctive, thought-provoking wine, it is minerally, citrusy and gently oaked, in a restrained, subtle style with good intensity and a long, crisp finish. Still very youthful, it is tightly structured and should be long-lived.

 DRY $65 –V

Black Estate Waipara Valley Chardonnay   ★★★★☆

The 2013 vintage (★★★★★) was estate-grown, hand-picked at 23.7 brix from 18-year-old vines, and fermented with indigenous yeasts in French oak barriques and puncheons (15 per cent new). Bright yellow, with a slightly smoky bouquet, it is rich, with fresh acidity threaded through its concentrated, vibrant, peachy flavours, which show excellent drive, complexity and length. Well worth cellaring.

 DRY $38 –V

Blackenbrook Family Reserve Nelson Chardonnay   ★★★★

The powerful 2014 vintage (★★★★) was matured for a year in American oak casks (43 per cent new). Pale straw, it has substantial body (15 per cent alcohol), with generous, peachy, citrusy flavours, strongly seasoned with oak, considerable complexity and a creamy-smooth finish. If you like a bold style of Chardonnay, try this.

DRY $38 –V

Blackenbrook Nelson Chardonnay ★★★★

The 2015 vintage (★★★★) is a sturdy wine, estate-grown, hand-picked and partly fermented and matured in French and American oak barrels. Light lemon/green, it is fresh and generous, with vibrant, citrusy, peachy, slightly biscuity flavours, showing good complexity, and a finely textured finish. Best drinking mid-2017+.

DRY $25 AV

Boneline, The, Sharkstone Waipara Chardonnay (★★★★★)

Showing excellent cellaring potential, the 2014 vintage (★★★★★) was hand-picked and matured in French oak barrels (20 per cent new). Mouthfilling, rich and finely balanced, it is youthful, with good weight, strong grapefruit and peach flavours, fresh acidity, a hint of butterscotch and a crisp, slightly creamy, lingering finish.

DRY $35 AV

Boundary Vineyards Tuki Tuki Road Hawke's Bay Chardonnay ★★★☆

Pernod Ricard NZ's wine is grown near the coast, at Te Awanga, fermented in Hungarian oak barriques, and much of the blend is given a softening malolactic fermentation. The 2015 vintage (★★★★) is a great buy. Bright, light yellow, it is mouthfilling and vibrantly fruity, with good concentration of peach and grapefruit flavours, a hint of butterscotch and a tight finish. Drink now or cellar.

DRY $20 AV

Brancott Estate Letter Series 'O' Marlborough Chardonnay ★★★★★

Named after the company's Omaka Vineyard, this typically refined wine is hand-picked at sites on the south side of the Wairau Valley, fermented with indigenous yeasts in French oak barriques (about 40 per cent new), and given a full, softening malolactic fermentation. The 2015 vintage (★★★★☆) has a fragrant, complex, nutty bouquet. Already very expressive, it is full-bodied, with very generous, ripe, peachy, slightly buttery and toasty flavours, showing excellent concentration and complexity. Drink now or cellar.

DRY $33 V+

Brancott Estate Marlborough Chardonnay (★★★☆)

Priced sharply, the 2015 vintage (★★★☆) is already drinking well. Full-bodied, it has peachy, slightly spicy and creamy flavours, showing good depth, a touch of complexity and a well-rounded finish.

DRY $17 V+

Brancott Estate Terroir Series Southern Valleys Marlborough Chardonnay (★★★★)

Delicious young, the debut 2014 vintage (★★★★) was grown in the Southern Valleys sub-region and fermented and matured for seven months in large new French oak cuves. Full-bodied, dry and sweet-fruited, it has strong, citrusy, peachy flavours, slightly buttery and smooth, a subtle seasoning of oak, and excellent depth and harmony.

DRY $20 V+

Brightside Nelson Chardonnay ★★★

From Kaimira, the 2014 vintage (★★★) was fermented in a 50:50 split of tanks and barrels. Light lemon/green, it is fresh, with good depth of citrusy, peachy, slightly nutty flavours, showing a touch of complexity. The 2015 vintage (★★★), also 50 per cent barrel-fermented, is mouthfilling, with peachy, slightly buttery flavours, fresh acidity and a smooth finish. Certified organic.

 DRY $18 AV

Brightwater Vineyards Lord Rutherford Barrique Chardonnay ★★★★☆

The 2013 vintage (★★★★☆) is a single-vineyard wine, hand-picked and fermented in French oak barriques (25 per cent new). Light lemon/green, it is fragrant and mouthfilling, with concentrated, youthful, citrusy, peachy flavours, integrated oak, and a tightly structured finish. Well worth cellaring.

Vintage	13	12	11	10
WR	6	7	NM	7
Drink	16-19	16-18	NM	P

 DRY $40 –V

Brightwater Vineyards Nelson Chardonnay ★★★★

The 2014 vintage (★★★★) was estate-grown, hand-picked, and fermented and matured for 11 months in French oak barriques (20 per cent new). Light lemon/green, it is mouthfilling and vibrantly fruity, with peach and grapefruit flavours, showing good concentration, a gentle seasoning of toasty oak, and a slightly buttery finish.

Vintage	14
WR	6
Drink	16-17

 DRY $25 AV

Brodie Estate Martinborough Chardonnay ★★★★

The 2015 vintage (★★★☆) was fermented and lees-aged in oak barrels (20 per cent new). Softly mouthfilling, it has good depth of fresh, ripe, peachy, slightly toasty flavours, showing considerable complexity, and a creamy-smooth finish.

 DRY $30 –V

Bronte Nelson Chardonnay (★★★☆)

From Rimu Grove, the 2015 vintage (★★★☆) is drinking well in its youth. Grown at Moutere and French oak-matured, it is full-bodied and moderately complex, with very good depth of citrusy, slightly peachy flavours, fresh acidity and a slightly buttery finish.

Vintage	15
WR	7
Drink	16-26

DRY $24 AV

Brookfields Bergman Chardonnay   ★★★☆

Named after the Ingrid Bergman roses in the estate garden, this wine is grown alongside the winery at Meeanee, in Hawke's Bay, hand-picked, and fermented and matured on its yeast lees in seasoned French and American oak casks. The 2015 vintage (★★★☆) is mouthfilling, with very good depth of youthful, peachy, slightly toasty flavours, showing considerable complexity. Best drinking mid-2017+.

Vintage	15	DRY $20 AV
WR	7	
Drink	18-20	

Brookfields Marshall Bank Chardonnay   ★★★★☆

Brookfields' top Chardonnay is named after proprietor Peter Robertson's grandfather's property in Otago. Grown in a vineyard adjacent to the winery at Meeanee and fermented and matured (with weekly stirring of its yeast lees) in French oak barriques (50 per cent new in 2015), it is a powerful, classy, concentrated Hawke's Bay wine. The 2015 vintage (★★★★☆), oak-matured for 10 months, is still very youthful. Fragrant, with rich, citrusy, peachy, biscuity, nutty flavours, ripe and rounded, it is savoury and complex, with obvious potential; best drinking 2018+.

Vintage	15	DRY $30 AV
WR	7	
Drink	18-21	

Byrne Northland Chardonnay   ★★★★

The attractive 2014 vintage (★★★★) was grown in the Fat Pig Vineyard and fermented with indigenous yeasts in French and American oak barriques (two-thirds new). It has a sweetly oaked bouquet, leading into a full-bodied wine with concentrated, ripe stone-fruit flavours, seasoned with toasty oak. Showing good weight, depth and texture, it's an age-worthy wine with balanced acidity and good complexity. The 2015 vintage (★★★★☆), labelled 'Puketotara Chardonnay', is even better. Light lemon/green, it is mouthfilling, concentrated and finely structured, with ripe stone-fruit flavours, seasoned with toasty oak, fresh acidity, good harmony and a lingering finish. Best drinking mid-2017+.

 DRY $29 AV

C.J. Pask Chardonnays – see Pask

Cable Bay Awatere Valley Marlborough Chardonnay   (★★★☆)

The 2014 vintage (★★★☆) is a fruit-driven style, mostly handled in tanks; 12 per cent of the blend was fermented and matured in new French oak barrels. Fresh, lively and weighty, it has citrusy, slightly appley flavours and a finely textured, slightly creamy finish.

Vintage	14	DRY $25 –V
WR	5	
Drink	16-25	

Cable Bay Waiheke Chardonnay ★★★★

Blended from three estate vineyards at the western end of the island, the 2015 vintage (★★★★) was fermented and matured for a year in French oak puncheons (20 per cent new). A youthful, creamy-textured wine, it is medium-bodied, with lively, citrusy, appley, mealy, slightly biscuity flavours, showing very good depth, vigour and complexity. Best drinking 2018+.

Vintage	15
WR	6
Drink	16-24

 DRY $45 –V

Carrick Bannockburn Central Otago Chardonnay ★★★★☆

This consistently impressive wine is estate-grown, fermented with indigenous yeasts, matured for almost a year in French oak barriques (15 per cent new in 2014), and bottled unfined and unfiltered. The 2014 (★★★★★) is a top vintage. Light lemon/green, it is a classy wine, mouthfilling, with concentrated, peachy, citrusy flavours that linger well. Showing excellent vibrancy, complexity and harmony, it should be at its best 2017+. Certified organic.

Vintage	14	13	12	11
WR	6	7	7	6
Drink	16-21	16-20	16-18	16-17

 DRY $36 –V

Carrick Cairnmuir Terraces EBM Chardonnay ★★★★★

From a region producing increasingly fine, often underrated Chardonnays, this is one of the best. EBM means 'extended barrel maturation'. The generous 2013 vintage (★★★★☆), estate-grown at Bannockburn, was fermented and matured for 18 months in French oak barrels (15 per cent new). Light lemon/green, it has deep, peachy, slightly toasty flavours, with yeasty notes adding complexity, and excellent harmony and potential. Drink now or cellar.

Vintage	13	12	11	10	09	08
WR	7	7	6	6	7	5
Drink	16-20	16-19	16-17	P	P	P

 DRY $42 AV

Chard Farm Closeburn Central Otago Chardonnay (★★★)

The 2014 vintage (★★★), a regional blend, was fermented and lees-aged in tanks, with no oak handling. Enjoyable young, it is full-bodied and smooth, with a slightly creamy texture and good depth of fresh, ripe, citrusy, peachy flavours.

DRY $26 –V

Charles Wiffen Marlborough Chardonnay ★★★★

Charles and Sandy Wiffen own a vineyard in the Wairau Valley. Their delicious 2013 vintage (★★★★), matured for 10 months in French oak, is mouthfilling, sweet-fruited and concentrated, with crisp, vibrant melon and peach flavours, lots of youthful impact, and a slightly buttery, toasty finish.

 DRY $24 V+

Church Road Grand Reserve Hawke's Bay Chardonnay ★★★★★

This wine sits above the McDonald Series (but below Tom) in the Church Road hierarchy. Hand-picked and fermented with indigenous yeasts in French oak barrels, the light yellow/green 2014 vintage (★★★★★) is a classic regional style, built to last. The bouquet is fragrant, smoky and complex; the palate is powerful (14.5 per cent alcohol), with highly concentrated stone-fruit and spice flavours, showing excellent ripeness and complexity, balanced acidity and a very long finish. Best drinking 2018+.

DRY $44 AV

Church Road Hawke's Bay Chardonnay ★★★★

This mouthfilling, rich wine is made by Pernod Ricard NZ at Church Road winery in Hawke's Bay. The juice is mostly fermented in French and Hungarian oak barrels; much of the wine undergoes a secondary, softening malolactic fermentation; and it is barrel-aged for about six months on its full yeast lees, with fortnightly stirring. Fleshy and rounded, it typically has substantial body and ripe stone-fruit flavours showing good texture, complexity and depth. The 2015 vintage (★★★★) is youthful, mouthfilling and smooth, with strong, ripe, peachy flavours, slightly toasty and buttery, and good complexity and harmony. As usual, a top buy.

Vintage	15	14	13	12	11	10
WR	7	7	7	5	5	7
Drink	16-19	16-18	16-17	P	P	P

DRY $20 V+

Church Road McDonald Series Hawke's Bay Chardonnay ★★★★★

Hand-picked and barrel-fermented with indigenous yeasts, the 2014 vintage (★★★★★) is a powerful, complex wine, offering great value. It has a highly fragrant, smoky bouquet, leading into a full-bodied wine with concentrated, ripe grapefruit-like flavours, gently seasoned with biscuity, toasty oak. Creamy-textured, with a long, harmonious finish, it's already delicious; drink now or cellar. The 2015 vintage (★★★★★) is another top buy. Mouthfilling, with a fragrant, slightly smoky bouquet, it is sweet-fruited, with rich, ripe citrus and stone-fruit flavours, showing excellent complexity, and a finely poised, lasting finish. It's still youthful, but already very open and expressive.

Vintage	15	14	13	12	11
WR	7	7	7	6	5
Drink	16-20	16-19	16-18	P	P

DRY $27 V+

Church Road Tom Chardonnay ★★★★★

Bright, light yellow/green, the 2013 vintage (★★★★★), released in 2016, is Chardonnay on the grand scale. Hand-picked in the company's Tuki Tuki Vineyard – cooled by afternoon sea breezes – it was fermented with indigenous yeasts and matured for 11 months on its full yeast lees, with periodic stirring, in French oak barriques and puncheons (54 per cent new). A memorable mouthful, it is richly fragrant and sturdy (14.5 per cent alcohol), with bottomless depth of youthful, citrusy, peachy, biscuity, smoky flavours, very complex and harmonious. Best drinking 2018+.

Vintage	13	12	11	10	09
WR	7	NM	NM	7	6
Drink	16-20	NM	NM	P	P

DRY $150 –V

Clearview Beachhead Hawke's Bay Chardonnay ★★★★☆

This Hawke's Bay winery has a reputation for powerful Chardonnays, and top vintages of this label are no exception. Estate-grown and hand-picked on the coast at Te Awanga, the 2015 vintage (★★★★★) was fermented and lees-stirred for six months in seasoned French oak barrels, with a strong, softening influence from malolactic fermentation. The bouquet is fragrant and complex; the palate is fleshy, vibrant, sweet-fruited and rich, with concentrated, peachy flavours, hints of toast and butterscotch, balanced acidity and a long, well-rounded finish. As a drink-young Chardonnay, this is hard to beat.

Vintage	15	14	13	12	11	10	09
WR	7	7	7	5	5	7	6
Drink	16-21	16-20	16-19	P	P	P	P

DRY $27 V+

Clearview Coastal Hawke's Bay Chardonnay ★★★☆

The debut 2015 vintage (★★★★) has replaced the former Clearview Te Awanga Chardonnay. A buoyantly fruity wine, grown at Te Awanga and partly barrel-fermented, it is mouthfilling, with fresh acidity woven through its peachy, slightly buttery and toasty flavours, which show very good depth and roundness. Fine value.

DRY $20 AV

Clearview Endeavour Hawke's Bay Chardonnay ★★★★☆

One of New Zealand's highest-priced Chardonnays, this wine is estate-grown at Te Awanga, hand-picked from vines planted in 1989, fermented with indigenous yeasts and matured for an unusually long period in new oak barrels. It typically makes a very bold statement. The 2013 vintage (★★★★☆) was matured for 30 months in all-new French oak barriques. Light lemon/green, it is a powerful, youthful wine, weighty and concentrated, with rich, grapefruit-like flavours, mealy and complex, and a very strong seasoning of toasty oak. Still unfolding, it shows excellent cellaring potential and should be at its best 2017+.

Vintage	13
WR	7
Drink	16-20

DRY $165 –V

Clearview Reserve Hawke's Bay Chardonnay ★★★★★

For his premium Chardonnay label, winemaker Tim Turvey aims for a 'big, grunty, upfront' style – and hits the target with ease. It's typically a hedonist's delight – an arrestingly bold, intense, savoury, mealy, complex wine with layers of flavour. Hand-harvested at Te Awanga and barrel-fermented (mostly in new French oak), the 2014 vintage (★★★★★) is a powerful, complex wine with a fragrant, mealy, slightly smoky bouquet. Classy and tight-knit, it has youthful, vibrant, grapefruit-like flavours, biscuity oak, and excellent complexity and concentration. Finely poised, it's very age-worthy.

Vintage	14	13	12	11	10	09	08
WR	7	7	6	6	7	7	7
Drink	16-25	16-23	16-21	16-20	16-20	16-19	16-18

DRY $39 AV

Clearview Te Awanga Hawke's Bay Chardonnay   ★★★☆

The 2014 vintage (★★★☆) was grown on the coast and fermented in tanks (mostly) and barrels. A full-bodied, citrusy, slightly buttery wine, with a touch of complexity and very good depth, it's enjoyable young. (This wine was recently replaced by the Coastal Chardonnay – see above.)

Clearview Three Rows Hawke's Bay Chardonnay   (★★★★☆)

The stylish, debut 2015 vintage (★★★★☆) was selected from three rows in the estate vineyard at Te Awanga, and fermented and lees-aged for 10 months in French oak puncheons (one and two years old). An elegant, youthful wine, it has generous, vibrant grapefruit and peach flavours, with biscuity, mealy notes adding complexity, and excellent drive and depth through the palate. Well worth cellaring, it should be in full stride 2018+.

Clearview White Caps Hawke's Bay Chardonnay   (★★★☆)

The 2014 vintage (★★★☆) was designed as a return 'to the excesses of the 1980s', with 'loads of oak'. Estate-grown and hand-picked at Te Awanga, and 'fermented with new French oak', it is full-bodied and vibrantly fruity. It lacks the complexity of its Beachhead stablemate from the same vintage, but offers strong, youthful, citrusy, peachy flavours.

Clifford Bay Marlborough Chardonnay   (★★★)

Enjoyable now, the bright light lemon/green 2014 vintage (★★★) is mouthfilling, with good depth of grapefruit and peach flavours, fresh acidity, and toasty, buttery notes adding a touch of complexity.

Clos de Ste Anne Chardonnay Naboth's Vineyard   ★★★★★

Millton's exceptional Chardonnay is based on ungrafted, unirrigated vines, over 25 years old, in the steep, north-east-facing Naboth's Vineyard in the Poverty Bay foothills. Grown biodynamically and hand-harvested, it is fermented with indigenous yeasts in mostly second-fill French oak barriques, and has usually not been put through malolactic fermentation, 'to leave a pure, crisp mineral flavour'. A powerful wine, it is also notably stylish and complete. The 2014 vintage (★★★★★) is fleshy, rich and sweet-fruited, with concentrated, vibrant, citrusy, peachy flavours, well-integrated oak, excellent complexity and a finely textured, very harmonious, lasting finish. Still youthful, it should be at its best 2018+.

Vintage	14	13	12	11	10	09	08	07	06	05
WR	7	7	NM	NM	7	7	6	7	7	7
Drink	16-29	16-28	NM	NM	16-25	16-21	16-17	16-17	P	P

Cloudy Bay Chardonnay   ★★★★★

A powerful Marlborough wine with impressively concentrated, savoury, lemony, mealy flavours and a proven ability to mature well over the long haul. The grapes, hand-picked, are sourced from numerous company-owned and growers' vineyards at Brancott, Fairhall, Benmorven and in the Central Wairau Valley. All of the wine is fermented (with a high proportion of indigenous yeasts) in French oak barriques (about 20 per cent new) and lees-aged in barrels for up to 15 months, and most goes through a softening malolactic fermentation. The 2012 vintage (★★★★☆) is richly fragrant, with a hint of butterscotch. Mouthfilling and savoury, it has citrusy, mealy, slightly toasty flavours, showing cool-climate vigour, firm acid spine, and a long finish. Drink now or cellar.

Vintage	12	11
WR	7	7
Drink	16-20	16-19

Collaboration Aurulent Hawke's Bay Chardonnay ★★★★☆

Hand-harvested at 'select vineyard sites', the 2014 vintage (★★★★☆) was fermented and lees-aged in French oak casks (25 per cent new). Still youthful, it is bright, light lemon/green, with a fragrant, complex, 'struck match' bouquet. Mouthfilling, it is fresh and rounded, with good concentration of ripe stone-fruit flavours, toasty and smoky notes adding interest, and obvious potential; best drinking 2017+. The finely poised 2015 vintage (★★★★☆) has a complex bouquet, leading into a full-bodied, elegant, tightly structured wine, with vibrant grapefruit and peach flavours, slightly smoky notes, and good complexity. Best drinking 2018+.

Vintage	15	14	13	12	11
WR	7	7	7	6	5
Drink	17-23	16-22	16-21	16-19	16-18

Coopers Creek Gisborne Chardonnay ★★★☆

Enjoyable young, the 2014 vintage (★★★☆) was tank-fermented and matured for eight months in seasoned oak. Full-bodied, it is sweet-fruited and vibrantly fruity, with good depth of ripe peach/melon flavours and a slightly creamy texture.

Vintage	14
WR	6
Drink	16-17

Coopers Creek SV Plainsman Hawke's Bay Chardonnay (★★★☆)

The 2015 vintage (★★★☆) is finely balanced for current drinking. Full-bodied, it was fermented in seasoned oak barrels and most (90 per cent) of the blend went through a softening malolactic fermentation. Fresh and weighty, it's a peachy, moderately complex style with a hint of butterscotch and satisfying depth.

Coopers Creek SV The Limeworks Hawke's Bay Chardonnay ★★★★

Estate-grown at Havelock North, this is crafted in a 'full-on' style. The vibrantly fruity 2015 vintage (★★★★) was fully barrel-fermented in American oak casks (50 per cent new). Fresh, tightly structured and moderately complex, it has a nutty oak influence and very good depth, vigour and harmony.

DRY $25 AV

Coopers Creek Swamp Reserve Chardonnay   ★★★★☆

Based on the winery's best Hawke's Bay grapes, this is typically a seductive wine with a finely judged balance of rich, citrusy, peachy fruit flavours and toasty oak. Hand-picked in the company's Middle Road Vineyard at Havelock North, it is fermented and matured in French oak barriques (30 per cent new in 2014), and given a full, softening malolactic fermentation. The 2014 vintage (★★★★★) is deliciously weighty and rich. A powerful wine, it has deep, ripe stone-fruit flavours, slightly buttery and toasty, impressive complexity and a harmonious, lasting finish. It's drinking well now.

Vintage	14	13
WR	7	7
Drink	16-20	16-18

DRY $39 –V

Cottier Estate Emily Chardonnay   (★★★★)

Tasted in late 2015, the 2012 vintage (★★★★) was grown at Gladstone, in the northern Wairarapa. It's a fleshy, generous wine, with ripe, concentrated flavours, slightly creamy and nutty, and good complexity and harmony. Good value.

DRY $24 V+

Craft Farm Home Vineyard Hawke's Bay Chardonnay   (★★★★☆)

Delicious young, the 2015 vintage (★★★★☆), estate-grown at Havelock North, was fermented with indigenous yeasts in French oak casks (30 per cent new) and given a full, softening malolactic fermentation. Light lemon/green, it is youthful, fragrant, weighty and concentrated, with ripe, rounded, peachy, biscuity flavours, showing excellent richness and harmony. Drink now onwards.

DRY $35 –V

Craggy Range Block 19 Gimblett Gravels Chardonnay   (★★★★★)

The very refined debut 2014 vintage (★★★★★) was hand-picked from seven-year-old vines and fermented with indigenous yeasts in French oak barriques (40 per cent new). Barrel-aged for 11 months, it's a full-bodied, finely textured wine, powerful yet subtle, with ripe stone-fruit flavours, a hint of toasty oak, and lovely mouthfeel, delicacy and depth. Best drinking 2017+.

DRY $60 –V

Craggy Range Gimblett Gravels Vineyard Hawke's Bay Chardonnay   ★★★★☆

This stylish wine is typically mouthfilling and savoury, with complexity from fermentation and maturation in French oak barriques (28 per cent new in 2015). The 2015 vintage (★★★★★) was hand-harvested, fermented with indigenous yeasts and barrel-aged for 10 months. The bouquet is fragrant and complex; the palate is mouthfilling, with subtle grapefruit and nut flavours, showing excellent vibrancy, delicacy, harmony and persistence. A very elegant, rather than high-impact, wine, it's already delicious, but well worth cellaring.

DRY $32 AV

Crazy by Nature Gisborne Shotberry Chardonnay   ★★★☆

From Millton, this is an unoaked style. The 2014 vintage (★★★☆) is light yellow, with mouthfilling body and generous, ripe, peachy flavours, slightly buttery and honeyed. It is drinking well now. The 2015 vintage (★★★☆) is a light lemon/green, medium-bodied wine, still youthful, with vibrant, peachy, citrusy flavours, fresh acidity and good depth. Certified organic.

Vintage	15	14
WR	6	5
Drink	16-19	16-18

DRY $22 AV

Crossroads Milestone Series Hawke's Bay Chardonnay   ★★★★

A consistently good buy, this is a classic regional style, weighty, ripe and rounded. The 2014 vintage (★★★★) was mostly grown inland, at Mangatahi, and predominantly (66 per cent) fermented in French oak barriques. Mouthfilling, it's a very harmonious wine, with strong, ripe stone-fruit flavours, finely integrated nutty oak, and good complexity.

Vintage	14	13
WR	6	6
Drink	16-24	16-20

DRY $20 V+

Crossroads Winemakers Collection Hawke's Bay Chardonnay   ★★★★☆

The 2014 vintage (★★★★★) was grown in the Kereru Vineyard, inland at Mangatahi, hand-picked and fermented and lees-aged for 10 months in French oak barriques (25 per cent new). A refined wine, it is fragrant and mouthfilling, youthful and tightly structured, with strong, vibrant, citrusy, peachy flavours, finely integrated oak, and very impressive delicacy, complexity and harmony. Well worth cellaring.

Vintage	14	13	12
WR	7	7	6
Drink	16-25	16-24	16-20

DRY $40 –V

Cypress Hawke's Bay Chardonnay   ★★★☆

The 2014 vintage (★★★☆) was estate-grown and gently oak-influenced (20 per cent of the blend was barrel-fermented). Full-bodied and buoyantly fruity, it has fresh, ripe, peachy flavours, showing a touch of complexity, and plenty of drink-young appeal.

Vintage	14	13	12
WR	7	7	6
Drink	16-17	P	P

DRY $21 AV

Cypress Terraces Hawke's Bay Chardonnay   ★★★★☆

From a sloping, 2-hectare site at Roys Hill, the 2014 vintage (★★★★☆) was hand-picked and barrel-fermented (40 per cent new oak). Powerful and very sweet-fruited, with fresh, ripe stone-fruit flavours, it shows excellent complexity and richness. Well worth cellaring.

Vintage	14	13	12
WR	7	7	6
Drink	16-19	16-18	P

 DRY $32 AV

Darling, The, Marlborough Chardonnay   (★★★★★)

Certified organic, the 2013 vintage (★★★★★) is a very elegant, tightly structured, single-vineyard wine, grown in the Southern Valleys and handled in seasoned oak casks. The bouquet is fragrant and complex; the palate is weighty, with penetrating grapefruit and nut flavours, good acid spine and a finely poised, lasting finish. Best drinking 2017+.

 DRY $33 V+

Dashwood Marlborough Chardonnay   ★★★☆

The 2014 vintage (★★★☆) is mouthfilling, with fresh, peachy, slightly buttery and toasty flavours, showing very good vigour and depth.

DRY $17 V+

De La Terre Hawke's Bay Chardonnay   (★★★★)

Handled without oak, the 2014 vintage (★★★★) was hand-picked on limestone terraces at Havelock North. It is freshly scented and youthful, with ripe, citrusy, peachy flavours in an elegant, slightly minerally style with obvious cellaring potential. Open 2017+.

 DRY $24 V+

De La Terre Hawke's Bay Chardonnay Barrique Ferment   (★★★★★)

Showing obvious potential, the classy 2015 vintage (★★★★★) was estate-grown at Havelock North and fermented in French oak barriques (15 per cent new). Light lemon/green, it has a fragrant, complex bouquet, leading into an elegant, tightly structured wine with excellent intensity of grapefruit-like flavours, mealy, biscuity notes adding complexity, good acid spine and a lengthy finish. Best drinking 2018+.

Vintage	15
WR	6
Drink	16-18

 DRY $30 V+

De La Terre Reserve Hawke's Bay Chardonnay   (★★★★★)

The classy, finely structured 2014 vintage (★★★★★) was hand-picked at 23 brix at Havelock North and fermented, partly with indigenous yeasts, in French oak barriques (50 per cent new). Full-bodied, with a minerally streak, it has intense, citrusy, peachy, spicy flavours, fresh acidity, well-integrated oak, and excellent complexity, vigour and length. Best drinking 2017+.

Vintage	14	13
WR	7	6
Drink	16-23	16-22

 DRY $40 AV

De Vine Central Otago Chardonnay   (★★★★)

The 2013 vintage (★★★★) offers outstanding value. Sold under a brand owned by Auckland retailer Manly Liquor, it was grown in the Cromwell Basin. Pale lemon in hue, it is fresh and elegant, with a citrusy bouquet, mouthfilling body, lemony, slightly spicy flavours, lively acidity and a lingering finish. Tightly structured, it's maturing very gracefully.

DRY $14 V+

Delegat Crownthorpe Terraces Chardonnay   ★★★★

Offering fine value, the 2014 vintage (★★★★) was grown at the company's elevated, inland site at Crownthorpe and fermented in French oak barrels (26 per cent new). Mouthfilling, it has strong, vibrant, grapefruit-like flavours, finely integrated oak adding complexity and a slightly creamy, finely textured finish. Bargain-priced.

DRY $20 V+

Dog Point Vineyard Marlborough Chardonnay   ★★★★★

This classy, single-vineyard wine is grown on the south side of the Wairau Valley, hand-picked, fermented and matured for 18 to 20 months in French oak barriques (15 to 25 per cent new), and given a full, softening malolactic fermentation. Bright, light lemon/green, the 2014 vintage (★★★★☆) is a sweet-fruited, bone-dry wine with very youthful, grapefruit-like flavours threaded with fresh acidity, slightly toasty notes, a minerally streak, and excellent vibrancy, delicacy, poise and length. A distinctly cool-climate style, it's well worth cellaring to mid-2017+.

Vintage	14	13	12	11	10	09	08
WR	7	7	5	7	6	5	7
Drink	16-26	16-21	16-17	16-19	16-17	16-17	P

 DRY $38 AV

Domaine Rewa Central Otago Chardonnay   ★★★★

The stylish 2013 vintage (★★★★) is a single-vineyard wine, grown and hand-picked at Pisa, in the Cromwell Basin, and fermented and matured for eight months in French oak barriques (25 per cent new). Full-bodied, it has strong, citrusy, mealy flavours, showing excellent freshness, depth and complexity.

Vintage	13	12
WR	7	7
Drink	16-19	16-18

 DRY $30 –V

Dry River Martinborough Chardonnay ★★★★★

Elegance, restraint and subtle power are the key qualities of this classic wine. It's not a bold, upfront style, but tight, savoury and seamless, with rich grapefruit and nut flavours that build in the bottle for several years. Based on low-cropping, Mendoza-clone vines in the Craighall and Dry River Estate vineyards, it is hand-harvested, whole-bunch pressed and fermented in French oak barrels (with a low percentage of new casks). The proportion of the blend that has gone through a softening malolactic fermentation has never exceeded 15 per cent. The 2014 vintage (★★★★★) is medium to full-bodied, with concentrated, ripe stone-fruit flavours, gently seasoned with toasty oak, good complexity, balanced acidity, and a deliciously rich, rounded finish. Offering lots of pleasure already, it's a drink-now or cellaring proposition.

Vintage	14	13	12	11	10	09	08	07	06
WR	7	7	5	7	7	7	7	7	7
Drink	16-24	16-23	16-22	16-20	16-20	16-20	16-17	16-18	P

Easthope Skeetfield Hawke's Bay Chardonnay ★★★★

Grown at Ohiti and fermented in French oak barrels (25 per cent new), the 2013 (★★★★) is an elegant, tightly structured wine, with a long finish. It's well worth cellaring. The 2014 vintage (★★★★) is more open and expressive in its youth, showing good complexity and richness.

DRY $35 –V

Elephant Hill Hawke's Bay Chardonnay ★★★★

Estate-grown near the coast at Te Awanga, the 2014 vintage (★★★★☆) is an elegant, age-worthy style. Hand-picked, fermented with indigenous yeasts in French oak barriques (25 per cent new) and lees-aged for 11 months, with no softening malolactic fermentation, it is mouthfilling and subtle, with good concentration of fresh, ripe grapefruit-like flavours, gently seasoned with biscuity oak. Tightly structured, with excellent delicacy and depth, it's approachable now, but well worth cellaring.

Vintage	14	13
WR	7	6
Drink	16-17	P

Elephant Hill Reserve Hawke's Bay Chardonnay ★★★★★

Estate-grown at Te Awanga, the weighty, generous 2013 vintage (★★★★★) was hand-harvested, fermented with indigenous yeasts, and matured for a year in French oak barrels (30 per cent new). A very classy wine, with a fragrant, complex, slightly smoky bouquet, it is mouthfilling and intense, with pure, vibrant, searching fruit flavours, well-integrated oak, and a long, creamy-smooth finish. Best drinking 2017+.

DRY $45 AV

Escarpment Kupe by Escarpment Chardonnay ★★★☆

The 2012 (★★★★☆) is markedly superior to the disappointing 2010 (★★) and 2011 (★★★) vintages. Grown on the Martinborough Terrace, it was fermented with indigenous yeasts and lees-aged for 10 months in French oak casks (20 per cent new). The bouquet is citrusy and gently toasty; the palate is full-bodied, with strong grapefruit/nut flavours, showing excellent delicacy and vibrancy, that build well across the palate to a lengthy, finely poised finish. A refined, tightly structured wine, it should mature very gracefully.

DRY $49 –V

Esk Valley Hawke's Bay Chardonnay ★★★★

Top vintages can offer irresistible value. The 2015 vintage (★★★★) was fully fermented and matured in French oak barriques (15 per cent new), and half the blend went through a softening malolactic fermentation. A classic regional style, it is a generous, sweet-fruited wine, mouthfilling, with youthful grapefruit and peach flavours, a subtle seasoning of oak, fresh acidity and a slightly mealy, finely textured finish. It's one of the best-value Chardonnays on the market.

Vintage	15	14	13	12	11	10
WR	7	6	6	5	5	6
Drink	16-19	16-18	P	P	P	P

DRY $20 V+

Esk Valley Winemakers Reserve Hawke's Bay Chardonnay ★★★★★

Often one of the region's most distinguished Chardonnays. Highly fragrant, with a hint of 'struck match', the classy 2015 vintage (★★★★★) was grown at two sites in northern Hawke's Bay (including the Esk Valley home block), and fermented and matured for 11 months in French oak barriques (30 per cent new). Elegant and weighty, it is youthful, with rich, peachy, citrusy and mealy flavours, impressive complexity and a sustained finish.

Vintage	15	14	13	12
WR	7	7	7	6
Drink	16-23	16-20	16-20	16-18

DRY $32 V+

Felton Road Bannockburn Central Otago Chardonnay ★★★★★

Forging ahead in quality, this classy, distinctive wine is grown at Bannockburn and matured in French oak barriques, with limited use of new oak. Light lemon/green, the 2015 vintage (★★★★★) was estate-grown in The Elms and Cornish Point vineyards, and barrel-aged for a year (6 per cent new). Already delicious, it is mouthfilling and vibrant, with a real sense of youthful drive. A finely structured, distinctly cool-climate style, it has fresh, pure, grapefruit-like flavours, a subtle seasoning of biscuity oak, and lovely delicacy and length. Best drinking 2018+.

Vintage	15	14	13	12	11	10	09	08
WR	7	7	7	7	6	7	7	6
Drink	16-29	16-28	16-24	16-26	16-22	16-22	16-20	16-18

DRY $43 AV

Felton Road Block 2 Central Otago Chardonnay   ★★★★★

This outstanding wine is grown in a 'special part of The Elms Vineyard in front of the winery', which has the oldest vines. Handled with no new oak influence, it is bottled unfined and unfiltered. The 2015 vintage (★★★★★) is bright, light lemon/green, mouthfilling, fresh and very youthful, with concentrated, grapefruit-evoking flavours, mealy notes adding complexity, a subtle seasoning of oak, and a very long finish. Best drinking 2018+.

Vintage	15	14	13	12
WR	7	7	7	7
Drink	16-31	16-30	16-27	16-26

DRY $56 AV

Felton Road Block 6 Central Otago Chardonnay   (★★★★★)

Estate-grown in The Elms Vineyard at Bannockburn, the debut 2015 vintage (★★★★★) was handled principally in seasoned oak casks (6 per cent new), and bottled unfined and unfiltered. Highly fragrant, it is full-bodied, with concentrated, citrusy, slightly peachy flavours, mealy, toasty notes adding complexity and a lasting finish. Still very youthful, it is slightly richer and rounder than its Block 2 stablemate, offering an intriguing style comparison.

Vintage	15
WR	7
Drink	16-31

DRY $56 AV

Framingham Marlborough Chardonnay   ★★★★

The 2014 vintage (★★★★) was fermented and matured for eight months in tanks (40 per cent) and barrels (60 per cent). An elegant wine, it is slightly creamy, with ripe grapefruit and peach flavours, a subtle seasoning of oak, and very good weight, texture and vibrancy. Well worth cellaring.

Vintage	14
WR	6
Drink	16-22

DRY $25 AV

French Peak Banks Peninsula Chardonnay   (★★★☆)

From 27-year-old vines in Canterbury, the 2015 vintage (★★★☆) was barrel-fermented. Light straw, with a creamy bouquet, it is a medium to full-bodied style, fresh and crisp, with peachy, slightly buttery flavours, showing very good depth, and firm acid spine. Already enjoyable, it should mature well; open mid-2017+.

DRY $35 –V

Frenchman's Hill Estate Waiheke Island Ted's Chardonnay   (★★★★)

Light gold, with a toasty bouquet, the 2014 vintage (★★★★) was grown at Te Rere Cove Vineyard and fermented and matured for a year in all-new French oak barriques. A powerful, full-bodied wine, it is sweet-fruited, with rich, ripe stone-fruit flavours, strongly seasoned with toasty oak. Best drinking 2017 onwards.

DRY $58 –V

Fromm Clayvin Vineyard Marlborough Chardonnay ★★★★★

Fromm's finest Chardonnay is grown on the southern flanks of the Wairau Valley, where the clay soils, says winemaker Hätsch Kalberer, give 'a less fruity, more minerally and tighter character'. Fermented with indigenous yeasts in French oak barriques, with little or no use of new wood, it is barrel-aged for well over a year. It is a rare wine – only three barrels were produced in 2013 – and top vintages mature well for a decade. The 2013 vintage (★★★★★) is pale lemon/green, with a highly fragrant, complex bouquet. It is very refined and harmonious, with concentrated, ripe grapefruit-like flavours, a subtle seasoning of oak, a slightly creamy texture, and lovely delicacy, poise and persistence. Best drinking 2017+.

Vintage	13	12	11	10	09	08
WR	7	NM	7	6	7	NM
Drink	16-23	NM	16-21	16-18	16-19	NM

DRY $68 AV

Fromm La Strada Marlborough Chardonnay ★★★★☆

The refined 2013 vintage (★★★★★) was grown in the Brancott Valley and matured for 16 months in French oak casks (10 per cent new). Weighty and fleshy, with strong, citrusy, peachy flavours and a subtle seasoning of oak, it has excellent freshness, delicacy, complexity and richness, in a very harmonious style, offering delicious drinking from now onwards.

Vintage	13	12	11	10	09
WR	7	7	7	7	6
Drink	16-19	16-17	16-17	P	P

DRY $37 –V

Fuder, The, Single Vineyard Selection Clayvin Marlborough Chardonnay ★★★★★

From Giesen, this wine is grown in the famous Clayvin Vineyard, in the Brancott Valley, and fermented and matured in 1000-litre German oak casks (fuders), which 'develop greater complexity and refinement, but the oak doesn't dominate'. The tight, youthful, age-worthy 2014 vintage (★★★★★) is bright, light lemon/green, with a fragrant, complex, slightly smoky bouquet. Mouthfilling, it is elegant, with concentrated grapefruit and peach flavours, integrated oak, fine acidity, and a powerful, lasting finish.

Vintage	14	13
WR	7	7
Drink	16-23	16-22

DRY $60 AV

Gibbston Highgate Estate Heartbreaker Central Otago Chardonnay ★★★

The 2013 vintage (★★★☆) was hand-picked at Gibbston and barrel-fermented (mostly in older oak). Light yellow, it's a weighty, fleshy wine with citrusy flavours, a hint of oak adding complexity, and a smooth finish.

DRY $25 –V

Gibbston Valley 95 China Terrace Central Otago Chardonnay   (★★★★★)

The debut 2014 vintage (★★★★★) is a single-vineyard Bendigo wine, estate-grown at 320 metres above sea level, and hand-picked solely from highly regarded, clone 95 vines. Fermented with indigenous yeasts in French oak barriques and puncheons (25 per cent new), and barrel-aged for a year, it is a pale, elegant, minerally wine, full-bodied and crisp. Taut and racy, with incisive, grapefruit-like flavours, nutty and smoky notes adding complexity, and a long finish, it is full of youthful vigour and potential; open 2018+.

DRY $55 –V

Gibbston Valley China Terrace Bendigo Single Vineyard Chardonnay   ★★★★☆

Here's more evidence that Central Otago has great Chardonnay potential. The 2015 vintage (★★★★☆) was estate-grown, at 320 metres above sea level, and fermented and matured for 11 months in French oak barriques and puncheons (25 per cent new). Light lemon/green, it is very fresh and poised, with an aromatic, slightly smoky bouquet. A distinctly cool-climate style, it is tightly structured, with strong, youthful, grapefruit-like flavours, a subtle seasoning of biscuity oak, and obvious cellaring potential. Best drinking 2018+.

DRY $39 –V

Giesen Hawke's Bay Chardonnay   (★★☆)

The youthful, pale lemon/green 2014 vintage (★★☆) is a fresh, medium-bodied wine, vibrant and fruity, with citrusy flavours and a smooth (4 grams/litre of residual sugar) finish.

Vintage	14
WR	4
Drink	16-17

DRY $17 –V

Giesen The Brothers Marlborough Chardonnay   ★★★★☆

The 2014 vintage (★★★★☆) is a fragrant, generous wine. Grown in the Wairau Valley and the Southern Valleys, it was fermented with indigenous yeasts in French and German oak fuders (big, 1000-litre barrels). The bouquet is complex, with ripe-fruit aromas and hints of toasty oak; the flavours are rich, peachy and slightly buttery, with excellent depth and harmony. Drink now or cellar.

DRY $30 AV

Glazebrook Regional Reserve Hawke's Bay Chardonnay   ★★★☆

Ngatarawa's second-tier Chardonnay is named after the Glazebrook family, once partners in the Hawke's Bay venture. A fruit-driven style, the 2015 vintage (★★★☆) is vibrant, with mouthfilling body, ripe, peachy flavours to the fore, and good freshness and depth.

DRY $20 AV

Goldie Chardonnay   ★★★★☆

Grown on Waiheke Island by Goldie Wines, owned by the University of Auckland, the 2013 vintage (★★★★★) was hand-picked and fermented with indigenous yeasts in French oak barriques (20 per cent new). A notably weighty, ripe, flavour-packed wine, it is sturdy (14.8 per cent alcohol) and very sweet-fruited, with highly concentrated stone-fruit flavours, barrel-ferment complexity, gentle acidity and a deliciously rich, well-rounded finish.

DRY $42 –V

Goldwater Wairau Valley Marlborough Chardonnay ★★★★

This is a consistently attractive, generous, sweet-fruited wine. The 2014 vintage (★★★★) is mouthfilling, with strong, fresh stone-fruit flavours, gently seasoned with toasty oak. It's a well-rounded, harmonious wine, delicious young.

DRY $22 V+

Greenhough Hope Vineyard Chardonnay ★★★★★

This impressive wine is estate-grown at Hope, in Nelson, hand-picked, barrel-fermented with indigenous yeasts and matured for well over a year in French oak barriques (25 per cent new in 2014). Certified organic, the 2014 vintage (★★★★★) is a refined, subtle wine, with pure, penetrating, citrusy flavours, gently seasoned with oak, and lovely freshness, drive and complexity. Tightly structured and intense, it's well worth cellaring.

Vintage	14	13	12	11	10	09	08
WR	7	6	6	6	NM	6	6
Drink	16-20	16-19	16-18	16-18	NM	P	P

DRY $36 AV

Greenhough Nelson Chardonnay ★★★☆

This consistently enjoyable wine is designed to express a 'fresh, taut' style, with background oak providing 'some subtle, savoury complexities'. Certified organic, the 2015 (★★★★) is a top vintage. Grown at Hope, it was barrel-fermented (19 per cent new) and oak-aged for 11 months. Pale straw, it is full-bodied, with peachy, citrusy flavours, integrated oak, good complexity and a finely balanced, tight, lingering finish. Best drinking mid-2017+.

Vintage	15	14	13	12	11	10
WR	6	6	6	6	6	6
Drink	17-20	16-19	16-18	16-18	16-17	P

DRY $24 AV

Greyrock Hawke's Bay Chardonnay (★★★)

From Sileni, the 2015 vintage (★★★) is a 'lightly oaked' style. Lemon-scented, it is mouthfilling and vibrantly fruity, with fresh acidity, a slightly creamy texure and good depth of citrusy, peachy flavours. Enjoyable young.

DRY $17 AV

Greystone Erin's Reserve Waipara Valley Chardonnay ★★★★★

Greystone views Chardonnay as 'the finest white wine variety'. The third 2013 vintage (★★★★★) is exceptionally rare – just 73 cases were produced. Grown on steep, north-facing limestone slopes, it was hand-picked at 24.6 brix, fermented with indigenous yeasts, and matured for 15 months in French oak casks (65 per cent new). Bright, light lemon/green, it is very rich and harmonious, with highly concentrated, citrusy, peachy flavours, mealy and biscuity notes adding complexity, and a well-rounded, lasting finish. A very generous wine, it has lapped up the new oak effortlessly, offering top-flight drinking from now onwards.

DRY $100 –V

Greystone Waipara Valley Chardonnay ★★★★☆

The classy 2015 vintage (★★★★★) was hand-picked, fermented with indigenous yeasts in French oak barrels (20 per cent new), and given a full, softening malolactic fermentation. Light yellow/green, it is full-bodied, with concentrated, peachy, slightly buttery flavours, finely integrated oak, good acid spine, excellent complexity and a long finish.

Vintage	15	14	13	12
WR	7	7	7	7
Drink	16-26	16-20	16-19	16-18

 DRY $42 -V

Greywacke Marlborough Chardonnay ★★★★★

The bright, light lemon/green 2014 vintage (★★★★☆) was hand-harvested in 'low-yielding, mature vineyards', fermented with indigenous yeasts in French barriques (20 per cent new) and oak-aged for 18 months. The bouquet is fragrant and complex; the palate is substantial (14.5 per cent alcohol) and sweet-fruited, with vibrant peach and grapefruit flavours, youthful and rich, and a subtle seasoning of oak. Best drinking 2018+.

Vintage	14	13	12	11	10	09
WR	6	6	5	6	6	5
Drink	17-24	17-23	17-20	17-20	17-20	17-18

 DRY $41 AV

Grove Mill Wairau Valley Marlborough Chardonnay ★★★☆

Enjoyable young, the 2015 vintage (★★★☆) is a pale yellow, full-bodied wine with smooth, peachy, citrusy flavours, slightly toasty and generous. It's drinking well now.

Vintage	14	13
WR	7	7
Drink	16-19	16-18

 DRY $22 AV

Gunn Estate Reserve Hawke's Bay Chardonnay ★★★☆

The slightly creamy, easy-drinking 2014 vintage (★★★☆) was 'fermented in stainless steel with French oak', and given a full, softening malolactic fermentation. Mouthfilling and vibrantly fruity, it has plenty of fresh, ripe, peachy flavour, a bare hint of oak, and a well-balanced, dry finish. Drink now. The 2015 vintage (★★★☆) was barrel-fermented. Pale straw, it has upfront appeal, with very good depth of peachy, slightly toasty flavours.

Vintage	15
WR	7
Drink	16-18

DRY $20 AV

Haha Marlborough Chardonnay ★★★

Already very enjoyable, the 2015 vintage (★★★☆) was partly oak-aged. Mouthfilling and creamy-textured, it is fresh and youthful, in an upfront style with good depth of grapefruit-like flavours, showing some savoury complexity.

Vintage	15	14	13
WR	7	7	7
Drink	16-19	16-18	16-17

 DRY $18 AV

Hans Herzog Marlborough Chardonnay ★★★★☆

At its best, this is a notably powerful wine with layers of peach, butterscotch, grapefruit and nut flavours. The pale straw 2013 vintage (★★★★☆) was hand-picked, fermented with indigenous yeasts in French oak puncheons, barrel-aged for 18 months and given a full, softening malolactic fermentation. A mouthfilling, youthful wine, it has rich, ripe grapefruit and peach flavours, seasoned with biscuity oak, and a tight, slightly creamy finish. Best drinking 2017+. Certified organic.

Vintage	13	12	11
WR	7	7	7
Drink	16-23	16-22	16-19

DRY $44 –V

Harakeke Farm Nelson Chardonnay ★★★★☆

This impressive, single-vineyard, Upper Moutere wine is hand-picked, fermented with indigenous yeasts in French oak puncheons and given a full, softening malolactic fermentation. The powerful 2014 vintage (★★★★★) is sturdy (14.5 per cent alcohol), sweet-fruited and rich, with concentrated, peachy, mealy, gently toasty and buttery flavours, balanced acidity and a highly fragrant, complex bouquet. Already delicious, it's a 'full-on' style, likely to be at its best 2017+.

Vintage	14	13	12
WR	7	7	6
Drink	16-18	16-17	P

DRY $30 AV

Harwood Hall Hawke's Bay Chardonnay (★★★☆)

The 2013 vintage (★★★☆) is an elegant, peachy wine in an easy-drinking, fruity style with a subtle oak influence, a creamy texture, and very good vibrancy and depth.

DRY $23 AV

Hawk's Nest Matakana Chardonnay (★★★★)

The 2013 vintage (★★★★) was grown at Matakana and fermented and matured in French oak casks (over 50 per cent new). It's a rare wine – only 33 cases were produced. Light yellow, it is powerful, weighty and well-rounded, with a slightly oily texture and very good ripeness and depth of peachy, biscuity flavour.

Vintage	13
WR	6
Drink	16-18

DRY $25 AV

Highfield Marlborough Chardonnay ★★★★

Typically a classy wine. The 2013 vintage (★★★★), barrel-fermented and lees-aged for 11 months, is youthful and mouthfilling, with strong, citrusy, peachy flavours, slightly mealy, buttery and toasty, in a complex style, worth cellaring.

Vintage	13	12	11	10
WR	6	7	6	7
Drink	16-18	P	P	P

DRY $33 –V

Hitchen Road Chardonnay ★★★☆

The 2014 vintage (★★★★) is a bargain. Estate-grown and hand-picked at 23.5 brix at Pokeno, in North Waikato, it was barrel-aged, with lees-stirring, for seven months. Mouthfilling, sweet-fruited and generous, it has strong, citrusy, peachy, slightly buttery flavours, integrated oak, considerable complexity and a well-rounded finish. Delicious young.

DRY $18 V+

Hopesgrove Estate Single Vineyard Hawke's Bay Chardonnay ★★★★

The elegant 2013 vintage (★★★★☆) was hand-picked and fermented and matured in French oak casks (35 per cent new). It is mouthfilling and rich, with concentrated peach and grapefruit flavours, finely integrated oak, good complexity and a slightly buttery, sustained finish. Very age-worthy.

DRY $35 –V

Huia Marlborough Chardonnay ★★★★

Certified organic, the 2014 vintage (★★★★☆) is a single-vineyard wine, mouthfilling and sweet-fruited, fleshy and youthful. It has deep, peachy, slightly biscuity flavours, showing excellent concentration and complexity. Best drinking 2017+.

DRY $34 –V

Hunter's Marlborough Chardonnay ★★★☆

This wine has traditionally placed its accent on vibrant fruit flavours, overlaid with very subtle wood-aging characters. The 2014 vintage (★★★★), estate-grown at Rapaura and Omaka, was fermented – with indigenous yeasts – and matured for 10 months in French oak casks (25 per cent new). Light lemon/green, it is an elegant, youthful wine with ripe grapefruit and peach flavours, showing good complexity, slightly smoky notes, and excellent vigour and harmony. Best drinking 2017.

Vintage	14	13	12	11	10
WR	7	6	6	5	6
Drink	16-19	16-18	16-17	P	P

DRY $21 AV

Hunter's Succession Marlborough Chardonnay (★★★★☆)

The debut 2013 vintage (★★★★☆) is a tightly structured, very elegant wine, likely to be long-lived. Matured in all-new French oak casks, it has youthful colour, with strong grapefruit-like flavours that have lapped up the new oak influence. Smoky and complex, with a long finish, it should be at its best 2017+.

DRY $39 –V

Hyperion Helios Matakana Chardonnay ★★★☆

The 2013 vintage (★★★☆), fermented in seasoned oak barrels, is a mouthfilling wine with ripe grapefruit-like flavours, showing very good ripeness and depth, and a gentle seasoning of biscuity oak.

DRY $27 –V

Invivo Gisborne Chardonnay   (★★★)

'There's nothing subtle in this bottle', says the back label on the easy-drinking, 'big, bold' 2016 vintage (★★★). Bright, light lemon/green, it is fresh, sweet-fruited and mouthfilling, with ripe, citrusy, peachy flavours, slightly creamy and toasty notes adding complexity, and a rounded finish.

DRY $20 –V

Invivo Michelle's Central Otago Chardonnay   (★★★★☆)

The impressive debut 2013 vintage (★★★★☆) was fermented in a 50:50 split of new French oak puncheons and seasoned French oak barriques. The bouquet is biscuity, with good complexity; the palate is mouthfilling and vibrant, with concentrated, peachy flavours, slightly spicy and yeasty notes, a hint of butterscotch, balanced oak and a long finish. A classy wine, it shows good cellaring potential.

Vintage	13
WR	7
Drink	16-20

DRY $30 AV

Jackson Estate Shelter Belt Single Vineyard Marlborough Chardonnay   ★★★★

The 2013 vintage (★★★★) was estate-grown in the Homestead Vineyard, in the heart of the Wairau Valley, fermented with indigenous yeasts, and fermented and lees-aged for 10 months in French oak barriques (25 per cent new). Light straw, it is mouthfilling, with concentrated, peachy flavours, finely balanced acidity, and subtle, mealy, toasty characters adding complexity. The 2014 vintage (★★★☆) is mouthfilling and rounded. Drinking well now, it is generous, with peachy, slightly buttery and toasty flavours.

Vintage	14	13
WR	6	6
Drink	16-18	16-17

DRY $26 AV

Johner Martinborough Chardonnay   ★★★☆

The 2015 vintage (★★★☆) was fermented and matured in French oak casks (25 per cent new). Light lemon/green, it is youthful, with fresh acidity and good depth of citrusy, slightly mealy and creamy flavours, showing considerable complexity. Best drinking mid-2017+.

Vintage	15
WR	5
Drink	16-19

DRY $26 –V

Johner Wairarapa Chardonnay   ★★★☆

Handled in seasoned oak, the 2016 vintage (★★★☆) is a fruit-driven style, lively and mouthfilling, with very good depth of grapefruit and spice flavours, leesy notes adding a touch of complexity, and lots of drink-young appeal.

Vintage	16
WR	6
Drink	16-21

DRY $26 –V

Jules Taylor Gisborne Chardonnay ★★★☆

The attractive 2014 vintage (★★★★) was partly barrel-fermented and made with some use of indigenous yeasts and malolactic fermentation. Mouthfilling and slightly creamy, it is a refined wine with strong grapefruit-like flavours, a hint of spice, fresh, balanced acidity, a subtle oak influence, and good weight, vibrancy, texture and harmony.

Vintage	14	
WR	5	
Drink	16-18	DRY $22 AV

Jules Taylor Marlborough Chardonnay ★★★★☆

Offering great value, the 2015 vintage (★★★★☆) was grown at two sites in the Southern Valleys and partly barrel-fermented. Fragrant, with a slightly creamy bouquet, showing good complexity, it's a 'serious' wine, but already delicious, with mouthfilling body, strong grapefruit and nut flavours, and a dry, well-rounded finish. Drink now or cellar.

Vintage	15	
WR	6	
Drink	16-20	DRY $22 V+

Junction Corner Post Central Hawke's Bay Chardonnay (★★★☆)

Grown in Central Hawke's Bay, the 2015 vintage (★★★☆) was barrel-fermented (30 per cent new) and given a full, softening malolactic fermentation. Fresh and lively, it has crisp, grapefruit-like flavours to the fore, a minerally streak and very good depth.

DRY $27 –V

Kaimira Estate Brightwater Chardonnay ★★★☆

Certified organic, the 2015 vintage (★★★☆) was estate-grown at Brightwater, in Nelson, fermented in French oak barrels (20 per cent new), and oak-aged for a year. A subtle, youthful wine with some elegance, it has moderately concentrated, grapefruit-like flavours, gently seasoned with toasty oak, balanced acidity, and cellaring potential; open mid-2017+.

Vintage	15	
WR	6	
Drink	16-20	DRY $25 –V

Kakapo Barrel Fermented Marlborough Chardonnay (★★★★)

Still very youthful, the 2015 vintage (★★★★) from wine distributor Sanz Global is a bright, light lemon/green, mouthfilling, vibrantly fruity wine. Showing good delicacy, it has ripe, peachy, citrusy flavours, strongly seasoned with nutty oak, and obvious potential; best drinking 2017+.

Vintage	15	
WR	4	
Drink	16-21	DRY $24 AV

Kalex Waipara Valley Chardonnay   (★★★★)

The 2013 vintage (★★★★) is a high-flavoured wine, hand-picked, fermented with indigenous yeasts and barrel-aged for a year. Pale yellow, it is mouthfilling, with ripe, peachy, mealy flavours, hints of toast and butterscotch, and impressive complexity, harmony and length.

DRY $36 –V

Karikari Estate Calypso Chardonnay   ★★★☆

Still drinking well in 2016, the 2013 vintage (★★★☆) of this Northland wine is sturdy (14.5 per cent alcohol), with very good depth of ripe grapefruit and peach flavours, a subtle seasoning of oak, and a slightly buttery, well-rounded finish. The 2014 vintage (★★★★) is fragrant and softly mouthfilling, with finely integrated oak and generous, ripe, peachy, slightly spicy flavours. It's an excellent example of the powerful northern style.

DRY $29 –V

Karikari Estate Chardonnay   ★★★★☆

Estate-grown in Northland, the 2013 vintage (★★★★☆) is a bright, light yellow/green, powerful wine (14.5 per cent alcohol), with strong personality. Robust, with concentrated stone-fruit and toasty oak flavours, a slightly creamy texture, and good complexity, it's a drink-now or cellaring proposition. The 2014 vintage (★★★★☆) is very similar. Mouthfilling, it is rich and well-rounded, with ripe, peachy, slightly toasty flavours, poised and lively, and excellent depth and complexity. It's already highly enjoyable, but worth cellaring.

DRY $45 –V

Kidnapper Cliffs Hawke's Bay Chardonnay   ★★★★★

From Te Awa (owned by Villa Maria), the outstanding 2013 vintage (★★★★★) was estate-grown in the Gimblett Gravels, hand-picked in multiple passes through the vineyard, fermented in French oak casks (30 per cent new), and given a full, softening malolactic fermentation. Full-bodied and fleshy, it has lovely concentration of fresh, ripe citrus and stone-fruit flavours, mealy, biscuity notes adding complexity, and a rich, well-rounded finish. Already delicious, it should mature well.

Vintage	13
WR	6
Drink	16-20

DRY $45 AV

Kumeu River Coddington Chardonnay   ★★★★★

Launched from the 2006 vintage, this powerful, rich wine is grown in the Coddington Vineyard, between Huapai and Waimauku. The grapes, cultivated on a clay hillside, achieve an advanced level of ripeness (described by Kumeu River as 'flamboyant, unctuous, peachy'). Mouthfilling, complex and slightly nutty, it's typically a lusher, softer wine than its Hunting Hill stablemate (below). The very age-worthy 2014 vintage (★★★★★) is a mouthfilling, elegant, tightly structured wine, with citrusy, peachy flavours, showing excellent complexity and length. The 2015 vintage (★★★★☆) is fresh and fragrant, with a slightly smoky bouquet and vibrant grapefruit and spice flavours, tight-knit and lasting. Woven with lively acidity, it's still very youthful; best drinking 2018+.

Vintage	15	14	13	12	11	10	09
WR	7	7	7	5	5	7	7
Drink	16-22	16-21	16-20	16-18	16-17	16-19	16-17

DRY $45 AV

Kumeu River Estate Chardonnay ★★★★★

This wine ranks fourth in the company's hierarchy of five Chardonnays, after three single-vineyard labels, but is still outstanding. Grown at Kumeu, in West Auckland, it is powerful, with rich, beautifully interwoven flavours and a seductively creamy texture, but also has good acid spine. The key to its quality lies in the vineyards, says winemaker Michael Brajkovich: 'We manage to get the grapes very ripe.' Grown in several blocks around Kumeu, hand-picked, fermented with indigenous yeasts and lees-aged (with weekly or twice-weekly lees-stirring) in Burgundy oak barriques (typically 25 per cent new), the wine normally undergoes a full, softening malolactic fermentation. The 2014 vintage (★★★★★) has a fragrant, complex bouquet, leading into a refined, youthful wine with excellent intensity of citrusy, mealy, biscuity flavours, lively and lingering. The 2015 vintage (★★★★★) is also a top buy. Open and expressive in its youth, it has fresh, ripe grapefruit, peach and spice flavours, gently seasoned with smoky, toasty oak, good complexity, a slightly minerally streak, lively acidity and impressive length. Best drinking mid-2017+.

Vintage	15	14	13	12	11	10	09
WR	6	7	7	5	5	7	7
Drink	16-20	16-20	16-19	P	P	16-19	16-17

DRY $30 V+

Kumeu River Hunting Hill Chardonnay ★★★★★

This outstanding, single-vineyard wine is grown on slopes above Mate's Vineyard, directly over the road from the winery at Kumeu (originally planted in 1982, the site was replanted in 2000). A notably elegant wine, in its youth it is generally less lush than its Coddington stablemate (above), but with good acidity and citrusy, complex flavours that build well across the palate. The 2014 vintage (★★★★★) is a very elegant, finely poised wine, citrusy, mealy, tightly structured and complex, with a crisp, long finish and excellent vigour and harmony. The 2015 vintage (★★★★★) is fresh, fragrant and mouthfilling, with impressive depth of citrus and stone-fruit flavours, good acid spine, excellent complexity and lovely drive through the palate. Best drinking 2018+.

Vintage	15	14	13	12	11	10	09
WR	7	7	7	5	5	7	6
Drink	16-22	16-21	16-20	16-18	16-17	16-19	16-17

DRY $50 AV

Kumeu River Mate's Vineyard Kumeu Chardonnay ★★★★★

This extremely classy single-vineyard wine is Kumeu River's flagship. It is made entirely from the best of the fruit harvested from Mate's Vineyard, planted in 1990 on the site of the original Kumeu River vineyard purchased by Mate Brajkovich in 1944. Strikingly similar to Kumeu River Estate Chardonnay, but slightly more opulent and concentrated, it offers the same rich and harmonious flavours of grapefruit, peach and butterscotch, typically with a stronger seasoning of new French oak (30 per cent in 2014). For winemaker Michael Brajkovich, the hallmark of Mate's Vineyard is 'a pear-like character on the nose, with richness and length on the palate after two to three years'. The 2014 vintage (★★★★★) has a rich, peachy, smoky bouquet. Mouthfilling, it is powerful and highly concentrated, with ripe stone-fruit flavours and a very sustained finish. The 2015 vintage (★★★★★) is still a baby. Full-bodied, it is tightly structured, with rich, vibrant, peachy, slightly spicy flavours, threaded with fresh acidity, smoky and toasty notes adding complexity, and a long, finely poised finish. Best drinking 2018+.

Vintage	15	14	13	12	11	10	09	08
WR	7	7	7	5	5	7	7	6
Drink	16-22	16-21	16-20	16-18	16-17	16-19	16-17	P

DRY $70 AV

Kumeu Village Chardonnay ★★★☆

Kumeu River's lower-tier, drink-young wine is hand-picked from heavier-bearing Chardonnay clones than the Mendoza commonly used for the top wines, and is typically fermented with indigenous yeasts in a mix of tanks (principally) and seasoned French oak casks. The 2015 vintage (★★★☆) was fully barrel-fermented, due to the ultra low-cropping season. Lemon-scented, it is youthful, with mouthfilling body, strong, citrusy flavours, a subtle oak influence and good acid spine. Fine value.

Landing, The, Bay of Islands Chardonnay ★★★★☆

From a coastal site in the northern Bay of Islands, the 2013 vintage (★★★★★), fermented and matured in French oak casks (40 per cent new), is outstanding. Showing real richness and class, it's a powerful wine with a fragrant, toasty, smoky bouquet and delicious stone-fruit flavours, concentrated, ripe and rounded.

Vintage	14	13
WR	5	6
Drink	16-19	16-17

Lawson's Dry Hills Marlborough Chardonnay ★★★☆

The 2014 vintage (★★★☆) is a very good example of the unoaked Chardonnay style. A single-vineyard wine, it was given a full, softening malolactic fermentation and lees-stirred weekly for four months. Freshly scented, it is mouthfilling, with strong, vibrant, citrusy, appley, slightly spicy flavours and lots of drink-young charm.

Vintage	14
WR	6
Drink	P

DRY $19 V+

Lawson's Dry Hills Reserve Marlborough Chardonnay ★★★★

Estate-grown in the Chaytors Road Vineyard, in the Wairau Valley, the 2014 vintage (★★★★) was fermented in French oak barriques (25 per cent new), and given a full, softening malolactic fermentation. Light lemon/green, it is mouthfilling, with a slightly creamy, biscuity bouquet. It has fresh, generous, grapefruit-like flavours, with a subtle seasoning of oak adding complexity, balanced acidity, and very good vigour and depth. Drink now or cellar.

Vintage	14	13
WR	6	6
Drink	16-20	16-18

Left Field Hawke's Bay Chardonnay   ★★★☆

From Te Awa, the 2015 vintage (★★★★) was fermented in an even split of tanks and French oak puncheons and hogsheads, fully barrel-aged for six months, and given a full, softening malolactic fermentation. Mouthfilling, it has strong, ripe, grapefruit-like flavours, woven with fresh acidity, savoury, smoky notes adding complexity, and a lingering finish. Fine value.

Vintage	15
WR	5
Drink	16-19

 DRY $18 V+

Leveret Estate Hawke's Bay Chardonnay   ★★★

Maturing well, the 2014 vintage (★★★★) is a fresh, elegant wine, offering good value. Mouthfilling and smooth, with a hint of gunflint, it is citrusy and peachy, slightly buttery and toasty, with lively acidity and good complexity and length.

 DRY $22 –V

Leveret Estate Reserve Hawke's Bay Chardonnay   ★★★★

The elegant, still youthful 2014 vintage (★★★★☆) was estate-grown at cool inland sites and barrel-fermented. Light lemon/green, it is mouthfilling and finely poised, with concentrated, grapefruit-like flavours, slightly smoky and toasty notes adding complexity, and a long, tightly structured finish. Best drinking 2017+.

 DRY $30 –V

Linden Estate Esk Valley Hawke's Bay Chardonnay   ★★★☆

The 2013 vintage (★★★☆) was estate-grown, hand-picked, and American oak-aged for 10 months. Citrusy and peachy, with a slightly buttery oak influence, it has very good flavour depth, a touch of complexity, and some elegance. Ready.

 DRY $25 –V

Lochiel Estate Chardonnay   (★★★★☆)

Estate-grown at Mangawhai, north of Auckland, the classy 2013 vintage (★★★★☆) was fermented and matured for 11 months in French oak barrels. The bouquet is slightly smoky; the palate is layered and complex, with sweet-fruit delights and concentrated stone-fruit flavours, enriched but not dominated by oak. Great value.

 DRY $25 V+

Longview Estate Unoaked Chardonnay   (★★★)

From a hillside vineyard in Northland, the 2014 vintage (★★★) is a youthful wine, mouthfilling and rounded, with ripe peach, apple and pear flavours. It's not a complex style, but shows good freshness, vigour and depth.

DRY $26 –V

Luna Eclipse Martinborough Chardonnay (★★★☆)

The 2015 vintage (★★★☆) is a distinctive, medium-bodied wine with a slightly creamy bouquet. Citrusy and appley, with fresh acidity and considerable complexity, it is lively and youthful, with cellaring potential. (From Murdoch James.)

 DRY $35 –V

Mad Dog Vineyard Bay of Islands Chardonnay (★★★★)

The 2014 vintage (★★★★), French oak-aged for 10 months, is a weighty, generous Northland style. Fleshy and creamy, it has fresh, strong grapefruit and peach flavours and a well-rounded finish. Enjoyable young.

DRY $24 AV

Mahi Alchemy Marlborough Chardonnay ★★★★☆

The 2013 vintage (★★★★☆) is a stylish, single-vineyard wine, grown at a warm site at Rapaura, hand-picked, and fermented and matured for 15 months in French oak barriques. Mouthfilling, with concentrated, ripe fruit flavours, gentle acidity, a slightly creamy texture, and excellent complexity and harmony, it's well worth cellaring.

Vintage	13
WR	6
Drink	16-21

 DRY $35 –V

Mahi Marlborough Chardonnay ★★★★

The 2015 vintage (★★★★) was hand-picked at four sites and fermented with indigenous yeasts in French oak barrels. Bright, light lemon/green, it is fresh and youthful, in a refined style with ripe, grapefruit-like, slightly mealy flavours, a subtle seasoning of oak, and very good delicacy, depth and complexity. Best drinking mid-2017+.

Vintage	15	14	13	12	11	10	09
WR	6	6	6	6	6	6	6
Drink	16-21	16-21	16-18	16-17	16-17	P	P

DRY $24 V+

Mahi Twin Valleys Vineyard Marlborough Chardonnay ★★★★★

Grown and hand-harvested in the Twin Valleys Vineyard, at the junction of the Wairau and Waihopai valleys, the 2014 vintage (★★★★☆) was fermented with indigenous yeasts and matured for 15 months in French oak barrels. Light lemon/green, it is still very youthful. Tightly structured and complex, it is full-bodied, with vibrant grapefruit and peach flavours, smoky and biscuity notes adding complexity, fresh acidity and obvious potential; open 2018+.

Vintage	14	13
WR	6	6
Drink	16-22	16-22

 DRY $35 AV

Mahurangi River Winery Field of Grace Chardonnay   ★★★★☆

Estate-grown at Matakana, this consistently impressive wine is grown in the Field of Grace Block, hand-harvested and matured in French oak barriques (8 per cent new in 2014). The 2014 vintage (★★★★☆) is a wine of subtle power. Sweet-fruited, it has deep, vibrant grapefruit and peach flavours, very subtle oak, good mouthfeel and complexity, and a slightly mealy, rounded finish. Open 2017+.

Vintage	14	13
WR	6	6
Drink	16-20	16-19

 DRY $36 –V

Mahurangi River Winery Field of Grace Reserve Chardonnay   ★★★★★

The 2014 vintage (★★★★★) was hand-picked at Matakana and fermented and matured in French oak barrels (64 per cent new). Fragrant, with a complex bouquet, it is a powerful, rich wine, with generous, ripe stone-fruit flavours, biscuity notes adding complexity, and a long, well-rounded finish. Distinctly classy, it should be at its best 2017+.

Vintage	14	13
WR	6	6
Drink	16-21	16-20

 DRY $58 AV

Main Divide Waipara Valley Chardonnay   ★★★☆

The Main Divide range is from Pegasus Bay. The 2014 vintage (★★★☆) was fermented with indigenous yeasts and lees-aged in old French oak casks, 'restricting any pick-up of oak flavours and allowing the fruit to express itself'. Already drinking well, it's a full-bodied, finely balanced wine with very good depth of grapefruit and peach flavours, fresh, lively acidity, and hints of honey and toast. Priced right.

Vintage	14	13
WR	6	6
Drink	16-17	P

 DRY $21 AV

Man O' War Valhalla Waiheke Island Chardonnay   ★★★★

This crisp, tautly structured wine is estate-grown at the eastern end of Waiheke Island. Hand-picked and fermented with indigenous yeasts in French oak casks, the 2012 vintage (★★★★) has a slightly smoky bouquet. Mouthfilling, crisp and tight, with strong, vibrant, mealy, biscuity flavours, showing good complexity, it is well worth cellaring. The 2011 (★★★★) is probably at its peak. A distinctive wine, nutty and toasty, with firm acid spine, it is mouthfilling and complex, with rich, citrusy, peachy flavours and a fractionally honeyed, tight, dry finish.

DRY $42 –V

Map Maker Marlborough Chardonnay Pure   ★★★★

From Staete Landt, the 2014 vintage (★★★★) was grown and hand-harvested at Rapaura, in the Wairau Valley. A weighty, creamy-textured wine, it was barrel-fermented, but not barrel-aged, and bottled young. An excellent drink-young style, it is fleshy and forward, with some complexity, and strong, citrusy, peachy, slightly nutty flavours. Fine value.

Vintage	14
WR	6
Drink	16-17

 DRY $20 V+

Marble Point Hanmer Springs Chardonnay   ★★★☆

The 2013 vintage (★★★☆) was estate-grown in North Canterbury and fermented with indigenous yeasts in French oak barrels (25 per cent new). Bright, light yellow, it is mouthfilling, with very good depth of peachy, lemony, slightly toasty flavours, woven with fresh acidity, and a minerally streak. Drink now to 2017.

Vintage	13
WR	6
Drink	16-20

 DRY $25 –V

Margrain Martinborough Chardonnay   ★★★☆

The 2012 vintage (★★★★) was fermented and matured for 11 months in French oak barrels (10 per cent new). Light lemon/green, it is full-bodied, with fresh, peachy, citrusy, slightly toasty flavours, woven with crisp acidity, and considerable complexity. Maturing gracefully, it's a drink-now or cellaring proposition.

Vintage	12	11	10
WR	5	6	7
Drink	16-17	P	16-17

 DRY $28 –V

Marsden Bay of Islands Black Rocks Chardonnay   ★★★★☆

Grown at Kerikeri, this Northland wine is impressive in favourably dry seasons – sturdy, with concentrated, ripe sweet-fruit flavours, well seasoned with toasty oak, in a typically lush, upfront, creamy-smooth style. The 2015 vintage (★★★★☆) was fermented and matured for 11 months in French oak barriques (30 per cent new). More tightly structured and restrained than most past releases, it is mouthfilling and creamy, with generous, peachy, citrusy, slightly smoky flavours, showing excellent vigour, complexity, harmony and length. Best drinking mid-2017+.

Vintage	15	14	13	12	11	10
WR	6	6	6	4	5	6
Drink	16-22	16-19	16-18	P	P	P

DRY $40 –V

Martinborough Vineyard Chardonnay ★★★★★

Mouthfilling, peachy and mealy, this is a powerful, harmonious wine, rich and complex. Made from grapes grown on the gravelly Martinborough Terrace, including the original Mendoza-clone vines planted in 1980, it is hand-picked, fermented with indigenous yeasts and lees-aged for a year in French oak barriques (20 per cent new in 2012). The 2013 vintage (★★★★☆) has a fragrant, stylish, complex bouquet. A finely poised wine with concentrated flavours of grapefruit, peach and biscuity oak, it is savoury and complex, with obvious potential; open 2017+.

Vintage	13	12	11	10	09	08
WR	7	6	6	7	7	7
Drink	16-19	16-17	P	P	P	P

DRY $39 AV

Martinborough Vineyard Home Block Chardonnay (★★★★★)

Already delicious, the 2014 vintage (★★★★★) is a fragrant, generous, age-worthy wine. Light lemon/green, it is finely poised, with rich, ripe stone-fruit flavours, showing good complexity, slightly smoky notes, finely integrated oak and a long finish. Best drinking mid-2017+.

DRY $40 AV

Matahiwi Estate Hawke's Bay Chardonnay ★★☆

The light lemon/green 2015 vintage (★★★) from this Wairarapa-based producer was grown at two sites in Hawke's Bay. Enjoyable young, it is fresh and vibrantly fruity, with good depth of ripe, peachy, slightly buttery and toasty flavours.

DRY $22 –V

Matahiwi Estate Holly Hawke's Bay Chardonnay ★★★★

The 2014 vintage (★★★★), barrel-fermented (35 per cent new), is fragrant, rich and rounded, with generous, slightly buttery flavours. The 2015 vintage (★★★★) is tightly structured, with mouthfilling body and ripe, peachy, slightly toasty flavours, woven with fresh acidity. Best drinking mid-2017+.

DRY $25 AV

Matakana Estate Matakana Chardonnay ★★★★☆

The 2014 vintage (★★★★☆) is a classy wine, fermented with indigenous yeasts in French oak casks (25 per cent new). It is full-bodied, with strong grapefruit and peach flavours, mingled with biscuity oak, fresh acidity, good complexity, and a long, savoury finish.

DRY $30 AV

Matawhero Church House Barrel Fermented Gisborne Chardonnay ★★★★

The 2015 vintage (★★★★☆) is a generous, 'upfront' style, already offering a lot of pleasure, but worth cellaring. Fermented in American oak casks (30 per cent new), and given a full, softening malolactic fermentation, it is full-bodied and sweet-fruited, with a hint of butterscotch and ripe, peachy, slightly creamy and toasty flavours, showing excellent vigour and richness.

DRY $26 AV

Matawhero Gisborne Chardonnay ★★★☆

Handled without oak, the 'unadulterated' 2014 vintage (★★★☆) was grown in the Tietjen and Leaderbrand vineyards, machine-harvested and fermented mostly with indigenous yeasts. Pale yellow, it is full-bodied and sweet-fruited, with strong, peachy, slightly buttery flavours in a smooth, traditional style with lots of drink-young appeal. Ready.

Vintage	14	13
WR	7	7
Drink	16-17	P

 DRY $23 AV

Matua Single Vineyard Marlborough Chardonnay ★★★★★

The 2014 vintage (★★★★★) was grown in the centre of the Wairau Valley and barrel-fermented, with some use of indigenous yeasts and new oak. The bouquet is fragrant, smoky and complex; the palate is mouthfilling and very savoury, with generous, peachy, citrusy flavours, integrated oak, and a very persistent finish. Best drinking 2017+.

 DRY $58 AV

Maude Mt Maude Vineyard Wanaka Chardonnay ★★★★☆

The 2014 vintage (★★★★☆), hand-picked from estate-grown, 20-year-old vines, was fermented and matured in seasoned French oak puncheons. Fragrant, full-bodied and youthful, it is a rich, elegant style with concentrated, citrusy, peachy flavours, slightly buttery notes, excellent complexity and a long finish. Best 2017+.

 DRY $28 V+

Milcrest Nelson Reserve Chardonnay ★★★

The 2014 vintage (★★★☆) is a single-vineyard wine, fermented and matured for 11 months in French and American oak barriques. It is full-bodied, with very good depth of peachy, citrusy, slightly yeasty and toasty flavours, showing considerable complexity. Enjoyable young.

 DRY $42 -V

Mills Reef Elspeth Gimblett Gravels Hawke's Bay Chardonnay ★★★★☆

Mills Reef's flagship Chardonnay is consistently rewarding and a classic regional style. The 2014 vintage (★★★★☆) was hand-picked and fermented, partly with indigenous yeasts, in French oak casks (23 per cent new). It is mouthfilling, with concentrated, peachy, toasty flavours, showing good complexity. A generous, tightly structured wine, it has obvious cellaring potential and should be at its best 2017+.

Vintage	15	14	13	12	11	10	09
WR	7	7	7	NM	7	7	6
Drink	16-21	16-20	16-18	NM	P	P	P

DRY $40 -V

Mills Reef Estate Hawke's Bay Chardonnay   ★★★

The 2015 vintage (★★★) was grown at Meeanee, Maraekakaho and Crownthorpe. A fruit-driven style, it was mostly handled in tanks; 14 per cent of the blend was barrel-fermented. Medium to full-bodied, it has lively, citrusy, appley, slightly spicy flavours, showing a touch of complexity, and a fresh, smooth finish. Enjoyable young.

Vintage	15	14
WR	7	6
Drink	16-18	16-17

Mills Reef Reserve Hawke's Bay Chardonnay   ★★★★

Mills Reef's middle-tier Chardonnay. The attractive 2015 vintage (★★★★) was mostly (93 per cent) fermented and matured for six months in barrels (76 per cent French, 24 per cent American, 24 per cent new). A very typical regional style, grown at several sites, it is mouthfilling, with strong, ripe stone-fruit flavours to the fore, fresh acidity, buttery and toasty notes adding complexity, and a slightly creamy texture. Enjoyable young, it should be at its best 2017+.

Vintage	15	14	13	12	11	10
WR	7	7	7	6	7	7
Drink	16-19	16-18	16-17	P	P	P

Millton Clos de Ste Anne Chardonnay – see Clos de Ste Anne Chardonnay

Millton Opou Vineyard Gisborne Chardonnay   ★★★★

Certified organic, the 2014 vintage (★★★★) was fermented with indigenous yeasts in French oak casks (23 per cent new). Bright, light gold, it is mouthfilling, with strong, peachy, slightly toasty flavours, balanced acidity, and current-drinking appeal. The impressive 2015 vintage (★★★★☆) was fermented with indigenous yeasts in French oak barrels (15 per cent new), and oak-aged for 15 months. Pale straw, it has a fragrant, complex bouquet. Mouthfilling, it is rich, sweet-fruited, peachy and biscuity, with a slightly oily texture and excellent depth and harmony.

Vintage	15	14
WR	6	6
Drink	16-25	16-24

Mission Hawke's Bay Chardonnay   ★★★

The 2015 vintage (★★★★) is a skilfully crafted wine with a slightly buttery bouquet. Full-bodied, it has peachy, slightly toasty flavours, showing excellent depth and harmony. Great value.

DRY $18 AV

Mission Huchet Hawke's Bay Chardonnay

Full of potential, the debut 2013 vintage (★★★★★) is a notably refined wine. Hand-harvested and fermented with indigenous yeasts in French oak casks (33 per cent new), it was given a full, softening malolactic fermentation. The bouquet is fragrant and complex; the palate is mouthfilling, rich and layered, with highly concentrated peach and grapefruit flavours, integrated oak, fine acidity, and a very persistent finish. Best drinking 2017+.

DRY $80 –V

Mission Jewelstone Hawke's Bay Chardonnay   ★★★★★

Hand-picked from mature vines, the 2015 vintage (★★★★★) was barrel-fermented (French, 26 per cent new) and lees-aged for 10 months. A powerful, rich wine with a real sense of drive and potential, it is weighty, with a hint of butterscotch, ripe, grapefruit-like flavours, finely integrated oak, a slightly creamy texture and a lengthy finish. Best drinking 2018+.

Vintage	15	14	13	12	11	10	09
WR	7	7	6	5	NM	7	6
Drink	17-22	16-21	16-20	16-17	NM	16-20	16-18

DRY $40 AV

Mission Reserve Hawke's Bay Chardonnay   ★★★★☆

For Mission's middle-tier Chardonnay, the style goal is a wine that 'emphasises fruit characters rather than oak, but offers some of the benefits of fermentation and maturation in wood'. The 2014 vintage (★★★★☆) offers good value. Partly hand-harvested, from 10 to 20-year-old vines, it was fermented and matured in French oak barrels (18 per cent new). Light lemon/green, with a slightly smoky bouquet, it is mouthfilling and sweet-fruited, with ripe, peachy, slightly buttery flavours, showing excellent vigour, concentration and complexity. Best drinking 2017+.

Vintage	15	14	13	12	11	10
WR	5	7	7	5	5	5
Drink	16-20	16-21	16-20	16-18	16-18	P

DRY $29 V+

Mission Vineyard Selection Hawke's Bay Chardonnay   ★★★☆

The pale yellow 2016 vintage (★★★☆) is a 'lightly oaked' style. Delicious young, it is mouthfilling, with ripe, citrusy flavours, showing very good vibrancy and depth.

DRY $20 AV

Misty Cove Signature Marlborough Chardonnay   ★★★☆

The 2014 vintage (★★★) was estate-grown at Rapaura, in the Wairau Valley. Mouthfilling and sweet-fruited, it has good depth of fresh, peachy, slightly toasty and buttery flavours, a hint of honey, and drink-young appeal.

DRY $30 –V

Moana Park Hawke's Bay Chardonnay ★★★

The disappointing 2014 vintage (★★) was estate-grown and barrel-fermented. A full-bodied (14.5 per cent alcohol) wine, I have tasted it on several occasions, but it lacks fragrance, delicacy and freshness.

DRY $20 –V

Moana Park Single Vineyard Reserve
Gimblett Road Hawke's Bay Chardonnay (★★★★)

Showing good complexity, the 2013 vintage (★★★★) was fermented and matured for a year in French oak barriques (30 per cent new). An elegant wine, it has peachy, slightly buttery and toasty flavours, fresh acidity and excellent depth.

Vintage	13
WR	5
Drink	16-18

 DRY $42 –V

Momo Marlborough Chardonnay ★★★★

BioGro-certified, the 2013 vintage (★★★☆) from Seresin was estate-grown in the Home and Raupo Creek vineyards, hand-picked, and fermented and matured for 11 months in French oak barriques and puncheons (30 per cent new). It is mouthfilling and slightly creamy, with strong, peachy, citrusy, slightly spicy flavours and a distinct hint of butterscotch. Enjoyable young.

DRY $20 V+

Monarch Estate Vineyard Matakana Chardonnay (★★★★)

The elegant 2014 vintage (★★★★) was estate-grown, hand-picked and barrel-fermented (33 per cent new oak). It's a full-bodied wine, with vibrant, citrusy, peachy flavours, integrated oak, savoury notes adding complexity and a tight finish. Well worth cellaring.

 DRY $25 AV

Mount Edward Central Otago Chardonnay (★★★★)

The 'lightly oaked' 2013 vintage (★★★★) is a lemon-scented, elegant wine, made in a vibrant, fruit-driven style with a touch of complexity. Weighty, it is ripely flavoured, with a subtle oak influence, fresh acid spine and good immediacy.

 DRY $25 AV

Mount Riley 17 Valley Marlborough Chardonnay ★★★★☆

The 2014 vintage (★★★★★) is very refined. Estate-grown at three sites, and fermented and matured in French oak barriques (30 per cent new), it is an immaculate wine, mouthfilling and rich, with concentrated, peachy, citrusy flavours, finely balanced oak, and a long, finely textured finish. Best drinking 2017+.

Vintage	14	13	12	11	10	09
WR	7	7	7	7	7	7
Drink	16-21	16-20	16-19	16-18	16-17	P

 DRY $31 AV

Mount Riley Marlborough Chardonnay   ★★★

The 2014 vintage (★★★) was mostly (70 per cent) fermented in French oak barriques; 30 per cent of the blend was tank-fermented. Grown in the Wairau Valley, it is a fruit-driven style, with mouthfilling body, vibrant, citrusy flavours to the fore, a very gentle seasoning of oak, fresh acidity, and good depth.

DRY $17 AV

Moutere Hills Nelson Chardonnay   (★★★★)

Sturdy and concentrated, the powerful, estate-grown 2014 vintage (★★★★) was hand-picked and French oak-fermented. Bright, light yellow/green, it is mouthfilling, with generous, ripe stone-fruit flavours, toasty and buttery notes adding complexity, and lots of current-drinking appeal.

DRY $34 –V

Moutere Hills Sarau Reserve Chardonnay   (★★★★)

The 2013 vintage (★★★★) is a single-vineyard Nelson wine, barrel-aged for 18 months, with a fragrant, toasty, buttery bouquet. A powerful, 'full-on' style with concentrated, peachy, toasty, slightly gingery and honeyed flavours, good complexity and strong personality, it's ready to roll.

DRY $55 –V

Mt Beautiful North Canterbury Chardonnay   ★★★☆

From young vines at Cheviot, the 2014 vintage (★★★☆) was partly (35 per cent) oak-aged. A medium-bodied wine, it is citrusy, slightly biscuity and buttery, in a cool-climate style with fresh acidity and a creamy texture.

Vintage	14
WR	5
Drink	16-20

DRY $27 –V

Mt Difficulty Grower's Series Lowburn Valley Chardonnay   (★★★★)

Lemon-scented, the 2014 vintage (★★★★) is mouthfilling (14.5 per cent alcohol), with strong, youthful, citrusy flavours, fresh acidity, smoky notes adding complexity and a slightly creamy finish. Drink now or cellar.

Vintage	14
WR	6
Drink	16-25

DRY $39 –V

Mud House Single Vineyard Hungry Hill Marlborough Chardonnay   ★★★★

Grown in the Ure Valley, half-way between Blenheim and Kaikoura, the 2013 vintage (★★★★) was fermented in French oak barrels (20 per cent new). Mouthfilling, sweet-fruited and slightly creamy, it shows good complexity, with ripe, citrusy, peachy, slightly biscuity and mealy flavours.

Vintage	13
WR	6
Drink	16-18

DRY $25 AV

Mudbrick Vineyard Reserve Waiheke Island Chardonnay ★★★★☆

The 2013 vintage (★★★★☆) was grown at three sites, hand-harvested, fermented with indigenous yeasts and lees-aged for seven months in French oak barriques (25 per cent new). It's a mouthfilling wine with ripe grapefruit-like flavours, nutty, biscuity notes adding complexity, balanced acidity, a slightly creamy texture, and obvious cellaring potential. Best drinking 2016 onwards.

Vintage	13	12	11	10	09	08
WR	7	7	NM	7	7	7
Drink	16-20	16-20	NM	P	P	P

DRY $45 –V

Muddy Water Waipara Chardonnay ★★★★☆

Certified organic, the elegant, youthful 2015 vintage (★★★★☆) was hand-picked from 22-year-old vines and fermented with indigenous yeasts in French oak puncheons (15 per cent new). Light lemon/green, it is weighty, with rich stone-fruit and spice flavours, a subtle seasoning of oak, fresh acidity, and strong personality. Best drinking 2018+.

Vintage	15	14	13	12	11	10
WR	7	6	6	6	6	6
Drink	16-26	16-22	16-21	16-20	16-18	16-18

DRY $38 AV

Nanny Goat Vineyard Central Otago Chardonnay ★★★☆

The 2014 vintage (★★★☆) is a mouthfilling, youthful, creamy wine with fresh acidity and very good depth of citrusy, slightly mealy and biscuity flavours. It should reward cellaring; open 2017+.

DRY $36 –V

Nautilus Marlborough Chardonnay ★★★★★

Hand-harvested, barrel-fermented and lees-stirred (in 25 per cent new oak), the 2015 (★★★★★) is a top vintage. Light lemon/green, it is fragrant, rich and harmonious, with fresh, ripe, peachy flavours, integrated oak and excellent complexity. A classy young wine, with lovely balance and freshness, it is very age-worthy; best drinking 2018+.

Vintage	15	14	13	12	11	10
WR	7	6	7	7	6	7
Drink	17-20	16-19	16-18	16-17	P	P

DRY $35 AV

Neudorf Moutere Chardonnay ★★★★★

Superbly rich but not overblown, with arrestingly intense flavours enlivened with fine acidity, this multi-faceted Nelson wine enjoys a reputation second to none among New Zealand Chardonnays. Grown in clay soils threaded with gravel at Upper Moutere, it is hand-harvested from mature vines, fermented with indigenous yeasts, and lees-aged, with regular stirring, for a year in French oak barriques. Bright, light lemon/green, the 2015 vintage (★★★★★) is a fragrant, weighty, fleshy, well-rounded wine, already delicious. It has concentrated, citrusy, mealy flavours, gently seasoned with oak (12 per cent new), a slightly creamy texture, and a persistent, very harmonious finish. A 'forward' vintage, highly expressive in its youth, it should be at its best mid-2017+.

Vintage	15	14	13	12	11	10	09	08
WR	7	6	6	7	6	7	7	6
Drink	18-22	16-21	16-20	16-20	16-18	16-18	16-17	P

DRY $74 AV

Neudorf Nelson Chardonnay   ★★★★☆

Overshadowed by its famous stablemate (above), this regional blend is a fine Chardonnay in its own right. Hand-picked mostly but not entirely at Upper Moutere, it was fermented with indigenous yeasts in French oak barriques (16 per cent new in 2014) and lees-aged for 10 months. The 2014 vintage (★★★★★) is a fragrant, elegant wine, citrusy and mealy, with grapefruit and toast flavours. Mouthfilling, it is youthful, with good concentration and acidity, excellent complexity and a long finish. (Note: since 2015 this label has been replaced by Neudorf Rosie's Block Chardonnay; see below.)

Vintage	14	13	12	11	10	09
WR	6	6	7	6	6	7
Drink	16-20	16-19	16-18	16-18	16-17	16-17

DRY $33 AV

Neudorf Rosie's Block Nelson Chardonnay   ★★★★☆

The 2015 vintage (★★★★☆) replaces the former Neudorf Nelson Chardonnay label, which was easily confused with the famous Moutere Chardonnay. Hand-harvested in Rosie's Block and other Moutere sites, it was fermented with indigenous yeasts and lees-aged for 10 months in French oak casks (15 per cent new), and given a full, softening malolactic fermentation. Fragrant, weighty and savoury, it has generous, youthful stone-fruit and smoky oak flavours, a minerally thread, excellent complexity and a finely poised, long finish. Drink now or cellar.

Vintage	15
WR	7
Drink	16-21

DRY $33 AV

Neudorf Twenty Five Rows Nelson Chardonnay   ★★★★☆

The 2014 vintage (★★★★☆) is a single-vineyard wine, estate-grown at Upper Moutere. Hand-harvested from the first 25 rows in Rosie's Block, it was fermented with indigenous yeasts in tanks, rather than barrels, then matured on its yeast lees, initially in tanks, then in old oak puncheons. A full-bodied, very youthful wine, it has strong, ripe, citrusy flavours, with mealy, faintly biscuity notes adding complexity, and good mouthfeel, delicacy and refinement. A subtle style of Chardonnay, it should be at its best 2017+.

Vintage	15	14	13
WR	7	6	6
Drink	17-20	16-19	16-18

DRY $33 AV

Nga Waka Home Block Chardonnay   ★★★★☆

This single-vineyard Martinborough wine is from vines planted in 1988. At its best, it is an authoritative wine, weighty and concentrated, with strong personality. Already drinking well, the 2015 vintage (★★★★☆) was fermented and matured for 10 months in French oak casks (30 per cent new), and given a full, softening malolactic fermentation. Pale gold, it is a generous wine, mouthfilling, ripe and rounded, with rich, citrusy, peachy, slightly toasty and buttery flavours. Drink now or cellar.

Vintage	15	14	13	12	11	10	09
WR	6	7	7	6	7	NM	7
Drink	16-21	16-20	16-17	P	P	NM	P

 DRY $40 -V

Nga Waka Martinborough Chardonnay   ★★★★

This is a consistently rewarding wine. The 2015 vintage (★★★★) was matured for 10 months in French oak casks (18 per cent new). Light lemon/green, it is mouthfilling and vibrantly fruity, with strong, peachy, citrusy, slightly mealy and buttery flavours, integrated oak, fresh acidity, and lots of drink-young appeal.

Vintage	15	14	13	12	11	10
WR	6	7	7	6	7	7
Drink	16-19	16-18	16-17	P	P	P

 DRY $30 -V

Ngatarawa Proprietors' Reserve Hawke's Bay Chardonnay   (★★★★★)

A very 'complete', generous, finely structured wine, the debut 2013 vintage (★★★★★) was grown at two sites in the Bridge Pa Triangle, fermented and lees-aged for 11 months in French oak barriques (33 per cent new), and given a full, softening malolactic fermentation. Fragrant, full-bodied, sweet-fruited and concentrated, it has rich stone-fruit flavours, toasty, buttery notes adding complexity, and a long, very harmonious finish. Currently delicious, it should also mature gracefully.

 DRY $35 AV

Ngatarawa Stables Reserve Hawke's Bay Chardonnay   ★★★

The 2014 vintage (★★★) is a mouthfilling, fresh, peachy, slightly toasty and buttery wine, with good depth and a dry, smooth finish. The 2015 vintage (★★★) is similar – full-bodied, with vibrant stone-fruit flavours, a touch of complexity, and plenty of drink-young appeal.

Vintage	15	14
WR	7	5
Drink	16-20	16-19

DRY $20 -V

Obsidian Reserve Waiheke Island Chardonnay   ★★★★☆

This reserve bottling, from 'small hillside vineyards', is based on 'the best fruit parcels and barrels'. Light lemon/green, the 2015 vintage (★★★★☆) is fragrant and mouthfilling, with layers of rich, ripe, peachy flavours, seasoned with toasty oak, excellent complexity, and a finely textured, harmonious finish. Delicious from the start, it should be at its best 2018+.

Vintage	15	14	13	12
WR	6	6	7	6
Drink	16-21	16-20	16-19	16-18

 DRY $48 -V

Obsidian Waiheke Island Chardonnay ★★★★

The 2014 vintage, matured in French oak barriques for 10 months, is mouthfilling, with fresh, generous peach and grapefruit flavours, gently seasoned with biscuity oak. A subtle, finely poised, youthful wine, it should be at its best 2017+.

 DRY $29 AV

Odyssey Gisborne Chardonnay ★★★

The 2014 vintage (★★★☆), grown in the Kawatiri Vineyard, was handled in tanks (60 per cent) and barrels (40 per cent). Full-bodied and fleshy, it has fresh, ripe, peachy, slightly nutty and buttery flavours, in a moderately complex style with a rounded finish – and lots of drink-young appeal.

DRY $20 –V

Odyssey Reserve Iliad Gisborne Chardonnay ★★★★☆

Top vintages represent Gisborne Chardonnay at its finest. Hand-picked from mature vines in the Kawatiri Vineyard at Hexton and fermented and lees-aged in French oak barriques (27 per cent new), the 2014 vintage (★★★★☆) is a mouthfilling wine with strong, ripe stone-fruit flavours, biscuity and nutty notes adding complexity, and good power and potential. Best drinking 2017+.

Vintage	14	13
WR	6	6
Drink	16-18	16-18

 DRY $34 AV

Ohinemuri Estate Patutahi Reserve Chardonnay ★★★★

The elegant, barrel-fermented 2014 vintage (★★★★) is one of the best yet. Mouthfilling, it has generous, ripe stone-fruit flavours, showing good complexity, a subtle oak influence, slightly buttery notes and excellent freshness and harmony. Retasted in mid-2016, it's maturing very gracefully; drink now or cellar.

Vintage	14
WR	6
Drink	16-21

DRY $25 AV

Old Coach Road Nelson Chardonnay ★★★

This affordable wine from Seifried Estate is an upfront, high-flavoured style that slides down very easily. The 2014 vintage (★★★), handled without oak, is sturdy (14 per cent alcohol), with ripe, peachy, slightly buttery flavours, showing good depth, and a smooth finish. An enjoyable, drink-young style.

Vintage	14	13
WR	6	6
Drink	16-21	16-21

 DRY $13 V+

Old Coach Road Unoaked Nelson Chardonnay   ★★☆

The 2016 vintage (★★☆) from Seifried is a very 'fruit-driven' wine, mouthfilling, with fresh, peachy, faintly buttery and spicy flavours and a smooth, off-dry (8 grams/litre of residual sugar) finish. Enjoyable young, it's priced right.

Vintage	16	15	14	13
WR	5	5	5	5
Drink	16-20	16-17	16-17	P

MED/DRY $13 V+

Omihi Hills Omihi Reserve Chardonnay   ★★★★☆

The 2013 vintage (★★★★☆) was grown in North Canterbury and matured in seasoned oak barrels. Mouthfilling, with concentrated, peachy, slightly buttery and toasty flavours, showing good complexity, it's a bold, expressive wine, drinking well now.

Vintage	13
WR	6
Drink	16-19

DRY $30 AV

Osawa Prestige Collection Hawke's Bay Chardonnay   ★★★☆

Grown at Maraekakaho, the 2015 vintage (★★★) is a citrusy, slightly limey wine with mouthfilling body, grapefruit-like flavours and a subtle oak seasoning.

DRY $50 –V

Osawa Winemakers Collection Hawke's Bay Chardonnay   (★★★★☆)

A rich, creamy style, the 2014 vintage (★★★★☆) was grown at Maraekakaho. The bouquet is fragrant and mealy, with a hint of maturity; the palate is softly textured, long and concentrated.

DRY $85 –V

Oyster Bay Marlborough Chardonnay   ★★★☆

From Delegat, this wine is designed to showcase Marlborough's incisive fruit flavours. Half the blend is handled solely in tanks; the other half is fermented, lees-stirred weekly and matured for six months in French oak barrels (20 per cent new). It typically offers ripe grapefruit-like flavours, slightly buttery and crisp, with creamy, toasty elements adding a touch of complexity. The attractive 2014 vintage (★★★☆), grown in the Wairau and Awatere valleys, is mouthfilling, citrusy and peachy, in an elegant style with fresh acidity, a subtle seasoning of oak adding complexity, and very good harmony and depth.

DRY $20 AV

Paddy Borthwick New Zealand Chardonnay   ★★★★

Grown in the Wairarapa, the 2015 vintage (★★★★) has a fragrant, slightly buttery and nutty bouquet. The palate is vibrant, with strong, peachy, mealy, slightly toasty flavours, woven with fresh acidity, good complexity, and some potential. Best drinking mid-2017+.

DRY $26 AV

Palliser Estate Martinborough Chardonnay ★★★★★

Rather than power, the key attributes of this wine are finesse and harmony. A celebration of rich, ripe fruit flavours, it is gently seasoned with oak (French, about 25 per cent new), producing a delicious wine with subtle winemaking input and concentrated varietal flavours. The 2014 (★★★★★) is clearly a top vintage. It has a fragrant, citrusy bouquet, leading into a generous palate with grapefruit-like flavours, finely integrated oak, and very impressive complexity, drive and elegance.

Vintage	14	13
WR	7	7
Drink	16-21	16-18

DRY $39 AV

Palliser Pencarrow Chardonnay – see Pencarrow Martinborough Chardonnay

Paritua Hawke's Bay Chardonnay ★★★★

The elegant 2013 vintage (★★★★) was matured for 11 months in French oak casks (60 per cent new). It is fragrant and sweet-fruited, with strong, citrusy, peachy flavours, biscuity oak adding complexity, fresh acidity, and a tightly structured finish.

Vintage	13
WR	6
Drink	16-20

DRY $35 –V

Paroa Bay Bay of Islands Chardonnay ★★★☆

The 2014 vintage (★★★☆) was estate-grown at Russell and barrel-fermented. Weighty, it has very good depth of ripe, peachy, citrusy flavours and a subtle seasoning of nutty, toasty oak.

DRY $35 –V

Parr & Simpson Limestone Bay Barrique Fermented Chardonnay ★★★☆

From a site at Puhara, overlooking Golden Bay, in Nelson, this wine has strong personality. The vigorous 2013 vintage (★★★☆), barrel-fermented in seasoned French oak, offers strong, citrusy, slightly mealy and buttery flavours, with a firm acid spine. Best drinking 2017+.

Vintage	13
WR	6
Drink	16-18

DRY $22 AV

Pask Declaration Gimblett Gravels Chardonnay ★★★★☆

The winery's top Chardonnay is estate-grown in the Gimblett Gravels, Hawke's Bay. The 2015 vintage (★★★★★) was fermented and matured for 11 months in French oak puncheons (78 per cent new). Bright, light lemon/green, it is weighty and youthful, with concentrated, ripe stone-fruit flavours, mealy and biscuity notes adding complexity, and excellent delicacy, texture and length. Best drinking 2018+.

Vintage	15	14	13	12	11	10
WR	6	7	7	5	6	NM
Drink	17-22	16-21	16-20	16-19	16-18	NM

DRY $40 –V

Pask Gimblett Gravels Chardonnay ★★★☆

This second-tier Hawke's Bay Chardonnay is designed to highlight its vibrant fruit characters, with a subtle wood influence from partial barrel fermentation. The 2015 vintage (★★★☆) is elegant and fruity, with ripe, peachy flavours, gently seasoned with oak, and fresh acidity keeping things lively.

Vintage	15	14	13	12	11	10	DRY $22 AV
WR	7	7	7	5	5	7	
Drink	16-20	16-19	16-18	P	P	P	

Pask Small Batch Gimblett Road Sur Lie Chardonnay ★★★☆

The debut 2013 vintage (★★★★) is a stylish wine from Hawke's Bay, matured in seasoned French oak casks. Fresh and lemony, it has some peachy and nutty notes adding complexity, balanced acidity and a long finish. The 2014 vintage (★★★☆) is a fresh, medium-bodied wine with a subtle oak influence and considerable elegance.

DRY $25 –V

Pask Small Batch Gimblett Road Wild Ferment Chardonnay ★★★★

The richly fragrant 2013 vintage (★★★★☆) is an estate-grown, Hawke's Bay wine, fermented with indigenous yeasts and matured in seasoned French oak casks. A classic regional style, it is weighty, with generous, ripe stone-fruit and nut flavours, showing excellent concentration and complexity. The 2014 vintage (★★★★) is fragrant and mouthfilling, with ripe-fruit flavours, impressive depth and complexity, and a lingering finish.

DRY $25 AV

Peacock Sky Waiheke Island Chardonnay (★★★)

The 2014 vintage (★★★) is mouthfilling and vibrantly fruity, in a moderately complex style with decent depth and a rounded finish.

DRY $39 –V

Pegasus Bay Chardonnay ★★★★★

Strapping yet delicate, richly flavoured yet subtle, this sophisticated wine is one of the country's best Chardonnays grown south of Marlborough. Muscular and taut, it typically offers a seamless array of fresh, crisp, citrusy, biscuity, complex flavours and great concentration and length. Estate-grown at Waipara, it is based on ungrafted, Mendoza-clone vines (30 years old), fermented with indigenous yeasts, given a full, softening malolactic fermentation and matured for a year on its yeast lees in barrels (French oak puncheons, 30 per cent new in 2013). The 2013 vintage (★★★★★) is mouthfilling, vibrantly fruity and finely poised. Likely to be long-lived, it has a fragrant, complex bouquet, leading into a peachy, citrusy, gently oaked wine, with slightly buttery notes, good acid spine, and a real sense of youthful vigour. Best drinking 2017+.

Vintage	13	12	11	10	09	08	DRY $39 AV
WR	7	6	6	6	7	6	
Drink	16-23	16-24	16-23	16-20	16-18	P	

Pegasus Bay Virtuoso Chardonnay   ★★★★★

Blended from several of the 'best barrels', this wine is hand-picked from the company's mature, Mendoza-clone vines at Waipara. Fermented with indigenous yeasts, it is lees-aged for a year in French oak puncheons (partly new), matured in tanks on light lees for several more months before bottling, and then bottle-aged for a year prior to its release. The 2013 vintage (★★★★☆) is very youthful, with strong, grapefruit-like flavours, balanced oak, and good drive through the palate. Rich and complex, it's crying out for more time.

 DRY $50 AV

Pencarrow Martinborough Chardonnay   ★★★☆

Pencarrow is Palliser Estate's second-tier label. The 2013 vintage (★★★☆) was fermented and matured for nine months in oak barriques (22 per cent new), and about one-third of the blend was handled with indigenous yeasts and malolactic fermentation. Fresh, vibrant and sweetly oaked, it has ripe stone-fruit flavours, slightly mealy and toasty, and lots of drink-young appeal.

 DRY $21 AV

People's, The, Chardonnay   ★★☆

From Constellation NZ, the 2013 vintage (★★☆) is a Hawke's Bay wine, fresh and vibrantly fruity, with citrusy, appley flavours, in an easy-drinking style.

 DRY $17 –V

Peregrine Central Otago Chardonnay   ★★★★

The 2013 vintage (★★★★) is a fleshy, citrusy, elegant wine, hand-picked at Pisa and matured for 10 months in oak puncheons and hogsheads. Vibrantly fruity, it shows excellent weight, ripeness and richness.

 DRY $35 –V

Peter Yealands Reserve Hawke's Bay Chardonnay   (★★★)

Made in a 'fruit-driven' style, the gently oak-influenced 2014 vintage (★★★) is an attractive, harmonious wine with ripe melon and peach flavours, mealy, biscuity notes adding a touch of complexity, and good harmony.

Vintage	14
WR	7
Drink	16-18

DRY $21 –V

Pukeora Estate Chardonnay   ★★★

Grown in Central Hawke's Bay, the 2013 vintage (★★★☆) was hand-harvested, fermented with indigenous yeasts in seasoned French barriques, and lees-aged in oak for 10 months. A powerful, full-bodied wine (14.9 per cent alcohol), it has fresh, vibrant, grapefruit-like flavours, a subtle oak influence, and very good vigour and depth.

Vintage	13	12
WR	6	6
Drink	16-18	16-17

 DRY $17 AV

Pukeora Estate Ruahine Range Chardonnay ★★★☆

Grown and hand-picked in Central Hawke's Bay, the 2013 vintage (★★★★) was fermented with indigenous yeasts and lees-aged for 10 months in French oak barriques (25 per cent new). Mouthfilling and concentrated, with vibrant, citrusy, peachy flavours and finely integrated oak, it's a powerful wine, but has the richness to carry its high (14.9 per cent) alcohol.

Vintage	13	12
WR	6	6
Drink	16-18	16-17

 DRY $26 –V

Pyramid Valley Growers Collection Marlborough Chardonnay (★★★★☆)

The stylish 2014 vintage (★★★★☆) was grown in Kerner Estate Vineyard, in the Waihopai Valley, and matured in seasoned French oak puncheons. Mouthfilling, it has deep, citrusy flavours, a restrained oak influence, and a very harmonious, smooth, slightly buttery finish. Drink now or cellar.

 DRY $48 –V

Pyramid Valley Vineyards Field of Fire Chardonnay ★★★★★

Estate-grown at Waikari, in North Canterbury, the 2013 vintage (★★★★★) is from vines on a north-facing slope of shallow clays over limestone. Fermented in a 50:50 split of old oak barriques and terracotta clay amphorae from Italy (viewed as a flavour-neutral vessel, compared to barrels), it is mouthfilling, with highly concentrated, youthful, citrusy flavours, good acid spine and a long, slightly buttery finish. Weighty, with a real sense of vigour and richness, it possesses strong personality; drink now or cellar.

Vintage	13	12	11
WR	7	7	7
Drink	16-22	16-21	16-20

 DRY $120 –V

Pyramid Valley Vineyards Lion's Tooth Chardonnay ★★★★★

Estate-grown on an east-facing slope at Waikari, in North Canterbury, the impressive 2013 vintage (★★★★★) was fermented in a 50:50 split of clay amphorae and seasoned French oak barriques (see above). Even richer than its Field of Fire stablemate, it is very powerful and sweet-fruited, with notably concentrated, peachy flavours, a subtle seasoning of oak, a distinct minerally streak and a long, harmonious finish. Drink now or cellar.

Vintage	13	12	11
WR	7	7	7
Drink	16-22	16-21	16-20

DRY $120 –V

Quarter Acre Hawke's Bay Chardonnay ★★★★☆

The 2014 vintage (★★★★☆), grown in the coastal Doc's Block Vineyard at Haumoana, was hand-picked from 20-year-old vines and fermented with indigenous yeasts in French oak barriques (60 per cent new). Mouthfilling, it has fresh, ripe, peachy flavours, showing excellent depth and complexity, and a slightly buttery, well-rounded finish. Best drinking 2017+.

 DRY $35 –V

Rapaura Springs Marlborough Chardonnay   ★★★

The 2015 vintage (★★★☆) is a full-bodied, oak-aged wine with ripe, citrusy and peachy flavours, showing a touch of complexity. Poised and lively, with a basically dry finish (4 grams/litre of residual sugar), it's good value at under $15.

Vintage	15
WR	7
Drink	16-21

DRY $14 V+

Rapaura Springs Reserve Marlborough Chardonnay   (★★★★)

Offering fine value, the 2015 vintage (★★★★) was barrel-fermented. Light lemon/green, it is mouthfilling, with generous, peachy, slightly toasty and smoky flavours, showing very good delicacy and complexity.

Vintage	15
WR	7
Drink	16-24

DRY $19 V+

Renato Nelson Chardonnay   ★★★★

Estate-grown on the Kina Peninsula, hand-picked and fermented and matured for 10 months in French oak barriques (15 per cent new), the 2014 vintage (★★★★) of this single-vineyard wine is sturdy and full-flavoured. Pale straw, it is mouthfilling, with peachy, slightly biscuity flavours, showing very good depth and complexity, a hint of butterscotch, fresh acidity and some potential.

Vintage	14	13	12	11	10	09
WR	6	NM	7	NM	6	7
Drink	16-20	NM	16-18	NM	16-17	16-17

DRY $25 AV

Richmond Plains Nelson Chardonnay   ★★★☆

Certified organic, the 2015 vintage (★★★★) was handled in a 2:1 mix of oak barrels (15 per cent new) and tanks. Light lemon/green, it is lemon-scented, with mouthfilling body, vibrant, citrusy, slightly buttery flavours, a subtle seasoning of oak, and good persistence. An elegant, youthful wine, it should be at its best mid-2017+.

DRY $25 –V

Rimu Grove Nelson Chardonnay   ★★★★☆

This wine is typically full of personality. Estate-grown near the coast in the Moutere hills and fermented and lees-matured for 11 months in French oak casks, the delicious 2015 vintage (★★★★★) is mouthfilling and sweet-fruited, with fresh, concentrated, peachy, slightly toasty flavours, a hint of butterscotch, a fine thread of acidity, and good complexity. Best drinking mid-2017+.

Vintage	15	14	13	12	11	10	09
WR	7	7	7	7	NM	7	6
Drink	16-30	16-25	16-28	16-27	NM	16-25	16-18

DRY $39 –V

Riverby Estate Marlborough Chardonnay ★★★☆

This single-vineyard wine is grown in Jacksons Road, Rapaura, in the heart of the Wairau Valley. The 2013 vintage (★★★☆), from mature vines, was fermented and matured in French oak casks (30 per cent new). Light lemon/green, it is medium to full-bodied, with fresh, citrusy flavours, a touch of complexity, and very good vigour and depth.

Vintage	13	12	11	10
WR	7	6	7	7
Drink	16-21	16-20	P	P

 DRY $25 –V

Rock Ferry 3rd Rock Marlborough Chardonnay ★★★★★

(This label recently replaced the former 'Rock Ferry Marlborough Chardonnay'.) Certified organic, the 2014 vintage (★★★★★), retasted in June 2016, is currently delicious. Estate-grown in The Corners Vineyard, at Rapaura, it was hand-picked, fermented with indigenous yeasts in a French oak cuve, and matured in French oak barriques (25 per cent new). Bright, light lemon/green, it is rich, ripe and rounded, with a fragrant bouquet, good weight and very generous, peachy, citrusy, mealy flavours, gently seasoned with oak. A very harmonious, creamy-textured wine, it's lovely now, but also worth cellaring. Fine value.

 DRY $30 V+

Rock Ferry The Corners Vineyard Marlborough Chardonnay (★★★★★)

Showing a real sense of 'completeness', the 2013 vintage (★★★★★) was estate-grown at Rapaura, hand-picked, fermented with indigenous yeasts in a French oak cuve, and then lees-aged for nine months in French oak barriques (30 per cent new). Richly scented, it has lovely depth of peachy, slightly buttery flavours, complex and subtle, and a long, well-rounded, very harmonious finish. Drink now or cellar.

 DRY $45 AV

Rongopai Hawke's Bay Chardonnay (★★☆)

The 2015 vintage (★★☆) is an uncomplicated wine, vibrantly fruity, with lemony, appley flavours, fresh and direct. (From Babich.)

 DRY $20 –V

Rossendale Marlborough Chardonnay ★★★

Priced sharply, the 2015 vintage (★★★) is a barrel-fermented, medium-bodied wine, with fresh, crisp, lively, citrusy flavours to the fore, slightly peachy and toasty notes, a touch of complexity and satisfying depth.

DRY $16 V+

Sacred Hill Halo Hawke's Bay Chardonnay ★★★☆

Past releases have been rewarding, but the 2015 vintage (★★☆) is disappointing. Estate-grown in the cool, elevated Riflemans Vineyard and barrel-fermented, it is pale gold and peachy, with slightly honeyed, toasty aromas and flavours, showing considerable development.

Vintage	15
WR	6
Drink	16-19

 DRY $28 –V

Sacred Hill Hawke's Bay Chardonnay ★★★☆

Enjoyable young, the 2015 vintage (★★★☆) is a moderately complex style with mouthfilling body and fresh, ripe, peachy, slightly toasty flavours. It shows very good depth and harmony.

Vintage	15
WR	6
Drink	16-18

DRY $20 AV

Sacred Hill Reserve Hawke's Bay Chardonnay ★★★☆

The 2015 vintage (★★★☆) is a fresh, citrusy, crisp wine, grown at the Riflemans Terraces Vineyard and barrel-fermented. A moderately complex style, it has a gentle oak influence and a finely textured, long finish.

Vintage	15
WR	5
Drink	16-17

DRY $25 –V

Sacred Hill Riflemans Chardonnay ★★★★★

Sacred Hill's flagship Chardonnay is one of New Zealand's greatest – powerful yet elegant, with striking intensity and outstanding cellaring potential. Grown in the cool, inland, elevated (100 metres above sea level) Riflemans Terraces Vineyard in the Dartmoor Valley of Hawke's Bay, it is hand-picked from mature, own-rooted, Mendoza-clone vines and fermented with indigenous yeasts in French oak barriques (new and one year old), with some malolactic fermentation. The 2015 vintage (★★★★★) is bright, light lemon/green. Lovely in its youth, it is finely poised, with pure, vibrant, peachy, citrusy flavours to the fore, very finely integrated oak, great harmony, and a very long finish. Best drinking 2018+.

Vintage	15	14	13	12	11	10	09
WR	6	7	7	NM	NM	7	7
Drink	16-22	16-20	16-19	NM	NM	16-17	P

DRY $70 AV

Sacred Hill Virgin Chardonnay   ★★★☆

This Chablis-style wine is hand-picked in the company's acclaimed Riflemans Terraces Vineyard, in the upper Dartmoor Valley, tank-fermented and lees-aged. Harvested relatively early to preserve its lively acidity, it is handled without oak or malolactic fermentation, and promoted as a 'pure, natural Chardonnay'. The 2014 vintage (★★★☆) is mouthfilling and vibrantly fruity, with ripe, peachy flavours, appetising acidity, good vigour and a tight, steely finish.

Vintage	14
WR	6
Drink	16-19

DRY $30 –V

Sacred Hill Wine Thief Hawke's Bay Chardonnay   ★★★★☆

Designed as a 'richer and toastier' style than the flagship Riflemans Chardonnay (above), this wine is grown in the same vineyard, hand-picked and fermented with indigenous yeasts in new and one-year-old French oak barriques. The 2015 vintage (★★★★☆) is an upfront, rich style, mouthfilling, vibrantly fruity, citrusy and creamy, with mealy, buttery notes adding complexity. Delicious young, it's still youthful.

Vintage	15
WR	6
Drink	16-19

DRY $35 –V

Saint Clair James Sinclair Marlborough Chardonnay   (★★★☆)

The 2014 vintage (★★★☆) is a mouthfilling, slightly creamy-textured wine, grown in the Southern Valleys and Awatere Valley and mostly barrel-fermented. Fresh and smooth, with citrusy, slightly biscuity flavours, a hint of sweet oak, and good depth and harmony, it's enjoyable now.

DRY $22 AV

Saint Clair Marlborough Chardonnay   ★★★☆

Well balanced for early drinking, the 2015 vintage (★★★☆) is a Wairau Valley wine, mostly fermented in French and American oak barrels. Pale lemon/green, it has a slightly creamy bouquet, with fresh acidity and good depth of peachy, slightly toasty flavours.

DRY $22 AV

Saint Clair Omaka Reserve Marlborough Chardonnay   ★★★★☆

This is a fat, creamy wine, weighty and rich, made in a bold, upfront style. It is partly hand-harvested in the Southern Valleys – mostly in the company's vineyard·in the Omaka Valley – and fermented and lees-aged in American oak casks (50 per cent new in 2014), with a full, softening malolactic fermentation. The 2014 vintage (★★★★) is full-bodied, with rich, peachy, citrusy flavours, seasoned with sweet oak, and a well-rounded finish.

Vintage	14	13	12	11	10
WR	7	7	7	7	7
Drink	17-18	16-17	P	P	P

DRY $38 AV

Saint Clair Pioneer Block 4 Sawcut Marlborough Chardonnay ★★★★☆

Grown in the Ure Valley, half-way between Blenheim and Kaikoura, this is a consistently classy wine. The 2014 vintage (★★★★) was hand-picked and fermented and lees-aged for 10 months in French oak barriques (25 per cent new). Slightly oaky in its youth, it is mouthfilling, with fresh, citrusy, peachy, toasty flavours, strong, vibrant and well-rounded.

DRY $34 AV

Saint Clair Pioneer Block 10 Twin Hills Marlborough Chardonnay ★★★★☆

This powerful wine is grown principally in the company's vineyard in the Omaka Valley, a warm site with clay-based soils. The 2014 vintage (★★★★☆), partly hand-harvested, was fermented and lees-aged for 10 months in French oak casks (50 per cent new). A stylish, mouthfilling wine, it has concentrated, peachy, citrusy, slightly biscuity and smoky flavours, good complexity, balanced acidity and a lingering finish.

DRY $33 AV

Saint Clair Pioneer Block 11 Cell Block Marlborough Chardonnay ★★★★☆

The classy 2014 vintage (★★★★☆) was grown at Dillons Point, in the lower Wairau Valley, and fermented and lees-aged for 10 months in new French oak barriques. Mouthfilling and sweet-fruited, with fresh, biscuity oak strongly in evidence, it has generous, peachy, citrusy flavours, good mouthfeel and texture, and a rich, rounded, long finish.

DRY $33 AV

Saint Clair Unoaked Marlborough Chardonnay ★★★

This refreshing wine is cool-fermented and lees-aged in tanks, using malolactic fermentation to add complexity and soften the acidity. Enjoyable young, the 2015 vintage (★★★) is a medium to full-bodied wine, with fresh, citrusy flavours, hints of apples and spices, a slightly creamy texture and a smooth (4.2 grams/litre of residual sugar) finish.

DRY $22 –V

Saint Clair Vicar's Choice Marlborough Chardonnay ★★★

The 2014 vintage (★★★☆), fermented in a 50:50 split of tanks and seasoned oak barrels, was matured on its yeast lees for several months and given a full, softening malolactic fermentation. Fresh and moderately complex, it's a highly attractive, drink-young style, with generous, vibrant, peachy flavours to the fore, a hint of sweet oak, and a creamy-smooth finish.

DRY $19 AV

Sanctuary Marlborough Chardonnay ★★★

The 2015 vintage (★★★) of this flavoursome, 'lightly oaked' wine is pale straw, with slightly buttery aromas and flavours. Vibrantly fruity, with spicy, toasty notes, it's enjoyable young.

Vintage	14
WR	7
Drink	16-20

DRY $18 AV

Satyr Kereru Hawke's Bay Chardonnay   (★★★★)

Bright, light lemon/green, the 2014 vintage (★★★★) is a mouthfilling wine, with ripe peach/grapefruit flavours, a slightly buttery, creamy texture, and good complexity. Still youthful, it's maturing gracefully; drink now onwards. (From Sileni.)

DRY $34 –V

Sea Level Home Block Nelson Chardonnay   ★★★★

The 2014 vintage (★★★★), estate-grown at Mariri, was matured for 10 months in seasoned French oak puncheons. Skilfully crafted, it is fragrant and finely poised, in a medium to full-bodied style with concentrated, vibrant, peachy flavours, showing good delicacy and length, balanced acidity and obvious cellaring potential. Best drinking 2017+.

Vintage	14
WR	6
Drink	16-20

DRY $25 AV

Seifried Nelson Chardonnay   ★★★☆

Priced sharply, the 2015 vintage (★★★☆) was fermented and matured for a year in one-year-old French oak barriques, and given a full, softening malolactic fermentation. Pale straw, it is mouthfilling, fresh and vibrantly fruity, with good depth of citrusy flavours, showing a touch of complexity, and a fully dry finish.

Vintage	15	14	13
WR	6	6	6
Drink	16-25	16-24	16-21

DRY $18 V+

Seifried Winemaker's Collection Nelson Barrique Fermented Chardonnay   ★★★★

This is typically a bold style, concentrated and creamy, with loads of flavour. The 2015 vintage (★★★★) was fermented and matured for a year in French oak barriques. Full-bodied, it is a generous wine with concentrated, ripe, peachy, slightly spicy flavours, showing good complexity, and a well-rounded finish. Drink now or cellar.

Vintage	15
WR	7
Drink	16-25

DRY $26 AV

Selaks Founders Limited Edition Hawke's Bay Chardonnay   (★★★★★)

The debut 2013 vintage (★★★★★) offers great value. Hand-picked at Moteo and fermented with indigenous yeasts in French oak barrels (21 per cent new), it has a fragrant, slightly smoky bouquet. Mouthfilling and fleshy, it has fresh, concentrated, citrusy, peachy flavours, ripe and generous, with well-integrated toasty oak, and excellent depth, complexity and harmony.

DRY $26 V+

Selaks Reserve Hawke's Bay Chardonnay ★★★

The 2013 vintage (★★★) is weighty, with fresh, grapefruit-like flavours to the fore, a touch of complexity and drink-young appeal.

Seresin Chardonnay Reserve ★★★★★

Finesse is the keynote quality of this organically certified Marlborough wine. Estate-grown in the Raupo Creek Vineyard, in the Omaka Valley, the classy 2013 vintage (★★★★★) was hand-picked, fermented with indigenous yeasts and lees-aged for 11 months in French oak barrels (20 per cent new), then blended and matured for a further four months in seasoned oak puncheons. It shows excellent depth, complexity and potential. Sweet-fruited, with concentrated, citrusy, slightly toasty flavours, a minerally streak, and impressive vigour and length, it should be at its best 2017+.

Vintage	13	12	11	10	09	08
WR	7	7	6	7	7	6
Drink	16-22	16-22	16-20	16-20	P	P

Seresin Marlborough Chardonnay ★★★★☆

This stylish, BioGro-certified wine is designed to 'focus on the textural element of the palate rather than emphasising primary fruit characters'. It is typically a full-bodied and complex wine with good mouthfeel, ripe melon/citrus characters shining through, subtle toasty oak and fresh acidity. The 2014 vintage (★★★★☆) was estate-grown in the Raupo Creek Vineyard, in the Omaka Valley, hand-picked, fermented with indigenous yeasts and lees-aged for 11 months in French oak barriques (8 per cent new), and given a full, softening malolactic fermentation. It's a mouthfilling, fleshy wine with generous, ripe grapefruit and peach flavours, finely integrated oak, good complexity and a well-rounded finish. Drink now or cellar.

Sherwood Estate Stoney Range Waipara Valley Chardonnay (★★★☆)

Offering fine value, the 2015 vintage (★★★☆) was partly handled in tanks, but 75 per cent of the blend was barrel-fermented with indigenous yeasts. Already drinking well, it is a full-bodied, fleshy wine with ripe peach/nectarine flavours and a slightly creamy finish.

Sileni Cellar Selection Hawke's Bay Chardonnay ★★★

Enjoyable young, the pale straw 2015 vintage (★★★☆) was mostly handled in tanks; 13 per cent of the blend was oak-aged and all of the wine went through a softening malolactic fermentation. Mouthfilling, it has strong, peachy, buttery, slightly toasty flavours, generous and well-rounded.

DRY $20 –V

Sileni Exceptional Vintage Hawke's Bay Chardonnay   ★★★★☆

Sileni's flagship Chardonnay is produced only in top vintages, such as 2010 and 2013. The 2013 vintage (★★★★★), fermented and matured in French oak casks (60 per cent new), is powerful, with a hint of butterscotch on the nose. Weighty, with rich stone-fruit flavours, buttery, toasty and nutty notes adding complexity, and lots of drink-young appeal, it's a drink-now or cellaring proposition.

Vintage	15	14	13	12	11	10
WR	NM	NM	6	NM	NM	7
Drink	NM	NM	16-22	NM	NM	16-19

 DRY $65 –V

Sileni The Lodge Hawke's Bay Chardonnay   ★★★★☆

The impressive 2015 vintage (★★★★☆) was fermented and matured in French oak barriques (30 per cent new). Pale lemon/green, it has a fragrant, slightly smoky bouquet, leading into a refined wine with concentrated, peachy, citrusy flavours, woven with fresh acidity, toasty notes adding complexity, and obvious cellaring potential. Best drinking mid-2017+.

Vintage	15	14	13	12	11	10
WR	6	6	6	5	5	6
Drink	16-21	16-21	16-19	16-19	16-17	16-17

 DRY $33 AV

Soho Carter Waiheke Island Chardonnay   ★★★★☆

The 2014 vintage (★★★★☆) is a fragrant, skilfully crafted wine, fermented in French oak barriques (28 per cent new). Mouthfilling and sweet-fruited, it has strong, citrusy, peachy flavours, mealy and biscuity notes adding complexity, a slightly creamy texture, and excellent depth and harmony. Best drinking 2017+.

 DRY $37 –V

Spade Oak Vineyard Voysey Series Gisborne Chardonnay   ★★★☆

The 2014 vintage (★★★☆) offers good value. Mouthfilling, it is a fleshy, sweet-fruited, moderately complex style with strong, ripe, peachy fruit flavours to the fore, gentle acidity and a well-rounded finish. Drink now to 2017.

 DRY $19 V+

Spinyback Nelson Chardonnay   ★★★

From Waimea Estates, the 2014 vintage (★★★) was tank-fermented and then 'aged with a selection of French oak'. Light lemon/green, it is mouthfilling and vibrantly fruity, with ripe, peachy, slightly spicy flavours, offering smooth, easy drinking.

 DRY $17 AV

Spy Valley Envoy Johnson Vineyard Marlborough Chardonnay   ★★★★★

This distinguished wine is estate-grown in the Waihopai Valley, hand-picked, fermented with indigenous yeasts and lees-aged in French oak barriques (mostly seasoned) for up to 20 months. Elegant and youthful, the 2014 vintage (★★★★☆) is fragrant and tightly structured, with fresh, concentrated, peachy, slightly toasty and creamy flavours, a minerally streak, good acid spine and obvious cellaring potential. Best drinking 2017+. (The subtle, refined 2011 vintage, tasted from a magnum in May 2016, was still tight, restrained and youthful.)

Vintage	14	13	12	11	10	09	08
WR	6	6	6	NM	6	6	6
Drink	16-20	16-21	16-18	NM	P	P	P

DRY $35 AV

Spy Valley Marlborough Chardonnay ★★★★

A consistently attractive, top-value wine. The 2015 vintage (★★★★) was hand-picked, barrel-fermented and oak-aged for nearly a year. Light lemon/green, it is fragrant and mouthfilling, with very youthful, vibrant, citrusy flavours to the fore, a subtle seasoning of oak, good acid spine and a bone-dry, slightly buttery, lingering finish.

Vintage	15	14	13	12
WR	6	7	7	7
Drink	16-20	16-20	16-19	16-18

DRY $23 V+

Staete Landt Josephine Marlborough Chardonnay ★★★★

This single-vineyard wine is estate-grown at Rapaura. The powerful, weighty 2013 vintage (★★★★☆) was hand-harvested and fermented in French oak barriques. It is mouthfilling, with rich, citrusy, peachy, slightly creamy and biscuity flavours, showing good ripeness, complexity and harmony. Drink now or cellar.

DRY $29 AV

Stanley Estates Reserve Single Vineyard
Awatere Valley Marlborough Chardonnay (★★★★)

The elegant, youthful 2014 vintage (★★★★) was fermented with indigenous yeasts in seasoned French oak barrels, and 60 per cent of the blend went through a softening malolactic fermentation. It is mouthfilling, with vibrant, peachy, citrusy flavours, hints of biscuity oak, slightly creamy notes, and good texture and concentration. Best drinking 2017+.

Vintage	14
WR	6
Drink	16-20

DRY $29 AV

Starborough Single Vineyard Awatere Valley Chardonnay (★★★★☆)

Delicious young, the lush 2015 vintage (★★★★☆) was estate-grown at Dashwood, hand-picked, fermented with indigenous yeasts in French oak casks (25 per cent new), and given a full, softening malolactic fermentation. Bright, light yellow/green, it is sturdy, rich and rounded, with generous, peachy, slightly buttery flavours, showing good complexity, and lots of drink-young appeal.

DRY $30 AV

Stone Paddock Hawke's Bay Chardonnay   ★★★

The 2013 vintage (★★★☆) from Paritua is mouthfilling, fresh and lively, with ripe, citrusy, peachy flavours, a touch of biscuity oak (half the blend was barrel-aged), moderate complexity and a crisp, dry finish. Ready; no rush.

Vintage	13
WR	6
Drink	16-20

DRY $20 –V

Stonecroft Gimblett Gravels Hawke's Bay Chardonnay   ★★★★

The 2014 vintage (★★★★) was estate-grown and matured for six months in seasoned French oak barrels. Fresh and weighty, with ripe, peachy, slightly spicy and nutty flavours, it is vibrantly fruity, with excellent mouthfeel and depth. Certified organic.

Vintage	15	14	13
WR	6	6	6
Drink	17-22	16-21	16-20

DRY $27 AV

Stonecroft Old Vine Gimblett Gravels Hawke's Bay Chardonnay   ★★★★☆

The youthful 2015 vintage (★★★★☆) is from vines planted in Mere Road in 1992. Hand-picked and fermented and matured for a year in French oak casks (two-thirds new), it is pale yellow, with a slightly buttery bouquet. Mouthfilling and creamy, it has concentrated, ripe stone-fruit flavours, seasoned with toasty oak, in a traditional regional style, well worth cellaring; open mid-2017+.

Vintage	15
WR	6
Drink	18-24

DRY $47 –V

Stoneleigh Latitude Marlborough Chardonnay   ★★★★

The 2014 vintage (★★★★) is a mouthfilling wine, grown at Rapaura. Softly textured, with strong, ripe grapefruit-like flavours and nutty, savoury elements adding complexity, it's enjoyable from the start.

DRY $23 V+

Stoneleigh Marlborough Chardonnay   ★★★☆

From Pernod Ricard NZ, this wine is always enjoyable and good value on special. It is typically about two-thirds wood-fermented, in French and Hungarian barrels, small and large; the rest is handled in tanks. The 2015 vintage (★★★) is bright, light yellow. Offering very easy drinking, it is fleshy, with satisfying depth of fresh, citrusy, slightly buttery flavours.

Vintage	15	14	13	12	11	10
WR	7	6	6	6	6	7
Drink	16-18	16-17	P	P	P	P

 DRY $17 V+

Stoneleigh Nature's Collection Marlborough Chardonnay   (★★★☆)

The debut 2014 vintage (★★★☆) was grown at Rapaura and fermented in large oak cuves. Enjoyable young, it is mouthfilling, with ripe, peachy, slightly buttery and toasty flavours, gentle acidity, a smooth, creamy texture and good depth.

DRY $18 V+

Stoneleigh Rapaura Series Marlborough Chardonnay   ★★★★

This single-vineyard wine is fermented and matured in new and one-year-old French oak casks. The 2015 vintage (★★★☆) is mouthfilling, with good depth of citrusy, slightly peachy and biscuity flavours, showing a touch of complexity.

Vintage	15	14	13	12	11
WR	7	6	6	6	6
Drink	16-18	16-17	P	P	P

DRY $28 AV

Stoneleigh Wild Valley Marlborough Chardonnay   (★★★☆)

The debut 2015 vintage (★★★☆) was grown at Rapaura, in the Wairau Valley, and fermented with indigenous ('wild') yeasts in a 50:50 split of tanks and French oak barrels. Mouthfilling and smooth, it has ripe, peachy, slightly toasty flavours and gentle acidity, in a moderately concentrated, creamy-textured style, already highly enjoyable. Priced right.

DRY $19 V+

Stonyridge Fallen Angel Hawke's Bay Chardonnay   (★★★★)

The 2014 vintage (★★★★) was barrel-fermented and lees-aged for 10 months. Pale straw, it is mouthfilling and creamy-textured, with generous, ripe, slightly spicy and toasty flavours, finely balanced for enjoyable, early drinking.

DRY $45 –V

Sugar Loaf Marlborough Chardonnay   (★★★★)

Delicious now, the 2014 vintage (★★★★) is a single-vineyard wine, hand-picked in the lower Wairau Valley and barrel-fermented. Full-bodied, ripe and rounded, it is vibrant and sweet-fruited, with strong, peachy, citrusy flavours, a hint of butterscotch, and good complexity and harmony. Priced sharply.

DRY $22 V+

Summerhouse Marlborough Chardonnay   ★★★★

The fine-value 2015 vintage (★★★★) was grown at four sites and barrel-fermented. Light lemon/green, it is mouthfilling and vibrantly fruity, with generous, citrusy, peachy flavours, finely integrated oak and good complexity. Best drinking mid-2017+.

Vintage	15	14
WR	7	7
Drink	16-23	16-22

DRY $19 V+

Supper Club Marlborough Chardonnay   (★★★☆)

Offering good value, the 2014 vintage (★★★☆) is a blend of upper Awatere Valley (principally) and lower Wairau Valley fruit, mostly handled in tanks, but 30 per cent barrel-fermented. Mouthfilling, it has citrusy, peachy flavours to the fore, with savoury, slightly buttery notes adding complexity, and very good depth and harmony.

DRY $19 V+

Tantalus Cachette Reserve Waiheke Island Chardonnay   (★★★★)

Estate-grown at Onetangi, the 2015 vintage (★★★★) was fermented and matured for 10 months in French oak casks. Light lemon/green, with a fragrant, creamy bouquet, it is mouthfilling, with fresh, ripe stone-fruit flavours, well-integrated oak and balanced acidity. Enjoyable young, it should be at its best mid-2017+.

Vintage	15
WR	5
Drink	16-19

DRY $45 -V

Te Awa Single Estate Hawke's Bay Chardonnay   ★★★★

Refined and subtle, the 2015 vintage (★★★★☆) was fermented in French oak hogsheads (30 per cent new) and lees-aged for 10 months. A mouthfilling, sweet-fruited wine with obvious potential, it has delicious, ripe peach and grapefruit flavours, showing excellent delicacy and depth, finely integrated oak, and lovely poise and harmony. Best drinking mid-2017+.

Vintage	15	14
WR	7	6
Drink	16-25	16-24

DRY $25 AV

Te Awanga Estate Hawke's Bay Chardonnay   ★★★★

Already delicious, the 2015 vintage (★★★★☆), from 12 to 19-year-old vines, was partly barrel-fermented with indigenous yeasts, given a full, softening malolactic fermentation, and lees-aged for 10 months. Bright, light lemon/green, it is mouthfilling and finely poised, with strong, vibrant grapefruit/peach flavours, a subtle seasoning of toasty oak, slightly buttery notes, and excellent harmony and drink-young appeal. Drink now or cellar.

DRY $25 AV

Te Kairanga John Martin Martinborough Chardonnay   ★★★★☆

The refined 2014 vintage (★★★★☆), from the 'best vineyard parcels', was fermented and matured in French oak puncheons (15 per cent new), and given a full, softening malolactic fermentation. It is an elegant, sweet-fruited wine with rich, youthful peach, grapefruit and subtle oak flavours, and a long, finely balanced finish. Best drinking 2017+.

Vintage	14	13
WR	7	7
Drink	16-22	16-22

DRY $37 AV

Te Kairanga Martinborough Chardonnay   ★★★★

The 2014 vintage (★★★★) was fermented in French oak puncheons (15 per cent new) and given a full, softening malolactic fermentation. It is mouthfilling and slightly creamy, with generous, ripe, peachy, slightly biscuity flavours and a well-rounded, harmonious finish.

Vintage	14	13
WR	7	6
Drink	16-20	16-20

DRY $24 V+

Te Mania Nelson Chardonnay   ★★★

The 2015 vintage (★★★☆) was handled in tanks (85 per cent) and barrels (15 per cent). Light lemon/green, it is mouthfilling and vibrantly fruity, with fresh, citrusy aromas and flavours to the fore, slightly creamy, buttery notes, lively acidity and very good depth.

DRY $22 –V

Te Mania Reserve Nelson Chardonnay   (★★★★)

Still youthful, the 2015 vintage (★★★★) was fermented and matured for 10 months in French oak barrels (25 per cent new). Fleshy, with strong, fresh grapefruit, peach and toasty oak flavours, balanced acidity and good complexity, it's well worth cellaring to 2018+.

DRY $30 –V

Te Mata Elston Chardonnay   ★★★★★

One of New Zealand's most illustrious Chardonnays, Elston is a stylish, intense, slowly evolving Hawke's Bay wine. At around four years old, it is notably complete, showing concentration and finesse. The grapes are grown and hand-picked principally at two sites in the Te Mata hills at Havelock North, and the wine is fully fermented in French oak barriques (35 per cent new), with full malolactic fermentation. The pale straw 2015 vintage (★★★★★) is mouthfilling and still very youthful. Weighty and sweet-fruited, it has peachy, slightly spicy flavours, integrated oak, balanced acidity, and a tightly structured, poised and persistent finish. Best drinking 2018+.

Vintage	15	14	13	12	11	10	09
WR	6	7	7	7	7	7	7
Drink	17-23	16-19	16-18	16-17	P	P	P

DRY $35 AV

🍇🍇🍇

Te Mata Estate Vineyards Hawke's Bay Chardonnay   ★★★☆

This consistently attractive wine is sourced from the company's vineyards at Woodthorpe Terraces, in the Dartmoor Valley, the Bridge Pa Triangle and at Havelock North. Fermented and lees-aged in a mix of tanks and French oak barrels, it is typically a harmonious wine with fresh, ripe grapefruit characters to the fore, a gentle seasoning of biscuity oak, very good depth and a touch of complexity. The 2014 vintage (★★★★), one-third barrel-fermented, is an elegant wine, full-bodied, with fresh acidity and vibrant, grapefruit-like flavours, showing good intensity.

Vintage	15
WR	6
Drink	16-19

DRY $22 AV

Te Rere Waiheke Island Chardonnay   (★★★★☆)

Delicious young, the 2014 vintage (★★★★☆) was grown at the western end of the island. It is mouthfilling, rich, sweet-fruited and creamy-textured, with impressively concentrated, ripe stone-fruit flavours and a nutty, fragrant bouquet.

 DRY $45 –V

Te Whau Vineyard Waiheke Island Chardonnay   ★★★★★

For its sheer vintage-to-vintage consistency, this has been Te Whau's finest wine. Full of personality, it has beautifully ripe fruit characters showing excellent concentration, nutty oak and a long, finely poised finish. The 2015 vintage (★★★★★) was hand-harvested and fermented and lees-aged for nine months in French oak barriques. Light lemon/green, it is fragrant and weighty, with youthful, rich, peachy, slightly toasty flavours, excellent complexity, and a well-rounded finish. Best drinking 2018+.

Vintage	15	14	13	12	11	10	09
WR	7	7	7	6	5	7	6
Drink	17-21	16-20	16-20	P	P	P	P

 DRY $95 –V

Terra Sancta Riverblock Bannockburn Central Otago Chardonnay   ★★★☆

The 2014 vintage (★★★☆) was fermented with indigenous yeasts and matured in French oak puncheons (20 per cent new). It is mouthfilling, with fresh acidity, a subtle oak influence, and peachy, citrusy flavours, showing considerable complexity.

Vintage	14
WR	7
Drink	16-22

 DRY $30 –V

TerraVin Hillside Reserve Marlborough Chardonnay   ★★★★

The 2013 vintage (★★★★☆) was grown in the Southern Valleys and barrel-fermented (only 5 per cent new oak). It is a more extroverted style than the non-reserve (below), with mouthfilling body and generous, ripe, peachy, slightly spicy and toasty flavours, showing good complexity.

Vintage	13
WR	6
Drink	16-20

 DRY $39 –V

Theory & Practice Hawke's Bay Chardonnay   (★★★★)

The 2014 vintage (★★★★) is an upfront style, enjoyable young. Grown in the Loughlin Vineyard and other sites, it was barrel-fermented (40 per cent new oak), and given a full, softening malolactic fermentation. A bold, powerful wine, it has fresh stone-fruit flavours, slightly buttery and toasty notes, and good vigour and potential.

DRY $25 AV

Thomas Waiheke Island Chardonnay (★★★★☆)

From Batch winery, the 2014 vintage (★★★★☆) was hand-picked at Onetangi and fermented and matured for 11 months in seasoned French oak barriques. The bouquet is fragrant and complex; the palate is mouthfilling and sweet-fruited, with strong, peachy, citrusy flavours, a gentle oak influence, excellent delicacy and harmony, and a lingering finish.

 DRY $45 –V

Thornbury Gisborne Chardonnay ★★★

The 2015 vintage (★★★☆) offers lots of drink-young charm. Fleshy and vibrantly fruity, with peachy, slightly toasty and buttery flavours, it shows a touch of complexity, gentle acidity and very good depth. (From Villa Maria.)

 DRY $16 V+

Three Paddles Martinborough Chardonnay ★★★

From Nga Waka, the 2016 vintage (★★★) is a 'fruit-driven' style. Mouthfilling, it has fresh, youthful, peachy flavours, slightly toasty and creamy notes, and lively acidity. Enjoyable young.

Vintage	16
WR	7
Drink	17-18

 DRY $18 AV

Ti Point Hawke's Bay Chardonnay ★★★☆

The 2015 vintage (★★★☆) has strong, drink-young appeal. Pale yellow, it is mouthfilling and slightly creamy, in a moderately complex style with generous, citrusy, peachy flavours, slightly buttery notes, and a dry finish. (From Sacred Hill.)

 DRY $23 AV

Tiki Hawke's Bay Chardonnay ★★★

The 2015 vintage (★★★) was given a full, softening malolactic fermentation. Light lemon/green, it is vibrantly fruity, with fresh, citrusy, slightly appley and buttery notes, and good depth. Enjoyable young.

 DRY $20 –V

Tiki Koro Hawke's Bay Chardonnay ★★★★

The 2015 vintage (★★★★) was hand-picked and fermented and lees-aged for 11 months in French oak barriques (70 per cent new). Light lemon/green, it is mouthfilling, sweet-fruited and creamy, with rich stone-fruit flavours, slightly buttery notes and a well-rounded finish. Delicious young.

 DRY $33 –V

Tiki Single Vineyard Hawke's Bay Chardonnay (★★★★)

The elegant, vibrantly fruity 2014 vintage (★★★★) was fermented in French oak barriques (40 per cent new). Fresh and finely balanced, it has strong grapefruit-like flavours, a subtle seasoning of oak, and very good vigour and depth.

DRY $23 AV

Tinpot Hut Marlborough Chardonnay   (★★★★)

The stylish, vibrantly fruity 2013 vintage (★★★★) was grown at Rapaura and in the Southern Valleys. Tightly structured, with good complexity, delicacy and harmony, it has strong, ripe, citrusy, slightly mealy flavours, threaded with fresh acidity.

DRY $25 AV

Tohu Gisborne Chardonnay   ★★★☆

Enjoyable young, the 2015 vintage (★★★☆) was partly barrel-fermented and given a full, softening malolactic fermentation. Pale straw, with a slightly buttery and toasty bouquet, it is mouthfilling and creamy, with ripe, peachy flavours, gentle acidity and very good depth.

DRY $22 AV

Tohu Hemi Reserve Marlborough Chardonnay   ★★★★☆

The very youthful 2015 vintage (★★★★☆) is a rare wine (60 cases), hand-picked from estate-grown vines in the Awatere Valley and handled in French oak barriques. Pale lemon/green, it is fragrant, mouthfilling and sweet-fruited, with strong, ripe stone-fruit flavours, a slightly creamy texture, and good delicacy and complexity. Best drinking 2018+.

DRY $35 –V

Tohu Single Vineyard Marlborough Chardonnay   ★★★

The 2014 vintage (★★★) was grown at Rapaura, in the Wairau Valley, handled entirely without oak, and given a full, softening malolactic fermentation. Mouthfilling, it is sweet-fruited, with fresh, ripe, peachy flavours and gentle acidity, in a very easy-drinking style.

DRY $22 –V

Toi Toi Gisborne Chardonnay   ★★☆

The easy-drinking 2016 vintage (★★☆) is a pale lemon/green, medium-bodied wine with peachy, slightly spicy flavours, fresh and smooth.

DRY $18 –V

Toi Toi Reserve New Zealand Chardonnay   ★★★☆

The 2015 vintage (★★★★) was grown in Marlborough and barrel-fermented. Fruit-driven, with well-integrated oak, it is full-bodied, with vibrant, ripe, citrusy, peachy, slightly buttery flavours. Showing considerable complexity and very good depth and harmony, it's enjoyable from the start.

Vintage	15	DRY $30 –V
WR	7	
Drink	16-20	

Tony Bish Skeetfield Vineyard Hawke's Bay Chardonnay   (★★★★☆)

The debut 2015 vintage (★★★★☆) is based on mature, Mendoza-clone vines at Ohiti. Hand-harvested, it was fermented in French oak barriques (60 per cent new), lees-aged for a year, and given a full, softening malolactic fermentation. Bright, light lemon/green, with a fragrant, slightly buttery bouquet, it is full-bodied and fleshy, with rich, ripe stone-fruit flavours, balanced acidity and a rounded, lasting finish. Powerful and finely poised, it's already enjoyable, but should be at its best 2018+.

DRY $55 –V

Trinity Hill Gimblett Gravels Chardonnay   ★★★★★

The winery's flagship 'black label' Chardonnay from Hawke's Bay is typically intense and finely structured. Grown in the Gimblett Gravels and fermented and matured for 10 months in French oak puncheons, the 2014 vintage (★★★★☆) is a tightly structured, youthful wine. The bouquet is fragrant and complex; the palate is mouthfilling, with fresh, ripe peach, melon and grapefruit flavours, biscuity, mealy notes adding complexity, and a long, finely balanced finish. Best drinking 2017+. The very youthful 2015 vintage (★★★★☆) was fermented and matured for a year in French oak puncheons. Light lemon/green, it is mouthfilling, with vibrant, citrusy, peachy flavours, biscuity, mealy and complex, and a dry, very harmonious finish. Best drinking 2018+.

Vintage	15	14	13	12	11	10
WR	6	7	7	6	6	6
Drink	17-23	16-21	16-20	16-18	P	P

DRY $35 AV

Trinity Hill Hawke's Bay Chardonnay   ★★★☆

From 'cooler' sites, the 2014 vintage (★★★☆) is a 'low oak-influenced' style. An elegant, mouthfilling wine, vibrantly fruity, it has subtle mealy, biscuity notes adding complexity and a finely poised, harmonious finish.

Vintage	14	13	12	11	10
WR	7	7	5	6	6
Drink	16-18	16-17	P	P	P

DRY $20 AV

Two Gates Hawke's Bay Chardonnay   (★★★★)

The 2013 vintage (★★★★) from Rod McDonald is a single-vineyard wine, grown inland at Maraekakaho, hand-picked and partly barrel-fermented. Mouthfilling, it has fresh, strong, citrusy flavours, showing good complexity, a gentle seasoning of toasty oak, and a creamy-smooth finish.

DRY $35 –V

Two Rivers Clos Des Pierres Marlborough Chardonnay   ★★★★

From a stony Wairau Valley site ('Clos des Pierres' means 'Place of Stones'), this wine is hand-picked, fermented with indigenous yeasts in French oak barrels (25 per cent new in 2015), and given a full, softening malolactic fermentation. The youthful 2015 vintage (★★★★) is pale yellow, with a fresh, buttery bouquet. Mouthfilling, it has strong, peachy, citrusy flavours, fresh acidity, buttery and toasty notes, and good complexity. Drink now or cellar.

Vintage	15
WR	6
Drink	16-21

DRY $36 –V

Unison Vineyard Reserve Hawke's Bay Chardonnay   (★★★☆)

The 2013 vintage (★★★☆) was grown in the Bridge Pa Triangle. Fermented in an even split of tanks and French oak barrels, it is citrusy and savoury, with some complexity, and very good texture and depth.

 DRY $30 –V

Vavasour Marlborough Chardonnay   ★★★★☆

This powerful, rich, creamy-textured wine is typically grown in the Awatere Valley, given a full, softening malolactic fermentation and lees-aged in French oak barrels. The 2014 vintage (★★★★☆) is weighty and harmonious, with citrusy, peachy, slightly biscuity flavours, showing excellent depth, harmony and cellaring potential. Best drinking 2017+.

 DRY $31 AV

Vidal Hawke's Bay Chardonnay   ★★★☆

The 2015 vintage (★★★☆) is a top buy. Fermented and matured in tanks (principally) and seasoned French oak barriques, it is mouthfilling, with strong, ripe, citrusy, peachy flavours to the fore and slightly smoky notes adding a touch of complexity. Showing excellent freshness, vigour and depth, it's delicious now.

Vintage	15	14	13
WR	6	7	7
Drink	16-18	16-17	P

 DRY $16 V+

Vidal Legacy Hawke's Bay Chardonnay   ★★★★★

The 2015 vintage (★★★★★) of Vidal's flagship Chardonnay was grown in the Lyons and Kokako vineyards, hand-picked, fermented with indigenous yeasts and matured for 10 months in French oak barriques (45 per cent new). Light lemon/green, it has a fragrant, smoky bouquet, with a hint of 'struck match'. Mouthfilling and sweet-fruited, it has lovely, pure citrus and stone-fruit flavours, showing excellent delicacy and depth. A complex, harmonious wine, subtle and lingering, it should flourish with cellaring.

Vintage	15	14	13	12	11	10
WR	7	7	7	7	6	7
Drink	16-25	16-23	16-20	16-19	16-17	16-17

 DRY $60 –V

Vidal Reserve Hawke's Bay Chardonnay   ★★★★

This middle-tier label offers great value. The 2015 vintage (★★★★) was grown at several sites – inland and coastal – and fermented and matured in French oak barriques (18 per cent new). Still youthful, it has a fragrant, smoky bouquet, leading into a mouthfilling, sweet-fruited wine with strong, ripe, peachy flavours, oak complexity and a dry, lengthy finish. At $20, it's a top buy.

Vintage	15	14	13	12
WR	7	7	7	6
Drink	16-20	16-18	16-18	P

 DRY $20 V+

Villa Maria Cellar Selection Gisborne Chardonnay   (★★★★)

Immediately appealing, the 2015 vintage (★★★★) is a weighty, dry wine, offering fine value. Almost entirely hand-picked (90 per cent), it was fully fermented in French and Hungarian oak casks (37 per cent new). Showing good complexity, it is mouthfilling and vibrantly fruity, with generous, ripe, peachy flavours and a long, dry finish.

 DRY $18 V+

Villa Maria Cellar Selection Hawke's Bay Chardonnay   ★★★★

A top buy. The 2015 vintage (★★★★) is a refined, youthful wine, grown at three sites – including the acclaimed Keltern Vineyard – 40 per cent hand-picked and almost entirely (95 per cent) fermented in French oak barrels (25 per cent new). Instantly appealing, it is fragrant, fresh and finely balanced, with ripe, citrusy, biscuity flavours, showing good complexity, a hint of 'struck match' and a finely textured, dry finish.

Vintage	15	14
WR	7	7
Drink	16-20	16-19

 DRY $18 V+

Villa Maria Cellar Selection Marlborough Chardonnay   ★★★★

A stylish, great-value wine. The 2015 vintage (★★★★☆) was grown in the Wairau and Awatere valleys, partly hand-picked, fully fermented in oak barriques (10 per cent new), and barrel-matured for eight months. A classy young wine, it is very fresh and elegant, with good intensity of grapefruit-like flavours, gentle mealy notes and a subtle seasoning of oak adding complexity, and excellent vibrancy, poise and depth.

Vintage	15	14	13	12	11	10
WR	6	6	6	6	6	6
Drink	16-20	16-20	16-18	16-17	P	P

DRY $18 V+

Villa Maria Library Release Hawke's Bay Chardonnay   (★★★★★)

The debut 2010 vintage (★★★★★) was released as a mature but still lively wine in 2015. Grown in the company's Ngakirikiri and Keltern vineyards, it was fermented, mostly with indigenous yeasts, and matured for 10 months in French oak barriques (38 per cent new). It's rare – only 190 cases were produced. It shows good maturity and complexity, with toasty, bottle-aged notes emerging, but also vibrant, citrusy, peachy fruit flavours. Still very lively, complex and long, it's a drink-now or cellaring proposition.

Vintage	10
WR	7
Drink	16-20

DRY $50 AV

Villa Maria Private Bin Gisborne Chardonnay   ★★★

The 2015 vintage (★★★) is fresh and flavourful. Mouthfilling, it is vibrant, peachy and slightly buttery, in a fruit-driven style with a well-rounded finish. Fine value at $12 on special.

 DRY $17 AV

Villa Maria Reserve Barrique Fermented Gisborne Chardonnay   ★★★★★

This acclaimed wine is usually sourced principally from the company's Katoa and McDiarmid Hill vineyards. The 2014 vintage (★★★★★) was fermented (56 per cent with indigenous yeasts) and matured in French oak barriques (40 per cent new). It's a sturdy, generous wine with concentrated, ripe stone-fruit flavours, a hint of struck match, excellent complexity and a rich, well-rounded finish. Drink now or cellar. The 2015 vintage (★★★★★) was grown at McDiarmid Hill (75 per cent), in the Patutahi district, and the Tietjens Vineyard, at Bushmere. Fermented in French oak casks (half new), and mostly (55 per cent) put through a softening malolactic fermentation, it is a concentrated, ripe, peachy, very generous wine, with slightly smoky notes, hints of butter and toast, and excellent complexity and length.

Vintage	15	14	13	12	11	10	09
WR	7	7	7	7	7	7	6
Drink	17-23	16-22	16-21	16-19	16-18	16-18	P

DRY $37 AV

Villa Maria Reserve Hawke's Bay Chardonnay   ★★★★★

The 2015 vintage (★★★★★) is an elegant, youthful wine, grown mostly (73 per cent) in the Lyons Vineyard, in the Gimblett Gravels, and barrel-fermented (French, 45 per cent new). Tightly structured, with obvious cellaring potential, it has a slightly smoky bouquet and ripe, grapefruit-like flavours, showing excellent delicacy and complexity.

Vintage	15	14	13	12	11	10	09	08
WR	7	7	7	6	6	7	7	7
Drink	17-23	16-22	16-21	16-19	16-18	16-18	P	P

DRY $33 AV

Villa Maria Reserve Marlborough Chardonnay   ★★★★★

With its rich, slightly mealy, citrusy flavours, this is a distinguished wine, concentrated and finely structured. A marriage of intense, ripe Marlborough fruit with French oak, it is one of the region's greatest Chardonnays. It is typically grown and hand-picked in the warmest sites supplying Chardonnay grapes to Villa Maria, in the Awatere and Wairau valleys. The highly refined 2015 vintage (★★★★★) was fermented and matured for nine months in French oak barriques and puncheons (30 per cent new), and given a full, softening malolactic fermentation. The bouquet is fragrant and complex; the palate is highly concentrated, with rich, peachy, citrusy flavours, integrated oak, and a long finish. Best drinking 2018+.

Vintage	15	14	13	12	11	10	09
WR	7	7	7	7	7	7	7
Drink	17-23	16-22	16-20	16-20	16-18	16-17	P

DRY $32 V+

Villa Maria Single Vineyard Ihumatao Chardonnay   ★★★★★

This impressive wine is estate-grown at Mangere, in South Auckland. The 2014 vintage (★★★★☆) was fermented (75 per cent indigenous yeasts) in French oak barriques (30 per cent new). It's an elegant wine, mouthfilling, with deep, youthful, citrusy, slightly biscuity flavours, showing good complexity, and a well-rounded finish. Best drinking 2017+.

Vintage	14	13	12	11	10	09
WR	7	7	6	6	7	6
Drink	16-22	16-21	16-19	16-18	16-18	P

DRY $35 AV

Villa Maria Single Vineyard Keltern Hawke's Bay Chardonnay ★★★★★

Grown at the Keltern Vineyard, a warm, inland site east of Maraekakaho, this consistently impressive wine is hand-picked, fermented with indigenous yeasts and lees-aged in French oak barriques (35 per cent new in 2015). Powerful, with youthful, vibrant, citrusy, peachy flavours, well-integrated oak and a long finish, the 2015 vintage (★★★★★) has slightly smoky notes adding complexity. Weighty, fresh, intense and tightly structured, it should be long-lived.

Vintage	15	14	13	12	11	10	09
WR	7	7	7	6	7	7	6
Drink	17-23	16-22	16-21	16-19	16-18	16-18	P

 DRY $40 AV

Villa Maria Single Vineyard Taylors Pass Chardonnay ★★★★★

Grown in the company's Taylors Pass Vineyard in Marlborough's Awatere Valley, this wine is hand-picked and barrel-fermented. The very refined 2015 vintage (★★★★☆) was fermented and lees-aged for nine months in French oak puncheons and barriques (25 per cent new), and given a full, softening malolactic fermentation. An elegant, tightly structured wine, it is citrusy and slightly smoky, with a subtle seasoning of oak and excellent vigour and potential. Open 2018+.

Vintage	15	14	13	12	11	10
WR	7	7	7	7	7	7
Drink	16-22	16-22	16-20	16-20	16-18	16-17

 DRY $35 AV

VNO Hawke's Bay Chardonnay ★★★

The 2015 vintage (★★★☆) is an upfront style from Constellation NZ, offering good value. Enjoyable young, it is a partly barrel-fermented style, fleshy and smooth, with ripe, peachy flavours, slightly buttery and toasty, and good depth.

 DRY $17 AV

Volcanic Hills Hawke's Bay Chardonnay ★★★☆

From Green Rocket, an Auckland-based company, the 2013 vintage (★★★☆) was fermented in mostly seasoned oak barrels (15 per cent new). It is fleshy, nutty and slightly buttery, with fresh acidity and plenty of flavour and drink-young appeal.

 DRY $27 –V

Waiheke Road Gisborne Reserve Chardonnay (★★★★)

From Awaroa, based on Waiheke Island, the 2015 vintage (★★★★) was grown in Gisborne and barrel-aged for nine months. Bright, light lemon/green, it is weighty, generous and youthful, with strong grapefruit and peach flavours, integrated oak, slightly buttery notes and lots of drink-young appeal. Best drinking mid-2017+.

Vintage	15
WR	6
Drink	18-20

 DRY $38 –V

Waiheke Road Waiheke Island Reserve Chardonnay   (★★★★☆)

The refined, youthful 2014 vintage (★★★★☆) has a fragrant, slightly creamy and biscuity bouquet. Full-bodied, with strong, ripe grapefruit and peach flavours, it has mealy and toasty notes adding complexity, and a finely balanced, long finish. Best drinking 2018+. (From Awaroa Vineyard.)

DRY $38 –V

Waimea Nelson Chardonnay   ★★★★

Enjoyable young, the 2014 vintage (★★★★) was fermented in French oak barriques and puncheons (partly new). Mouthfilling, it is creamy-textured, with fresh acidity, strong, ripe, peachy flavours, gently seasoned with biscuity oak, and good harmony.

Vintage	14	13	12	11	10
WR	6	6	6	6	7
Drink	16-18	16-17	P	P	P

DRY $23 V+

Waipara Hills Equinox Waipara Valley Chardonnay   ★★★☆

The 2013 vintage (★★★★) was estate-grown in the Home Block Vineyard, hand-picked and barrel-fermented, with some use of indigenous yeasts. An elegant, mouthfilling, finely poised wine, it is freshly scented, with strong, vibrant, citrusy, peachy flavours, a very subtle seasoning of oak, slighty creamy notes and a tight, lengthy finish.

DRY $32 –V

Wairau River Marlborough Chardonnay   ★★★☆

The 2014 vintage (★★★☆) was handled in a 50:50 split of tanks and French oak casks (20 per cent new). It is a fruit-driven style, mouthfilling and vibrantly fruity, with a subtle seasoning of oak and a smooth, creamy-textured finish. The 2015 vintage (★★★☆) is fresh and lively, with citrusy, slightly peachy flavours, showing a touch of complexity, and very good vigour and depth.

Vintage	15	14	13	12	11
WR	6	6	6	5	6
Drink	16-19	16-19	16-17	P	P

DRY $20 AV

Wairau River Reserve Marlborough Chardonnay   ★★★★

Grown at two sites adjacent to the Wairau River, on the north side of the valley, the 2014 vintage (★★★★☆) was fermented in French and American oak barrels (33 per cent new). It's a powerful wine, with a complex bouquet leading into a full-bodied palate with concentrated, ripe, peachy flavours, hints of toasty oak and butterscotch, and obvious potential. The 2015 vintage (★★★★) is lemon-scented, mouthfilling and sweet-fruited, with a subtle seasoning of oak, good complexity, and a slightly buttery finish. Best drinking mid-2017+.

Vintage	15	14
WR	6	6
Drink	16-22	16-19

DRY $30 –V

Walnut Block Nutcracker Marlborough Chardonnay   ★★★★

Certified organic, the 2013 vintage (★★★★) is a single-vineyard, Wairau Valley wine, hand-picked and fermented and matured for a year in French oak barrels (25 per cent new). Mouthfilling, slightly toasty and buttery, it has concentrated grapefruit and peach flavours, fresh acidity, and very good depth and potential.

DRY $30 –V

Whitehaven Marlborough Chardonnay   ★★★★

The 2014 vintage (★★★★) was grown at Rapaura and Brancott, French oak-matured and given a full, softening malolactic fermentation. The bouquet is creamy; the palate is mouthfilling and smooth, with vibrant peach and grapefruit flavours, woven with fresh acidity, and very good depth.

Vintage	14	13	12	11	10
WR	6	6	7	6	7
Drink	16-19	16-18	16-17	16-17	P

DRY $25 AV

Wither Hills Single Vineyard Benmorven Marlborough Chardonnay   (★★★★☆)

The fine-value 2015 vintage (★★★★☆) was hand-picked and fermented in oak hogsheads and barriques (40 per cent new). The bouquet is savoury; the palate is mouthfilling, with concentrated, vibrant, citrusy, peachy flavours, showing excellent harmony, and a well-rounded finish. Best drinking mid-2017+.

DRY $25 V+

Wooing Tree Central Otago Chardonnay   ★★★★

The 2014 vintage (★★★★) was hand-picked and barrel-fermented. It is mouthfilling and slightly creamy, with strong, peachy flavours, integrated oak, good complexity, and lots of drink-young appeal. The 2015 vintage (★★★★) was estate-grown, hand-picked and French oak-fermented. Pale lemon/green, it is mouthfilling, fleshy and creamy-textured, with youthful peach and grapefruit flavours, a subtle seasoning of oak and considerable complexity.

DRY $30 –V

Zephyr Marlborough Chardonnay   (★★★★)

The 2014 vintage (★★★★) is a subtle wine, estate-grown in the lower Wairau Valley, hand-picked and fermented with indigenous yeasts in large oak barrels. Light lemon/green, it is full-bodied and fleshy, with generous, ripe, citrusy flavours, a gentle seasoning of nutty oak, and a finely textured, lengthy finish. Drink now or cellar.

DRY $32 –V

Chenin Blanc

Today's Chenin Blancs are markedly riper, rounder and more enjoyable to drink than the sharply acidic, austere wines of the 1980s, when Chenin Blanc was far more extensively planted in New Zealand. Yet this classic grape variety is still struggling for an identity. In recent years, several labels have been discontinued – not for lack of quality or value, but lack of buyer interest.

A good New Zealand Chenin Blanc is fresh and buoyantly fruity, with melon and pineapple-evoking flavours and a crisp finish. In the cooler parts of the country, the variety's naturally high acidity (an asset in the warmer viticultural regions of South Africa, the United States and Australia) can be a distinct handicap. But when the grapes achieve full ripeness here, this classic grape of Vouvray, in the Loire Valley, yields sturdy wines that are satisfying in their youth yet can mature for many years, gradually unfolding a delicious, honeyed richness.

Only three wineries have consistently made impressive Chenin Blancs over the past decade: Millton, Margrain and Esk Valley. Many growers, put off by the variety's late-ripening nature and the susceptibility of its tight bunches to botrytis rot, have uprooted their vines. Plantings have plummeted from 372 hectares in 1983 to 24 hectares of bearing vines in 2017.

Chenin Blanc is the country's thirteenth most widely planted white-wine variety (behind Albariño and Arneis), with plantings concentrated in Hawke's Bay, Marlborough and Gisborne. In the future, winemakers who plant Chenin Blanc in warm, sunny vineyard sites with devigorating soils, where the variety's vigorous growth can be controlled and yields reduced, can be expected to produce the ripest, most concentrated wines. New Zealand winemakers have yet to get to grips with Chenin Blanc.

Amisfield Central Otago Chenin Blanc (★★★★)

The debut 2014 vintage (★★★★) was estate-grown at Pisa, in the Cromwell Basin, hand-picked and mostly tank-fermented, with a small percentage of barrel fermentation. Finely scented, it is a crisp, off-dry style (7.3 grams/litre of residual sugar), with vibrant, ripe flavours, a minerally streak, and excellent delicacy and poise. Best drinking 2017+.

MED/DRY $30 –V

Astrolabe Vineyards Wrekin Vineyard Chenin Blanc ★★★★

Showing good personality, the 2014 vintage (★★★★) was hand-picked on the south side of the Wairau Valley and partly fermented with indigenous yeasts in old oak barrels. A fully dry style (3 grams/litre of residual sugar), it is mouthfilling and finely textured, with strong, ripe, peachy flavours, showing good complexity, gentle acidity (for Chenin Blanc) and a dry, slightly creamy, lingering finish.

DRY $25 AV

Bishop's Head Waipara Valley Chenin Blanc (★★★★)

Fresh and age-worthy, the 2015 vintage (★★★★) was hand-picked, fermented with indigenous yeasts and lees-aged for 11 months in oak barrels (20 per cent new). Vibrant and youthful, with peachy, slightly mealy and toasty flavours, it shows good complexity, with a slightly buttery, dry, lingering finish.

DRY $30 –V

Black Estate Home Chenin Blanc (★★★★☆)

The first 2014 vintage (★★★★☆) is from young, first-crop vines in the Home Vineyard at Omihi, Waipara. From botrytised grapes (80 per cent), hand-picked at over 28 brix, it's a finely balanced wine, fermented and matured in oak barrels. Delicious young, with gentle acidity and moderate sweetness (40 grams/litre of residual sugar), it has excellent complexity and depth of vibrant, peachy, lightly honeyed flavour. An auspicious debut.

MED $28 (375ML) –V

Clos de Ste Anne La Bas Chenin Blanc   ★★★★★

Certified biodynamic, the 2014 vintage (★★★★★) is already delicious. From a section of the vineyard 'down there' (La Bas), it was grown in Millton's Clos de Ste Anne hillside vineyard at Manutuke, in Gisborne, and fermented – with indigenous yeasts – and matured for nine months in large, 600-litre oak barrels ('demi-muids'). Bright, light yellow/green, it is a mouthfilling, fleshy wine, unusually ripe and well-rounded for Chenin Blanc, with concentrated peach and pineapple flavours, showing excellent complexity, gentle acidity, and a long, dry (2.1 grams/litre of residual sugar) finish. Drink now or cellar.

DRY $75 AV

Crazy by Nature Dry Flint Gisborne Chenin Blanc   ★★★★

From Millton and certified organic, the 2013 vintage (★★★★☆) offers terrific value. Mouthfilling and vibrantly fruity, it has pure, ripe, peachy flavours, showing excellent delicacy, depth and harmony. Chenin Blanc is often austere in its youth, but this delicious wine is scented and slightly creamy, with gentle acidity and an off-dry finish (6.4 grams/litre of residual sugar). A great introduction to the variety's charms.

MED/DRY $22 V+

Esk Valley Hawke's Bay Chenin Blanc   ★★★★

This is one of New Zealand's few convincing Chenin Blancs, with an ability to mature gracefully for several years. The 2013 vintage (★★★★), fermented in tanks (80 per cent) and barrels (20 per cent), is a fractionally off-dry style (5.4 grams/litre of residual sugar). Grown in the inland, organically certified Moteo Terraces Vineyard, it is a weighty wine with strong, youthful lemon/apple flavours, a touch of barrel-ferment complexity, and a slightly creamy and nutty, dryish, lingering finish. (There is no 2014.)

Vintage	14	13	12	11	10
WR	NM	7	5	6	6
Drink	NM	16-18	16-17	P	P

MED/DRY $20 V+

Esk Valley Winemakers Reserve Hawke's Bay Chenin Blanc   (★★★★☆)

The 2013 vintage (★★★★☆) was grown in the Moteo Ridge Vineyard and fermented with indigenous yeasts in seasoned French oak casks. A fully dry style (2 grams/litre of residual sugar), it's a powerful (14.5 per cent alcohol) wine, with concentrated, vibrant pear, citrus-fruit and spice flavours, showing good complexity, and obvious potential.

Vintage	13
WR	7
Drink	16-20

DRY $29 AV

Forrest Marlborough Chenin Blanc   ★★★☆

This is a rare beast – a Chenin Blanc from the South Island. Estate-grown in the Wairau Valley, the 2013 vintage (★★★☆) is a medium-bodied wine with fresh melon, citrus-fruit and lime flavours, a gentle splash of sweetness, and tangy acidity. A lively, finely balanced wine, it should reward cellaring.

 MED/DRY $25 –V

Lazy Dog, The, Queensbury Chenin Blanc   ★★★☆

Grown at Queensberry, midway between Cromwell and Wanaka, the 2013 vintage (★★★), handled entirely in tanks, is a fresh, medium-bodied wine with lively, lemony, appley, slightly peachy flavours, a sliver of sweetness (11 grams/litre of residual sugar) and balanced acidity. It's worth cellaring. (Note: the 2014 vintage is sold under the brand Queensberry – see under that brand.)

Vintage	13	12	11
WR	4	5	4
Drink	16-18	16-18	16-17

MED/DRY $23 –V

Margrain Martinborough Chenin Blanc   ★★★★

When Margrain bought the neighbouring Chifney property, they acquired Chenin Blanc vines now around 30 years old. The 2015 vintage (★★★★) is a youthful wine, handled without oak. It has strong, peachy, slightly spicy flavours, with a gentle splash of sweetness (23 grams/litre of residual sugar), appetising acidity and a long finish. Open mid-2017+. The 2016 vintage (★★★★) has a real sense of youthful vigour. Crisp and gently sweet (22 grams/litre of residual sugar), it has very good depth of peach, lemon and pear flavours, lively acidity, good balance and obvious potential. Best drinking 2018+.

Vintage	16	15
WR	7	6
Drink	16-26	16-25

MED $38 –V

Matawhero Church House Gisborne Chenin Blanc   ★★★★

The 2015 vintage (★★★★☆) is a fresh, medium-bodied, finely balanced wine, enjoyable from the start. Clearly varietal, with vibrant, peachy, slightly sweet flavours, lively acidity and impressive poise and depth, it should be at its best 2018+.

Vintage	15	14	13
WR	7	7	6
Drink	16-18	16-17	P

 MED/DRY $28 –V

Millton Chenin Blanc Te Arai Vineyard   ★★★★★

Certified organic, this Gisborne wine is New Zealand's best-known Chenin Blanc. It's a richly varietal wine with concentrated, fresh, vibrant fruit flavours to the fore in some vintages (2010, 2013, 2014), nectareous scents and flavours in others (2005, 2008). The grapes are hand-picked at up to four stages of ripening, culminating in some years ('It's in the lap of the gods,' says James Millton) in a final harvest of botrytis-affected fruit. Fermentation is in tanks and large, 600-litre French oak casks, used in the Loire for Chenin Blanc. The 2014 vintage (★★★★★)

is a highly scented, off-dry style (7 grams/litre of residual sugar) with rich, ripe, peachy, slightly limey and honeyed flavours, woven with appetising acidity, and good complexity. Mouthfilling and full of youthful vigour, it is already highly approachable, but should flourish with cellaring. The 2015 vintage (★★★★☆) is fragrant and finely poised, with very youthful, finely balanced peach, pear and spice flavours, slightly sweet and woven with fresh acidity. Vibrantly fruity and long, it's already approachable, but well worth cellaring.

Vintage	15	14	13	12	11	10	09	08
WR	6	7	7	NM	6	7	6	6
Drink	16-25	16-26	16-25	NM	P	16-22	16-21	P

MED/DRY $30 AV

Queensbury Central Otago Chenin Blanc ★★★☆

The impressive 2014 vintage (★★★★) was estate-grown at Queensberry, midway between Cromwell and Wanaka, hand-picked and fermented in tanks and barrels. Crisp and vibrantly fruity, with strong, citrusy flavours, showing excellent depth, delicacy and purity, a touch of complexity and a finely balanced, off-dry finish (12.5 grams/litre of residual sugar), it is well worth cellaring. (Note: past vintages were sold under The Lazy Dog brand.)

Vintage	14
WR	6
Drink	16-19

MED/DRY $23 –V

Fiano

A traditional low-yielding variety of Campania, in south-west Italy, Fiano is also grown in Sicily, Argentina and Australia. It is not listed separately in New Zealand Winegrowers' *Vineyard Register Report 2015–2018*, but its age-worthy wines have been praised by UK writer Oz Clarke as 'exciting' and 'distinctive'.

Bushhawk Vineyard Bella's Block Hawke's Bay Fiano ★★★★☆

The 2013 vintage (★★★★★) was a top debut, full of personality, and the 2014 vintage (★★★★☆) is again impressive. Grown in the Bridge Pa Triangle, hand-picked, and fermented and lees-aged for six months in small stainless steel 'barrels', it is full-bodied, with finely balanced acidity and a powerful surge of fresh, ripe fruit flavours, reminiscent of peaches and pineapples. Sturdy and dry, it's a drink-now or cellaring proposition.

DRY $25 V+

Flora

A California crossing of Gewürztraminer and Sémillon, in cool-climate regions Flora produces aromatic, spicy wine. Some of New Zealand's 'Pinot Gris' vines were more than a decade ago positively identified as Flora, but the country's total area of bearing Flora vines in 2017 will be just 3 hectares, almost all in Auckland and Northland.

Shipwreck Bay Northland Flora (★★★)

The 2014 vintage (★★★) is a fresh, full-bodied, slightly sweet wine, balanced for easy drinking, with ripe, peachy, gently spicy flavours. (From Okahu Estate.)

 MED/DRY $20 –V

Thomas & Sons Reserve Collection Waiheke Flora (★★★★)

The 2013 vintage (★★★★), made in a distinctly medium style (30 grams/litre of residual sugar), was fermented with indigenous yeasts and handled entirely in tanks. It is full-bodied, with strong, fresh, ripe flavours of peaches, lychees and spices that linger well.

MED $45 –V

Gewürztraminer

Only a trickle of Gewürztraminer is exported (0.01 per cent of our total wine shipments), and the majority of New Zealand bottlings lack the power and richness of the great Alsace model. Yet this classic grape is starting to get the respect it deserves from grape-growers and winemakers here.

For most of the 1990s, Gewürztraminer's popularity was on the wane. Between 1983 and 1996, New Zealand's plantings of Gewürztraminer dropped by almost two-thirds. A key problem is that Gewürztraminer is a temperamental performer in the vineyard, being particularly vulnerable to adverse weather at flowering, which can decimate grape yields. Now there is proof of a strong renewal of interest: the area of bearing vines has surged from 85 hectares in 1998 to 256 hectares in 2017. Most of the plantings are in Marlborough (34 per cent of the national total), Hawke's Bay (19 per cent) and Gisborne (18 per cent), but there are also significant pockets in Nelson, Canterbury and Otago. Gewürztraminer is a high-impact wine, brimming with scents and flavours. 'Spicy' is the most common adjective used to pinpoint its distinctive, heady aromas and flavours; tasters also find nuances of gingerbread, freshly ground black pepper, cinnamon, cloves, mint, lychees and mangoes. Once you've tasted one or two Gewürztraminers, you won't have any trouble recognising it in a blind tasting – it's one of the most forthright, distinctive white-wine varieties of all.

Anchorage Family Estate Nelson Gewürztraminer ★★★☆

Offering good value, the 2014 vintage (★★★★) is mouthfilling and fleshy, with ripe-fruit flavours and a slightly oily texture. Made in a medium style, it is harmonious, well-rounded and ripely perfumed.

MED/DRY $19 V+

Aronui Nelson Gewürztraminer ★★★☆

The 2015 vintage (★★★☆) is a single-vineyard wine, hand-picked in the Moutere hills. Mouthfilling (14 per cent alcohol), it is a dryish style (5 grams/litre of residual sugar), still very youthful, with fresh, delicate peach, lychee and spice flavours, showing good varietal character, and a perfumed bouquet. Best drinking mid-2017+.

MED/DRY $22 AV

Askerne Hawke's Bay Gewürztraminer ★★★★

Partly barrel-fermented, this is a consistently good, easy-drinking wine, priced right. The 2015 vintage (★★★★) is gently perfumed, mouthfilling and well-rounded, with a gentle splash of sweetness (11 grams/litre of residual sugar), plenty of ripe, citrusy, spicy flavour, and excellent harmony.

MED/DRY $22 V+

Ataahua Waipara Gewürztraminer ★★★★☆

Exotically perfumed and mouthfilling, the 2014 vintage (★★★★☆) is a partly barrel-fermented wine (20 per cent) with soft, rich flavours. Peachy, spicy and slightly gingery, it is concentrated, with good complexity, gentle sweetness and a seductively smooth finish.

Vintage	14	13	12	11	10
WR	6	6	7	7	6
Drink	16-19	16-20	16-19	16-18	P

MED/DRY $26 AV

Babich Family Estates Gimblett Gravels Gewürztraminer ★★★☆

Grown in Hawke's Bay, the 2014 vintage (★★★★) is very open and expressive from the start. Mouthfilling, it has ripe, peachy, slightly spicy flavours in a strongly varietal style, showing good body and fragrance.

Vintage	14	13	12	11
WR	7	7	5	7
Drink	16-18	16-17	P	P

DRY $25 –V

Blackenbrook Vineyard Nelson Gewürztraminer ★★★★☆

A consistently attractive wine. The refined 2016 vintage (★★★★) was mostly handled in tanks, but 10 per cent of the blend was oak-matured. Pale and mouthfilling, it is a medium-dry style (11 grams/litre of residual sugar), with youthful, vibrant pear, lychee and spice flavours, showing excellent freshness, delicacy and depth. Best drinking 2018+.

Vintage	16
WR	5
Drink	16-20

 MED/DRY $24 V+

Bladen Marlborough Gewürztraminer ★★★★☆

Hand-harvested in the Tilly Vineyard, the 2015 vintage (★★★★☆) is very expressive in its youth. Exotically perfumed, it is mouthfilling (14.5 per cent alcohol), with concentrated, peachy, spicy flavours, a hint of apricots, gentle sweetness (12 grams/litre of residual sugar), and lots of drink-young appeal.

 MED/DRY $25 V+

Brancott Estate Letter Series 'P' Marlborough Gewürztraminer ★★★★☆

The 2014 vintage (★★★★☆) is a weighty, fleshy wine, with ripe, peachy, spicy flavours, showing excellent concentration and complexity, and an off-dry, finely balanced finish. The 2015 vintage (★★★★) is a highly perfumed, strongly varietal wine, with fresh, pure, well-spiced flavours. Mouthfilling, it has a lush, oily texture and a gently sweet finish.

MED/DRY $33 –V

Charcoal Gully Sally's Pinch Central Otago Gewürztraminer ★★★☆

The 2014 vintage (★★★☆) was hand-picked at Pisa, in the Cromwell Basin. Offering good drinkability, it's a fresh, medium-dry style (8 grams/litre of residual sugar), with a slightly oily texture, good depth of lively, finely balanced lemon, apple and spice flavours, and a floral, spicy bouquet.

Vintage	14
WR	6
Drink	16-19

 MED/DRY $21 AV

Cicada Marlborough Gewürztraminer ★★★★

The refined 2014 vintage (★★★★☆) is a perfumed, mouthfilling, vibrantly fruity wine with deep, peachy, spicy flavours. A strongly varietal wine, it has good vigour and harmony, with a gentle splash of sweetness (9 grams/litre of residual sugar) and a slightly oily richness. (From Riverby Estate.)

MED/DRY $25 AV

Clearview Te Awanga Gewürztraminer ★★★★

Exotically perfumed, the 2015 vintage (★★★★) is a refined wine with fresh pear and spice flavours, showing good balance of sweetness and acidity. A strongly varietal wine, with excellent delicacy and depth, it should mature well.

MED/DRY $19 V+

Craft Farm Home Vineyard Hawke's Bay Gewürztraminer (★★★★☆)

The 2014 vintage (★★★★☆) is enticingly perfumed. Full-bodied (14.5 per cent alcohol), it's a medium style (17 grams/litre of residual sugar) with impressive weight, concentrated lychee and spice flavours, gentle acidity and a slightly oily richness.

MED $32 –V

Crossroads Milestone Series Hawke's Bay Gewürztraminer ★★★★

The 2014 vintage (★★★★), grown at Fernhill, is perfumed, with mouthfilling body, delicate lychee and spice flavours and a dryish (5 grams/litre of residual sugar) finish. An intensely varietal wine, it should blossom in the bottle.

Vintage	14
WR	6
Drink	16-24

MED/DRY $20 V+

Dry River Lovat Vineyard Gewürztraminer ★★★★★

The delicious 2015 vintage (★★★★★) is from mature, 23-year-old vines in Martinborough. Highly expressive in its infancy, it is pale straw, with a fragrant, well-spiced bouquet. A mouthfilling, medium style (20 grams/litre of residual sugar), it has concentrated, peachy, gingery flavours, with a vague hint of honey, distinctly spicy notes, moderate acidity and excellent complexity. Drink now or cellar.

Vintage	15	14	13
WR	6	6	6
Drink	16-27	16-26	16-25

MED $47 AV

Dunstan Road Central Otago Gewürztraminer (★★★☆)

From a single row of vines, in a 2-hectare vineyard between Clyde and Alexandra, the easy-drinking 2014 vintage (★★★☆) was briefly wood-aged (for a month) and made in a medium style. Fresh, lively and harmonious, it is mouthfilling, with good depth of ripe lychee and spice flavours, showing a touch of complexity, a gentle splash of sweetness, and a rounded finish.

MED $20 AV

Ellero Central Otago Gewürztraminer   ★★★☆

The 2014 vintage (★★★☆) was grown in two neighbouring vineyards at Pisa, in the Cromwell Basin, and fermented in a tank and an old oak puncheon. Full-bodied and fresh, it has pear, lychee and spice flavours, gentle acidity and a dry (4 grams/litre of residual sugar), lingering, spicy finish.

DRY $27 –V

Forrest Marlborough Gewürztraminer   (★★★☆)

The 2014 vintage (★★★☆) is full-bodied and fresh, with pear and spice flavours, gentle sweetness (9 grams/litre of residual sugar), hints of lychees and ginger, moderate acidity and good depth.

 MED/DRY $20 AV

Framingham Marlborough Gewürztraminer   ★★★★★

This label is consistently impressive. Made in a medium style, it is handled in tanks and old barrels – the 2013 vintage (★★★★★) was mostly (60 per cent) fermented with indigenous yeasts in old oak casks. Exotically perfumed, it is fleshy and gently sweet (15 grams/litre of residual sugar), in a full-bodied style (14 per cent alcohol), with concentrated lychee, peach and spice flavours, a hint of ginger, impressive complexity and a finely textured, rounded finish. Delicious drinking now onwards.

Vintage	13	12	11	10	09
WR	7	6	6	6	7
Drink	16-18	16-17	P	P	P

MED $30 AV

Gibson Bridge Reserve Marlborough Gewürztraminer   ★★★★

The 2013 vintage (★★★★) of this single-vineyard, hand-picked Renwick wine is fleshy, with strong, vibrant, citrusy, spicy flavours, hints of apricot and ginger, and a slightly sweet, well-rounded finish. Drink now or cellar.

MED/DRY $28 –V

Giesen The Brothers Marlborough Gewürztraminer   (★★★★☆)

From sites at Rapaura and in the lower Wairau Valley, the 2014 vintage (★★★★☆) is exotically perfumed and fleshy. It has concentrated, gently sweet lychee, pear and spice flavours, showing a touch of complexity, and a slightly oily richness.

MED/DRY $33 –V

Greystone Waipara Valley Gewürztraminer   ★★★★★

An emerging star. The 2015 vintage (★★★★☆) was estate-grown, hand-picked and briefly matured on its yeast lees. Bright, light lemon/green, it is beautifully perfumed and very full-bodied (14.5 per cent alcohol). Still very youthful, it is a powerful wine, with deep, delicate lychee, pear and spice flavours, an oily texture and obvious potential; open 2018+.

Vintage	15	14	13	12	11
WR	7	6	7	7	7
Drink	16-25	16-18	16-17	P	P

MED/DRY $33 AV

Grove Mill Wairau Valley Marlborough Gewürztraminer   (★★★★☆)

The exotically perfumed 2013 vintage (★★★★☆) was fermented in tanks (90 per cent) and seasoned oak barrels (10 per cent). Mouthfilling and gently sweet, it has excellent depth of peach, lychee, spice and ginger flavours, a slightly oily texture, and a finely balanced, soft finish. Great value.

 MED/DRY $20 V+

Huia Marlborough Gewürztraminer   ★★★★☆

The 2014 vintage (★★★★★) is a striking wine. Estate-grown in the lower Wairau Valley and certified organic, it was partly fermented and fully matured for 10 months in old French oak puncheons. Fragrant and softly mouthfilling, it has rich, ripe, peachy, spicy, faintly gingery flavours, showing excellent complexity, and loads of personality. Delicious young, it is a dry style (4 grams/litre of residual sugar), finely textured, with good potential and notable harmony.

 DRY $28 V+

Hunter's Marlborough Gewürztraminer   ★★★★☆

The 2015 vintage (★★★★★), estate-grown at Rapaura, on the north side of the Wairau Valley, is full-bodied (14 per cent alcohol) and exotically perfumed. A classy young wine, delicious young, it has gentle sweetness (12.5 grams/litre of residual sugar) and a strong surge of lychee, peach and spice flavours. A very harmonious wine, it should be at its best 2017+.

 MED/DRY $25 V+

Johanneshof Cellars Marlborough Gewürztraminer   ★★★★★

This beauty is one of the country's greatest Gewürztraminers. The 2014 vintage (★★★★★) is a single-vineyard wine, hand-picked and made in a medium style (20 grams/litre of residual sugar). Very exotically perfumed, it is medium to full-bodied, with peachy, spicy, intensely varietal flavours, showing lovely delicacy and richness, hints of ginger and apricot, and a deliciously harmonious, well-rounded, lasting finish.

Vintage	14	13	12	11	10	09	08
WR	7	7	7	6	7	6	6
Drink	16-24	16-23	16-21	16-20	16-20	16-17	P

 MED $29 V+

Kaimira Estate Brightwater Gewürztraminer   ★★★☆

The 2015 vintage (★★★☆), certified organic, is a perfumed, strongly varietal wine with lively acidity and very good depth of peachy, spicy flavour, fresh and slightly sweet (7 grams/litre of residual sugar). Drink now or cellar.

 MED/DRY $22 AV

Konrad Marlborough Gewürztraminer   ★★★

Estate-grown and hand-picked in the Waihopai Valley, the 2014 vintage (★★★☆) is mouthfilling, with a spicy bouquet, strong, citrusy, spicy flavours and a dryish finish. Showing good varietal character, it's certified organic.

MED/DRY $19 AV

Kumeu River Estate Gewürztraminer ★★★★

The 2014 vintage (★★★☆) was hand-picked from mature vines at Kumeu, in West Auckland, and fermented with indigenous yeasts in tanks. Full-bodied, it is gently sweet, with fresh lychee and spice flavours, balanced acidity and good length.

 MED/DRY $25 AV

Lawson's Dry Hills Marlborough Gewürztraminer ★★★★★

One of the country's most impressive Gewürztraminers. Grown in the Home Block and nearby Woodward Vineyard, at the foot of the Wither Hills, it is typically harvested at about 24 brix and mostly fermented in stainless steel tanks; a key part of the blend (about 15 per cent) is given 'the full treatment', with a high-solids, indigenous yeast ferment in seasoned French oak barriques, malolactic fermentation and lees-stirring. The youthful 2015 vintage (★★★★☆) is light lemon/green, ripely scented and mouthfilling, with gentle sweetness (8 grams/litre of residual sugar), strong pear, lychee and spice flavours, and a tightly structured finish. Open mid-2017+.

Vintage	15	14	13	12	11	10	09
WR	7	6	7	7	7	7	7
Drink	17-24	16-22	16-20	16-18	16-17	16-18	P

 MED/DRY $24 V+

Lawson's Dry Hills The Pioneer Marlborough Gewürztraminer ★★★★★

The instantly seductive 2014 vintage (★★★★★) is a weighty (14.5 per cent alcohol), fleshy, Alsace-style wine, estate-grown in the Home Block and French oak-aged. Bright, light yellow/green, it is sturdy and creamy-textured, with abundant sweetness (26 grams/litre of residual sugar) and soft, rich, peachy, spicy flavours, showing lovely ripeness, depth, complexity and harmony.

Vintage	14	13
WR	6	7
Drink	16-24	16-20

 MED $35 AV

Linden Estate Esk Valley Hawke's Bay Gewürztraminer (★★★)

The 2014 vintage (★★★) is aromatic and fleshy, with strong pear, lychee and spice flavours and a dry (4 grams/litre of residual sugar) finish. It shows a slight lack of delicacy, but plenty of body and flavour.

 DRY $20 –V

Loveblock Marlborough Gewürztraminer ★★★★

Certified organic, the 2014 vintage (★★★★) was harvested at a hilltop site in the lower Awatere Valley and made in a medium-dry style (14 grams/litre of residual sugar). Light lemon/green, it is fleshy and soft, with gentle acidity and strong, ripe peach, lychee and spice flavours. A harmonious wine with good varietal character, it's drinking well now.

 MED/DRY $25 AV

Mahi Twin Valleys Marlborough Gewürztraminer ★★★★

The 2015 vintage (★★★★) is a single-vineyard wine, grown at the junction of the Wairau and Waihopai valleys, hand-picked and fermented with indigenous yeasts in tanks (60 per cent) and seasoned French oak barriques (40 per cent). It has a perfumed, strongly varietal bouquet, leading into a mouthfilling, fleshy, dry palate (3 grams/litre of residual sugar), with rich, youthful lychee and spice flavours, showing considerable complexity, and a softly textured finish.

Vintage	15
WR	7
Drink	16-20

DRY $24 AV

Main Divide Marlborough Gewürztraminer (★★★☆)

The 2015 vintage (★★★☆) has a perfumed, distinctly spicy bouquet, leading into a mouthfilling wine (14 per cent alcohol), with strong, peachy, spicy, slightly gingery flavours and a dryish finish. (From Pegasus Bay.)

MED/DRY $21 AV

Main Divide Waipara Valley Gewürztraminer ★★★★

Partly barrel-fermented, the 2013 vintage (★★★★) is exotically perfumed, with mouthfilling body, a slightly oily texture, and rich stone-fruit, ginger and spice flavours. Fine value. (From Pegasus Bay.)

Vintage	13	12
WR	7	7
Drink	16-20	16-19

MED $20 V+

Margrain Martinborough Gewürztraminer (★★★★)

Pale straw, the 2016 vintage (★★★★) is a distinctly medium style (31 grams/litre of residual sugar). Full-bodied, with a strong surge of peachy, spicy flavours, and hints of ginger and honey, it's already drinking well.

Vintage	16
WR	7
Drink	16-23

MED $38 –V

Marsden Bay of Islands Gewürztraminer (★★★★)

Who says you can't make good Gewürztraminer in the north? Grown at Mangawhai, the 2015 vintage (★★★★) is a pale straw, faintly pink wine with a spicy, gingery bouquet. Mouthfilling, it is gently sweet (21 grams/litre of residual sugar), with strong, peachy, spicy, vaguely honeyed flavours, ripe and fresh, and a long, well-spiced finish.

Vintage	15
WR	6
Drink	16-18

MED $29 –V

Matawhero Gisborne Gewürztraminer ★★★★

Grown in the Matawhero Vineyard, the 2014 vintage (★★★★) is medium to full-bodied, with good varietal character and strong, ripe, peachy, spicy flavours, slightly sweet (10 grams/litre of residual sugar) and finely balanced. Best drinking now onwards.

Vintage	14	13
WR	7	6
Drink	16-17	P

MED/DRY $24 AV

Mills Reef Reserve Gisborne Gewürztraminer (★★★★)

Released in mid to late 2015, the 2013 vintage (★★★★) was grown at Patutahi. It is mouthfilling and fleshy, with strong, ripe, peachy, spicy flavours, hints of lychees and ginger, and a perfumed bouquet.

DRY $25 AV

Millton Riverpoint Vineyard Gewürztraminer ★★★★

The 2013 vintage (★★★★) of this Gisborne wine was hand-harvested over a month, with three passes through the vineyard, and made in a deliciously smooth, off-dry style (9 grams/litre of residual sugar). Certified organic, it is mouthfilling, with strong, ripe, peachy, spicy flavours, gentle acidity and a long, soft, slightly gingery finish. It's a very harmonious wine; drink now or cellar. The 2014 vintage (★★★★☆), partly oak-aged, is a light gold, mouthfilling, fleshy wine with concentrated, spicy, gingery flavours, a sliver of sweetness, and strong personality. Drinking well now, it's certified organic.

Vintage	14
WR	6
Drink	16-18

MED/DRY $26 –V

Misha's Vineyard The Gallery Central Otago Gewürztraminer ★★★★☆

The 2014 vintage (★★★★☆), estate-grown and hand-harvested at Bendigo, was fermented in seasoned French oak casks, partly (25 per cent) with indigenous yeasts. Weighty (14.5 per cent alcohol), it has strong, ripe lychee and spice flavours, showing excellent delicacy and depth, good complexity, gentle acidity, and a slightly sweet (13 grams/litre of residual sugar), well-rounded finish. Drink now or cellar.

Vintage	14	13	12	11	10	09	08
WR	6	6	7	6	6	6	7
Drink	16-23	16-23	16-21	16-20	16-20	16-18	16-18

MED/DRY $32 –V

Mission Hawke's Bay Gewürztraminer ★★★★

Bargain-priced, the 2015 vintage (★★★★) is a full-bodied, medium style (15 grams/litre of residual sugar), with an attractively perfumed bouquet, lively acidity and strong, fresh, youthful, well-spiced flavours.

Vintage	13
WR	5
Drink	16-18

MED $18 V+

Mount Riley Marlborough Gewürztraminer ★★★☆

The 2014 vintage (★★★☆), grown in the Omaka Valley, was mostly handled in tanks; 10 per cent of the blend was barrel-fermented. Mouthfilling, it is weighty and smooth, with a sliver of sweetness (8 grams/litre of residual sugar) and very good depth of fresh, citrusy, peachy, spicy flavour.

MED/DRY $17 V+

Mt Difficulty Growers Series Station Block Pisa Range
Central Otago Gewürztraminer (★★★★)

The 2014 vintage (★★★★) is a single-vineyard wine, grown in the Cromwell Basin. The bouquet is gently spicy; the palate is mouthfilling and fleshy, with gentle sweetness (25 grams/litre of residual sugar), strong lychee, pear and spice flavours, fresh acidity, and a long, spicy finish. It shows good varietal character, vigour and depth; open now or cellar.

MED $26 –V

Ohinemuri Estate Matawhero Gewürztraminer ★★★☆

The 2015 vintage (★★★★) was grown in Gisborne and mostly handled in tanks, but 10 per cent of the blend was fermented and matured for four months in oak barrels. It is already drinking well, but worth cellaring. Light lemon/green, it is mouthfilling, slightly sweet (15 grams/litre of residual sugar) and smooth, with fresh, peachy, gently spicy flavours. Finely balanced, it's a strongly varietal wine, youthful and enticingly perfumed.

Vintage	15
WR	5
Drink	16-19

MED $24 –V

Old Coach Road Nelson Gewürztraminer ★★★☆

From Seifried, the bargain-priced 2015 vintage (★★★☆) is medium to full-bodied, with good depth of citrusy, gently spicy flavours. Slighty sweet (8 grams/litre of residual sugar), it's a strongly varietal wine, drinking well now. The 2016 vintage (★★★☆) is similar – fresh, citrusy and gently spicy, with a sliver of sweetness (11 grams/litre of residual sugar), balanced acidity, and good varietal definition and depth. Fine value.

MED/DRY $13 V+

Pegasus Bay Gewürztraminer ★★★★★

Grown at Waipara and fermented with indigenous yeasts in large old barrels, the distinctive 2014 vintage (★★★★★) was made from 'very ripe' grapes, with 'a lot of noble botrytis'. Light gold, with honeyed, spicy aromas and flavours, it is mouthfilling and complex, with concentrated, vibrant, peachy, spicy flavours, enriched but not dominated by botrytis. A youthful wine with fresh acidity and powerful personality, it should be long-lived.

Vintage	14	13	12	11	10
WR	7	7	7	6	6
Drink	16-22	16-21	16-20	16-17	P

MED $30 AV

Rimu Grove Nelson Gewürztraminer ★★★★

Still unfolding, the 2015 vintage (★★★★) is a strongly varietal wine, perfumed and softly mouthfilling, with gentle sweetness (15 grams/litre of residual sugar) and youthful, ripe lychee, pear and spice flavours that linger well.

Vintage	15	14
WR	7	7
Drink	16-26	16-25

MED $26 –V

Rippon Gewürztraminer ★★★★

The 2013 vintage (★★★☆) is from mature vines at Lake Wanaka, Central Otago. Fermented with indigenous yeasts and lees-aged in tanks, it has a fresh, spicy bouquet, mouthfilling body, and slightly sweet lychee and spice flavours, showing good delicacy and depth, with a touch of complexity.

MED/DRY $33 –V

Ruru Central Otago Gewürztraminer (★★★)

The 2015 vintage (★★★) is a full-bodied and fresh, slightly sweet wine, grown at Alexandra. Lightly scented, it has attractive, lemony, appley, gently spicy flavours, with earthy notes adding a touch of complexity.

MED/DRY $19 AV

Saint Clair Marlborough Gewürztraminer ★★★☆

Attractively perfumed, the 2014 vintage (★★★★) is grown at two sites in the Wairau Valley. It's a richly varietal wine with very good depth of fresh, ripe lychee, pear and spice flavours, a slightly oily texture, gentle acidity and a slightly sweet (9 grams/litre of residual sugar), soft finish. Delicious young.

MED/DRY $22 AV

Saint Clair Pioneer Block 12 Lone Gum Marlborough Gewürztraminer ★★★★☆

Grown at a warm site in the lower Omaka Valley, the 2015 vintage (★★★★☆) is an attractively perfumed, softly seductive wine, already delicious. It is fleshy and smooth, with concentrated, peachy, spicy flavours, a slightly oily texture, and a gently sweet (16 grams/litre of residual sugar), rich finish.

MED $27 AV

Saint Clair Vicar's Choice Marlborough Gewürztraminer ★★★

Enjoyable young, the 2014 vintage (★★★) is full-bodied, fresh and smooth, with good depth of vibrant lychee, peach and spice flavours, and a dryish (7 grams/litre of residual sugar), well-rounded finish.

MED/DRY $19 AV

Sea Level Home Block Nelson Gewürztraminer   ★★★★☆

Estate-grown at Mariri, the 2013 vintage (★★★★☆) is a richly perfumed, medium style (15 grams/litre of residual sugar), with concentrated, fresh lychee, pear and spice flavours, pure and strong, a slightly oily texture and excellent harmony.

Vintage	13
WR	6
Drink	16-20

 MED $24 V+

Seifried Nelson Gewürztraminer   ★★★★

Typically a floral, well-spiced wine, offering excellent quality and value. The 2015 vintage (★★★★) is a richly perfumed, mouthfilling, strongly varietal wine with pear, lychee and spice flavours, showing very good delicacy and richness, and a finely textured, off-dry finish. The 2016 vintage (★★★★) is fresh and finely poised, with a sliver of sweetness (7 grams/litre of residual sugar) amid its youthful, vibrant peach, pear and spice flavours. Tightly structured, with good potential, it should be at its best mid-2017+.

Vintage	16	15	14	13	12
WR	6	6	6	6	6
Drink	16-20	16-20	16-17	P	P

 MED/DRY $18 V+

Seifried Winemaker's Collection Nelson Gewürztraminer   ★★★★★

This is typically a powerful wine with loads of personality. The 2016 vintage (★★★★☆) is richly perfumed and full-bodied, with concentrated, fresh, strongly spicy, slightly gingery flavours and a bone-dry finish. It's already very expressive; drink now or cellar.

Vintage	16	15	14	13
WR	7	6	6	6
Drink	16-21	16-21	16-19	16-18

 DRY $26 V+

Sherwood Estate Waipara Valley Gewürztraminer   (★★★★)

The pale gold 2014 vintage (★★★★) is enticingly scented and mouthfilling, with strong, peachy, slightly gingery and honeyed flavours. Made in a medium style (25 grams/litre of residual sugar) with finely balanced acidity, it's a powerful wine, drinking well young.

 MED $19 V+

Sileni Estate Selection 1,000 Vines Hawke's Bay Gewürztraminer   (★★★★)

The debut 2015 vintage (★★★★) has a musky perfume, good weight and strong, fresh lychee, pear and spice flavours. Fleshy and dryish (7 grams/litre of residual sugar), with a touch of complexity, it's well worth cellaring; open 2017+.

Vintage	15
WR	6
Drink	16-23

MED/DRY $28 –V

Sileni G2 Hawke's Bay Gewürztraminer   (★★★★)

The 'G2' refers to Graeme Avery (the owner) and Grant Edmonds (chief winemaker), the two key figures at Sileni. Grown in the Bridge Pa Triangle, the 2014 vintage (★★★★) is a mouthfilling, fleshy, soft wine with off-dry (6 grams/litre of residual sugar) flavours of peaches, apricots, lychees and spices, a slightly oily texture, and loads of drink-young charm.

Vintage	14
WR	6
Drink	16-22

 MED/DRY $35 –V

Spy Valley Envoy Johnson Vineyard Marlborough Gewürztraminer   ★★★★★

Estate-grown in the lower Waihopai Valley, hand-harvested from mature vines and fermented in small oak vessels, the 2015 vintage (★★★★★) is a deliciously perfumed, complex and harmonious wine. Already very open and expressive, it is mouthfilling and smooth, with gentle sweetness (25 grams/litre of residual sugar), highly concentrated, spicy, peachy, slightly toasty and gingery flavours, and a long, well-rounded finish.

Vintage	15	14	13	12
WR	7	6	7	5
Drink	16-20	16-19	16-20	16-18

 MED $32 AV

Spy Valley Marlborough Gewürztraminer   ★★★★☆

Estate-grown in the Waihopai Valley and fermented in tanks and old oak vessels, this wine is consistently impressive. Pale straw, the 2015 vintage (★★★★) is a perfumed, mouthfilling wine. Richly varietal and weighty, it has generous, ripe, peachy, gingery flavours, gentle acidity, and a slightly sweet (10 grams/litre of residual sugar), seductively soft finish.

Vintage	15	14	13	12	11	10
WR	6	7	6	6	7	6
Drink	16-19	16-18	16-17	P	P	P

 MED/DRY $23 V+

Stonecroft Gimblett Gravels Hawke's Bay Gewürztraminer   ★★★★☆

Certified organic, the 2015 vintage (★★★★☆) was estate-grown and a small part of the blend was fermented in old oak casks. Sturdy (14.5 per cent alcohol) and gently sweet (10 grams/litre of residual sugar), it has concentrated, ripe, citrusy, spicy flavours, with hints of ginger and honey, and a well-rounded finish. Already delicious, it should mature gracefully.

Vintage	15	14	13
WR	6	5	5
Drink	16-22	16-21	16-20

MED/DRY $27 AV

Stonecroft Old Vine Gewürztraminer   ★★★★★

The Gewürztraminers from this tiny Hawke's Bay winery are among the finest in the country. This 'Old Vine' wine is made entirely from grapes hand-picked from the original Mere Road plantings in 1983. Certified organic, the 2015 vintage (★★★★★) is a pale gold, mouthfilling (14.5 per cent alcohol), very rich wine, with lush, ripe, peachy, spicy flavours, gentle acidity, and a smooth, gently sweet (20 grams/litre of residual sugar), lasting finish. Drink now or cellar.

Vintage	15	14
WR	6	6
Drink	17-24	16-23

 MED $47 AV

Te Awanga Estate Hawke's Bay Gewürztraminer   (★★★★)

The 2014 vintage (★★★★) was hand-harvested at an inland site, tank-fermented and matured on its yeast lees. It has a perfumed, spicy bouquet, leading into a mouthfilling, off-dry wine with strong, citrusy, peachy, spicy flavours, fresh, harmonious and long. Drink now or cellar.

MED/DRY $25 AV

Te Mania Nelson Gewürztraminer   ★★★☆

The 2014 vintage (★★★) is a charming wine with lemony, gently spicy flavours in a fresh, off-dry style, well balanced for early appeal.

 MED/DRY $23 -V

Two Gates Hawke's Bay Gewürztraminer   (★★★☆)

Grown at Maraekakaho, the 2014 vintage (★★★☆) is a single-vineyard wine, hand-picked and fermented with indigenous yeasts in tanks and French oak puncheons. The bouquet is spicy, with some 'funky' notes; the palate is medium-bodied, with good depth of peachy, spicy, slightly gingery, dryish flavours.

 MED/DRY $28 -V

Villa Maria Private Bin East Coast Gewürztraminer   ★★★☆

This regional blend, grown at sites stretching from Auckland to Waipara, typically offers very good value. The 2015 vintage (★★★☆) has a fragrant, well-spiced bouquet. Enjoyable young, it's a medium-dry style (7.5 grams/litre of residual sugar) with very good depth of peach, lychee and spice flavours. Priced sharply. The 2016 vintage (★★★★) is a great buy. The bouquet is fragrant and well-spiced; the palate is mouthfilling, with a sliver of sweetness (7.8 grams/litre of residual sugar) and rich peach, spice and ginger flavours. Delicious from the start.

Vintage	16	15	14	13	12
WR	7	6	7	7	6
Drink	16-19	16-17	16-17	P	P

 MED/DRY $17 V+

Villa Maria Private Bin Hawke's Bay Organic Gewürztraminer   ★★★☆

The 2014 vintage (★★★★) is an off-dry style (7 grams/litre of residual sugar). Mouthfilling (14 per cent alcohol), it has fresh, rich stone-fruit and spice flavours, finely balanced and lingering. Certified organic, it offers top value.

Vintage	16	15	14
WR	7	6	7
Drink	16-19	16-17	16-17

 MED/DRY $17 V+

Villa Maria Single Vineyard Ihumatao Gewürztraminer   ★★★★★

Estate-grown in South Auckland, this wine is partly fermented with indigenous yeasts in seasoned French oak barriques; the rest is handled in tanks. The 2014 vintage (★★★★☆), 10 per cent barrel-fermented, is perfumed and weighty, with concentrated, ripe pear and lychee flavours, showing excellent delicacy and richness. An off-dry style (7 grams/litre of residual sugar), it has an oily texture and good cellaring potential.

Vintage	14	13
WR	7	7
Drink	16-20	P

 MED/DRY $28 V+

Vinoptima Ormond Reserve Gewürztraminer   ★★★★★

This wine, launched from 2003, is from Nick Nobilo's vineyard at Ormond, in Gisborne, devoted exclusively to the variety, and is fermented in tanks and large 1200-litre German oak ovals. The 2010 vintage (★★★★★), dubbed 'Delicatum', is fleshy, with strong, peachy, citrusy, gently spicy flavours, showing good vigour and bottle-aged complexity. Released in October 2015, it's probably at its peak now to 2018.

Vintage	10	09	08
WR	7	NM	6
Drink	16-20	NM	16-18

 MED $75 –V

Waimea Nelson Gewürztraminer   ★★★★

The 2014 vintage (★★★★) is a tightly structured wine with mouthfilling body, lively acidity and strong, peachy, spicy flavours, with hints of ginger and apricot. Made in a medium-dry style (10 grams/litre of residual sugar), it shows good richness and potential.

 MED/DRY $23 AV

Wairau River Marlborough Gewürztraminer   ★★★☆

The 2015 vintage (★★★☆) is ripely scented and mouthfilling, with vibrant peach, lychee and spice flavours and a dry, smooth finish. The 2016 vintage (★★★☆) is a pale, youthful wine with mouthfilling body and very good depth of fresh, ripe, peachy, spicy flavours. Made in an off-dry style (8 grams/litre of residual sugar), it's best opened mid-2017+.

Vintage	16	15	14	13
WR	6	5	5	6
Drink	16-19	16-18	16-17	P

MED/DRY $20 AV

Whitehaven Marlborough Gewürztraminer   ★★★★☆

The 2014 vintage (★★★★★) was hand-harvested, fermented in tanks and a large oak oval, and made in a medium style (22 grams/litre of residual sugar). Exotically perfumed, it is mouthfilling, with a lovely array of ripe peach, pear, lychee and spice flavours, vague hints of ginger, a touch of complexity, gentle acidity and a lasting finish. Refined, with great drink-young appeal, it's a very harmonious wine, priced sharply.

Vintage	14	13
WR	7	7
Drink	16-19	16-18

 MED $23 V+

Yealands Estate Single Vineyard Awatere Valley Marlborough Gewürztraminer   ★★★☆

Estate-grown at Seaview, the 2013 vintage (★★★☆) is mouthfilling and slightly creamy, with a sliver of sweetness (6.5 grams/litre of residual sugar) and very good depth of well-balanced lychee and spice flavours.

Vintage	13
WR	6
Drink	16-17

 MED/DRY $23 –V

Zephyr Marlborough Gewürztraminer   ★★★★☆

Richly perfumed, the youthful 2015 vintage (★★★★☆) was estate-grown in the lower Wairau Valley and mostly tank-fermented; 5 per cent was handled in old oak. Light lemon/green, it is sturdy (14.5 per cent alcohol) and smooth, with ripe pear, lychee and spice flavours, showing excellent delicacy and depth. A powerful, harmonious wine with a touch of complexity, it shows strong personality.

MED/DRY $24 V+

Grüner Veltliner

Grüner Veltliner, Austria's favourite white-wine variety, is currently stirring up interest in New Zealand, especially in the south. 'Grü-Vee' is a fairly late ripener in Austria, where it yields medium-bodied wines, fruity, crisp and dry, with a spicy, slightly musky aroma. Most are drunk young, but the finest wines, with an Alsace-like substance and perfume, are more age-worthy. Coopers Creek produced New Zealand's first Grüner Veltliner from the 2008 vintage. Of the country's 46 hectares of bearing Grüner Veltliner vines in 2017, most are now clustered in Marlborough (33 hectares), with Nelson (6 hectares) a distant second.

Aronui Single Vineyard Nelson Grüner Veltliner (★★★)

The debut 2014 vintage (★★★) was estate-grown at Upper Moutere, hand-harvested and tank-fermented. Mouthfilling, it's a fully dry style with vibrant, citrusy, slightly appley and spicy flavours, moderate acidity and good vigour.

DRY $25 –V

Ata Mara Central Otago Grüner Veltliner (★★★)

The 2014 vintage (★★★) is a basically dry style (4.2 grams/litre of residual sugar), from vines planted in 2008. Medium-bodied, it has good freshness and vigour, with crisp, slightly appley flavours that linger well.

DRY $20 –V

Babich Family Estates Headwaters Organic Block Marlborough Grüner Veltliner ★★★☆

Certified organic, the 2015 vintage (★★★☆) is a tasty, lively, medium-bodied wine. It offers good depth of citrusy, slightly spicy flavours, with fresh acidity and a dry, persistent finish.

Vintage	15	14	13
WR	7	7	7
Drink	16-18	16-17	P

DRY $27 –V

Bannock Brae Marlene's Central Otago Grüner Veltliner ★★★★

The 2015 vintage (★★★★☆) is the best yet. Hand-harvested at Bannockburn, it was fermented in a mix of tanks and seasoned French oak barriques. Pale lemon/green, it's a bone-dry style, weighty and finely textured, with fresh, strong, yet delicate flavours, citrusy, peachy and slightly spicy, a salty streak, balanced acidity, good complexity and a lasting finish.

Vintage	15	14
WR	7	6
Drink	16-21	16-20

DRY $25 AV

Hans Herzog Marlborough Grüner Veltliner ★★★★

Estate-grown on the north side of the Wairau Valley, the age-worthy 2013 vintage (★★★★) was fermented and matured for 18 months in French oak puncheons. A dry style (3 grams/litre of residual sugar), it is medium to full-bodied, with vibrant grapefruit, peach and spice flavours, gently seasoned with oak, fresh acidity and good cellaring potential. Certified organic.

Vintage	13	12
WR	7	7
Drink	16-20	16-17

DRY $44 –V

Jules Taylor Marlborough Grüner Veltliner   ★★★★

The 2015 vintage (★★★★) is a refined, single-vineyard wine, handled without oak and produced in a dryish (5 grams/litre of residual sugar) style. Mouthfilling and vibrantly fruity, it has balanced acidity and very good depth of ripe, peachy, slightly spicy flavours. A fresh, very harmonious wine, it's enjoyable from the start.

Vintage	15	14
WR	6	5
Drink	16-19	16-18

MED/DRY $22 V+

Margrain Martinborough Grüner Veltliner   ★★★

Promoted as a sort of 'potbellied Riesling', the 2015 vintage (★★★) is a crisp wine, fermented in tanks (60 per cent) and old oak casks (40 per cent). Medium-bodied, it's a gently sweet style (19 grams/litre of residual sugar), with peachy, slightly limey flavours. The 2016 vintage (★★★☆) was partly barrel-fermented. Light lemon/green, it is a medium to full-bodied, slightly sweet style (20 grams/litre of residual sugar), with lively, peachy, appley flavours, crisp acidity, and good depth. Best drinking mid-2017+.

Vintage	16
WR	6
Drink	16-22

MED $30 –V

Nautilus Marlborough Grüner Veltliner   ★★★★☆

Showing good personality, the 2015 vintage (★★★★☆) was handled without oak and made in a bone-dry style. Weighty and tangy, with strong, citrusy, slightly spicy flavours, it is very fresh and lively, with a crisp, finely balanced, lasting finish. Drink now or cellar.

Vintage	15	14
WR	7	6
Drink	16-19	16-18

DRY $29 AV

Riverby Estate Marlborough Grüner Veltliner   ★★★☆

A single-vineyard wine, grown and hand-picked in the heart of the Wairau Valley, the 2014 vintage (★★★☆) was handled in stainless steel tanks and made in a dry style (3.9 grams/litre of residual sugar). Medium to full-bodied, it has finely balanced acidity and very good depth of fresh, citrusy, slightly spicy flavours. Enjoyable young.

Vintage	14	13
WR	6	6
Drink	16-19	16-18

DRY $24 –V

Saint Clair Marlborough Grüner Veltliner   ★★★★

Already delicious, the 2015 vintage (★★★★) is a full-bodied, dry wine (2.5 grams/litre of residual sugar), grown in the Omaka and Wairau valleys, and made with some use of old oak and malolactic fermentation. Vibrantly fruity, it shows very good vigour and depth of citrusy, spicy flavours, with hints of peaches and ginger, gentle acidity and a well-rounded finish.

DRY $21 V+

Seifried Nelson Grüner Veltliner   ★★★☆

The 2016 vintage (★★★☆) is medium to full-bodied, with fresh, citrusy, slightly spicy and peachy flavours, showing very good vibrancy and depth. Made in a fully dry style, it's still very youthful; open mid-2017 onwards.

Vintage	16	15	14	13	12
WR	6	6	6	6	6
Drink	16-18	16-18	P	P	P

DRY $25 –V

Waimea Nelson Grüner Veltliner   ★★★★

The 2015 vintage (★★★★) is mouthfilling, vibrantly fruity and dry (4 grams/litre of residual sugar), with finely balanced acidity and fresh, citrusy, peachy, slightly spicy flavours, showing very good depth and harmony. Enjoyable young, it should be at its best 2017+.

DRY $23 AV

Wairau River Marlborough Grüner Veltliner   (★★★☆)

A single-vineyard, estate-grown wine, the 2014 vintage (★★★☆) is mouthfilling and dry (2 grams/litre of residual sugar), with citrusy, slightly peachy and spicy flavours, showing good freshness and vigour.

DRY $25 –V

Whitehaven Marlborough Grüner Veltliner   (★★★★)

The fragrant 2015 vintage (★★★★) is enjoyable from the start. Full-bodied, with gentle acidity, it has strong, vibrant, peachy, spicy flavours, with a slightly creamy texture and a dry (4.7 grams/litre of residual sugar), well-rounded finish.

DRY $23 AV

Yealands Estate Single Vineyard Awatere Valley Marlborough Grüner Veltliner   ★★★★☆

Consistently good. The 2015 vintage (★★★★☆) is mouthfilling, fleshy and dry (3 grams/litre of residual sugar), with rich, ripe stone-fruit and spice flavours, strong, vibrant, finely balanced and lingering. It's already very open and expressive.

Vintage	15	14
WR	7	7
Drink	16-19	16-18

DRY $23 V+

Marsanne

Cultivated extensively in the northern Rhône Valley of France, where it is often blended with Roussanne, Marsanne yields powerful, sturdy wines with rich pear, spice and nut flavours. Although grown in Victoria since the 1860s, it is extremely rare in New Zealand, with 0.3 hectares of bearing vines in 2017, clustered in Gisborne and Auckland.

Coopers Creek SV Gisborne Allison Marsanne ★★★★

The 2014 vintage (★★★☆), made without oak, is mouthfilling, dry and slightly creamy, with fresh, peachy, citrusy, slightly spicy flavours and good texture and mouthfeel.

		DRY $24 AV
Vintage	14	
WR	7	
Drink	16-17	

Trinity Hill Gimblett Gravels Marsanne/Viognier ★★★★☆

Deliciously weighty, rich and rounded, the 2014 vintage (★★★★★) is a powerful blend of Marsanne (55 per cent) and Viognier (45 per cent), fermented and matured for 15 months in old oak puncheons. Sturdy (14.5 per cent alcohol), it has concentrated, ripe stone-fruit and spice flavours, finely integrated oak, good complexity, a slightly oily texture and a long, dry, seductively smooth finish. The 2015 vintage (★★★★☆) is a blend of Marsanne (51 per cent) and Viognier (49 per cent), fermented and matured for a year in seasoned French oak casks. A dry style (4 grams/litre of residual sugar), it is mouthfilling and smooth, with very youthful, peachy, citrusy flavours, gentle acidity, good complexity and a long finish. Well worth cellaring.

			DRY $35 –V
Vintage	15	14	
WR	6	6	
Drink	17-20	16-20	

Muscat

Muscat vines grow all over the Mediterranean, but Muscat is rarely seen in New Zealand as a varietal wine, because it ripens late in the season, without the lushness and intensity achieved in warmer regions. Of the country's 37 hectares of bearing Muscat vines in 2017, 30 hectares are clustered in Gisborne. Most of the grapes are used to add an inviting, musky perfume to low-priced sparklings, modelled on the Asti Spumantes of northern Italy.

Blackenbrook Nelson Muscat ★★★★

The 2014 vintage (★★★★) is a rare example of South Island Muscat (the 2010 was the first). Estate-grown, hand-picked at 22.6 brix and lees-aged in tanks, it is scented and vibrant, with good body, poise and richness. Made in an off-dry style (5 grams/litre of residual sugar), it is full-bodied, with lychee, pear and orange flavours, showing excellent purity, delicacy and varietal precision.

Vintage	14	MED/DRY $24 AV
WR	6	
Drink	P	

Millton Te Arai Vineyard Gisborne Muskats at Dawn ★★★★

Certified organic, the 2015 vintage (★★★★) is 'just off-dry', according to the label, but it tastes a lot sweeter than that. Highly perfumed, it is vibrantly fruity, with rich peach, pear and lychee flavours, balanced acidity, and lots of drink-young charm. Imagine an Asti Spumante, without the bubbles . . .

Vintage	15	SW $22 V+
WR	6	
Drink	16-17	

Pinot Blanc

If you love Chardonnay, try Pinot Blanc. A white mutation of Pinot Noir, Pinot Blanc is highly regarded in Italy and California for its generous extract and moderate acidity, although in Alsace and Germany the more aromatic Pinot Gris finds greater favour.

With its fullness of weight and subtle aromatics, Pinot Blanc can easily be mistaken for Chardonnay in a blind tasting. The variety is still rare in New Zealand, but in 2017 there will be 12 hectares of bearing vines, mostly in Marlborough and Central Otago.

Gibbston Valley Red Shed Bendigo Single Vineyard
Central Otago Pinot Blanc ★★★★★

The classy 2015 vintage (★★★★★) was estate-grown and hand-picked at Bendigo, fermented with indigenous yeasts in old French barriques, lees-aged in oak for 10 months, and given a full, softening malolactic fermentation. Pale lemon/green, it is mouthfilling, with concentrated, peachy, citrusy flavours, slightly biscuity and buttery notes adding complexity, and a bone-dry, very long and harmonious finish. A subtle, finely poised, very youthful wine, it should be at its best 2018+.

DRY $39 AV

Greenhough Hope Vineyard Nelson Pinot Blanc ★★★★☆

Based principally on Pinot Blanc vines planted at Hope, in Nelson, in 1976, the 2013 vintage (★★★★☆) is a blend of Pinot Blanc (90 per cent) and Pinot Gris (10 per cent), hand-harvested at 23.1 brix and fermented and matured for 18 months in seasoned French oak casks. Fleshy and mouthfilling, it has rich, ripe lemon, apple and spice flavours, showing good complexity, and a smooth, creamy texture. A very age-worthy, slightly Chardonnay-like, fully dry wine, it should be at its best mid-2016+.

Vintage	13	12
WR	7	6
Drink	16-18	16-17

DRY $34 –V

Kaimira Estate Brightwater Nelson Pinot Blanc ★★★☆

Certified organic, the 2014 vintage (★★★★) was estate-grown, fermented in seasoned oak barrels and made in a dry style (3 grams/litre of residual sugar). Light lemon/green, it has a slightly creamy bouquet, leading into a mouthfilling, slightly Chardonnay-like wine with concentrated, peachy, slightly biscuity flavours and a well-rounded finish. Drink now onwards.

DRY $25 –V

Nevis Bluff Merrill's Block Central Otago Pinot Blanc (★★★★)

The fresh, full-bodied 2014 vintage (★★★★) was grown at Pisa and fermented in an even split of tanks and old oak casks. Dryish, with delicate, citrusy, appley, slightly spicy flavours, showing a touch of complexity, a hint of nectarines, balanced acidity and a lingering finish, it's well worth cellaring.

MED/DRY $35 –V

Pyramid Valley Growers Collection Kerner Estate Vineyard
Marlborough Pinot Blanc   ★★★★☆

Grown in the Waihopai Valley, the 2014 vintage (★★★★) was hand-picked and fermented with indigenous yeasts in seasoned French oak puncheons. It is mouthfilling and fleshy, with strong, ripe, youthful, peachy flavours, showing considerable complexity, balanced acidity and a dry, slightly creamy finish. Best drinking 2017+.

DRY $32 –V

Rock Ferry Marlborough Pinot Blanc   ★★★★

Certified organic, the 2013 vintage (★★★★) is a single-vineyard wine, fermented in tanks (88 per cent) and barrels (12 per cent). Mouthfilling and dryish (6 grams/litre of residual sugar), with strong, ripe, peachy, faintly toasty flavours, and a slightly creamy texture, it's delicious young, but also worth cellaring.

MED/DRY $27 –V

Pinot Gris

New Zealanders' love affair with Pinot Gris shows no signs of abating, and the wines are also starting to win an international reputation. The variety is spreading like wildfire – from 130 hectares of bearing vines in 2000 to 2480 hectares in 2017 – and accounts for nearly 7 per cent of the total producing vineyard area. New Zealand's third most extensively planted white-wine variety, with plantings more than triple those of Riesling, Pinot Gris is trailing only Sauvignon Blanc and Chardonnay.

A mutation of Pinot Noir, Pinot Gris has skin colours ranging from blue-grey to reddish-pink, sturdy extract and a fairly subtle, spicy aroma. It is not a difficult variety to cultivate, adapting well to most soils, and ripens with fairly low acidity to high sugar levels. In Alsace, the best Pinot Gris are matured in large casks, but the wood is old, so as not to interfere with the grape's subtle flavour.

What does Pinot Gris taste like? Imagine a wine that couples the satisfying weight and roundness of Chardonnay with some of the aromatic spiciness of Gewürztraminer. A popular and versatile wine, Pinot Gris is well worth getting to know.

In terms of style and quality, however, New Zealand Pinot Gris vary widely. Many of the wines lack the enticing perfume, mouthfilling body, flavour richness and softness of the benchmark wines from Alsace. These lesser wines, typically made from heavily cropped vines, are much leaner and crisper – more in the tradition of cheap Italian Pinot Grigio.

Popular in Germany, Alsace and Italy, Pinot Gris is now playing an important role here too. Well over half of the country's plantings are concentrated in Marlborough (41 per cent) and Hawke's Bay (17 per cent), but there are also significant pockets of Pinot Gris in Gisborne, Otago, Canterbury, Nelson, Wairarapa and Auckland.

8 Ranges Tussock Ridge Central Otago Pinot Gris ★★★☆

From Tussock Ridge Vineyard, between Alexandra and Clyde, the 2015 vintage (★★★☆) was estate-grown and hand-picked. A floral, vibrantly fruity wine, it has very good depth of fresh pear, lychee and peach flavours, with finely balanced acidity and a dryish finish.

MED/DRY $25 –V

12,000 Miles Wairarapa Pinot Gris ★★★☆

From Gladstone Vineyard, the 2015 vintage (★★★☆) was grown in the northern Wairarapa, briefly lees-aged and handled without oak. Fresh and full-bodied, it's enjoyable young, with ripe, peachy, slightly spicy flavours, balanced acidity and a basically dry (4.7 grams/litre of residual sugar) finish.

DRY $20 AV

Akarua Central Otago Pinot Gris ★★★☆

Estate-grown at Bannockburn, the 2016 vintage (★★★☆) is freshly scented and mouthfilling. Still very youthful, it is an off-dry style, vibrantly fruity, with good depth of citrusy, peachy flavours, hints of lychees and pears, a sliver of sweetness and appetising acidity. Best drinking mid-2017+.

MED/DRY $28 –V

Akarua Rua Central Otago Pinot Gris (★★★)

The easy-drinking 2015 vintage (★★★) is medium to full-bodied, with fresh, citrusy, slightly peachy flavours and an off-dry finish. Enjoyable young.

MED/DRY $23 –V

Ake Ake Vineyard Northland Pinot Gris ★★★☆

Hand-picked at Kerikeri, the 2015 vintage (★★★) was handled without oak and made in a medium-dry style (7 grams/litre of residual sugar). It's a fresh, medium to full-bodied wine, with finely balanced acidity and lively, peachy, slightly spicy flavours. Good, easy drinking.

MED/DRY $25 –V

Alexandra Wine Company alex.gold Pinot Gris ★★★

Grown in Central Otago, the 2014 vintage (★★☆) is a lively, citrusy, appley wine with a sliver of sweetness (11 grams/litre of residual sugar) and fresh, crisp acidity.

MED/DRY $17 AV

Allan Scott Marlborough Pinot Gris ★★★

Very pale pink, the easy-drinking 2016 vintage (★★★) was produced with a 'short period of skin contact, to extract colour and flavour'. Full-bodied, it is a smooth, off-dry style, with plenty of fresh, peachy, slightly spicy flavour. Enjoyable young, it's already very open and expressive.

MED/DRY $18 AV

Amisfield Central Otago Pinot Gris ★★★★

The 2015 vintage (★★★★), estate-grown and hand-picked at Pisa, in the Cromwell Basin, was mostly fermented and lees-aged in tanks; part of the blend was fermented with indigenous yeasts in large, seasoned French oak barrels. Drinking well from the start, it is a weighty, off-dry style (9.8 grams/litre of residual sugar), with excellent depth of peachy, spicy flavours, showing a touch of complexity, and a harmonious, well-rounded finish.

MED/DRY $30 –V

Anchorage Family Estate Nelson Pinot Gris ★★★

The 2015 vintage (★★★) is mouthfilling and well-rounded, with a sliver of sweetness (5.8 grams/litre of residual sugar) amid its ripe, peachy, slightly spicy flavours, and hints of pears and ginger. Fresh and finely balanced, it's enjoyable young.

MED/DRY $17 AV

Ant Moore Signature Series Marlborough Pinot Gris (★★★)

The 2015 vintage (★★★) is a peachy, spicy, gingery wine, slightly Gewürztraminer-like, with fresh acidity, a sliver of sweetness, and drink-young charm.

MED/DRY $23 –V

Ara Select Blocks Marlborough Pinot Gris (★★★★)

Still on sale, the 2013 vintage (★★★★) is a dry style (3.5 grams/litre of residual sugar), drinking well now. Light yellow/green, it is maturing gracefully, with concentrated peach, pear and spice flavours, showing good vigour, and slightly toasty, bottle-aged notes emerging.

Vintage	13
WR	6
Drink	16-17

DRY $26 –V

Ara Single Estate Marlborough Pinot Gris ★★★☆

Estate-grown in the lower Waihopai Valley, the 2015 vintage (★★★★) has a very pale straw colour. Drinking well now, it has excellent depth of fresh pear and spice flavours, hints of peaches and honey, a gentle splash of sweetness (8 grams/litre of residual sugar) and lively acidity.

Vintage	15
WR	6
Drink	16-17

MED/DRY $22 AV

Archangel Central Otago Pinot Gris ★★★★

The highly attractive 2014 vintage (★★★★) is scented and full-bodied, with strong lychee, pear and apple flavours, showing excellent freshness, delicacy and purity. Fleshy, with a dryish (5 grams/litre of residual sugar), well-rounded finish, it's a drink-now or cellaring proposition.

MED/DRY $25 AV

Aronui Single Vineyard Nelson Pinot Gris ★★★☆

From Kono – also owner of the Tohu brand – the 2016 vintage (★★★☆) was estate-grown and hand-picked at Upper Moutere, and briefly lees-aged. Made in an off-dry style (5.5 grams/litre of residual sugar), it is full-bodied and vibrantly fruity, with youthful citrus-fruit and lychee flavours, hints of apples, pears and spices, and good depth. Best drinking mid-2017+.

MED/DRY $22 AV

Ashwood Late Harvest Gisborne Pinot Gris (★★★☆)

The 2013 vintage (★★★☆) is a weighty wine (14.6 per cent alcohol), late-picked, fermented in large oak cuves and made in a medium-sweet style (47 grams/litre of residual sugar). Mouthfilling, it has ripe pear, lychee and spice flavours, showing very good depth, and a smooth finish. It should mature well.

MED $28 (375ML) –V

Askerne Hawke's Bay Pinot Gris ★★★☆

The 2015 vintage (★★★★) is soft and generous, in a finely textured style with mouthfilling body, concentrated, peachy flavours, gentle sweetness, and a floral, slightly honeyed and toasty bouquet.

MED/DRY $22 AV

Astrolabe Province Marlborough Pinot Gris ★★★☆

The 2015 vintage (★★★☆) is mouthfilling and vibrant, with strong, fresh citrus-fruit, pear, lychee and spice flavours, and a fully dry (2 grams/litre of residual sugar), lingering finish.

DRY $21 AV

Astrolabe Valleys Kekerengu Coast Pinot Gris ★★★★

The elegant 2015 vintage (★★★★) is a single-vineyard, hand-picked wine with mouthfilling body and vibrant lychee, apple and spice flavours, showing excellent delicacy and depth. A finely balanced, basically dry wine (4 grams/litre of residual sugar), it should be at its best 2017+.

DRY $24 AV

Ata Mara Central Otago Pinot Gris

(★★★★)

From estate-grown, 12-year-old vines in the Cromwell Basin, the 2014 vintage (★★★★) was made in an 'Alsace' style. Fragrant pear and spice aromas lead into a full-bodied wine (13.4 per cent alcohol) with strong, vibrant fruit flavours, a sliver of sweetness (6.5 grams/litre of residual sugar), gentle acidity and loads of drink-young charm.

 MED/DRY $19 V+

Ata Rangi Lismore Pinot Gris

★★★★☆

Grown in the Lismore Vineyard in Martinborough, 400 metres from the Ata Rangi winery, the 2014 vintage (★★★★★) was partly (20 per cent) barrel-fermented. Scented and mouthfilling, it has excellent depth of ripe stone-fruit and spice flavours, showing good complexity, a slightly oily texture, and a long, dryish (6 grams/litre of residual sugar) finish. Delicious young.

Vintage	14	13	12	11	10
WR	7	7	6	6	7
Drink	16-18	16-17	P	P	P

 MED/DRY $28 AV

Aurum Central Otago Pinot Gris

★★★☆

Certified organic, the 2014 vintage (★★★☆) was estate-grown and hand-picked at Lowburn, tank-fermented and lees-stirred. A mouthfilling wine, it has youthful, citrusy flavours, hints of apples, pears and spices, and a dryish (7 grams/litre of residual sugar), tightly structured finish.

Vintage	14	13	12	11	10
WR	5	6	6	6	7
Drink	16-20	16-18	16-17	P	P

 MED/DRY $26 –V

Awatere River by Louis Vavasour Marlborough Pinot Gris

★★★☆

The 2015 vintage (★★★★) is an elegant, youthful wine, partly oak-aged. Fleshy, with a slightly creamy texture, it has good weight and depth of pear, lychee and spice flavours, showing a touch of oak-derived complexity, and excellent delicacy and harmony.

 MED/DRY $25 –V

Babich Black Label Marlborough Pinot Gris

★★★★

Sold principally in restaurants, the 2015 vintage (★★★★) was grown in the Waihopai and Wairau valleys and mostly handled in tanks; 15 per cent of the blend spent four months in old oak. A mouthfilling, fleshy wine, it has rich, ripe peach, pear and spice flavours, a hint of almonds, and a balanced, dry finish.

 DRY $25 AV

Babich Marlborough Pinot Gris

★★★☆

The 2015 vintage (★★★☆) was tank-fermented and made in a dryish style. Fleshy, with peachy, spicy, slightly gingery flavours, showing very good depth, it's a drink-now or cellaring proposition.

MED/DRY $22 AV

Bald Hills Central Otago Pinot Gris   (★★★★)

Maturing gracefully, the 2015 vintage (★★★★) was grown at Bannockburn and made in an off-dry (7 grams/litre of residual sugar) style. Floral and fleshy, it is mouthfilling, fresh and vibrant, with strong peach, lychee, pear and spice flavours, showing good delicacy and purity, and a dryish finish (7.6 grams/litre of residual sugar).

Vintage	15
WR	5
Drink	16-21

 MED/DRY $28 –V

Beach House Ohiti Road Hawke's Bay Pinot Gris   (★★★☆)

The 2014 vintage (★★★☆) was partly barrel-fermented. Mouthfilling, with generous, ripe peach, pear, lychee and spice flavours and a sliver of sweetness, balanced by fresh acidity, it's enjoyable young.

MED/DRY $20 AV

Bellbird Spring Block Eight Pinot Gris   ★★★★

The 2013 vintage (★★★★) was estate-grown at Waipara, hand-harvested, and fermented and lees-aged in old oak casks. Showing good complexity, it is medium to full-bodied, with concentrated, ripe stone-fruit flavours, a distinct splash of sweetness (40 grams/litre of residual sugar), and a soft, faintly honeyed finish. Drink now or cellar.

 MED $32 –V

Bilancia Reserve Hawke's Bay Pinot Gris   (★★★★★)

The impressive 2013 vintage (★★★★★) is notably fragrant and weighty, with ripe sweet-fruit characters and rich stone-fruit/spice flavours. It shows good complexity and lovely depth and harmony. Made in a dry style (3 grams/litre of residual sugar), it is highly concentrated, with a long, spicy, rounded finish.

Vintage	13
WR	7
Drink	16-20

 DRY $35 AV

Bird Gisborne Pinot Gris   (★★★☆)

Enjoyable young, the 2015 vintage (★★★☆) is a medium-bodied wine with ripe, peachy, slightly spicy flavours. Made in an off-dry style, with balanced acidity, it is youthful, fresh and lively, with good depth.

MED/DRY $20 AV

Black Barn Single Vineyard Hawke's Bay Pinot Gris   ★★★☆

Estate-grown at Havelock North, the 2014 vintage (★★★) is a good, all-purpose wine, medium-bodied, with pear and gentle spice flavours, fresh, crisp and lively.

 MED/DRY $26 –V

Black Cottage Marlborough Pinot Gris ★★★

From Two Rivers, the 2016 vintage (★★★☆) is a gently floral, dry style, with pear, lychee and spice flavours, lively acidity, and very good freshness, delicacy and depth.

DRY $18 AV

Blackenbrook Nelson Pinot Gris ★★★★★

An emerging classic. Estate-grown and hand-picked, the 2016 vintage (★★★★) was handled in tanks (92 per cent) and old oak barrels (8 per cent). Pale lemon/green, it is mouthfilling and slightly sweet (10 grams/litre of residual sugar), in a strongly varietal style with generous, peachy, slightly spicy flavours, showing excellent depth and harmony. Best drinking mid-2017+.

Vintage	16	15	14	13	12	11	10
WR	5	6	7	5	7	6	7
Drink	17-19	16-19	16-19	P	P	P	P

MED/DRY $24 V+

Bladen Marlborough Pinot Gris ★★★☆

Estate-grown and hand-picked, the 2015 vintage (★★★★) is mouthfilling, with excellent varietal character and strong, vibrant peach, pear and spice flavours. Made in an off-dry style (5.6 grams/litre of residual sugar), with fresh, balanced acidity, it's a very harmonious wine.

MED/DRY $25 –V

Boundary Vineyards Paper Lane Waipara Pinot Gris ★★★★

The 2014 vintage (★★★★) from Pernod Ricard NZ is attractively scented, with mouthfilling body and fresh, vibrant, citrusy, slightly sweet flavours, showing excellent depth and harmony.

MED/DRY $21 V+

Brancott Estate Flight Marlborough Pinot Gris ★★☆

This low-alcohol wine is harvested early and made in a medium style, with high acidity. The 2015 vintage (★★☆) is light-bodied (9 per cent alcohol), with fresh, simple, appley flavours.

MED $17 –V

Brancott Estate Hawke's Bay Pinot Gris ★★★

The 2016 vintage (★★★☆) is full-bodied and fresh, with generous pear/spice aromas and flavours. Made in an off-dry style, it's enjoyable young. Fine value.

MED/DRY $17 AV

Brancott Estate Letter Series 'F' Fairhall Marlborough Pinot Gris ★★★★☆

The 2015 vintage (★★★★★) is a powerful, full-bodied wine (14.5 per cent alcohol), grown on the south side of the Wairau Valley, mostly hand-picked, and fermented in a mix of large, old, 10,000-litre oak cuves (85 per cent) and oak puncheons (15 per cent). Fleshy and sweet-fruited, with concentrated stone-fruit and spice flavours, it shows excellent delicacy, harmony and depth. Richly varietal, with good complexity and a long, off-dry finish (9.7 grams/litre of residual sugar), it's delicious from the start, but well worth cellaring.

MED/DRY $33 –V

Brancott Estate Living Land Series Marlborough Pinot Gris

Certified organic, the 2014 vintage (★★★☆) is a full-bodied, off-dry wine with good depth of fresh, citrusy, slightly peachy and spicy flavours, and a smooth, harmonious finish. Enjoyable young.

MED/DRY $20 AV

Brancott Estate Terroir Series Awatere Valley Marlborough Pinot Gris

Delicious young, the 2015 vintage (★★★★) is a scented, mouthfilling, vibrantly fruity wine, with ripe pear, peach and spice flavours, showing clear-cut varietal character, and a dryish, well-rounded finish.

MED/DRY $20 AV

Brick Bay Matakana Pinot Gris

At its best, this estate-grown wine is weighty, rich and rounded. Hand-harvested and lees-aged, it is made in an off-dry style. The 2014 vintage (★★★☆) is medium-bodied, fresh and tightly structured, with pear, lychee and spice flavours, a hint of apricot, and crisp acidity.

MED/DRY $32 –V

Brightside New Zealand Organic Pinot Gris

Certified organic, the 2016 vintage (★★★☆) was produced by Kaimira Estate, based in Nelson. Made in an off-dry style (10 grams/litre of residual sugar), it is a pale lemon/green, medium to full-bodied wine, with good varietal character and depth of vibrant pear, lychee and spice flavours. Best drinking mid-2017+.

MED/DRY $18 V+

Brightwater Vineyards Lord Rutherford Nelson Pinot Gris (★★★★☆)

The instantly attractive 2014 vintage (★★★★☆) is finely textured, with a long finish. Hand-picked and made in a medium style (28 grams/litre of residual sugar), it is fresh and lively, with concentrated, ripe peach, pear and spice flavours. Best drinking 2017+.

MED $30 –V

Brightwater Vineyards Nelson Pinot Gris

Grown inland at Hope and matured briefly on its yeast lees, the 2015 vintage (★★★★) is a medium to full-bodied wine. Bright, light lemon/green, it is youthful and vibrantly fruity, with fresh peach, lychee and pear flavours showing good intensity, and a slightly sweet (16 grams/litre of residual sugar), finely balanced finish.

MED $20 V+

Vintage	15	14	13	12	11	10
WR	7	6	6	6	6	5
Drink	16-18	16-18	16-17	P	P	P

Bronte Nelson Pinot Gris   ★★★☆

Rimu Grove's second-tier label. Hand-picked in the Moutere hills and mostly handled in tanks (6 per cent French oak-aged), the 2015 vintage (★★★★) is an off-dry style (11 grams/litre of residual sugar), attractively scented and mouthfilling, with vibrant, peachy, slightly spicy flavours, showing good concentration. Delicious young.

MED/DRY $22 AV

Brookfields Robertson Hawke's Bay Pinot Gris   ★★★★

Bright, light lemon/green, the 2016 vintage (★★★★) is a mouthfilling, off-dry wine (6 grams/litre of residual sugar). Full-bodied, it's an Alsace-style wine, with strong, ripe peach, lychee and spice flavours, gentle sweetness and a rich, rounded finish. Best drinking mid-2017+.

Vintage	16
WR	7
Drink	18-20

MED/DRY $20 V+

Cable Bay Awatere Valley Marlborough Pinot Gris   ★★★★

The pale gold 2015 vintage (★★★★) is a characterful, estate-grown wine, 'pushed' for fruit ripeness, given 'lots of skin contact', and lees-aged for seven months. Full-bodied and dry, it has strong, peachy, spicy, gingery, vaguely honeyed flavours, a touch of tannins, and loads of interest and personality. Drink now to 2017.

Vintage	15
WR	5
Drink	16-17

DRY $23 AV

Carrick Bannockburn Central Otago Pinot Gris   ★★★★

Certified organic, the 2015 vintage (★★★★) was estate-grown and fermented in tanks (60 per cent) and old French barriques (40 per cent). Mouthfilling, with strong, ripe, peachy, slightly toasty flavours, showing good complexity, and a dryish finish, it should be at its best 2017+.

MED/DRY $29 –V

Catalina Sounds Marlborough Pinot Gris   ★★★★

The distinctive 2015 vintage (★★★★) was estate-grown in the Waihopai Valley, hand-picked and fermented in tanks (80 per cent) and seasoned French oak puncheons (20 per cent). Made in a dry style, it is full-bodied, with concentrated, ripe peach, pear and spice flavours, oak and lees-aging notes adding a touch of complexity, and a finely balanced finish. Drink now or cellar.

DRY $25 AV

Ceres Composition Central Otago Pinot Gris   ★★★★

Drinking well now, the 2014 vintage (★★★★) is a mouthfilling, fleshy wine with strong, ripe peach, lychee and pear flavours, gentle acidity and a slightly spicy, off-dry (9 grams/litre of residual sugar), smooth finish.

MED/DRY $28 –V

Ceres Swansong Vineyard Central Otago Pinot Gris   ★★★☆

From two sites at Bannockburn, the powerful, age-worthy 2015 vintage (★★★★) is sturdy (14.5 per cent alcohol), with strong, peachy, citrusy, spicy flavours and an off-dry, creamy-textured finish.

Chard Farm Sur Lie Central Otago Pinot Gris   ★★★★

The 2015 vintage (★★★★☆) of this consistently enjoyable wine was hand-picked at Parkburn, in the Cromwell Basin, and fermented and lees-aged in tanks. It is attractively scented and mouthfilling, with vibrant, pure lychee, pear and spice flavours, showing excellent delicacy and richness, gentle acidity, a slightly oily texture and a dry (2 grams/litre of residual sugar), well-rounded finish. Delicious young.

Church Road Hawke's Bay Pinot Gris   ★★★★☆

Estate-grown in Pernod Ricard NZ's relatively cool, elevated, inland site at Matapiro, this is a consistently impressive and enjoyable, Alsace-style wine, bargain-priced. Delicious from the start, the 2015 vintage (★★★★☆) is fleshy, with concentrated, ripe, peachy, slightly spicy flavours, gentle sweetness and a rich, rounded finish. Fine value.

Church Road McDonald Series Hawke's Bay Pinot Gris   ★★★★★

If you like Alsace-style Pinot Gris, try the 2015 vintage (★★★★★). Instantly engaging, it is fragrant and full-bodied (14.5 per cent alcohol), in a rich, ripe, slightly sweet style with lovely depth of peach, pear and spice flavours. Slightly honeyed, with complexity from some indigenous yeast fermentation in old French oak cuves, and gentle acidity, it's a delicious, very finely balanced wine, already drinking well.

Circuit North Canterbury Pinot Gris   (★★★★)

Full of personality, the debut 2015 vintage (★★★★) was hand-picked in the Falcon Crest Vineyard at Waipara, and mostly fermented with indigenous yeasts in old French oak puncheons; 10 per cent of the blend was co-fermented on its skins with Riesling from the same vineyard and held on its skins for seven months, before pressing. Pale straw, with a fragrant, spicy bouquet, it is rich and peachy, with excellent flavour depth, good complexity and a slightly sweet (9 grams/litre of residual sugar), faintly honeyed finish. (From Black Estate.)

Clark Estate Single Vineyard Upper Awatere Marlborough Pinot Gris   ★★★☆

The 2014 vintage (★★★) is an easy-drinking style, with fresh, ripe, peachy, slightly spicy and gingery flavours and an off-dry, smooth finish. Ready.

MED/DRY $23 –V

Clearview Haumoana Hawke's Bay Pinot Gris   ★★★

The 2015 vintage (★★★☆) is a fresh, lively, medium to full-bodied wine, hand-picked and fermented in seasoned oak barrels. Made in an off-dry style (11 grams/litre of residual sugar), it has appetising acidity and very good depth of finely balanced, ripe, peachy, slightly spicy flavours. Drink now or cellar.

MED/DRY $19 AV

Clifford Bay East Coast Pinot Gris   ★★★☆

The 2015 vintage (★★★) is a light lemon/green, fresh, medium-bodied wine, vibrantly fruity, with good depth of pear, lychee and spice flavours, slightly sweet and crisp.

MED/DRY $20 AV

Coopers Creek New Zealand Pinot Gris   ★★★

The 2014 vintage (★★★) is a blend of Auckland (Huapai) and Marlborough grapes, made in a dryish (7 grams/litre of residual sugar) style. Fresh and vibrantly fruity, it is full-bodied, with good depth of peachy, citrusy, slightly appley and spicy flavours, balanced acidity, and a smooth, easy-drinking charm.

MED/DRY $17 AV

Coopers Creek SV The Pointer Marlborough Pinot Gris   ★★★☆

The 2014 vintage (★★★☆) is a single-vineyard, Brancott Valley wine, tank-fermented. Full-bodied, it is a medium-dry style (9.5 grams/litre of residual sugar), scented, with good depth of pear, lychee, peach and spice flavours, fresh acidity and a finely balanced finish. Very easy drinking.

Vintage	14
WR	7
Drink	16-17

MED/DRY $25 –V

Couper's Shed Hawke's Bay Pinot Gris   ★★★★

Grown at Pernod Ricard NZ's elevated, inland Matapiro site, the 2015 vintage (★★★★) is a pale yellow, weighty (14.5 per cent alcohol), Alsace-style Pinot Gris. It has generous, peachy, slightly spicy aromas and flavours and a slightly sweet, smooth finish. Good value.

MED/DRY $20 V+

Crab Farm Winery Hawke's Bay Pinot Gris   ★★★

The 2014 vintage (★★★) is a sturdy, fleshy wine with ripe, peachy, slightly yeasty flavours and a fully dry finish. It's ready to roll.

DRY $17 AV

Craggy Range Te Muna Road Vineyard Martinborough Pinot Gris   ★★★★

Hand-harvested at over 23 brix, the 2015 vintage (★★★★) is a full-bodied, dry style (4 grams/litre of residual sugar). Attractively scented and fleshy, with fresh, vibrant pear, lychee and spice flavours, and finely balanced acidity, it should be at its best 2017+.

DRY $27 –V

Crossings, The, Awatere Valley Marlborough Pinot Gris ★★★☆

Enjoyable young, the 2015 vintage (★★★) is mouthfilling, with fresh, lively, peachy, spicy flavours and a finely balanced, dryish (5 grams/litre of residual sugar) finish.

Vintage	15
WR	6
Drink	16-17

MED/DRY $20 AV

Crossroads Milestone Series Hawke's Bay Pinot Gris ★★★☆

Fermented in tanks (92 per cent) and barrels (8 per cent), the 2014 vintage (★★★☆) is a scented, medium to full-bodied wine with peach, apricot and spice flavours, showing good depth, a touch of complexity and a finely balanced, dry (4 grams/litre of residual sugar) finish.

Vintage	15	14	13	12
WR	6	6	7	5
Drink	16-19	16-19	16-18	P

DRY $20 AV

Cypress Hawke's Bay Pinot Gris (★★★★)

The 2014 vintage (★★★★) is a dry style (3 grams/litre of residual sugar), mostly handled in tanks, but 20 per cent of the blend was barrel-fermented, with lots of lees-stirring. Grown at Bridge Pa, it is lively, with strong, ripe stone-fruit and spice flavours, a touch of complexity, and a finely textured, well-rounded finish.

DRY $26 AV

Dashwood Marlborough Pinot Gris ★★★★

The 2015 vintage (★★★★) is a tightly structured, youthful wine with good weight, fresh, strong pear, apple and spice flavours, and a finely textured, lengthy finish. Excellent value.

MED/DRY $19 V+

De Vine Dry Nelson Pinot Gris (★★★☆)

The 2015 vintage (★★★☆) offers fine value. Medium to full-bodied, it's a dryish wine with balanced acidity and fresh peach, pear and spice flavours, showing very good vigour and depth.

MED/DRY $16 V+

Domain Road Vineyard Central Otago Pinot Gris ★★★★

Fleshy and mouthfilling, the 2013 vintage (★★★★) is a single-vineyard, Bannockburn wine, hand-picked and partly barrel-fermented. It has generous stone-fruit and spice flavours, with a touch of complexity and dryish (6 grams/litre of residual sugar), slightly spicy, finely textured finish.

Vintage	13
WR	6
Drink	16-17

MED/DRY $25 AV

Drumsara Central Otago Pinot Gris   ★★★★

Estate-grown at Alexandra and handled without oak, the 2013 vintage (★★★★) is scented and mouthfilling, with ripe stone-fruit flavours to the fore, citrusy and spicy notes, a sliver of sweetness (9 grams/litre of residual sugar), and good harmony and immediacy.

MED/DRY $29 –V

Dry River Martinborough Pinot Gris   ★★★★★

From the first vintage in 1986, for many years Dry River towered over other New Zealand Pinot Gris, by virtue of its exceptional body, flavour richness and longevity. A sturdy Martinborough wine, it has peachy, spicy characters that can develop great subtlety and richness with maturity (at around five years old for top vintages, which also hold well for a decade). It is grown in the estate and nearby Craighall vineyards, where the majority of the vines are over 25 years old. To avoid any loss of varietal flavour, it is not oak-aged. The 2015 vintage (★★★★★) is already delicious. Bright, light lemon/green, it is fleshy, concentrated and rounded, with generous, ripe stone-fruit and spice flavours, a vague hint of honey, gentle sweetness (20 grams/litre of residual sugar), balanced acidity and a very long, peachy, spicy, harmonious finish. Best drinking 2017+.

Vintage	15	14	13	12	11	10	09	08
WR	7	7	6	7	7	7	7	7
Drink	16-27	16-26	16-25	16-22	16-21	16-20	16-19	16-18

MED $55 AV

Dunstan Road Central Otago Pinot Gris   (★★★☆)

From a single row of vines in a small vineyard, between Clyde and Alexandra, the 2014 vintage (★★★☆) was briefly oak-aged. It is light-bodied (10.5 per cent alcohol), with strong, peachy, spicy flavours, showing a touch of complexity, plentiful sweetness (46 grams/litre of residual sugar) and a smooth finish.

MED $20 AV

Durvillea D by Astrolabe Marlborough Pinot Gris   (★★★)

The 2015 vintage (★★★) was grown in the Awatere and Waihopai valleys. Mouthfilling, fresh and dry (2 grams/litre of residual sugar), it has pear, lychee and spice flavours, with moderate acidity and a smooth finish. A good, all-purpose wine, it's priced sharply.

DRY $15 V+

Easthope Blackhawk Hawke's Bay Dry Pinot Gris   (★★★★)

Grown in the Te Awanga and Bridge Pa Triangle sub-regions, the 2015 vintage (★★★★) is an attractively scented, dry style (3 grams/litre of residual sugar). It has mouthfilling body, balanced acidity, and strong, vibrant lychee, pear and spice flavours.

DRY $25 AV

Elder, The, Martinborough Pinot Gris   ★★★★☆

The 2015 vintage (★★★★) is a distinctive, youthful, single-vineyard wine, tank-fermented with indigenous yeasts and lees-aged for six months in old barriques. Mouthfilling, it has vibrant, pure lychee, pear and spice flavours, showing excellent delicacy and depth, a very subtle oak influence, and a dry, lingering finish.

Vintage	15	14	13	12	11
WR	6	7	6	7	6
Drink	16-20	16-20	16-19	16-18	16-17

 DRY $45 –V

Eradus Awatere Valley Single Vineyard Marlborough Pinot Gris   ★★★☆

The 2015 vintage (★★★☆) is a mouthfilling wine, vibrantly fruity, with good depth of fresh peach, pear and spice flavours and a dryish, finely balanced finish.

 DRY $19 V+

Esk Valley Hawke's Bay Pinot Gris   ★★★★

Winemaker Gordon Russell says this wine 'stylistically hints more at the fuller end of Pinot Grigio than the original Alsace model'. Fermented in tanks (70 per cent) and old oak barriques, the 2016 vintage (★★★☆) has a spicy bouquet, leading into a softly mouthfilling wine with fresh stone-fruit flavours, gently seasoned with oak, moderate acidity and a dry (3.7 grams/litre of residual sugar) finish.

 DRY $20 V+

Fairmont Estate Pinot Gris   (★★★★)

Grown in the northern Wairarapa, the 2014 vintage (★★★★) is a full-bodied, fleshy wine, with generous, ripe, peachy flavours, showing a touch of complexity. Priced sharply.

 DRY $18 V+

Falconhead Hawke's Bay Pinot Gris   (★★☆)

The 2014 vintage (★★☆) is faintly pink. Medium-bodied, it's an easy-drinking style with solid depth of peachy, slightly spicy flavours and a fresh, slightly sweet (7 grams/litre of residual sugar), smooth finish.

Vintage	14
WR	6
Drink	P

MED/DRY $16 AV

Fern Ridge Hawke's Bay Pinot Gris   (★★★)

The pale 2015 vintage (★★★) is a fresh, dryish wine with mouthfilling body and vibrant, citrusy, slightly appley and spicy flavours. It's a very easy-drinking wine, priced sharply.

 MED/DRY $16 V+

Framingham Marlborough Pinot Gris ★★★★☆

The 2014 vintage (★★★★☆) is mouthfilling and dryish (9 grams/litre of residual sugar). Fermented in tanks (55 per cent) and old oak barrels (45 per cent), it's an Alsace-style wine, weighty and soft, with ripe, peachy flavours, gentle acidity, a touch of complexity, and excellent harmony and depth. Delicious drinking now onwards.

Vintage	14	13	12	11	10
WR	5	6	6	6	6
Drink	16-20	16-17	16-17	P	P

 MED/DRY $25 V+

French Peak Banks Peninsula Pinot Grigio (★★★☆)

Hand-harvested at French Farm, on the shores of Akaroa Harbour, the pale 2015 vintage (★★★☆) is medium-bodied and smooth. Fresh and finely balanced, it has good depth of lemony, slightly appley flavours, with hints of pears and lychees, lively acidity and a dryish (5 grams/litre of residual sugar) finish. Drink now to 2017.

MED/DRY $28 –V

Fromm La Strada Marlborough Pinot Gris ★★★★☆

Certified organic, the 2015 vintage (★★★★) was two-thirds barrel-fermented. Light lemon/green, it is medium to full-bodied, with fresh, concentrated, peachy, spicy flavours, showing a touch of complexity, and a dryish (5.6 grams/litre of residual sugar), well-rounded finish. Enjoyable young.

Vintage	15	14	13
WR	7	6	6
Drink	16-18	16-17	16-17

 MED/DRY $28 AV

Georges Road Selection Waipara Pinot Gris ★★★★☆

Full of personality, the 2015 vintage (★★★★★) is a powerful, rich wine, estate-grown, hand-picked and fermented with indigenous yeasts in seasoned oak barrels. Fragrant, fleshy and creamy-textured, it is full-bodied (14.5 per cent alcohol), with concentrated, ripe stone-fruit flavours, hints of ginger and spice, and good complexity. Made in a dryish style, it's already very open and expressive.

MED/DRY $24 V+

Gibbston Valley Central Otago Pinot Gris ★★★★

At its best, this wine is full of personality. The 2014 vintage (★★★★) is mouthfilling, with vibrant peach, citrus-fruit and spice flavours, showing good concentration, a sliver of sweetness (5.9 grams/litre of residual sugar), fresh acidity, and a tight, slightly creamy finish. Well worth cellaring. (This label was recently replaced by the GV Collection Pinot Gris – see that wine.)

Vintage	14	13
WR	7	7
Drink	16-20	16-20

MED/DRY $28 –V

Gibbston Valley Gold River Central Otago Pinot Gris   ★★★★

Delicious now, the 2015 vintage (★★★★) is mouthfilling, fresh and finely balanced. From hand-picked grapes, it has strong, lively, peachy, slightly spicy flavours, a gentle splash of sweetness (8 grams/litre of residual sugar) and appetising acidity. Drink now or cellar.

MED/DRY $23 AV

Gibbston Valley GV Collection Central Otago Pinot Gris   ★★★★

Hand-picked at Bendigo, the 2015 vintage (★★★★) replaces the former Gibbston Valley Central Otago Pinot Gris label. Pale and mouthfilling, it is fresh and youthful, with generous pear, lychee and spice flavours, showing good delicacy and purity, and a dryish (6 grams/litre of residual sugar), lengthy finish. Best drinking 2017+.

MED/DRY $28 –V

Gibbston Valley La Dulcinée Bendigo Single Vineyard Pinot Gris   ★★★★★

Estate-grown and hand-picked at over 350 metres above sea level, in the La Dulcinée Vineyard at Bendigo, in Central Otago, the 2015 vintage (★★★★★) was fermented and lees-aged for a year in stainless steel barriques (85 per cent) and French acacia puncheons (15 per cent). A powerful, very youthful wine, it is full-bodied (14.5 per cent alcohol), with concentrated pear, lychee, peach and spice flavours, a distinct touch of complexity, and a dryish (5.7 grams/litre of residual sugar), lasting finish. Best drinking mid-2017+. Certified organic.

MED/DRY $39 AV

Gibson Bridge Reserve Marlborough Pinot Gris   ★★★★☆

The 2015 vintage (★★★★☆), an estate-grown, single-vineyard wine, was hand-picked in the Wairau Valley and lees-aged in tanks. Pale lemon/green, it is fragrant, sturdy and vibrantly fruity, with generous stone-fruit flavours, slightly spicy notes, good concentration, a touch of complexity, and a finely balanced, basically dry (4.3 grams/litre of residual sugar) finish. It's still unfolding; best drinking 2017+.

DRY $34 –V

Giesen New Zealand Pinot Gris   ★★★

The easy-drinking 2015 vintage (★★★) is a blend of Marlborough and Hawke's Bay grapes. Tank-fermented and lees-aged, it is fresh and medium-bodied, with citrusy, peachy, slightly spicy flavours, slightly sweet and crisp, and satisfying depth. Enjoyable young. The 2016 vintage (★★★) is fresh, medium-bodied and smooth, with lively peach, pear and spice flavours, a gentle splash of sweetness (8 grams/litre of residual sugar), and balanced acidity.

Vintage	16
WR	5
Drink	16-17

MED/DRY $17 AV

Gladstone Vineyard Pinot Gris   ★★★★

The 2015 vintage (★★★★) was grown in the northern Wairarapa and fermented and lees-aged in a mix of tanks (mostly) and old French oak barrels. Ripely scented, it is an elegant, vibrantly fruity wine, with good concentration of lychee, peach, pear and spice flavours and a dry (4 grams/litre of residual sugar), well-rounded finish. Best drinking mid-2017+.

DRY $25 AV

Gold Star XIV Pinot Gris   (★★★)

The 2014 vintage (★★★) from Pukeora Estate, in Central Hawke's Bay, was predominantly (73 per cent) barrel-fermented with indigenous yeasts; the rest was handled in tanks. It's a weighty, fully dry wine, with a touch of complexity and good depth of peachy, spicy, slightly buttery flavours. Ready.

DRY $23 –V

Goldwater Wairau Valley Pinot Gris   ★★★☆

Drinking well now, the light lemon/green 2015 vintage (★★★☆) is ripely scented and fleshy, with generous, vaguely honeyed, stone-fruit and spice flavours.

MED/DRY $22 AV

Greyrock Hawke's Bay Pinot Gris   ★★★

From Sileni, the 2015 vintage (★★★) is an easy-drinking, medium-bodied style, with good depth of fresh peach, pear and spice flavours and an off-dry finish. Priced right.

MED/DRY $14 V+

Greystone Sand Dollar Waipara Pinot Gris   ★★★★☆

The 2015 vintage (★★★★☆) is a fragrant, fleshy, basically dry style (4 grams/litre of residual sugar), mostly lees-aged in tanks, but 10 per cent of the blend was fermented with indigenous yeasts in old French oak barrels. Mouthfilling and richly varietal, it has pure, delicate peach, pear and lychee flavours to the fore, hints of ginger and spice, and a poised, long, very harmonious finish. Drink now or cellar.

Vintage	15
WR	7
Drink	16-22

DRY $28 AV

Greystone Waipara Valley Pinot Gris   ★★★★★

At its best, this is one of the finest Pinot Gris in the country. Estate-grown and hand-picked, it is mostly handled in tanks; about 5 per cent of the blend is barrel-fermented with indigenous yeasts. The 2015 vintage (★★★★☆) is a mouthfilling (13.5 per cent alcohol), Alsace-style wine, off-dry in style (10 grams/litre of residual sugar), with rich, youthful peach, pear and spice flavours, a slightly oily texture, and excellent concentration, complexity and harmony. Best drinking 2017+.

Vintage	15	14	13	12	11	10
WR	7	7	7	7	6	6
Drink	16-19	16-17	P	P	P	P

MED/DRY $25 V+

🍇🍇

Greywacke Marlborough Pinot Gris ★★★★★

Grown in the Brancott Valley (principally) and at Rapaura, the 2015 vintage (★★★★★) was mostly (80 per cent) fermented with indigenous yeasts in old oak barrels and wood-matured for seven months; 20 per cent of the blend was handled with cultured yeasts in tanks. A lovely young wine, showing greater complexity than most Pinot Gris, it is fleshy and vibrantly fruity, with mouthfilling body and deep, ripe peach/pear flavours, slightly sweet (10 grams/litre of residual sugar) and well-rounded. A rich, subtle, finely poised wine, it should be at its best 2018+.

Vintage	15	14	13	12	11	10
WR	6	6	6	6	5	5
Drink	17-21	17-20	17-20	17-19	16-17	17-18

 MED/DRY $29 V+

Grove Mill Marlborough Pinot Gris ★★★☆

The fresh, mouthfilling 2014 vintage (★★★★) was grown in the Wairau Valley. It has ripe stone-fruit flavours, with a gentle splash of sweetness, balanced acidity, an oily texture, and excellent delicacy and depth.

 MED/DRY $20 AV

Gunn Estate Reserve Marlborough Pinot Gris ★★★☆

The 2016 vintage (★★★☆) is a fleshy style, grown in the Southern Valleys and blended with a small amount of Chardonnay (10 per cent). Mouthfilling, it has a hint of sweetness and very good depth of ripe, peachy, slightly gingery and spicy flavours.

Vintage	16
WR	6
Drink	16-18

 MED/DRY $20 AV

Haha Hawke's Bay Pinot Gris ★★★☆

The 2015 vintage (★★★☆) is a vivacious, medium-bodied wine with an attractive, aromatic bouquet, crisp, lively pear and spice flavours and an off-dry finish. Priced sharply.

MED/DRY $16 V+

Hans Herzog Marlborough Pinot Gris ★★★★☆

Prepare for something different! Estate-grown on the north side of the Wairau Valley, the 2015 vintage (★★★★★) is a thought-provoking wine, hand-harvested and mostly handled in tanks; 20 per cent of the blend spent nine months in French oak puncheons. Made in a fully dry style, it is full-bodied, with a light apricot colour and a peachy, spicy, fragrant bouquet. Sweet-fruited and complex, it offers concentrated, ripe stone-fruit and spice flavours, with a gentle touch of tannin, finely balanced acidity, and loads of personality. Certified organic.

 DRY $39 –V

Harwood Hall Marlborough Pinot Gris ★★★

The 2014 vintage (★★★☆) was blended from Awatere Valley (90 per cent) and Rarangi (10 per cent) fruit, and mostly handled in tanks; 10 per cent was barrel-fermented. It's a fleshy, full-bodied style with very good depth of lemon, apple and pear flavours, balanced acidity, and a dryish, slightly nutty finish. Enjoyable young.

 MED/DRY $19 AV

Hawkshead Central Otago Pinot Gris ★★★★

Estate-grown and hand-picked at Gibbston, the 2014 vintage (★★★★) is fully dry (2 grams/litre of residual sugar). Mouthfilling and smooth, it has strong, ripe peach/pear flavours, gentle acidity, a slightly creamy texture and a floral bouquet.

Vintage	14	13	12
WR	7	7	5
Drink	16-17	P	P

 DRY $26 –V

Hills & Rivers Hawke's Bay Pinot Gris (★★★☆)

The 2015 vintage (★★★☆) is a top buy. Pale pink, with a fragrant bouquet of pears and spices, it has very good body, ripeness and flavour depth, in an off-dry (6 grams/litre of residual sugar) style, delicious young. (From Ash Ridge.)

 MED/DRY $14 V+

Huia Marlborough Pinot Gris ★★★★

Certified organic, the stylish 2013 vintage (★★★☆) is a weighty, barrel-aged wine. Made in a dry style, it has strong, citrusy, appley flavours, with fresh acidity, and slightly toasty notes adding complexity.

Vintage	13	12	11	10
WR	7	6	6	6
Drink	16-23	16-22	16-21	16-20

 DRY $28 –V

Hunter's Marlborough Pinot Gris ★★★★

A consistently good buy. The 2015 vintage (★★★★), estate-grown at Rapaura, is full-bodied (14.5 per cent alcohol), with generous, ripe flavours of peaches, lychees and spices, a hint of apricots, gentle acidity and a dry, well-spiced finish. The 2016 vintage (★★★★) was mostly handled in tanks, but a small part of the blend was fermented with indigenous yeasts in seasoned French oak casks. Aromatic and fleshy, it is sturdy (14.5 per cent alcohol), with strong, peachy, spicy flavours, a vague hint of honey, a harmonious, dry finish (3 grams/litre of residual sugar) and plenty of personality. Drink now or cellar.

DRY $21 V+

Hyperion Phoebe Matakana Pinot Gris (★★★★)

The 2014 vintage (★★★★) is a sturdy, dry style, with fresh, strong, citrusy, slightly spicy flavours, a slightly oily texture and a lingering finish.

 DRY $27 –V

Invivo Marlborough Pinot Gris
★★★☆

The scented, mouthfilling 2015 vintage (★★★☆) was grown at Rarangi, on the Wairau Valley coast. Vibrantly fruity, it offers good depth of peach, pear and slightly spicy flavours, fresh and finely balanced. The 2016 vintage (★★★☆) is full-bodied and fresh, with clear-cut varietal character. A dryish wine (5.8 grams/litre of residual sugar), it has pear, lychee and spice flavours, showing good depth, and a smooth finish.

MED/DRY $19 V+

Johanneshof Marlborough Pinot Gris
★★★★

The freshly scented 2015 vintage (★★★★) is a single-vineyard wine, hand-picked and made in a gently sweet style (17 grams/litre of residual sugar). Medium to full-bodied, it has ripe, peachy, distinctly spicy flavours, showing good concentration, and a smooth finish. Delicious young.

MED $28 –V

Johner Estate Wairarapa Pinot Gris
★★★★

The 2016 vintage (★★★★) was fully fermented in seasoned oak barrels and made in a dry style (4 grams/litre of residual sugar). Pale, it is vibrantly fruity, with strong pear, lychee and spice flavours, showing very good delicacy and harmony, and a touch of complexity. Well worth cellaring, it should be at its best mid-2017+.

Vintage	16	15	14	13	12
WR	6	6	6	6	6
Drink	16-21	16-20	P	P	P

DRY $24 AV

Jules Taylor Marlborough Pinot Gris
★★★★

Grown in the Awatere and Wairau valleys, the 2016 vintage (★★★★) was made with some use of hand-picking, indigenous yeasts and old barrel fermentation. Produced in a dry style (2.4 grams/litre of residual sugar), it is mouthfilling and vibrantly fruity, with finely poised, peachy, slightly spicy flavours, a creamy texture, and very good freshness, delicacy and depth. Best drinking mid-2017+.

Vintage	16
WR	6
Drink	16-19

DRY $22 V+

Junction Pastime Central Hawke's Bay Pinot Gris
(★★★☆)

Ripely scented, the 2015 vintage (★★★☆) has mouthfilling body and very good depth of fresh, slightly sweet, peachy, spicy flavours.

MED/DRY $22 AV

Kaimira Estate Brightwater Pinot Gris
★★★☆

Certified organic, the 2015 vintage (★★★★) is fleshy and dry (4.8 grams/litre of residual sugar), with ripe peach, pear and spice flavours, finely balanced and generous. Enjoyable from the start.

DRY $22 AV

Kainui Road Bay of Islands Pinot Gris   ★★★

The 2015 vintage (★★★) was estate-grown and hand-picked at Kerikeri. Faintly pink, it's an easy-drinking wine with fresh, peachy, spicy flavours and an off-dry finish.

MED/DRY $25 –V

Kakapo Central Otago Pinot Gris   (★★★★)

The 2015 vintage (★★★★) from distributor Sanz Global is full-bodied and vibrantly fruity. Mouthfilling, it has fresh, strong pear, lychee and spice flavours and a dryish, very harmonious finish. Drink now or cellar.

MED/DRY $24 AV

Kapiro Vineyard Northland Pinot Gris   ★★★☆

Hand-harvested at Kerikeri, the 2015 vintage (★★★☆) is a mouthfilling wine with fresh, ripe peach, lychee and spice flavours, a gentle splash of sweetness (13 grams/litre of residual sugar), balanced acidity and very good depth.

Vintage	14	13	12	11	10
WR	7	7	6	5	7
Drink	16-17	P	P	P	P

MED/DRY $25 –V

Kate Radburnd Sun Kissed Hawke's Bay Pinot Gris   ★★☆

From Pask, the 2014 vintage (★★☆) was grown in the Gimblett Gravels. It's a light-bodied, off-dry wine with decent depth of pear and spice flavours.

MED/DRY $18 –V

Kim Crawford Reserve Marlborough Pinot Gris   ★★★

The 2015 vintage (★★★☆) has the word 'Reserve' only on the screwcap. The bouquet is fresh and ripely scented; the palate is mouthfilling and vibrantly fruity, with good varietal character and depth of ripe peach, pear and spice flavours, balanced acidity, and a slightly sweet, smooth finish. Enjoyable young.

MED/DRY $17 AV

Kina Cliffs Nelson Pinot Gris   ★★★★

Grown in a coastal vineyard, the 2015 vintage (★★★☆) was hand-picked at 23.7 brix and mostly handled in tanks; 10 per cent was barrel-fermented. A youthful, medium to full-bodied wine, it has vibrant pear, nectarine and spice flavours, fresh acidity and a finely balanced, dryish finish.

MED/DRY $22 V+

Kumeu River Pinot Gris   ★★★★

This consistently attractive wine is grown at Kumeu, in West Auckland, aged on its yeast lees, but not oak-matured. Made in a medium-dry style, it is typically floral and weighty, with a slightly oily texture, finely balanced acidity and peach, pear and spice aromas and flavours, vibrant and rich. The 2014 vintage (★★★★) is fleshy, ripe and rounded, in a mouthfilling style with a touch of complexity, excellent depth of peachy, slightly spicy flavours and an off-dry (9 grams/litre of residual sugar) finish.

Vintage	15	14	13	12	11	10
WR	7	7	7	5	5	7
Drink	16-19	16-18	16-17	P	P	P

MED/DRY $25 AV

Kumeu Village Pinot Gris   ★★★☆

From Kumeu River, the 2014 vintage (★★★☆) was hand-picked, fermented in tanks with indigenous yeasts and matured on its yeast lees. An ideal, all-purpose wine, it is full-bodied, with vibrant peach, pear and slight spice flavours, showing very good depth, balanced acidity, and a dryish finish. Bargain-priced.

MED/DRY $15 V+

Lake Chalice Marlborough Pinot Gris   ★★★☆

The 2014 vintage (★★★☆) was grown at three sites in the Wairau Valley. It's a fresh, vibrant, medium to full-bodied wine with peach, pear, lychee and spice flavours, showing good depth, and a dryish (5 grams/litre of residual sugar) finish.

MED/DRY $21 AV

Lake Hayes Central Otago Pinot Gris   ★★★☆

From Amisfield, the 2016 vintage (★★★☆) is freshly scented and mouthfilling, with very good depth of peach, lychee and spice flavours, and a slightly sweet (10 grams/litre of residual sugar), smooth finish. Enjoyable from the start.

MED/DRY $20 AV

Lawson's Dry Hills Marlborough Pinot Gris   ★★★★

Grown in the Waihopai Valley, the 2015 vintage (★★★★) was principally handled in tanks, but 10 per cent of the blend was fermented in seasoned French oak barrels. Mouthfilling, it has fresh, youthful pear, lychee and spice flavours, gentle acidity, a sliver of sweetness (9 grams/litre of residual sugar), and excellent balance and depth. A strongly varietal wine, it's delicious young.

Vintage	15	14	13	12	11	10
WR	7	7	7	7	6	7
Drink	16-20	16-17	P	P	P	P

MED/DRY $24 AV

Left Field Hawke's Bay Pinot Gris ★★★☆

The easy-drinking 2016 vintage (★★★) was fermented in tanks and stainless steel barrels. Medium-bodied, it has vibrant pear and spice flavours, fractional sweetness (5.5 grams/litre of residual sugar) and lots of drink-young appeal. (From Te Awa.)

Vintage	16	MED/DRY $18 V+
WR	5	
Drink	16-19	

Linden Estate Hawke's Bay Pinot Gris ★★★☆

Enjoyable young, the 2015 vintage (★★★☆) was grown at Te Awanga. Pale straw, it's a medium-dry style (13 grams/litre of residual sugar), with good body and depth of peachy, spicy, slightly gingery flavours.

MED/DRY $20 AV

Little Black Shag Nelson Pinot Gris (★★★)

Priced sharply, the non-vintage wine (★★★) on the market in 2016 is medium-bodied, with good depth of peachy, citrusy flavours, a sliver of sweetness and crisp acidity. Fresh, lively and finely balanced, it's a good, all-purpose wine, drinking well now to 2017.

MED/DRY $11 V+

Loveblock Marlborough Pinot Gris ★★★☆

The 2014 vintage (★★★☆) was estate-grown in the lower Awatere Valley. Full-bodied and creamy-textured, it has smooth, dryish, peachy, gently spicy flavours (13 per cent Gewürztraminer), hints of lemons and apples, and drink-young appeal. Certified organic.

MED/DRY $27 –V

Lynfer Estate Wairarapa Pinot Gris ★★★★

Grown at Gladstone, the 2014 vintage (★★★★) is mouthfilling, with good intensity of ripe, peachy, slightly spicy flavours, hints of lychees and pears, a touch of complexity, and a dry (3 grams/litre of residual sugar), slightly honeyed finish.

DRY $21 V+

Mahi Marlborough Pinot Gris ★★★★

The 2016 vintage (★★★★) is a single-vineyard wine, hand-picked near Ward, in the Awatere Valley, and mostly handled in tanks; 10 per cent of the blend was barrel-fermented. Mouthfilling and fleshy, with a touch of complexity, it is vibrantly fruity, with moderate acidity and generous, ripe peach, pear and spice flavours, dry (2 grams/litre of residual sugar) and smooth. Best drinking mid-2017+.

Vintage	16	15	14	DRY $20 V+
WR	6	NM	6	
Drink	16-20	NM	16-20	

Mahi Ward Farm Marlborough Pinot Gris (★★★★☆)

The 2015 vintage (★★★★☆) is a single-vineyard wine, grown near Ward, in the Awatere Valley. Hand-picked, it was fermented with indigenous yeasts in French oak barriques and matured on its yeast lees in oak for over a year. Light lemon/green, it is a mouthfilling, dry style (3 grams/litre of residual sugar), in a 'serious', slightly Chardonnay-like style. Showing plenty of personality, it is finely textured, with strong stone-fruit and spice flavours, a hint of toasty oak, and good complexity. Best drinking mid-2017+.

Vintage	15
WR	7
Drink	16-21

 DRY $35 –V

Main Divide Waipara Valley Pinot Gris ★★★★

From Pegasus Bay, this is consistently a great buy. The 2014 vintage (★★★★) is a powerful, Alsace-style wine, with 'noble botrytis and lees-aging' influences. Pale yellow, with a fragrant, slightly honeyed bouquet, it is mouthfilling, with fresh acidity, strong, peachy, spicy, gently sweet and honeyed flavours, a hint of ginger, and a long, distinctly spicy finish.

Vintage	14	13	12	11	10
WR	7	5	7	6	6
Drink	16-20	16-19	16-18	16-18	P

 MED $20 V+

Man O' War Exiled Pinot Gris ★★★★

Grown on Ponui Island, off the eastern end of Waiheke Island, in Auckland, the 2015 vintage (★★★★☆) is a powerful, fleshy, concentrated wine, still youthful. Handled in tanks (80 per cent) and seasoned French oak barrels (20 per cent), it is mouthfilling and vibrant, with strong peach, pear and spice flavours. Made in a medium style (28 grams/litre of residual sugar), it should mature well. The 2016 vintage (★★★☆) was grown on Waiheke and Ponui islands, and 20 per cent of the blend was handled in seasoned French oak casks. Pale straw, it is medium-bodied and gently sweet (28 grams/litre of residual sugar), with vibrant peach, pear and ginger flavours, fresh acidity, and very good drive and depth. Best drinking mid-2017+.

Vintage	16	15
WR	7	6
Drink	16-22	16-19

 MED $34 –V

Man O' War Paradise Pinot Gris (★★★★)

Still a baby, the 2016 vintage (★★★★) was grown on Ponui Island, off the eastern end of Waiheke Island, and made in a medium style (15 grams/litre of residual sugar). Pale lemon/green, it is fresh and light-bodied (10.5 per cent alcohol), with strong pear and lychee flavours, hints of peaches and spices, and obvious potential. Best drinking 2018+.

Vintage	16
WR	6
Drink	16-21

MED $29 –V

Maori Point Central Otago Pinot Gris   ★★★☆

Scented, mouthfilling and crisp, the 2014 vintage (★★★★) is a single-vineyard, Cromwell Basin wine, fermented in a 50:50 split of tanks and seasoned French oak barrels, and bottled unfined and unfiltered. Made in an off-dry style, it is fresh and youthful, with tightly structured peach, pear, lychee and spice flavours, showing very good drive and length. The easy-drinking 2015 vintage (★★★☆) was fully fermented in neutral oak casks. Pale lemon/green, it is medium-bodied, with good depth of fresh, citrusy, peachy flavours, hints of ginger and spice, a sliver of sweetness and an appetisingly crisp finish.

 MED/DRY $24 –V

Map Maker Marlborough Pinot Gris   ★★★★

From Staete Landt, the easy-drinking 2015 vintage (★★★☆) was estate-grown at Rapaura, in the Wairau Valley, and part of the blend was fermented in old French oak puncheons. Faintly pink, with a fresh, spicy bouquet, it is mouthfilling and smooth, with good depth of ripe, peachy, spicy flavours, showing a touch of complexity, and a dry finish.

 DRY $21 V+

Margrain Martinborough Pinot Gris   ★★★☆

The 2014 vintage (★★★★) is a bone-dry style, mostly handled in tanks; 15 per cent of the blend was fermented in old barrels. Light lemon/green, it is full-bodied and fleshy, with generous, ripe, peachy flavours, slightly toasty, bottle-aged notes adding complexity, and a slightly creamy texture. A distinctive wine, it's drinking well now.

Vintage	14	13
WR	6	5
Drink	16-26	16-20

 DRY $24 –V

Marsden Bay of Islands Pinot Gris   ★★★★

In favourable seasons, this Kerikeri, Northland winery produces an impressive Pinot Gris. The 2015 vintage (★★★★) is mouthfilling, fresh and generous, with a gently spicy bouquet. Showing good varietal character, it has vibrant, peachy, citrusy, spicy flavours, a sliver of sweetness (8 grams/litre of residual sugar), balanced acidity, and good concentration.

Vintage	15	14	13
WR	6	5	6
Drink	16-18	P	P

 MED/DRY $28 –V

Martinborough Vineyard Te Tera Martinborough Pinot Gris   ★★★

The light lemon/green 2016 vintage (★★★☆) is full-bodied and fresh, with good weight, ripe peach, pear and spice flavours, a sliver of sweetness, and very good vibrancy and depth.

MED/DRY $18 AV

Matahiwi Estate Wairarapa Pinot Gris   ★★★

The 2015 vintage (★★★) is an off-dry style, full-bodied, with a slightly minerally streak and good depth of peachy, spicy flavours.

 MED/DRY $22 –V

Matawhero Gisborne Pinot Gris   ★★★☆

The 2014 vintage (★★★★) is attractively scented, full-bodied and vibrantly fruity, with a sliver of sweetness (5.7 grams/litre of residual sugar) and ripe stone-fruit, citrus-fruit and spice flavours, showing good concentration. Instantly appealing, it's the best vintage yet.

Vintage	14	13
WR	7	6
Drink	16-17	P

 MED/DRY $24 –V

Maude Central Otago Pinot Gris   ★★★★

Grown at several sites – including Mount Maude Vineyard at Wanaka – and partly barrel-fermented, the 2015 vintage (★★★★) was fermented in tanks (60 per cent) and barrels (40 per cent). Scented, very fresh and vibrant, it has peach, pear, lychee and spice flavours, showing a touch of complexity, and a dryish (5 grams/litre of residual sugar), finely balanced finish.

 MED/DRY $25 AV

Maui Marlborough Pinot Gris   (★★★☆)

The fine-value 2016 vintage (★★★☆) was estate-grown in the upper Wairau Valley. Mouthfilling and fleshy, with very good depth of fresh peachy, spicy, slightly gingery flavours, it's already drinking well. (From Tiki.)

 MED/DRY $19 V+

Milcrest Estate Nelson Pinot Gris   ★★★

The 2014 vintage (★★★☆) was grown at Hope and mostly handled in tanks; 4 per cent of the blend was French oak-aged. It is mouthfilling, with very good depth of ripe, peachy, slightly appley and spicy flavours, a gentle splash of sweetness (14 grams/litre of residual sugar) and balanced acidity.

 MED/DRY $24 –V

Mills Reef Estate Hawke's Bay Pinot Gris   ★★★

The 2015 vintage (★★★☆) is a medium to full-bodied, finely balanced wine, fresh and vibrantly fruity, with citrusy, peachy, slightly spicy flavours, showing very good depth. It's ready to roll.

DRY $18 AV

Mills Reef Reserve Hawke's Bay Pinot Gris   ★★★☆

The 2015 vintage (★★★★), a single-vineyard wine grown at Maraekakaho, was fermented and aged for 10 weeks in seasoned French oak casks. Light straw, it is mouthfilling, with generous, peachy, spicy flavours, showing a touch of complexity, and a well-rounded finish. Enjoyable young.

 DRY $25 –V

Misha's Vineyard Dress Circle Central Otago Pinot Gris   ★★★★★

The outstanding 2015 vintage (★★★★★) was estate-grown and hand-harvested at 23.4 to 24 brix at Bendigo. It was mostly handled in tanks, but 39 per cent of the blend was fermented with indigenous yeasts in old French oak barrels. Made in an off-dry style (6 grams/litre of residual sugar), it is mouthfilling and well-rounded, fleshy and rich, with a strong surge of peach, pear, lychee and ginger flavours, a bare hint of biscuity oak, a slightly oily texture and excellent harmony, depth and fragrance. Drink now or cellar.

Vintage	15	14	13	12	11	10
WR	7	6	6	7	6	6
Drink	16-23	16-22	16-21	16-20	16-19	16-18

 MED/DRY $28 V+

Mission Hawke's Bay Pinot Gris   ★★★

The Mission has long been a standard-bearer for Pinot Gris. The 2015 vintage (★★★☆) is full-bodied, with very good depth of ripe, peachy, spicy flavours, fresh acidity and a smooth, dryish (5 grams/litre of residual sugar) finish.

 MED/DRY $18 AV

Mission Pinot Gris Lighter in Alcohol   ★★☆

The light lemon/green 2016 vintage (★★☆) is not labelled by region, but is mostly from grapes estate-grown and hand-harvested early in the vintage at Taradale, in Hawke's Bay. Stop-fermented with low alcohol (10 per cent), it is an off-dry style (8 grams/litre of residual sugar), light-bodied, with fresh, crisp, lemony flavours.

 MED/DRY $16 AV

Mission Vineyard Selection Marlborough Pinot Gris   ★★★☆

The 2015 vintage (★★★☆) was estate-grown in the Awatere Valley. Made in an off-dry style (6 grams/litre of residual sugar), it's an easy-drinking style, full-bodied and fleshy, with generous, citrusy, slightly spicy and appley flavours and a smooth finish. The 2016 vintage (★★★☆) is still very youthful. It has citrusy, slightly sweet flavours, balanced by appetising acidity, and very good vibrancy and depth. Best drinking mid-2017+.

 MED/DRY $20 AV

Momo Marlborough Pinot Gris   ★★★★

From Seresin, the organically certified 2014 vintage (★★★★☆) is a wonderful buy. Estate-grown, it was hand-harvested and fermented with indigenous yeasts in a mix of tanks and old French oak barriques. A distinctly 'Alsace style' Pinot Gris, it is full-bodied, with a sliver of sweetness and strong, ripe stone-fruit and spice flavours. A very harmonious wine, with a slightly oily texture, complexity and excellent richness, it's already delicious, but also worth cellaring.

 MED/DRY $23 AV

Montana Festival Block Waipara Pinot Gris   ★★★☆

The 2014 vintage (★★★☆) is mouthfilling, with generous, ripe, citrusy, peachy flavours, slightly sweet and smooth. Enjoyable from the start.

MED/DRY $20 AV

Montana Winemakers' Series Hawke's Bay Pinot Gris ★★★

The 2016 vintage (★★★) is mouthfilling, vibrantly fruity and smooth, with fresh pear, lychee and spice flavours, skilfully balanced for early drinking.

MED/DRY $15 V+

Morepork Vineyard Northland Pinot Gris ★★★★

Estate-grown and hand-picked in a small, single-variety vineyard at Kerikeri, the finely poised 2015 vintage (★★★★) is a mouthfilling, youthful wine, dryish (5 grams/litre of residual sugar), with vibrant pear, lychee and spice flavours, showing excellent freshness, delicacy, purity and length.

MED/DRY $24 AV

Mount Brown Grand Reserve Waipara Pinot Gris (★★★★★)

The 2015 vintage (★★★★★) is a full-bodied, Alsace-style wine, partly barrel-fermented. The bouquet is fragrant and lush; the palate is sturdy, with deep, ripe, peachy, spicy flavours and a gently sweet (10 grams/litre of residual sugar), very harmonious, persistent finish. A concentrated, richly varietal wine, it offers great value.

Vintage	15
WR	7
Drink	16-20

MED/DRY $24 V+

Mount Brown Waipara Valley Pinot Gris ★★★☆

Priced sharply, the 2015 vintage (★★★☆) is an off-dry style (8 grams/litre of residual sugar), attractively scented, with good concentration of stone-fruit and spice flavours and a creamy-textured finish. It's drinking well now.

Vintage	15
WR	6
Drink	16-20

MED/DRY $16 V+

Mount Riley Marlborough Pinot Gris ★★★★

Showing good personality, the 2015 vintage (★★★★) is a mouthfilling wine with fresh, strongly varietal flavours of pears, lychees and spices, a touch of complexity (from 10 per cent barrel fermentation), and an off-dry, very harmonious finish. Fine value.

Vintage	15	14
WR	7	6
Drink	16-18	16-17

MED/DRY $17 V+

Mount Vernon Marlborough Pinot Gris ★★★

The pale straw 2015 vintage (★★★) is a fresh, medium to full-bodied wine with good depth of ripe, peachy, slightly spicy and gingery flavours, and a dryish (5 grams/litre of residual sugar) finish. (From Lawson's Dry Hills.)

MED/DRY $19 AV

Moutere Hills Nelson Pinot Gris ★★★★

The 'lightly oaked' 2015 vintage (★★★☆) is a single-vineyard, Upper Moutere wine, full-bodied, with a gentle splash of sweetness in its citrus-fruit, pear and apple flavours, woven with fresh acidity. Slightly minerally, with good depth, it's for drinking now or cellaring.

MED/DRY $23 AV

Mt Beautiful North Canterbury Pinot Gris ★★★☆

The 2014 vintage (★★★★) was estate-grown at Cheviot and handled in tanks (90 per cent) and old oak casks (10 per cent). Fragrant and fleshy, it is powerful (14.5 per cent alcohol) and creamy-textured, with balanced acidity and strong, bone-dry stone-fruit and spice flavours.

Vintage	14	DRY $27 –V
WR	6	
Drink	16-18	

Mt Difficulty Bannockburn Pinot Gris ★★★★

Grown and hand-picked at several sites at Bannockburn, in Central Otago, and lees-aged in tanks, the 2015 vintage (★★★★) is a pale lemon/green, weighty wine (14.5 per cent alcohol), with generous, pure pear, lychee and spice flavours, showing excellent freshness and depth, and an off-dry, well-rounded finish. Drink now or cellar.

MED/DRY $23 AV

Mt Hector Wairarapa Pinot Gris ★★☆

From Matahiwi, the 2014 vintage (★★☆) is a slightly sweet, drink-young style with decent depth of peachy, lemony, spicy flavours, fresh acidity and a slightly buttery finish.

MED/DRY $15 AV

Mud House Marlborough Pinot Gris ★★★★

The 2015 vintage (★★★★) is mouthfilling and vibrantly fruity, with a fragrant bouquet, good intensity of ripe, peachy, spicy flavours, and an off-dry, smooth finish. Delicious young.

MED/DRY $18 V+

Mud House Single Vineyard Home Block Waipara Valley Pinot Gris ★★★★

The 2014 vintage (★★★★) was partly barrel-fermented and made in a dry style (4 grams/litre of residual sugar). Mouthfilling, it is vibrantly fruity, with strong yet delicate flavours of lychees, pears and spices, hints of peaches and nectarines, a touch of complexity, and excellent freshness and length.

DRY $24 AV

Nautilus Marlborough Pinot Gris   ★★★★

The impressive 2015 vintage (★★★★☆) is a full-bodied, dry style (4 grams/litre of residual sugar), grown mostly in the Awatere Valley, hand-picked, and mostly tank-fermented (8 per cent of the blend was fermented in old oak casks). Refined and youthful, it is ripely scented, fleshy and well-rounded, with strong, pure peach, pear and lychee flavours, showing excellent delicacy and depth. Best drinking mid-2017+.

Vintage	15	14	13	12	11	10
WR	7	7	7	7	6	7
Drink	16-19	16-17	16-17	P	P	P

 DRY $29 –V

Neudorf Maggie's Block Nelson Pinot Gris   ★★★★

The 2015 vintage (★★★★) was grown in the Balquidder Vineyard, at Brightwater, on the Waimea Plains, hand-picked, and fermented in tanks (79 per cent) and old oak puncheons (21 per cent). Made in an off-dry style (7 grams/litre of residual sugar), it is freshly scented and mouthfilling, with youthful, citrusy, peachy, slightly spicy flavours, showing a touch of complexity, and very good vigour, harmony and depth. Best drinking 2017+.

Vintage	15	14	13	12	11	10
WR	6	6	6	6	6	6
Drink	16-20	16-19	16-18	16-18	P	P

 MED/DRY $25 AV

Neudorf Moutere Pinot Gris   ★★★★★

The 2015 vintage (★★★★☆) was hand-picked from mature vines in the Home Vineyard at 22.1 to 23.4 brix and fermented with indigenous yeasts in tanks (75 per cent) and old French oak puncheons (25 per cent). An off-dry style (7.1 grams/litre of residual sugar), it is mouthfilling, with strong, ripe stone-fruit and spice flavours, showing excellent delicacy, texture and length. Still very youthful, it's a complex, age-worthy style, likely to be at its best 2017+.

Vintage	15	14	13	12
WR	7	6	7	6
Drink	16-20	16-19	16-18	16-18

 MED/DRY $29 V+

Nevis Bluff Central Otago Pinot Gris   ★★★★

Drinking well now, the distinctive 2013 vintage (★★★★) was estate-grown at Pisa, in the Cromwell Basin, and 20 per cent barrel-fermented. Fragrant, with an inviting, complex bouquet, it is mouthfilling and fleshy, with lively peach, lychee and spice flavours, and a fully dry, harmonious finish. Drink now or cellar.

 DRY $33 –V

Nevis Bluff Oak Aged Central Otago Pinot Gris   ★★★★

The 2013 vintage (★★★★) was hand-picked at Pisa, in the Cromwell Basin, and fermented and matured for nine months in seasoned oak casks. Fleshy, it has strong, ripe peach, pear and spice flavours, showing good complexity, and a fully dry, rounded finish. A distinctive wine, it's drinking well now.

 DRY $35 –V

Nevis Bluff Vendanges Tardives Central Otago Pinot Gris (★★★★☆)

The 2014 vintage (★★★★☆) is a floral, gently sweet wine (55 grams/litre of residual sugar) picked at Pisa, in the Cromwell Basin, six weeks after the main harvest. Bright, light lemon/green, it is weighty, with vibrant, peachy, spicy flavours, hints of pears and ginger, a slightly oily texture, and excellent richness and roundness.

MED $35 (500ML) –V

Ngatarawa Stables Reserve Hawke's Bay Pinot Gris (★★★☆)

The 2015 vintage (★★★☆) is weighty and finely textured, with good depth of vibrant peach, pear and spice flavours, and a fully dry finish. Enjoyable from the start.

Vintage	15
WR	7
Drink	16-17

DRY $20 AV

Obsidian Waiheke Island Pinot Gris ★★★☆

The 2015 vintage (★★★☆) is a single-vineyard wine, attractively scented. Full-bodied and fleshy, it is a dryish style, with youthful, ripe, citrusy, peachy flavours, showing good depth, and a well-rounded finish. Best drinking mid-2016+.

MED/DRY $27 –V

Odyssey Marlborough Pinot Gris ★★★☆

Estate-grown in the Brancott Valley, the characterful 2014 vintage (★★★★) was hand-picked and fermented in old French oak casks. It's a sturdy, fleshy wine with peachy, slightly spicy and toasty flavours, showing more complexity than most Pinot Gris, and a well-rounded, dry (3.5 grams/litre of residual sugar) finish. Certified organic.

DRY $25 –V

Ohinemuri Estate Central Valley Poverty Bay Pinot Gris ★★★☆

The 2015 vintage (★★★☆) was fermented with indigenous yeasts in seasoned oak barrels. Made in a medium-dry style (11 grams/litre of residual sugar), it is a fresh, medium to full-bodied wine, with very good depth of peachy, slightly spicy flavours.

Vintage	15
WR	6
Drink	16-22

MED/DRY $27 –V

Old Coach Road Nelson Pinot Gris ★★★

From Seifried, the 2015 vintage (★★★) is a mouthfilling, medium-dry style (8 grams/litre of residual sugar) with fresh, peachy, spicy flavours, a hint of apricot, and lots of drink-young appeal. Priced sharply.

MED/DRY $13 V+

Omaha Bay Vineyard Matakana Pinot Gris ★★★★

The 2014 vintage (★★★★) is impressive – fleshy, ripe and rounded, with good concentration of stone-fruit and spice flavours, a slightly creamy texture and a dry finish.

Vintage	14	13
WR	6	6
Drink	16-19	16-17

 DRY $30 –V

Omata Estate Russell Pinot Gris (★★★★)

Grown in Northland, the 2014 vintage (★★★★) is a full-bodied, fleshy wine with pear, lychee and spice flavours, showing excellent depth.

 MED/DRY $27 –V

Opawa Marlborough Pinot Gris ★★★☆

This wine is made in a 'lighter, crisper' style than its Nautilus Estate stablemate. Hand-picked in the Wairau Valley and tank-fermented, the 2015 vintage (★★★☆) is lightly scented, mouthfilling and vibrantly fruity, with peach, lychee and spice flavours, showing good delicacy and depth, and a finely balanced, dry finish. The 2016 vintage (★★★☆) is mouthfilling and dry (3 grams/litre of residual sugar), with vibrant, peachy, slightly spicy flavours, showing very good depth. Enjoyable from the start.

DRY $22 AV

Ostler Audrey's Waitaki Valley Pinot Gris ★★★★

The 2013 vintage (★★★☆) was estate-grown, harvested in May and June, and mostly handled in tanks; 25 per cent was barrel-fermented with indigenous yeasts, using large, old oak. It is fleshy, with peachy, slightly spicy flavours, showing very good vibrancy and depth, and a dryish (5 grams/litre of residual sugar) finish.

Vintage	13
WR	6
Drink	16-19

 MED/DRY $35 –V

Ostler Lakeside Vines Waitaki Valley Pinot Gris ★★★★

The 2013 vintage (★★★★) was grown at Lake Waitaki and partly (20 per cent) fermented with indigenous yeasts in old oak barriques. It is fragrant and fleshy, with good weight and depth of vibrant, citrusy, peachy flavours, a touch of complexity, and an off-dry (9 grams/litre of residual sugar), tightly structured finish. Drink now or cellar.

Vintage	13	12
WR	6	6
Drink	16-19	P

MED/DRY $30 –V

Overstone Hawke's Bay Pinot Gris ★★☆

The 2015 vintage (★★☆) is a decent, dryish wine, medium-bodied, with fresh acidity and ripe, peachy, spicy flavours, balanced for easy drinking. Good value from Sileni.

 MED/DRY $13 V+

Oyster Bay Hawke's Bay Pinot Gris   ★★★☆

Grown mostly at Crownthorpe, a relatively cool, elevated, inland district, this is a good, all-purpose wine, modelled on dry Italian Pinot Grigio rather than the richer, sweeter Pinot Gris of Alsace. Handled without oak, it is typically medium to full-bodied, with peach, pear and spice flavours, showing very good depth and harmony, gentle acidity, and a dry finish.

DRY $20 AV

Paddy Borthwick Wairarapa Pinot Gris   ★★★★

Estate-grown at Gladstone, in the northern Wairarapa, the 2015 vintage (★★★★) is fleshy, ripe and rounded. It has strong stone-fruit and spice flavours, in a dry style (3 grams/litre of residual sugar), inviting current drinking or cellaring.

DRY $24 AV

Palliser Estate Martinborough Pinot Gris   ★★★☆

The 2015 vintage (★★★★) is weighty and fleshy, with generous, ripe lychee, pear and spice flavours, fresh, slightly sweet and well-rounded.

MED/DRY $28 –V

Pass, The, Gisborne Pinot Gris   (★★☆)

From Vavasour, the easy-drinking 2016 vintage (★★☆) is fresh-scented and mouthfilling, with gentle acidity and pleasant peach, pear and spice flavours, ripe and smooth.

MED/DRY $17 –V

Paulownia Estate Pinot Gris   (★★★☆)

Grown in the northern Wairarapa, the 2014 vintage (★★★☆) is mouthfilling and dry, with very good depth of ripe, peachy, slightly spicy flavours. Priced sharply.

DRY $18 V+

People's, The, Hawke's Bay Pinot Gris   ★★★

Offering very easy drinking, the 2014 vintage (★★★) includes a splash (3 per cent) of Gewürztraminer. It is smooth and mouthfilling, with plenty of citrusy, peachy, slightly spicy flavour, dryish and well-rounded. Ready. (From Constellation New Zealand.)

MED/DRY $16 V+

Peregrine Central Otago Pinot Gris   (★★★☆)

Grown at Bendigo and Pisa, the 2014 vintage (★★★☆) was mostly handled in tanks; 10 per cent of the blend was fermented in French oak puncheons. It's a fleshy wine with good depth of ripe peach and pear flavours, and an off-dry (6.5 grams/litre of residual sugar), gently spiced finish.

MED/DRY $27 –V

Peter Yealands Lighter in Alcohol Marlborough Pinot Gris

The 2015 vintage (★★) is fresh, light (9.5 per cent alcohol), lemony and slightly appley, with a slightly sweet (6 grams/litre of residual sugar), crisp finish. Pleasant, but plain.

Vintage	15
WR	7
Drink	16-17

MED/DRY $16 –V

Peter Yealands Marlborough Pinot Gris

The 2015 vintage (★★★) is a good, all-purpose wine, full-bodied, fresh and rounded. Moderately priced, it has vibrant, ripe, peachy, slightly spicy flavours, well-balanced, smooth and dry (4 grams/litre of residual sugar).

Vintage	15	14
WR	7	7
Drink	16-17	P

DRY $16 V+

Peter Yealands Reserve Awatere Valley Marlborough Pinot Gris

The 2015 vintage (★★★☆) is mouthfilling and fleshy, with generous, peachy, spicy flavours, a slightly creamy texture and a well-rounded, dry (4 grams/litre of residual sugar) finish. Enjoyable young.

Vintage	15	14
WR	7	6
Drink	16-17	P

DRY $21 AV

Pied Stilt Nelson Pinot Gris

A single-vineyard Motueka wine, the 2014 vintage (★★★) is sturdy and creamy-textured, with peach, pear, lychee and spice flavours, and a dry (3 grams/litre of residual sugar) finish. Ready.

DRY $20 –V

Prophet's Rock Central Otago Pinot Gris ★★★★☆

Estate-grown and hand-picked at two Bendigo sites, in the Cromwell Basin, the 2015 vintage (★★★★★) is full of personality. Fermented with indigenous yeasts and made with some use of old oak, it is fleshy, with rich, peachy, citrusy, slightly spicy flavours, showing a distinct touch of complexity, gentle sweetness (12 grams/litre of residual sugar), and lovely vigour and harmony. Drink now or cellar.

Vintage	15
WR	6
Drink	16-22

MED/DRY $35 –V

Quartz Reef Bendigo Single Vineyard Pinot Gris   ★★★★

Certified biodynamic, the refined and youthful 2015 vintage (★★★★☆) was estate-grown at Bendigo, in Central Otago, hand-picked and fermented and lees-aged in tanks. Bright, light lemon/green, it is freshly scented, mouthfilling, weighty and dry, with strong, vibrant, pure, citrusy, peachy, spicy flavours, very finely textured and harmonious. Drink now or cellar.

Vintage	15	14	13	12	11	10
WR	7	7	6	7	7	7
Drink	16-19	16-18	16-17	P	P	P

 DRY $29 –V

Quest Farm Silver Lining Central Otago Pinot Gris   (★★★☆)

The 2014 vintage (★★★☆) is a fully dry style (2 grams/litre of residual sugar), with a small portion (about 5 per cent) of Gewürztraminer and Viognier in the blend. Full-bodied, it is vibrantly fruity, with stone-fruit and pear flavours, fresh, appetising acidity, and very good depth and immediacy.

 DRY $25 –V

Ransom Clos De Valerie Pinot Gris   ★★★★

Estate-grown at Mahurangi, north of Auckland, the 2013 vintage (★★★★) is on sale now. A full-bodied, bone-dry style, it has a richly scented bouquet, showing a touch of bottle-aged complexity. Sweet-fruited, with fresh, citrusy, slightly peachy and spicy flavours and a well-rounded finish, it shows good personality. Ready; no rush.

 DRY $24 AV

Rapaura Springs Marlborough Pinot Gris   ★★★☆

The easy-drinking 2016 vintage (★★★) is full-bodied and vibrantly fruity, with peachy, slightly spicy flavours, fresh, dryish (9 grams/litre of residual sugar) and finely balanced.

Vintage	16	15	14
WR	7	7	7
Drink	16-19	16-18	16-18

 MED/DRY $14 V+

Rapaura Springs Reserve Marlborough Pinot Gris   (★★★★)

Already very open and expressive, the dryish 2016 vintage (★★★★) was mostly handled in tanks; 5 per cent of the blend was barrel-fermented. Full-bodied, it has generous stone-fruit and spice flavours, with a hint of ginger, slight sweetness (5 grams/litre of residual sugar), a touch of complexity, and lots of drink-young appeal.

Vintage	16
WR	7
Drink	16-20

MED/DRY $19 V+

Renato Nelson Pinot Gris ★★★☆

Estate-grown at Kina, on the coast, hand-picked and lees-aged, the 2015 vintage (★★★★) is fleshy, with ripe pear, lychee and spice flavours, showing excellent vibrancy and depth, and an off-dry (7 grams/litre of residual sugar), rounded finish.

Vintage	15	14	13	12	11	10
WR	6	7	NM	6	6	7
Drink	16-20	16-20	NM	16-19	16-17	16-17

MED/DRY $20 AV

Ribbonwood Marlborough Pinot Gris ★★★☆

From Framingham, the 2014 vintage (★★★☆) was partly (15 per cent) barrel-matured. Full-bodied (14 per cent alcohol), it is a dryish style (6 grams/litre of residual sugar), with citrusy, slightly peachy and spicy flavours, showing good depth, and a scented bouquet. An attractive, all-purpose wine.

MED/DRY $20 AV

Richmond Plains Nelson Pinot Gris ★★★☆

Certified organic, the youthful 2015 vintage (★★★☆) was barrel-aged and made in an off-dry (7 grams/litre of residual sugar) style. It's an easy-drinking wine, full-bodied, with plenty of peachy, citrusy, slightly gingery flavour. Drink now or cellar.

MED/DRY $23 –V

Rimu Grove Bronte Pinot Gris – see Bronte Pinot Gris

Riverby Estate Marlborough Pinot Gris ★★★☆

A single-vineyard wine, grown in the heart of the Wairau Valley, the 2014 vintage (★★★) is full-bodied, with fresh, moderately concentrated pear, lychee and spice flavours and an off-dry (8 grams/litre of residual sugar), smooth finish.

Vintage	13
WR	7
Drink	16-20

MED/DRY $22 AV

Roaring Meg Central Otago Pinot Gris ★★★☆

From Mt Difficulty, the bright, light lemon/green 2015 vintage (★★★☆) is scented and mouthfilling, with fresh peach, pear and spice flavours, showing very good vibrancy and depth. An off-dry style, it's enjoyable from the start.

MED/DRY $23 –V

Rock Ferry Marlborough Pinot Gris ★★★★☆

Certified organic, the 2013 vintage (★★★★☆) is sturdy and generous, with good complexity from handling in tanks and barrels. A concentrated wine, with an array of peach, pear, ginger and spice flavours and a finely textured, dry (3 grams/litre of residual sugar) finish, it's drinking well now.

DRY $27 AV

Rock Ferry Trig Hill Vineyard Central Otago Pinot Gris   ★★★★☆

Certified organic, the elegant 2013 vintage (★★★★☆) is mouthfilling and rich. It is concentrated, with vibrant, peachy, slightly spicy and gingery flavours, good acid spine, complexity from handling in tanks and seasoned oak puncheons, and obvious potential.

 MED/DRY $33 –V

Rockburn Central Otago Pinot Gris   ★★★

Grown at Parkburn, in the Cromwell Basin, and at Gibbston, the 2015 vintage (★★☆) is a pale straw, medium-bodied wine, crisp and dry (4 grams/litre of residual sugar), but slightly austere, showing a slight lack of ripeness, richness and roundness.

 DRY $25 –V

Rocky Point Central Otago Pinot Gris   (★★★☆)

The 2013 vintage (★★★☆) was estate-grown at Bendigo, hand-picked, and fermented with indigenous yeasts in tanks. Attractively scented, it is full-bodied, with a sliver of sweetness and very good depth of fresh, crisp, citrusy, peachy flavours, slightly spicy and gingery.

 MED/DRY $26 –V

Rod McDonald One Off Hawke's Bay Pinot Gris Rhymes With Orange   (★★★☆)

The debut 2015 vintage (★★★☆) is described by the producer as 'a typical orange wine, with sweet upfront fruit and drying finish'. Hand-picked at Maraekakaho and held on its skins for nine months, it is medium to full-bodied, with an onion skin hue and a spicy, peachy bouquet. The flavours are strong, with stone-fruit and spice notes, a hint of apricots, more personality than most Pinot Gris, and a firm, dry finish. Worth trying.

 DRY $25 –V

Rossendale Marlborough Pinot Gris   ★★☆

Priced sharply, the estate-grown 2016 vintage (★★☆) is a sound but not memorable wine, with fresh lemon, apple and spice flavours, and a dryish finish.

 MED/DRY $14 AV

Runner Duck Pinot Gris   (★★★)

Grown at Waimauku, the high-priced 2014 vintage (★★★) offers good depth of peachy, spicy flavour, with a gentle splash of sweetness and fresh acidity. Ready.

MED/DRY $38 –V

Ruru Central Otago Pinot Gris   (★★★)

Grown and hand-picked at Alexandra, the 2016 vintage (★★★) is a medium-bodied wine, with fresh, lively pear and lychee flavours, a sliver of sweetness, and good vigour and immediacy.

 MED/DRY $19 AV

Sacred Hill Marlborough Pinot Gris   ★★★★

The 2016 vintage (★★★★) is a sturdy, Alsace-style Pinot Gris (blended with 11 per cent Gewürztraminer), grown in the Southern Valleys. Fleshy, with strong, ripe, peachy, spicy flavours, gentle acidity and a dryish, rich, rounded finish, it's delicious from the start.

MED/DRY $20 V+

Sailfish Cove Northland Pinot Gris   (★★☆)

The 2014 vintage (★★☆) includes a splash (10 per cent) of Flora. It's an easy-drinking wine with citrusy, slightly appley flavours and a smooth, dry finish.

DRY $19 –V

Saint Clair Godfrey's Creek Reserve Marlborough Pinot Gris   ★★★☆

Made in a full-bodied, dry style (4.5 grams/litre of residual sugar), the 2014 vintage (★★★★) is a single-vineyard, Brancott Valley wine, tank-fermented and lees-aged. It is mouthfilling, with fresh, strong pear, lychee and spice flavours, showing very good vigour and depth.

DRY $31 –V

Saint Clair James Sinclair Marlborough Pinot Gris   (★★★)

The debut 2015 vintage (★★★) is a blend of Pinot Gris (87.5 per cent) with small amounts of Gewürztraminer, Riesling, Grüner Veltliner and Muscat. Grown in the Southern Valleys and Awatere Valley, it is fresh and full-bodied, in a dryish (4.5 grams/litre of residual sugar), 'grigio' style, with plenty of crisp, slightly spicy flavour.

DRY $22 –V

Saint Clair Pioneer Block 5 Bull Block Marlborough Pinot Gris   ★★★★

Grown in the lower Omaka Valley, the 2014 vintage (★★★★) was made in a 'tardive' (late-harvest) style. An elegant wine with citrusy, appley aromas and flavours, it has good vigour and delicacy, with hints of peaches, spices and ginger, gentle acidity and a finely balanced, slightly sweet (10 grams/litre of residual sugar) finish. Very age-worthy.

MED/DRY $27 –V

Saint Clair Vicars Choice Bright Light Marlborough Pinot Gris   (★★☆)

The 2014 vintage (★★☆) is a pleasant, light wine (9.5 per cent alcohol), with fresh pear, lychee and spice flavours and a slightly sweet (8.6 grams/litre of residual sugar) finish. It's a clearly varietal wine, offering smooth, easy, no-fuss drinking.

MED/DRY $19 –V

Saint Clair Vicar's Choice Marlborough Pinot Gris   ★★★

The 2015 vintage (★★★) includes splashes of Grüner Veltliner (7 per cent) and Viognier (6 per cent) in the blend. Made in a 'grigio' style, it is medium-bodied, fresh and crisp, with pear, citrus and spice flavours and a dry finish.

 DRY $19 AV

Sanctuary Gisborne Pinot Gris

(★★☆)

The 2016 vintage (★★☆) is a medium-bodied wine with decent depth of fresh, ripe citrus-fruit, pear and spice flavours, balanced for easy drinking.

MED/DRY $18 –V

Satyr Hawke's Bay Pinot Gris

★★☆

From Sileni, the easy-drinking 2015 vintage (★★☆) is a medium-bodied, crisp and lively wine with dryish, citrusy, appley flavours. Priced sharply.

MED/DRY $14 AV

Sea Level Home Block Nelson Pinot Gris

★★★★

The 2014 vintage (★★★★) was estate-grown at Mariri. Freshly scented, it is mouthfilling, with strong, vibrant pear, lychee and spice flavours, showing excellent varietal character, and a finely balanced, off-dry (6 grams/litre of residual sugar) finish.

Vintage	14
WR	7
Drink	P

MED/DRY $18 V+

Seifried Nelson Pinot Gris

★★★

The 2016 vintage (★★★) is a fresh, medium-bodied wine with good depth of citrusy, peachy, slightly spicy flavours, lively acidity and a dry (4 grams/litre of residual sugar) finish. Best drinking mid-2017+.

Vintage	16	15	14	13
WR	6	6	5	6
Drink	16-18	16-17	P	P

DRY $18 AV

Selaks Founders Limited Edition Hawke's Bay Pinot Gris

(★★★★)

The refined 2014 vintage (★★★★), grown mostly at Moteo, is a mouthfilling, dry style (3 grams/litre of residual sugar). It is ripely flavoured, peachy and spicy, with balanced acidity and very good drive, delicacy and depth through the palate.

DRY $26 –V

Selaks Reserve Marlborough Pinot Gris

★★★

Grown in the Awatere Valley, the 2014 vintage (★★★) is fragrant and mouthfilling, with satisfying depth of fresh, peachy, slightly spicy flavour and an off-dry, smooth finish.

MED/DRY $17 AV

Seresin Marlborough Pinot Gris   ★★★★★

One of the region's most distinctive Pinot Gris. The 2015 vintage (★★★★) was estate-grown in the Omaka and Wairau valleys, hand-picked, fermented with indigenous yeasts, and lees-aged for five months in seasoned French oak puncheons and barriques. Certified organic, it's a distinctive, mouthfilling wine, with good concentration of peachy, spicy flavours, oak-derived complexity, gentle acidity and a dry (4.6 grams/litre of residual sugar) finish.

DRY $25 V+

Sherwood Signature Family Waipara Pinot Gris   (★★★★)

Showing good complexity, the 2015 vintage (★★★★) is an aromatic, fleshy wine, partly barrel-fermented. It has strongly varietal pear/spice flavours, woven with fresh acidity, and an off-dry, finely textured finish.

MED/DRY $19 V+

Sileni Cellar Selection Hawke's Bay Pinot Gris   ★★☆

The 2015 vintage (★★☆) is a light-bodied (11 per cent alcohol), 'grigio' style, with crisp, citrusy flavours, fresh and lively, and a dryish (5 grams/litre of residual sugar) finish. The 2016 vintage (★★☆) is similar – light and lively, with solid depth of lemony, spicy flavours.

MED/DRY $20 –V

Sileni Wisp Cellar Selection Lo Cal Pinot Gris   (★★☆)

The 2014 vintage (★★☆) is a light style (9.5 per cent alcohol), with pleasant, lemony, appley flavours, hints of pears and peaches, and a smooth, slightly sweet (7 grams/litre of residual sugar) finish. Forward, easy drinking.

MED/DRY $17 –V

Silver Fern Marlborough Pinot Gris   (★★★☆)

The 2014 vintage (★★★☆) is full-bodied and creamy-textured, in a very easy-drinking style with stone-fruit, pear and spice flavours, showing very good freshness and depth. (From Yealands.)

MED/DRY $21 AV

Soho Jagger Marlborough Pinot Gris   ★★★★

The 2015 vintage (★★★★) was mostly handled in tanks; 5 per cent of the blend was fermented in seasoned French oak barrels. A scented, mouthfilling wine, it has very good depth of pear, lychee, peach and spice flavours, showing a touch of complexity, and a smooth, dryish finish.

MED/DRY $26 –V

Vintage	15
WR	5
Drink	16-18

Soho White Collection Marlborough Pinot Gris ★★★☆

The 2015 vintage (★★★☆) is fragrant and full-bodied, with fresh acidity woven through its peachy, slightly spicy flavours, which show good depth. An off-dry style, it's skilfully balanced for enjoyable, early drinking.

Vintage	15
WR	4
Drink	16-17

MED/DRY $20 AV

Soljans Kumeu Pinot Gris ★★★

Estate-grown and hand-picked in West Auckland and tank-fermented, the 2014 vintage (★★★) is a freshly scented, medium-bodied wine with ripe, peachy, slightly spicy and gingery flavours, a touch of sweetness (12 grams/litre of residual sugar), and an easy-drinking charm.

Vintage	14
WR	7
Drink	16-17

MED/DRY $19 AV

Spade Oak Vineyard Voysey Gisborne Pinot Gris ★★★

The 2014 vintage (★★☆) is an easy-drinking style, peachy and slightly spicy, with considerable sweetness (16 grams/litre of residual sugar), gentle acidity and a smooth finish.

MED $19 AV

Spinyback Nelson Pinot Gris ★★★☆

From Waimea Estate, the 2014 vintage (★★★) is a medium-bodied, vibrant wine with good depth of peach, pear and spice flavours, a sliver of sweetness (6 grams/litre of residual sugar), fresh acidity and plenty of drink-young appeal.

MED/DRY $18 V+

Spy Valley Envoy Marlborough Pinot Gris ★★★★★

Estate-grown in the Waihopai Valley, the 2014 vintage (★★★★★) was harvested from vines planted in 1999 and fermented in small oak vessels. Made from the 'very ripest grapes', it's a powerful, Alsace-style wine, strapping (15.5 per cent alcohol), with concentrated, still youthful peach, lychee and pear flavours, a distinct touch of complexity, and a gently sweet (25 grams/litre of residual sugar), lasting finish. Best drinking 2018.

Vintage	14	13
WR	7	6
Drink	16-21	16-20

MED $32 –V

Spy Valley Marlborough Pinot Gris ★★★★☆

The 2015 vintage (★★★★☆) was hand-picked at 22 to 24 brix and most of the blend (60 per cent) was fermented and matured for five months in old oak barrels and ovals. Richly fragrant, it's a sturdy wine, intensely varietal, with rich, peachy, spicy, slightly toasty flavours, a sliver of sweetness (7 grams/litre of residual sugar), and strong personality. Already delicious, it's also worth cellaring.

Vintage	15	14	13	12	11	10
WR	7	7	6	6	6	6
Drink	16-20	16-19	P	P	P	P

MED/DRY $23 V+

Starborough Family Estate Marlborough Pinot Gris ★★★☆

The 2015 vintage (★★★★) was estate-grown in the Wairau (two-thirds) and Awatere valleys, and 10 per cent of the blend was barrel-fermented. Mouthfilling, it is fresh and vibrantly fruity, with clearly defined varietal characteristics, concentrated peach, pear and spice flavours, and a dryish (5.5 grams/litre of residual sugar) finish. Best drinking 2017+. The 2016 vintage (★★★☆) is a 2:1 blend of Wairau Valley and Awatere Valley grapes, mostly handled in tanks; 10 per cent of the blend was barrel-aged. Pale, it shows good varietal character, with good depth of fresh, delicate pear and lychee flavours, fractional sweetness (5.5 grams/litre of residual sugar) and balanced acidity.

MED/DRY $20 AV

Stoneleigh Latitude Marlborough Pinot Gris ★★★★

Estate-grown on the northern side of the Wairau Valley, the 2015 vintage (★★★★) is attractively scented and vibrantly fruity, with excellent depth of stone-fruit, lychee and spice flavours, a slightly oily texture and a smooth, lengthy finish. Already enjoyable, the 2016 vintage (★★★★) is mouthfilling and generous, with strong, fresh, peachy, slightly spicy flavours, a sliver of sweetness and a very harmonious finish.

MED/DRY $23 AV

Stoneleigh Marlborough Lighter Pinot Gris (★★)

The 2016 vintage (★★) is a light style (9.8 per cent alcohol). Freshly scented, with lemony, appley flavours and a sliver of sweetness (7.6 grams/litre of residual sugar), it's a pleasant lunchtime sipper, but lacks real body, ripeness and richness.

MED/DRY $17 –V

Stoneleigh Marlborough Pinot Gris ★★★☆

Offering excellent value, the 2015 vintage (★★★★) is an aromatic, full-bodied wine with very good intensity of pear/spice flavours, fresh and harmonious.

MED/DRY $17 V+

Stoneleigh Rapaura Series Marlborough Pinot Gris ★★★★☆

The 2015 vintage (★★★★) of this single-vineyard wine has a spicy bouquet, leading into a mouthfilling, fleshy palate with strong, fresh peach, lychee, pear and spice flavours, and an off-dry, finely textured finish.

MED/DRY $28 AV

Summerhouse Marlborough Pinot Gris   (★★★★)

The attractive 2014 vintage (★★★★) was fermented in tanks and old oak casks. Ripely scented, it is mouthfilling and gently sweet (15 grams/litre of residual sugar), with fresh, strong pear and spice flavours, showing a touch of complexity, and a well-rounded, rich finish.

Vintage 14
WR 5
Drink 16-17

 MED $19 V+

Takatu Matakana Pinot Gris   ★★★★

Grown on a north-facing hillside, this is a sophisticated wine. The 2014 vintage (★★★★) was handled in a mix of seasoned oak puncheons and barriques (60 per cent of the blend) and stainless steel tanks. Mouthfilling, it is richly scented, with strong, vibrant, citrusy, peachy flavours, balanced acidity and a tight, dry finish (1.5 grams/litre of residual sugar).

 DRY $35 –V

Tantalus Estate Waiheke Island Pinot Gris   (★★★★)

Grown at Onetangi, the 2015 vintage (★★★★) was French oak-aged for six months. Fleshy and well-rounded, it is youthful in colour, with strong, ripe pear and lychee flavours, showing good varietal character, a touch of complexity and a dry (3 grams/litre of residual sugar) finish. Drink now or cellar.

Vintage 15
WR 5
Drink 16-18

 DRY $35 –V

Tarras Vineyards Central Otago Pinot Gris   (★★★★)

Grown at Alexandra, the 2014 vintage (★★★★) is a gently perfumed wine, displaying good varietal character. It has dryish pear and quince flavours, showing excellent balance and length.

 MED/DRY $29 –V

Te Awanga Estate Hawke's Bay Pinot Gris   ★★★

The 2014 vintage (★★★) was hand-picked at an inland site, tank-fermented and lees-aged. It's a mouthfilling wine with vibrant pear, lychee and spice flavours and a dry (under 3 grams/litre of residual sugar) finish.

 DRY $25 –V

Te Kairanga Martinborough Pinot Gris   ★★★★

The 2015 vintage (★★★☆) was fermented in tanks (85 per cent) and old French oak barrels (15 per cent). Made in a dry style (2.6 grams/litre of residual sugar), it is a mouthfilling, creamy-textured wine with ripe peach, pear and spice flavours and a well-rounded finish. The excellent 2016 vintage (★★★★☆) is full-bodied, with concentrated, ripe stone-fruit and spice flavours, a touch of complexity, and a fresh, lasting finish. Best drinking mid-2017+.

DRY $22 V+

Te Mania Nelson Pinot Gris   ★★★★

The 2015 vintage (★★★★) was grown at two sites, on the plains and in the hills. Light lemon/
green, it is full-bodied and vibrantly fruity, with strong pear, lychee and spice flavours, fractional
sweetness (6.5 grams/litre of residual sugar), and very good varietal character and harmony. Best
drinking 2017+.

MED/DRY $22 V+

Terra Sancta Lola's Block Bannockburn Central Otago Pinot Gris   ★★★★

The 2015 vintage (★★★☆) was estate-grown, hand-picked and fermented and matured for 10
months in old oak barrels. Full-bodied, it has a subtle bouquet, with good depth of ripe, citrusy,
appley, spicy flavours, a touch of complexity, and a dryish (5 grams/litre of residual sugar), smooth
finish.

MED/DRY $27 –V

Terra Sancta Mysterious Diggings Bannockburn Central Otago Pinot Gris   ★★★★

Estate-grown and hand-picked, the 2015 vintage (★★★★) is an attractively scented wine,
fleshy and vibrantly fruity, with fresh pear and lychee flavours, slightly peachy and spicy notes,
gentle acidity and a dryish, smooth finish. It's an excellent, all-purpose wine. The 2016 vintage
(★★★★) is mouthfilling, fresh and smooth, with very good depth of ripe, peachy, slightly spicy
flavours, fractional sweetness and finely balanced acidity. Drink now or cellar.

MED/DRY $23 AV

Terrace Edge Waipara Valley Pinot Gris   ★★★★

The fleshy 2015 vintage (★★★★) was hand-picked and fermented with indigenous yeasts in
a mix of seasoned oak barrels (60 per cent) and tanks (40 per cent). Bright, light lemon/green,
it's a medium style (15 grams/litre of residual sugar), full-bodied (14.5 per cent alcohol), with
rich, citrusy, slightly peachy and spicy flavours, good complexity and a rounded finish. Drink
now onwards.

Vintage	15	14	13	12	11
WR	7	6	7	7	6
Drink	16-22	16-19	16-18	16-17	P

MED $25 AV

Thornbury Waipara Pinot Gris   ★★★

The very easy-drinking 2016 vintage (★★★) is a full-bodied, dryish style (5 grams/litre of
residual sugar), with gentle acidity and good depth of fresh, vibrant pear/lychee flavours. (From
Villa Maria.)

Vintage	16	15	14	13
WR	7	7	5	7
Drink	16-18	16-18	16-17	P

MED/DRY $16 V+

Tiki Estate Marlborough Pinot Gris   ★★★☆

Estate-grown in the upper Wairau Valley, the 2016 vintage (★★★★) is attractively scented, with
mouthfilling body and strong, ripe peach, pear, lychee and spice flavours, showing good varietal
character. Made in a dryish style, it's a drink-now or cellaring proposition.

MED/DRY $20 AV

Tinpot Hut Marlborough Pinot Gris ★★★

Fresh and lively, the 2014 vintage (★★★) was grown in the Home Block and neighbouring McKee Vineyard, in the Awatere Valley. Mouthfilling, it has decent depth of vibrant, ripe citrus-fruit and pear flavours, with hints of apples and spices, and a dry (3.9 grams/litre of residual sugar) finish.

DRY $22 –V

Tohu Awatere Valley Marlborough Pinot Gris ★★★☆

The 2015 vintage (★★★★) was grown at several sites in the Awatere Valley. Mouthfilling and vibrantly fruity, it has strong, peachy, citrusy, spicy flavours and a finely balanced, dryish (5.5 grams/litre of residual sugar) finish. A good, all-purpose wine. The youthful 2016 vintage (★★★☆) is full-bodied, with vibrant, peachy, spicy flavours, showing very good depth, and an off-dry (5 grams/litre of residual sugar) finish. Best drinking mid-2017+.

MED/DRY $22 AV

Toi Toi Brookdale Reserve Marlborough Pinot Gris ★★★☆

The 2016 vintage (★★★☆) has gentle pear, lychee and spice aromas. Mouthfilling, fleshy and rounded, it has fresh, moderately concentrated flavours, showing a touch of complexity, and a finely textured, dryish (6 grams/litre of residual sugar) finish.

Vintage	16
WR	7
Drink	16-20

MED/DRY $22 AV

Toi Toi Marlborough Pinot Gris ★★☆

The easy-drinking 2016 vintage (★★☆) is mouthfilling and smooth, in a 'grigio' style with solid depth of pear and lychee flavours, a hint of spice and a dryish finish.

MED/DRY $18 –V

Torea Marlborough Pinot Gris ★★★☆

From an Auckland-based company, the 2014 vintage (★★★☆) is a fleshy, very easy-drinking wine with good depth of ripe, peachy flavours and a slightly sweet, creamy-smooth finish.

MED/DRY $17 V+

Torrent Bay Nelson Pinot Gris ★★☆

The 2014 vintage (★★☆) is medium-bodied, with decent depth of vibrant lemon, apple and spice flavours, slightly sweet and crisp. Fresh, easy drinking.

MED/DRY $17 –V

Trinity Hill Hawke's Bay Pinot Gris ★★★☆

Still on sale, the light yellow/green 2014 vintage (★★★☆) is a medium-bodied style, with dry, peachy, spicy flavours, showing very good depth, and toasty, bottle-aged notes emerging. Ready.

DRY $22 AV

Triplebank Awatere Valley Marlborough Pinot Gris   ★★★☆

Pernod Ricard NZ's wine is typically aromatic and flavourful. The 2016 vintage (★★★★) is scented and mouthfilling, with vibrant pear, lychee and spice flavours, gentle acidity and a well-rounded finish. Delicious young.

MED/DRY $20 AV

Tupari Awatere Valley Marlborough Pinot Gris   ★★★★

A single-vineyard wine, the 2015 vintage (★★★☆) is fresh, balanced and lively, with an aromatic, appley, spicy bouquet, fresh acidity and ripe, smooth flavours.

Vintage	15	14	13
WR	6	6	6
Drink	16-18	16-17	P

MED/DRY $27 –V

Two Rivers of Marlborough Brookby Hill Pinot Gris   (★★★★)

From 16-year-old vines in the Southern Valleys, the 2016 vintage (★★★☆) was partly (10 per cent) barrel-fermented. Fresh, with citrus-fruit and pear-like flavours, it is lively and youthful, with a touch of complexity and a dry (4 grams/litre of residual sugar) impression. Best drinking mid-2017+.

Vintage	16
WR	6
Drink	17-20

DRY $24 AV

Two Rivers of Marlborough Wairau Selection Pinot Gris   ★★★☆

The 2015 vintage (★★★) is medium to full-bodied, with vibrant pear and apple flavours, and a fresh, dryish (5 grams/litre of residual sugar), finely balanced finish.

Vintage	15	14	13
WR	6	6	7
Drink	16-17	P	P

MED/DRY $25 –V

Two Sisters Central Otago Pinot Gris   ★★★★

The impressive 2015 vintage (★★★★☆) is a single-vineyard wine, hand-harvested at Lowburn, in the Cromwell Basin, and fermented in seasoned oak casks. Fragrant and weighty (14.5 per cent alcohol), it is intensely varietal, with ripe, peachy, citrusy, spicy flavours, showing excellent delicacy and depth. Made in a fully dry style, with a slightly creamy texture, it's a drink-now or cellaring proposition.

DRY $29 –V

Urlar Gladstone Pinot Gris   ★★★★

Weighty and rich, this northern Wairarapa wine is hand-picked and fermented and matured in seasoned French oak casks, with extended lees-aging and lees-stirring. Still youthful, the 2014 vintage (★★★★☆) is mouthfilling and sweet-fruited, with vibrant, peachy, slightly spicy flavours, savoury notes adding complexity and a dry, lingering finish.

DRY $28 –V

Valli Gibbston Vineyard Central Otago Pinot Gris ★★★★

The 2016 vintage (★★★★☆) was estate-grown at Gibbston and handled entirely in tanks. A pale, scented wine, it is a dry style (4 grams/litre of residual sugar), full-bodied and vibrantly fruity, with fresh, rich pear, lychee and spice flavours, showing excellent purity, depth and harmony. Still very youthful, it's well worth cellaring; open 2018+.

Vintage	16
WR	7
Drink	16-24

 DRY $30 –V

Vavasour Awatere Valley Marlborough Pinot Gris ★★★★☆

A consistently impressive wine. Invitingly scented, the 2015 vintage (★★★★☆) is mouthfilling and vibrantly fruity, with concentrated peach, pear, lychee and spice flavours, showing excellent varietal character. An off-dry style with balanced acidity and good harmony, it's drinking well from the start.

 MED/DRY $23 V+

Vidal East Coast Pinot Gris ★★★

The 2014 vintage (★★★) was grown in Marlborough and Waipara and made in a dry style (4.7 grams/litre of residual sugar). It's a very easy-drinking wine, with gentle acidity and soft, ripe, peachy flavours.

Vintage	14	13	12
WR	5	6	6
Drink	P	P	P

 DRY $15 V+

Villa Maria Cellar Selection Marlborough Pinot Gris ★★★★

The 2015 vintage (★★★★) was mostly handled in tanks; 5 per cent of the blend was oak-aged. It's a fleshy, dryish wine (5.8 grams/litre of residual sugar) with strong stone-fruit and spice flavours, ripe, finely balanced and lingering. A top buy. The 2016 vintage (★★★★☆) was also 5 per cent oak-aged. Grown in the Wairau and Awatere valleys, it's an off-dry style (7.8 grams/litre of residual sugar), with mouthfilling body and rich stone-fruit and spice flavours, finely textured and well-rounded. A very harmonious wine, it's a drink-now or cellaring proposition. Fine value.

Vintage	16	15	14	13
WR	6	6	6	6
Drink	16-19	16-18	16-18	16-17

MED/DRY $20 V+

Villa Maria Private Bin East Coast Pinot Gris   ★★★☆

The 2015 vintage (★★★☆), grown in Marlborough, Gisborne and Waipara, is fragrant and mouthfilling, with fresh pear, lychee and spice aromas and flavours, showing good varietal character and depth, and an off-dry finish. Fine value. The 2016 vintage (★★★★) is delicious from the start. Full-bodied, it is generous, with fresh, off-dry peach, pear and spice flavours, vibrant, strong and finely balanced. Good, sharply priced drinking for the summer of 2016–17.

Vintage	16	15	14	13
WR	6	7	7	7
Drink	16-18	16-18	16-17	P

 MED/DRY $17 V+

Villa Maria Single Vineyard Seddon Marlborough Pinot Gris   ★★★★★

One of the country's top Pinot Gris, this Awatere Valley wine is typically sturdy, beautifully scented and intense. Hand-picked and fermented in tanks (80 per cent) and seasoned French oak casks (20 per cent), the youthful, tight-knit 2015 vintage (★★★★★) is a dryish style (6 grams/litre of residual sugar), highly fragrant and fleshy, with strong, luscious pear and spice flavours, showing a touch of nutty complexity, and good length. Best drinking 2017 onwards.

Vintage	15	14	13
WR	7	7	7
Drink	16-20	16-18	16-19

 MED/DRY $33 AV

Vista Nelson Pinot Gris   ★★★☆

Priced right, the 2015 vintage (★★★☆) is a single-vineyard wine, grown at Kina. Mouthfilling and dry (4 grams/litre of residual sugar), it has very good depth of peach, pear and spice flavours, woven with appetising acidity.

 DRY $18 V+

VNO Hawke's Bay Pinot Gris   ★★★

Mouthfilling, with a slightly oily texture, the 2015 vintage (★★★☆) includes a splash of Gewürztraminer (5 per cent). Well balanced for easy drinking, it has good depth of pear, lychee and spice flavours, with a dryish, very smooth finish. Good value.

 MED/DRY $17 AV

VNO Skinny Hawke's Bay Pinot Gris   (★★)

The pale, easy-drinking 2015 vintage (★★) is a light style (9 per cent alcohol). It has gentle pear and spice flavours, fresh acidity, a sliver of sweetness and a smooth finish.

MED/DRY $17 –V

Waimea Nelson Pinot Gris   ★★★★

In top seasons, this is one of the country's best-value Pinot Gris. The 2015 vintage (★★★★), estate-grown on the Waimea Plains, is mouthfilling and well-rounded, with strong peach and pear flavours, hints of ginger and spice, gentle acidity, and a slightly sweet (11 grams/litre of residual sugar), smooth finish.

 MED/DRY $17 V+

Waipara Hills Waipara Valley Pinot Gris   ★★★★

The 2015 vintage (★★★★) is an attractively scented, off-dry style with mouthfilling body and youthful, peachy, gently spicy, slightly gingery flavours. Showing very good varietal character and depth, it's a finely textured wine, likely to be at its best 2017+.

 MED/DRY $22 V+

Wairau River Marlborough Pinot Gris   ★★★★

The 2015 vintage (★★★☆) was mostly handled in tanks, but 5 per cent was barrel-aged. It is mouthfilling and vibrantly fruity, with peach, pear and spice flavours, showing good depth, and a finely balanced, dry (2.8 grams/litre of residual sugar) finish. The 2016 vintage (★★★★) is mouthfilling and slightly creamy-textured, with a sliver of sweetness (7 grams/litre of residual sugar) and vibrant, citrusy, slightly peachy and spicy flavours, showing very good vigour and depth. Best drinking mid-2017+.

Vintage	16	15	14	13
WR	6	7	7	5
Drink	16-19	16-20	16-19	16-18

 MED/DRY $20 V+

Whitehaven Marlborough Pinot Gris   ★★★★

The 2014 vintage (★★★★) is a fragrant, full-bodied, vibrantly fruity wine, partly hand-harvested, with strong, peachy, slightly spicy and gingery flavours, and a dryish (6 grams/litre of residual sugar), finely balanced finish. Delicious in its youth.

 MED/DRY $23 AV

Wither Hills Early Light Marlborough Pinot Gris   (★★★☆)

The 2014 vintage (★★★☆) is clearly one of the best low-alcohol Pinot Gris on the market. Peachy and slightly spicy, it shows clear-cut varietal character, and a small amount of wood handling has even given it a touch of complexity. Light-bodied (9.5 per cent alcohol), it is fragrant, fresh, lively and flavoursome, with a slightly sweet, crisp, finely balanced finish. Drink now to 2017.

MED/DRY $17 V+

Wooing Tree Central Otago Pinot Gris   (★★★☆)

Grown at Alexandra, the 2015 vintage (★★★☆) was hand-picked, tank-fermented and made in an off-dry (7.8 grams/litre of residual sugar) style. Pale, it is mouthfilling, vibrantly fruity and smooth, with fresh, citrusy, peachy flavours, showing good depth, and a smooth finish. Drink now onwards.

 MED/DRY $32 –V

Yealands Estate Land Made Marlborough Pinot Gris ★★★☆

The 2015 vintage (★★★☆) is mouthfilling and dry (4 grams/litre of residual sugar), with fresh acidity and vibrant pear/spice flavours that linger well.

Vintage	15	14
WR	6	7
Drink	16-17	P

 DRY $20 AV

Yealands Estate Single Vineyard Marlborough Pinot Gris ★★★★

Estate-grown in the Seaview Vineyard, in the Awatere Valley, the 2015 vintage (★★★★) is scented and full-bodied, with lychee, pear, peach and spice flavours, fresh, lively and generous. Made in a dry style (4 grams/litre of residual sugar), it's delicious young.

Vintage	15	14
WR	6	6
Drink	16-17	16-17

DRY $23 AV

Riesling

Riesling isn't yet one of New Zealand's great successes in overseas markets and most New Zealand wine lovers also ignore Riesling. The favourite white-wine variety of many winemakers, Riesling barely registers on the wine sales charts in supermarkets, generating about 1 per cent of the dollar turnover.

Around the world, Riesling has traditionally been regarded as Chardonnay's great rival in the white-wine quality stakes, well ahead of Sauvignon Blanc. So why are wine lovers here slow to appreciate Riesling's stature?

Riesling is usually made in a slightly sweet style, to balance the grape's natural high acidity, but this obvious touch of sweetness runs counter to the fashion for dry wines. And fine Riesling demands time (at the very least, a couple of years) to unfold its full potential; drunk in its infancy, as it so often is, it lacks the toasty, minerally, honeyed richness that is the real glory of Riesling.

After being overhauled by Pinot Gris in 2007, Riesling ranks as New Zealand's fourth most extensively planted white-wine variety. Between 2007 and 2017, its total area of bearing vines has contracted slightly, from 868 to 768 hectares.

The great grape of Germany, Riesling is a classic cool-climate variety, particularly well suited to the cooler growing temperatures and lower humidity of the South Island. Its two strongholds are Marlborough (where 40 per cent of the vines are clustered) and Canterbury (38 per cent), but the grape is also extensively planted in Otago, Nelson and Wairarapa.

Riesling styles vary markedly around the world. Most Marlborough wines are medium to full-bodied (12 to 13.5 per cent alcohol), with just a touch of sweetness. However, a new breed of Riesling has emerged in the past decade – lighter (only 7.5 to 10 per cent alcohol) and markedly sweeter. These refreshingly light, sweet Rieslings offer a more vivid contrast in style to New Zealand's other major white wines, and are much closer in style to the classic German model.

36 Bottles Central Otago Riesling ★★★★

Grown at Bannockburn, in the Cromwell Basin, the 2014 vintage (★★★★) has good intensity of lemony, limey, slightly spicy flavour, a sliver of sweetness (6.5 grams/litre of residual sugar), lively acidity, and obvious potential.

Vintage	14	13
WR	6	7
Drink	16-21	16-22

MED/DRY $25 AV

Abbey Cellars Hawke's Bay Medium Dry Riesling ★★★☆

Estate-grown and hand-picked in the Bridge Pa Triangle, the 2014 vintage (★★★★) is a tightly structured, medium-bodied (11 per cent alcohol) wine, with citrusy flavours, showing excellent vibrancy and depth.

MED/DRY $22 AV

Akarua Central Otago Riesling ★★★☆

The pale 2015 vintage (★★★) was hand-picked at Bannockburn at 19.8 brix. Still very youthful, it is an off-dry style (9 grams/litre of residual sugar) with fresh, restrained, citrusy, appley flavours. Best drinking mid-2017 onwards.

MED/DRY $28 –V

Allan Scott Family Winemakers Marlborough Riesling   ★★★★

The 2015 vintage (★★★☆) is a mouthfilling (13 per cent alcohol), medium-dry wine with a slightly minerally bouquet. Showing some early development, it is fleshy, ripe and citrusy, with slightly toasty notes and a rounded finish. Priced right.

MED/DRY $18 V+

Allan Scott Generations Marlborough Dry Riesling   (★★★★)

The debut 2015 vintage (★★★★) is a generous, youthful wine, estate-grown in the Moorlands Vineyard, in the heart of the Wairau Valley. Mouthfilling, with a dry feel (5 grams/litre of residual sugar), it has strong, ripe, citrusy, slightly peachy flavours, balanced acidity, and lots of drink-young appeal, but should also reward cellaring.

MED/DRY $26 –V

Allan Scott Generations Marlborough Riesling   (★★★★)

Launched from the 2015 vintage (★★★★), this estate-grown wine is from the Moorlands Vineyard, in the heart of the Wairau Valley, with some botrytis-affected grapes in the blend. Pale lemon/green, with a gently honeyed bouquet, it has moderate acidity, gentle sweetness (34 grams/litre of residual sugar), and strong, peachy, slightly spicy flavours. An age-worthy wine, it's already delicious.

MED $26 –V

Amisfield Dry Central Otago Riesling   ★★★★☆

Estate-grown at Pisa, in the Cromwell Basin, the 2014 vintage (★★★★☆) was hand-picked and fermented with cultured and indigenous yeasts. Bright, light lemon/green, it is tightly structured, with strong, vibrant lemon/lime flavours, tense acidity, minerally, toasty notes adding complexity and a finely balanced, dryish (9.5 grams/litre of residual sugar), lingering finish. A classic 'dry' style. It's very age-worthy, but already full of interest.

MED/DRY $25 V+

Amisfield Lowburn Terrace Central Otago Riesling   ★★★★☆

Estate-grown in the Cromwell Basin, the 2014 vintage (★★★★☆) was hand-picked and made in a low-alcohol (9 per cent), sweetish style (56 grams/litre of residual sugar). A Mosel-like wine, with firm acid spine, it is citrusy, poised and lively, with strong, lemony, slightly peachy flavours, finely balanced and already delicious.

SW $25 V+

Anchorage Family Estate Classic Nelson Riesling   ★★★☆

Light and lively, with low alcohol (9 per cent), the 2015 vintage (★★★☆) has strong, crisp lemon/lime flavours, a sliver of sweetness (7.1 grams/litre of residual sugar) and tangy acidity. Finely balanced for early drinking, it's priced sharply.

MED/DRY $17 V+

Anchorage St Urbanus Nelson Riesling   (★★★)

The 2014 vintage (★★★) is a partly barrel-fermented, dry wine (2.5 grams/litre of residual sugar). Medium-bodied, it is citrusy, with moderate acidity (for Riesling) and good freshness, depth and drinkability.

DRY $19 AV

Aronui Single Vineyard Nelson Riesling (★★★★)

The finely balanced 2014 vintage (★★★★) was grown on the Waimea Plains and made in a medium-dry style (11 grams/litre of residual sugar). It has moderate acidity for Riesling and strong, lively, citrusy, slightly spicy and gingery flavours, showing good vigour, depth and harmony.

 MED/DRY $25 AV

Astrolabe Province Marlborough Dry Riesling ★★★★

The 2015 vintage (★★★★) was hand-picked at Grovetown, in the lower Wairau Valley, and tank-fermented to dryness (4 grams/litre of residual sugar). It is very finely poised, with good intensity of fresh, lemony, slightly appley and spicy flavours, lively but not high acidity, a minerally streak, and obvious cellaring potential. Best drinking 2017+.

 DRY $23 AV

Astrolabe Valleys Wairau Valley Marlborough Riesling ★★★★

The 2014 vintage (★★★★) was grown at Grovetown, in the lower Wairau Valley, and tank-fermented. Made in a medium-dry style (6.8 grams/litre of residual sugar), it has strong, ripe grapefruit/lime flavours, fresh, balanced acidity, slightly toasty, bottle-aged characters emerging and good harmony.

 MED/DRY $20 V+

Ata Mara Central Otago Riesling (★★★★)

The 2014 vintage (★★★★) is a youthful, tightly structured and vigorous wine, with good intensity of fresh, lemony, limey flavours, slightly sweet (17 grams/litre of residual sugar), crisp and strong. Best drinking 2017+.

 MED $27 –V

Ataahua Waipara Riesling ★★★★

Light lemon/green, the 2015 vintage (★★★☆) is a youthful, medium-bodied wine, slightly sweet, with good depth of ripe, citrusy, limey flavours, hints of peaches and passionfruit, fresh acidity and a tight finish. Good drinking mid-2017+.

 MED $26 –V

Aurum Central Otago Riesling ★★★★☆

Freshly scented, lively and tangy, the 2014 vintage (★★★★★) is a medium-bodied wine with intense lemon/lime flavours, a minerally streak and a finely poised, dryish, very long finish. Full of personality and potential, it's certified organic.

Vintage	14
WR	6
Drink	18-24

MED/DRY $26 AV

Babich Family Estates Cowslip Valley Marlborough Riesling ★★★☆

Estate-grown in the Waihopai Valley, the youthful 2015 vintage (★★★☆) is a medium-bodied, dryish style, with a scented, lemony bouquet. Light lemon/green, it is peachy and citrusy, with hints of spices and ginger, and an appetisingly crisp finish. Best drinking 2018+.

 MED/DRY $25 –V

Bald Hills Central Otago Riesling (★★★★☆)

The 2015 vintage (★★★★☆) was grown at Bannockburn. An elegant, tightly structured, youthful wine, it has excellent depth of vibrant, delicate lemon/lime flavours, in a medium style (23 grams/litre of residual sugar) with finely balanced acidity. Delicious young, it should be at its best 2017+.

MED $28 AV

Bannock Brae Central Otago Riesling ★★★★

Grown at Bannockburn and fermented in seasoned French oak barriques, the youthful 2015 vintage (★★★★) is a medium-bodied, finely poised wine with strong, peachy, citrusy, slightly spicy flavours, showing a touch of complexity, and an off-dry (14 grams/litre of residual sugar), crisp finish. Showing good intensity and harmony, it's a drink-now or cellaring proposition.

MED/DRY $25 AV

Beach House Stoney Beach Gravels Hawke's Bay Riesling (★★★★)

The 2014 vintage (★★★★) was hand-picked at Te Awanga. A top example of Hawke's Bay Riesling, it is crisp and light-bodied (9 per cent alcohol), with lively, penetrating lemon/apple flavours, a hint of apricot, and a slightly sweet, racy finish.

MED $20 V+

Black Estate Damsteep Waipara Valley Riesling (★★★★☆)

From vines planted in 1999, the 2015 vintage (★★★★☆) was hand-picked at 19.8 to 23.6 brix and fermented with indigenous yeasts in tanks (95 per cent) and old 500-litre barrels (5 per cent). Pale straw, it is mouthfilling and fleshy, in a dryish style (6 grams/litre of residual sugar) with concentrated, peachy flavours, slightly spicy, gingery and honeyed, finely balanced acidity, and excellent vigour and harmony. Drink now or cellar.

MED/DRY $28 AV

Black Estate Waipara Valley Riesling ★★★★

For the 2014 vintage (★★★★), Black Estate 'sourced a parcel of local, hand-harvested fruit'. A slightly honeyed wine, it's drinking well in its youth, with rich, citrusy, peachy, spicy flavours, good complexity, and a dryish finish.

MED/DRY $24 AV

Black Peak Wanaka Central Otago Riesling ★★★★

The 2015 vintage (★★★★) is an instantly appealing, vivacious wine, light (8.9 per cent alcohol) and gently sweet (48 grams/litre of residual sugar), with a freshly scented bouquet, strong, vibrant lemon/lime flavours, good acid spine and a lengthy finish. Drink now or cellar.

MED $26 –V

Black Stilt Waitaki Valley Riesling ★★★☆

Priced sharply, the 2014 vintage (★★★☆) is a medium-bodied North Otago wine with good depth of lemony, slightly peachy and appley flavours and a finely balanced, off-dry, smooth finish. Enjoyable young.

MED/DRY $18 V+

Brancott Estate Flight Waipara Riesling   ★★★

Offering very easy drinking, the 2015 vintage (★★☆) is a light wine (9 per cent alcohol), gently sweet, with decent depth of tangy, citrusy, limey flavours.

MED $17 AV

Brancott Estate Waipara Riesling   ★★★☆

Priced right, the 2016 vintage (★★★☆) is a vibrantly fruity, crisp, medium-bodied wine with a sliver of sweetness and good depth of citrusy, slightly spicy flavours. Fresh, youthful and finely balanced, it should be at its best mid-2017+.

MED/DRY $17 V+

Brightside Nelson Riesling   ★★★☆

From Kaimira Estate, the 2014 vintage (★★★☆) is a medium-dry style (10 grams/litre of residual sugar), lemon-scented, with strong, citrusy, slightly peachy and spicy flavours, finely balanced for very enjoyable early drinking. Certified organic, it's priced sharply.

MED/DRY $15 V+

Brightwater Vineyards Nelson Riesling   ★★★★☆

Estate-grown and hand-picked on the Waimea Plains, the classy 2015 vintage (★★★★★) is richly scented, with incisive lemon, lime and passionfruit flavours, and an off-dry (14 grams/litre of residual sugar), mouth-wateringly crisp finish. Very fresh and concentrated, with a minerally streak, it's a beautifully poised wine, already highly expressive, but well worth cellaring. A top buy.

Vintage	15	14
WR	6	5
Drink	16-19	16-18

MED/DRY $20 V+

Burn Cottage Central Otago Riesling/Grüner Veltliner   (★★★★☆)

Launched in 2016, the debut 2014 vintage (★★★★☆) is an estate-grown blend of Riesling (53 per cent) and Grüner Veltliner (47 per cent), fermented and matured for 11 months in stainless steel barrels and old oak barriques. Light lemon/green, it is medium-bodied, with penetrating, vibrant, citrusy flavours and a tightly structured, sustained finish. A dryish style (5.6 grams/litre of residual sugar) with finely balanced acidity, a minerally thread and plenty of personality, it's still developing and likely to be at its best 2018+.

MED/DRY $55 –V

Camshorn Classic Riesling   ★★★★

The 2015 vintage (★★★★) from Pernod Ricard is a good buy. Bright, light lemon/green, it is attractively scented and light-bodied (10.5 per cent alcohol), with generous, ripe, peachy flavours, moderate acidity and a smooth finish. It's already drinking well.

MED $20 V+

Carrick Bannockburn Central Otago Riesling   ★★★★★

Estate-grown, the youthful 2014 vintage (★★★★★) is intense and tangy, with fresh, vibrant lemon/lime flavours, slightly sweet (18 grams/litre of residual sugar), crisp, finely poised and lasting. Delicious young, it should be long-lived. Certified organic.

Vintage	14	13	12	11	10
WR	7	7	7	6	7
Drink	16-20	16-18	16-18	16-17	16-17

MED $25 V+

Carrick Central Otago Dry Riesling   ★★★★☆

Grown at Bannockburn, the 2014 vintage (★★★★☆) is a full-bodied wine, youthful, with strong, citrusy, limey flavours and a crisp, long, dry (5 grams/litre of residual sugar) but not austere finish. Certified organic. Best drinking 2018+.

MED/DRY $25 V+

Carrick Josephine Central Otago Riesling   ★★★★★

Estate-grown at Bannockburn, hand-harvested, and stop-fermented in a low-alcohol (9 per cent) style, the 2015 vintage (★★★★★) is a very fresh and vibrant, sweetish wine (68 grams/litre of residual sugar), with lovely poise, vigour and intensity of grapefruit/lime flavours. Offering a lovely interplay of sweetness and acidity, it's delicious from the start. Certified organic.

Vintage	15	14	13	12	11	10
WR	7	7	7	7	6	7
Drink	16-20	16-19	16-18	16-18	16-17	16-17

SW $27 V+

Ceres Black Rabbit Vineyard Central Otago Riesling   (★★★★★)

Already enjoyable, the 2015 vintage (★★★★★) is a highly scented, vivacious wine, grown at Bannockburn. Showing lovely vibrancy and depth, it has intense lemon/lime flavours, a minerally streak and a long, slightly sweet (30 grams/litre of residual sugar) and spicy, tangy finish. Great value.

MED $23 V+

Ceres Composition Central Otago Riesling   (★★★★)

The 2014 vintage (★★★★) is a fragrant Bannockburn wine with strong, citrusy, limey aromas and flavours, showing good freshness and vigour, tangy acidity, and a finely balanced, slightly sweet, appetisingly crisp finish.

MED/DRY $23 AV

Chard Farm Central Otago Riesling   (★★★☆)

The 2014 vintage (★★★☆) was estate-grown in the Viper Vineyard, at Parkburn, in the Cromwell Basin. An off-dry wine, it is medium-bodied, with fresh, citrusy, slightly spicy flavours, tangy acidity, and very good balance and length.

MED/DRY $24 –V

Clark Estate Upper Awatere Block 8 Marlborough Riesling   ★★★★

The 2015 vintage (★★★★) of this single-vineyard Riesling is fresh-scented, light (8 per cent alcohol) and lively, with good acid spine and strong, citrusy, appley, slightly peachy flavours. Delicious young, it's also worth cellaring.

MED $28 –V

Coney The Ritz Martinborough Riesling   ★★★☆

The 2014 vintage (★★★☆) is a 'spritzig' (faintly sparkling) wine, light (9 per cent alcohol) and crisp, with a splash of sweetness (31 grams/litre of residual sugar) amid its tangy, lemony, limey flavours, which show good freshness, balance and depth.

MED $20 AV

Coopers Creek Marlborough Riesling   ★★★☆

The 2015 vintage (★★★☆) is medium-bodied and tangy, in an off-dry style with fresh, lemony, slightly limey flavours, showing very good depth and vigour.

MED/DRY $18 V+

Craggy Range Te Muna Road Vineyard Martinborough Riesling   ★★★☆

The 2014 vintage (★★★☆) was hand-picked at 19.8 brix and fermented with some use of indigenous yeasts. Aromatic, it is fresh, light (11.5 per cent alcohol) and lively, with very good vigour and depth of lemony, limey flavours, dryish (7 grams/litre of residual sugar) and racy. Best drinking 2017+.

MED/DRY $27 –V

Dashwood Marlborough Riesling   ★★★☆

The 2015 vintage (★★★★) is a floral, medium-bodied, reasonably dry but not austere wine, vibrantly fruity. It has finely balanced acidity, with citrusy, limey flavours, showing very good delicacy and depth.

MED/DRY $19 V+

Doctors', The, Marlborough Riesling   ★★★★

From Forrest, this is a low-alcohol style. The 2014 vintage (★★★★) is an elegant, tightly structured wine, light-bodied (9 per cent alcohol), with youthful, vibrant, citrusy, limey flavours, finely poised and lingering. Drink now or cellar.

Vintage	14	13	12	11	10
WR	6	6	6	6	6
Drink	16-23	16-22	16-21	16-20	16-20

 MED $22 V+

Drowsy Fish by Crown Range Cellar Waipara Riesling   (★★★★)

Already drinking well, the 2015 vintage (★★★★) was hand-harvested and produced in a distinctly medium style (23 grams/litre of residual sugar). Pale straw, it is fleshy, with peachy, slightly spicy flavours, showing a touch of complexity, finely balanced acidity, and a long, harmonious finish.

 MED $50 –V

Dry River Craighall Vineyard Martinborough Riesling   ★★★★★

One of the finest Rieslings in the country, this is typically a wine of exceptional purity, delicacy and depth, with a proven ability to flourish in the cellar for many years. The grapes are sourced from a small block of mature vines, mostly over 20 years old, in the Craighall Vineyard, with yields limited to an average of 6 tonnes per hectare, and the wine is stop-fermented just short of dryness. The 2015 vintage (★★★★★) is full-bodied, with deep, citrusy, peachy, slightly limey and biscuity flavours, that build across the palate to a very harmonious and lasting finish. Not at all austere, it's already very expressive, but well worth cellaring.

MED/DRY $47 AV

Dry River Craighall Vineyard Selection Martinborough Riesling   ★★★★★

From the 'ripest parcels of fruit, picked later', this wine is made to 'produce a Riesling with low alcohol, high residual sugar and high acidity, in order to create a tension between these components'. The 2015 vintage (★★★★★) is already very open, expressive and enjoyable. Harbouring just 8 per cent alcohol, it has concentrated, ripe, peachy, slightly lemony and spicy flavours, abundant sweetness (70 grams/litre of residual sugar), lively acidity and a finely balanced, very persistent finish. Drink now or cellar.

SW $59 AV

Esk Valley Marlborough Riesling   ★★★★

The 2015 vintage (★★★★) is from mature vines, grown in the Wairau Valley. Made in an appetisingly crisp, dryish style (6.5 grams/litre of residual sugar), it is lemon-scented, with good intensity of finely balanced, citrusy, slightly limey flavours.

MED/DRY $20 V+

Falconhead Marlborough Riesling   (★★★)

Still on sale, the 2011 vintage (★★★) is ready to roll. Bright, light lemon/green, it's an easy-drinking wine, mouthfilling, with citrusy, slightly sweet and toasty flavours, hints of peaches and spices, and a touch of bottle-aged complexity.

MED/DRY $16 V+

Felton Road Bannockburn Central Otago Riesling   ★★★★★

Estate-grown in The Elms Vineyard, this gently sweet style has deep flavours woven with fresh acidity. It offers more drink-young appeal than its Dry Riesling stablemate, but invites long-term cellaring. Hand-picked and tank-fermented with indigenous yeasts, it is bottled with a high level of residual sugar (63 grams/litre in 2016). The 2016 vintage (★★★★★) is bright, light lemon/green. A Mosel-like wine, it is light (9.5 per cent alcohol), with vibrant lemon/lime flavours, a hint of sherbet, and lovely depth, balance and freshness. Delicious from the start, it's a drink-now or cellaring proposition.

Vintage	16
WR	7
Drink	16-36

SW $35 AV

Felton Road Block 1 Riesling – see Sweet White Wines

Felton Road Dry Riesling ★★★★★

Based on low-yielding vines in schisty soils at Bannockburn, in Central Otago, this wine is hand-picked in The Elms Vineyard and fermented with indigenous yeasts. The 2015 vintage (★★★★★) is beautifully scented and finely poised, with deep, peachy, slightly spicy flavours, showing notable vigour and richness. The 2016 vintage (★★★★★) is pale/lemon green, with an inviting fragrance. Mouthfilling (13.5 per cent alcohol) and vibrant, it is finely balanced, with intense, citrusy, slightly spicy flavours, fresh acidity, a whisker of sweetness (5.3 grams/litre of residual sugar), and a lasting finish. Best drinking 2018+.

Vintage	16
WR	7
Drink	16-31

 DRY $35 V+

Framingham Classic Marlborough Riesling ★★★★★

Top vintages of this Marlborough wine are strikingly aromatic, richly flavoured and zesty. The 2014 vintage (★★★★☆) is a full-bodied wine, with concentrated, lemony, limey, slightly spicy flavours, a gentle splash of sweetness (17 grams/litre of residual sugar), and fresh, tangy acidity. It's highly enjoyable in its youth, but also has obvious potential; best drinking 2017+.

Vintage	14
WR	6
Drink	16-22

 MED $25 V+

Framingham F-Series Old Vine Marlborough Riesling ★★★★★

From estate vines planted at Renwick over 30 years ago, the 2014 vintage (★★★★★) of this organically certified wine is promoted as an 'Old World style, with more texture and complexity'. Full-bodied, it has fresh, ripe, peachy flavours, gentle acidity for Riesling, and a distinct touch of complexity (19 per cent of the blend was matured for 10 months in old oak barrels). Weighty, finely textured and lingering, it's a distinctive, dryish (8.5 grams/litre of residual sugar), 'food-worthy' Riesling, for drinking now or cellaring.

Vintage	14
WR	7
Drink	16-21

 MED/DRY $40 AV

Framingham F-Series Riesling Kabinett ★★★★☆

The 2015 is only the second vintage of this label, after the slightly sweeter 2011. The 2015 vintage (★★★★☆) is a medium-sweet style (48 grams/litre of residual sugar), handled in tanks (60 per cent) and old oak casks (40 per cent). Light-bodied (9 per cent alcohol), it has fresh, incisive, lemony, appley, slightly peachy and spicy flavours, gentle sweetness (48 grams/litre of residual sugar), good acid spine, a minerally streak, and a long finish. Still youthful, it should mature gracefully; best drinking 2017+.

MED $35 –V

Gibbston Valley Central Otago Riesling ★★★★

Estate-grown in the Red Shed Vineyard, at Bendigo, the 2014 vintage (★★★☆) is mouthfilling, with very good depth of citrusy, slightly peachy and spicy flavours, a touch of sweetness (8.7 grams/litre of residual sugar), lively acidity and obvious potential. (This label has been replaced by the GV Collection Central Otago Riesling – see below.)

Vintage	14	13
WR	7	7
Drink	16-25	16-20

MED/DRY $28 –V

Gibbston Valley GV Collection Central Otago Riesling ★★★★

The debut 2016 vintage (★★★★) is an estate-grown, single-vineyard wine, hand-picked at Bendigo. Light lemon/green, it's still a baby, with good intensity of vibrant, citrusy, appley, slightly spicy flavours, showing excellent delicacy, and a finely poised dryish (8 grams/litre of residual sugar) finish. Best drinking 2018+.

MED/DRY $28 –V

Gibbston Valley Le Fou Riesling ★★★★★

Estate-grown in the Red Shed Vineyard, at Bendigo, in Central Otago, the 2015 (★★★★★) is the first vintage not based on old vines at Gibbston. Hand-picked, it is pale lemon/green, with lovely freshness, delicacy and poise. It has concentrated, citrusy, slightly limey and spicy flavours that build across the palate to a very harmonious, lasting finish. A very classy, medium wine (28 grams/litre of residual sugar), it's already delicious; drink now or cellar.

Vintage	15	14	13	12	11	10	09	08	07
WR	7	7	7	7	NM	7	6	7	7
Drink	16-26	16-25	16-25	16-25	NM	16-23	16-20	16-20	16-18

MED $39 AV

Giesen Marlborough Riesling ★★★★

The 2015 vintage (★★★★) is a low-alcohol (10 per cent), medium-sweet style (44 grams/litre of residual sugar). Grown in Marlborough and Waipara, it is fresh and vibrantly fruity, with crisp, citrusy flavours, showing good intensity. A poised, vivacious wine, it's a drink-now or cellaring proposition.

MED $17 V+

Giesen The Brothers Marlborough Riesling (★★★★☆)

The 2013 vintage (★★★★☆) is delicious now. Although packaged in a full-size bottle, it could easily be in the Sweet White Wines section of the book, given its abundant sweetness (80 grams/litre of residual sugar). Scented and rich, it is still youthful, with concentrated, citrusy flavours, lively acidity, toasty, bottle-aged notes starting to emerge, and a long, smooth finish. Drink now or cellar.

Vintage	13
WR	6
Drink	16-20

SW $33 V+

Grava Martinborough Riesling   (★★★★)

The 2015 vintage (★★★★) was estate-grown south of Martinborough, at a site formerly called Hudson Vineyard. Light lemon/green, it's an instantly appealing, off-dry style (12 grams/litre of residual sugar), medium-bodied, with vibrant, citrusy, peachy flavours, a hint of passionfruit, and excellent freshness and harmony. Drink now or cellar.

 MED/DRY $30 –V

Greenhough Apple Valley Nelson Riesling   ★★★★

Grown and hand-picked at Upper Moutere, the 2015 vintage (★★★★) is light-bodied (9.5 per cent alcohol) and gently sweet (36 grams/litre of residual sugar). Pale and lively, it is youthful, with appetising acidity, a minerally streak and good intensity of fresh, citrusy, appley flavours. Best drinking mid-2017+.

Vintage	15	14	13	12	11	10	09
WR	6	7	7	7	7	6	6
Drink	16-20	16-20	16-19	16-18	16-17	P	P

 MED $22 V+

Greenhough Hope Vineyard Riesling   ★★★★☆

This Nelson wine is hand-picked from vines that average over 20 years old. The 2013 vintage (★★★★☆) is tightly structured, tense and tangy, with strong lemon, lime, apple and spice flavours, fractional sweetness (7 grams/litre of residual sugar), and a lasting finish. Certified organic.

Vintage	13	12	11	10	09
WR	6	6	6	7	7
Drink	16-20	16-19	16-17	P	P

 MED/DRY $24 V+

Greystone Waipara Valley Riesling   ★★★★★

Greystone sees this wine as 'the truest expression of the variety for us'. Estate-grown and hand-harvested at over 23 brix, with a small percentage of 'noble rot', the 2015 vintage (★★★★★) is a medium style (23 grams/litre of residual sugar). A lovely young wine, it is full-bodied, with strong, ripe, citrusy, peachy flavours, hints of lime, spice and honey, and excellent concentration and harmony. Instantly appealing.

Vintage	15	14	13	12	11	10	09	08	07
WR	7	5	7	6	7	7	6	6	5
Drink	16-30	16-20	16-22	16-20	16-21	16-20	P	P	P

 MED $27 V+

Greywacke Marlborough Riesling ★★★★★

The 2015 vintage (★★★★☆) was hand-picked from mature vines at Fairhall. Half of the juice was fermented with indigenous yeasts in old French oak barrels, and all of the wine was oak-aged for five months. Made in a medium style (20 grams/litre of residual sugar), it is instantly attractive, with ripe-fruit flavours of peaches, passionfruit and limes, gentle sweetness, a touch of complexity, and excellent harmony and concentration. Best drinking 2018+.

Vintage	15	14	13	12	11	10	09
WR	5	5	6	5	6	5	6
Drink	17-21	17-21	17-20	17-18	17-19	17-20	16-17

 MED $29 V+

Grove Mill Wairau Valley Marlborough Riesling ★★★☆

The 2015 vintage (★★★☆) is fragrant and fleshy, with strong, ripe, citrusy, limey flavours, showing good freshness, acidity and length.

MED $21 AV

Hans Herzog Marlborough Riesling ★★★★☆

Certified organic, the characterful 2013 vintage (★★★★★) was estate-grown in the Wairau Valley and matured for a year in French oak puncheons. Bright, light lemon/green, it is mouthfilling and vibrantly fruity, with good intensity of grapefruit and lime flavours, a very subtle seasoning of oak adding richness, inconspicuous sweetness (6 grams/litre of residual sugar) and excellent harmony. Best drinking 2018+.

Vintage	13
WR	7
Drink	16-23

 MED/DRY $44 –V

Hawkshead Central Otago Riesling ★★★★

Grown at Lowburn, hand-picked and tank-fermented, the 2014 vintage (★★★★) is a slightly sweet style (10 grams/litre of residual sugar). Full-bodied, it is still youthful, with generous citrusy, limey flavours, a minerally streak, good acid spine, and a lingering finish. Finely balanced for easy drinking, it's a drink-now or cellaring proposition.

Vintage	14	13	12
WR	6	6	6
Drink	16-19	16-18	16-17

MED/DRY $23 AV

Highfield Marlborough Riesling ★★★★

The 2015 vintage (★★★★) is already drinking well. Made in a gently sweet style (24 grams/litre of residual sugar), it is a light lemon/green, medium-bodied wine, vaguely honeyed, with ripe, peachy, slightly limey and toasty flavours, showing good concentration.

Vintage	15
WR	6
Drink	16-19

MED $21 V+

Huia Marlborough Dry Riesling (★★★★)

The distinctive 2014 vintage (★★★★) is a single-vineyard wine, certified organic. Fleshy, ripe and rounded, with a touch of complexity, it is weighty, peachy and slightly spicy, with moderate acidity and a slightly creamy texture. Good food wine.

DRY $25 AV

Hunter's Marlborough Riesling ★★★★

This wine is consistently good and bargain-priced. The youthful 2016 vintage (★★★★) is an off-dry style (7 grams/litre of residual sugar), pale lemon/green, with good intensity of lively, citrusy, slightly spicy flavours, tightly structured and tangy.

MED/DRY $20 V+

Invivo Central Otago Riesling ★★★★

The 2014 vintage (★★★★) is a tangy, medium style (25 grams/litre of residual sugar), with punchy, ripe, peachy, slightly limey and spicy flavours, strong, fresh and finely balanced for early enjoyment. Retasted in September 2016, it is drinking well, with toasty, bottle-aged aromas and flavours emerging.

Vintage	14
WR	6
Drink	16-24

MED $22 V+

Jackson Estate Homestead Marlborough Dry Riesling ★★★★

Drinking well now, but worth cellaring, the 2015 vintage (★★★★) is a bone-dry but not austere style, estate-grown in the Wairau Valley. Full-bodied, with strong, ripe, citrusy, slightly spicy flavours, woven with fresh acidity, it has very good vigour, balance and depth.

DRY $24 AV

Johanneshof Marlborough Riesling ★★★★

From hand-picked grapes, the 2015 vintage (★★★★) is a single-vineyard wine, full-bodied, with strong, citrusy, peachy flavours, a gentle splash of sweetness (15 grams/litre of residual sugar) and appetising acidity. Finely balanced, with a touch of complexity, it's already drinking well.

MED $25 AV

Johner Estate Wairarapa Riesling ★★★★

The pale lemon/green 2016 vintage (★★★★) is a tangy, vivacious wine, medium-dry (11 grams/litre of residual sugar), with lively, citrusy, appley flavours, showing good intensity and harmony. Best drinking 2018+.

Vintage	16	15
WR	6	7
Drink	16-22	16-25

MED/DRY $24 AV

Julicher Martinborough Riesling ★★★★

The 2014 vintage (★★★★) was estate-grown at Te Muna. Light-bodied (10.5 per cent alcohol), it is a vivacious, youthful wine with moderate acidity – for Riesling – and very good depth of ripe, peachy, gently sweet (11 grams/litre of residual sugar), slightly spicy flavours. Delicious young.

MED/DRY $20 V+

Junction Runaway Riesling (★★★☆)

Grown in Central Hawke's Bay, the attractively scented 2015 vintage (★★★☆) is an off-dry style, with lively acidity threaded through its vibrant, grapefruit-like flavours, which show good freshness and depth.

MED/DRY $22 AV

Kaimira Estate Brightwater Riesling ★★★☆

This estate-grown, Nelson wine typically matures well. The 2015 vintage (★★★☆) is fresh and vibrant, with lemon/lime flavours, slightly peachy notes, good depth and a finely balanced, dry finish. Certified organic.

Vintage	15	14	13
WR	5	5	5
Drink	16-21	16-20	16-19

DRY $20 AV

Kaimira Estate Iti Selection Brightwater Riesling ★★★☆

Made in a low-alcohol style ('Iti' is Maori for 'Small'), the 2015 vintage (★★★) is light-bodied (10 per cent), with ripe, lemony, slightly peachy and spicy flavours, gentle sweetness and fresh acidity keeping things lively. Offering very easy drinking, it's certified organic.

MED $20 AV

Kalex Central Otago Riesling ★★★★

Instantly appealing, the 2014 vintage (★★★★) is a light (9.5 per cent alcohol), gently sweet style, grown at Bendigo, in the Cromwell Basin. Tangy, ripe, peachy and slightly spicy, it has good concentration and harmony, in a very expressive style, enjoyable young.

MED $26 –V

Lake Chalice The Falcon Marlborough Riesling ★★★★

The 2014 vintage (★★★★) is a single-vineyard, Awatere Valley wine, harvested early and stop-fermented to produce a low-alcohol (9.5 per cent) style. Delicious young, it is light-bodied, very vibrant and racy, with a splash of sweetness (30 grams/litre of residual sugar), strong lemon/apple flavours, a hint of sherbet, and a finely poised, tangy finish.

MED $21 V+

Lawson's Dry Hills Marlborough Riesling ★★★★☆

The 2015 vintage (★★★★☆) is a single-vineyard wine, grown in the Waihopai Valley. A medium-dry style (10 grams/litre of residual sugar), it is bright, light lemon/green, with excellent intensity of lemon/lime flavours, slightly toasty bottle-aged notes starting to add complexity, good acid spine, and a long finish.

Vintage	15	14
WR	7	6
Drink	16-22	16-20

 MED/DRY $20 V+

Linden Estate Martinborough Riesling (★★★★)

Drinking well now, the 2014 vintage (★★★★) is a pale lemon/green, ripely scented wine, crisp and lively. Light-bodied (10.2 per cent alcohol), it has good intensity of lemon/lime flavours, with a sliver of sweetness (8 grams/litre of residual sugar), fresh, appetising acidity and toasty, bottle-aged complexities starting to emerge.

 MED/DRY $20 V+

Loveblock Bone Dry Marlborough Riesling (★★★★)

Still on sale, with toasty, bottle-aged aromas emerging, the 2011 vintage (★★★★) is a 'real Riesling drinker's Riesling', according to the back label. From young vines in the lower Awatere Valley, it is fully dry (1.4 grams/litre of residual sugar), but not sharp or austere. The bouquet is minerally; the palate is mouthfilling and rich, with finely balanced acidity and grapefruit-like, slightly spicy flavours. Still very lively, it's drinking well now.

 DRY $27 –V

Main Divide Waipara Valley Riesling ★★★★

From Pegasus Bay, this is a bargain. Showing good personality, the 2014 vintage (★★★★) is medium-bodied and tangy, with strong citrus and passionfruit flavours, a hint of oranges, gentle sweetness and lively acidity. Drink now or cellar.

Vintage	14	13
WR	6	7
Drink	16-20	16-22

 MED $21 V+

Marble Point Hanmer Springs Riesling Dry ★★★★

Estate-grown in North Canterbury and matured for two months in old barrels, the 2014 vintage (★★★★) has a fragrant, citrusy, slightly honeyed bouquet. It shows very good freshness, vigour and depth, with strong, lemony flavours, hints of peaches, limes and spices, mouth-watering acidity, good sugar/acid balance (13 grams/litre of residual sugar), and lots of personality.

Vintage	14
WR	6
Drink	16-25

MED/DRY $22 V+

Margrain Proprietor's Selection Martinborough Riesling (★★★★)

Well worth cellaring, the pale lemon/green 2016 vintage (★★★★) is a medium-dry style (9 grams/litre of residual sugar). Medium to full-bodied, it is fresh, crisp and youthful, with good intensity of lemon, apple and lime flavours, slightly sweet and tangy. Best drinking 2018+.

Vintage	16
WR	7
Drink	16-26

 MED/DRY $24 AV

Martinborough Vineyard Manu Riesling ★★★★

The 2014 vintage (★★★☆) is a ripely scented, easy-drinking style of Riesling, with youthful, slightly sweet (15 grams/litre of residual sugar), moderately intense flavours of citrus fruits, pears and peaches. Drink now or cellar. The pale lemon/green 2016 vintage (★★★★☆) is quietly classy. Still a baby, it's a medium-dry style (14 grams/litre of residual sugar), fresh and finely poised, with ripe, citrusy, peachy flavours, showing excellent delicacy, richness and harmony. Best drinking mid-2018+.

 MED/DRY $28 –V

Maude Mt Maude Vineyard East Block Wanaka Riesling ★★★★☆

From vines planted in 1994 on a steep, north-facing slope at Wanaka, in Central Otago, the attractively scented 2015 vintage (★★★★) is a light-bodied (9 per cent alcohol), medium-sweet wine. It has youthful, finely poised, lemony, appley flavours, showing excellent delicacy and harmony. Still a baby, the 2016 vintage (★★★★★) is highly aromatic, light and vivacious, with strong lemon/apple flavours, gentle sweetness (34 grams/litre of residual sugar), racy acidity and obvious potential; open 2019+.

 MED $32 –V

Maude Mt Maude Vineyard Wanaka Dry Riesling ★★★★☆

Crying out for cellaring, the 2015 vintage (★★★★) was hand-picked from vines planted in 1994. Tightly structured, it's a dryish, minerally wine with good acid spine and strong, immaculate lemon/apple flavours. Best drinking mid-2017+. The richly scented 2016 vintage (★★★★★) is even better. Pale lemon/green, it is very refined, intense and minerally, with deep lemon, apple and spice flavours, a sliver of sweetness (9 grams/litre of residual sugar) and mouth-watering acidity. Best drinking 2019+.

 MED/DRY $32 –V

Millton Opou Vineyard Riesling ★★★★☆

Typically scented, with rich, lemony, often honeyed flavours, this is the country's northernmost fine-quality Riesling. Harvested from Gisborne vines of varying ages – the oldest planted in 1981 – it is gently sweet, in a less racy style than South Island wines. The grapes, grown in the Opou Vineyard at Manutuke, are hand-picked over a month at three stages of ripening, usually culminating in a final pick of botrytis-affected fruit. The 2014 vintage (★★★★★) is a low-alcohol (9.5 per cent), gently sweet wine. Light lemon/green, with a fragrant bouquet, it is rich and rounded, with concentrated, peachy, slightly limey flavours, lively and lingering. A top vintage, it's a delicious, very harmonious wine, already drinking well. Certified organic.

Vintage	14	13	12
WR	6	7	6
Drink	16-25	16-22	16-20

MED $28 AV

Misha's Vineyard Limelight Riesling ★★★★★

This single-vineyard wine is hand-harvested at Bendigo, in Central Otago. The 2014 vintage (★★★★) is a highly scented, vibrantly fruity wine, made in a medium style (33 grams/litre of residual sugar), with complexity gained by fermenting 25 per cent of the blend with indigenous yeasts in old French oak barrels. Fleshy, with concentrated, citrusy, limey flavours, appetising acidity and a rich, finely poised finish, it's already delicious, but likely to be at its best 2017+.

Vintage	14	13	12	11	10	09	08
WR	6	7	7	6	6	7	6
Drink	16-21	16-20	16-18	16-19	16-18	16-18	16-17

MED $28 V+

Misha's Vineyard Lyric Riesling ★★★★★

This is the sort of 'dry' Riesling New Zealand needs a lot more of. Estate-grown at Bendigo, in Central Otago, the 2013 vintage (★★★★) is fractionally off-dry (5.5 grams/litre of residual sugar). It was mostly handled in tanks, but 41 per cent of the blend was fermented with indigenous yeasts in old French oak barrels. Lemon-scented, it is elegant and tightly structured, with rich, citrusy, appley, slightly spicy flavours. Weighty, with good complexity and harmony and a long, dry finish, it's already enjoyable but also very age-worthy. (There is no 2014, but the label returns from the 2015 vintage.)

Vintage	14	13	12	11	10	09
WR	NM	7	7	6	6	7
Drink	NM	16-22	16-21	16-20	16-19	16-18

MED/DRY $27 V+

Mission Hawke's Bay Riesling ★★★☆

Finely balanced for easy drinking, the 2015 vintage (★★★★) is a single-vineyard wine, showing good intensity. Aromatic, with strong, ripe, citrusy flavours and a harmonious, off-dry (13 grams/litre of residual sugar), lingering finish, it offers top value.

MED/DRY $18 V+

Misty Cove Marlborough Riesling (★★★★)

The fleshy, full-bodied 2015 vintage (★★★★), branded 'Signature' on the back label, was hand-picked at Rapaura and lees-aged for 16 weeks. It has generous, ripe grapefruit/lime flavours, with a hint of honey, gentle sweetness and balanced acidity. Already enjoyable, it's a drink-now or cellaring proposition.

MED/DRY $24 AV

Mondillo Central Otago Riesling ★★★★

Estate-grown at Bendigo, the 2015 vintage (★★★★) is an almost fully dry style (2.6 grams/litre of residual sugar). Light lemon/green, it is mouthfilling, with strong, youthful lemon/lime flavours, crisp acidity, a minerally streak and good vigour and length. Best drinking 2018+.

Vintage	15	14	13	12	11	10
WR	7	7	7	NM	7	NM
Drink	16-21	16-24	16-22	NM	16-20	NM

DRY $30 –V

Montana Waipara Riesling ★★★

The 2014 vintage (★★★) offers great value, with moderate alcohol (11 per cent) and plenty of fresh, lively, lemony flavour.

MED $12 V+

Mount Edward Central Otago Riesling ★★★★☆

The 2014 vintage (★★★★☆) is a single-vineyard wine, grown at Lowburn. It is a youthful, tight, medium-bodied style with good intensity of vibrant lemon/lime flavours, a minerally streak, and a gently sweet, racy finish. Open 2017+.

MED/DRY $25 V+

Mount Riley Marlborough Riesling ★★★☆

The 2015 vintage (★★★☆), grown in the Wairau Valley, is medium-bodied, with strong, lemony, slightly limey flavours and an off-dry (7.9 grams/litre of residual sugar), crisp finish. It's still youthful; best drinking 2017+.

Vintage	15	14
WR	6	6
Drink	16-18	16-17

MED/DRY $17 V+

Moutere Hills Single Vineyard Nelson Riesling ★★★☆

The 2014 vintage (★★★☆) was grown and hand-picked on the Waimea Plains. A finely balanced, lively, light-bodied wine (under 10 per cent alcohol), it has good depth of fresh, peachy, spicy flavours, a hint of apricot, and gentle sweetness (21 grams/litre of residual sugar) balanced by appetising acidity.

MED $29 –V

Mt Beautiful North Canterbury Riesling ★★★★

Estate-grown at Cheviot, the 2015 vintage (★★★★) is a bright, light lemon/green, attractively scented, very lively wine, medium-bodied, with incisive, citrusy, limey flavours and a gently sweet (14.8 grams/litre of residual sugar) finish. Best drinking mid-2017+.

Vintage	15
WR	7
Drink	16-25

MED/DRY $31 –V

Mt Difficulty Bannockburn Dry Riesling ★★★★

Grown at Bannockburn, this is a wine for purists – steely and austere when young, but rewarding (almost demanding) time. The tightly structured 2015 vintage (★★★★) is pale lemon/green, crisp and dryish, with punchy lemon/lime flavours and obvious potential. Best drinking 2018+.

MED/DRY $26 –V

Mt Difficulty Growers Series Packspur Vineyard Lowburn Riesling (★★★★)

From a late-ripening site, the 2014 vintage (★★★★) is medium-bodied, with a slightly honeyed bouquet and palate. Medium-bodied, it has good intensity of lemon/apple flavours, with a hint of peaches, abundant sweetness (60 grams/litre of residual sugar) balanced by lively acidity, and excellent harmony. Delicious young.

SW $26 –V

Mt Difficulty Target Bannockburn Medium Riesling ★★★★☆

From Central Otago, the 2015 vintage (★★★★☆) is a vibrantly fruity, gently sweet style (43 grams/litre of residual sugar). Light lemon/green, it is a finely poised, medium-bodied wine, with lively acidity and incisive lemon, passionfruit and lime flavours.

MED $26 AV

Mud House Single Vineyard The Mound Waipara Valley Riesling ★★★★

The 2014 vintage (★★★☆) is a poised, vibrantly fruity wine with lemon/lime flavours, showing very good depth, and a slightly sweet, mouth-wateringly crisp finish. Drink now or cellar.

Vintage	14	13
WR	5	7
Drink	16-18	16-18

MED/DRY $24 AV

Mud House Waipara Valley Riesling ★★★★

The lemon-scented 2014 vintage (★★★★) is a single-vineyard, estate-grown wine. A medium-dry style (14 grams/litre of residual sugar), it is lively and finely balanced, with strong citrus-fruit, lime and passionfruit flavours, showing excellent vigour and length.

MED/DRY $18 V+

Muddy Water James Hardwick Waipara Riesling ★★★★★

Certified organic, the youthful 2015 vintage (★★★★☆) is a medium-dry style, hand-harvested (with a touch of botrytis) and fermented with indigenous yeasts. The bouquet is scented; the palate is rich, citrusy and peachy, with a hint of passionfruit, a minerally streak, and excellent complexity and depth. Best drinking 2018+.

Vintage	15
WR	7
Drink	16-30

MED/DRY $28 V+

Neudorf Moutere Riesling ★★★★★

A copybook cool-climate style with excellent intensity, estate-grown at Upper Moutere. The 2014 vintage (★★★★★) was hand-picked in Rosie's Block at 19.7 brix, fermented with indigenous yeasts, and stop-fermented in a medium-sweet style, with just 9.5 per cent alcohol and 48 grams per litre of residual sugar. It is already very expressive, with a slightly minerally streak and deep, peachy, slightly spicy flavours. Drink now or cellar.

MED $30 AV

Neudorf Moutere Riesling Dry   ★★★★☆

The 2015 vintage (★★★★☆) was estate-grown in Rosie's Block, hand-harvested and fermented with indigenous yeasts in tanks (93 per cent) and old oak puncheons (7 per cent). Pale lemon/lime, it is an elegant, tightly structured wine, medium to full-bodied, with strong, citrusy, limey, vaguely biscuity flavours, a gentle splash of sweetness (7.7 grams/litre of residual sugar) and fresh, balanced acidity. Already enjoyable, it should be at its best 2018+.

Vintage	15	MED/DRY $27 AV
WR	7	
Drink	17-25	

Nga Waka Martinborough Dry Riesling   ★★★★☆

Still on sale, the 2013 vintage (★★★★☆) is fleshy, generous and slightly minerally, with strong, ripe, citrusy flavours, hints of peaches and limes, and a finely textured, long finish. A good food wine, it should be at its best 2017+.

Vintage	13	MED/DRY $22 V+
WR	7	
Drink	16-26	

Ohinemuri Estate Waikato Riesling   ★★★

Karangahake Gorge-based winemaker Horst Hillerich usually draws his Riesling grapes from Gisborne, but the 2014 vintage (★★★) was hand-picked near Cambridge in the Waikato. Fermented in tanks (mostly) and old oak barrels (7 per cent), it is fresh, crisp, lemony and appley, with slight sweetness (12 grams/litre of residual sugar), lively acidity and a tight, youthful finish. Best drinking mid-2017+.

Vintage	14	MED/DRY $20 –V
WR	6	
Drink	16-21	

Old Coach Road Lighter in Alcohol Nelson Riesling   (★★★)

From Seifried, the 2015 vintage (★★★) is crisp and slightly sweet (17 grams/litre of residual sugar), with a low level of alcohol (9.5 per cent), vibrant, lemony, appley, limey flavours, firm acid spine, and lots of drink-young charm.

Vintage	16	MED $13 V+
WR	7	
Drink	16-22	

Old Coach Road Nelson Riesling ★★★

From Seifried, this is an enjoyable, drink-young style, priced sharply. The 2015 vintage (★★★☆) is a medium-dry style (8.5 grams/litre of residual sugar). Mouthfilling, it is crisp and lively, with plenty of fresh, citrusy, slightly spicy flavour.

Vintage	15
WR	6
Drink	16-22

MED/DRY $13 V+

Omeo Blackman's Gully Central Otago Riesling (★★★☆)

Grown at Alexandra, the 2014 vintage (★★★☆) is a light lemon/green, slightly sweet style (15 grams/litre of residual sugar), with firm acid spine and youthful lemon/apple flavours, crisp, lively and racy. Best drinking 2017+.

Vintage	14
WR	5
Drink	16-22

MED $21 AV

Ostler Lakeside Vines Waitaki Valley North Otago Riesling ★★★★

Grown at Lake Waitaki, the 2013 vintage (★★★★) is a peachy, citrusy wine, woven with cool-climate acidity, with very good depth and an off-dry, tangy finish. It's a strongly varietal wine, for drinking now or cellaring.

Vintage	13
WR	6
Drink	16-25

MED/DRY $30 –V

Paddy Borthwick New Zealand Riesling ★★★☆

Balanced for easy drinking, the 2015 vintage (★★★★) was grown at Gladstone, in the Wairarapa. Fleshy, it has generous peach and grapefruit flavours, hints of passionfruit and spices, lively acidity, a gentle splash of sweetness (6.6 grams/litre of residual sugar), and lots of drink-young appeal.

MED/DRY $22 AV

Palliser Estate Martinborough Riesling ★★★☆

Instantly attractive, the 2015 vintage (★★★★) is a finely scented wine with fresh, citrusy, limey, slightly sweet flavours that linger well. Skilfully crafted for early enjoyment, it's also well worth cellaring.

MED/DRY $23 –V

Paulownia Estate Riesling (★★★★)

Estate-grown near Masterton, in the northern Wairarapa, the generous 2013 vintage (★★★★) is still on sale. Bright, light yellow/green, it is fleshy and rich, with mouthfilling body and strong grapefruit and lime flavours, acquiring bottle-aged complexity. Fine value.

MED/DRY $20 V+

Pegasus Bay Aria Late Picked Riesling – see Sweet White Wines

Pegasus Bay Bel Canto Riesling Dry   ★★★★★

Bel Canto means 'Beautiful Singing'. Late-harvested at Waipara from mature vines and made with 'a good portion' of noble rot, the distinctive 2014 vintage (★★★★) is a very powerful and fleshy wine (14.5 per cent alcohol), with generous, ripe, peachy, slightly honeyed flavours, a vague hint of oak adding complexity, and lots of drink-young appeal.

 DRY $33 AV

Pegasus Bay Riesling   ★★★★★

Classy stuff. Estate-grown at Waipara, in North Canterbury, in top vintages it is richly fragrant and thrillingly intense, with flavours of citrus fruits and honey, complex and luscious. Based on mature vines and stop-fermented in a distinctly medium style, it breaks into full stride at about three years old and can mature well for a decade. The 2013 vintage (★★★★☆) was harvested in May with a 'good portion of lovely, clean botrytis'. Light gold, it is full-bodied, fresh and lively, with slightly honeyed aromas and flavours, crisp, peachy and slightly spicy, with good concentration. It's already quite expressive; drink now or cellar. The 2014 vintage (★★★★★) is bright, light lemon/green. Mouthfilling, it is gently sweet, with a hint of honey and penetrating, peachy, slightly spicy flavours, showing lovely freshness, depth and harmony.

Vintage	14	13	12	11	10
WR	7	6	7	6	7
Drink	16-28	16-27	16-27	16-25	16-22

 MED $30 AV

Peter Yealands Marlborough Riesling   ★★★

The 2015 vintage (★★★☆) is a lively, medium-bodied wine with lemony, limey flavours, gentle sweetness (7 grams/litre of residual sugar), fresh acidity, and very good varietal character, depth and harmony. Priced right.

Vintage	15	14
WR	7	5
Drink	16-18	16-18

 MED/DRY $16 V+

Pisa Range Estate Pisa Central Otago Riesling   ★★★★

The 2014 vintage (★★★☆) was grown at Pisa, tank-fermented and lees-aged in tanks. It is a dry style (4 grams/litre of residual sugar), with strong, lemony, slightly peachy and spicy flavours.

Vintage	14
WR	7
Drink	16-18

 DRY $28 –V

Prophet's Rock Central Otago Dry Riesling   ★★★★☆

Estate-grown and hand-picked at Pisa, in the Cromwell Basin, the classy 2014 vintage (★★★★★) was fermented with indigenous yeasts and lees-aged in old oak barrels. Light lemon/ green, it has a scented, citrusy bouquet, revealing good complexity. Medium-bodied, it has rich, vibrant lemon, grapefruit and lime flavours, a bare hint of sweetness (8 grams/litre of residual sugar), good acid spine and a finely poised, lasting finish. A wine of strong personality, it is delicious now, but should also be long-lived.

Vintage	14
WR	6
Drink	16-26

MED/DRY $35 –V

Ribbonwood Marlborough Riesling ★★★☆

From Framingham, the 2014 vintage (★★★) is a freshly scented wine. It has good depth of lemon, lime and apple flavours, in a medium-dry style (12 grams/litre of residual sugar), with tangy acidity and drink-young appeal.

MED/DRY $20 AV

Rimu Grove Nelson Riesling ★★★★

The light lemon/green 2015 vintage (★★★★) is fresh and vivacious, in a light-bodied (10 per cent alcohol) style with strong, lemony flavours, good acid spine and an off-dry (12 grams/litre of residual sugar), tangy finish. Still youthful, it should be at its best mid-2017+.

Vintage	15	14	13	12	11
WR	7	6	7	7	6
Drink	16-26	16-25	16-21	16-20	16-19

MED/DRY $26 –V

Rippon Mature Vine Riesling ★★★★★

This single-vineyard, Lake Wanaka, Central Otago wine is a distinctly cool-climate style, steely, long-lived and penetratingly flavoured. Based on mature vines, it is fermented with indigenous yeasts and given extended lees-aging. Still on sale, the 2013 vintage (★★★★☆) is a medium-bodied wine, fleshy and ripe, with grapefruit and peach flavours, good acid spine, a hint of sweetness (8 grams/litre of residual sugar), and excellent depth, complexity and harmony. 'More Rheingau than Mosel', I jotted down.

Vintage	13
WR	7
Drink	16-20

MED/DRY $35 AV

Riverby Estate Eliza Marlborough Riesling ★★★★☆

Instantly appealing, the 2014 vintage (★★★★) is an estate-grown, Wairau Valley wine, hand-picked from vines planted in 1990. A distinctly medium style (40 grams/litre of residual sugar), it has a slightly honeyed bouquet, leading into a medium to full-bodied wine with strong, ripe, peachy, slightly gingery and honeyed flavours, and a smooth finish. A characterful wine, it's drinking well now.

Vintage	14	13
WR	6	7
Drink	16-20	16-20

MED $27 AV

Riverby Estate Sali's Block Marlborough Riesling   ★★★☆

The 2014 vintage (★★★) is a mouthfilling, medium-dry style (14 grams/litre of residual sugar), with lemony aromas and flavours, slightly spicy notes, fresh acidity and good depth.

Vintage	14	13
WR	6	7
Drink	16-20	16-20

MED/DRY $22 AV

Rock Ferry Marlborough Riesling   ★★★☆

The 2013 vintage (★★★★) is a mouthfilling, concentrated, dryish wine (6 grams/litre of residual sugar), with strong, ripe flavours, showing a touch of complexity, and a well-rounded finish. Good food wine. Certified organic.

MED/DRY $27 –V

Rockburn Central Otago Tigermoth Riesling   ★★★★

Estate-grown at Parkburn and made in a low-alcohol (8.4 per cent) style, the 2014 vintage (★★★★☆) is already very open and expressive. A gently sweet style (56 grams/litre of residual sugar), it has lovely lightness of body, with excellent vigour and intensity of citrusy, slightly peachy flavours, woven with lively acidity. Drink now or cellar. The 2015 vintage (★★★☆) is light and gently sweet, with crisp, lemony, appley flavours, showing very good vibrancy and depth.

Vintage	15	14	13	12	11
WR	6	6	6	6	7
Drink	16-30	16-30	16-30	16-25	16-25

SW $39 –V

Sailfish Cove Northland Riesling   (★★☆)

A rare example of Riesling from the north, the 2014 vintage (★★☆) is less scented than Rieslings grown in cooler regions to the south, but very sound, with decent depth of crisp, dry, citrusy flavours.

DRY $19 –V

Saint Clair Marlborough Riesling   ★★★★

Typically an attractive, finely balanced wine. The 2015 vintage (★★★★) – which has minor amounts of Grüner Veltliner, Chardonnay, Pinot Gris and Sauvignon Blanc, totalling 9 per cent of the blend – is very open and expressive in its youth. Lively, tangy and slightly sweet (8.5 grams/litre of residual sugar), it is medium-bodied, with penetrating, lemony, spicy, slightly gingery flavours, woven with steely acidity. Best drinking 2017+.

MED/DRY $22 V+

Saint Clair Pioneer Block 9 Big John Marlborough Riesling ★★★★★

Still very youthful, the 2014 vintage (★★★★) was grown in the lower Brancott Valley and stop-fermented with low alcohol (8.5 per cent) and abundant sweetness (53.6 grams/litre of residual sugar). Fresh and light-bodied, it is slightly minerally, with vibrant, citrusy, appley, peachy flavours, showing very good delicacy and depth. It should be at its best 2018+.

SW $27 AV

Saint Clair Vicar's Choice Marlborough Riesling Bright Light (★★★)

The debut 2014 vintage (★★★) is a low-alcohol style (9 per cent), from grapes harvested early in the Awatere Valley. Fresh and light, with lemony, appley flavours, it is a medium style (26 grams/litre of residual sugar) with lively acidity. Slightly sweet and tangy, with an easy-drinking balance, it's enjoyable young.

MED $19 AV

Sanctuary Marlborough Riesling (★★★☆)

The 2014 vintage (★★★☆) is a crisp, lively, medium-bodied wine with very good depth of fresh lemon/lime flavours, slightly sweet and tangy. A strongly varietal wine, it should be at its best 2017+.

MED/DRY $18 V+

Seifried Nelson Riesling ★★★★

From a pioneer of Riesling in New Zealand, the 2015 vintage (★★★☆) is typically good value. Light lemon/green, it is crisp and mouthfilling, with strong, youthful, citrusy, limey, slightly spicy flavours, gentle sweetness (7 grams/litre of residual sugar) and firm acid spine. Still youthful, it should be at its best mid-2017+.

Vintage	15	14	13	12	11	10	09
WR	6	6	6	6	6	6	6
Drink	16-25	16-21	16-20	16-19	P	P	P

MED/DRY $18 V+

Seresin Memento Riesling ★★★★

Harvested by hand from mature vines in Marlborough, this is a medium style. Pale lemon/green, the 2013 vintage (★★★★☆) has an invitingly fragrant bouquet, with slightly toasty, bottle-aged notes emerging. It has intense, citrusy, slightly spicy flavours, a gentle splash of sweetness (23 grams/litre of residual sugar), appetising acidity and strong personality. Drink now or cellar.

Vintage	13	12	11	10	09	08
WR	7	6	6	7	7	5
Drink	16-20	16-20	16-19	16-17	16-18	16-18

MED $25 AV

Soho Maren Marlborough Riesling ★★★★

The 2015 vintage (★★★☆) is a lively, medium-bodied wine with strong, slightly sweet, lemony, appley flavours. Finely poised, it's a very youthful wine with good depth, vigour and harmony. Best drinking 2017+.

Vintage	15
WR	6
Drink	16-28

 MED/DRY $26 –V

Spinyback Nelson Riesling ★★★

The 2014 vintage (★★★) from Waimea Estates is a vibrantly fruity, medium-bodied wine with ripe, peachy, limey flavours, a sliver of sweetness (13.5 grams/litre of residual sugar), fresh, appetising acidity and satisfying depth. Ready.

 MED/DRY $15 V+

Spy Valley Envoy Marlborough Dry Riesling ★★★★★

Estate-grown and hand-picked in the Waihopai Valley, the 2014 vintage (★★★★★) is a bright, light lemon/green, dry wine (3 grams/litre of residual sugar), fermented with indigenous yeasts and matured for five months in oak, then held on its yeast lees for another five months in tanks. Promoted as 'more reminiscent of Old World wines', it is mouthfilling and fleshy, with rich, ripe, peachy, slightly spicy flavours, showing good complexity, and excellent drinkability.

Vintage	14	13
WR	6	7
Drink	16-21	16-20

DRY $30 AV

Spy Valley Envoy Single Vineyard Marlborough Riesling (★★★★☆)

Currently on sale, the 2012 vintage (★★★★☆) is a sweetish style (65 grams/litre of residual sugar), estate-grown in the lower Waihopai Valley and barrel-fermented. Pale lemon/green, it is youthful and tightly structured, with strong lemon, apple and lime flavours, a minerally streak, firm acid spine and good complexity. A distinctive wine, it should be long-lived.

 SW $32 –V

Spy Valley Marlborough Riesling ★★★★

The 2015 vintage (★★★★) is a mouthfilling, dry style (4.7 grams/litre of residual sugar), fermented in tanks and old oak vessels. Bright, light lemon/green, with good body and depth of ripe, citrusy, slightly peachy and spicy flavours, moderate acidity and a touch of complexity, it's a distinctive, age-worthy Riesling, unusually fleshy and dry for New Zealand.

Vintage	15	14	13	12
WR	7	6	6	6
Drink	16-23	16-20	16-17	P

 DRY $23 V+

Stoneleigh Marlborough Riesling ★★★★

Priced sharply, the 2015 vintage (★★★★) is a scented, youthful wine with vibrant, crisp, citrusy, slightly limey flavours, showing very good sugar/acid balance and depth. Tightly focused, it should unfold well. The 2016 vintage (★★★☆) is medium-bodied and vibrantly fruity, with a gentle splash of sweetness and good depth of fresh, citrusy, limey flavours.

MED/DRY $17 V+

Stoney Range Waipara Riesling ★★★☆

The 2015 vintage (★★★) from Sherwood Estate is a lively, finely poised wine with strong, lemony, slightly sweet flavours and a slightly funky bouquet.

MED $17 V+

Stonyridge Fallen Angel Marlborough Riesling (★★★★)

Already drinking well, the 2014 vintage (★★★★) is a generous, tangy wine with strong lemon/lime flavours, a minerally streak, slightly toasty, bottle-aged notes adding complexity and an off-dry (11 grams/litre of residual sugar), crisp finish.

MED/DRY $30 –V

Te Kairanga Martinborough Riesling ★★★★

The 2015 vintage (★★★) has a moderately fresh bouquet, leading into a mouthfilling, dryish style with citrusy, limey flavours, firm acid spine and a minerally streak.

MED/DRY $23 AV

Te Mania Nelson Riesling ★★★☆

The 2015 vintage (★★★★) is delicious now. Pale lemon/green, it is medium-bodied, with appetising acidity, generous, ripe, lemony, slightly peachy and spicy flavours, and a slightly sweet, finely balanced finish.

MED/DRY $22 AV

Terra Sancta Miro's Block Bannockburn Central Otago Dry Riesling ★★★★☆

The 2014 vintage (★★★★) was estate-grown and harvested from 'seven rows of old vines'. A dryish style, it has citrusy, slightly limey and spicy flavours, a minerally streak, slightly toasty notes emerging and good complexity. Drink now or cellar.

MED/DRY $28 AV

Terrace Edge Classic Waipara Valley Riesling ★★★★

Currently on sale, the 2013 vintage (★★★☆) is light lemon/green, with a fragrant, slightly toasty bouquet. An off-dry style (12.5 grams/litre of residual sugar), it has good depth of citrusy flavours, hints of passionfruit and spice, and lively acidity. Drink now or cellar.

Vintage	13
WR	7
Drink	16-24

MED/DRY $19 V+

Terrace Edge Liquid Geography Waipara Valley Riesling ★★★★

Produced in a delicious, distinctly medium style (35 grams/litre of residual sugar), the 2015 vintage (★★★★) is certified organic. Bright, light lemon/green, it has strong, fresh lemon, lime and passionfruit flavours, lively acidity, and excellent balance and depth. Drink now onwards.

Vintage	15
WR	7
Drink	16-24

 MED $19 V+

Thornbury Waipara Riesling ★★★☆

The 2016 vintage (★★★☆) is a medium style (18 grams/litre of residual sugar), fresh and lively, with good depth of citrusy, slightly spicy flavours, woven with appetising acidity. Finely balanced for early drinking, it offers good value. (From Villa Maria.)

Vintage	16
WR	6
Drink	16-21

 MED $16 V+

Three Paddles Martinborough Riesling ★★★☆

The 2014 vintage (★★★★) from Nga Waka is medium-bodied, very fresh and lively, in a slightly sweet style (10 grams/litre of residual sugar) with strong lemon/lime flavours. Showing good intensity and harmony, it's delicious young. Fine value.

Vintage	14
WR	7
Drink	16-20

 MED/DRY $18 V+

Tohu Single Vineyard Marlborough Riesling ★★★☆

Estate-grown in the upper Awatere Valley, the 2015 vintage (★★★☆) is a dryish style (8.5 grams/litre of residual sugar). Pale, with a slightly toasty bouquet, it is tangy and lively, with citrusy, slightly limey flavours, a minerally streak, and good depth. Best drinking mid-2017+.

Vintage	14	13	12	11
WR	6	7	6	7
Drink	16-18	16-18	16-17	P

 MED/DRY $22 AV

Toi Toi Reserve Marlborough Riesling ★★★☆

The 2014 vintage (★★★★) is a ripely scented, medium-bodied wine with strong, citrusy flavours, a gentle splash of sweetness, lively acidity, and very good freshness, balance and length. Drink now or cellar.

MED $22 AV

Two Paddocks Central Otago Riesling ★★★★

Estate-grown at Earnscleugh, near Alexandra, in the Red Bank Vineyard, the 2014 vintage (★★★☆) has fresh lemon/lime flavours, showing very good vigour and depth, and an off-dry (10 grams/litre of residual sugar) finish. Enjoyable young.

MED/DRY $30 –V

Two Paddocks Picnic Central Otago Riesling ★★★★

Estate-grown in the Red Banks Vineyard, at Earnscleugh, near Alexandra, the 2015 vintage (★★★★) is an off-dry style. Lemon-scented, it is a medium-bodied, citrusy, appley wine, fresh, finely balanced and full-flavoured.

MED/DRY $22 V+

Two Rivers of Marlborough Juliet Riesling ★★★★

The 2016 vintage (★★★★) was harvested from 16-year-old vines in the Wairau Valley. Tangy and lively, it has ripe, peachy, slightly sweet flavours (12.5 grams/litre of residual sugar), with a hint of passionfruit, and very good vigour and depth. Already approachable, it should be at its best 2016+.

Vintage	16
WR	6
Drink	17-21

MED/DRY $25 AV

Two Sisters Central Otago Riesling ★★★★★

Estate-grown on a steeply sloping site at Lowburn, in the Cromwell Basin, the finely balanced 2010 vintage (★★★★★) was released in 2016. Finely scented and mouthfilling, it is lively, with moderate acidity and peachy, slightly toasty flavours, showing excellent ripeness, delicacy, depth and harmony. A medium style (18 grams/litre of residual sugar), it's a drink-now or cellaring proposition.

MED $29 V+

Valli Old Vine Central Otago Riesling ★★★★★

Harvested from ultra low-cropping vines planted at Black Ridge, in Alexandra, in 1981, this distinctive, classy wine is made in an unusually dry style, tautly structured, racy and long – a classic for the cellar. The 2013 vintage (★★★★★) is weighty and dry, with deep, citrusy, limey flavours, leesy notes adding complexity, and a long, slightly spicy finish. A 'serious' wine with a sense of youthful power and potential, it's well worth cellaring.

Vintage	13	12	11	10	09	08
WR	7	7	7	7	7	7
Drink	16-23	16-22	16-20	P	16-20	16-19

DRY $30 AV

🍇🍇

Vavasour Marlborough Riesling (★★★☆)

Fleshy and sweet-fruited, the 2015 vintage (★★★☆) has very good depth of lemon/lime flavours and lots of drink-young appeal.

MED/DRY $21 AV

Vidal Marlborough Dry Riesling ★★★☆

Grown in the Wairau and Awatere valleys, the 2014 vintage (★★★☆) is scented, with plenty of fresh, off-dry (9 grams/litre of residual sugar), citrusy, slightly appley flavour.

Vintage	16	15	14	13
WR	6	6	7	7
Drink	16-22	16-23	16-20	16-18

MED/DRY $15 V+

Villa Maria Cellar Selection Marlborough Dry Riesling ★★★★

The 2014 vintage (★★★★) is a dryish style (7 grams/litre of residual sugar), grown and partly hand-picked in the Wairau and Awatere valleys. It has fresh, limey, minerally aromas, leading into a crisp, youthful wine with good intensity of citrusy, limey, slightly spicy flavours, finely poised and lingering, and a bare hint of bottle-aged toastiness. The 2015 vintage (★★★★) was grown in the Wairau and Awatere valleys and made in an off-dry (8.4 grams/litre of residual sugar) style. Highly aromatic, it is vibrantly fruity, with strong, ripe, citrusy, slightly peachy flavours, skifully balanced for early enjoyment. Drink now or cellar.

Vintage	15	14	13	12	11	10	09
WR	7	7	6	6	6	6	7
Drink	16-22	16-20	16-18	16-17	16-17	P	16-17

MED/DRY $20 V+

Villa Maria Private Bin Marlborough Dry Riesling ★★★☆

Grown in the Awatere and Wairau valleys, the 2015 vintage (★★★☆) is a slightly sweet style (8.5 grams/litre of residual sugar), with fresh, ripe, citrusy and limey flavours, crisp acidity and a finely balanced finish. Enjoyable young.

Vintage	16	15	14	13	12	11	10
WR	5	6	6	6	6	6	6
Drink	16-20	16-20	16-18	16-17	P	P	P

MED/DRY $17 V+

Waimea Classic Nelson Riesling ★★★★

This luscious wine is balanced for easy drinking, consistently impressive – and good value. Estate-grown on the Waimea Plains, the 2014 vintage (★★★★) is tightly structured, in a medium-bodied style with fresh, lively peach, passionfruit and spice flavours, mouth-watering acidity and an off-dry (13 grams/litre of residual sugar) finish.

MED/DRY $20 V+

Waipara Hills Waipara Valley Riesling ★★★★

The youthful 2015 vintage (★★★★) is drinking well from the start. Freshly scented, it is vibrant and tangy, with citrusy, limey, slightly peachy and spicy flavours, a gentle splash of sweetness, and excellent vigour, balance and depth.

MED/DRY $22 V+

Waipara Springs Waipara Riesling ★★★☆

The 2015 vintage (★★★★) is medium-bodied, with strong, ripe, citrusy flavours, a gentle splash of sweetness, and excellent depth and harmony.

MED $19 V+

Wairau River Marlborough Riesling ★★★☆

A single-vineyard wine from 23-year-old vines in the Wairau Valley, the 2015 vintage (★★★☆) is an off-dry style (7 grams/litre of residual sugar). Full-bodied, it has fresh, ripe, youthful lemon/lime flavours, crisp and strong.

Vintage	15	14	13
WR	7	6	5
Drink	16-22	16-21	16-20

MED/DRY $20 AV

Wairau River Summer Marlborough Riesling ★★★★

The 2015 vintage (★★★★) is light-bodied (10 per cent alcohol) and vivacious, with very good depth of citrusy, limey flavours, gently sweet (36 grams/litre of residual sugar), tangy, and instantly appealing. The 2016 vintage (★★★★) was made 'to be supped with frivolous frivolity'. Pale, fresh and light-bodied (9.5 per cent alcohol), it is medium-sweet (41 grams/litre of residual sugar), with good intensity of peachy, citrusy flavours, fresh and tangy. Delicious from the start.

Vintage	16	15	14	13
WR	6	7	6	5
Drink	16-19	16-18	16-17	16-17

MED $20 V+

Whitehaven Marlborough Riesling ★★★★

The 2015 vintage (★★★★☆) is an excellent example of the dryish (6 grams/litre of residual sugar) style, made mostly from hand-picked grapes. Attractively scented, it shows excellent intensity, with fresh, strong lemon/lime flavours, crisp and vibrant. Well worth cellaring.

MED/DRY $23 AV

Yealands Estate Land Made Marlborough Riesling ★★★☆

The 2015 vintage (★★★☆) is a fragrant wine, slightly sweet (7 grams/litre of residual sugar) and crisp, with strong lemon/lime flavours, a minerally streak and a tangy finish. Best drinking 2017+.

Vintage	15	14
WR	7	5
Drink	16-18	16-18

MED/DRY $20 AV

Yealands Estate Single Vineyard Awatere Valley Marlborough Riesling   ★★★☆

Estate-grown and hand-picked in the Seaview Vineyard, the 2014 vintage (★★★☆) is a basically dry style (5 grams/litre of residual sugar), with vibrant, citrusy, slightly gingery flavours, fresh acidity and good depth. Worth cellaring.

Vintage	14	MED/DRY $23 –V
WR	7	
Drink	16-20	

Zephyr Marlborough Riesling   ★★★★

Estate-grown by the Glover family at Dillons Point, in the lower Wairau Valley, the 2014 vintage (★★★★) is a medium-dry style, finely poised, with fresh acidity, strong, citrusy, slightly spicy flavours and good harmony.

MED/DRY $25 AV

Roussanne

Roussanne is a traditional ingredient in the white wines of France's northern Rhône Valley, where typically it is blended with the more widely grown Marsanne. Known for its fine acidity and 'haunting aroma', likened by some tasters to herbal tea, it is also found in the south of France, Italy and Australia, but this late-ripening variety is extremely scarce in New Zealand, with only 0.2 hectares bearing in 2017, north of Auckland.

Mahurangi River Winery Roussanne/Viognier ★★★★☆

The elegant 2014 vintage (★★★★) was estate-grown and hand-picked near Matakana. A blend of Roussanne (54 per cent) and Viognier (46 per cent), it is very youthful, with fresh, strong pear and citrus-fruit flavours, good acid spine and a tight finish. A powerful, dry wine, showing good delicacy and complexity, it's well worth cellaring.

Vintage	14	13
WR	5	6
Drink	16-20	16-20

DRY $39 –V

Ransom Roussanne Matakana (★★★★)

Delicious now, the vibrantly fruity 2014 vintage (★★★★) was made from bought-in grapes and handled entirely in tanks. Full-bodied, it is sweet-fruited, with ripe stone-fruit flavours, fresh and strong, and a dry finish. Drink now or cellar.

DRY $26 –V

Sauvignon Blanc

Sauvignon Blanc is New Zealand's major calling card in the wine markets of the world, often – but not always, due to the rising challenge from Chile – winning trophies at big competitions in the UK. For countless wine lovers overseas, New Zealand 'is' Sauvignon Blanc, almost invariably from Marlborough. The rise to international stardom of New Zealand Sauvignon Blanc was remarkably swift. Government Viticulturist Romeo Bragato imported the first Sauvignon Blanc vines from Italy in 1906, but it was not until 1974 that Matua Valley marketed New Zealand's first varietal Sauvignon Blanc, grown in West Auckland. Montana first planted Sauvignon Blanc vines in Marlborough in 1975; its first bottling of Marlborough Sauvignon Blanc flowed in 1979. In 2015, 86.5 per cent by volume of all New Zealand's wine exports were based on Sauvignon Blanc.

Sauvignon Blanc is by far New Zealand's most extensively planted variety, in 2017 comprising 58 per cent of the bearing national vineyard. Well over 90 per cent of the vines are concentrated in Marlborough, with further significant plantings in Hawke's Bay, Nelson, Canterbury and Waipara. Between 2005 and 2017, the area of bearing Sauvignon Blanc vines will surge from 7277 hectares to 21,352 hectares.

The flavour of New Zealand Sauvignon Blanc varies according to fruit ripeness. At the herbaceous, under-ripe end of the spectrum, vegetal and fresh-cut grass aromas hold sway; riper wines show capsicum, gooseberry and melon-like characters; very ripe fruit displays tropical-fruit flavours.

Intensely herbaceous Sauvignon Blancs are not hard to make in the viticulturally cool climate of the South Island and the lower North Island (Wairarapa). 'The challenge faced by New Zealand winemakers is to keep those herbaceous characters in check,' says Kevin Judd, of Greywacke Vineyards, formerly chief winemaker at Cloudy Bay. 'It would be foolish to suggest that these herbaceous notes detract from the wines; in fact I am sure that this fresh edge and intense varietal aroma are the reason for its international popularity. The better of these wines have these herbaceous characters in context and in balance with the more tropical-fruit characters associated with riper fruit.'

There are two key styles of Sauvignon Blanc produced in New Zealand. Wines handled entirely in stainless steel tanks – by far the most common – place their accent squarely on their fresh, direct fruit flavours. Alternatively, many top labels are handled principally in tanks, but 5 to 15 per cent of the blend is barrel-fermented, adding a touch of complexity without subduing the wine's fresh, punchy fruit aromas and flavours.

Another major style difference is regionally based: the crisp, incisively flavoured wines of Marlborough contrast with the softer, less pungently herbaceous Hawke's Bay style. These are wines to drink young (traditionally within 18 months of the vintage) while they are irresistibly fresh, aromatic and tangy, although the oak-matured, more complex wines can mature well for several years.

The swing since the 2001 vintage from corks to screw-caps has also boosted the longevity of the wines. Rather than running out of steam, many are still highly enjoyable at two years old.

12,000 Miles Gladstone Sauvignon Blanc ★★★

From Gladstone Vineyard, in the northern Wairarapa, the 2015 vintage (★★★) was grown at four sites, partly hand-picked, tank-fermented and lees-aged. Crisp and dry, it has fresh, ripe tropical-fruit aromas and flavours, vaguely toasty notes and good depth.

DRY $20 –V

Ake Ake Marlborough Sauvignon Blanc

The 2015 vintage (★★★☆) from this Northland-based winery is freshly aromatic and tangy, in a medium-bodied style with ripely herbaceous flavours, showing very good vigour and depth.

DRY $22 –V

Allan Scott Generations Marlborough Sauvignon Blanc

Released in mid to late 2016, the 2015 vintage (★★★★☆) is a single-vineyard wine, estate-grown in the Wairau Valley. Pale lemon/green, it is freshly scented, mouthfilling and dry, with generous, ripe tropical-fruit flavours, finely balanced acidity, and excellent drinkability.

DRY $26 AV

Allan Scott Marlborough Sauvignon Blanc

Grown in the central Wairau Valley, the 2016 vintage (★★★☆) is a fresh, medium-bodied wine with vibrant, ripe melon/lime flavours, showing very good delicacy and length. Handled without oak, it's a fully dry style (2.1 grams/litre of residual sugar), crisp and lively. Good value.

DRY $18 V+

Alluviale Hawke's Bay Sauvignon Blanc/Sémillon

The mouthfilling, fleshy 2015 vintage (★★★★☆) was grown at the Craft Farm and Askerne vineyards at Havelock North. A blend of Sauvignon Blanc (81 per cent), Sémillon (14 per cent) and Muscat (5 per cent), partly barrel-fermented, it has strong, ripe tropical-fruit flavours, a very subtle seasoning of oak, good complexity, and a crisp, dry, lingering finish.

DRY $24 V+

Alluviale Marlborough Sauvignon Blanc

Ripely scented, the 2016 vintage (★★★★) was grown at sites in the lower Wairau Valley and Waihopai Valley, and lees-aged for three months. Weighty and sweet-fruited, it has generous melon, passionfruit and lime flavours, lively acidity, and a dry (2.8 grams/litre of residual sugar) finish. Good value.

DRY $20 V+

Amisfield Central Otago Sauvignon Blanc

The 2016 vintage (★★★★), estate-grown at Lowburn, was mostly handled in tanks, but a small portion of the blend was fermented with indigenous yeasts in old French oak barriques. Aromatic and tangy, it is bone-dry, with good intensity of tropical-fruit and herbaceous flavours, a touch of complexity, and very good balance, vigour and depth.

DRY $25 AV

Amisfield Fumé Central Otago Sauvignon Blanc

The 2014 vintage (★★★★) was estate-grown at Lowburn, hand-harvested at 24–25 brix, barrel-fermented with indigenous yeasts, and oak-aged for well over a year. Light lemon/green, it's a 'serious', full-bodied style, with fresh, concentrated, ripely herbaceous flavours and a smooth (5 grams/litre of residual sugar), finely balanced finish.

MED/DRY $35 –V

Anchorage Family Estate Nelson Sauvignon Blanc   ★★★☆

The 2015 vintage (★★★) is a fresh, lively, medium-bodied wine with herbaceous and tropical-fruit characters. Made in an off-dry style (7.1 grams/litre of residual sugar), with gentle sweetness balanced by appetising acidity, it is flavoursome and tangy, in a very easy-drinking style.

 MED/DRY $17 V+

Aotea Nelson Sauvignon Blanc   ★★★★

From Seifried Estate, the 2016 vintage (★★★★) is ripely scented, weighty and concentrated, with fresh, crisp tropical-fruit flavours, dry (3.8 grams/litre of residual sugar) and lingering.

 DRY $29 –V

Ara Pathway Marlborough Sauvignon Blanc   ★★★☆

Still on sale, the light lemon/green 2014 vintage (★★★☆) is a tangy, lively, ripely herbaceous wine, estate-grown in the lower Waihopai Valley. Showing very good depth, it's still drinking well.

Vintage	14
WR	5
Drink	P

 DRY $20 AV

Ara Resolute Marlborough Sauvignon Blanc   ★★★★☆

Still on sale, the 2014 vintage (★★★★☆) was estate-grown in the lower Waihopai Valley, hand-harvested and fermented with indigenous yeasts. Light lemon/green, it is a youthful, tightly structured wine with ripe tropical-fruit flavours, slightly toasty and nutty notes adding complexity, fresh acidity and a dryish (5 grams/litre of residual sugar) finish. Drink now or cellar.

Vintage	14
WR	7
Drink	16-18

 MED/DRY $40 –V

Ara Select Blocks Marlborough Sauvignon Blanc   ★★★★☆

This single-vineyard, Waihopai Valley wine is from 'older vines, cropped lower', and made with some use of hand-picking and barrel fermentation. Still on sale, the 2013 vintage (★★★★★) is weighty, mouthfilling and vibrant, with excellent drive and depth of ripe melon/lime flavours, a hint of passionfruit, good acid spine and a finely textured, long finish.

Vintage	13
WR	6
Drink	16-17

DRY $26 AV

Ara Single Estate Marlborough Sauvignon Blanc   ★★★★

Ara in a glass, the 2015 vintage (★★★★) from this Waihopai Valley producer is bright, light lemon/green, with a freshly aromatic bouquet. Crisp and lively, it has strong passionfruit/lime flavours, a touch of bottle-aged complexity, and a dry (3.5 grams/litre of residual sugar), lingering finish.

Vintage	15
WR	6
Drink	16-17

DRY $22 V+

Aronui Single Vineyard Nelson Sauvignon Blanc   ★★★☆

Still on sale, the 2014 vintage (★★★) is a lively wine, grown at Brightwater, on the Waimea Plains. Freshly herbaceous, it has good depth of melon/lime flavours, crisp and dry (2.6 grams/litre of residual sugar).

DRY $22 AV

Ash Ridge Hawke's Bay Estate Sauvignon Blanc   ★★★☆

The 2015 vintage (★★★☆) was fermented in old barrels and lees-aged in oak for several months. Medium-bodied, it is dry, with melon, spice and capsicum flavours, threaded with fresh acidity, a touch of complexity and good length.

DRY $20 AV

Ashwell Martinborough Sauvignon Blanc   ★★★☆

Grown on the Martinborough Terraces, the 2016 vintage (★★★☆) is freshly scented and mouthfilling, with good depth of ripely herbaceous flavours, moderate acidity and a smooth finish. Enjoyable young.

DRY $20 AV

Astrolabe Province Marlborough Sauvignon Blanc   (★★★★)

The 2015 vintage (★★★★) is a regional blend, made in a bone-dry style. Mouthfilling, it is concentrated, with tropical-fruit and herbaceous flavours, showing good delicacy and a touch of complexity, and a green-edged, persistent finish.

DRY $21 V+

Astrolabe Valleys Awatere Valley Sauvignon Blanc   ★★★★

Grown at two sites in the Awatere Valley, the 2015 vintage (★★★★☆) is a very typical sub-regional style, with punchy, herbaceous aromas, leading into a mouthfilling, tangy wine with good intensity of melon, capsicum and lime flavours, slightly minerally, dry (1 gram/litre of residual sugar) and long.

DRY $24 AV

Ata Rangi Martinborough Sauvignon Blanc   ★★★★☆

A consistently attractive wine, with ripe tropical-fruit rather than herbaceous flavours. The 2014 vintage (★★★★☆) was hand-picked and mostly handled in tanks, but part of the blend was fermented and lees-aged in seasoned French oak barrels. Mouthfilling, it is vibrantly fruity, with ripe melon/lime fruit flavours, showing good complexity, and a long, dry finish.

 DRY $27 AV

Ataahua Waipara Sauvignon Blanc   ★★★★

Drinking well now, the 2014 vintage (★★★★) is a pale lemon/green, mouthfilling wine with strong, ripe melon, passionfruit and lime flavours, woven with fresh acidity, and a crisp, dry (less than 3 grams/litre of residual sugar) finish.

 DRY $26 –V

Auntsfield Single Vineyard Southern Valleys
Marlborough Sauvignon Blanc   ★★★★★

Estate-grown on the south side of the Wairau Valley, on the site where the region's first wines were made in the 1870s, the 2016 vintage (★★★★☆) was mostly fermented in tanks; a small percentage was handled in old oak casks. Bright, light lemon/green, it is freshly scented, mouthfilling and dry, with excellent intensity of tropical-fruit flavours, tight and youthful. Best drinking mid-2017+.

 DRY $23 V+

Auntsfield South Oaks Barrel Fermented Southern Valleys
Marlborough Sauvignon Blanc   ★★★★☆

Currently on sale, the impressive 2013 vintage (★★★★★) was estate-grown on the south side of the Wairau Valley and matured for a year in seasoned oak casks. Light lemon/green, it is fragrant, full-bodied and sweet-fruited, with excellent concentration of tropical-fruit flavours, lively, rich and complex. Probably approaching its peak, it's a tightly structured wine with a lasting finish.

Vintage	13
WR	6
Drink	16-21

 DRY $39 –V

Babich Black Label Marlborough Sauvignon Blanc   ★★★★

The 'Black Label' wines are mostly seen in restaurants. The 2015 vintage (★★★★) is a bold, highly aromatic wine with good weight and concentration of vibrant passionfruit, melon and capsicum flavours, woven with appetising acidity.

 DRY $25 AV

Babich Family Estates Cowslip Valley Marlborough Sauvignon Blanc ★★★★

Estate-grown in the Waihopai Valley, the 2015 vintage (★★★☆) is medium to full-bodied, with crisp, lively, melon and capsicum flavours that linger well.

Babich Family Estates Headwaters Organic Block
Marlborough Sauvignon Blanc ★★★★

This subtle, fully dry wine is grown in the Wairau Valley. The 2016 vintage (★★★★) is mouthfilling, with good vigour and depth of ripe tropical-fruit flavours, slightly spicy and minerally notes, and a long, tight finish. Best drinking mid-2017+. Certified organic.

Babich Family Estates Wakefield Downs Marlborough Sauvignon Blanc ★★★☆

From the Awatere Valley, the 2015 vintage (★★★) is a fresh, aromatic, clearly herbaceous wine with good depth of lively, slightly peachy, green-edged flavours.

Babich Hawke's Bay Sauvignon Blanc ★★★☆

Drinking well now, the 2015 vintage (★★★) is a fresh, lively, medium to full-bodied wine with ripe tropical-fruit flavours, crisp and dry.

Babich Marlborough Sauvignon Blanc ★★★★

Babich favours 'a fuller, riper, softer' Sauvignon Blanc. 'It's not a jump out of the glass style, but the wines develop well.' The latest releases reflect a rising input of grapes from the company's Cowslip Valley Vineyard in the Waihopai Valley, which gives less herbaceous fruit characters than its other Marlborough vineyards. The 2016 vintage (★★★★) is typical. The bouquet is fresh, with ripe tropical-fruit aromas; the palate is mouthfilling, with strong, vibrant, passionfruit-evoking flavours, in a non-herbaceous, but still lively and appetisingly crisp, style.

Babich Winemakers Reserve Marlborough Sauvignon Blanc ★★★★☆

A stylish example of gently oaked Sauvignon Blanc. Estate-grown in the Waihopai and Awatere valleys, it is mostly handled in tanks, but part of the blend (20 per cent in 2015) is fermented and lees-aged in French oak barriques. The 2015 vintage (★★★★) is mouthfilling and smooth, with strong, ripe tropical-fruit flavours to the fore, nutty and creamy notes adding richness and complexity, and a dry, finely textured finish. It shows good potential; open mid-2017+.

DRY $30 –V

Baby Doll Marlborough Sauvignon Blanc ★★★☆

The 2015 vintage (★★★★) has an aromatic, freshly herbaceous bouquet. Mouthfilling, it is vibrantly fruity, with strong melon, lime and green-capsicum flavours, and some tropical-fruit notes. A 'greener' style, it shows good intensity, with a powerful finish. (From Yealands.)

DRY $19 V+

Bel Echo by Clos Henri Marlborough Sauvignon Blanc ★★★★☆

This well-priced wine is grown in the more clay-based soils at Clos Henri (the top wine, sold as 'Clos Henri', is from the stoniest blocks). The 2014 vintage (★★★★☆) was hand-picked, tank-fermented and matured on its yeast lees for six months. Bright, light lemon/green, it is attractively scented, mouthfilling and fleshy, with good intensity of ripe tropical-fruit flavours, a minerally streak, and a long, rounded, bone-dry finish. Certified organic.

Vintage	14
WR	7
Drink	16-20

DRY $25 V+

Bellbird Spring Block Eight Waipara Sauvignon Blanc ★★★★

This distinctive wine is hand-picked and fermented with indigenous yeasts in old oak barriques. The 2014 vintage (★★★★), barrel-aged for 10 months, is light yellow/green, with strong, ripe tropical-fruit flavours, a subtle seasoning of toasty oak adding complexity, and a tight, dry finish. A highly distinctive wine, it's a drink-now or cellaring proposition. (In a short vertical tasting of the 2011–2013 vintages, held in August 2015, the older wines were still drinking well.)

Vintage	14	13	12	11
WR	6	6	6	7
Drink	16-18	16-17	16-18	P

DRY $32 –V

Bird Marlborough Sauvignon Blanc ★★★★

Showing good vigour and intensity, the 2015 vintage (★★★★) is a single-vineyard wine, grown at Rapaura. Full-bodied, it has ripe, strongly varietal melon/lime flavours, fresh, tangy and strong.

DRY $20 V+

Bishops Head Waipara Valley Fumé Blanc ★★★

The 2015 vintage (★★★☆) was hand-picked and fermented with indigenous yeasts in acacia barrels, which give 'a nice, lifted sweetness on the palate'. Full-bodied, with fresh acidity and generous, ripely herbal, slightly nutty flavours, it's a distinctly cool-climate expression of Sauvignon Blanc, showing considerable complexity.

DRY $30 –V

Black Cottage Marlborough Sauvignon Blanc ★★★☆

From Two Rivers, the 2016 vintage (★★★☆) is a blend of fruit from the Wairau and Awatere valleys. A good-value wine, with lots of drink-young appeal, it is mouthfilling and finely balanced, with a fresh, aromatic bouquet and good depth of ripely herbaceous flavours, crisp and lively.

Vintage	16
WR	5
Drink	16-17

 DRY $18 V+

Blackenbrook Nelson Sauvignon Blanc ★★★★

Estate-grown at Tasman, hand-harvested and lees-aged in tanks (mostly) and old oak barrels (4 per cent), the 2016 vintage (★★★★) is dryish (5 grams/litre of residual sugar), with a freshly aromatic, intensely varietal bouquet. Showing good vigour and intensity, it is tangy, with tropical-fruit and green-capsicum flavours, fresh and tangy.

Vintage	16	15	14	13
WR	6	5	7	6
Drink	16-17	P	P	P

 MED/DRY $21 V+

Bladen Marlborough Sauvignon Blanc ★★★★

This label has shown good form recently. The 2015 vintage (★★★★) was grown at two sites at Renwick, in the Wairau Valley. Freshly aromatic, it is mouthfilling, with ripe, punchy tropical-fruit flavours, showing very good vibrancy and depth, and a crisp, dry (3.7 grams/litre of residual sugar), finely balanced finish.

 DRY $21 V+

Boatshed Bay Marlborough Sauvignon Blanc ★★★☆

Pale lemon/green, the 2016 vintage (★★★☆) is mouthfilling and vibrantly fruity, with good weight and depth of fresh passionfruit, melon and green-capsicum flavours, crisp and lively. (From Foley Family Wines.)

DRY $20 AV

Boundary Vineyards Rapaura Road Marlborough Sauvignon Blanc ★★★★☆

The 2015 vintage (★★★★☆) from Pernod Ricard NZ offers great value. Still fresh and youthful, it is mouthfilling and tightly structured, with generous, ripe tropical-fruit flavours, appetisingly crisp, finely poised and long.

 DRY $20 V+

Brancott Estate Chosen Rows Marlborough Sauvignon Blanc   ★★★★★

From the company that planted the region's first Sauvignon Blanc vines in 1975, Chosen Rows is promoted as 'the ultimate expression of Marlborough Sauvignon Blanc'. The goal is to create 'an age-worthy wine with great palate weight and texture . . . a sophisticated, thought-provoking wine'. The second, 2013, vintage (★★★★★) was grown in the historic Brancott Vineyard, hand-picked from 15 to 17-year-old vines, fermented with indigenous yeasts in large French oak cuves, and lees-aged for eight months. Bottled in June 2014 and released in December 2015, it is a powerful (14.5 per cent alcohol) wine, weighty and fleshy, with firm acid spine, very ripe melon/lime flavours, showing excellent concentration and complexity, and a dry, lasting finish. Drink now or cellar.

Vintage	13	12	11	10
WR	7	NM	NM	7
Drink	16-20	NM	NM	16-17

DRY $80 –V

Brancott Estate Flight Marlborough Sauvignon Blanc   ★★☆

This is a low-alcohol style (9 per cent) with a gentle splash of sweetness. The 2015 vintage (★★☆) is light-bodied, with citrusy, appley flavours, fresh and tart.

MED/DRY $17 –V

Brancott Estate Letter Series 'B' Brancott Marlborough Sauvignon Blanc   ★★★★★

This wine is promoted by Pernod Ricard NZ as 'our finest expression of Marlborough's most famous variety' – and lives up to its billing. 'Palate weight, concentration and longevity' are the goals. It has traditionally been grown in the company's sweeping Brancott Vineyard, on the south, slightly cooler side of the Wairau Valley, and a significant portion (40 per cent in 2015) is fermented and lees-aged in French oak puncheons and large Frenc oak cuves, to add 'some toast and spice as well as palate richness'. The 2015 vintage (★★★★☆) is fleshy, crisp and dry, with good weight, concentrated, ripe tropical-fruit flavours, a subtle seasoning of oak adding complexity, and a finely textured, slightly creamy, lingering finish.

DRY $33 AV

Brancott Estate Living Land Series Marlborough Sauvignon Blanc   ★★★☆

Certified organic, the 2016 vintage (★★★★) is from vineyards on the south side of the Wairau Valley. Intensely aromatic, it is mouthfilling and vibrantly fruity, with rich, incisive, ripely herbaceous flavours. Fine value.

DRY $20 AV

Brancott Estate Marlborough Sauvignon Blanc   ★★★☆

This famous wine is promoted as 'the original Marlborough Sauvignon Blanc', since it is descended directly from the pioneering label, Montana Marlborough Sauvignon Blanc, launched in 1979 . The impressive 2016 vintage (★★★★) has a highly aromatic, punchy bouquet, pure, incisive tropical-fruit and herbaceous flavours, good acid spine and a long, dry finish. Fine value.

DRY $17 V+

Brightside Nelson Sauvignon Blanc ★★★

The 2015 vintage (★★★) from Kaimira Estate has a strong, freshly herbaceous bouquet. Light lemon/green, it has tropical-fruit and herbal flavours, with a crisp, dry (2.3 grams/litre of residual sugar) finish. Certified organic.

DRY $18 AV

Brightwater Vineyards Lord Rutherford Barrique
Nelson Sauvignon Blanc (★★★★)

The debut 2015 vintage (★★★★), estate-grown at Hope, was fermented with indigenous yeasts and lees-aged for six months in seasoned French oak barrels. Bright, light lemon/green, it's a mouthfilling, sweet-fruited wine, still youthful, with fresh, strong tropical-fruit flavours, seasoned with slightly biscuity oak, and a crisp, dry finish. Best drinking mid-2017+.

DRY $30 –V

Brightwater Vineyards Lord Rutherford Nelson Sauvignon Blanc ★★★★☆

The impressive 2015 vintage (★★★★★), grown at Hope, on the Waimea Plains, was low-cropped, bunch-thinned and briefly matured on its yeast lees. Mouthfilling and fleshy, with strong, ripe melon and passionfruit aromas and flavours, showing some leesy complexity, it's a dry (1.5 grams/litre of residual sugar), non-herbaceous style with balanced acidity and a lasting, smooth finish. Drink now or cellar.

Vintage	15	14	13	12
WR	6	6	6	7
Drink	16-20	16-19	16-18	16-17

DRY $25 V+

Brightwater Vineyards Nelson Sauvignon Blanc ★★★★

Grown at Hope, on the Waimea Plains, this is a consistently attractive, ripely flavoured wine, fresh and punchy. The 2016 vintage (★★★★), harvested from vines up to 23 years old, is dry (2 grams/litre of residual sugar) and ripely scented, with generous passionfruit and lime flavours, vibrant and appetisingly crisp. Enjoyable from the start.

Vintage	15	14
WR	7	6
Drink	16-17	P

DRY $20 V+

Byrne Northland Sauvignon Blanc ★★★☆

Grown at Kerikeri, in the Bay of Islands, the 2015 vintage (★★★☆) is a mouthfilling, sweet-fruited wine, partly (40 per cent) fermented with indigenous yeasts in French oak barrels. It has good body and depth of ripe tropical-fruit flavours, showing a touch of complexity, and a smooth finish.

DRY $23 –V

Cable Bay Awatere Valley Marlborough Sauvignon Blanc   ★★★☆

Estate-grown, the 2015 vintage (★★★☆) is a mouthfilling, herbaceous wine with strong melon, lime and capsicum flavours, produced deliberately in a traditional 'greener' style. A generous, high-impact wine, it's ready to roll.

Vintage	15
WR	4
Drink	16-17

DRY $23 –V

Cable Bay Reserve Marlborough Sauvignon Blanc   (★★★★)

A complex style, still unfolding, the 2015 vintage (★★★★) was estate-grown in the Awatere Valley and fermented with indigenous yeasts in French oak barrels (15 per cent new). Mouthfilling, it has impressive weight and depth of youthful, ripe tropical-fruit flavours and a slightly creamy texture.

Vintage	15
WR	6
Drink	16-22

DRY $28 –V

Carrick Central Otago Sauvignon Blanc   ★★★☆

Grown and hand-picked at Bannockburn, this wine is handled in tanks and old barrels (40 per cent in 2014). The 2014 vintage (★★★☆) is mouthfilling, with ripe melon, lime and green-capsicum flavours, a touch of complexity, and a smooth finish. Certified organic.

DRY $22 AV

Catalina Sounds Marlborough Sauvignon Blanc   ★★★★

Tightly structured and youthful, the 2015 vintage (★★★★☆) is a richly scented wine, mostly handled in tanks; 5 per cent of the blend was barrel-fermented. Mouthfilling, it is crisp, with intense, vibrant melon, lime and capsicum flavours, showing a touch of complexity, and excellent delicacy and length.

DRY $24 AV

Catalina Sounds Sound of White Marlborough Sauvignon Blanc   ★★★★☆

The 2015 vintage (★★★★☆) is a complex, very youthful, estate-grown wine from the Waihopai Valley, hand-picked and barrel-fermented. Light lemon/green, it has mouthfilling body and concentrated, ripe grapefruit/lime flavours, seasoned with nutty oak. Tightly structured, it shows excellent vigour, depth and potential.

DRY $31 –V

Caythorpe Family Estate Marlborough Sauvignon Blanc   ★★★★☆

Grown in the 'heart of the Wairau Plains', the impressive 2015 vintage (★★★★★) was harvested on 31 March and handled entirely in tanks. Weighty and dry (2.3 grams/litre of residual sugar), it's a distinctly non-herbaceous style, sweet-fruited, with good mouthfeel, balanced acidity and rich passionfruit/lime flavours. An immaculate, tightly structured wine with a long finish, it's a top-flight debut. The youthful 2016 vintage (★★★★) is full-bodied, with strong, ripe tropical-fruit flavours, a hint of spice, good acid spine and a dry (3.5 grams/litre of residual sugar), lengthy finish. Best drinking mid-2017+.

DRY $20 V+

Church Road Grand Reserve Barrel Fermented
Hawke's Bay Sauvignon Blanc   ★★★★★

The powerful, thought-provoking 2014 vintage (★★★★★) was estate-grown in the Redstone Vineyard, in the Bridge Pa Triangle, hand-picked and barrel-fermented with indigenous yeasts. Bright, light lemon/green, it is multi-faceted, with a very fragrant, ripe bouquet leading into a mouthfilling (14.5 per cent alcohol), tropical fruit-flavoured wine, deliciously sweet-fruited, complex, rich and rounded. Best drinking 2017+.

DRY $44 –V

Church Road Hawke's Bay Sauvignon Blanc   ★★★★

Aiming for a wine that is 'more refined and softer than a typical New Zealand Sauvignon Blanc, with restrained varietal characters', this wine is based mostly on aromatic fruit from Pernod Ricard NZ's inland, elevated, cool site at Matapiro (300 metres above sea level). The 2015 vintage (★★★★) is full-bodied and dry. Vibrantly fruity, it is a ripely herbaceous style with passionfruit, peach and lime flavours, balanced acidity and good intensity. Drink now to 2017.

Vintage	15	14	13	12	11	10
WR	7	7	7	5	6	7
Drink	16-19	16-18	16-17	P	P	P

DRY $20 V+

Church Road McDonald Series Hawke's Bay Sauvignon Blanc   ★★★☆

The 2014 vintage (★★★★) is designed as a 'more complex style of Sauvignon Blanc without relying on new oak'. Hand-picked and partly barrel-fermented, it is mouthfilling, with concentrated, ripe tropical-fruit flavours, slightly creamy notes and a dry, tight finish.

DRY $27 –V

Churton Best End Marlborough Sauvignon Blanc   (★★★★★)

The debut 2013 vintage (★★★★★) is Churton's 'first single block, organic Sauvignon Blanc'. From a north-facing slope, 185 metres above sea level, in the Waihopai Valley, it was fermented and lees-aged for a year in French oak puncheons (40 per cent new). A highly distinctive wine, it is very tight, elegant and minerally, with penetrating melon/lime flavours, a hint of nutty oak adding complexity, steely acidity and a lasting finish. Retasted in early 2016, it is maturing superbly. (There is no 2014, but the label returns from the 2015 vintage.)

Vintage	13
WR	7
Drink	16-26

DRY $47 AV

Churton Marlborough Sauvignon Blanc ★★★★★

This producer aims for a style that 'combines the renowned flavour and aromatic intensity of Marlborough fruit with the finesse and complexity of fine European wines'. Estate-grown on an elevated site in the Waihopai Valley, it is hand-harvested and part of the blend (10 per cent in 2014) is fermented in large French oak casks. The delicious 2014 vintage (★★★★★) is a light lemon/green, ripely scented wine, mouthfilling and fleshy, with concentrated melon/lime flavours, showing a distinct touch of complexity, a minerally streak, and a well-rounded, bone-dry finish. Drink now or cellar. Certified organic.

Vintage	14	13	12	11	10
WR	6	7	5	6	7
Drink	16-23	16-25	16-19	16-19	16-23

DRY $27 V+

Clark Estate Marlborough Sauvignon Blanc ★★★

The 2015 vintage (★★★) is a single-vineyard wine from the upper Awatere Valley. Mouthfilling, it has tropical-fruit and herbaceous flavours, with hints of herbs and passionfruit, firm acid spine, and a finely balanced finish.

Vintage	15	14
WR	7	7
Drink	16-17	P

Clearview Reserve Hawke's Bay Barrique Fermented Sauvignon Blanc ★★★☆

The 2014 vintage (★★★☆) was grown at Te Awanga, hand-harvested, blended with a small percentage of Sémillon, and fermented and matured in oak barrels. A tangy, medium-bodied wine, it is fresh, vibrant and ripely herbaceous, with gentle biscuity, nutty flavours adding complexity, good vigour and depth, and a crisp, dry finish.

Clearview Te Awanga Hawke's Bay Sauvignon Blanc ★★★☆

Pale, with a fresh, limey bouquet, the 2016 vintage (★★★) is a medium-bodied wine, with good depth of ripely herbaceous flavours and a well-rounded finish.

DRY $19 V+

Clearwater Cove by Peter Yealands Marlborough Sauvignon Blanc (★★★☆)

The 2015 vintage (★★★☆) offers fine value. A vibrantly fruity, herbaceous style, with some tropical-fruit notes and a minerally streak, it has very good depth and lots of drink-young appeal.

Clifford Bay Marlborough Sauvignon Blanc ★★★

Bright, light lemon/green, the 2016 vintage (★★★) is fresh and vibrant, with good depth of tropical-fruit and herbaceous flavours, crisp and lively. Fine value.

Clos Henri Marlborough Sauvignon Blanc   ★★★★★

The Clos Henri Vineyard near Renwick is owned by Henri Bourgeois, a leading, family-owned producer in the Loire Valley, which feels this wine expresses 'a unique terroir . . . and French winemaking approach'. A sophisticated and distinctive Sauvignon Blanc, in top years it's a joy to drink. The 2014 vintage (★★★★☆) was hand-picked and mostly fermented and matured for eight months on its yeast lees in tanks; 10 per cent was fermented in old barrels. Mouthfilling, it is sweet-fruited, with ripe tropical-fruit flavours, showing good intensity, a slightly biscuity complexity, good mouthfeel and texture, and a dry, rounded finish. Certified organic.

Vintage	14	13	12	11	10	09
WR	6	7	7	6	7	6
Drink	16-21	16-21	16-20	16-17	P	P

Clos Marguerite Marlborough Sauvignon Blanc   ★★★★★

Estate-grown and hand-picked in the Awatere Valley, the 2015 vintage (★★★★★) is typically classy. Most of the wine was lees-aged in tanks, but 8 per cent was barrel-fermented. Weighty, fleshy and rich, it is full of personality, with concentrated tropical-fruit flavours, a herbaceous undercurrent, good complexity and a crisp, dry, very persistent finish.

Cloudy Bay Sauvignon Blanc   ★★★★★

New Zealand's most internationally acclaimed wine is sought after from Sydney to New York and London. Its irresistibly aromatic and zesty style and intense flavours stem from 'the fruit characters that are in the grapes when they arrive at the winery'. It is sourced from company-owned and several long-term contract growers' vineyards in the Rapaura, Fairhall, Renwick and Brancott districts of the Wairau Valley, Marlborough. The juice is mostly cool-fermented with cultured and indigenous yeasts in stainless steel tanks and aged on its yeast lees, and a small percentage of the blend (3 per cent in 2016) is fermented at warmer temperatures in old French oak barriques and large oak vats. The 2016 vintage (★★★★★) is delicious from the start. Bright, light lemon/green, it is weighty, with mouthfilling body (13.5 per cent alcohol) and concentrated, ripe tropical-fruit flavours, showing a distinct touch of biscuity, oak-derived complexity. A sophisticated wine, rich, lively and long, it should break into full stride mid-2017+.

Vintage	16	15	14	13	12
WR	7	7	7	7	7
Drink	16-18	16-17	P	P	P

Cloudy Bay Te Koko – see the Branded and Other White Wines section

Coopers Creek Marlborough Sauvignon Blanc   ★★★☆

The 2015 vintage (★★★) is a light, lively wine with good depth of clearly herbaceous flavours, woven with appetising acidity.

DRY $18 V+

Couper's Shed Hawke's Bay Sauvignon Blanc   ★★★☆

Mouthfilling and smooth, the 2015 vintage (★★★) is bright, light lemon/green, with good depth of fresh, clearly herbaceous flavours. Ready. (From Pernod Ricard NZ.)

DRY $20 AV

Craggy Range Te Muna Road Vineyard Martinborough Sauvignon Blanc   ★★★☆

Grown a few kilometres south of Martinborough township, this wine is fermented in tanks, barriques and oak cuves. The 2014 vintage (★★★) is medium-bodied, with fresh melon, lime and capsicum flavours, crisp and lively.

DRY $24 –V

Crossings, The, Awatere Valley Marlborough Sauvignon Blanc   ★★★★

The 2015 vintage (★★★★) is a mouthfilling, weighty wine with good intensity of fresh melon/ lime flavours, a slightly minerally streak, and a dry (3.6 grams/litre of residual sugar), lingering finish.

Vintage	15
WR	7
Drink	16-17

DRY $20 V+

Crowded House Marlborough Sauvignon Blanc   ★★★☆

Delicious young, the 2015 vintage (★★★★) is a tangy, punchy wine with melon, green-capsicum and lime flavours, very fresh and strong.

DRY $20 AV

Dashwood Marlborough Sauvignon Blanc   ★★★☆

Typically great value. The 2016 vintage (★★★☆) is very fresh and lively, with appetisingly crisp tropical-fruit and herbaceous flavours, showing very good vigour and depth.

DRY $18 V+

Delegat Awatere Valley Sauvignon Blanc   ★★★★

Offering fine value, the 2015 vintage (★★★★) is mouthfilling and rounded, with good weight, strong, peachy, limey flavours, moderate acidity and a very harmonious, dry (1.4 grams/litre of residual sugar), lingering finish. Delicious young.

DRY $20 V+

Delta Hatters Hill Marlborough Sauvignon Blanc   (★★★★★)

The immaculate 2014 vintage (★★★★★) is a single-vineyard wine from Dillons Point, in the lower Wairau Valley. Pale lemon/green, it is weighty and sweet-fruited, with ripe melon, capsicum and lime flavours, showing excellent delicacy and length, a slightly 'salty' streak, and a crisp, dry (3 grams/litre of residual sugar) finish.

DRY $28 V+

Discovery Point Marlborough Sauvignon Blanc   (★★★★☆)

Offering outstanding value, the 2015 vintage (★★★★☆) from wine distributor Steve Bennett was blended from three sites in the Wairau and lower Waihopai valleys. Ripely scented, it is vibrant, with excellent body, vigour and depth of ripe melon, lime and capsicum flavours. A bone-dry style, it shows strong personality, building to a crisp, lasting finish. Drink now to 2018.

DRY $17 V+

Dog Point Vineyard Marlborough Sauvignon Blanc   ★★★★★

This wine offers a clear style contrast to Section 94, Dog Point's complex, barrel-aged Sauvignon Blanc (see the Branded and Other White Wines section). Hand-harvested at several sites in the Wairau Valley, it is lees-aged in tanks but handled without oak. The classy 2016 vintage (★★★★★) is highly scented, very fresh and vibrant. Weighty, it has searching, ripe grapefruit/lime flavours, firm acid spine and a dry (3 grams/litre of residual sugar), lasting finish. Highly concentrated and tightly structured, it's a very harmonious wine, arguably the best vintage yet.

Vintage	16	15	14	13	12
WR	7	7	6	7	5
Drink	16-21	16-20	16-18	16-19	P

DRY $27 V+

Drowsy Fish by Crown Range Cellar Nelson Sauvignon Blanc   (★★★★)

The 2015 vintage (★★★★) was grown inland and handled without oak. Ripely scented, it is weighty, with strong melon/lime flavours, a hint of green capsicum, and a fully dry (1.3 grams/litre of residual sugar), appetisingly crisp finish. Drink now to 2017.

DRY $30 –V

Durvillea 'D' by Astrolabe Marlborough Sauvignon Blanc   (★★★)

Offering fine value, the 2015 vintage (★★★) was grown in the Awatere, Wairau and Southern valleys. It has freshly herbaceous aromas and flavours, in a strongly varietal style with lively melon and green-capsicum flavours, balanced acidity and a dry (2 grams/litre of residual sugar) finish.

DRY $15 V+

Elephant Hill Reserve Hawke's Bay Sauvignon Blanc   (★★★☆)

The 2014 vintage (★★★☆) was estate-grown at Te Awanga, hand-picked, fermented in a 50:50 split of tanks and old oak puncheons, then blended and matured for eight months in seasoned oak casks. Medium-bodied, it is fresh and lively, in a minerally, dry style (2.5 grams/litre of residual sugar) with melon/lime flavours, showing good intensity.

DRY $35 –V

Eradus Awatere Valley Marlborough Sauvignon Blanc   ★★★☆

The 2015 vintage (★★★☆) is light lemon/green, mouthfilling and fleshy, with tropical-fruit and herbaceous flavours, showing very good depth, and a green-edged finish. Priced right.

DRY $19 V+

Esk Valley Marlborough Sauvignon Blanc   ★★★★

The 2016 vintage (★★★★) was grown in the Wairau Valley (75 per cent) and Awatere Valley (25 per cent). Very fresh and punchy, it is a fully dry style (1.7 grams/litre of residual sugar), with ripely herbaceous flavours, finely balanced and rich.

Fairbourne Marlborough Sauvignon Blanc   ★★★★☆

From elevated, north-facing slopes in the Wairau Valley, the 2015 vintage (★★★★) of this single-vineyard wine was hand-picked and fermented to full dryness (1.4 grams/litre of residual sugar), mostly in tanks, but a small portion of the blend was French oak-fermented. Light lemon/green, it is full-bodied, with strong, crisp, ripely herbaceous flavours, a minerally streak and a tight finish. Best drinking mid-2017+.

Vintage	15	14	13	12	11	10
WR	6	7	7	6	7	6
Drink	16-21	16-20	16-19	16-18	16-18	P

Fairhall Downs Single Vineyard Marlborough Sauvignon Blanc   ★★★★

The 2015 vintage (★★★★) was estate-grown on the south side of the Wairau Valley. The bouquet is fresh and herbaceous; the palate is mouthfilling and buoyantly fruity, with strong melon, lime and green-capsicum flavours. A 'Marlborough in a glass' style, it shows excellent weight, vibrancy and depth.

Falcon Ridge Estate Nelson Sauvignon Blanc   (★★★☆)

Estate-grown in the Wai-iti Valley, the 2015 vintage (★★★☆) is light lemon/green, mouthfilling and vibrantly fruity, with fresh, lively, clearly herbaceous flavours, showing very good depth, and a dry (2 grams/litre of residual sugar) finish.

Vintage	15
WR	5
Drink	16-17

DRY $30 –V

Falconhead Marlborough Sauvignon Blanc   ★★☆

The 2015 vintage (★★★) is a medium-bodied wine, with an aromatic, freshly herbaceous bouquet. It has vibrant melon and green capsicum-like flavours, slightly leesy notes and a smooth finish. Priced right.

DRY $16 AV

Folium Reserve Marlborough Sauvignon Blanc   ★★★★☆

The 2014 vintage (★★★★★) was hand-picked in the Brancott Valley and handled almost entirely in tanks; a small parcel was barrel-fermented. Weighty, it's a very elegant wine, sweet-fruited, tightly structured and crisp, with fresh, delicate melon, lime and capsicum flavours, intense, dry (1.8 grams/litre of residual sugar), racy and long.

Vintage	14
WR	6
Drink	16-25

 DRY $32 –V

Folium Vineyard Marlborough Sauvignon Blanc   ★★★★

The 2014 vintage (★★★★) was hand-picked in the Brancott Valley and handled entirely in tanks. Bright, light lemon/green, it is aromatic, crisp and lively, with mouthfilling body and vibrant, racy melon, lime and capsicum flavours that linger well.

Vintage	14
WR	6
Drink	16-18

 DRY $28 –V

Framingham F-Series Marlborough Sauvignon Blanc   ★★★★☆

Estate-grown and hand-picked, the classy 2014 vintage (★★★★★) was 50 per cent fermented and matured for 10 months in old oak barrels; the rest was handled in tanks. Light lemon/green, it is tight and elegant, in a highly refined, dry style (2.5 grams/litre of residual sugar), with a very subtle oak influence and lovely delicacy, poise and intensity.

Vintage	14	13
WR	5	7
Drink	16-20	16-20

 DRY $35 –V

Framingham Marlborough Sauvignon Blanc   ★★★★

Consistently impressive and fine value. Grown in the Wairau Valley, the 2015 vintage (★★★★☆) was mostly handled in tanks, but a small portion of the blend (7 per cent) was barrel-fermented. It has a fresh, ripely scented bouquet, showing good intensity. Weighty, tightly structured and dry (3 grams/litre of residual sugar), it has strong, ripe melon/lime flavours, showing a distinct touch of complexity, a crisp, minerally edge and a finely textured, long finish.

Vintage	15	14	13	12
WR	6	6	6	6
Drink	16-18	16-17	P	P

DRY $21 V+

Fromm La Strada Marlborough Sauvignon Blanc ★★★★☆

After 16 vintages, the Fromm winery, renowned for Pinot Noir, finally produced its first Sauvignon Blanc in 2008 – mostly for export markets. Certified organic, the outstanding 2015 vintage (★★★★★) was hand-picked and fermented with indigenous yeasts in tanks (mostly) and seasoned French oak casks. Light lemon/green, it is fragrant and weighty, with ripe tropical-fruit flavours to the fore, good complexity, layers of flavour, and a finely textured, dry, long finish. Full of personality.

Vintage	15	14	13
WR	7	7	6
Drink	16-20	16-19	P

 DRY $28 AV

Fuder, The, Single Vineyard Selection Dillons Point Marlborough Sauvignon Blanc ★★★★☆

Currently on sale, the 2013 vintage (★★★★☆) from Giesen was grown in the lower Wairau Valley and handled in large German oak barrels, 'which develop a greater complexity and refinement but the oak doesn't dominate'. Bright, light lemon/green, it's a finely textured wine, dry (3 grams/litre of residual sugar), with mouthfilling body (14.5 per cent alcohol) and concentrated, ripely herbaceous flavours, showing a subtle seasoning of oak and excellent complexity. Drink now to 2017.

Vintage	13
WR	7
Drink	16-20

 DRY $45 –V

Fuder, The, Single Vineyard Selection Matthews Lane Marlborough Sauvignon Blanc ★★★★☆

Now on sale, the classy 2013 vintage (★★★★★) was grown at Rapaura, in the central Wairau Valley, and handled in large German oak fuders. Bright, light yellow-green, it is mouthfilling and dry (3 grams/litre of residual sugar), with deep, ripe tropical-fruit flavours, showing excellent complexity and harmony, and a finely poised, long finish. A powerful wine with strong personality, it's delicious now.

Vintage	13
WR	7
Drink	16-22

DRY $45 –V

Giesen Marlborough Sauvignon Blanc ★★★☆

This huge-volume wine from Giesen enjoys major export success. Still fresh and lively, the 2015 vintage (★★★☆) was grown in estate-owned and contract growers' vineyards, mostly in the Wairau Valley, with a small portion from the Awatere Valley. Light lemon/green, it is medium to full-bodied, with good depth of tropical-fruit flavours, a herbaceous undercurrent, and a finely balanced (4 grams/litre of residual sugar) finish. Drink now.

Vintage	15
WR	4
Drink	16-17

 DRY $17 V+

Giesen Marlborough Sauvignon Blanc The August 1888   ★★★★★

This distinctive wine is named after the Giesen brothers' grandfather, August (pronounced 'Ow-goost') Giesen. The 2013 vintage (★★★★★) was hand-picked and barrel-fermented with indigenous yeasts. Light yellow/green, it is a commanding, weighty wine (14.5 per cent alcohol), complex and dry, with highly concentrated tropical-fruit flavours, slightly nutty, tight and long. Maturing gracefully, it's a very harmonious wine, likely to be at its best 2017+.

Vintage	13
WR	7
Drink	16-20

 DRY $44 AV

Giesen Marlborough Sauvignon Blanc The Brothers   ★★★★

The 2014 vintage (★★★★) is made from Giesen's 'most expressive parcels', which typically include grapes from the Wairau and Awatere valleys. Pale lemon/green, it is mouthfilling, fresh and vibrantly fruity, in a clearly herbaceous style with good intensity and a crisp, dry (4 grams/litre of residual sugar), lingering finish.

Vintage	14
WR	5
Drink	16-18

 DRY $25 AV

Giesen Organic Marlborough Sauvignon Blanc   ★★★☆

Certified organic, the 2015 vintage (★★★☆) is drinking well now. Pale lemon/green, it is medium-bodied, lively and crisp, in a basically dry style (4 grams/litre of residual sugar) with ripely herbaceous, intensely varietal flavours, showing very good vigour and depth.

Vintage	15
WR	5
Drink	16-17

 DRY $20 AV

Gladstone Vineyard Sauvignon Blanc   ★★★★

The 2015 vintage (★★★★) was grown in the northern Wairarapa and 40 per cent barrel-fermented; the rest was handled in tanks. Made in a fully dry style (1.4 grams/litre of residual sugar), it is mouthfilling, with fresh, finely balanced acidity, concentrated, ripe tropical-fruit flavours and slightly toasty notes adding complexity. Drink now to 2017.

 DRY $25 AV

Gladstone Vineyard Sophie's Choice Barrel Fermented Sauvignon Blanc   ★★★★

The impressive, age-worthy 2014 vintage (★★★★☆) was estate-grown in the northern Wairarapa and fermented in barrels (76 per cent) and tanks (24 per cent). A complex style, it is fragrant and full-bodied, with fresh tropical-fruit flavours, finely integrated oak, balanced acidity and a bone-dry (1.6 grams/litre of residual sugar), long finish.

DRY $35 –V

Goldwater Wairau Valley Marlborough Sauvignon Blanc   ★★★★

Light lemon/green, the 2016 vintage (★★★★) is a fresh, medium to full-bodied wine with ripe tropical-fruit flavours, woven with fresh acidity. Crisp and lively, it shows good intensity, with a dry finish.

Vintage	14
WR	7
Drink	16-17

 DRY $21 V+

Graham Norton's Own Marlborough Sauvignon Blanc   ★★★★

From 'chief winemaker Graham Norton', Invivo's 2016 vintage (★★★★) has a punchy, aromatic bouquet. Medium to full-bodied, it is vibrantly fruity, with strong, ripe melon, lime and capsicum flavours, a slightly salty streak, a faint suggestion of sweetness (4.1 grams/litre of residual sugar) and a crisp, lingering finish.

 DRY $19 V+

Grava Martinborough Sauvignon Blanc   (★★★★★)

The very impressive 2015 vintage (★★★★★) was estate-grown south of Martinborough, at a site formerly known as Hudson Vineyard. Hand-picked, tank-fermented and lees-aged for four months (with some exposure to oak), it is richly scented, vibrantly fruity and tightly structured, in a medium to full-bodied style with intense, ripe non-herbaceous flavours. Crisp and minerally, with a dry, very long finish, it's full of personality. A top debut.

 DRY $27 V+

Greenhough Hope Vineyard Nelson Sauvignon Blanc   ★★★★☆

Certified organic, the age-worthy 2015 vintage (★★★★) was estate-grown, hand-harvested and fermented with indigenous yeasts in French oak barriques (20 per cent new). Full-bodied, it has strong, ripe tropical-fruit flavours, gently seasoned with biscuity oak, good complexity and a tight, dry finish. Still youthful, it should be at its best mid-2017+.

 DRY $30 –V

Greenhough Nelson Sauvignon Blanc   ★★★★

Certified organic, this consistently rewarding wine is mostly handled in tanks, but a minor portion (5 per cent of the blend in 2016) is fermented with indigenous yeasts in French oak casks. The 2016 vintage (★★★★) is fresh, crisp and lively, with strong passionfruit/lime flavours, showing a touch of complexity, and a fully dry (1.9 grams/litre of residual sugar) finish. Best drinking mid-2017+.

 DRY $22 V+

Greyrock Marlborough Sauvignon Blanc   (★★)

Solid but plain, the 2016 vintage (★★) is a pale lemon/green, medium-bodied wine with crisp green-apple flavours and a smooth (4 grams/litre of residual sugar) finish. (From Sileni.)

DRY $17 –V

Greystone Waipara Valley Sauvignon Blanc ★★★★

The 2015 vintage (★★★★☆) was fermented with indigenous yeasts in old oak barrels and matured on its full yeast lees for six months. Pale yellow/green, it is mouthfilling and fleshy, with concentrated, ripe tropical-fruit flavours, good complexity, and a faintly buttery, rounded finish. Already drinking well, it's a top vintage of this label.

Vintage	15	14	13	12
WR	7	6	6	5
Drink	16-20	16-20	16-19	P

 DRY $22 V+

Greywacke Marlborough Sauvignon Blanc ★★★★★

The very classy 2016 vintage (★★★★★), grown at sites in the central Wairau Valley and the Southern Valleys, was fermented entirely in tanks (with some indigenous yeast fermentation at relatively warm temperatures). Weighty, punchy and dry, it is overflowing with vibrant, ripe melon/lime flavours, with good acid spine and a long, tight finish. Explosively flavoured, it offers great value.

Vintage	16	15	14	13	12
WR	6	6	6	6	5
Drink	17-22	17-21	17-20	17-19	P

 DRY $26 V+

Greywacke Marlborough Wild Sauvignon ★★★★★

Still very youthful, the 2014 vintage (★★★★★) is a leading example of Marlborough Sauvignon Blanc from well outside the mainstream. Grown in the Southern Valleys and the central Wairau Valley, it was fermented with indigenous yeasts in mostly old French oak barriques (8 per cent new), wood-matured for a year, and finally lees-aged in tanks for five months before bottling. Weighty, it has rich, vibrant tropical-fruit flavours, showing excellent complexity, and a long, dry, well-rounded finish. (In a recent vertical tasting of the 2009–2014 vintages, all of the wines showed impressive freshness and vigour, highlighted by the 2009 and 2010, both seemingly in full stride, and the 2013, exceptionally elegant, rich and persistent.)

Vintage	14	13	12	11	10	09
WR	6	6	5	6	6	5
Drink	17-24	17-23	17-20	17-21	17-20	17-18

 DRY $37 AV

Grove Mill Wairau Valley Marlborough Sauvignon Blanc ★★★★

The 2016 vintage (★★★★) is a mouthfilling, dry wine with balanced acidity and generous, ripe tropical-fruit flavours that linger well.

DRY $22 V+

Gunn Estate Reserve Marlborough Sauvignon Blanc ★★★☆

Offering good, easy drinking, the freshly scented 2015 vintage (★★★☆) is mouthfilling and vibrantly fruity, with ripe tropical-fruit flavours and a gentle splash of sweetness (6 grams/litre of residual sugar), well balanced by fresh, tangy acidity.

Vintage	15
WR	6
Drink	16-17

 MED/DRY $20 AV

Haha Marlborough Sauvignon Blanc   ★★★☆

From Fern Ridge, based in Hawke's Bay, this is a consistently good buy. Grown in the Wairau and Waihopai valleys, the 2015 vintage (★★★☆) is ripely scented, with good depth of passionfruit/lime flavours, lively but not high acidity, and a smooth, dry (1.7 grams/litre of residual sugar) finish.

 DRY $16 V+

Hans Herzog Marlborough Sauvignon Blanc Barrel Fermented Sur Lie   ★★★★★

Far outside the mainstream regional style, the 2015 vintage (★★★★★) was estate-grown and hand-picked on the north side of the Wairau Valley, fermented with indigenous yeasts in French oak puncheons, and wood-aged for 15 months. Bright, light yellow/green, it is mouthfilling and ripely herbaceous, with generous, highly concentrated grapefruit, lime and slight capsicum flavours, a subtle seasoning of oak, and a dry, lasting finish. Drink now or cellar. Certified organic.

 DRY $44 AV

Hans Herzog Marlborough Sauvignon Blanc Grand Duchess   ★★★★☆

Currently on sale, the 2013 vintage (★★★★☆) was estate-grown on the north side of the Wairau Valley and fermented and matured for 18 months in French oak puncheons. Light yellow/green, it is mouthfilling, with fresh, concentrated tropical-fruit flavours to the fore, some herbaceous notes, a subtle seasoning of oak adding complexity, and a fully dry, rounded finish. Drink now or cellar. Certified organic.

 DRY $64 –V

Highfield Marlborough Sauvignon Blanc   ★★★☆

The 2015 vintage (★★★☆), handled without oak, was given extended aging on its yeast lees. Full-bodied, it is crisp and lively, with tropical-fruit and herbaceous flavours, dry and tangy.

Vintage	15	14	13	12
WR	6	6	6	6
Drink	16-17	16-18	16-17	P

DRY $24 –V

Huia Marlborough Sauvignon Blanc   ★★★★

The 2015 vintage (★★★★), grown in the Wairau Valley, was handled in a 50:50 split of tanks and old oak casks. Bright, light lemon/green, it is mouthfilling and sweet-fruited, with generous, ripe tropical-fruit flavours, a touch of complexity, and a persistent, dry (3.8 grams/litre of residual sugar) finish. Certified organic.

 DRY $30 –V

Hunky Dory Marlborough Sauvignon Blanc ★★★☆

From Huia, the finely balanced 2015 vintage (★★★★) was grown in the Wairau Valley. Handled entirely in tanks, it is mouthfilling and sweet-fruited, with fresh tropical-fruit flavours, a herbaceous undercurrent, and a lively, dry (3.8 grams/litre of residual sugar), lingering finish. Certified organic.

DRY $18 V+

Hunter's Kaho Roa Marlborough Sauvignon Blanc ★★★★

Based on the ripest, least-herbaceous grapes, this wine is estate-grown in stony vineyards along Rapaura Road, on the relatively warm, north side of the Wairau Valley. Maturing gracefully, 60 per cent of the 2013 vintage (★★★★) was handled in stainless steel tanks, but 40 per cent was fermented in an even split of new and seasoned French oak casks. A mouthfilling, sweet-fruited wine with generous tropical-fruit flavours and a twist of oak, it has considerable complexity, with balanced acidity and a slightly buttery, rounded finish.

DRY $25 AV

Hunter's Marlborough Sauvignon Blanc ★★★☆

Hunter's fame rests on this dry wine, which has the intense aromas of cool-climate grapes, uncluttered by oak handling. The goal is 'a strong expression of Marlborough fruit – a bell-clear wine with a mix of tropical and searing gooseberry characters'. The grapes are sourced from numerous sites in the Wairau Valley, and to retain their fresh, vibrant characters they are processed very quickly, with protective anaerobic techniques and minimal handling. The wine is usually at its best between one and two years old. The 2015 vintage (★★★☆) is dry (1.8 grams/litre of residual sugar), with mouthfilling body, delicate, ripe melon/lime flavours, a minerally streak and a lingering finish.

DRY $21 AV

Invivo Belle Marlborough Sauvignon Blanc (★★★)

The 2015 vintage (★★★) is a good example of the low-alchohol style (9.5 per cent). Pale lemon/green, it is light, lemony, appley and crisp, with lively, green-edged flavours, a slightly off-dry finish (5.4 grams/litre of residual sugar) and plenty of flavour.

Vintage	15
WR	7
Drink	16-18

MED/DRY $18 AV

Invivo Marlborough Sauvignon Blanc ★★★★

The 2016 vintage (★★★★☆) is a medium to full-bodied, intensely varietal wine, full of youthful vigour, with punchy melon, gooseberry, lime and capsicum flavours, crisp, dry (4.2 grams/litre of residual sugar) and lasting.

Vintage	16	15	14
WR	7	7	5
Drink	16-19	16-18	16-17

DRY $19 V+

Invivo Organic Marlborough Sauvignon Blanc   (★★★★☆)

The 2015 vintage (★★★★☆) is a top buy. Grown at Renwick, in the Wairau Valley, and 50 per cent barrel-fermented, it has a freshly scented bouquet, showing good complexity. Mouthfilling and tightly structured, it has strong, ripe melon/lime flavours, enriched by subtle oak/lees characters, and a long, dry (2.9 grams/litre of residual sugar), finely balanced finish.

DRY $19 V+

Jackson Estate Grey Ghost Barrique Wairau Valley
Marlborough Sauvignon Blanc   ★★★★★

Currently on sale, the outstanding 2013 vintage (★★★★★) was hand-picked from vines planted in 1988. Half the blend was handled in tanks; the other half was fermented with indigenous yeasts in seasoned French oak barriques and oak-aged for 10 months. Light lemon/green, it is mouthfilling, sweet-fruited and very harmonious, with strong, ripe tropical-fruit and slightly nutty flavours, very finely integrated oak, notable delicacy and complexity, and a finely poised, dry (1.9 grams/litre of residual sugar), persistent finish. Delicious now.

Vintage	13	12	11	10
WR	5	6	7	7
Drink	16-22	16-19	16-21	16-20

DRY $27 V+

Jackson Estate Stich Marlborough Sauvignon Blanc   ★★★★★

Estate-grown at three sites in the Wairau and Waihopai valleys (including some vines over 25 years old), this is typically a lush, ripe and rounded wine with concentration and huge drinkability. It has excellent aging ability, and the latest releases are often outstanding. The impressive 2015 vintage (★★★★★) is highly aromatic, mouthfilling and sweet-fruited, with excellent intensity of melon, lime and green-capsicum flavours, finely balanced acidity, and a long, dry (2.1 grams/litre of residual sugar) finish, zingy and harmonious.

Vintage	15	14	13	12
WR	6	5	5	6
Drink	16-18	P-17	P	P

DRY $21 V+

Johanneshof Cellars Marlborough Sauvignon Blanc   ★★★

Ready to roll, the 2015 vintage (★★★☆) from this small producer is fleshy and smooth. A single-vineyard wine, made from hand-harvested grapes, it is an easy-drinking, off-dry style (6.6 grams/litre of residual sugar), with balanced acidity and strong passionfruit and lime flavours.

MED/DRY $24 –V

Johner Estate Gladstone Sur Lie Sauvignon Blanc   ★★★★

Maturing well, the 2015 vintage (★★★★) was grown in the northern Wairarapa and fermented with indigenous yeasts in tanks (90 per cent) and old oak barrels (10 per cent). Lees-aged for seven months, it's a sweet-fruited wine, crisp, lively and dry (3 grams/litre of residual sugar), with youthful vigour and good intensity of melon, citrus-fruit and lime flavours. Best drinking 2017.

Vintage	15
WR	5
Drink	16-19

DRY $24 AV

Johner Estate Wairarapa Sauvignon Blanc   ★★★☆

The light lemon/green 2016 vintage (★★★★) is medium to full-bodied, with strong, lively tropical-fruit flavours, a herbaceous undercurrent, and a dry (4 grams/litre of residual sugar) appetisingly crisp finish. Good value.

Vintage	16	15	14	13
WR	6	5	6	6
Drink	16-18	16-17	P	P

DRY $20 AV

Jules Taylor Marlborough Sauvignon Blanc   ★★★★☆

Grown in the Wairau and Awatere valleys, the vibrant, punchy 2016 vintage (★★★★☆) was handled entirely in tanks and made in a fully dry (1.1 grams/litre of residual sugar) style. Pale, it is highly aromatic, with an array of melon, grapefruit, lime and green-capsicum flavours, in an intensely varietal style with pure, penetrating flavours.

Vintage	16
WR	5
Drink	16-18

DRY $22 V+

Jules Taylor OTQ Series Marlborough Sauvignon Blanc   ★★★★★

Made 'On The Quiet', the classy 2015 vintage (★★★★★) is a single-vineyard wine, grown at Dillons Point, in the lower Wairau Valley. Hand-picked and fermented with indigenous yeasts in old French oak barrels, it was matured on its yeast lees in wood for nearly a year. Bright, light lemon/green, it is ripely scented, mouthfilling and sweet-fruited, with concentrated tropical-fruit flavours, a subtle seasoning of oak, excellent complexity and a long, dry (2.2 grams/litre of residual sugar), rounded finish. Already delicious, it's a drink-now or cellaring proposition.

Vintage	15
WR	6
Drink	16-20

DRY $30 AV

Kaimira Estate Brightwater Sauvignon Blanc   ★★★☆

Certified organic, the 2015 vintage (★★★☆) was estate-grown. Light lemon/green, it is full-bodied, lively and freshly herbaceous, with some tropical-fruit notes, in a crisp, dry style (3.2 grams/litre of residual sugar), showing good depth. Drink now.

DRY $21 AV

Kainui Road Bay of Islands Sauvignon Blanc ★★★

The 2015 vintage (★★★) of this Northland wine is mouthfilling, with gentle, ripe melon/lime flavours, hints of lychees and pears, fresh acidity, and a finely balanced finish.

Kim Crawford Reserve Marlborough Sauvignon Blanc ★★★☆

The mouthfilling, smooth 2015 vintage (★★★☆) is a 3:1 blend of Wairau Valley and Awatere Valley grapes. It has fresh, strong passionfruit/lime flavours to the fore, a herbaceous undercurrent, and a crisp, dryish (5 grams/litre of residual sugar) finish. Priced sharply. (Note: the word 'Reserve' is only on the capsule.)

Kina Cliffs Nelson Sauvignon Blanc ★★★

From a single coastal site, the 2015 vintage (★★★) is full-bodied, with good depth of fresh, ripe tropical-fruit flavours and a distinct splash of sweetness, balanced by lively acidity.

Konrad Marlborough Sauvignon Blanc ★★★☆

Certified organic, the 2014 vintage (★★★☆) was estate-grown in the Waihopai Valley and mostly handled in tanks; a small part of the blend was barrel-fermented. It is full-bodied, with ripe tropical-fruit flavours to the fore, slightly spicy and toasty notes adding a touch of complexity, and a dryish (4.8 grams/litre of residual sugar), crisp finish.

Lake Hayes Central Otago Sauvignon Blanc ★★☆

The 2016 vintage (★★☆) is an easy-drinking, light-bodied wine with fresh, citrusy, appley flavours, dry (2 grams/litre of residual sugar) and crisp. (From Amisfield.)

DRY $20 –V

Lawson's Dry Hills Marlborough Sauvignon Blanc ★★★★★

One of the region's best, widely available Sauvignon Blancs, this stylish wine is vibrant, intense and finely structured. The grapes are grown at several sites, mostly in the Southern Valleys, and to add a subtle extra dimension, 4 to 8 per cent of the blend (7 per cent in 2015) is fermented in seasoned French oak barriques. The wine typically has great impact in its youth, but also has a proven ability to age, acquiring toasty, minerally complexities. The 2015 vintage (★★★★) is light lemon/green, with a fresh, aromatic, ripely herbaceous bouquet. Mouthfilling, it is vibrantly fruity, with pure melon/herb flavours, tangy, dry (2 grams/litre of residual sugar) and lingering.

Vintage	15
WR	7
Drink	16-20

Lawson's Dry Hills Wairau Reserve Marlborough Sauvignon Blanc ★★★★★

The impressive 2015 vintage (★★★★), grown at several sites around the Wairau Valley, was fermented in tanks (85 per cent) and old French oak barriques (15 per cent). Mouthfilling and fleshy, it is sweet-fruited, with concentrated tropical-fruit scents and flavours, a gentle hint of oak, and a crisp, dry (1.5 grams/litre of residual sugar) finish.

Vintage	15	
WR	7	DRY $24 V+
Drink	16-20	

Left Field Nelson Sauvignon Blanc ★★★☆

Offering good value, the 2016 vintage (★★★☆) is lively, with fresh, strong tropical-fruit flavours and a dry (4.3 grams/litre of residual sugar), appetisingly crisp finish. (From Te Awa.)

Vintage	16	
WR	5	DRY $18 V+
Drink	16-19	

Little Black Shag Nelson Sauvignon Blanc (★★☆)

Priced sharply, the 2015 vintage (★★☆) is a medium-bodied wine with fresh, moderately ripe, melon and green-capsicum flavours, woven with tangy acidity. A 'greener' style, it's ready to roll.

DRY $11 V+

Little Darling Organic Marlborough Sauvignon Blanc (★★★☆)

From organically certified vineyards, the 2015 vintage (★★★☆) is a strongly varietal wine, with a herbaceous bouquet. Lively, it shows good depth of crisp melon, lime and capsicum flavours, fresh and tangy.

DRY $20 AV

Loveblock Marlborough Sauvignon Blanc ★★★★

Still on sale, the 2014 vintage (★★★★) is maturing gracefully and drinking well now. Estate-grown in the lower Awatere Valley, it is a weighty, ripe style, with strong, lively passionfruit-like flavours, hints of pineapples and spices, fresh, balanced acidity and a lingering finish. Certified organic.

DRY $27 –V

Luminary, The, Martinborough Sauvignon Blanc ★★★☆

From Palliser Estate, the 2014 vintage (★★★☆) currently on sale has a strong, ripely herbaceous bouquet. Still fresh, it is mouthfilling and sweet-fruited, with generous, ripe flavours and a smooth finish. Ready.

DRY $17 V+

Mahi Boundary Farm Sauvignon Blanc ★★★★☆

Grown on the lower slopes of the Wither Hills, the 2014 vintage (★★★★☆) is a single-vineyard wine, hand-picked, fermented with indigenous yeasts and lees-aged for 10 months in French oak barriques. Pale lemon/green, it is a complex, dry style (3.1 grams/litre of residual sugar), still very fresh and vibrant, with lively acidity and very good intensity of tropical-fruit flavours. Worth cellaring, it should be at its best 2017+.

Vintage	14	13	12
WR	6	6	6
Drink	16-21	16-21	16-20

DRY $29 AV

Mahi Marlborough Sauvignon Blanc ★★★★

The 2015 vintage (★★★★), a regional blend, was mostly handled in tanks; 12 per cent (the ripest, hand-picked fruit) was barrel-fermented with indigenous yeasts. Light lemon/green, it is crisp and dry (1.4 grams/litre of residual sugar), with very good vigour and depth of ripely herbaceous flavours, slightly minerally and toasty.

Vintage	15	14	13	12
WR	6	6	6	6
Drink	16-18	16-18	16-17	P

DRY $20 V+

Main Divide Waipara Valley Sauvignon Blanc ★★★★

The 2015 vintage (★★★★) offers fine value. It has a fresh, strong, ripely herbaceous bouquet, leading into a weighty wine (14 per cent alcohol) with passionfruit, melon and lime flavours, crisp, dry and sustained. (From Pegasus Bay.)

Vintage	15	14	13	12
WR	7	6	7	7
Drink	16-20	16-18	16-18	P

DRY $20 V+

Man O' War Waiheke Island Sauvignon Blanc ★★★☆

The 2015 vintage (★★★★) was estate-grown, hand-picked, blended with a small portion of Sémillon, and partly barrel-fermented. Bright, light lemon/green, it is a powerful, full-bodied (14.5 per cent alcohol), dry wine (4 grams/litre of residual sugar), with tropical-fruit flavours, gently seasoned with toasty oak, good complexity and strong personality.

Vintage	15	14
WR	6	5
Drink	16-19	16-18

DRY $24 –V

Margrain Martinborough Sauvignon Blanc   ★★★☆

This wine is typically made in an easy-drinking, off-dry style. The 2016 vintage (★★★☆) is fresh and lively, with strong melon, grapefruit and lime flavours, a sliver of sweetness (6 grams/litre of residual sugar) and appetising acidity. The 2015 vintage (★★★☆) is a fleshy, slightly developed wine with good depth of tropical-fruit flavours, a herbaceous undercurrent, and a slightly sweet (7 grams/litre of residual sugar), smooth finish. Ready.

Vintage	16	15
WR	6	6
Drink	16-20	16-20

 MED/DRY $24 –V

Marsden Marlborough Sauvignon Blanc   ★★★

Drinking well now, the 2015 vintage (★★★☆) is a strongly varietal wine, fresh, crisp and lively. Medium-bodied, it is dry (2 grams/litre of residual sugar), with tropical-fruit and herbaceous flavours, showing good vigour and depth.

 DRY $27 –V

Martinborough Vineyard Martinborough Sauvignon Blanc   ★★★★

The 2016 vintage (★★★★) was partly barrel-aged. Light lemon/green, it is fleshy and dry, with rich, ripe tropical-fruit flavours, gently seasoned with nutty oak, and good complexity. Delicious drinking now onwards.

 DRY $23 AV

Martinborough Vineyard Te Tera Sauvignon Blanc   ★★★☆

The 2015 vintage (★★★☆) is a freshly scented, mouthfilling wine with tropical-fruit and herbaceous flavours, strong and smooth.

 DRY $18 V+

Matahiwi Holly Wairarapa Sauvignon Blanc   ★★★★

The youthful 2015 vintage (★★★★) was barrel-fermented. Bright, light lemon/green in hue, it is a full-bodied, age-worthy wine with fresh, ripe tropical-fruit flavours, a subtle seasoning of oak adding complexity, and a dry, appetisingly crisp finish. Best drinking 2017+.

 DRY $29 –V

Matahiwi Wairarapa Sauvignon Blanc   ★★★☆

The 2015 vintage (★★★★), handled without oak, is a fleshy, generous wine, drinking well now. Sweet-fruited, it has strong, vibrant, well-ripened tropical-fruit flavours, balanced acidity, and a dry, finely balanced finish.

DRY $20 AV

Matua Single Vineyard Awatere Valley Sauvignon Blanc ★★★★☆

Full of personality, the 2015 vintage (★★★★★) is a highly aromatic, tightly structured and slightly minerally wine, with intense, crisp melon and green-capsicum flavours, and slightly smoky notes adding complexity. A dry style (2.8 grams/litre of residual sugar) with mouth-watering acidity and a lasting finish, it's drinking well now.

DRY $36 –V

Maui Marlborough Sauvignon Blanc ★★★☆

The 2016 vintage (★★★☆) is a crisp, mouthfilling wine with good depth of fresh melon, lime and green-capsicum flavours, lively, tangy, and skilfully balanced for easy drinking. (From Tiki.)

DRY $19 V+

Mills Reef Estate Marlborough Sauvignon Blanc ★★☆

The easy-drinking 2016 vintage (★★☆) was grown in the Awatere Valley. Fresh and lively, it is medium-bodied, with melon and green-capsicum flavours and a smooth (4 grams/litre of residual sugar) finish.

Vintage	16	15
WR	7	7
Drink	16-18	16-17

DRY $19 –V

Mills Reef Reserve Hawke's Bay Sauvignon Blanc ★★★☆

Grown in the inland, elevated Puketapu district, the 2016 vintage (★★★☆) is aromatic, fresh and lively, with good depth of melon/lime flavours, dry (2 grams/litre of residual sugar) and crisp. Enjoyable young.

Vintage	16
WR	7
Drink	16-18

DRY $23 –V

Misha's Vineyard The Starlet Central Otago Sauvignon Blanc ★★★★

Still on sale, the 2014 vintage (★★★★) was estate-grown in the Cromwell Basin. It was hand-picked and 21 per cent of the blend was fermented with indigenous yeasts in old French oak casks. Weighty, with strong, vibrant melon/lime flavours, it shows a touch of complexity, with moderate acidity and a dryish (5 grams/litre of residual sugar) finish.

Vintage	14	13	12	11
WR	6	7	7	6
Drink	16-20	16-19	16-18	P

MED/DRY $27 –V

Mission Marlborough Sauvignon Blanc ★★★☆

The 2016 vintage (★★★☆) is already drinking well. Bright, light lemon/green, it is mouthfilling and finely balanced, with good depth of vibrant melon and green-capsicum flavours, a sliver of sweetness (5 grams/litre of residual sugar) and tangy acidity.

MED/DRY $18 V+

Mission Reserve Marlborough Sauvignon Blanc   (★★★★)

The 2015 vintage (★★★★) is a single-vineyard, Awatere Valley wine, barrel-fermented. Mouthfilling, it has fresh, strong tropical-fruit and herbaceous flavours, with a touch of oak-derived complexity, and a dry, appetisingly crisp finish.

DRY $30 –V

Mission Vineyard Selection Marlborough Sauvignon Blanc   ★★★☆

The 2016 vintage (★★★★) was estate-grown in the Awatere Valley. Mouthfilling, it is sweet-fruited, with fresh, ripe melon, grapefruit, lime and capsicum flavours, dryish (5 grams/litre of residual sugar) and crisp. Instantly appealing.

MED/DRY $20 AV

Misty Cove Ella Maria Limited Edition Marlborough Sauvignon Blanc   ★★★★

Showing considerable complexity, the 2014 vintage (★★★★) was estate-grown and hand-picked at Rapaura and fermented and lees-aged for nine months in French oak casks (20 per cent new). Full-bodied and dry, it has good concentration of ripe tropical-fruit flavours, toasty oak in evidence, balanced acidity and obvious potential. Drink now to 2017.

DRY $30 –V

Misty Cove Marlborough Sauvignon Blanc   ★★★☆

Mouthfilling, crisp and dry, the 2015 vintage (★★★☆) of this 'Signature' wine was hand-picked at Rapaura and Omaka and lees-aged for nine months. Lively, it has fresh, strong passionfruit/lime flavours, firm acid spine and very good length.

DRY $24 –V

Misty Cove Organic Marlborough Sauvignon Blanc   ★★★

The crisp, medium-bodied 2015 vintage (★★★) was grown in the Wairau Valley and 10 per cent barrel-fermented. Distinctly citrusy, it is slightly limey and appley, with a touch of complexity and good acid spine. Certified organic.

DRY $24 –V

Momo Marlborough Organic Sauvignon Blanc   ★★★☆

From Seresin, the 2015 vintage (★★★☆) is an organically certified wine, fermented with indigenous yeasts and bottled unfined. Grown at company-owned and growers' sites in the Wairau Valley and Waihopai Valley, it is full-bodied and dry (3.7 grams/litre of residual sugar), with ripe tropical-fruit flavours, a vague suggestion of honey, fresh acidity and very good depth. Enjoyable now.

DRY $20 AV

Montana Marlborough Sauvignon Blanc   ★★☆

The 2015 vintage (★★☆) of this classic label (now sold only in New Zealand, since its replacement overseas by the Brancott Estate brand) is medium-bodied, fresh, herbaceous and smooth. Ready.

DRY $12 V+

Mouku Marlborough Sauvignon Blanc (★★★)

Offering good value, the 2015 vintage (★★★) is a clearly varietal, mouthfilling wine with fresh tropical-fruit and herbaceous flavours, and a dryish, tangy finish. (From Toi Toi.)

DRY $15 V+

Mount Brown Estates Grand Reserve Sauvignon Blanc (★★★★)

Offering good value, the 2015 vintage (★★★★) is a freshly aromatic, barrel-fermented wine with mouthfilling body and a dryish (5 grams/litre of residual sugar) blend of tropical fruit and lively, cut-grass flavours that linger well.

Vintage	15
WR	6
Drink	16-17

MED/DRY $20 V+

Mount Brown Waipara Valley Sauvignon Blanc ★★★

The 2015 vintage (★★★) is mouthfilling, with fresh tropical-fruit and herbaceous flavours, dry (4 grams/litre of residual sugar) and crisp. Priced sharply.

DRY $16 V+

Mount Riley Limited Release Marlborough Sauvignon Blanc ★★★★

The 2015 vintage (★★★★) is Mount Riley's 'best effort' from the vintage. A 50:50 blend of Awatere Valley and Wairau Valley fruit, it is an elegant, mouthfilling wine, tightly structured, with melon/lime flavours, a slightly 'salty' note and a dry, lingering finish.

DRY $18 V+

Mount Riley Marlborough Sauvignon Blanc ★★★☆

Fine value. The 2015 vintage (★★★☆), grown in the Wairau Valley (70 per cent) and the Awatere Valley (30 per cent), is full-bodied, with good depth of fresh, ripe passionfruit/lime flavours and a dry (4 grams/litre of residual sugar), finely balanced finish.

DRY $17 V+

Mount Riley Seventeen Valley Marlborough Sauvignon Blanc ★★★★

The 2014 vintage (★★★★☆) was hand-harvested in the Anderson Vineyard, in the central Wairau Valley, and fermented and lees-aged for eight months in seasoned French oak barrels. The bouquet is ripely scented, with a gentle twist of oak; the palate is fleshy and dry, with strong, ripe tropical-fruit flavours, complexity from the wood handling, finely balanced acidity and a lingering finish. A very age-worthy wine, it offers fine value.

DRY $22 V+

Mount Vernon Marlborough Sauvignon Blanc ★★★★

From Lawson's Dry Hills, the 2016 vintage (★★★★☆) is a pale lemon/green, medium to full-bodied wine. Highly aromatic, it is freshly herbaceous, with penetrating melon, lime and green capsicum-evoking flavours, slightly nettley, youthful and lively, and a dry (4 grams/litre of residual sugar) finish. A top buy.

DRY $19 V+

Mountain Road Taranaki Sauvignon Blanc   ★★★

Grown north of New Plymouth, this rare wine is from vines planted in 2004. Designed to be enjoyed 'with cobbers', and made with some use of barrel fermentation and lees-stirring, the 2014 vintage (★★★), retasted in 2016, is maturing well. Light lemon/green, it's a medium to full-bodied wine with ripely herbaceous flavours, showing a touch of complexity, and a smooth finish. Ready.

Moutere Hills Nelson Sauvignon Blanc   ★★★

The 2015 vintage (★★★) is a single-vineyard wine, medium-bodied, lemony, appley and dry, with a minerally streak and a lively, slightly spicy finish.

Mt Beautiful North Canterbury Sauvignon Blanc   ★★★☆

Estate-grown at Cheviot, north of Waipara, the 2015 vintage (★★★☆) is light lemon/green, mouthfilling and freshly herbaceous, with some tropical-fruit notes. Weighty (14.5 per cent alcohol), it is a green-edged style, dry (2 grams/litre of residual sugar),with good intensity. Ready.

Vintage	15
WR	6
Drink	16-18

Mt Difficulty Bannockburn Sauvignon Blanc   ★★★☆

The 2015 vintage (★★★☆) of this Central Otago wine is pale and full-bodied (14.5 per cent alcohol), with fresh melon, lime and capsicum flavours, strong and youthful. Best drinking now to 2017.

Mud House Marlborough Sauvignon Blanc   ★★★★

This is typically a lively, herbaceous wine, offering a clear style contrast to its riper stablemate under the Waipara Hills Marlborough Sauvignon Blanc label. The highly attractive 2015 vintage (★★★★☆) is mouthfilling and finely balanced, with excellent intensity of vibrant melon, lime and capsicum flavours, fresh and lingering. Great value.

Mud House Single Vineyard The Woolshed Marlborough Sauvignon Blanc   ★★★★☆

Estate-grown in the upper Wairau Valley, the 2014 vintage (★★★★☆) is fully dry (1.5 grams/litre of residual sugar), highly scented, tight and elegant, with mouthfilling body, vibrant melon/lime flavours, showing excellent delicacy and depth, and a minerally, persistent finish.

Vintage	14
WR	6
Drink	16-17

DRY $25 V+

Nautilus Marlborough Sauvignon Blanc   ★★★★☆

This is typically a fragrant, sweet-fruited wine with mouthfilling body and crisp, concentrated flavours. The 2016 vintage (★★★★☆) is ripely scented, punchy and dry (2 grams/litre of residual sugar), with good weight, appetising acidity and fresh, strong tropical-fruit flavours.

Vintage	16	15	14	13
WR	7	7	7	7
Drink	16-19	16-18	16-17	P

 DRY $25 V+

Nautilus The Paper Marlborough Sauvignon Blanc   (★★★★★)

Named after a paper-thin shell, the debut 2015 vintage (★★★★★) was estate-grown, hand-picked and fermented in a single, seasoned French oak cuve. Made in a dry style (2 grams/litre of residual sugar), it has a complex bouquet. Mouthfilling, it is ripely herbaceous, with a subtle seasoning of oak, a sense of youthful drive, and lovely complexity, delicacy and harmony. Youthful and tight-knit, it's already very approachable.

 DRY $35 AV

Neudorf Nelson Sauvignon Blanc   ★★★★

Grown on the Waimea Plains, the 2015 vintage (★★★★☆) was mostly handled in tanks; 20 per cent of the blend was fermented and matured in old French oak barriques. Light lemon/green, it is fresh and full-bodied, with concentrated tropical-fruit flavours to the fore, some herbaceous notes, a touch of complexity, balanced acidity and a dry, persistent finish. Best drinking this summer.

 DRY $25 AV

Nga Waka Martinborough Sauvignon Blanc   ★★★★

The 2015 vintage (★★★★) is a mouthfilling, dry wine, fermented in tanks (60 per cent) and seasoned oak barrels (40 per cent). Crisp and lively, it has strong tropical-fruit flavours, with a minerally streak and a persistent finish.

Vintage	15
WR	7
Drink	16-17

 DRY $25 AV

Old Coach Road Lighter Alcohol Nelson Sauvignon Blanc   ★★☆

The 2016 vintage (★★☆) from Seifried is light and lively, with low alcohol (9.5 per cent), a gentle splash of sweetness (5 grams/litre of residual sugar), and tangy, citrusy, appley flavours.

MED/DRY $13 V+

Old Coach Road Nelson Sauvignon Blanc   ★★★

This is Seifried Estate's lowest-tier Sauvignon, priced right and enjoyable young. The 2016 vintage (★★★) is full-bodied, with ripely herbaceous flavours, showing good depth, and a dry (3 grams/litre of residual sugar) finish.

DRY $13 V+

Omihi Hills Limestone Ridge Sauvignon Blanc   ★★★☆

The 2014 vintage (★★★☆), grown at Omihi, in North Canterbury, has fresh, ripe tropical-fruit flavours, a minerally streak, and a dry (3 grams/litre of residual sugar) finish.

Vintage	14
WR	6
Drink	16-18

DRY $15 V+

Opawa Marlborough Sauvignon Blanc   ★★★★

From Nautilus, the stylish, bargain-priced 2016 vintage (★★★★☆) was grown in the Wairau Valley and mostly handled in tanks, but 10 per cent was fermented with indigenous yeasts in large oak cuves. Bright, light lemon/green, it is mouthfilling and sweet-fruited, with strong, vibrant passionfruit/lime flavours, showing a distinct touch of complexity, lively acidity and a dry (2 grams/litre of residual sugar), persistent finish. Instantly appealing.

DRY $22 V+

Overstone Marlborough Sauvignon Blanc   (★★★)

Enjoyable young, the 2016 vintage (★★★) is fresh, lively and smooth, with good depth of ripely herbaceous flavours and a dry (4 grams/litre of residual sugar) finish. (From Sileni.)

DRY $16 V+

Oyster Bay Marlborough Sauvignon Blanc   ★★★☆

Oyster Bay is a Delegat brand, focused mostly but not entirely on Marlborough wines and enjoying huge success in international markets. Handled entirely in stainless steel tanks, this wine is grown at dozens of sites around the Wairau (mostly) and Awatere valleys, and made in a dry style with tropical-fruit and herbaceous flavours, crisp and punchy. It is typically full-bodied, with fresh, dry melon, lime, passionfruit and green-capsicum flavours. The 2015 vintage (★★★☆) is mouthfilling and sweet-fruited, with ripe, gently herbaceous flavours and a dry (3 grams/litre of residual sugar), rounded finish.

DRY $20 AV

Paddy Borthwick Wairarapa Sauvignon Blanc   ★★★☆

Grown at Gladstone, in the Wairarapa, the 2014 vintage (★★★☆) is a strongly varietal wine with a punchy, aromatic bouquet. Crisp and lively, it has a hint of spice and very good depth of melon/lime flavours.

DRY $22 AV

Palliser Estate Martinborough Sauvignon Blanc   ★★★★★

At its best, this is a seductive wine, one of the best Sauvignons in the country. A distinctly cool-climate style, it offers an exquisite harmony of crisp acidity, mouthfilling body and fresh, penetrating fruit characters. The grapes are mostly estate-grown, but are also purchased from growers on the Martinborough Terrace and at Te Muna. The fruit gives the intensity of flavour – there's no blending with Sémillon, no barrel fermentation, no oak-aging. The 2015 vintage (★★★★☆) is aromatic, full-bodied, crisp and zingy, with finely balanced tropical-fruit flavours of passionfruit and lime, fresh, dry (4 grams/litre of residual sugar) and lingering.

DRY $27 V+

Paroa Bay Bay of Islands Sauvignon Blanc   ★★★★

Estate-grown on a steep, south-facing slope at Russell, in Northland, the 2015 vintage (★★★★) is very fresh and vibrant, in a sweet-fruited style with tight melon/lime flavours, balanced acidity, and impressive vigour, depth and immediacy.

DRY $29 –V

Pask Gimblett Road Barrique-Fermented Sauvignon Blanc   ★★★★

The 2014 vintage (★★★★) is an aromatic Hawke's Bay wine, handled in old French oak barriques. It's an elegant, mouthfilling wine with crisp, ripe tropical-fruit flavours to the fore, a subtle seasoning of oak adding complexity, and good length.

Vintage	14
WR	6
Drink	16-18

DRY $22 V+

Pegasus Bay Sauvignon/Sémillon   ★★★★★

At its best, this Waipara, North Canterbury wine is concentrated and complex, with loads of personality. From vines almost 30 years old, the 2014 vintage (★★★★☆) is a blend of Sauvignon Blanc and Sémillon, fermented in a mix of tanks and French oak barrels, old and new, and lees-aged for eight months. Bright yellow/green, it is a powerful wine, very full-bodied, with concentrated, ripe peach and passionfruit flavours, a vague hint of honey, exellent complexity and a dry, rich finish. A very distinctive wine, it's drinking well now.

DRY $31 AV

Peter Yealands Lighter in Alcohol Marlborough Sauvignon Blanc   ★★★

The 2015 vintage (★★★) is dry (4 grams/litre of residual sugar) and light-bodied (9 per cent alcohol), with crisp, citrusy, appley flavours, showing good depth, and a freshly aromatic bouquet.

Vintage	15	14
WR	6	5
Drink	16-17	P

DRY $16 V+

Peter Yealands Marlborough Sauvignon Blanc ★★★☆

The 2015 vintage (★★★★) is a punchy, intensely varietal wine, blended from Awatere Valley (70 per cent) and Wairau Valley (30 per cent) grapes. Crisp, tightly structured and slightly minerally, it is dry (4 grams/litre of residual sugar), with fresh, strong melon and green-capsicum flavours, and the incisive, nettley notes typical of the Awatere Valley. The 2016 vintage (★★★☆) offers fine value. Light lemon/green, it is aromatic and vividly varietal, with a slightly 'salty' streak and very good depth of fresh melon, capsicum and lime flavours.

Vintage	16	15	14
WR	7	7	7
Drink	16-18	16-17	P

DRY $15 V+

Peter Yealands Reserve Awatere Valley Marlborough Sauvignon Blanc ★★★★

Offering great value, the pale lemon/green 2016 vintage (★★★★) is a classic Awatere Valley style. Medium to full-bodied, it has fresh, vibrant melon, lime and green-capsicum flavours, showing good intensity, a slightly minerally streak and a tangy, dry (3.6 grams/litre of residual sugar), persistent finish.

Vintage	16	15	14
WR	7	6	6
Drink	16-18	16-17	P

DRY $18 V+

Petit Clos by Clos Henri Marlborough Sauvignon Blanc ★★★★

Certified organic, the 2015 vintage (★★★★) is from young vines, estate-grown in the Wairau Valley and tank-fermented. Full-bodied, it has generous, ripe tropical-fruit flavours, with lees-aging adding a touch of complexity, and a crisp, dry, lingering finish. Priced sharply.

Vintage	15	14	13	12
WR	7	6	7	6
Drink	16-18	16-17	P	P

DRY $20 V+

Pruner's Reward, The, Waipara Sauvignon Blanc ★★★☆

From Bellbird Spring, the 2016 vintage (★★★★) was fermented in tanks (80 per cent) and old oak casks (20 per cent). The best yet, it is medium to full-bodied, fresh and lively, with very good vigour and depth of ripe tropical-fruit flavours, showing a touch of complexity, and a dry, crisp finish.

DRY $22 AV

Rapaura Springs Marlborough Sauvignon Blanc ★★★☆

Bargain-priced, the 2016 vintage (★★★☆) is pale, fresh and punchy, with ripe passionfruit/lime flavours and a finely balanced, dry (4 grams/litre of residual sugar), appetisingly crisp finish. It's already quite open and expressive.

Vintage	16	15	14	13
WR	7	7	6	7
Drink	16-19	16-18	16-18	P

DRY $14 V+

Rapaura Springs Reserve Marlborough Sauvignon Blanc   ★★★★

Grown in the Wairau Valley, the 2015 vintage (★★★★☆) is aromatic, fleshy and sweet-fruited, with fresh, ripe melon/lime flavours, showing good intensity, and a finely poised, crisp, dry (2.9 grams/litre of residual sugar) finish. Fine value.

Vintage	15	14	13
WR	7	7	7
Drink	16-18	16-18	P

DRY $20 V+

Renato Nelson Sauvignon Blanc   ★★★★

The 2015 vintage (★★★★), grown on the Waimea Plains, has a freshly aromatic, herbaceous bouquet. Showing strong varietal characteristics, it is mouthfilling, with tropical-fruit and herbaceous flavours, and a dry (3 grams/litre of residual sugar), lingering finish.

Vintage	15	14	13
WR	6	7	6
Drink	16-18	16-18	16-17

DRY $18 V+

Richmond Plains Blue Moon Nelson Sauvignon Blanc   ★★★★

Certified biodynamic, the very age-worthy 2015 vintage (★★★★) was fermented and matured for 10 months in French oak hogsheads. Slightly oaky in its youth, it is youthful, with mouthfilling body and ripe tropical-fruit flavours, showing good complexity and length. Best drinking 2017+.

DRY $25 AV

Richmond Plains Nelson Sauvignon Blanc   ★★★★

Certified organic, the 2015 vintage (★★★★) is an attractive, lively wine with good weight and depth. Offering fresh, strong tropical-fruit and herbaceous flavours, with a well-rounded, lingering finish, it's a delicious mouthful.

DRY $22 V+

Roaring Meg Central Otago Sauvignon Blanc   ★★★☆

From Mt Difficulty, the 2015 vintage (★★★) is pale, mouthfilling, fleshy and smooth, with fresh melon, lime and capsicum flavours. Ready.

DRY $23 –V

Rock Ferry 3rd Rock Marlborough Sauvignon Blanc   ★★★★☆

(This label recently replaced the former Rock Ferry Marlborough Sauvignon Blanc.) Certified organic, the stylish, tightly structured 2015 vintage (★★★★★) was estate-grown at Rapaura and mostly handled in tanks; 12 per cent of the blend was fermented with indigenous yeasts in seasoned oak casks. Ripely scented and weighty, it is vibrant and intense, with tropical-fruit flavours to the fore, showing excellent delicacy and depth, firm acid spine, barrel-ferment complexity and a crisp, lasting finish. A fresh, concentrated, harmonious wine with strong personality, it's still youthful; drink now or cellar.

DRY $25 V+

Rock Ferry The Corners Vineyard Marlborough Sauvignon Blanc   (★★★★☆)

Still on sale, the 2013 vintage (★★★★☆) is certified organic. Hand-picked at Rapaura, it was fermented with indigenous yeasts and lees-aged for eight months in French oak barriques (8 per cent new). Maturing very gracefully, it is an elegant, tightly structured wine with rich tropical-fruit flavours, well-integrated oak adding complexity and a finely textured, bone-dry, lingering finish. Drink now to 2017.

DRY $30 –V

Rockburn Central Otago Fumé Blanc   (★★★★)

Showing good personality, the 2014 vintage (★★★★) currently on sale is a single-vineyard wine, estate-grown at Parkburn, in the Cromwell Basin. Fermented with indigenous yeasts in French oak barrels, it was wood-aged for the unusually long period of 18 months, and bottled without fining or filtration. Bright, light yellow/green, it is a complex, finely balanced wine, still fresh and lively, with strong, ripe tropical-fruit flavours, a gentle oak influence, good acid spine and a long, dry finish. Drink now to 2017.

DRY $40 –V

Rockburn Central Otago Sauvignon Blanc   ★★★

Currently on sale, the 2014 vintage (★★☆) was fermented with indigenous yeasts in French oak barrels. Bright, light lemon/green, it is mouthfilling and moderately fresh, but slightly tart, with canned peas and asparagus notes emerging. Ready.

DRY $24 –V

Rossendale Marlborough Sauvignon Blanc   ★★☆

The low-priced 2016 vintage (★★☆) is pale lemon/green, with freshly herbaceous aromas. Medium-bodied, it has lively melon, lime and capsicum flavours, with a green-edged, smooth finish.

DRY $14 AV

Russian Jack Marlborough Sauvignon Blanc   ★★★

Offering fine value, the 2015 vintage (★★★) from Martinborough Vineyard is mouthfilling, with good depth of ripely herbaceous flavours, fresh acidity and a smooth finish. It's enjoyable now.

DRY $15 V+

Sacred Hill Halo Marlborough Sauvignon Blanc   ★★★★

The 2015 vintage (★★★★) is attractively scented, with lively, herbaceous aromas leading into a mouthfilling, smooth wine (4 grams/litre of residual sugar), with an array of melon, lime and green-capsicum flavours. Intensely varietal, it is appetisingly crisp and green-edged, with very good intensity, delicacy and length.

Vintage	15
WR	6
Drink	16-18

DRY $25 AV

Sacred Hill Marlborough Sauvignon Blanc   ★★★★

The 2016 vintage (★★★☆) is a freshly herbaceous, strongly varietal style. Medium-bodied, it has crisp melon, lime and green-capsicum flavours, showing very good balance, vigour and depth, and a dry (3 grams/litre of residual sugar) finish.

Vintage	16
WR	6
Drink	16-18

DRY $20 V+

Saint Clair James Sinclair Marlborough Sauvignon Blanc   (★★★☆)

Grown in the lower Wairau Valley, the debut 2015 vintage (★★★☆) is a herbaceous style with an aromatic, slightly nettley bouquet. Full-flavoured, with a slightly salty streak, it's a strongly varietal wine, ready to roll.

DRY $22 AV

Saint Clair Marlborough Sauvignon Blanc   ★★★★☆

In top years, this label is a great buy. The 2015 vintage (★★★★☆), from sites in the lower Wairau Valley, is mouthfilling, fresh and tightly structured, with punchy, vibrant tropical-fruit and herbaceous flavours, showing excellent purity and depth, slightly 'salty' notes and a long, dry (3 grams/litre of residual sugar) finish.

DRY $22 V+

Saint Clair Pioneer Block 1 Foundation Marlborough Sauvignon Blanc   ★★★★

This single-vineyard Marlborough wine is grown east of Blenheim, at Dillons Point, in the lower Wairau Valley, at a site formerly the source of the Wairau Reserve Sauvignon Blanc. The 2015 vintage (★★★★☆) is a characterful wine, with good intensity of vibrant melon, lime and passionfruit flavours, a slightly salty note and a dry (2.2 dry grams/litre of residual sugar), lingering finish.

DRY $27 –V

Saint Clair Pioneer Block 20 Cash Block Marlborough Sauvignon Blanc   ★★★★☆

From vines close to the sea, at Dillons Point, in the lower Wairau Valley, the 2015 vintage (★★★★☆) is highly scented. A mouthfilling wine with penetrating, ripe melon, capsicum and lime flavour, slightly peachy and nutty, it is very fresh, harmonious, dry (3 grams/litre of residual sugar) and lingering.

DRY $27 AV

Saint Clair Pioneer Block 25 Point Five Marlborough Sauvignon Blanc   (★★★★☆)

Grown in the lower Wairau Valley at 0.5 metres above sea level (hence the 'Point Five' in the name), the 2015 vintage (★★★★) is a mouthfilling, rich, vibrant wine with fresh, concentrated melon/capsicum flavours, dry (2.9 grams/litre of residual sugar), and very open and expressive from the start.

DRY $27 AV

Saint Clair Pioneer Block 3 43 Degrees Marlborough Sauvignon Blanc   ★★★★☆

This Marlborough wine is grown at Dillons Point, in the lower Wairau Valley, at a site with rows 'running at an unusual angle of 43 degrees north-east to south-west', giving 'a slightly more herbaceous Sauvignon Blanc'. The 2015 vintage (★★★★☆) is very aromatic, fresh and vibrant. Mouthfilling, with some tropical-fruit notes, a slightly salty streak and a crisp, dry (3.2 grams/litre of residual sugar), persistent finish, it shows excellent intensity and vigour.

DRY $27 AV

Saint Clair Vicar's Choice Marlborough Sauvignon Blanc   ★★★☆

Vicars, like many of us, will gladly worship a bargain – and this easy-drinking wine delivers the goods. Drinking well from the start, the 2015 vintage (★★★★) is an aromatic, freshly herbaceous wine with good intensity of melon and green-capsicum flavours, a slightly minerally streak and a crisp, dry (3.3 grams/litre of residual sugar), lingering finish. Fine value.

DRY $19 V+

Saint Clair Vicar's Choice Marlborough Sauvignon Blanc Bright Light   ★★☆

The 2015 vintage (★★☆) is a low-alcohol (9.5 per cent), off-dry wine (10 grams/litre of residual sugar). Light, fruity and smooth, it has fresh tropical-fruit and herbaceous flavours, in an easy-drinking style.

MED/DRY $19 –V

Saint Clair Wairau Reserve Marlborough Sauvignon Blanc   ★★★★★

Marlborough's largest family-owned wine producer has an extensive array of Sauvignon Blancs. This is not the region's most complex Savvy, but in terms of sheer pungency, it's a star, having won countless gold medals and trophies since the first 2001 vintage. Grown in the cooler, coastal end of the Wairau Valley and handled entirely in stainless steel tanks, it is typically super-charged, in an exuberantly fruity, very pure and zesty style. The classy 2015 vintage (★★★★★), grown at Dillons Point, is a deliciously pure and sweet-fruited wine. Weighty, it has concentrated melon, grapefruit and lime flavours that build across the palate to a powerful, dry (3.1 grams/litre of residual sugar), harmonious finish.

DRY $34 AV

Sanctuary Marlborough Sauvignon Blanc   ★★★

The easy-drinking 2016 vintage (★★★) is fresh and full-bodied, with ripe tropical-fruit flavours to the fore and a smooth finish. (From Foley Family Wines.)

DRY $15 V+

Satellite Marlborough Sauvignon Blanc   ★★★

From Spy Valley, the 2016 vintage (★★★☆) offers fine value. Fresh and full-bodied, it offers good depth of ripe tropical-fruit flavours, crisp, lively and dry (2.4 grams/litre of residual sugar). Enjoyable young.

Vintage	16	15
WR	5	5
Drink	16-17	P

 DRY $16 V+

Satyr by Sileni Marlborough Sauvignon Blanc   (★★★)

The easy-drinking 2016 vintage (★★★) is a fresh, medium-bodied wine with good depth of lively, ripely herbaceous flavours, balanced acidity, and a dry (4 grams/litre of residual sugar), smooth finish.

 DRY $20 –V

Satyr by Sileni Valiant Marlborough Sauvignon Blanc   (★★★★)

Showing a touch of bottle-aged complexity, the 2015 vintage (★★★★) is mouthfilling, with a ripely herbaceous bouquet and flavours, showing good intensity. Vibrant and sweet-fruited, it is crisp and harmonious, with lots of current-drinking appeal.

 DRY $18 V+

Seifried Nelson Sauvignon Blanc   ★★★☆

Priced right, the 2016 vintage (★★★☆) is crisp and lively, with good body, punchy, ripely herbaceous flavours and a dry (2.4 grams/litre of residual sugar) finish.

Vintage	16	15	14	13
WR	6	6	6	6
Drink	16-18	16-17	P	P

 DRY $18 V+

Seresin Marama Sauvignon Blanc   ★★★★★

This multi-faceted style of Sauvignon Blanc is hand-picked from the oldest vines in the estate vineyard at Renwick, in Marlborough, fermented with indigenous yeasts in French oak barriques (7 per cent new in 2013), and wood-matured for well over a year. Pale yellow, the 2013 vintage (★★★★★) is fragrant and weighty, with rich, ripe, complex flavours of passionfruit and pineapple, enriched with biscuity oak. Slightly buttery, with a long, dry (2.9 grams/litre of residual sugar), harmonious finish, it's already delicious. Certified organic.

Vintage	13	12	11	10
WR	7	6	6	7
Drink	16-22	16-22	16-20	16-18

 DRY $45 AV

Seresin Marlborough Sauvignon Blanc ★★★★★

This is one of the region's most sophisticated, subtle and satisfying Sauvignons. It's also one of the most important, given its widespread international distribution and certified BioGro status. The grapes are grown in the original estate vineyard near Renwick, and in the company's younger vineyards, especially Raupo Creek, on an elevated slope in the Omaka Valley. The wine (which includes 5 to 9 per cent Sémillon) is mostly fermented in tanks with indigenous yeasts, but 15 to 20 per cent of the blend is fermented and lees-aged in seasoned French oak casks. Full of personality, the lively 2015 vintage (★★★★☆) has an aromatic bouquet, with hints of melons, limes and nuts. Pale straw, it has strong, fully dry flavours (1.6 grams/litre of residual sugar), in a minerally style with good complexity and a lingering, slightly flinty finish.

DRY $25 V+

Seresin OSIP Organic Marlborough Sauvignon Blanc (★★★☆)

The debut 2015 vintage (★★★☆) was grown organically and biodynamically and made with no use of sulphur in the winery. The bouquet has no real delights, lacking the fresh, lifted aromatics typical of the variety and region, but the palate is interesting – full-bodied, dry and crisp, with very good weight and depth of ripe tropical-fruit flavours, a touch of complexity, and plenty of personality. Drink now.

DRY $30 –V

Sherwood Estate Stoney Range Waipara Valley Sauvignon Blanc (★★★☆)

Priced sharply, the 2015 vintage (★★★☆) has plenty of personality. Weighty, crisp and lively, it is strongly varietal, in a clearly herbaceous style with with very good depth of melon and lime flavours, a hint of asparagus, and lots of drink-young appeal.

DRY $13 V+

Sileni Cellar Selection Hawke's Bay Sauvignon Blanc ★★★

The easy-drinking 2016 vintage (★★★) is fresh and light, with passionfruit-like aromas, moderate acidity and lively, ripely herbaceous flavours.

DRY $20 –V

Sileni Cellar Selection Marlborough Sauvignon Blanc ★★★☆

The 2016 vintage (★★★☆) is an aromatic, fresh, medium-bodied wine, dry (4 grams/litre of residual sugar), with lively, ripe melon, capsicum and lime flavours, showing very good depth and immediacy.

DRY $20 AV

Sileni Estate Selection Cape Hawke's Bay Sauvignon Blanc   (★★★★)

This is Sileni's top Sauvignon Blanc from Hawke's Bay. The 2015 vintage (★★★★), hand-harvested at Mangatahi, was handled entirely in stainless steel tanks. Mouthfilling, it has lively, ripe melon, capsicum and lime flavours, with leesy notes adding complexity, moderate acidity and a dry (2.9 grams/litre of residual sugar) finish. A subtle style, it should be at its best now to 2017.

Vintage	15
WR	7
Drink	16-19

Sileni Estate Selection Straits Marlborough Sauvignon Blanc   ★★★★☆

The impressive 2016 vintage (★★★★☆) is highly aromatic, mouthfilling and lively, with vibrant melon, lime and capsicum flavours, very fresh, tangy, finely poised (3.5 grams/litre of residual sugar) and punchy.

Vintage	16	15	14	13
WR	6	7	6	6
Drink	16-18	16-17	16-17	P

Snapper Rock Marlborough Sauvignon Blanc   (★★★☆)

Still on sale in 2016, the 2014 vintage (★★★☆) is at its peak. Aromatic, mouthfilling and sweet-fruited, with ripe melon/lime flavours, it is still lively, with balanced acidity and very good freshness and depth. Fine value.

Soho Stella Marlborough Sauvignon Blanc   ★★★☆

'Inspired by eco conscious fashionistas', the 2016 vintage (★★★☆) is a fresh, smooth, medium to full-bodied style, clearly herbaceous, with melon, lime and green-capsicum flavours, crisp and dry.

Vintage	16	15
WR	6	5
Drink	16-18	16-17

Spinyback Nelson Sauvignon Blanc   ★★★★

From Waimea Estates, this is typically a great buy. The 2015 vintage (★★★★) is mouthfilling and punchy, with ripe tropical-fruit flavours, showing good freshness and intensity, and a dry (3.9 grams/litre of residual sugar), crisp finish. Delicious young.

Spy Valley Easy Tiger Marlborough Sauvignon Blanc   ★★★

The 2016 vintage (★★★) is light-bodied, with green-edged flavours. Low in alcohol (9 per cent), it is tasty and dry (3.9 grams/litre of residual sugar), with a hint of passionfruit, firm acid spine, and a touch of complexity (from some barrel fermentation).

Vintage	16	15
WR	6	7
Drink	16-18	16-17

Spy Valley Envoy Johnson Vineyard Marlborough Sauvignon Blanc ★★★★★

Estate-grown in the lower Waihopai Valley, the classy 2015 vintage (★★★★★) was hand-picked from vines over 20 years old and fermented and lees-aged in oak (mostly new) for almost a year. Bright, light lemon/green, it is mouthfilling and sweet-fruited,, with vibrant, ripe, non-herbaceous flavours, crisp, intense, dry (2.9 grams/litre of residual sugar), tightly structured and long. Still youthful, with excellent complexity and harmony, it should be at its best mid-2017+.

Vintage	15	14	13	12	11	10
WR	7	7	7	6	5	6
Drink	16-23	16-20	16-19	16-17	P	P

 DRY $32 AV

Spy Valley Marlborough Sauvignon Blanc ★★★★

Always a good buy. Showing good intensity, the 2016 vintage (★★★★) was partly barrel-fermented and made in a crisp, dry (2.3 grams/litre of residual sugar) style. Mouthfilling, it has lively tropical-fruit and herbaceous flavours, with a touch of complexity, and a lengthy finish. Already drinking well.

Vintage	16	15	14	13
WR	7	6	7	7
Drink	16-18	16-17	P	P

 DRY $19 V+

Staete Landt Annabel Marlborough Sauvignon Blanc ★★★★★

Estate-grown at Rapaura, on the relatively warm north side of the Wairau Valley, the 2014 vintage (★★★★☆) is a weighty, single-vineyard wine. It has fresh, ripe, concentrated passionfruit/lime flavours, with a dry, finely textured, long finish.

 DRY $22 V+

Staete Landt Duchess Marlborough Sauvignon Blanc (★★★★★)

A rich, very ripe style, the 2014 vintage (★★★★★) was estate-grown and hand-picked at Rapaura, and fermented and matured for 10 months in old French oak casks. Mouthfilling, with passionfruit, pineapple and lime flavours, fresh acidity and a hint of toasty, buttery oak, it has excellent vigour, complexity and personality.

DRY $25 V+

Starborough Family Estate Marlborough Sauvignon Blanc ★★★★☆

This label consistently offers great value. Estate-grown, the 2016 vintage (★★★★☆) is from two vineyards in the Awatere Valley (accounting for 60 per cent of the final blend), and a third site in the Wairau Valley (40 per cent). Highly aromatic, it is mouthfilling and vibrantly fruity, with excellent intensity of melon, lime and capsicum flavours, slightly minerally, dry (3 grams/litre of residual sugar) and tangy.

 DRY $20 V+

Stoneburn Marlborough Sauvignon Blanc ★★★

Priced sharply, the 2015 vintage (★★★☆) from Hunter's is mouthfilling, fresh and lively, with good depth of ripely herbaceous flavours and a finely balanced, dry (1.8 grams/litre of residual sugar) finish. Enjoyable from the start.

DRY $16 V+

Stonecroft Hawke's Bay Sauvignon Blanc ★★★☆

The attractive 2016 vintage (★★★★) was fermented in a mix of tanks (90 per cent) and barrels (10 per cent). Mouthfilling, it has good concentration of ripe tropical-fruit flavours, with a touch of toasty oak adding complexity and a crisp, dryish (5 grams/litre of residual sugar) finish. Best drinking mid-2017+.

MED/DRY $22 AV

Stoneleigh Latitude Marlborough Sauvignon Blanc ★★★★

From 'vineyards on the Golden Mile' (Rapaura Road, on the north side of the Wairau Valley), the 2015 vintage (★★★★) is a classic Rapaura style, with ripe tropical-fruit aromas and flavours. Crisp and punchy, it has good freshness, vigour and intensity.

DRY $23 AV

Stoneleigh Lighter Marlborough Sauvignon Blanc (★★☆)

Picked early and made in a low-alcohol style (9.6 per cent), the 2016 vintage (★★☆) is light and crisp, with citrusy, appley flavours, pleasant and smooth.

MED/DRY $17 –V

Stoneleigh Marlborough Sauvignon Blanc ★★★☆

From Pernod Ricard NZ, this consistently good wine flows from the stony, relatively warm Rapaura district of the Wairau Valley, which produces a ripe style of Sauvignon Blanc, yet retains good acidity and vigour. Over 300,000 cases are produced. The 2015 vintage (★★★★) is lively, with strong passionfruit, melon and capsicum flavours, in an intensely varietal style with a slightly salty note and a refreshing, crisp and persistent finish.

Vintage	15	14
WR	7	7
Drink	16-17	P

DRY $17 V+

Stoneleigh Rapaura Series Marlborough Sauvignon Blanc ★★★★☆

This richly flavoured wine is grown in the warm, shingly soils of the Rapaura district and briefly lees-aged, with regular stirring. The 2015 vintage (★★★★☆) is a vigorous, tangy wine, with good intensity of melon, grapefruit and green-capsicum flavours, a slightly oily texture and flinty notes adding complexity.

DRY $28 AV

Stoneleigh Wild Valley Marlborough Sauvignon Blanc   (★★★★)

Showing lots of personality, the 2015 vintage (★★★★) was 'wild fermented by the micro-flora that occur naturally in the Rapaura environment' and partly (10 per cent) barrel-fermented. The bouquet is punchy, with some complexity; the palate is mouthfilling, very fresh and vibrant, with incisive, ripe tropical-fruit flavours, crisp, dry (4.4 grams/litre of residual sugar) and lingering.

 DRY $19 V+

Stonyridge Fallen Angel Marlborough Sauvignon Blanc   (★★★☆)

The 2015 vintage (★★★☆) is drinking well now. Light lemon/green, it is full-bodied, with ripe, gently herbaceous flavours, balanced acidity, very good depth and a fresh, dry finish.

DRY $30 –V

Summerhouse Marlborough Sauvignon Blanc   ★★★★☆

The 2015 vintage (★★★★☆) is mouthfilling, crisp and vibrantly fruity, with good intensity of melon, lime and capsicum flavours, dry (2.6 grams/litre of residual sugar), racy and long. Fine value.

Vintage	15
WR	7
Drink	16-18

 DRY $19 V+

Supper Club Marlborough Sauvignon Blanc   ★★★☆

The 2015 vintage (★★★★) is very fresh and lively. Grown at Dillons Point and Rapaura, in the Wairau Valley, it is aromatic, with very good depth of melon/lime flavours, slightly peachy and spicy notes, tangy acidity and a lingering finish. Enjoyable young, it offers great value.

 DRY $15 V+

Taraire Block Sauvignon Blanc   (★)

Grown at Kaikohe, in Northland, the 2015 vintage (★) is very plain.

DRY $21 –V

Te Awa Single Estate Hawke's Bay Sauvignon Blanc   (★★★★)

The 2015 vintage (★★★★) is fleshy, with strong, ripe tropical-fruit flavours, fresh acidity and a dry, rich finish. Enjoyable from the start.

 DRY $25 AV

Te Kairanga Estate Martinborough Sauvignon Blanc   ★★★★

The 2015 vintage (★★★☆) is ripely scented and mouthfilling, with fresh gooseberry and lime flavours. It shows good weight and texture, with a subtle seasoning of oak from 10 per cent barrel fermentation. The 2016 vintage (★★★★) is aromatic, mouthfilling, vibrantly fruity and dry, with ripely herbaceous flavours, crisp and finely poised. Best drinking 2017+.

 DRY $20 V+

Te Mania Nelson Sauvignon Blanc   ★★★☆

Typically a very good wine – full-flavoured, with tropical-fruit characters, nettley notes and
appetising acidity. The 2015 vintage (★★★☆) has a fresh, clearly herbaceous bouquet, leading
into a mouthfilling, lively wine with ripe tropical-fruit and grassy flavours, crisp and strong.
Certified organic.

Te Mata Cape Crest Sauvignon Blanc   ★★★★★

This oak-aged Hawke's Bay label is impressive for its ripely herbal, complex, sustained flavours.
Most of the grapes are hand-picked in the company's relatively warm Bullnose Vineyard,
inland from Hastings (the rest is grown at Woodthorpe, in the Dartmoor Valley), and the
blend includes small proportions of Sémillon (to add longevity) and Sauvignon Gris (which
contributes weight and mouthfeel). The wine is fully fermented and lees-aged for eight months
in French oak barriques (partly new). In a vertical tasting, the two to four-year-old wines look
best – still fresh, but very harmonious. The impressive 2014 vintage (★★★★★) is powerful,
weighty and concentrated, with rich, ripe fruit flavours, oak-derived complexity, balanced
acidity and a long finish. Well worth cellaring, it should be at its peak 2017+.

Vintage	15	14
WR	7	7
Drink	17-27	16-19

Te Mata Estate Vineyards Hawke's Bay Sauvignon Blanc   ★★★☆

The 2016 vintage (★★★★) is a pale lemon/green, weighty, rounded wine, grown in the Bridge
Pa Triangle and at the Woodthorpe Terraces Vineyard, in the Dartmoor Valley. Handled without
oak, it is sweet-fruited, with ripe tropical-fruit flavours and a smooth finish. Instantly appealing.

Ten Sisters Single Vineyard Marlborough Sauvignon Blanc   ★★★☆

Grown in the Southern Valleys, the 2015 vintage (★★★☆) is a medium-bodied, tightly
structured wine with gooseberry, melon and lime flavours, and a crisp, dry finish.

TerraVin Marlborough Sauvignon Blanc   ★★★★

Showing plenty of personality, the mouthfilling, rich 2015 vintage (★★★★☆) is drinking well
now. Grown in the Southern Valleys, it was partly (21 per cent) fermented with indigenous
yeasts in old French oak casks. Pale yellow, it is weighty and complex, with fresh acidity, slightly
toasty and buttery notes, and concentrated, ripely herbaceous flavours.

TerraVin Te Ahu Marlborough Sauvignon Blanc   ★★★★★

This thought-provoking wine is grown in the Southern Valleys, barrel-fermented with indigenous yeasts and oak-matured (60 per cent new in 2013). The 2013 vintage (★★★★★) has youthful, light lemon/green colour. Powerful, it is lively and complex, with highly concentrated tropical-fruit, spice and nut flavours, and a fragrant bouquet of ripe fruit and oak. Drink now to 2017.

Vintage	13	12	11	10
WR	7	4	7	7
Drink	16-20	16-17	16-20	P

 DRY $40 AV

Thornbury Marlborough Sauvignon Blanc   ★★★☆

The 2016 vintage (★★★☆) is aromatic, with good body and depth of fresh, ripely herbaceous flavours, dry (3.7 grams/litre of residual sugar) and smooth. Fine value.

Vintage	16	15	14
WR	6	7	6
Drink	16-18	16-17	P

 DRY $15 V+

Three Paddles Martinborough Sauvignon Blanc   ★★★☆

From Nga Waka, the 2015 vintage (★★★) is a medium to full-bodied wine with satisfying depth of fresh, ripe melon/lime flavours, dry and lively.

Vintage	15	14	13
WR	7	7	7
Drink	16-18	16-17	P

 DRY $18 V+

Tiki Marlborough Sauvignon Blanc   ★★★☆

The 2016 vintage (★★★☆), grown in the Wairau Valley, is is fresh and lively, with very good depth of melon, lime and capsicum flavours, and a finely balanced, smooth finish. Enjoyable from the start.

 DRY $20 AV

Tiki Single Vineyard Marlborough Sauvignon Blanc   ★★★★

Estate-grown in the upper Wairau Valley, the 2016 vintage (★★★★) is mouthfilling, fresh and vibrantly fruity, with strong tropical-fruit and herbaceous flavours, woven with appetising acidity, and a finely balanced, smooth finish.

DRY $23 AV

Tohu Mugwi Reserve Marlborough Sauvignon Blanc ★★★★☆

Drinking well now, the 2014 vintage (★★★★☆) was estate-grown in the upper Awatere Valley and fermented with indigenous yeasts in old French oak barriques. The bouquet is complex; the palate is mouthfilling, with balanced acidity and strong, non-herbaceous flavours, savoury and lingering. The 2015 vintage (★★★★) is still youthful. Light lemon/green, it is vibrant, with ripe fruit flavours, slightly nutty notes adding complexity, and a bone-dry, lingering finish. Best drinking mid-2017+.

 DRY $30 –V

Tohu Single Vineyard Marlborough Sauvignon Blanc ★★★★

This consistently enjoyable wine is estate-grown in the upper Awatere Valley. Delicious young, the 2016 vintage (★★★★) is strongly aromatic and full-bodied, with incisive, pure, ripely herbaceous flavours, dry (3.9 grams/litre of residual sugar), crisp and long.

 DRY $20 V+

Tohu Single Vineyard Naturally Lighter Alcohol
Marlborough Sauvignon Blanc (★★★)

The lively, aromatic 2015 vintage (★★★) is light-bodied (10 per cent), with vibrant, green-edged flavours. Citrusy, appley and limey, with a sliver of sweetness (5.7 grams/litre of residual sugar) and tangy acidity, it has more flavour interest than most low-alcohol Sauvignons.

 MED/DRY $20 –V

Toi Toi Brookdale Organic Marlborough Sauvignon Blanc ★★★★

Still on sale, the 2014 vintage (★★★☆) was estate-grown in the Brookdale Vineyard, in the Omaka Valley. It is crisp and tangy, with melon, lime and green-capsicum flavours, clearly herbaceous, lively and lingering. Certified organic.

Vintage	14
WR	7
Drink	16-23

 DRY $24 AV

Toi Toi Marlborough Sauvignon Blanc ★★★

The 2016 vintage (★★★) is a fresh, mouthfilling wine with ripe tropical-fruit flavours, lively acidity, an easy-drinking balance and satisfying depth.

 DRY $18 AV

Toi Toi Reserve Marlborough Sauvignon Blanc ★★★☆

Still on sale, the 2014 vintage (★★★★) is a blend of Awatere Valley and Wairau Valley grapes, partly barrel-fermented. Mouthfilling and smooth (5 grams/litre of residual sugar), it has generous, ripely herbaceous flavours, with a hint of green capsicums, a very subtle oak influence, lees-aging notes adding complexity and good length.

Vintage	14
WR	7
Drink	16-19

MED/DRY $22 AV

Trinity Hill Hawke's Bay Sauvignon Blanc   ★★★

This wine is grown in several vineyards, coastal and inland, and tank-fermented. The 2015 vintage (★★★) is medium-bodied, with fresh, ripe tropical-fruit and herbaceous flavours, lively acidity and a smooth finish. Enjoyable now.

DRY $20 –V

Triplebank Awatere Valley Marlborough Sauvignon Blanc   ★★★☆

Drinking well now, the 2015 vintage (★★★★) is a classic Awatere Valley style – freshly aromatic, with vibrant tropical-fruit and green-capsicum flavours, a hint of 'tomato stalk', mouth-watering acidity and a finely poised finish. (From Pernod Ricard NZ.)

DRY $20 AV

Tupari Awatere Valley Marlborough Sauvignon Blanc   ★★★★

Estate-grown in the upper Awatere Valley, this single-vineyard wine is partly oak-matured (10 per cent was handled in old barrels in 2013). The 2013 vintage (★★★★) has an aromatic, nettley bouquet, leading into a mouthfilling, strongly varietal wine, with good weight and ripe, citrusy, limey flavours, dry (2.6 grams/litre of residual sugar) and lingering.

Vintage	13
WR	6
Drink	P

DRY $27 –V

Tupari Boulder Rows Marlborough Sauvignon Blanc   (★★★☆)

Maturing gracefully, the 2014 vintage (★★★☆) is a barrel-fermented wine, weighty and lively, with peach, melon and capsicum flavours, showing considerable complexity, and a finely textured, lengthy finish.

DRY $34 –V

Twin Islands Marlborough Sauvignon Blanc   ★★★☆

Negociants' wine offers highly attractive, easy drinking. The 2016 vintage (★★★☆) is medium to full-bodied, very fresh and vibrant, with melon and green-capsicum flavours, showing good depth and immediacy, and a dry finish (3 grams/litre of residual sugar).

DRY $18 V+

Two Rivers of Marlborough Altitude Sauvignon Blanc   (★★★★★)

Still unfolding, the impressive 2015 vintage (★★★★★) is a single-vineyard wine, grown in the Southern Valleys and matured for 10 months in a concrete egg-shaped tank (40 per cent) and seasoned oak hogsheads (60 per cent). Light lemon/green, it is weighty and unusually complex, with rich, ripe tropical-fruit flavours, a subtle seasoning of oak, and a harmonious, dry (2.7 grams/litre of residual sugar), long finish. Best drinking mid-2017+.

Vintage	15
WR	6
Drink	16-21

DRY $36 AV

Two Rivers of Marlborough Convergence Sauvignon Blanc ★★★★☆

The classy 2016 vintage (★★★★☆) is from five sites, in the Awatere and Southern valleys, and at Rapaura, in the Wairau Valley. Fresh and sweet-fruited, it has strong, vibrant melon, lime and green-capsicum flavours, a slightly salty streak, a touch of complexity, and a finely balanced, dry (2.8 grams/litre of residual sugar), persistent finish.

Vintage	16	15
WR	6	6
Drink	16-19	16-18

 DRY $24 V+

Two Tails Marlborough Sauvignon Blanc ★★★★

From Fairbourne, the distinctive 2015 vintage (★★★★) was grown at sites in the Southern Valleys and partly hand-picked. Medium to full-bodied, it is dry (1.4 grams/litre of residual sugar), with ripe, citrusy, slightly appley flavours, showing good intensity, a minerally streak, and a crisp, lingering finish. It's drinking well now.

Vintage	15	14	13	12
WR	6	5	6	6
Drink	16-18	16-17	16-17	P

 DRY $22 V+

Urlar Gladstone Sauvignon Blanc ★★★★

Partly barrel-fermented, the 2015 vintage (★★★☆) is mouthfilling and sweet-fruited, with ripe tropical-fruit flavours, showing a touch of complexity, and a slightly creamy finish. Certified organic.

 DRY $23 AV

Vavasour Awatere Valley Marlborough Sauvignon Blanc ★★★☆

The 2015 vintage (★★★☆) is tangy and slightly salty, in a vibrant, herbaceous style with very good depth of fresh, crisp, citrus-fruit and green-capsicum flavours. (From Foley Family Wines.)

Vintage	15	14	13
WR	7	7	6
Drink	16-18	16-17	P

 DRY $21 AV

Vidal Marlborough Sauvignon Blanc ★★★☆

The 2016 vintage (★★★★) was grown in the Wairau Valley (mostly) and Awatere Valley. Aromatic, it is full-bodied, with good intensity of ripely herbaceous flavours, appetisingly crisp and dry (2.7 grams/litre of residual sugar), and lots of drink-young appeal. Fine value.

Vintage	16	15	14
WR	7	6	6
Drink	16-17	P	P

DRY $16 V+

Vidal Reserve Marlborough Sauvignon Blanc   ★★★★

Offering great value, the 2015 vintage (★★★★☆) was grown in the Wairau (78 per cent) and Awatere (22 per cent) valleys, and tank-fermented. It's a vivacious wine, highly aromatic and weighty, with vibrant, ripe passionfruit and green-capsicum flavours, showing excellent delicacy and intensity, and a dry (3.3 grams/litre of residual sugar), crisp finish.

Vintage	15
WR	7
Drink	16-17

DRY $20 V+

Villa Maria Cellar Selection Marlborough Sauvignon Blanc   ★★★★☆

An intensely flavoured wine, typically of a high standard, blended from Wairau Valley and Awatere Valley grapes. The striking 2016 vintage (★★★★★) is ripely scented, weighty and punchy, with deliciously rich, tropical-fruit flavours, a hint of 'sweat', and lovely vibrancy, harmony and length. Appetisingly crisp and dry (3.7 grams/litre of residual sugar), it offers top quality and irresistible value.

Vintage	16	15
WR	6	6
Drink	16-19	16-18

DRY $20 V+

Villa Maria Private Bin Marlborough Sauvignon Blanc   ★★★★

This huge-volume label offers consistently good quality and value. The 2016 vintage (★★★★) was grown in the Wairau and Awatere valleys. Pale lemon/green, it is highly aromatic, with a ripely herbaceous bouquet, showing good freshness and intensity. Mouthfilling, it is instantly attractive, with an array of melon, lime, passionfruit and green-capsicum flavours, balanced acidity, and a lengthy, dry (3.9 grams/litre of residual sugar) finish.

Vintage	16	15	14
WR	6	6	6
Drink	16-19	16-17	P

DRY $17 V+

Villa Maria Private Bin Organic Marlborough Sauvignon Blanc   ★★★★

The 2016 vintage (★★★★) is crisp and dry (3.8 grams/litre of residual sugar). Freshly aromatic, it is mouthfilling and sweet-fruited, with lively acidity and good intensity, vigour and harmony. Priced sharply.

Vintage	16	15
WR	6	6
Drink	16-19	16-17

DRY $17 V+

Villa Maria Reserve Clifford Bay Sauvignon Blanc   ★★★★★

Grown in the Awatere Valley (although the label refers only to 'Clifford Bay', into which the Awatere River empties), this is a very classy Marlborough wine. Seddon Vineyards and the Taylors Pass Vineyard – both managed but not owned by Villa Maria – are the key sources of fruit. Handled entirely in stainless steel tanks and aged on its light yeast lees for several months, the wine typically exhibits the leap-out-of-the-glass fragrance and zingy, explosive flavour of Marlborough Sauvignon Blanc at its best. The 2015 vintage (★★★★☆) is full-flavoured, with fresh, crisp tropical-fruit characters to the fore, a herbaceous undercurrent, minerally notes, and excellent balance and length.

Vintage	15	14
WR	7	7
Drink	16-18	P

DRY $28 V+

Villa Maria Reserve Wairau Valley Sauvignon Blanc   ★★★★★

An authoritative wine, it is typically ripe and zingy, with impressive weight and length of flavour, and tends to be fuller in body, less herbaceous and rounder than its Clifford Bay stablemate (above). The contributing vineyards vary from vintage to vintage, but Peter and Deborah Jackson's warm, stony vineyard in the heart of the valley has long been a key source of grapes, and sometimes a small part of the blend is barrel-fermented, to enhance its complexity and texture. The 2015 vintage (★★★★★) is a powerful, mouthfilling wine, with excellent weight on the palate, strong, ripe passionfruit and lime flavours, and a dry, long finish. The 2016 vintage (★★★★★) is fragrant and lively, with slightly 'sweaty' tropical-fruit aromas leading into a mouthfilling wine (13.5 per cent alcohol) with concentrated, ripely herbaceous flavours and a dry (3.4 grams/litre of residual sugar), finely poised, rich finish.

Vintage	16	15	14
WR	7	7	7
Drink	16-19	16-18	P

DRY $28 V+

Villa Maria Single Vineyard Graham Marlborough Sauvignon Blanc   ★★★★★

Grown in the Awatere Valley, near the coast, this wine has strong 'tomato stalk' aromas and flavours, crisp, zingy and incisive. The 2015 vintage (★★★★★) is a very refined, dry wine (2.8 grams/litre of residual sugar), sweet-fruited, with fresh melon, lime and capsicum flavours, showing lovely purity, delicacy and depth.

Vintage	15	14
WR	7	7
Drink	16-18	16-17

DRY $28 V+

Villa Maria Single Vineyard Taylors Pass Marlborough Sauvignon Blanc   ★★★★★

Taylors Pass Vineyard lies 100 metres above sea level in the Awatere Valley. This is typically a classic example of the sub-regional style – vibrant, punchy, minerally and herbal, with intense capsicum and 'tomato stalk' aromas and a long, dry, racy finish. The 2015 vintage (★★★★★)

shows lovely delicacy and poise, in a dry (2.5 grams/litre of residual sugar), ripely herbaceous style. It is slightly nettley, with deep melon/lime flavours, a minerally streak, and obvious cellaring potential.

Vintage	15	14
WR	7	7
Drink	16-18	16-17

DRY $28 V+

Villa Maria Single Vineyard Templar Sauvignon Blanc   ★★★★☆

Grown in the Awatere Valley and certified organic, the 2015 vintage (★★★★) is full-bodied, with fresh, strong melon and green-capsicum flavours, crisp, dry (4 grams/litre of residual sugar) and lingering.

Vintage	15	14
WR	7	7
Drink	16-18	16-17

DRY $28 AV

VNO Marlborough Sauvignon Blanc   ★★★☆

Fresh and lively, the 2015 vintage (★★★☆) is a medium to full-bodied wine, strongly varietal, with very good depth of ripe passionfruit/lime flavours and a smooth finish. (From Constellation NZ.)

DRY $17 V+

VNO Skinny Marlborough Sauvignon Blanc   (★★)

From early-picked grapes, the 2015 vintage (★★) is light (9 per cent alcohol) and lively, with crisp, lemony, appley flavours, showing moderate depth, and a slightly sweet (10 grams/litre of residual sugar) finish. (From Constellation NZ.)

MED/DRY $17 –V

Waiheke Road Marlborough Sauvignon Blanc   (★★★★)

Still on sale, the 2014 vintage (★★★★) from Awaroa Vineyard is drinking well now. Bright lemon/green, it has a fragrant, ripely herbaceous bouquet, showing bottle-aged complexity. Mouthfilling, it is full-flavoured and sweet-fruited, with generous tropical-fruit and herbaceous characters.

DRY $26 –V

Waimea Nelson Sauvignon Blanc   ★★★★

Always a good buy. The 2015 vintage (★★★★), estate-grown at five sites on the Waimea Plains, is mouthfilling and vibrantly fruity, with good intensity of melon, passionfruit and lime flavours, dry (3.8 grams/litre of residual sugar) and crisp.

DRY $17 V+

Wairau River Marlborough Sauvignon Blanc   ★★★☆

The 2016 vintage (★★★★) is mouthfilling and vibrantly fruity, with good intensity of passionfruit/lime flavours, dry (1.9 grams/litre of residual sugar) and mouth-wateringly crisp. Enjoyably young.

Vintage	16	15	14
WR	6	7	6
Drink	16-18	16-17	P

DRY $20 AV

Wairau River Reserve Marlborough Sauvignon Blanc   ★★★★☆

The 2016 vintage (★★★★☆) is a single-vineyard wine, grown on the north side of the Wairau Valley. Weighty, it has concentrated, ripe tropical-fruit flavours, in a fresh, tightly structured, classic sub-regional style with balanced acidity and a long, dry (2.5 grams/litre of residual sugar) finish. Best drinking mid-2017+.

Vintage	16	15
WR	6	6
Drink	16-18	16-18

DRY $30 –V

Walnut Block Collectables Marlborough Sauvignon Blanc   ★★★☆

Balanced for easy drinking, the 2015 vintage (★★★☆) is a mouthfilling wine with fresh, ripe tropical-fruit flavours, lively acidity and good depth. Certified organic.

DRY $20 AV

Walnut Block Nutcracker Marlborough Sauvignon Blanc   ★★★★☆

Certified organic, the delicious 2015 vintage (★★★★☆) is a weighty, finely textured wine, hand-harvested and partly (30 per cent) fermented with indigenous yeasts in old barrels. Sweet-fruited, it is mouthfilling and dry (2.3 grams/litre of residual sugar), with excellent delicacy and depth of fresh tropical-fruit flavours, balanced acidity and a smooth finish.

Vintage	15	14
WR	7	5
Drink	16-20	16-18

DRY $24 V+

Whitehaven Greg Marlborough Sauvignon Blanc   ★★★★☆

Dedicated to the memory of founder Greg White, the 2015 vintage (★★★★★) is a single-vineyard wine, grown in the Awatere Valley. Mouthfilling, it is vibrantly fruity, with intense melon, lime and capsicum flavours, a minerally streak, and a dry (3.5 grams/litre of residual sugar), long finish.

DRY $27 AV

Whitehaven Marlborough Sauvignon Blanc   ★★★★☆

This consistently rewarding wine is a big seller in the US, where it is distributed by one of its shareholders, global wine giant E & J Gallo. The grapes are grown at more than a dozen sites in the Wairau and Awatere valleys, and the wine is handled entirely in tanks. The instantly appealing 2015 vintage (★★★★) is mouthfilling, with strong, punchy tropical-fruit and herbaceous flavours and a crisp, dry (3.8 grams/litre of residual sugar) finish.

DRY $23 V+

Wild Grace Marlborough Sauvignon Blanc   (★★☆)

The debut 2016 vintage (★★☆) is disappointing – mouthfilling and crisp, with ripe tropical-fruit flavours, but lacking in fragrance and harmony. (From Constellation NZ.)

DRY $27 –V

Wild South Marlborough Sauvignon Blanc   ★★★☆

Zesty and finely balanced, the 2016 vintage (★★★☆) is a crisp, medium-bodied wine, strongly varietal, with vibrant melon, lime and green-capsicum flavours.

DRY $18 V+

Wither Hills Early Light Marlborough Sauvignon Blanc   (★★★)

The 2015 vintage (★★★) is a fresh, light-bodied wine (9.5 per cent alcohol), with zesty, clearly varietal lemon and green-capsicum flavours, a sliver of sweetness, crisp acidity and good depth.

MED/DRY $15 V+

Wither Hills Single Vineyard Rarangi Marlborough Sauvignon Blanc   ★★★★★

Grown at Rarangi, on the Wairau Valley coast, the classy 2015 vintage (★★★★★) perfectly captures the 'unique sense of place' promised on the back label. From a low-fertility district, where the vines develop small canopies, it is a ripely scented, tangy, bone-dry wine with pure, penetrating grapefruit, green-capsicum and lime flavours, a distinctive salty streak and a very long finish. Matured on its yeast lees for six months, with no stirring, and handled without oak, it's full of personality. Drink now to 2017.

DRY $25 V+

Yealands Estate Land Made Marlborough Sauvignon Blanc   ★★★☆

Grown in the Awatere and Wairau valleys, the 2015 vintage (★★★☆) is mouthfilling and sweet-fruited, with lively peach, melon and capsicum flavours, dry (4 grams/litre of residual sugar), crisp and balanced for early appeal.

Vintage	15	14
WR	6	6
Drink	16-17	P

DRY $20 AV

Yealands Estate Single Block L5 Awatere Valley
Marlborough Sauvignon Blanc   ★★★★

The 2014 vintage (★★★★★) was estate-grown 900 metres from the ocean, on the coastal edge of the sweeping Seaview Vineyard. Fresh and punchy, with nettley and salty notes, it shows excellent intensity, with penetrating melon, grapefruit, lime and green-capsicum flavours, deliciously vibrant, delicate, dry (2.5 grams/litre of residual sugar) and sustained.

Vintage	14
WR	6
Drink	16-17

DRY $25 AV

Yealands Estate Single Block M2 Wairau Valley
Marlborough Sauvignon Blanc   ★★★★

The 2014 vintage (★★★★☆) was estate-grown in the Mills & Ford Vineyard, in the lower Wairau Valley. Tank-fermented, it is finely scented, weighty and fleshy, with fresh, concentrated tropical-fruit flavours and a dry (2.5 grams/litre of residual sugar), rich, rounded finish. Certified organic.

Vintage	14
WR	7
Drink	16-17

 DRY $25 AV

Yealands Estate Single Block S1 Awatere Valley
Marlborough Sauvignon Blanc   ★★★★★

The 2014 vintage (★★★★★) was estate-grown inland in the sweeping Seaview Vineyard, 3.5 kilometres from the coast. Mouthfilling and vibrant, it shows excellent intensity of ripe tropical-fruit flavours, slightly salty notes, and a long, dry (2.5 grams/litre of residual sugar), finely textured finish. Pure and penetrating, it's a classic Awatere Valley style.

Vintage	14
WR	6
Drink	16-17

 DRY $25 V+

Yealands Estate Single Vineyard Awatere
Valley Marlborough Sauvignon Blanc   ★★★★☆

Estate-grown at Seaview, in the lower Awatere Valley, the 2015 vintage (★★★★★) is pale and mouthfilling, with an almost ethereal delicacy and purity. It has excellent intensity of melon, lime and capsicum flavours that build across the palate to a finely balanced, dry (2.5 grams/litre of residual sugar), lasting finish. A classic Awatere Valley style.

Vintage	15
WR	6
Drink	16-18

 DRY $23 V+

Yealands Estate Winemakers Reserve Awatere
Valley Marlborough Sauvignon Blanc   ★★★★☆

The 2014 vintage (★★★★☆) is a richly scented, clearly herbaceous style, estate-grown and fermented in a mix of tanks (70 per cent) and French oak puncheons (30 per cent). Mouthfilling and vibrant, it has concentrated tropical-fruit and herbaceous flavours, a subtle seasoning of oak and a crisp, dry (1.5 grams/litre of residual sugar), very persistent finish.

Vintage	14	13
WR	7	7
Drink	16-19	16-18

DRY $25 V+

Sauvignon Gris

Pernod Ricard NZ launched New Zealand's first commercial bottlings of an old French variety, Sauvignon Gris, from the 2009 vintage. Also known as Sauvignon Rosé – due to its pink skin – Sauvignon Gris typically produces less aromatic, but more substantial, wines than Sauvignon Blanc.

Sauvignon Gris is not a blend of Sauvignon Blanc and Pinot Gris (watch out for the confusing 'Sauvignon Blanc/Pinot Gris' under several brands); nor is it a new vine, bred by crossing those grapes. Sauvignon Gris is a variety in its own right.

In Bordeaux, Sauvignon Gris is commonly used as a minority partner in dry white blends dominated by Sauvignon Blanc, but in Chile – like New Zealand – producers are bottling and exporting Sauvignon Gris as a varietal wine. In Marlborough, where the majority of the vines are planted, Sauvignon Gris has proved to be fairly disease-resistant, ripening in the middle of the Sauvignon Blanc harvest. Of New Zealand's 104 hectares of bearing vines in 2017, 102 hectares are in Marlborough, with the rest in Hawke's Bay.

Brancott Estate Letter Series 'R' Sauvignon Gris ★★★★☆

The 2015 vintage (★★★★) is instantly appealing. Mouthfilling (14.5 per cent alcohol), it is very smooth, with fresh, ripely herbaceous aromas and flavours, stone-fruit notes, some oak-derived complexity, and lots of youthful impact.

MED/DRY $33 –V

Brancott Estate Marlborough Sauvignon Gris ★★★☆

The 2014 vintage (★★★☆) is full-bodied (14.5 per cent alcohol), fresh, crisp and lively, with ripely herbaceous flavours of melon, passionfruit and lime. An ideal, all-purpose, dryish wine with good acid spine, it shows very good vibrancy and depth.

MED/DRY $17 V+

Clearview Te Awanga Hawke's Bay Sauvignon Gris (★★★★)

The 2014 vintage (★★★★) is a generous, instantly appealing wine, estate-grown, hand-picked and fermented in old French oak casks. Weighty, sweet-fruited and well-rounded, it has vibrant, ripe stone-fruit flavours, a subtle seasoning of oak and a sustained finish.

DRY $21 V+

Waimea Nelson Sauvignon Gris ★★★★

Enjoyable young, the 2015 vintage (★★★★) was estate-grown at Hope. Full-bodied and fleshy, it has strong, ripe tropical-fruit flavours to the fore, a herbal undercurrent, fresh acidity and a dryish (4.8 grams/litre of residual sugar), finely balanced finish.

DRY $23 AV

Sémillon

You'd never guess it from the tiny selection of labels on the shelves, but Sémillon is New Zealand's eighth most widely planted white-wine variety. The few winemakers who once played around with Sémillon could hardly give it away, so aggressively stemmy and spiky was its flavour. Now, there is a new breed of riper, richer, rounder Sémillons on the market – and they are ten times more enjoyable to drink.

The Sémillon variety is beset by a similar problem to Chenin Blanc. Despite being the foundation of outstanding white wines in Bordeaux and Australia, Sémillon is out of fashion in the rest of the world, and in New Zealand its potential is still largely untapped. The area of bearing Sémillon vines has contracted markedly between 2007 and 2017, from 230 to 48 hectares.

Sémillon is highly prized in Bordeaux, where as one of the two key varieties both in dry wines, most notably white Graves, and the inimitable sweet Sauternes, its high levels of alcohol and extract are perfect foils for Sauvignon Blanc's verdant aroma and tartness. With its propensity to rot 'nobly', Sémillon forms about 80 per cent of a classic Sauternes.

Cooler climates like those of New Zealand's South Island, however, bring out a grassy-green character in Sémillon which, coupled with its higher acidity in these regions, can give the variety strikingly Sauvignon-like characteristics.

Grown principally in Hawke's Bay, Gisborne and Marlborough, Sémillon is mostly used in New Zealand not as a varietal wine, but as a minor (and anonymous) partner in wines labelled Sauvignon Blanc, contributing complexity and aging potential. By curbing the variety's natural tendency to grow vigorously and crop bountifully, winemakers are now overcoming the aggressive cut-grass characters that in the past plagued the majority of New Zealand's unblended Sémillons. The spread of clones capable of giving riper fruit characters has also contributed to quality advances.

However, very few wineries in New Zealand are exploring Sémillon's potential to produce complex, long-lived dry whites.

Clearview Reserve Hawke's Bay Sémillon ★★★☆

The 2014 vintage (★★★☆) is a mouthfilling wine, hand-picked at Te Awanga and fermented and matured in American oak barriques (partly new). It's lively, with good depth of ripe-fruit flavours, a strong seasoning of biscuity oak, and considerable complexity. Best drinking 2017+.

DRY $27 –V

Man O' War South Three Sémillon (★★★☆)

Estate-grown on Waiheke Island and barrel-aged for nine months, the 2015 vintage (★★★☆) has a slightly nettley, nutty bouquet. Full-flavoured, it has moderately ripe flavours, showing good complexity, crisp acidity and a dry finish. Best drinking 2017+.

Vintage	15
WR	7
Drink	16-21

DRY $34 –V

Poverty Bay Young Vines Sémillon ★★★☆

Estate-grown in the Bridge Estate Vineyard at Matawhero, in Gisborne, the 2014 vintage (★★★☆) is light yellow, mouthfilling and dry. It has moderately fresh, ripe, peachy flavours, balanced acidity, a touch of complexity and a rounded finish. Ready.

DRY $30 –V

Sileni The Circle Hawke's Bay Sémillon   ★★★☆

The 2013 (★★★★), partly barrel-fermented, is a top vintage – ripely scented, crisp and lively, with ripe tropical-fruit flavours, showing very good depth. Made in a basically dry style (4.6 grams/litre of residual sugar), it's drinking well now.

Vintage	13	DRY $24 –V
WR	6	
Drink	16-23	

Verdelho

A Portuguese variety traditionally grown on the island of Madeira, Verdelho preserves its acidity well in hot regions, yielding enjoyably full-bodied, lively, lemony table wines in Australia. It is still extremely rare in New Zealand, with only 7 hectares of bearing Verdelho vines in 2017, mostly in Hawke's Bay and Auckland.

Esk Valley Gimblett Gravels Verdelho ★★★★

The 2015 vintage (★★★★) was hand-picked in the company's Omahu Gravels Vineyard and 40 per cent barrel-fermented. Fleshy, with strong, ripe tropical-fruit flavours to the fore and a very subtle seasoning of oak, it is vibrantly fruity, mouthfilling and finely balanced, with fresh acidity and a smooth, dryish (4.6 grams/litre of residual sugar) finish. Worth cellaring. The 2016 vintage (★★★★) was partly barrel-fermented and made in a dry style (2.5 grams/litre of residual sugar). Mouthfilling, it is vibrantly fruity, with strong tropical-fruit flavours, woven with fresh acidity, and clear-cut varietal characters. Best drinking mid-2017+.

Vintage	16	15	14	13	12	11	10	DRY $20 V+
WR	7	7	7	7	7	7	6	
Drink	17-19	16-18	16-17	16-17	P	P	P	

Summerhouse Marlborough Verdelho ★★★★

The 2014 vintage (★★★★) is a fleshy, weighty wine (14.5 per cent alcohol), barrel-fermented. It has fresh, ripe stone-fruit flavours, gently seasoned with oak, good complexity and a dry (4 grams/litre of residual sugar), rounded finish. The 2015 vintage (★★★★) was barrel-fermented. Bright, light lemon/green, it is sturdy (14.5 per cent alcohol) and fleshy, with rich, ripe tropical-fruit flavours, showing good complexity, and a dry finish. Delicious now, it's also worth cellaring. Fine value.

Vintage	15	14	DRY $19 V+
WR	7	7	
Drink	16-21	16-20	

Villa Maria Single Vineyard Ihumatao Vineyard Auckland Verdelho ★★★★★

Estate-grown at Mangere, in South Auckland, the organically certified 2014 vintage (★★★★★) is a notably varietal wine. Highly fragrant and mouthfilling, it has fresh, concentrated tropical-fruit flavours, with hints of pears and spices, and a long, dry finish.

Vintage	13	12	11	10	DRY $30 AV
WR	7	6	6	6	
Drink	16-17	P	P	P	

Vermentino

Extremely rare in New Zealand, this aromatic variety is grown extensively on Sardinia and Corsica, and is also well known in north-west Italy and southern France. Often compared to Sauvignon Blanc, it yields dry, light-bodied wines, with peach, lemon and dried-herb flavours, woven with fresh acidity. According to New Zealand Winegrowers' *Vineyard Register Report 2015–2018*, only 0.1 hectares will be bearing in 2017, planted in Northland.

Doubtless Vermentino (★★★☆)

The debut 2015 vintage (★★★☆) was grown at Doubtless Bay, in Northland. New Zealand's first example of a variety associated with coastal European wine regions, it is a light lemon/green, mouthfilling wine (13.5 per cent alcohol), with ripe, dry, slightly peachy and spicy flavours, balanced acidity, and very good texture and depth. It's already quite open and expressive.

DRY $23 AV

Viognier

A classic grape of the Rhône Valley, in France, Viognier is renowned for its exotically perfumed, substantial, peach and apricot-flavoured dry whites. A delicious alternative to Chardonnay, Viognier (pronounced Vee-yon-yay) is an internationally modish variety, popping up with increasing frequency in shops and restaurants here.

Viognier accounts for only 0.3 per cent of the national vineyard, but the area of bearing vines has expanded from 15 hectares in 2002 to 125 hectares in 2017. Over 70 per cent of the vines are clustered in Hawke's Bay and Gisborne, with further significant plantings in Marlborough (14 per cent) and Auckland (7 per cent).

As in the Rhône, Viognier's flowering and fruit set have been highly variable here. The deeply coloured grapes go through bud-burst, flowering and 'veraison' (the start of the final stage of ripening) slightly behind Chardonnay and are harvested about the same time as Pinot Noir.

The wine is often fermented in seasoned oak barrels, yielding scented, substantial, richly alcoholic wines with gentle acidity and subtle flavours. If you enjoy mouthfilling, softly textured, dry or dryish white wines, but feel like a change from Chardonnay and Pinot Gris, try Viognier. You won't be disappointed.

Alpha Domus The Wingwalker Hawke's Bay Viognier ★★★★

The 2014 vintage (★★★★) was estate-grown in the Bridge Pa Triangle and barrel-fermented. Mouthfilling, fleshy and fully dry (1.4 grams/litre of residual sugar), it has concentrated, ripe, peachy, slightly spicy flavours, gently seasoned with oak, soft acidity, good complexity and a well-rounded finish. Delicious young.

DRY $26 –V

Ascension The Vestal Virgin Matakana Viognier ★★★☆

The 2014 vintage (★★★☆) was estate-grown at Matakana. It's a vibrantly fruity, attractively scented wine with good depth of stone-fruit and spice flavours, crisp and lively.

DRY $40 –V

Ash Ridge Premium Estate Hawke's Bay Viognier ★★★☆

The 2015 vintage (★★★★), grown in the Bridge Pa Triangle, was fermented in seasoned French and American oak barrels, and 'using the orange technique', 15 per cent of the blend was fermented on its skins. Mouthfilling and dry, it is a distinctive wine, highly aromatic, with strong, citrusy, peachy, slightly spicy flavours, showing excellent freshness and complexity.

DRY $30 –V

Askerne Hawke's Bay Viognier ★★★★

The 2015 vintage (★★★★) is a rich, weighty, complex wine, fully barrel-fermented (20 per cent new oak). It has a fragrant bouquet, with a slightly creamy texture and concentrated stone-fruit flavours, gently seasoned with toasty oak.

DRY $22 V+

Babich Family Estates Fernhill Hawke's Bay Viognier ★★★☆

The 2014 vintage (★★★☆) is an estate-grown wine, mouthfilling and dry, with generous, ripe peach, pear and spice flavours, gentle acidity, a slightly creamy texture, and very good delicacy and depth.

DRY $25 –V

Byrne Northland Waingaro Viognier ★★★★

The 2015 vintage (★★★★), grown at Kerikeri, is a pale yellow, mouthfilling wine, creamy-textured, with good concentration of ripe, peachy, slightly spicy and toasty flavours, considerable complexity and a dry finish. Best drinking mid-2017+.

DRY $36 –V

Cable Bay Waiheke Island Viognier ★★★★

The 2015 vintage (★★★★) was hand-picked and handled in French oak and acacia barriques. Pale lemon/green, with a fragrant, slightly buttery bouquet, it is mouthfilling, with fresh, ripe pear, stone-fruit and spice flavours. Highly enjoyable in its youth, it is creamy-textured, with a sliver of sweetness (5 grams/litre of residual sugar) and very good depth and harmony.

Vintage	15	14
WR	6	6
Drink	16-20	16-19

MED/DRY $34 –V

Churton Marlborough Viognier ★★★★☆

The 2014 vintage (★★★★☆) was estate-grown and hand-picked in the Waihopai Valley, and fermented and matured for nearly a year in large, 600-litre French oak casks. It is mouthfilling, with vibrant, concentrated, ripe, peachy flavours, showing good complexity, a slightly creamy texture, and a long, fully dry finish. Certified organic.

Vintage	14	13
WR	6	7
Drink	16-20	16-22

DRY $40 –V

Clos de Ste Anne Viognier Les Arbres ★★★★★

This biodynamically certified Gisborne wine from Millton shows impressive richness and complexity. Hill-grown, it is hand-harvested and fermented with indigenous yeasts in large, 600-litre oak barrels. The light lemon/green 2014 vintage (★★★★☆) is a powerful (14 per cent alcohol) wine, rich and rounded, with generous, ripe stone-fruit flavours, gentle acidity, good complexity and a basically dry (4.9 grams/litre of residual sugar), creamy-smooth finish. Delicious drinking now onwards.

DRY $60 AV

Coopers Creek SV Chalk Ridge Hawke's Bay Viognier ★★★★

Floral and full-bodied, the barrel-fermented 2014 vintage (★★★☆) is vibrantly fruity, with fresh, ripe, peachy, slightly spicy flavours, a very subtle seasoning of oak, and very good delicacy and depth.

DRY $20 V+

Coopers Creek SV Cook County Gisborne Viognier   (★★★★)

Pale, weighty and dry, the 2015 vintage (★★★★) has peachy, spicy flavours, showing good balance and concentration, a hint of apricot, and a lifted, floral bouquet.

DRY $25 AV

De La Terre Reserve Hawke's Bay Viognier   ★★★★☆

The 2014 vintage (★★★★☆) was grown on limestone terraces at Havelock North, hand-picked at 23 brix, and fermented in seasoned French oak barriques. Powerful and fleshy, it was slightly oaky in its youth, but sturdy and fleshy, with good concentration of stone-fruit and spice flavours, nutty, complex and rich. Open 2017+.

Vintage	14
WR	6
Drink	16-20

DRY $40 –V

De La Terre Ridgeline Hawke's Bay Viognier   (★★★★)

Handled without oak, the refined, youthful 2015 vintage (★★★★) was estate-grown at Havelock North. Pale lemon/green, it is mouthfilling and vibrantly fruity, with concentrated peach, pear and lychee flavours, showing excellent delicacy, a sliver of sweetness (5 grams/litre of residual sugar), and a well-rounded finish. Best drinking 2018+.

Vintage	15
WR	6
Drink	16-19

MED/DRY $40 –V

Dry River Estate Martinborough Viognier   ★★★★☆

Handled without oak, the 2015 vintage (★★★★☆) is fragrant and fleshy, with rich, vibrant, peachy, citrusy flavours, a faint suggestion of sweetness, and a well-rounded finish. It's still youthful, but delicious young; drink now or cellar.

MED/DRY $47 –V

Falconhead Hawke's Bay Viognier   ★★★☆

The 2014 vintage (★★★★) offers top value. Barrel-fermented, it is fragrant, mouthfilling (14.5 per cent alcohol), sweet-fruited and smooth, with generous, peachy, slightly buttery and spicy flavours, soft acidity and a well-rounded finish. A good Chardonnay alternative, it's ready now.

MED/DRY $16 V+

Framingham F-Series Marlborough Viognier   ★★★★☆

Certified organic, the rare 2015 vintage (★★★★★) was hand-picked and partly barrel-fermented. It is mouthfilling (14.5 per cent alcohol), fleshy and harmonious, with concentrated, ripe, peachy flavours, a subtle seasoning of oak, a slightly oily texture and a dry, well-rounded finish. Already delicious, it's a drink-now or cellaring proposition. Only 533 bottles were made.

DRY $35 –V

Gladstone Vineyard Viognier   ★★★★

Instantly appealing, the 2014 vintage (★★★★) was hand-picked in the northern Wairarapa and mostly tank-fermented; 20 per cent of the blend was fermented in seasoned French oak barrels. Full-bodied, it is soft and creamy, with concentrated, ripe, peachy, slightly nutty flavours, gentle acidity and a bone-dry, well-rounded finish.

DRY $25 AV

Hans Herzog Marlborough Viognier   ★★★★★

Certified organic, the youthful 2014 vintage (★★★★) was hand-harvested from mature, estate-grown vines on the north side of the Wairau Valley, and fermented and matured for 18 months in French oak puncheons. Mouthfilling and dry, it is fleshy and well-rounded, with concentrated, citrusy, peachy, slightly spicy flavours, integrated oak, good complexity and a smooth finish. It's still developing; best drinking mid-2017+.

DRY $44 AV

Hopesgrove Estate Single Vineyard Hawke's Bay Viognier   (★★★★)

The 2014 vintage (★★★★) was estate-grown, hand-picked, and fermented and matured in French oak casks (25 per cent new). It's a full-bodied, well-rounded wine with ripe stone-fruit flavours, seasoned with toasty oak, good concentration and a dry, finely textured finish.

DRY $30 –V

Kaimira Estate Brightwater Viognier   (★★★★☆)

Certified organic, the impressive 2014 vintage (★★★★☆) was estate-grown, hand-picked and fermented in seasoned oak casks. Light lemon/green, it is fragrant, with concentrated stone-fruit flavours, finely integrated oak adding complexity, and a rich, dry (1.6 grams/litre of residual sugar) finish. Drink now or cellar. Fine value.

DRY $25 V+

Kainui Road Bay of Islands Viognier   ★★☆

Hand-picked at Kerikeri, in Northland, the easy-drinking 2015 vintage (★★★☆) is mouthfilling and sweet-fruited, with vibrant, peachy, gently spicy flavours, showing good delicacy and moderate richness.

DRY $25 –V

La Collina Viognier   ★★★★★

The classy 2014 vintage (★★★★★) from Bilancia, in Hawke's Bay, was fermented in very old French oak barriques. It is sturdy (14.5 per cent alcohol), with deep stone-fruit and spice flavours, a very subtle seasoning of oak, impressive complexity and a slightly creamy, long finish. Best drinking 2017+.

Vintage	14
WR	7
Drink	16-20

DRY $45 AV

Linden Estate Hawke's Bay Viognier ★★★★

The 2014 vintage (★★★★) was grown in the Dartmoor Valley and fermented in tanks and barrels. Bright, light yellow/green, it is full-bodied, with strong, peachy, slightly spicy flavours, creamy and buttery notes adding a touch of complexity, fresh acidity and a slightly off-dry (6 grams/litre of residual sugar), finely balanced finish. Drink now to 2017.

MED/DRY $25 AV

Marsden Bay of Islands Viognier ★★★☆

The mouthfilling 2015 vintage (★★★☆) was hand-picked and matured in seasoned oak barrels. Still youthful, it has ripe, peachy, slightly spicy flavours, in a vibrant, fruity style with a dry (3 grams/litre of residual sugar), seductively smooth finish. Best drinking 2017+.

Vintage	15
WR	6
Drink	16-17

DRY $27 –V

Millton Clos de Ste Anne Viognier Les Arbres – see Clos de Ste Anne Viognier Les Arbres

Millton Riverpoint Vineyard Gisborne Viognier ★★★★

Still youthful, the 2015 vintage (★★★★) was handled in tanks and French oak hogsheads. Certified organic, it is full-bodied, with fresh, ripe, peachy, spicy, slightly toasty flavours, showing very good complexity, gentle acidity and a dry finish. The powerful 2014 vintage (★★★★☆) is sturdy (14.5 per cent alcohol) and lively, with concentrated, ripe stone-fruit and spice flavours, a gentle seasoning of toasty oak, and a dry, lasting finish. Drink now or cellar.

Vintage	15	14
WR	6	7
Drink	16-21	16-20

DRY $26 AV

Obsidian Reserve Waiheke Island Viognier ★★★★

Hand-harvested at Onetangi and fermented and lees-aged for 10 months in seasoned French oak casks, the 2014 vintage (★★★★) is mouthfilling, with good concentration of vibrant, well-ripened, peachy, slightly spicy flavours, balanced acidity, and a subtle seasoning of oak adding complexity. Drink now or cellar.

DRY $45 –V

Okahu Estate Viognier ★★★☆

Grown at Kaitaia, in Northland, and handled without oak, the 2014 vintage (★★★☆) is a weighty wine with ripe, peachy, slightly spicy flavours, showing good depth.

DRY $39 –V

Quarter Acre Hawke's Bay Viognier ★★★★

The 2014 vintage (★★★★☆) was hand-picked in the Bridge Pa Triangle and fermented with indigenous yeasts in French oak barriques. It is mouthfilling and sweet-fruited, with ripe stone-fruit flavours, well-integrated oak and a slightly oily texture. Strongly varietal and dry, it has lots of drink-young appeal.

DRY $27 –V

Saint Clair Hawke's Bay Viognier   (★★★☆)

Vibrantly fruity and softly textured, the 2015 vintage (★★★☆) was estate-grown in the Gimblett Gravels and tank-fermented. Attractive in its youth, it is mouthfilling and well-rounded, with ripe, peachy, slightly spicy flavours, showing good freshness and depth, and a dry (2.8 grams/litre of residual sugar) finish.

DRY $22 AV

Sileni Estate Selection Hedonist Hawke's Bay Viognier   (★★★★)

Already delicious, the 2015 vintage (★★★★) was hand-picked at Te Awanga and fermented in seasoned oak casks. Mouthfilling and sweet-fruited, it has ripe stone-fruit and pear flavours, with a soft, dry (4.7 grams/litre of residual sugar), creamy-textured finish. Drink now to 2018.

Vintage	15
WR	6
Drink	16-22

DRY $25 AV

Staete Landt State of Surrender Marlborough Viognier   ★★★★

Estate-grown at Rapaura, the 2014 vintage (★★★★) was hand-picked and matured on its yeast lees for eight months. Fleshy and soft, it is vibrantly fruity, with pure, ripe, peachy flavours, showing excellent depth, and a slightly oily texture.

Vintage	14	13	12
WR	6	6	6
Drink	16-20	16-19	16-18

DRY $39 –V

Te Mata Zara Viognier   ★★★★★

This estate-grown wine is from Woodthorpe Terraces, on the south side of the Dartmoor Valley in Hawke's Bay. Hand-picked, it is partly fermented and lees-aged in seasoned French oak barrels. The 2015 vintage (★★★★★) is bright, light lemon/green. Powerful, sturdy (14.5 per cent alcohol) and softly seductive, it is floral and very sweet-fruited, with rich, lush, peachy flavours to the fore, a subtle seasoning of oak adding complexity, and lots of drink-young appeal.

Vintage	15
WR	6
Drink	17-23

DRY $30 AV

Tohu Single Vineyard Marlborough Viognier   (★★★☆)

The easy-drinking 2015 vintage (★★★☆) is a single-vineyard wine, grown in the upper Awatere Valley and partly barrel-fermented. Pale and freshly scented, it is mouthfilling and slightly creamy, with strong, citrusy, appley flavours, gentle sweetness (10 grams/litre of residual sugar) and a smooth finish.

MED/DRY $20 AV

Villa Maria Cellar Selection Gisborne Viognier   (★★★★)

Bargain-priced, the powerful 2015 vintage (★★★★) is sturdy (14.5 per cent alcohol) and fleshy, with strong, ripe, peachy, slightly biscuity flavours, a hint of honeysuckle, gentle acidity and a dry finish. Drink now onwards.

DRY $18 V+

Villa Maria Cellar Selection Hawke's Bay Viognier ★★★★☆

The fine-value 2015 vintage (★★★★☆) was partly hand-picked and fermented with indigenous yeasts in tanks (40 per cent) and seasoned French oak barriques (60 per cent). Mouthfilling (14.5 per cent alcohol) and fleshy, it has fresh stone-fruit and spice flavours, showing excellent ripeness and richness, gentle acidity, and a fully dry (2 grams/litre of residual sugar) finish. Drink now or cellar.

Vintage	15	14	13
WR	7	7	7
Drink	16-20	16-19	16-17

 DRY $18 V+

Villa Maria Private Bin Gisborne Viognier ★★★☆

The 2015 vintage (★★★☆), handled without oak, is mouthfilling and vibrantly fruity, with fresh, ripe, peachy flavours and a bone-dry (2 grams/litre of residual sugar) finish.

Vintage	15	14	13
WR	7	7	7
Drink	16-18	16-17	P

 DRY $17 V+

Waimea Nelson Viognier ★★★★

The 2014 vintage (★★★★) was estate-grown on the Waimea Plains, hand-picked and tank-fermented. Delicious young, it is scented and smooth, in a fleshy, finely textured style with strong, peachy flavours to the fore, a slightly creamy texture and an off-dry (8 grams/litre of residual sugar) finish.

MED/DRY $23 AV

Wairau River Reserve Marlborough Viognier ★★★★

The 2014 vintage (★★★★) was estate-grown on the banks of the Wairau River, and fermented and lees-aged in seasoned French oak barriques. It has mouthfilling body (14.5 per cent alcohol) and strong, ripe, fully dry stone-fruit flavours, gently seasoned with toasty oak. Showing a touch of complexity, it's well worth cellaring. The youthful 2015 vintage (★★★★) was oak-aged. Light lemon/green, it is mouthfilling and vibrantly fruity, with rich, peachy flavours, a touch of complexity, and a smooth (4.9 grams/litre of residual sugar) finish. Best drinking mid-2017+.

Vintage	15	14	13	12	11
WR	6	7	7	6	6
Drink	16-20	16-18	16-17	P	P

 DRY $30 –V

Sweet White Wines

New Zealand's sweet white wines (often called dessert wines) are hardly taking the world by storm, with only about 10,000 cases exported each year. Yet around the country, winemakers work hard to produce some ravishingly beautiful, honey-sweet white wines that are worth discovering and can certainly hold their own internationally. New Zealand's most luscious, concentrated and honeyish sweet whites are made from grapes which have been shrivelled and dehydrated on the vines by 'noble rot', the dry form of the 'Botrytis cinerea' mould. Misty mornings, followed by clear, fine days with light winds and low humidity, are ideal conditions for the spread of noble rot, but in New Zealand this favourable interplay of weather factors occurs irregularly.

Some enjoyable but rarely exciting dessert wines are made by the 'freeze-concentration' method, whereby a proportion of the natural water content in the grape juice is frozen out, leaving a sweet, concentrated juice to be fermented.

Marlborough has so far yielded a majority of the finest sweet whites. Most of the other wine regions can also point to the successful production of botrytised sweet whites in favourable vintages.

Riesling has been the foundation of the majority of New Zealand's most opulent sweet whites, but Sauvignon Blanc, Sémillon, Gewürztraminer, Pinot Gris, Chenin Blanc, Viognier and Chardonnay have all yielded fine dessert styles. With their high levels of extract and firm acidity, most of these wines mature well for two to three years, although few are very long-lived.

Ake Ake La Douce   (★★★)

The 2014 vintage (★★★) is a Northland blend of Pinot Gris (90 per cent) and Sauvignon Blanc (10 per cent). It is mouthfilling, with gentle sweetness (120 grams/litre of residual sugar) and good depth of ripe, peachy, slightly spicy flavours.

SW $25 (750ML) AV

Allan Scott Marlborough Late Harvest Riesling   (★★★★★)

The luscious 2014 vintage (★★★★★) is golden, with rich honey and apricot scents and flavours. Delicious now, it harbours just 7.5 per cent alcohol, but is a highly botrytised, concentrated wine with abundant sweetness and good acid spine. Intense and oily, with lovely vibrancy, richness and harmony, it's a drink-now or cellaring proposition.

SW $28 (375ML) V+

Alpha Domus AD Noble Selection   ★★★★★

A pale gold beauty, the botrytis-affected 2015 vintage (★★★★★) was made from Sémillon grapes, grown in the Bridge Pa Triangle and mostly harvested with soaring sugar contents (45–47 brix). French oak-aged, it is fresh and full-bodied (although only 10 per cent alcohol), with rich, ripe flavours, showing good complexity, plentiful sweetness (248 grams/litre of residual sugar), and an oily, honeyed richness.

SW $38 (375ML) AV

Ara Select Block Limited Release Cut Cane Sauvignon Blanc   (★★★★☆)

Light gold, the refined 2014 vintage (★★★★☆) has an inviting, honeyed bouquet and ripe, peachy, nectareous flavours. Finely balanced, with abundant sweetness (200 grams/litre of residual sugar), it has excellent vibrancy and depth.

Vintage	14
WR	7
Drink	16-18

SW $30 (375ML) AV

Ash Ridge Premium Estate Late Harvest Chardonnay   (★★★☆)

Harvested at 32 brix in early April, three weeks after the main crop, but with very little botrytis, the 2015 vintage (★★★☆) has pure, vibrant, sweet (120 grams/litre of residual sugar), grapey flavours. Worth cellaring.

SW $25 (375ML) –V

Ataahua Waipara Late Harvest Gewürztraminer   (★★★★★)

The pale gold 2014 vintage (★★★★★) is packed with personality. From grapes hand-harvested in early winter and barrel-fermented with indigenous yeasts, it is perfumed and weighty, with sweet, concentrated stone-fruit and spice flavours, showing lovely complexity, richness and harmony. Drink now or cellar.

SW $26 (375ML) V+

Awatere River by Louis Vavasour Marlborough
Late Harvest Gewürztraminer   (★★★★★)

The golden, honey-sweet 2014 vintage (★★★★★) was picked in mid-May at over 40 brix, with an 'extensive' botrytis infection, and barrel-fermented. The bouquet is perfumed, honeyish and spicy; the palate is fresh and rich, with peach, apricot and spice flavours, good sugar/acid balance (213 grams/litre of residual sugar), and great drink-young appeal.

SW $40 (375ML) AV

Babich Family Estates Gimblett Gravels
Hawke's Bay Noble Gewürztraminer   (★★★★☆)

Showing strong personality, the 2014 vintage (★★★★☆) is an amber-hued, honeyed dessert wine, hand-harvested at 42 brix. Mouthfilling (14.5 per cent alcohol), with rich peach, spice and apricot flavours, it's a sweet but not super-sweet style (115 grams/litre of residual sugar) with a powerful botrytis influence. Drink now onwards.

SW $25 (375ML) V+

Brancott Estate Letter Series 'B' Late Harvest
Marlborough Sauvignon Blanc   ★★★★☆

The 2014 vintage (★★★★☆) has a gently honeyed, faintly herbal bouquet, leading into a luscious wine with rich passionfruit, ginger and apricot-like flavours, woven with fresh acidity, excellent drive and depth through the palate, and a long, sweet finish.

SW $36 (375ML) –V

Brookfields Indulgence Hawke's Bay Viognier (★★★★☆)

Already hard to resist, the 2016 vintage (★★★★☆) was made from botrytis-enriched grapes, handled without oak. Bright, light yellow/green, it has a scented, peachy bouquet, leading into a youthful, vibrantly fruity wine, deliciously concentrated and soft, with ripe stone-fruit and slight honey flavours, abundant sweetness (250 grams/litre of residual sugar), and an oily richness.

Vintage	16	SW $25 (375ML) V+
WR	7	
Drink	18-20	

Charcoal Gully Late Harvest Central Otago Gewürztraminer (★★★★)

The 2014 vintage (★★★★) is a full-bodied, generous, gently sweet wine (57 grams/litre of residual sugar), hand-picked at 27 brix, six weeks after the normal harvest. Attractively scented, with ripe stone-fruit, lychee and spice flavours, concentrated and soft, it's drinking well now and starting to develop bottle-aged complexity.

SW $28 (750ML) V+

De La Terre Late Harvest Hawke's Bay Viognier (★★★★)

The pale yellow 2015 vintage (★★★★) was estate-grown at Havelock North and handled without oak. A gently sweet style (55 grams/litre of residual sugar), it is finely balanced, with vibrant, peachy flavours, showing a touch of complexity, and very good ripeness and concentration. Already drinking well, it should be at its best mid-2017+.

Vintage	15	SW $24 (375ML) V+
WR	5	
Drink	16-18	

De La Terre Noble Hawke's Bay Viognier ★★★★☆

The delicious 2015 vintage (★★★★☆) was estate-grown at Havelock North and handled without oak. Bright lemon/green, it is rich and rounded, with concentrated, peachy, slightly spicy and honeyed flavours, sweet (125 grams/litre of residual sugar), finely balanced and youthful. Best drinking 2018+.

Vintage	15	SW $34 (375ML) AV
WR	6	
Drink	16-20	

Esk Valley Late Harvest Chenin Blanc (★★★★★)

The 2013 vintage (★★★★★) is pale gold, with a deliciously honeyed, strongly botrytis-influenced bouquet. Hand-picked in late May in the Joseph Soler Vineyard, near Hastings, and partly (33 per cent) barrel-fermented, it has luscious, sweet (204 grams/litre of residual sugar) peach, pear and apricot flavours, fresh and vibrant, with a slightly oily richness and lovely harmony.

Vintage	14	13	SW $30 (375ML) V+
WR	NM	7	
Drink	NM	16-20	

Felton Road Block 1 Central Otago Riesling   ★★★★★

Estate-grown in The Elms Vineyard, from mature vines on a 'steeper slope' which yields 'riper fruit' without noble rot, this Bannockburn wine is made in a style 'similar to a late-harvest, Mosel spätlese'. The 2015 vintage (★★★★★) is light (9 per cent alcohol) and vivacious, with gentle sweetness, crisp acidity and citrusy, appley, limey flavours, showing lovely purity, poise and persistence. The 2016 vintage (★★★★★) is already delicious. Pale lemon/green, it is light (9 per cent alcohol) and lively, with rich, ripe, lemony, peachy, slightly spicy flavours, gentle sweetness (66.5 grams/litre of residual sugar), appetising acidity, and lovely depth and harmony.

Vintage	16	15	14	13
WR	7	7	6	7
Drink	16-41	16-40	16-28	16-28

SW $43 (750ML) V+

Framingham F-Series Gewürztraminer VT   ★★★★★

'VT' stands for Vendange Tardive. This wine is typically made from dehydrated Marlborough grapes, hand-harvested with a touch of botrytis and fermented with indigenous yeasts in old oak barrels. The outstanding 2014 vintage (★★★★★) is slightly fuller-bodied (11 per cent alcohol) and sweeter (217 grams/litre of residual sugar) than the 2013 vintage (★★★★☆). Light gold, it is oily-textured and rich, with a complex bouquet leading into a concentrated, peachy, spicy, gently honeyed wine, showing lovely complexity, depth and harmony.

SW $40 (375ML) AV

Framingham F-Series Marlborough Riesling Spätlese   (★★★★★)

The 2014 vintage (★★★★★) is rare – only 507 bottles were made. Hand-picked at 21.9 brix, it is finely scented and light (8.5 per cent alcohol), with gentle sweetness (63 grams/litre of residual sugar) and intense flavours of peaches, apples and lemons, woven with fresh acidity. Vivacious and tangy, it's a beautifully poised, lovely young wine; drink now or cellar.

SW $35 (750ML) V+

Framingham F-Series Riesling Auslese   ★★★★★

The 2015 vintage (★★★★★), handled in tanks (57 per cent) and old oak casks (43 per cent), is bright yellow/green, with a honeyed bouquet. Already delicious, it is light (9 per cent alcohol) and rich, with sweet (120 grams/litre of residual sugar), ripe, peachy, spicy flavours, honeyed and highly concentrated. Drink now or cellar.

Vintage	15
WR	7
Drink	16-20

SW $45 (375ML) AV

Framingham F-Series Riesling Trockenbeerenauslese ★★★★★

Hand-harvested in Marlborough when all the berries were botrytis-affected and dried out, the memorable 2015 vintage (★★★★★) was handled in tanks (65 per cent) and old oak casks (35 per cent). Bright lemon/green, with advanced sweetness (260 grams/litre of residual sugar) and finely balanced acidity, it is vibrantly fruity, with concentrated lemon, apricot and honey flavours, showing lovely harmony, and a notably rich, lasting finish.

Vintage	15
WR	7
Drink	16-20

 SW $70 (375ML) AV

Framingham Noble Riesling ★★★★★

Bright yellow/green, the 2015 vintage (★★★★★) was handled in tanks (67 per cent) and old oak barrels (33 per cent). Highly expressive in its youth, it is deliciously rich and rounded, with abundant sweetness (185 grams/litre of residual sugar) and highly concentrated stone-fruit and honey flavours, fresh and long. Drink now or cellar.

Vintage	15
WR	6
Drink	16-20

 SW $40 (375ML) AV

Framingham Select Marlborough Riesling ★★★★★

'Inspired by the German Spätlese style', the lemon/green 2015 vintage (★★★★★) was handled entirely in tanks. Richly scented, it is a vivacious, light-bodied style (8.5 per cent alcohol) with gentle sweetness (70 grams/litre of residual sugar), appetising acidity and fresh, concentrated, peachy, slightly spicy flavours. Intense, tangy and long, it's already delicious.

Vintage	15	14
WR	6	6
Drink	16-22	16-21

 SW $35 (750ML) V+

Fromm Riesling Spätlese ★★★★☆

This vivacious Marlborough wine is made from the ripest hand-picked grapes with no botrytis infection, in an intense, low-alcohol style with plentiful sweetness (typically around 80–90 grams/litre of residual sugar). The 2014 vintage (★★★★★) is scented, light (7 per cent alcohol) and lively, with lovely poise and immediacy. It has pure, penetrating, lemony, appley flavours, good acid spine, delicious sugar/acid balance and a long, racy finish. Already delicious, it should mature well.

Vintage	14	13	12	11	10	09
WR	7	7	7	6	7	7
Drink	16-24	16-23	16-22	16-21	16-20	16-19

 SW $35 (750ML) V+

Gibbston Valley Late Harvest   ★★★★

Grown at Bendigo, in Central Otago, the 2014 vintage (★★★☆) is not labelled by variety, but was blended from Riesling (70 per cent) and Pinot Blanc (30 per cent). It is light-bodied (8.5 per cent alcohol), with good depth of fresh, peachy, slightly spicy and honeyed flavours, sweet (138 grams/litre of residual sugar) and smooth. Enjoyable young.

Vintage	14	13
WR	7	6
Drink	16-25	16-25

SW $35 (375ML) –V

Giesen The Brothers Late Harvest Marlborough Sauvignon Blanc   ★★★★★

The lovely 2014 vintage (★★★★★) is a single-vineyard, hand-picked wine. Golden, honeyed and rich, with an oily texture, it is highly concentrated, with peachy, unabashedly sweet flavours (252 grams/litre of residual sugar), balanced acidity, a strong botrytis influence, and lots of current-drinking appeal.

Vintage	14
WR	7
Drink	16-18

SW $30 (375ML) V+

Greystone Brittle Star Waipara Valley Riesling   ★★★★☆

Very expressive in its youth, the 2015 vintage (★★★★☆) was hand-picked at high natural sugar levels (26.9 to 30.6 brix), when 70 per cent of the bunches were botrytis-infected. Pale gold, with a gently honeyed bouquet, it is medium-bodied, with strong, ripe peach, apricot and marmalade flavours, a hint of honey, and a sweet (108 grams/litre of residual sugar), rounded finish. Drink now or cellar.

Vintage	15
WR	7
Drink	16-25

SW $38 (750ML) V+

Greywacke Botrytis Marlborough Pinot Gris   (★★★★☆)

Released in 2016, the bright, light lemon/green 2013 vintage (★★★★☆) is a single-vineyard wine, grown at Woodbourne, in the Wairau Valley. From botrytis-affected grapes, it is a sweet but not super-sweet style, still fresh and youthful, with mouthfilling body (13 per cent alcohol), rich lemon, peach and slight honey flavours, and good complexity. It should be long-lived; drink now or cellar.

SW $38 (375ML) –V

Hunter's Hukapapa Marlborough Riesling Dessert Wine   ★★★☆

The 2014 vintage (★★★☆) is a freeze-concentrated wine. It has strong, lemony, slightly limey flavours, sweet (130 grams/litre of residual sugar) and crisp, showing very good depth and harmony. Drink now or cellar.

SW $24 (375ML) AV

Jackson Estate Botrytis Marlborough Riesling   (★★★★★)

Estate-grown in the heart of the Wairau Valley, the 2014 vintage (★★★★★) is delicious now. Amber-hued, with a honeyed bouquet, it has concentrated, apricot-like flavours, abundant sweetness (260 grams/litre of residual sugar), good acid spine, and lovely richness and harmony.

SW $45 (375ML) AV

Johner Estate Gladstone Noble Pinot Noir   ★★★

Estate-grown in the northern Wairarapa, the 2014 vintage (★★★☆) is a sweet (140 grams/litre of residual sugar), light pink/orange wine. Mouthfilling and smooth, it is slightly honeyed, with strawberry, peach and spice flavours, woven with fresh acidity, good depth, and lots of drink-young charm.

Vintage	14
WR	6
Drink	16-20

SW $22 (375ML) –V

Johner Estate Gladstone Noble Sauvignon Blanc   ★★★☆

Estate-grown in the northern Wairarapa, the 2016 vintage (★★★☆) is still very youthful. Handled without oak, it is light lemon/green, with vibrant, ripe, peachy, vaguely honeyed flavours, gentle sweetness (140 grams/litre of residual sugar), crisp acidity and very good poise and depth.

Vintage	16
WR	6
Drink	16-22

SW $22 (375ML) AV

Johner Estate Wairarapa Noble Lynder Cabernet   (★★★☆)

The light red 2014 vintage (★★★☆) is mouthfilling (13.5 per cent alcohol), with raspberry/plum flavours, fresh, sweet (140 grams/litre of residual sugar) and strong. It's a distinctive wine, ready to roll.

Vintage	14
WR	5
Drink	16-20

SW $22 (375ML) AV

Jules Taylor Late Harvest Marlborough Sauvignon Blanc   ★★★★☆

The bright light yellow/green 2015 vintage (★★★★) was handled without oak. It has a gently honeyed bouquet, leading into a finely balanced wine with rich, ripe, peachy, non-herbaceous flavours, slightly honeyed, sweet (169 grams/litre of residual sugar) and youthful. Well worth cellaring.

SW $33 (375ML) AV

Loveblock Marlborough Noble Chenin Blanc (★★★★★)

Full of youthful vigour, but already delicious, the 2014 vintage (★★★★★) was estate-grown and hand-picked in the Awatere Valley at 42 brix, with 100 per cent botrytis infection. Light gold, deliciously peachy and honeyed, it has abundant sweetness (230 grams/litre of residual sugar), balanced by firm acidity, and a slightly oily, lasting finish.

 SW $30 (500ML) V+

Loveblock Marlborough Sweet Moscato (★★★★)

Estate-grown in the Awatere Valley, the 2014 vintage (★★★★) is a full-bodied (13.5 per cent alcohol), sweet but not super-sweet wine, fortified with grain alcohol, 'in true Muscat de Beaumes-de-Venise style'. Light lemon/green, it is invitingly perfumed, with fresh, pure Muscat aromas and strong, vibrant peach, lemon, orange and grape flavours.

 SW $30 (500ML) V+

Margrain Botrytis Selection Martinborough Chenin Blanc (★★★★★)

The lovely 2014 vintage (★★★★★) is light gold, with a gently honeyed bouquet. Already delicious, it has intense, vibrant peach, apricot and honey flavours, abundant sweetness, good acid spine, and excellent richness and poise. Enriched but not swamped by botrytis, it's a drink-now or cellaring proposition.

 SW $38 (375ML) AV

Millton Clos Samuel Special Bunch Selection Viognier (★★★★★)

Certified organic, the 2013 vintage (★★★★★) is an amber-hued Gisborne wine, handled in French oak half barrels (114 litres). Richly fragrant, with apricot/honey aromas and flavours, it is youthful, with an oily texture and lovely vigour, concentration and complexity. Drink now or cellar.

Vintage	13
WR	7
Drink	16-24

 SW $36 (375ML) AV

Misha's Vineyard The Cadenza Late Harvest Gewürztraminer ★★★★☆

The 2015 vintage (★★★★☆) was hand-harvested at Bendigo, in Central Otago, at 29.3 brix, with a 25 per cent botrytis infection, and handled without oak. A very pale gold, weighty wine (although only 10 per cent alcohol), it has excellent depth of ripe, peachy, gingery, spicy flavours, sweet (135 grams/litre of residual sugar) and smooth. Showing lovely delicacy and balance, it's delicious young.

Vintage	15	14
WR	7	6
Drink	16-23	16-22

 SW $32 (375ML) AV

Mission Estate Late Harvest ★★★

The 2014 vintage (★★★☆), grown in Hawke's Bay and Gisborne, is a pale gold, sweetish Gewürztraminer, full-bodied, with good depth of ripe, gentle, moderately spicy flavours and an invitingly perfumed bouquet. Best drinking 2017+.

SW $18 (375ML) AV

Mondillo Nina Late Harvest Riesling   ★★★★☆

Estate-grown at Bendigo, in Central Otago, the 2014 vintage (★★★★) has lemony, appley scents and flavours, a hint of honey, good acid spine, abundant sweetness (110 grams/litre of residual sugar), and a finely poised, lengthy finish.

Vintage	14	12	11
WR	7	7	7
Drink	16-20	16-19	16-18

SW $35 (375ML) –V

Nevis Bluff Selection De Grains Noble Pinot Gris   (★★★★☆)

The 2014 vintage (★★★★☆) has a lovely honeyed, botrytis-enriched bouquet, leading into a concentrated Central Otago wine with sweet pear and marmalade flavours, enlivened by fresh acidity, impressive complexity and length.

SW $35 (375ML) –V

Ngatarawa Proprietors' Reserve Noble Riesling   (★★★★★)

The ravishing 2014 vintage (★★★★★) is from a Hawke's Bay producer with a decades-long commitment to dessert wines. Hand-picked in two passes through the vineyard, at 42 and 44 brix, it is golden and richly scented, with highly concentrated, sweet (204 grams/litre of residual sugar), peachy, citrusy, gently honeyed flavours, enriched but not swamped by botrytis. A very elegant wine, it's hard to resist.

SW $40 (375ML) AV

O:TU Barrel Reserve Marlborough Sauvignon Blanc   (★★★☆)

Still very fresh and lively, the pale straw 2013 vintage (★★★☆) has gently herbaceous aromas. Full-bodied (although only 10 per cent alcohol), it is vibrantly fruity, with moderately ripe and rich, lightly oaked, sweetish flavours (67 grams/litre of residual sugar), finely balanced for current drinking. Pricey.

SW $70 (375ML) –V

Omaha Bay Vineyard Late Harvest Matakana Flora/ Viognier   (★★★☆)

Still on sale, the 2010 vintage (★★★☆) is probably at its peak. Light gold, it is peachy and gently sweet, with ripe, slightly honeyed flavours, showing a touch of bottle-aged complexity, and a well-rounded finish.

SW $25 (375ML) –V

Osawa Prestige Collection Late Harvest Gewürztraminer   ★★★★☆

Gold, with a hint of amber, the 2013 vintage (★★★★), still on sale, is a soft, sweet wine, grown at Maraekakaho, in Hawke's Bay. Drinking well now, it is floral, peachy and spicy, with bottle-aged complexity and a rich, well-rounded finish.

SW $29 (375ML) V+

Pegasus Bay Aria Late Picked Riesling ★★★★★

From 'a great botrytis year', the 2014 vintage (★★★★☆) is a sweet but not super-sweet Waipara, North Canterbury wine. Bright, light lemon/green, with a honeyed, complex bouquet, it is finely poised, with fresh, citrusy, peachy, honeyed flavours, concentrated and long. Drink now or cellar.

Vintage	14	13	12
WR	6	7	6
Drink	16-26	16-25	16-25

SW $39 (375ML) AV

Pegasus Bay Encore Noble Riesling ★★★★★

Grown at Waipara, in North Canterbury, this beauty is from hand-selected, botrytised bunches and berries, harvested late in the season in multiple passes through the vineyard. The 2014 vintage (★★★★★) is light gold, with beautifully intense, apricot/honey aromas and flavours. Notably concentrated, it has marmalade-like notes and a lush, super-rich finish.

SW $39 (375ML) AV

Pegasus Bay Finale Noble Sémillon/Sauvignon Blanc Barrique Matured   (★★★★★)

Currently on sale, the 2011 vintage (★★★★★) is a striking Waipara, North Canterbury dessert wine, given lengthy barrel aging. Deep amber, with notable complexity on the nose and palate, it has substantial body (14.5 per cent alcohol), with super-rich peach and apricot flavours, an oily texture and a lush, raisiny, superbly sustained finish. A wine to ponder over.

SW $37 (375ML) AV

Riverby Estate Marlborough Noble Riesling ★★★★☆

The strongly botrytis-affected 2014 vintage (★★★★★) is liquid honey. Delicious in its youth, it is light gold, with concentrated peach and apricot flavours, an oily texture, abundant sweetness (200 grams/litre of residual sugar) and good acid spine. A top year.

SW $35 (375ML) –V

Rock Ferry Botrytised Riesling ★★★★☆

Certified organic, the 2015 vintage (★★★★☆) was hand-picked at 33 brix in Marlborough and fermented with indigenous yeasts, partly in old oak casks. Light gold, with a hint of straw, it has an inviting, richly honeyed bouquet. Delicious from the start, it is full-bodied (13 per cent alcohol), lush and sweet (138 grams/litre of residual sugar), with peachy, honeyed flavours, gentle acidity, and excellent concentration and roundness.

SW $35 (375ML) –V

Saint Clair Godfrey's Creek Reserve Noble Gewürztraminer   (★★★★)

Light gold, with a spicy, honeyed bouquet, the 2014 vintage (★★★★) is a single-vineyard Marlborough wine, hand-picked in the Wairau Valley. Delicious young, it is medium to full-bodied, in a vividly varietal style with abundant sweetness (161 grams/litre of residual sugar), gentle acidity and peachy, spicy flavours, rich and soft.

SW $29 (375ML) AV

Saint Clair Godfrey's Creek Reserve Noble Pinot Gris   (★★★★)

The 2014 vintage (★★★★) is an amber-hued, single-vineyard Marlborough dessert wine, hand-picked and handled entirely in tanks. A strongly botrytised style, it is sweet but not super-sweet (97 grams/litre of residual sugar), with a nectareous bouquet, good acid spine and rich apricot and honey flavours.

SW $29 (375ML) AV

Seifried Winemaker's Collection Sweet Agnes Nelson Riesling   ★★★★☆

Seifried's most celebrated wine. The 2015 vintage (★★★★☆) has a strong surge of lemony, sweet flavours (172 grams/litre of residual sugar), peachy and spicy notes, a hint of honey, good acid spine, and excellent intensity, vigour and richness. The 2016 vintage (★★★★★) is highly impressive. Bright, light lemon/green, it is refined and tightly structured, with concentrated peach and pear flavours, a hint of honey, abundant sweetness (175 grams/litre of residual sugar), and a crisp, lasting finish. Still a baby, it has a real sense of vigour and potential.

Vintage	16	15
WR	7	6
Drink	16-26	16-24

SW $29 (375ML) V+

Sileni Estate Selection Late Harvest Hawke's Bay Sémillon   ★★★☆

The 2014 vintage (★★★) is an unoaked style, with fresh, ripe·peach flavours, showing good depth, hints of pears and lemons, gentle sweetness (92 grams/litre of residual sugar), and a smooth finish. Enjoyable young.

Vintage	14	13	12
WR	6	5	7
Drink	16-20	16-18	16-17

SW $20 (375ML) AV

Sileni Exceptional Vintage Marlborough Pourriture Noble   ★★★★☆

The lovely 2014 vintage (★★★★★) is light gold, very honeyed and rich, with lush stone-fruit flavours, advanced sweetness (245 grams/litre of residual sugar), an oily texture and good acid spine. (Although not labelled by variety, it was made from botrytised Sauvignon Blanc grapes, picked in Marlborough at 46 brix.) Drink now or cellar.

Vintage	14
WR	7
Drink	16-22

SW $32 (375ML) AV

Spy Valley Iced Marlborough Sauvignon Blanc   ★★★★☆

The 2015 vintage (★★★★) was picked at 34 brix and fermented in tanks and barrels. Light yellow/green, it is fresh and sweet (157 grams/litre of residual sugar), with vibrant, citrusy, peachy flavours, balanced acidity, and a rich, harmonious finish. Delicious young.

Vintage	15	14
WR	6	6
Drink	16-20	16-19

SW $23 (375ML) V+

Staete Landt State of Love Marlborough Sweet Riesling   (★★★★☆)

The 2014 vintage (★★★★☆) is amber-hued, with a honeyed bouquet. A richly botrytised style, it is sweet, with strong, peachy, honeyed flavours, good acid spine, an oily texture, lovely intensity, and plenty of drink-young appeal.

SW $29 (375ML) V+

TerraVin Late Harvest Marlborough Pinot Gris   ★★★★

Ensconced in a full-sized bottle, the light gold 2013 vintage (★★★★) has strong personality. A sweetish style (73 grams/litre of residual sugar), it is peachy and slightly honeyed, with some maturity showing, and good complexity and richness. Ready.

SW $40 (750ML) V+

Tohu Raiha Reserve Limited Release Marlborough Noble Riesling   ★★★★☆

Delicious young, the 2014 vintage (★★★★☆) is an amber-hued, Awatere Valley wine, strongly botrytis-affected. It has a richly honeyed bouquet, moderate acidity, and vibrant peach, apricot and honey flavours, sweet (175 grams/litre of residual sugar) and concentrated.

SW $28 (375ML) V+

Toi Toi Late Harvest New Zealand Dessert Wine   (★★★)

The 2014 vintage (★★★) is a Waipara, North Canterbury Riesling. Light yellow/green, it is citrusy and sweet, with balanced acidity and slightly toasty, bottle-aged notes emerging. Ready.

SW $18 (375ML) AV

Tupari Late Harvest Marlborough Riesling   (★★★★)

The 2014 vintage (★★★★) is a pale gold, Awatere Valley wine with a honeyed bouquet and good intensity and drive on the palate. Fresh, sweet and finely balanced, it has lemon, apricot, honey and marmalade flavours, showing a strong botrytis influence.

SW $29 (375ML) AV

Urlar Noble Riesling   ★★★★☆

The lovely 2015 vintage (★★★★★) was estate-grown in the northern Wairarapa. Bright light/green, it has a scented, citrusy, honeyed bouquet. Beautifully poised, it has strong, delicate lemon/lime flavours, enriched but not dominated by botrytis, a touch of complexity, fresh acidity and a very long finish.

SW $30 (375ML) AV

Valli Late Harvest Waitaki North Otago Riesling   (★★★★★)

The highly refined 2014 vintage (★★★★★) is light-bodied (9 per cent alcohol), with a gently honeyed bouquet. Delicious from the start, it has rich, citrusy flavours, sweet and crisp, with a lovely interplay of fruit and botrytis, a hint of sherbet, and a long, honeyed finish.

SW $45 (750ML) V+

Villa Maria Reserve Marlborough Noble Riesling Botrytis Selection ★★★★★

One of New Zealand's top sweet wines on the show circuit. It is typically stunningly perfumed, weighty and oily, with intense, very sweet honey/citrus flavours and a lush, long finish. The grapes are grown mainly in the Fletcher Vineyard, in the centre of Marlborough's Wairau Plains, where trees create a 'humidity crib' around the vines and sprinklers along the vines' fruit zone create ideal conditions for the spread of noble rot. The 2015 vintage (★★★★★), hand-harvested in mid-May, is a pale gold wine, light (10 per cent alcohol), peachy, sweet (240 grams/litre of residual sugar), oily-textured and long, with instant appeal.

Vintage	15
WR	7
Drink	16-25

SW $37 (375ML) AV

🍇🍇🍇

Wairau River Botrytised Reserve Riesling ★★★★☆

The 2016 vintage (★★★★☆) is a light gold, honeyed, low-alcohol (10 per cent) wine, with abundant sweetness (213 grams/litre of residual sugar). It has rich, vibrant, peachy flavours, hints of apricot and honey, and obvious potential; open 2018+.

Vintage	16	15
WR	6	6
Drink	16-20	16-18

SW $30 (375ML) AV

Whitehaven Marlborough Noble Riesling ★★★★☆

The classy, green/gold 2014 vintage (★★★★★) has a fragrant, honeyed bouquet. Concentrated and oily-textured, it is light-bodied (8.3 per cent alcohol), with a strong surge of rich peach and apricot flavours, sweet, crisp and very harmonious. It's already hard to resist.

SW $28 (375ML) V+

Wooing Tree Tickled Pink ★★★★

The delightful, bright pink/pale red 2015 vintage (★★★★) was made from Pinot Noir, late-picked on 13 May in the Cromwell Basin, Central Otago. The fermentation, in tanks, was arrested when the wine had reached 9.5 per cent alcohol, leaving 105 grams per litre of residual sugar. Light and vibrantly fruity, it has concentrated, cherryish flavours, deliciously fresh, sweet and smooth.

SW $35 (375ML) –V

Yealands Estate Single Vineyard Awatere Valley Noble Sauvignon Blanc (★★★★)

The golden 2014 vintage (★★★★) was estate-grown at Seaview and handled without oak. From botrytised grapes, it is sweet (160 grams/litre of residual sugar), peachy and honeyed, very open and expressive, with fresh acidity, a slightly oily texture and loads of drink-young charm.

Vintage	14
WR	7
Drink	16-18

SW $23 (375ML) V+

Sparkling Wines

Fizz, bubbly, méthode traditionnelle, sparkling – whatever name you call it by (the word Champagne is reserved for the wines of that most famous of all wine regions), wine with bubbles in it is universally adored.

How good are Kiwi bubblies? Good enough for the industry to export about 160,000 cases per year, although that accounts for less than 1 per cent of New Zealand's overseas wine shipments.

The selection of New Zealand bubblies is not wide, but has been boosted in recent years by an influx of low-priced sparkling Sauvignon Blancs, sparkling Pinot Gris and the like. Most small wineries find the production of bottle-fermented sparkling wine too time-consuming and costly, and the domestic demand for premium bubbly is limited. The vast majority of purchases are under $15.

New Zealand's sparkling wines can be divided into two key classes. The bottom end of the market is dominated by extremely sweet, simple wines which acquire their bubbles by simply having carbon dioxide pumped into them. Upon pouring, the bubbles race out of the glass. A few other sparklings are made by the 'Charmat' method, which involves a secondary fermentation in a sealed tank.

At the middle and top end of the market are the much drier, bottle-fermented, méthode traditionnelle (formerly méthode Champenoise, until the French got upset) labels, in which the wine undergoes its secondary, bubble-creating fermentation not in a tank but in the bottle, as in Champagne itself. Ultimately, the quality of any fine sparkling wine is a reflection both of the standard of its base wine and of its later period of maturation in the bottle in contact with its yeast lees. Only bottle-fermented sparkling wines possess the additional flavour richness and complexity derived from extended lees-aging.

Pinot Noir and Chardonnay, both varieties of key importance in Champagne, are also the foundation of New Zealand's top sparkling wines. Pinot Meunier, also extensively planted in Champagne, is still rare here, with 21 hectares of bearing vines in 2017.

Marlborough, with its cool nights preserving the grapes' fresh natural acidity, has emerged as the country's premier region for bottle-fermented sparkling wines (10 producers launched a promotional group, Méthode Marlborough, in 2013), but there are also some very stylish examples flowing from Central Otago.

The vast majority of sparkling wines are ready to drink when marketed, and need no extra maturation. A short spell in the cellar, however, can benefit the very best bottle-fermented sparklings.

Akarua Central Otago Brut NV ★★★★

This non-vintage wine (★★★★) is a blend of Pinot Noir (55–70 per cent) and Chardonnay (30–45 per cent), estate-grown at Bannockburn and disgorged after 18 months to two years on its yeast lees. The bouquet is typically fresh and yeasty; the palate is crisp and vigorous, with strong, lemony, appley, yeasty, slightly nutty flavours and a finely balanced finish.

MED/DRY $33 –V

Akarua Central Otago Rosé Brut NV ★★★★

This non-vintage wine (★★★★) is a pale pink, vivacious blend of Pinot Noir (55–75 per cent) and Chardonnay (25–45 per cent), estate-grown at Bannockburn and disgorged after 18 months to two years on its yeast lees. It is typically crisp and dryish, with fresh, gentle strawberry and spice flavours, showing excellent complexity and length.

MED/DRY $42 –V

Akarua Central Otago Vintage Brut   ★★★★☆

The 2011 vintage (★★★★) is a pale, light and vivacious blend of Pinot Noir (61 per cent) and Chardonnay (39 per cent), estate-grown at Bannockburn and disgorged after a minimum of three years on its yeast lees. It has a yeasty bouquet and crisp, racy palate, showing good complexity.

MED/DRY $45 –V

Aurum Blanc de Blancs Vintage   (★★★★☆)

Currently on sale, the 2008 vintage (★★★★☆) is a distinctive, bone-dry style from Central Otago Chardonnay, disgorged after six years of maturation on its yeast lees. Crisp and zesty, it has good intensity of lively, citrusy flavour, yeasty and toasty notes adding complexity, and excellent vigour and length.

Vintage	08
WR	6
Drink	16-20

DRY $39 –V

Aurum Rosé Vintage   (★★★★)

The 2011 vintage (★★★★), currently on sale, was estate-grown in Central Otago, bottle-fermented and disgorged after three years on its yeast lees. A blend of Pinot Gris and Pinot Noir, it is pale pink, mouthfilling and dryish (5 grams/litre of residual sugar), with berryish, yeasty flavours, hints of apricots and spices, and good intensity, vigour and complexity.

Vintage	11
WR	5
Drink	16-18

MED/DRY $34 –V

Black Barn Blanc de Blancs   (★★★★)

Currently on sale, the 2010 vintage (★★★★) is a scented, citrusy sparkling, from Chardonnay grapes hand-picked in the Havelock hills, and was disgorged after nearly four years on its yeast lees. Showing considerable complexity, it is yeasty, very crisp and lively.

MED/DRY $70 –V

Cloudy Bay Pelorus NV   ★★★★☆

Cloudy Bay's non-vintage Marlborough bubbly is a Chardonnay-dominant style, with 30 per cent Pinot Noir, matured for at least two years on its yeast lees. Refined, tightly structured and elegant, it typically has strong, citrusy, peachy, yeasty flavours, showing excellent depth and harmony.

MED/DRY $34 AV

Cuvée No. 1 Marlborough Méthode Traditionnelle   ★★★★☆

This is a non-vintage 'blanc de blancs', based entirely on Marlborough Chardonnay. Made by Daniel Le Brun (in his family company) and matured for two years on its yeast lees, it is typically a stylish wine, fresh-scented, with tight-knit, delicate flavours, citrusy, yeasty and biscuity, and a crisp, dryish finish.

MED/DRY $35 –V

Daniel Le Brun Méthode Traditionnelle Brut NV   ★★★★☆

The Daniel Le Brun brand is owned by the beer giant Lion – which owns Wither Hills. A non-vintage blend of Chardonnay and Pinot Noir, grown in Marlborough, it is disgorged after at least two years on its yeast lees. Top batches are highly impressive – tight and rich, with lovely vibrancy and depth of citrusy, appley, peachy flavours, yeasty, bready notes adding real complexity, and a finely balanced, lasting finish.

 MED/DRY $29 V+

Deutz Marlborough Cuvée Blanc de Blancs   ★★★★★

New Zealand's most awarded bubbly on the show circuit. This Chardonnay-predominant blend is hand-harvested on the south side of the Wairau Valley, at Renwick Estate and in the Brancott Vineyard, and matured for up to three years on its yeast lees. It is typically a very classy wine with delicate, piercing, lemony, appley flavours, well-integrated yeastiness and a slightly creamy finish. The very elegant 2013 vintage (★★★★★) has a rich, citrusy, yeasty bouquet, leading into an intense, vibrant, tightly structured wine, yeasty, complex and long.

 MED/DRY $33 V+

Deutz Marlborough Cuvée Brut NV   ★★★★

The marriage of Pernod Ricard NZ's fruit at Marlborough with the Champagne house of Deutz's 150 years of experience created an instant winner. Bottled-fermented and matured on its yeast lees for two to three years, this non-vintage wine has evolved over the past decade into a less overtly fruity, more delicate and flinty style. The Pinot Noir grapes are drawn principally from Kaituna Estate, on the north side of the Wairau Valley; the Chardonnay comes mostly from Renwick Estate, in the middle of the valley. Before being bottled, the base wine is lees-aged for up to three months and given a full malolactic fermentation. Reserve wines, a year or two older than the rest, are added to each batch, contributing consistency and complexity to the final blend. The wine I tasted in August 2016 (★★★★☆) was bright, light lemon/green, fresh and finely balanced, with crisp, citrusy, peachy, slightly toasty flavours, showing good complexity and length.

 MED/DRY $27 AV

Deutz Marlborough Cuvée Prestige   ★★★★★

This is typically a very classy, Chardonnay-predominant style, disgorged after three years on its yeast lees. Light lemon/green, the lovely 2012 vintage (★★★★★) is finely scented, very elegant and rich, with intense, vibrant, citrusy, yeasty flavours.

MED/DRY $33 V+

Deutz Marlborough Cuvée Rosé   ★★★★☆

The 2013 vintage (★★★★), made predominantly from Pinot Noir, is a pink/pale orange wine, with strong, peachy, yeasty flavours, showing good complexity, and a finely balanced, appetisingly crisp finish.

 MED/DRY $33 AV

Elstree Marlborough Cuveé Brut   ★★★★

Still on sale, the 2010 vintage (★★★★☆) was made from hand-picked Chardonnay and Pinot Noir, and disgorged after three years on its yeast lees. Pale lemon/green, it is a drier style than most sparklings (5 grams/litre of residual sugar), lemon-scented, punchy and vivacious, with strong citrusy, toasty flavours, tight and lively.

Vintage	10
WR	7
Drink	16-17

 MED/DRY $38 –V

En Rose   ★★★★☆

From Margrain, the 2012 vintage (★★★★☆) is a dry style, made from Pinot Noir grown in Martinborough. Pink, with a hint of orange, it is fresh and crisp, with strong strawberry/spice flavours, a hint of apricot, good yeast-derived complexity and a lively, long finish. The 2013 vintage (★★★★☆) is similar. Very pale pink, it is crisp, tight and dry (4 grams/litre of residual sugar), with strong peach, strawberry and spice flavours, showing good complexity, and a long finish.

Vintage	13
WR	7
Drink	16-21

 DRY $45 –V

Gibbston Valley Méthode Traditionnelle NV Extra Brut   ★★★★☆

The wine on sale in 2016 (★★★★★), from grapes hand-picked in Central Otago, was disgorged in July 2016, after 28 months on its yeast lees. Pale straw, with an invitingly fragrant, complex bouquet, it has penetrating, citrusy, biscuity, yeasty flavours, dry, crisp and rich. Floating very smoothly across the palate, it shows excellent delicacy, complexity and harmony.

 MED/DRY $45 –V

Giesen Classic Cuvée   (★★★)

The fresh, crisp and lively 2014 vintage (★★★) was made from Chardonnay, grown in the Wairau Valley, Marlborough. It's a stimulating apéritif, not complex, but citrusy and slightly sweet, in a very attractive, refreshing style.

MED/DRY $20 –V

Gold Digger Frizzante Naturally Sparkling Pinot Gris   (★★★☆)

Ensconced in a beer bottle with a crown seal, the non-vintage wine (★★★☆) currently on sale is from Maori Point Vineyard, at Tarras, in Central Otago. Promoted as a 'prosecco style', it was made from grapes grown in 2016, tank-fermented, and bottled at Wanaka Beer Works. Pale, it is gently sparkling, light and lively, with citrusy, appley, slightly spicy and gingery flavours, and a slightly sweet (14 grams/litre of residual sugar), crisp finish. Ready to roll.

MED/DRY $11 AV

Haha Brut Cuvée   (★★★)

The non-vintage (★★★) launched in 2016 was blended from Chardonnay and Pinot Noir. Pale lemon/green, it is fresh and lively, with good depth of citrusy, slightly peachy flavours, showing a touch of complexity, and a crisp, dryish (6.7 grams/litre of residual sugar) finish.

MED/DRY $22 –V

Hans Herzog Cuvée Thérèse Rosé Méthode Traditionnelle   ★★★★☆

This highly distinctive Marlborough wine is made occasionally. The 2011 vintage (★★★★) is a blend of Pinot Noir (80 per cent) and Chardonnay (20 per cent). The base wines were barrel-aged for eight months and then blended, before the wine was bottled for its lengthy maturation on yeast lees. It has a light red hue and cherryish, slightly nutty flavours, crisp and dry (4 grams/litre of residual sugar), with plenty of yeast-derived complexity. A distinctive style, it's a good food wine. Certified organic.

Vintage	11
WR	7
Drink	16-18

DRY $64 –V

Highfield Marlborough Cuveé Rosé   (★★)

Still on sale, the 2008 vintage (★★) was made from Chardonnay and Pinot Noir. Pink/orange, it is slightly sweet (10 grams/litre of residual sugar), with strawberry and peach flavours, but lacks real fragrance and finesse.

MED/DRY $29 –V

Huia Marlborough Brut   ★★★★☆

The 2009 vintage (★★★★★), the best yet, is a blend of Chardonnay (52 per cent) and Pinot Noir (48 per cent). Disgorged after three years on its yeast lees (a year earlier than for past releases, to create a slightly fresher style), it is richly fragrant, very crisp and lively, with vibrant, peachy, nutty flavours, deliciously rich, vivacious and long. Ready.

MED/DRY $38 –V

Hunter's Miru Miru NV   ★★★★

'Miru Miru' means 'Bubbles'. This wine is disgorged earlier than its Reserve stablemate (below), has a lower Pinot Noir content and a crisper finish. A blend of Chardonnay, Pinot Noir and Pinot Meunier, it is typically fresh and aromatic, with an attractive lightness and vivacity. It has crisp, citrusy, appley, yeasty flavours, showing good tightness, delicacy and complexity.

MED/DRY $27 AV

Hunter's Miru Miru Reserve ★★★★

This has long been one of Marlborough's finest sparklings, full and lively, with loads of citrusy, yeasty, nutty flavour and a creamy, long finish. It is matured on its yeast lees for an average of three and a half years. The 2010 vintage (★★★★☆) is a blend of Pinot Noir (55 per cent), Chardonnay (44 per cent) and Pinot Meunier (1 per cent). It has a refined, gently yeasty bouquet, with a hint of cashew nuts. Strongly flavoured, it is peachy and slightly biscuity, with excellent complexity and harmony, and a crisp, dryish (6.5 grams/litre of residual sugar), lasting finish.

Vintage	10	09	08
WR	6	6	6
Drink	16-18	16-17	P

Johanneshof Cellars Blanc de Blancs ★★★★☆

Released after a minimum of five years' maturation on its yeast lees, this wine is made from hand-picked, barrel-fermented Marlborough Chardonnay and Pinot Blanc. The 2008 vintage (★★★★) is a vivacious wine, crisp and lively, with citrusy, slightly appley, biscuity and nutty flavours, showing excellent depth, and a dryish, very smooth finish.

Johner Blanc de Blancs (★★★★☆)

The stylish, tightly structured 2012 vintage (★★★★☆) was made from Wairarapa Chardonnay, with some use of old barrels. Fragrant, it is crisp and elegant, very lively and finely balanced, with lemony, faintly nutty flavours, a subtle yeastiness, and good intensity and persistence.

Johner Blanc de Noirs (★★★☆)

Grown at Gladstone, in the northern Wairarapa, the 2012 vintage (★★★☆) was made with some use of old barrels. Pale straw, with a steady eruption of small bubbles, it is peachy and spicy, with a slightly creamy texture and a smooth, dryish, harmonious finish.

Joiy (★★★)

This freshly scented, gently sparkling wine is made from Riesling and packaged in 250-ml bottles. The non-vintage wine I tasted in mid-2016 (★★★) was light (10 per cent alcohol) and lively, with strong, lemony, appley flavours. It offers crisp, slightly sweet, very easy drinking.

MED $6 AV

Junction Persistence (★★★☆)

Made from Riesling, Flora and Gewürztraminer, the 2014 vintage (★★★☆) was grown in Central Hawke's Bay, barrel-fermented and oak-aged for nine months. It's a vivacious wine, very fresh and lively, with crisp, dryish, citrusy, slightly limey and spicy flavours.

June Nelson Méthode Traditionnelle   (★★★☆)

From Kaimira Estate, the still youthful 2009 vintage (★★★☆) is a pale straw blend of Chardonnay (78 per cent) and Pinot Noir (22 per cent), grown at Brightwater and disgorged after six years aging on its yeast lees. The bouquet is citrusy; the palate is tightly structured, crisp and lemony, with considerable complexity and a dryish (6 grams/litre of residual sugar), smooth finish.

MED/DRY $39 –V

La Michelle   ★★★★

From Margrain, the 2013 vintage (★★★★) is a bottle-fermented bubbly, blended from Pinot Noir (66 per cent) and Chardonnay (34 per cent), grown in Martinborough and made in an unusually dry (4 grams/litre of residual sugar) but not austere style. Disgorged after 30 months on its yeast lees, it is pale, fresh and lively, with vibrant, citrusy, moderately yeasty flavours, in a youthful, very elegant style, showing good intensity.

Vintage	13
WR	7
Drink	16-21

 DRY $45 –V

Leveret IQ 3 Méthode Traditionnelle   ★★★☆

The non-vintage wine (★★★☆) I tasted in early 2016 is a blend of Chardonnay (98 per cent) and Pinot Noir (2 per cent), grown in Hawke's Bay and disgorged after a minimum of three years on its yeast lees. Light gold, it is mature-tasting, with strong, lemony flavours to the fore, yeasty and slightly toasty, with moderate complexity and a crisp, dryish finish.

 MED/DRY $25 –V

Leveret IQ Premium Brut NV   ★★★

The batch of this bottle-fermented sparkling on sale in 2016 (★★★) is a pale straw, Hawke's Bay blend of Pinot Noir, Chardonnay and Pinot Meunier, disgorged after a minimum of 18 months on its yeast lees. Crisp and fruity, it has citrusy, slightly buttery and toasty flavours, showing moderate complexity and good depth.

MED/DRY $22 –V

Leveret IQ Rosé Méthode Traditionnelle   ★★★☆

Showing some maturity, the non-vintage wine (★★★☆) on sale in 2016 is a Hawke's Bay blend of Pinot Noir, Chardonnay and Pinot Meunier. Orange-hued, with a hint of apricot, it is crisp, flavoursome and dry, with berry and spice flavours, showing considerable complexity, and a smooth, gently yeasty finish.

 MED/DRY $22 AV

Lindauer Brut Cuvée NV ★★★

Given its track record of very good quality, low price and huge volumes (batch variation is inevitable), this non-vintage bubbly has been a miracle of modern winemaking. Made from Pinot Noir and Chardonnay, grown in Gisborne and Hawke's Bay, it is matured for a year on its yeast lees, and blended with some reserve wine from past vintages. Fractionally sweet (12 grams/litre of residual sugar), it typically has good vigour and depth in a refined style, crisp and finely balanced, with lively, lemony, slightly nutty and yeasty flavours. The wine I tasted in April 2016 (★★★☆) was pale straw, with a steady bead. A moderately complex style, it showed very good freshness, with citrusy, slightly toasty flavours and a medium-dry, crisp, harmonious finish. Fine value.

 MED/DRY $10 V+

Lindauer Enlighten Moscato Rosé (★★★☆)

'Enlighten' is – you guessed it – a range of light wines, and this recently launched charmer is just 8.5 per cent alcohol. Based on Muscat grapes, grown in Gisborne, it was blended with a splash of Pinotage (hence its enticing, pale pink hue). Deliciously light and lively, it is unabashedly sweet (60 grams/litre of residual sugar), but very crisp, fruity and well-balanced, in a simple but vivacious style that offers plenty of pleasure.

SW $13 V+

Lindauer Enlighten Sauvignon Blanc (★★)

The non-vintage wine (★★) I tasted in April 2016 is light (8.5 per cent alcohol), with herbaceous aromas and flavours, fresh and simple.

MED/DRY $13 –V

Lindauer Special Reserve Brut Cuveé ★★★★

The non-vintage wine I tasted in April 2016 (★★★★) was a blend of Pinot Noir (70 per cent) and Chardonnay (30 per cent), grown in Gisborne and Hawke's Bay. Disgorged after two years maturing on its yeast lees, with a portion of reserve wine added from previous vintages, it is pale pink, with a steady bead. Smooth, with strawberryish, yeasty flavours, fresh and crisp, it shows good complexity, with a finely balanced, lengthy finish. Great value on special at around $13.

 MED/DRY $20 V+

Loveblock Marlborough Moscato Brut (★★★☆)

Pale yellow, with a perfumed bouquet, the 2014 vintage (★★★☆) is an easy-drinking wine, estate-grown in the lower Awatere Valley. Crisp and lively, it has fresh peach and orange-like flavours, with a hint of Turkish delight and a dryish (7 grams/litre of residual sugar) finish.

 MED/DRY $25 –V

Man O' War Tulia ★★★☆

The 2012 vintage (★★★☆) was made from Waiheke Island Chardonnay grapes, hand-harvested. The base wine was partly barrel-fermented and all barrel-aged, followed by secondary fermentation in the bottle and nine months' lees-aging. Tight and elegant, it is bone-dry, with vibrant, citrusy, appley flavours, showing moderate complexity, and a well-balanced, lengthy finish.

 DRY $45 –V

Matahiwi Estate Hawke's Bay Blanc de Blancs   (★★★)

The non-vintage wine (★★★) on sale in 2016 was made from Chardonnay. Crisp and lively, it has citrusy, moderately yeasty flavours, with a slightly buttery finish.

MED/DRY $22 –V

Matahiwi Estate Wairarapa Cuvée   (★★★)

The non-vintage wine (★★★) on sale in 2016 was made from Pinot Gris. Showing clear-cut varietal characters, it has fresh lemon, pear and apple aromas and flavours, in a refreshing, crisp and vivacious style.

MED/DRY $22 –V

Nautilus Cuvée Marlborough   ★★★★★

Recent releases of this non-vintage, bottle-fermented sparkling have generally revealed an intensity and refinement that positions the label among the finest in the country. Made with Pinot Noir (mostly) and Chardonnay, it is blended with older, reserve stocks held in old oak barriques and disgorged after a minimum of three years aging on its yeast lees. Lean and crisp, piercing and long, it's a beautifully tight, vivacious and refined wine, its Marlborough fruit characters enriched with intense, bready aromas and flavours. The sample I tasted in August 2016 (★★★★☆) was – as the back label indicates helpfully – bottled in September 2012 and disgorged in May 2016. A blend of Pinot Noir (71 per cent) and Chardonnay (29 per cent), it was blended with 12.5 per cent reserve stocks. Pale straw, it is fragrant, with finely poised, citrusy, biscuity, slightly limey flavours, yeasty and complex, and a crisp, tightly structured, dryish (6 grams/litre of residual sugar) finish.

MED/DRY $39 AV

Nautilus Cuvée Marlborough Vintage Rosé   ★★★★☆

The 2013 vintage (★★★★☆) was made entirely from Pinot Noir, bottle-fermented and disgorged after two years on its yeast lees. Pale pink, it is dryish (7 grams/litre of residual sugar), very fresh and lively, with strawberry and spice flavours, yeasty and complex, and a smooth, finely balanced finish.

MED/DRY $49 –V

Omaha Bay Vineyard FAB Matakana Sparkling Flora   ★★☆

'FAB' stands for Flora Avec Bulles (Flora With Bubbles). An enjoyable summer sipper, the 2014 vintage (★★★) is a slightly sweet (15 grams/litre of residual sugar) style with fresh, vibrant fruit flavours to the fore, showing good harmony and depth.

MED $27 –V

Osawa Prestige Collection Méthode Traditionnelle NV   (★★★★)

The wine on sale in 2016 (★★★★) is a fragrant, complex Hawke's Bay blend of equal portions of Chardonnay and Pinot Noir, grown at Maraekakaho. Attractively scented, it has crisp, lively, citrusy, yeasty, slightly toasty flavours, showing good intensity.

MED/DRY $60 –V

Oyster Bay Sparkling Cuvée Brut   ★★★

Chardonnay-based, this Hawke's Bay wine has vibrant, lemony flavours to the fore, fresh, crisp and slightly sweet. Made by the 'Charmat' method (where the secondary, bubble-inducing fermentation occurs in tanks, rather than the individual bottles), it is typically attractive, although not complex.

MED/DRY $19 AV

Oyster Bay Sparkling Cuvée Rosé   ★★★☆

Pale pink, with a hint of onion skin, this wine is blended from Hawke's Bay Chardonnay (80 per cent) and Marlborough Pinot Noir (20 per cent). Fragrant, with hints of peaches and spices, it is typically crisp and lively, with strong peach and strawberry flavours and an off-dry (8 grams/ litre of residual sugar) finish. Worth trying.

MED/DRY $19 V+

Palliser Estate Martinborough Méthode Traditionnelle   ★★★★☆

This is the district's finest sparkling (although very few are produced). The 2010 vintage (★★★★) is a blend of Chardonnay (54 per cent) and Pinot Noir (46 per cent). Pale gold, with a fragrant, toasty bouquet, it has strong, peachy, yeasty flavours, showing good complexity, and a creamy, dryish, lingering finish.

MED/DRY $49 –V

Peregrine Vintage   (★★★★)

The 2012 vintage (★★★★), grown at Gibbston, in Central Otago, is a full-flavoured blend of Pinot Noir (50 per cent) and Chardonnay (47 per cent), with a touch of Pinot Meunier. Disgorged after two years on its yeast lees, it has strong, crisp, citrusy, yeasty flavours, in a tightly structured style with good complexity and a lingering finish.

MED/DRY $50 –V

Peter Yealands Sparkling Marlborough Pinot Gris Blush   ★★★

This non-vintage wine is typically pink, fresh and lively, with good depth of peachy, slightly spicy flavours, a sliver of sweetness and balanced acidity. It's an attractive, very easy-drinking style.

MED/DRY $17 AV

Peter Yealands Sparkling Marlborough Sauvignon Blanc   ★★☆

This non-vintage wine typically has strongly herbaceous aromas, leading into a slightly sweet wine with fresh, crisp, direct, distinctly green-edged flavours.

MED/DRY $17 –V

Quartz Reef Méthode Traditionnelle [Vintage]   ★★★★★

Top vintages are outstanding, showing great vigour and complexity in a Champagne-like style, intense and highly refined. The 2010 (★★★★★) is a blend of Chardonnay (93 per cent) and Pinot Noir (7 per cent), estate-grown and hand-picked at Bendigo, in Central Otago, and disgorged after maturing for nearly four years on its yeast lees. Light straw, it is elegant and racy, with intense, citrusy, slightly peachy and nutty flavours that float very harmoniously to a lively, lasting finish.

Quartz Reef Méthode Traditionnelle Brut NV   ★★★★☆

This increasingly Champagne-like, non-vintage bubbly is estate-grown at Bendigo, in Central Otago, and lees-aged for at least two years. The batches vary in their varietal composition, but the release I tasted in September 2016 (★★★★) is a blend of Pinot Noir (64 per cent) and Chardonnay (36 per cent), disgorged from autumn 2016 onwards. Very faintly pink, with a steady bead, it floats smoothly across the palate, with lively, lemony, slightly appley flavours, and yeasty, biscuity notes adding complexity. Certified biodynamic.

Quartz Reef Méthode Traditionnelle Rosé   ★★★★☆

The lively, non-vintage wine (★★★★☆) on the market in mid-2016 was estate-grown at Bendigo, in Central Otago. Made entirely from Pinot Noir and disgorged after at least two years on its yeast lees, it is bright, pale pink, vivacious and smooth, with dryish, strawberryish, slightly spicy, yeasty flavours, showing excellent complexity. Certified biodynamic.

MED/DRY $37 –V

Rock Ferry Brut NV   (★★★★★)

Full of personality, the generous, non-vintage (★★★★★) released in 2016 is a blend of Marlborough and Central Otago base wines, fermented initially in old oak and stainless steel barrels. Disgorged after three and a half years on its yeast lees, it is pale straw, with a fine, persistent bead. The bouquet is fragrant, yeasty and biscuity; the palate is rich, lively and appetisingly crisp, with strong, peachy, citrusy, biscuity, yeasty flavours, showing excellent complexity and richness, and a dryish (6 grams/litre of residual sugar), finely balanced finish.

Rock Ferry Central Otago Brut Rosé   ★★★★☆

The salmon pink 2011 vintage (★★★★☆) was made from Pinot Noir, hand-picked at Bendigo, and disgorged after three years on its yeast lees. Delicious now, it is mouthfilling and smooth, with strong strawberry and spice flavours, hints of peaches and apricots, excellent complexity, appetising acidity, and a long, dryish (5 grams/litre of residual sugar), harmonious finish.

Rock Ferry Marlborough Blanc de Blancs   ★★★★

The elegant, vivacious, Chardonnay-based 2010 vintage (★★★★☆) was fermented in old oak and stainless steel barrels, bottled for its secondary fermentation and then disgorged after four years on its yeast lees. Light lemon/green, it is lemon-scented, with strong, crisp, citrusy, yeasty flavours, showing good vigour and complexity, and a lingering, unusually dry (4.5 grams/litre of residual sugar) finish. Certified organic.

DRY $40 –V

Saint Clair Dawn   (★★★★★)

The vivacious 2012 vintage (★★★★★) is a top-flight debut. Full of personality, it is a blend of Marlborough Pinot Noir and Chardonnay, hand-picked, partly barrel-fermented, and disgorged after nearly three years aging on its yeast lees. Pale straw, it is fragrant, with fresh, crisp, toasty, yeasty flavours, showing excellent intensity and complexity, and a finely poised, dryish (6.5 grams/litre of residual sugar), lasting finish.

MED/DRY $45 AV

Saint Clair Vicar's Choice Marlborough Sauvignon Blanc Bubbles   ★★★

The 2016 vintage (★★★) is a fresh, crisp, lively, carbonated sparkling, from grapes grown in the Wairau Valley and Ure Valley. Aromatic and vivacious, with ripely herbaceous flavours, it tastes just like you would expect – Sauvignon Blanc with bubbles.

MED/DRY $19 AV

Satyr Sparkling Sauvignon Blanc   (★★☆)

From Sileni, the non-vintage wine (★★☆) on sale in late 2016 was grown in Hawke's Bay. Fresh and punchy, it has ripely herbaceous flavours, crisp, dryish (7.5 grams/litre of residual sugar) and direct.

MED/DRY $20 –V

Seresin Moana Blanc Marlborough Méthode Traditionnelle   (★★★★☆)

Currently on sale, the highly distinctive 2009 vintage (★★★★☆) is a bone-dry blend of Pinot Noir (59 per cent) and Chardonnay (41 per cent). Disgorged after three years on its yeast lees, it has a scented, lemony, yeasty, complex bouquet. Tightly structured, it is lively, with strong, crisp, citrusy, slightly toasty flavours, showing good complexity. Certified organic.

DRY $45 –V

Seresin Moana Rosé Marlborough Méthode Traditionnelle   (★★★★★)

Certified organic, the 2009 vintage (★★★★★) currently on sale is a distinctive blend of Pinot Noir (62 per cent) and Chardonnay (38 per cent), oak-aged for two months and disgorged after three years on its yeast lees. Pale orange, it is crisp and dry (5.4 grams/litre of residual sugar), with rich, mature flavours of strawberries, oranges and spices, intense, yeasty and complex. Showing strong personality, it is an unusually complex, dry and persistent wine, worth discovering.

MED/DRY $45 AV

Sileni Art Deco Sparkling (★★★)

This non-vintage wine (★★★) is a sparking Pinot Gris. Offering fresh, easy drinking, it has crisp, dryish, citrus-fruit and pear flavours, with slightly yeasty and nutty notes adding a touch of complexity.

MED/DRY $25 –V

Sileni Sparkling Cuvée Brut (★★★)

The non-vintage wine (★★★) now on sale was grown in Hawke's Bay. Light lemon/green, it is lively and smooth, offering vibrantly fruity and fresh, very easy, slightly sweet (6 grams/litre of residual sugar) drinking.

MED/DRY $20 –V

Sileni Sparkling Cuvée Pinot Gris (★★★)

The easy-drinking, non-vintage wine (★★★) released in 2016 was grown in Hawke's Bay, briefly lees-aged and carbonated. Light lemon/green, it tastes like Pinot Gris with bubbles, in a simple but very lively style, with strong, peachy, slightly spicy flavours and a crisp, dryish (6.5 grams/litre of residual sugar) finish.

MED/DRY $19 AV

Sileni Sparkling Cuvée Rosé (★)

The non-vintage wine (★) I tasted in September 2016 was grown in Hawke's Bay. The colour is developed and slightly brown; the palate is berryish and crisp, but dull.

MED/DRY $20 –V

Snapper Rock Marlborough Sparkling Rosé (★★★☆)

The charming 2015 vintage (★★★☆) was made solely from Pinot Noir. Bright pink, it is lively and smooth, with fresh, attractive red-berry, strawberry and spice flavours, crisp acidity and a dryish finish.

MED/DRY $20 AV

Soljans Fusion Sparkling Sauvignon Blanc (★★★)

This non-vintage wine (★★★) is typically crisp and gently sweet. Grown in Marlborough and made in a very easy-drinking style, it has tropical-fruit and herbaceous flavours, lively and smooth.

MED $20 –V

Spy Valley Echelon Marlborough Méthode Traditionnelle ★★★★

The 2011 vintage (★★★★☆) is an elegant blend of Pinot Noir (59 per cent) and Chardonnay (41 per cent), aged in old oak casks for a year before bottling and then disgorged after three and a half years maturing on its yeast lees. Tightly structured, it is very crisp and lively, with good intensity of citrusy, yeasty, slightly nutty flavours, unusually dry (2.8 grams/litre of residual sugar) and persistent.

DRY $37 –V

Vintage	11	10	09	08
WR	5	7	7	6
Drink	16-20	16-17	P	P

Taraire Block Bubbles of Kaikohe   (★★)

From Palomino grapes grown in Northland, the pale, non-vintage wine (★★) I tasted in early 2016 is citrusy and very crisp, with dry, slightly appley flavours, clean and direct. (From Ivana Wines.)

MED/DRY $22 –V

Tohu Rewa Marlborough Blanc de Blancs   ★★★★

The 2013 vintage (★★★★) is a fresh, elegant sparkling, from Chardonnay grapes grown at Rapaura. Disgorged after 20 months on its yeast lees, it is refined and poised, with citrusy, appley, dry (4 grams/litre of residual sugar) flavours, slightly yeasty and nutty, and very good delicacy and length.

DRY $34 –V

Tohu Rewa Méthode Traditionnelle Blanc de Noir   (★★★★☆)

The debut 2012 vintage (★★★★☆) is based entirely on Marlborough Pinot Noir, hand-picked in the Waihopai Valley and disgorged after 20 months on its yeast lees. Instantly attractive, it is a finely balanced, dryish style (6 grams/litre of residual sugar) with generous, peachy, nutty, yeasty flavours, showing excellent vigour, complexity, harmony and length.

MED/DRY $39 –V

Toi Toi Marlborough Sparkling Sauvignon Blanc   ★★☆

The non-vintage wine (★★☆) on sale in mid to late 2016 is pale lemon/green, crisp and lively, in an aromatic, clearly herbaceous style with a sliver of sweetness and fresh, direct flavours.

MED/DRY $17 –V

Toi Toi New Zealand Sparkling Rosé   ★★★

The non-vintage wine (★★★) on sale in mid to late 2016 is bright pink/red, very fresh, crisp and lively, with berry and plum flavours, off-dry and vivacious.

MED $17 AV

Twin Islands Chardonnay/Pinot Noir Brut NV   ★★★★

'A great bottle to be seen with in some of the classiest bars and restaurants', Nautilus's lower-priced sparkling is a bottle-fermented, non-vintage style. The batch I tasted in mid to late 2016 (★★★☆) is pale lemon/green, with a citrusy, peachy, gently yeasty bouquet and generous, smooth (10 grams/litre of residual sugar), slightly toasty, moderately complex flavours.

MED/DRY $25 AV

Rosé Wines

The number of rosé labels on the market has exploded recently, as drinkers discover that rosé is not an inherently inferior lolly water, but a worthwhile and delicious wine style in its own right. New Zealand rosé is even finding offshore markets and collecting overseas awards.

In Europe many pink or copper-coloured wines, such as the rosés of Provence, Anjou and Tavel, are produced from red-wine varieties. (Dark-skinned grapes are even used to make white wines: Champagne, heavily based on Pinot Meunier and Pinot Noir, is a classic case.) To make a rosé, after the grapes are crushed, the time the juice spends in contact with its skins is crucial; the longer the contact, the greater the diffusion of colour, tannin and flavour from the skins into the juice.

'Saignée' (bled) is a French term that is seen occasionally on rosé labels. A technique designed to produce a pink wine or a more concentrated red wine – or both – it involves running off or 'bleeding' free-run juice from crushed, dark-skinned grapes after a brief, pre-ferment maceration on skins. An alternative is to commence the fermentation as for a red wine, then after 12 or 24 hours, when its colour starts to deepen, drain part of the juice for rosé production and vinify the rest as a red wine.

Pinot Noir and Merlot are the grape varieties most commonly used in New Zealand to produce rosé wines. Regional differences are emerging. South Island and Wairarapa rosés, usually made from Pinot Noir, are typically fresh, slightly sweet and crisp, while those from the middle and upper North Island – Hawke's Bay, Gisborne and Auckland – tend to be Merlot-based, fuller-bodied and drier.

These are typically charming, 'now-or-never' wines, peaking in their first six to 18 months with seductive strawberry/raspberry-like fruit flavours. Freshness is the essence of the wines' appeal.

8 Ranges Tussock Ridge Central Otago Pinot Rosé ★★★★

Estate-grown near Alexandra, hand-picked and made in an off-dry style, the 2015 vintage (★★★★) is delicious young. Bright, light pink, it is very finely balanced, with vibrant watermelon and strawberry flavours, hints of peaches and spices, and good freshness, delicacy and depth.

MED/DRY $25 AV

36 Bottles Central Otago Pinot Rosé ★★★★

Grown in the Cromwell Basin, the 2015 vintage (★★★★) was made entirely from Pinot Noir. Pink/pale red, it is floral and vibrantly fruity, with strong, ripe plum and red-berry flavours, a sliver of sweetness and a very smooth finish. Delicious young.

MED/DRY $20 V+

Aitken's Folly Riverbank Road Central Otago Rosé (★★★★)

The 2014 vintage (★★★★) is maturing well. Made from Pinot Noir grapes, estate-grown at Wanaka, it is bright pink/red, fresh and lively, with very satisfying depth of watermelon and spice flavours, woven with appetising acidity, and instant appeal.

DRY $20 V+

Akarua Rua Pinot Rosé (★★★★)

The 2015 vintage (★★★★) is from Pinot Noir grapes, estate-grown at Bannockburn and Lowburn. Bright pink, it is floral and charming, with gentle plum, strawberry and spice flavours, a sliver of sweetness (9 grams/litre of residual sugar) balanced by fresh acidity, and excellent delicacy, vivacity and immediacy.

MED/DRY $21 V+

Ake Ake The Wild Rosé ★★★

The bright pink/pale red 2015 vintage (★★★) is a blend of Syrah and Merlot, grown in Northland. Fresh and lively, it is medium-bodied, with berryish flavours, hints of strawberry and peach, and a smooth, dry (4 grams/litre of residual sugar) finish.

DRY $20 –V

Allan Scott Marlborough Rosé ★★★☆

The 2016 vintage (★★★) has an appealing, bright pink hue. Fresh and lively, it is berryish and plummy, with slightly earthy notes, hints of strawberry and watermelon, and a dryish finish.

MED/DRY $18 V+

Alluviale Hawke's Bay Rosé (★★★★)

The 2016 vintage (★★★★) is a blend of Merlot (85 per cent) and Malbec (15 per cent), grown in the Bridge Pa Triangle and fermented in an old oak vat. Bright pink, it is full-bodied, dry (2 grams/litre of residual sugar) and smooth, with fresh, berryish, spicy flavours, showing good harmony. Delicious young.

DRY $24 AV

Alpha Domus The Heroines Hawke's Bay Rosé (★★★)

The 2015 vintage (★★★), made from Merlot, is light pink, with a hint of orange. A fully dry style (1 gram/litre of residual sugar), it is peachy, with hints of strawberries and spices and a smooth finish. Ready.

DRY $24 –V

Amisfield Central Otago Pinot Noir Rosé ★★★★

Estate-grown in the Cromwell Basin and fermented in tanks (mostly) and barrels, the highly attractive 2016 vintage (★★★★) is bright pink, with strong, vibrant strawberry and spice flavours, showing a distinct touch of complexity. Made in a basically dry style (4.6 grams/litre of residual sugar), it's a good food wine.

DRY $30 –V

Anchorage Family Estate Montepulciano Rosé (★★★☆)

The refreshing, buoyantly fruity 2015 vintage (★★★☆) is a dry style (1.6 grams/litre of residual sugar), grown at Brightwater. Bright pink, it is light-bodied (11.5 per cent alcohol), with vibrant, berryish flavours, hints of spices and watermelon, and crisp acidity keeping things lively.

DRY $18 V+

Ant Moore Central Otago Rosé (★★★☆)

Fresh and lively, with an inviting, light pink hue, the 2015 vintage (★★★☆) is a medium-bodied style with strawberryish flavours, hints of peaches and plums, appetising acidity and a smooth finish.

MED/DRY $19 V+

Ara Single Estate Limited Release Marlborough Pinot Noir Rosé ★★★☆

Drinking well now, the 2015 vintage (★★★) is pale red, with a hint of development. Still fairly fresh, it has good depth of cherryish, slightly spicy flavours and a smooth, dryish (5.7 grams/litre of residual sugar) finish.

MED/DRY $25 –V

Aronui Single Vineyard Nelson Pinot Rosé ★★★☆

The 2016 vintage (★★★) was made from Pinot Noir, estate-grown at Upper Moutere. Salmon pink, it is full-bodied and smooth (12 grams/litre of residual sugar), with plummy, slightly spicy flavours, balanced acidity and good depth.

MED/DRY $22 AV

Ashwell Martinborough Rosé ★★★☆

The 2016 vintage (★★★★) is bright pink/pale red, with a fragrant, floral bouquet. Full-bodied and vibrantly fruity, with strong, fresh, berryish, slightly spicy flavours, it's a very smooth and harmonious wine, delicious young.

DRY $20 AV

Astrolabe Vineyards Beacon Hill Vineyard Marlborough Pinot Rosé (★★★★)

The instantly appealing 2015 vintage (★★★★) is a blend of Pinot Noir (75 per cent) and Pinot Gris (25 per cent). Bright, light pink, it is lively, with peachy, strawberryish, spicy flavours, showing good delicacy and depth, and a smooth, fully dry, lingering finish.

DRY $24 AV

Ataahua Waipara Rosé ★★★★☆

A 'serious' but delicious wine, the 2015 vintage (★★★★☆) was made from estate-grown Pinot Noir. Pale pink, it is full-bodied, with excellent depth of fresh strawberry, peach, spice and apricot flavours, a sliver of sweetness, gentle tannins and plenty of personality.

MED/DRY $26 AV

Aurum Central Otago Pinot Gris Rosé ★★★☆

Certified organic, the very pale pink 2015 vintage (★★★★) is delicious young. Made from estate-grown Pinot Gris, it is attractively scented and mouthfilling, with strong strawberry, peach and spice flavours and a dry (2 grams/litre of residual sugar), well-rounded finish.

DRY $26 –V

Babich Marlborough Rosé   (★★★☆)

Pale pink, the lively 2015 vintage (★★★☆) is freshly scented, with ripe strawberry, peach and spice flavours. Medium-bodied, it is a dry style, with very good delicacy, balance and depth.

 DRY $20 AV

Bellbird Spring Pinot Noir Rosé   ★★★★

Grown at Waipara, the 2016 vintage (★★★★) was fermented in old oak casks. Pale pink/slight orange, it is full-bodied, with good depth of ripe, peachy and spicy flavours, showing a touch of complexity, and a dry, rounded finish. Drink this summer.

 DRY $28 –V

Black Barn Hawke's Bay Rosé   (★★★★)

Merlot-based, the 2015 vintage (★★★★) is a pale pink, medium-bodied wine with fresh strawberry, peach and spice flavours, lively and sustained. A 'serious' but approachable wine, it shows more complexity than most rosés, with a dry finish.

 DRY $23 AV

Black Cottage Marlborough Rosé   ★★★☆

The pale pink, medium-bodied 2016 vintage (★★★☆) is a dryish blend of Pinot Noir and Pinot Gris. Fresh and smooth, it has lively peach, watermelon, lychee and pear flavours, showing very good delicacy and harmony. (From Two Rivers of Marlborough.)

 MED/DRY $18 V+

Black Estate Netherwood Rosé   ★★★☆

The 2015 vintage (★★★☆) is from mature vines in the Netherwood Vineyard at Omihi, in Waipara. Blended from hand-picked, co-fermented Pinot Noir (60 per cent) and Chardonnay (40 per cent), it was matured for five months in large, seasoned oak casks. Made in a dry style (3.4 grams/litre of residual sugar), it is pale red, with ripe red-berry flavours, hints of plums and spices, a touch of complexity, and a fresh, smooth finish. Good food wine.

 DRY $29 –V

Blackenbrook Nelson Pinot Rosé   ★★★★

The weighty 2015 vintage (★★★★) was partly estate-grown, hand-picked and partly (15 per cent) oak-aged. Pale pink, it is vivacious, with generous, peachy, strawberryish flavours, in a slightly sweet style (6 grams/litre of residual sugar), with good body.

Vintage	15	14
WR	7	7
Drink	16-17	P

MED/DRY $23 AV

Brancott Estate Flight Rosé   ★★☆

Pale pink, the 2015 vintage (★★☆) is lively and light (9 per cent alcohol), with fresh, gentle, berryish flavours, hints of peach and watermelon, a sliver of sweetness and appetising acidity.

 MED/DRY $17 –V

Brick Bay Matakana Rosé   ★★★☆

Estate-grown, the 2015 vintage (★★★☆) was made principally from Cabernet Sauvignon. Bright pink, it is fresh and lively, in a medium-bodied style with vibrant berry and spice flavours, a gentle touch of tannin, and an off-dry finish.

MED/DRY $24 –V

Brodie Estate The Angel's Sigh Rosé   ★★☆

Grown in Martinborough, the 2015 vintage (★★☆) is a pale pink wine, made from Pinot Noir. Medium-bodied, it has solid depth of strawberry/spice flavours, with an off-dry finish.

MED/DRY $27 –V

Byrne Northland Rosé   ★★★☆

Grown at Kerikeri, the 2015 vintage (★★★★) is full of flavour and interest. A pink-hued Syrah, it is mouthfilling and buoyantly fruity, with strong strawberry and spice flavours and a dryish finish. A good food wine.

MED/DRY $22 AV

Cambridge Road Papillon Rosé   (★★★★)

Pink/slight orange, the 2015 vintage (★★★★) is a full-bodied, generous, slightly peachy Wairarapa wine with strawberry and spice aromas and flavours. A 'serious' style, it has excellent depth, with a smooth, dry finish.

DRY $25 AV

Carrick Central Otago Rosé   ★★★★

The pink-hued 2015 vintage (★★★★), made from Pinot Noir, was aged briefly in old barrels. It's a weighty wine (13.5 per cent alcohol), with generous strawberry and spice flavours, a hint of peaches, a touch of complexity, and a harmonious, dry finish. Certified organic.

DRY $25 AV

Church Road Hawke's Bay Rosé   ★★★★

Delicious young, the 2015 vintage (★★★★) was blended from Merlot, Syrah, Cabernet Sauvignon and Malbec. Mouthfilling, it has strong red-berry/plum flavours, with hints of strawberries and spices, and excellent freshness, delicacy and depth. The 2016 vintage (★★★★) is a bright pink, full-bodied wine, fragrant and fresh, with vibrant berry and spice flavours, a hint of watermelon and a dryish finish.

MED/DRY $20 V+

Clearview Black Reef Blush   ★★★★

The 2016 vintage (★★★★) is an instantly appealing Hawke's Bay wine, with Chambourcin, a well-regarded French hybrid, contributing bright pink/pale red colour. Fleshy and vibrantly fruity, it has fresh, berryish, plummy flavours and a smooth, long finish.

MED/DRY $21 V+

Coopers Creek Huapai Rosé ★★★☆

The 2015 vintage (★★★) was made from estate-grown, hand-picked Malbec (76 per cent) and Merlot (24 per cent). Bright, light pink, it is vibrantly fruity, with gentle peach, strawberry and spice flavours, and a dry (2.5 grams/litre of residual sugar), smooth finish.

Vintage	15
WR	7
Drink	16-17

 DRY $18 V+

Craggy Range Gimblett Gravels Vineyard Hawke's Bay Rosé ★★★★

The light pink 2015 vintage (★★★★) is a blend of 'different red varieties' (usually Merlot and Syrah), fermented in old French oak barrels. Full-bodied, it has good complexity, with peach, strawberry, watermelon and spice flavours, showing excellent freshness and depth.

 DRY $30 –V

Elder, The, Martinborough Rosé (★★★★☆)

The delicious 2016 vintage (★★★★☆) was made from Pinot Noir grapes, estate-grown at Te Muna. Bright pink, it is freshly scented and weighty, with strong, vibrant plum/cherry flavours, hints of strawberries and spices, and a finely balanced, dry (2 grams/litre of residual sugar) finish.

 DRY $33 –V

Esk Valley Hawke's Bay Merlot Rosé ★★★★

For many years, this was New Zealand's most successful rosé on the show circuit. The 2016 vintage (★★★☆) is a bright, tasty, Merlot-based wine, vibrantly fruity, with red-berry, watermelon and spice flavours and a fresh, crisp, almost bone-dry (2.6 grams/litre of residual sugar) finish.

 DRY $20 V+

French Peak Banks Peninsula Rosé (★★★★)

The pale pink 2015 vintage (★★★★) was made from Pinot Noir, estate-grown in Canterbury. Tasted in mid-2016, it is maturing very gracefully. Fresh and smooth, with a touch of complexity, it shows very good weight, delicacy and depth of peach, apricot, strawberry and spice flavours.

 MED/DRY $25 AV

Fromm La Strada Marlborough Rosé ★★★★☆

Bargain-priced, the instantly appealing 2015 vintage (★★★★☆) is based on Pinot Noir, blended with Syrah and Malbec. Bright pink, it is floral and vibrantly fruity, with good body, strong, fresh, strawberryish flavours, hints of peaches and spices, and a dry, lingering finish.

DRY $19 V+

Gibbston Valley GV Collection Central Otago Rosé   ★★★☆

The floral, vivacious 2016 vintage (★★★★), grown at Gibbston, is a bright pink, off-dry wine (6.5 grams/litre of residual sugar), made from Pinot Noir. Mouthfilling and smooth, it is vibrantly fruity, with gentle plum, strawberry and spice flavours and a finely balanced finish. Delicious drinking this summer.

MED/DRY $28 –V

Giesen Hawke's Bay Rosé   (★★★☆)

Already drinking well, the 2016 vintage (★★★☆) is a pale pink, Merlot-based wine. It has fresh, ripe peach, watermelon and spice flavours, showing good depth, and a dryish (5.6 grams/litre of residual sugar) finish.

MED/DRY $20 AV

Gladstone Vineyard Rosé   ★★★★

Grown in the northern Wairarapa, the 2015 vintage (★★★★) is a pale pink blend of Merlot (35 per cent), Cabernet Franc (36 per cent) and Pinot Noir (29 per cent), made in a dry (2.3 grams/litre of residual sugar) style. Mouthfilling and very smooth, it has ripe strawberry, peach and spice flavours, a hint of apricot, gentle acidity and excellent depth.

DRY $25 AV

Grava Martinborough Rosé   (★★★★)

The 2015 vintage (★★★★) was grown at a site south of Martinborough – formerly known as Hudson Vineyard – and fermented in oak puncheons. Pale pink, it's a medium-dry style, with good intensity of fresh, peachy, slightly spicy flavour, balanced acidity, a distinct touch of complexity and a smooth finish. A distinctive wine, it's drinking well in 2016.

MED/DRY $30 –V

Greyrock Hawke's Bay Rosé   (★★★☆)

The attractive 2016 vintage (★★★☆) is bright pink, mouthfilling and smooth, with vibrant red-berry and spice flavours, showing good delicacy and harmony. A basically dry style (4 grams/litre of residual sugar), it's sharply priced. (From Sileni.)

DRY $17 V+

Hawkshead Central Otago Rosé   (★★☆)

The debut 2015 vintage (★★☆) was grown at Gibbston. Very pale red/orange, it is smooth and gently sweet (6 grams/litre of residual sugar), with moderately fresh, slightly herbal flavours. Ready.

MED/DRY $26 –V

Hunter's Pinot Noir Marlborough Rosé   ★★★☆

Good summer sipping, the 2016 vintage (★★★☆) has a pale, delicate pink hue. Grown at Rapaura and made in a fully dry (1.1 grams/litre of residual sugar) style, it is medium-bodied, very fresh and vibrant, with gentle peach, strawberry and spice flavours, lively and refreshing.

DRY $20 AV

Invivo Sophie's Marlborough Rosé   ★★★★

The 2015 vintage (★★★★) was made from Pinot Noir. Bright pink, it is attractively scented and full of vibrant, berryish flavour, with hints of plums and watermelon, and a sliver of sweetness (5.8 grams/litre of residual sugar). Fresh and finely balanced, it's packed with charm.

Vintage	15	
WR	7	
Drink	16-17	

MED/DRY $19 V+

Johner Estate Gladstone Pinot Noir Rosé   ★★★★

The 2015 vintage (★★★☆) is mouthfilling (14.5 per cent alcohol), with good depth of plum and spice flavours, crisp and lively, hints of peach and watermelon, and a fractionally off-dry (4 grams/litre of residual sugar) finish. The 2016 vintage (★★★★) is bright pink, appetisingly crisp and lively, with generous, plummy, berryish flavours and a slightly spicy, dryish (5 grams/litre of residual sugar) finish. Delicious young.

Vintage	16	15
WR	6	6
Drink	16-18	16-18

MED/DRY $20 V+

Jules Taylor Gisborne Rosé   ★★★★

The vivacious 2016 vintage (★★★★) has an inviting, bright pink hue. Merlot-based (with 3 per cent Pinot Noir), it is a dry style (2.1 grams/litre of residual sugar), with fresh, lively, plummy, gently spicy flavours, crisp and strong.

Vintage	16	
WR	5	
Drink	16-18	

DRY $22 V+

Lawson's Dry Hills Pinot Rosé   ★★★☆

The 2015 vintage (★★★★) of this Marlborough wine was made from early-picked Pinot Noir. Pink/pale red, it is fresh and vibrantly fruity, with strong plum, red-berry and spice flavours, and a finely balanced, dryish (5 grams/litre of residual sugar) finish.

MED/DRY $20 AV

Left Field Hawke's Bay Rosé   ★★★☆

The sharply priced 2015 vintage (★★★☆) is a blend of Merlot, Pinotage and Arneis. Bright pink, it is vibrantly fruity, with lively, fresh plum and strawberry flavours, slightly sweet (6 grams/litre of residual sugar) and smooth. The 2016 vintage (★★★☆) is a blend of Pinotage (65 per cent), Arneis and Pinot Gris. Bright pink, it is a dryish style (5.9 grams/litre of residual sugar), full-bodied, with vibrant cherry/plum flavours and a smooth finish. (From Te Awa.)

Vintage	16	
WR	6	
Drink	16-19	

MED/DRY $18 V+

Locharburn Central Otago Pinot Noir Rosé ★★★★

The bright pink, attractively scented 2015 vintage (★★★★☆) was estate-grown and mostly handled in tanks; 15 per cent was fermented in seasoned French oak puncheons. Very floral, vibrantly fruity and smooth, with a strong surge of ripe, plummy flavours, woven with fresh acidity, it's full of drink-young charm.

 MED/DRY $28 AV

Mahi Marlborough Rosé (★★★★★)

Ensconced in a tall, slender, see-through bottle, the delicious 2015 vintage (★★★★★) is a single-vineyard wine, hand-picked at the junction of the Waihopai and Wairau valleys, and tank-fermented to full dryness. Pale pink, it is highly fragrant, with fresh, seductive strawberry, watermelon and spice flavours, very delicate and deep. Instantly appealing, it's priced sharply.

Vintage	16	15
WR	7	7
Drink	16-18	16-18

 DRY $20 V+

Mahurangi River Winery Pretty in Pink Rosé ★★★★

Estate-grown at Matakana, the 2015 vintage (★★★★) was blended from Merlot (90 per cent) and Malbec (10 per cent). Pink/pale red, it is vivacious, with fresh, plummy flavours, showing excellent delicacy and depth, gentle sweetness, and lots of drink-young appeal.

 MED $24 AV

Man O' War Waiheke Island Pinque ★★★☆

The refreshing 2016 vintage (★★★☆) is a blend of equal portions of Syrah, Merlot and Malbec, estate-grown on Waiheke Island. Made in a fully dry style, it is pale pink and medium-bodied, with peach, spice and watermelon flavours, very fresh and crisp.

Vintage	16	15
WR	6	5
Drink	16-19	16-17

 DRY $29 -V

Maori Point Central Otago Pinot Noir Rosé ★★★☆

The attractive 2015 vintage (★★★☆) is a bright pink, freshly scented wine, with very good depth of strawberry and spice flavours and a smooth, off-dry (7.5 grams/litre of residual sugar) finish.

 MED/DRY $24 -V

Margrain Martinborough Pinot Rosé ★★★☆

The easy-drinking 2016 vintage (★★★☆) was made from Pinot Noir. Bright pink/pale red, it is full-bodied, with fresh, vibrant red-berry and spice flavours, a splash of sweetness (8 grams/litre of residual sugar), appetising acidity and a finely balanced, smooth finish.

Vintage	16
WR	7
Drink	16-18

MED/DRY $24 -V

Matawhero Gisborne Pinot Rosé ★★★☆

The easy-drinking 2015 vintage (★★★☆), made from Pinot Noir, is light pink, mouthfilling and smooth (6 grams/litre of residual sugar), with good depth of fresh, ripe, plummy, slightly spicy and peachy flavours.

MED/DRY $23 –V

Millton Te Arai Vineyard Rosé ★★★★

Certified organic, the 2016 vintage (★★★★) is pale pink, mouthfilling and smooth, with fresh peach, spice and strawberry flavours, showing a touch of complexity, a sliver of sweetness and good personality. Delicious drinking this summer.

Vintage	16
WR	6
Drink	16-18

MED/DRY $26 –V

Misha's Vineyard The Soloist Central Otago Pinot Rosé (★★★★☆)

Instantly appealing, the debut 2016 vintage (★★★★☆) was made from Pinot Noir, estate-grown at Bendigo. Bright pink, it is invitingly scented and mouthfilling, with notably vibrant plum, spice and strawberry flavours, showing excellent delicacy and depth, and a very smooth, dry (4 grams/litre of residual sugar) finish.

DRY $27 AV

Mission Hawke's Bay Rosé ★★★☆

The 2016 vintage (★★★) is an attractive, bright pink blend of Merlot (55 per cent), with smaller amounts of Syrah, Malbec, Cabernet Franc and Cabernet Sauvignon. Fresh, light, berryish and smooth (6 grams/litre of residual sugar), it's a drink-young charmer.

MED/DRY $18 V+

Mission Vineyard Selection Hawke's Bay Rosé (★★★)

The 2016 vintage (★★★) is Merlot-based (77 per cent), with minor portions of Cabernet Franc, Cabernet Sauvignon and Syrah. Bright, light pink, it is lively, with fresh, gentle berry and spice flavours, a hint of herbs, and a smooth, dryish (6 grams/litre of residual sugar) finish.

MED/DRY $20 –V

Mount Riley Limited Release The Bonnie Marlborough Rosé ★★★☆

The 2015 vintage (★★★☆), produced from Pinot Noir, is bright pink, fresh, crisp and lively, with berryish, slightly spicy flavours and a dryish finish.

MED/DRY $18 V+

Neudorf Nelson Pinot Rosé ★★★★☆

The 2016 vintage (★★★★) was hand-picked at Upper Moutere and mostly handled in tanks; 10 per cent was handled in old barriques. Pale pink, it is mouthfilling and smooth, with gentle watermelon and spice flavours, showing a touch of complexity, a hint of apricot and a dry finish.

DRY $25 V+

Nevis Bluff Central Otago Pinot Noir Rosé   (★★☆)

The 2015 vintage (★★☆) was made from Pinot Noir grapes, estate-grown in the Cromwell Basin. Bright, light red, it is fresh and fruity, with slightly earthy notes, crisp acidity and a dry (3 grams/litre of residual sugar) finish.

DRY $30 –V

Nga Waka Martinborough Rosé   (★★★☆)

From Pinot Noir grapes, the debut 2016 vintage (★★★☆) has a bright pink, pale red hue. Fresh and vibrantly fruity, it offers very good depth of plummy, slightly cherryish flavours, threaded with lively acidity, and a dry finish.

DRY $25 –V

Obsidian Waiheke Island Rosé   ★★★★

The 2015 vintage (★★★★) was made from estate-grown, hand-picked Merlot. A dry style, with inviting bright pink/pale red colour, it is mouthfilling, fleshy and vibrantly fruity, with generous, berryish, spicy, slightly peachy flavours. A 'serious' style with a touch of complexity, it's an ideal food wine.

DRY $27 –V

Opawa Marlborough Rosé   (★★★★)

Grown at Rapaura, in the Wairau Valley, the attractive 2016 vintage (★★★★) was hand-harvested and handled in tanks (mostly) and old barrels. Pale pink, it has fresh, gentle strawberry/spice flavours, a hint of apricot and a smooth, finely poised, dryish (5 grams/litre of residual sugar) finish.

MED/DRY $22 V+

Palliser Estate Special Release Martinborough Rosé   (★★★☆)

Bright, pale pink, the 2015 vintage (★★★☆) is a freshly scented, medium-bodied wine with lively strawberry/spice flavours, a gentle touch of tannin and a crisp, dryish finish.

MED/DRY $23 –V

Poverty Bay Old Vines Rosé   ★★★☆

Estate-grown in the Bridge Estate Vineyard at Matawhero, in Gisborne, the 2015 vintage (★★★☆) is a blend of Merlot (80 per cent) and Malbec (20 per cent). Pink/orange, it is less buoyantly fruity than more southern styles, but full-bodied, with generous, peachy, spicy flavours, showing greater complexity than most rosés. Ready.

DRY $30 –V

Ransom Matakana Vin Gris   (★★★★)

The 2015 vintage (★★★★) was made from red varieties (Cabernet Sauvignon, Malbec and Syrah), crushed and pressed immediately to minimise colour extraction, and bottled early. Pale pink, it is full-bodied and dry, with fresh acidity and lively, refreshing strawberry and spice flavours, with hints of watermelon and apricot. A 'serious' but vivacious wine, it's delicious from the start.

DRY $21 V+

Rapaura Springs Reserve Marlborough Pinot Rosé (★★★★☆)

Delicious from the start, the generous 2016 vintage (★★★★☆) is bright, pale pink, with a fresh, scented bouquet. Mouthfilling, with strawberry and spice flavours, it is slightly peachy, with very good weight and depth and a dryish (6 grams/litre of residual sugar), well-rounded finish.

Vintage	16
WR	6
Drink	16-18

DRY $19 V+

Redmetal Vineyards Hawke's Bay Cabernet Franc Rosé ★★★

Grown in the Bridge Pa Triangle, the 2016 vintage (★★★☆) is a pale pink wine, based on Cabernet Franc. Full-bodied (14 per cent alcohol), it is fleshy, with generous, peachy, slightly spicy flavours and a smooth, dry (4 grams/litre of residual sugar) finish. Ready to roll.

 DRY $19 AV

Rocky Point Central Otago Pinot Noir Rosé (★★★★)

Drier than most rosés, the 2015 vintage (★★★★) was made from Pinot Noir grapes, hand-picked at Bendigo and fermented with indigenous yeasts in tanks (80 per cent) and old barrels (20 per cent). Pink, with a hint of orange, it is attractively scented, with cherry, watermelon and spice flavours, showing good freshness and delicacy, and a dry (less than 4 grams/litre of residual sugar), lengthy finish. (From Prophet's Rock.)

DRY $22 V+

Rod McDonald One Off Syrah/Viognier Rosé (★★★★☆)

Showing good personality, the fresh, vibrantly fruity 2015 vintage (★★★★☆) is a blend of Syrah (93 per cent) and Viognier (7 per cent), fermented with indigenous yeasts in seasoned oak barriques. Light pink, it is mouthfilling, with gentle strawberry/spice flavours, peachy notes, a touch of complexity and a long, basically dry finish.

 DRY $25 V+

Ruru Central Otago Rosé ★★★★

From Immigrant's Vineyard, at Alexandra, the charming 2015 vintage (★★★★) is a pale pink, delicious summer wine, made from Pinot Noir. Very fresh and vibrant, it has strawberry, peach and slight apricot flavours, a sliver of sweetness and appetising acidity. The 2016 vintage (★★★★), also Pinot Noir-based, is bright, pale pink. Floral, it is very fresh, with vivacious watermelon, peach and spice flavours, just a hint of sweetness (6.4 grams/litre of residual sugar), and mouth-watering acidity.

 MED/DRY $22 V+

Saint Clair Marlborough Pinot Gris Rosé ★★★★

The 2015 vintage (★★★★) is a bright pink blend of Pinot Gris (mostly) and Pinot Noir. It has dryish (5 grams/litre of residual sugar) strawberry, peach and spice flavours, showing very good body, freshness, balance and depth.

 MED/DRY $22 V+

Saint Clair Vicar's Choice Marlborough Bright Light Sauvignon Blanc Rosé   ★★★

The 2015 vintage (★★★), which includes a splash of Malbec, is a light style (9.5 per cent), bright pink, with fresh, delicate watermelon and spice flavours and an off-dry (7.6 grams/litre of residual sugar) finish.

MED/DRY $19 AV

Sherwood Estate Stoney Range Saignée Pinot Noir Rosé   (★★★☆)

Pink/slight orange, the 2015 vintage (★★★☆) is full-bodied and dry (2 grams/litre of residual sugar), with good personality and depth of peach, strawberry, watermelon and spice flavours. Ready.

DRY $20 AV

Sileni Cellar Selection Hawke's Bay Cabernet Franc Rosé   ★★★☆

Pink/pale red, the lively 2016 vintage (★★★☆) is mouthfilling, with fresh, plummy, slightly spicy flavours, showing good depth, and a dryish (4.7 grams/litre of residual sugar) finish.

DRY $20 AV

Sileni Estate Selection Hawke's Bay Ridge Rosé   (★★★★★)

Delicious from the start, the 2016 vintage (★★★★★) is made from Pinot Noir. Bright pink, it is very attractively scented, mouthfilling and smooth, with strong, fresh strawberry, peach and spice flavours and a finely balanced, dry (3.6 grams/litre of residual sugar) finish.

DRY $25 V+

Soho Westwood Waiheke Island Rosé   ★★★★

The 2015 vintage (★★★★), grown at Onetangi, is a bright pink/pale red rosé, Merlot-based. Medium-bodied, it is slightly sweeter than most (14 grams/litre of residual sugar), with strong, plummy, berryish, slightly spicy flavours, crisp, tightly structured and vivacious.

Vintage	15
WR	5
Drink	16-17

MED/DRY $26 –V

Spy Valley Marlborough Pinot Noir Rosé   ★★★☆

The pale pink 2016 vintage (★★★☆) was made from hand-picked Pinot Noir grapes, with some use of barrel fermentation. It has fresh watermelon, peach and spice flavours, crisp and dry (2.7 grams/litre of residual sugar), showing very good depth.

Vintage	16	15	14	13
WR	6	7	7	6
Drink	16-18	16-17	P	P

DRY $23 –V

Stonecroft Gimblett Gravels Hawke's Bay Rosé   (★★★☆)

Offering very easy drinking, the debut 2016 vintage (★★★☆) was grown at Fernhill. Light pink, it is medium-bodied, with good depth of fresh, lively, plummy flavours and a smooth (6 grams/litre of residual sugar), harmonious finish.

MED/DRY $22 AV

Stoneleigh Latitude Marlborough Rosé   ★★★★

The delicious 2015 vintage (★★★★☆) is an inviting, pale pink rosé, grown at Rapaura, in the Wairau Valley. Floral, full-bodied and smooth, it has fresh strawberry, spice and apricot flavours, showing excellent delicacy and depth, and a dryish, finely balanced, long finish.

MED/DRY $23 AV

Stoneleigh Lighter Marlborough Rosé   (★★☆)

From early-picked grapes, the youthful 2016 vintage (★★☆) is a very pale pink, light-bodied wine (9.9 per cent alcohol), with vibrant, peachy flavours and a crisp, slightly sweet finish.

MED/DRY $17 –V

Stoneleigh Marlborough Pinot Noir Rosé   ★★★☆.

The very easy-drinking 2016 vintage (★★★☆) is a bright pink, fresh-scented, full-bodied wine, with good depth of vibrant strawberry, peach and spice flavours and a smooth finish. Fine value.

MED/DRY $17 V+

Sugar Loaf Harriet Marlborough Pinot Noir Rosé   (★★★☆)

The 2015 vintage (★★★☆) is a pale pink wine, fresh and smooth, with gentle, berryish flavours and a finely balanced, slightly spicy finish.

MED/DRY $18 V+

Summerhouse Marlborough Pinot Noir Rosé   (★★★★)

Already delicious, the 2016 vintage (★★★★) is a pale pink, mouthfilling rosé with strong strawberry, peach and spice flavours, showing good delicacy, and a dry (2.8 grams/litre of residual sugar), well-rounded finish.

DRY $19 V+

Te Mania Nelson Pinot Noir Rosé   ★★★☆

Certified organic, the 2016 vintage (★★★) is a pink-hued, dryish style (5 grams/litre of residual sugar), with red-berry, peach and spice flavours, fresh and smooth. Good drinking this summer.

MED/DRY $22 AV

Terra Sancta Bannockburn Central Otago Pinot Noir Rosé   ★★★★★

From one vintage to the next, this is one of the country's leading rosés. Bursting with freshness, the 2016 vintage (★★★★★) was mostly handled in tanks; 10 per cent was fermented in old oak casks. Bright pink, it is floral and vivacious, with vibrant strawberry and spice flavours, woven with fresh acidity, a sliver of sweetness (4 grams/litre of residual sugar), and lovely poise, delicacy and flow.

DRY $27 V+

Thornbury Hawke's Bay Rosé   (★★★☆)

The 2015 vintage (★★★☆) is bright pink, with fresh, lively red-berry and watermelon flavours, slightly sweet and very smooth. Lots of drink-young charm. Good value.

Vintage	16
WR	6
Drink	16-18

MED/DRY $16 V+

Ti Point Ruby Hawke's Bay Rosé   (★★★☆)

Light pink, the 2016 vintage (★★★☆) is Merlot-based. Made in a crisp, dry style, it has gentle peach, watermelon and spice flavours, showing good delicacy and depth.

DRY $23 –V

Ti Point Tess Hawke's Bay White Merlot   (★★☆)

A rosé in all but name, the 2016 vintage (★★☆) is a pale pink wine, made entirely from Merlot. Medium-bodied, it has fresh watermelon and spice flavours, dry and slightly earthy, but lacks a bit of charm and fragrance.

DRY $23 –V

Tiki Estate Marlborough Pinot Noir Rosé   ★★★★

The 2016 vintage (★★★☆) is bright pink, mouthfilling and smooth, with cherryish flavours, a gentle splash of sweetness, balanced acidity and good vigour and freshness.

MED/DRY $23 AV

Tohu Nelson Pinot Rosé   (★★★)

Estate-grown at Upper Moutere, the 2016 vintage (★★★) is a basically dry style (3 grams/litre of residual sugar). Medium-bodied, it is lively, with balanced acidity and fresh peach, strawberry and spice flavours.

DRY $22 –V

Trinity Hill Hawke's Bay Rosé   (★★★★)

Bright, light pink, the 2015 vintage (★★★★) has excellent depth and freshness. A blend of Pinot Noir (50 per cent), Merlot (25 per cent) and Montepulciano (25 per cent), it is dry (4 grams/litre of residual sugar), with mouthfilling body and strong, lively berry, spice and slight apricot flavours.

DRY $20 V+

True North Rosé   ★★☆

From Doubtless Bay, in Northland, the 2014 vintage (★★☆) is a dry wine, robust (14.5 per cent alcohol), with some complexity, but slightly heavy and starting to lose freshness. The lighter-bodied 2015 vintage (★★★), fermented in old oak casks, is pale red, with satisfying depth of fresh red-berry and spice flavours, and a dry finish. Priced right.

Vintage	15	14
WR	5	6
Drink	16-19	16-21

DRY $16 AV

Two Rivers of Marlborough L'Ile de Beauté Rosé   ★★★★

Grown in the Southern Valleys, the 2016 vintage (★★★★) is a pale pink, medium-bodied wine, based on hand-picked Pinot Noir. Attractively scented, it is vibrantly fruity, with fresh, strong strawberry and spice flavours, and a crisp, dry (3 grams/litre of residual sugar) finish.

Vintage	16
WR	6
Drink	16-17

DRY $24 AV

Villa Maria Private Bin Hawke's Bay Rosé   ★★★☆

The 2016 vintage (★★★☆) is a pale pink, off-dry style (5 grams/litre of residual sugar), based on Merlot. Finely balanced, it is smooth, with plum, watermelon and spice flavours, showing very good delicacy, vibrancy and depth.

Vintage	16	15	14
WR	7	6	6
Drink	16-18	16-17	P

MED/DRY $17 V+

Villa Maria Private Bin Lighter Hawke's Bay Rosé   ★★★

This wine is for those looking for 'a quality wine with less calories'. The 2015 vintage (★★★) is a bright pink, light-bodied wine (9 per cent alcohol), with vibrant, strawberryish, peachy flavours, gently sweet, crisp and lively. The 2016 vintage (★★★) was blended from Pinot Noir, Arneis and Merlot. Bright pink, it is light-bodied (10 per cent alcohol), with a floral bouquet and vibrant strawberry and watermelon flavours, fresh, slightly sweet (8.6 grams/litre of residual sugar) and crisp.

Vintage	16	15
WR	6	6
Drink	16-17	16-17

MED/DRY $17 AV

VNO Skinny Hawke's Bay Rosé   (★★☆)

The 2015 vintage (★★☆) is a low-alcohol (9 per cent) blend of Pinot Gris (91 per cent), Merlot (6 per cent) and other varieties. Pink/pale red, it is light, fresh and raspberryish, with lively acidity and an off-dry finish.

MED/DRY $17 –V

Wairau River Marlborough Rosé   ★★★☆

The 2015 vintage (★★★☆), made from Pinot Noir, is an off-dry style (8 grams/litre of residual sugar), bright, pale pink. It's a vivacious wine, light and lively, with very refreshing strawberry, spice and peach flavours. The 2016 vintage (★★★★) is already delicious. Pale pink, it shows excellent vibrancy and delicacy, with strong strawberry, watermelon and spice flavours, slightly sweet (7.9 grams/litre of residual sugar), lively and smooth.

Vintage	16	15	14	13
WR	6	7	7	4
Drink	16-18	16-17	P	P

MED/DRY $20 AV

Whitehaven Marlborough Pinot Rosé   ★★★★

The delicious 2016 vintage (★★★★☆) is bright, light pink. Fragrant and full-bodied, it is vibrantly fruity, with fresh, delicate strawberryish, spicy, slightly peachy flavours, and a very finely balanced, dry (3.8 grams/litre of residual sugar) finish. Top drinking for the summer of 2016–17.

DRY $23 AV

Wild Grace Central Otago Pinot Noir Rosé   (★★★★)

Launched from the 2016 vintage (★★★★), this is a bright pink, freshly scented wine, instantly appealing. Full-bodied, it has vibrant strawberry, watermelon and slightly spicy flavours, threaded with appetising acidity, and a dryish, finely balanced finish. Good drinking for the summer of 2016–17. (From Constellation NZ.)

MED/DRY $27 –V

Wooing Tree Central Otago Rosé   ★★★★

From estate-grown Pinot Noir grapes, hand-picked in the Cromwell Basin, the 2016 vintage (★★★★) is a bright pink, scented, dryish wine (4.9 grams/litre of residual sugar), full-bodied and vibrantly fruity, with strong, fresh strawberry, watermelon and spice flavours, lively acidity and a smooth finish. Delicious from the start.

DRY $25 AV

Yealands Estate Single Vineyard Awatere Valley
Marlborough Pinot Noir Rosé   ★★★☆

The 2015 vintage (★★★) is a lively wine from young, estate-grown vines at Seaview. Pink and smooth, it has fresh red-berry flavours to the fore, hints of spices and herbs, balanced acidity and a dry (3 grams/litre of residual sugar) finish.

Vintage	15
WR	7
Drink	16-18

DRY $23 –V

Red Wines

Barbera

One of Italy's most widely planted red-wine varieties – particularly in Piedmont, in the north-west – Barbera is known for its generous yields of robust, full-coloured reds, typically with lively acidity. Although increasingly popular in California, it is extremely rare in New Zealand and is not listed separately in New Zealand Winegrowers' *Vineyard Register Report 2015–2018.*

De La Terre Hawke's Bay Barbera ★★★★

The 2013 vintage (★★★☆) is rare – fewer than 900 bottles were produced. From grapes hand-picked at 25 brix at Havelock North, it was matured for 15 months in seasoned French oak barriques. The colour is fullish, with a hint of development; the palate is sturdy (14.5 per cent alcohol), with strong cherry/spice flavours, hints of tamarillo and nuts, good complexity, and a firm foundation of tannin. The 2014 vintage (★★★★) was matured for 18 months in seasoned French oak barriques. Full and fairly youthful in colour, it is mouthfilling, with concentrated, ripe, plummy, gently spicy flavours, firm tannins beneath, and good complexity. Best drinking 2018+.

Vintage	14	13
WR	6	5
Drink	16-20	16-18

DRY $40 –V

Branded and Other Red Wines

Most New Zealand red wines carry a varietal label, such as Pinot Noir, Syrah, Merlot or Cabernet Sauvignon (or blends of the last two). Those not labelled prominently by their principal grape varieties – often prestigious wines such as Esk Valley The Terraces or Destiny Bay Magna Praemia – can be found here.

Although not varietally labelled, these wines are mostly of high quality and sometimes outstanding.

Alluviale ★★★★★

Often a great buy. The 2012 vintage (★★★★), blended from Merlot (mostly) and Cabernet Sauvignon, was grown at two sites, both certified organic, in the Gimblett Gravels, Hawke's Bay, and matured without sulphur dioxide for 14 months in French oak barriques (30 per cent new). Deeply coloured, with a fragrant, spicy bouquet, it is mouthfilling and supple, with fresh acidity, vibrant, blackcurrant-like flavours to the fore, and hints of plums, spices and coffee. Showing good concentration, it is silky-textured and currently drinking well.

Vintage	12	11	10	09	08
WR	5	NM	7	7	6
Drink	16-18	NM	16-19	16-18	16-17

DRY $33 V+

Alpha Domus AD The Aviator ★★★★★

Estate-grown in the Bridge Pa Triangle, this is a blend of classic Bordeaux varieties. The outstanding 2013 vintage (★★★★★) is a marriage of Cabernet Sauvignon (37 per cent), Cabernet Franc (27 per cent), Merlot (18 per cent) and Malbec (18 per cent). Matured for 20 months in French oak barriques (75 per cent new), it is dark and purple-flushed, with an enticingly fragrant bouquet. Mouthfilling and supple, it has fresh, beautifully ripe blackcurrant, plum and spice flavours, with silky tannins. Showing lovely richness, purity, delicacy and structure, it should flourish for a decade. Best drinking 2020+.

Vintage	13
WR	7
Drink	16-23

DRY $72 AV

Alpha Domus The Navigator ★★★★☆

The refined, very youthful 2013 vintage (★★★★☆) is a blend of Merlot (69 per cent), Cabernet Sauvignon (17 per cent), Cabernet Franc (7 per cent), Malbec (5 per cent) and Petit Verdot (2 per cent), estate-grown in the Bridge Pa Triangle of Hawke's Bay, and matured in seasoned French (80 per cent) and American (20 per cent) oak casks. Full-coloured, it is mouthfilling, rich and finely poised, with strong, vibrant blackcurrant, plum and spice flavours, good complexity, gentle tannins and a persistent finish. Best drinking 2017+.

DRY $29 V+

Ash Ridge Vintner's Reserve The Blend (★★★★☆)

The stylish, debut 2013 vintage (★★★★☆) is based principally (85 per cent) on Merlot and Cabernet Sauvignon, blended with smaller portions of Malbec, Cabernet Franc and Syrah. Grown in the Bridge Pa Triangle, Hawke's Bay, it was matured in seasoned French and new American oak casks. Full-coloured and fragrant, it is mouthfilling and savoury, with strong, berryish, plummy, spicy flavours, a hint of dark chocolate, good complexity and ripe, supple tannins. (There is no 2014, but the label returns from the 2015 vintage.)

DRY $45 -V

Ata Rangi Martinborough Célèbre   ★★★★☆

Pronounced 'say-lebr', this is a blend of Merlot, Syrah and Cabernet Sauvignon. It typically has impressive weight and depth of plummy, spicy flavours in a complex style that matures well. The impressive 2014 vintage (★★★★☆) is a blend of Merlot (55 per cent), Syrah (35 per cent) and Cabernet Sauvignon (10 per cent). An elegant, notably drinkable red, it is fragrant and full-coloured, with strong, fresh, well-ripened berry, plum and spice flavours, to which the Syrah makes a noticeable, but not pungent, contribution. A distinctive wine, complex and harmonious, it is already delicious, but should be at its best 2018+.

Vintage	14	13	12	11	10	09	08	07	06
WR	7	7	NM	6	NM	6	7	7	7
Drink	16-26	16-25	NM	16-20	NM	16-20	16-20	16-19	16-18

DRY $40 –V

Babich The Patriarch   ★★★★★

This is promoted as Babich's finest red, regardless of the variety or region of origin, but all vintages have been grown in the company's shingly vineyards in Gimblett Road, Hawke's Bay. It is typically a dark, ripe and complex, deliciously rich red, matured in mostly French oak barriques (30–35 per cent new). The 2013 vintage (★★★★★) is a blend of Cabernet Sauvignon, Merlot and Malbec. Deeply coloured, it is concentrated and firmly structured, with deep, still very youthful blackcurrant, plum and spice flavours, ripe, nutty and savoury. It should age superbly. The 2014 vintage (★★★★☆) is a dark, sturdy, concentrated blend of Cabernet Sauvignon, Merlot and Malbec. Sweet-fruited and tightly structured, it has a rich array of blackcurrant, plum, spice and herb flavours, with a lingering finish.

Vintage	14	13	12	11	10	09	08
WR	7	7	5	5	7	7	5
Drink	16-25	16-25	16-21	16-20	16-22	16-21	16-18

DRY $70 AV

Cable Bay Five Hills   (★★★★)

The 2014 vintage (★★★★) is a Waiheke Island blend of Malbec (63 per cent), Merlot (25 per cent) and Cabernet Sauvignon (12 per cent), hand-picked at several sites and matured in French and Hungarian oak casks (30 per cent new). Fresh plum and spice aromas lead into a mouthfilling, vibrantly fruity red with generous, youthful plum and blackcurrant flavours, gentle tannins, and a long, spicy, smooth finish.

Vintage	14
WR	6
Drink	16-25

DRY $48 –V

Clearview Enigma   ★★★★☆

The 2013 vintage (★★★★★) is a dense, classy Hawke's Bay blend of Merlot (80 per cent), Malbec (10 per cent) and Cabernet Franc (10 per cent), grown at Te Awanga and matured in French and American oak barriques. A powerful, sturdy (14.5 per cent alcohol) wine, it has bold, youthful blackcurrant, plum and spice flavours, with hints of nuts and coffee, and ripe, fine-grained tannins. Savoury, complex and notably concentrated, it should be long-lived. The 2014 vintage (★★★★) is a fragrant, dark blend of Merlot (67 per cent), Malbec (17 per cent) and Cabernet Franc (16 per cent), barrel-aged (40 per cent new). Deeply coloured, it has strong plum, blackcurrant and herb flavours, savoury notes, and a firmly structured finish.

DRY $55 –V

Clearview Old Olive Block ★★★★★

This Hawke's Bay red is named after the estate vineyard at Te Awanga, which has a very old olive tree in the centre. It is grown there and in the Gimblett Gravels. The 2013 vintage (★★★★☆) is a youthful, generous Hawke's Bay blend of Cabernet Sauvignon (46 per cent), Merlot (38 per cent), Cabernet Franc (11 per cent) and Malbec (5 per cent), grown at Te Awanga (mostly) and in the Gimblett Gravels. Deeply coloured, it is mouthfilling and smooth, with strong, ripe blackcurrant, plum, herb and spice flavours, oak complexity and obvious potential. The 2014 vintage (★★★★☆) is a bold, youthful blend of Cabernet Sauvignon (73 per cent), Merlot (21 per cent) and Malbec (6 per cent). Well worth cellaring, it has blackcurrant, plum and spice flavours, a hint of herbs, and excellent structure and density.

DRY $36 AV

Clearview The Basket Press ★★★★★

The distinguished 2013 vintage (★★★★★) is a youthful blend of 35 per cent Cabernet Sauvignon, grown in the Gimblett Gravels, with coastal Te Awanga fruit: Merlot (30 per cent), Cabernet Franc (30 per cent) and Malbec (5 per cent). Hand-picked and matured for over two years in all-new French oak barriques, it is deeply coloured, with dense, pure blackcurrant, plum and spice flavours that build to a lasting, finely poised finish. Weighty and highly concentrated, with a backbone of ripe, supple tannins, it has lapped up the new oak influence, creating a savoury, multi-faceted red. Already delicious, it should flourish for a decade – or longer.

DRY $165 –V

Clearview Two Pinnacles ★★★★

The 2013 vintage (★★★★) is a rich, vibrantly fruity Hawke's Bay blend of Malbec and Cabernet Franc, estate-grown on the coast, at Te Awanga, and matured for a year in seasoned French and American barriques. Full-coloured, it has fresh, ripe blackcurrant, plum and spice flavours, firm tannins and good density. Drink now or cellar.

DRY $31 –V

Coopers Creek Four Daughters ★★★

The 2013 vintage (★★★) is a youthful Hawke's Bay blend of roughly equal portions of Malbec, Cabernet Franc, Syrah (25 per cent) and Merlot. Fullish in colour, it has ripe, moderately rich berry and spice flavours, a smooth finish and a fragrant bouquet.

DRY $18 AV

Crab Farm La Somme Rouge (★★★★☆)

The 2013 vintage (★★★★☆) is a densely packed Hawke's Bay blend of equal portions of Cabernet Franc, Merlot and Malbec, with a splash of Cabernet Sauvignon. Matured in French and American oak casks, it is deeply coloured, fresh and supple, with bold, vibrant plum and spice flavours. Sweet-fruited, with excellent delicacy and depth, it shows good aging potential.

DRY $25 V+

Crab Farm Pukera Reserve Blend   ★★★★☆

Deeply coloured, the 2013 vintage (★★★★) was grown in Hawke's Bay and matured in French and American oak barrels. Rich and smooth, it's a gutsy red with bold, ripe plum, spice and blackcurrant flavours, and a firm backbone of tannin.

DRY $30 AV

Craggy Range Aroha   ★★★★★

From a warm, early-ripening season, the 2014 vintage (★★★★★) is a single-vineyard Pinot Noir, estate-grown at Te Muna, on the edge of Martinborough. Hand-picked at 24.2 brix, it was fermented with indigenous yeasts and matured for 10 months in French oak barriques (30 per cent new). A very 'complete' wine, it is deep ruby, full-bodied and notably savoury, with generous, well-ripened cherry, plum and nut flavours, good tannin support, and lovely complexity and harmony. Best drinking 2019+.

Vintage	14	13	12	11	10	09	08	07
WR	7	7	7	7	NM	6	7	7
Drink	16-25	16-25	16-24	16-23	NM	16-20	16-21	16-18

DRY $120 –V

Craggy Range Le Sol   ★★★★★

This famous Syrah impresses with its lovely fragrance and finesse. Estate-grown in the Gimblett Gravels of Hawke's Bay, the floral 2014 vintage (★★★★★) was hand-picked at 23.9 brix and matured for 18 months in French oak barriques (35 per cent new). The colour is dense and purple-flushed; the palate is dense but not tough, with highly concentrated, very youthful plum, spice and black-pepper flavours, framed by ripe, supple tannins, and obvious cellaring potential. Best drinking 2020+.

Vintage	14	13	12	11	10	09	08	07	06	05
WR	7	7	NM	7	7	7	7	7	6	7
Drink	16-30	16-30	NM	16-25	16-27	16-26	16-23	16-22	16-20	P

DRY $120 AV

Craggy Range Sophia   ★★★★★

This is Craggy Range's premier Merlot-based red. The 2014 vintage (★★★★★) is a Gimblett Gravels, Hawke's Bay blend of Merlot (61 per cent), Cabernet Sauvignon (20 per cent) and Cabernet Franc (19 per cent), hand-picked at 24 brix and matured for 19 months in French oak barriques (40 per cent new). A lovely young red, it is highly fragrant, with deep colour, substantial body, generous, ripe blackcurrant, plum and spice flavours, very fine-grained tannins and a complex, lingering finish. Best drinking 2019+.

Vintage	14	13	12	11	10	09	08	07	06	05
WR	7	7	NM	7	7	7	7	7	7	7
Drink	16-30	16-30	NM	16-25	16-27	16-26	16-23	16-27	16-26	16-20

DRY $95 AV

Craggy Range Te Kahu ★★★★

Estate-grown in the Gimblett Gravels, the 2014 vintage (★★★★) of this Hawke's Bay red is Merlot-based (68 per cent), with smaller portions of Cabernet Sauvignon (18 per cent), Malbec (8 per cent) and Cabernet Franc (6 per cent). Matured for 17 months in oak barriques (28 per cent new), it is deeply coloured and full-bodied, with youthful, well-ripened blackcurrant, plum and spice flavours, showing good concentration and complexity, and a fairly firm finish. Well worth cellaring to 2018+.

Vintage	14	13	12	11	10	09	08	07	06	DRY $32 –V
WR	7	7	NM	5	6	6	6	7	6	
Drink	16-23	16-23	NM	16-18	16-20	16-18	P	16-22	16-20	

Craggy Range The Quarry ★★★★★

This is Craggy Range's top Cabernet-based red. The 2011 vintage (★★★★☆), estate-grown in the Gimblett Gravels district of Hawke's Bay, was made principally from Cabernet Sauvignon (95 per cent), but includes splashes of Merlot (4 per cent) and Cabernet Franc (1 per cent). From grapes hand-harvested at an average of 22.9 brix, the wine was matured for 19 months in French oak barriques (50 per cent new). Deeply coloured, with concentrated blackcurrant, herb and nut flavours, strongly seasoned with oak, it is slightly less striking than the notably classy, rich 2009 (★★★★★), but still youthful, and well worth cellaring. (Not produced 2012–2015).

Vintage	15	14	13	12	11	10	09	08	07	06	DRY $70 AV
WR	NM	NM	NM	NM	7	NM	7	7	7	7	
Drink	NM	NM	NM	NM	16-25	NM	16-26	16-23	16-27	16-26	

Crazy by Nature Gisborne Cosmo Red ★★★☆

Certified organic, the 2014 vintage (★★★★) from Millton is a blend of Malbec, Syrah and Viognier, matured for 11 months in American oak barrels. Full-coloured, it is mouthfilling, with strong berry, plum and spice flavours, good tannin backbone, and a tight, lingering finish. Still very youthful, it should be at its best mid-2017+.

Vintage	14	DRY $26 –V
WR	5	
Drink	16-20	

Crossroads Hawke's Bay Talisman ★★★★☆

A blend of several red varieties whose identities the winery delights in concealing (I see Malbec and Syrah as prime suspects), Talisman has long been estate-grown in the Origin Vineyard at Fernhill, in Hawke's Bay, but now also includes fruit from sites in the Gimblett Gravels. The 2013 vintage (★★★★☆) has bold, purple-flushed colour. Barrique-aged for 16 months, it is mouthfilling, vibrant and supple, in a youthful but approachable style with strong, plummy, spicy flavours, showing good complexity, and a rich, smooth finish.

Vintage	13	12	11	10	09	08	DRY $56 –V
WR	7	5	5	7	6	6	
Drink	16-23	16-23	16-22	16-22	16-20	P	

Destiny Bay Destinae   ★★★★★

The 2013 vintage (★★★★★) is a perfect introduction to the Destiny Bay range. Estate-grown on Waiheke Island, it is a blend of Cabernet Sauvignon (38 per cent), Merlot (36 per cent), Cabernet Franc (12 per cent), Malbec (8 per cent) and Petit Verdot (6 per cent), harvested at 24–25.6 brix and matured in a 50:50 split of French and American oak casks (40 per cent new). A distinguished but already very approachable red, it is deeply coloured, fleshy, rich and softly textured, with blackcurrant, plum, dried-herb and spice flavours, showing excellent concentration, complexity and harmony. Best drinking 2018+. ($60 to Patron Club members.)

DRY $125 –V

Destiny Bay Magna Praemia   ★★★★★

The powerful, lush 2013 vintage (★★★★★), harvested at 24–25.6 brix, is a blend of Cabernet Sauvignon (71 per cent) and Merlot (16 per cent), with minor portions of Cabernet Franc, Petit Verdot and Malbec. Matured for up to 15 months in an even split of French and American oak casks (60 per cent new), it is dark and full-bodied (14.5 per cent alcohol), with deliciously dense, ripe blackcurrant, plum and spice flavours, fine-grained tannins, excellent complexity and a lasting finish. A classy, youthful, savoury, highly concentrated red, it's already approachable, but likely to be long-lived; best drinking 2020+. ($195 to Patron Club members.)

DRY $355 –V

Destiny Bay Mystae   ★★★★★

The 2013 vintage (★★★★★) of this Waiheke Island blend is Cabernet Sauvignon-based (52 per cent), with Merlot (25 per cent), Cabernet Franc (9 per cent), Malbec (8 per cent) and Petit Verdot (6 per cent). Harvested at 24–25.6 brix, it was matured in an even split of French and American oak casks (60 per cent new). Dark and youthful in colour, it is a powerful red (14.5 per cent alcohol), fleshy and rich, sweet-fruited and lush, with concentrated blackcurrant and spice flavours, a hint of sweet oak, and fine-grained tannins. A very age-worthy wine, it should be at its best 2020+. ($85 to Patron Club members.)

DRY $155 –V

Elephant Hill Hawke's Bay Le Phant   ★★★★

The 2014 vintage (★★★★) is a dark, purple-flushed blend of Merlot (61 per cent), Syrah (26 per cent) and Cabernet Sauvignon (13 per cent), grown in the Gimblett Gravels, at Te Awanga and in the Bridge Pa Triangle. Mouthfilling, it is vibrantly fruity, with strong, fresh, ripe plum and spice flavours, a subtle seasoning of oak, a slightly earthy streak adding complexity, and gentle tannins. An excellent, drink-young style.

DRY $24 V+

Elephant Hill Hieronymus   (★★★★★)

The dense, flowing 2013 vintage (★★★★★) is a blend of Cabernet Sauvignon, Malbec and Merlot, grown in the Gimblett Gravels and the Bridge Pa Triangle, and matured for 17 months in French oak casks (80 per cent new). Dark and purple-flushed, it is mouthfilling, with ripe sweet-fruit characters and highly concentrated plum, spice, blackcurrant and coffee flavours. Lush and approachable in its youth, it should flourish for a decade; open 2017+.

Esk Valley Heipipi The Terraces   ★★★★★

Grown on the steep, terraced, north-facing hillside flanking the winery at Bay View, in Hawke's Bay, this is a strikingly bold, dark wine with bottomless depth of blackcurrant, plum and strongly spicy flavour. Malbec (43 per cent of the vines) and Merlot (35 per cent) are typically the major ingredients, supplemented by Cabernet Franc; the Malbec gives 'perfume, spice, tannin and brilliant colour'. Yields in the 1-hectare vineyard are very low, and the wine is matured for 17 to 22 months in all-new French oak barriques. 'En primeur' (payment at a reduced price of $99, in advance of delivery) has been the best way to buy. It typically matures well, developing a beautiful fragrance and spicy, Rhône-like complexity. Matured for 18 months in French oak barriques (100 per cent new), the 2013 vintage (★★★★★) is a notably 'complete' wine. The colour is dense and inky; the flavours are highly concentrated, youthful, plummy and spicy, with fine-grained tannins and a deliciously smooth, rich finish. A powerful (14.5 per cent alcohol), very harmonious red, with a wow factor, it should flourish for many years. The 2014 vintage (★★★★★) – the first to be named after the former site of Heipipi Pa, above the vineyard – is a blend of Malbec (46 per cent), Merlot (31 per cent) and Cabernet Franc (23 per cent). Deeply coloured, with a welcoming, ripe, spicy bouquet, it has dense blackcurrant, plum and spice flavours, very complex and savoury. Already delicious, it should break into full stride 2019+.

Vintage	14	13	12	11	10	09	08	07	06
WR	7	7	NM	NM	NM	7	NM	NM	7
Drink	16-30	16-35	NM	NM	NM	16-25	NM	NM	16-20

Frenchmans Hill Estate Waiheke Island Blood Creek 8   ★★★★★

The highly concentrated 2012 (★★★★★) is a blend of eight varieties, with a 'core' of Cabernet Sauvignon (35 per cent), Merlot (20 per cent) and Petit Verdot (20 per cent), plus minor portions of Syrah, Cabernet Franc, Tannat, Viognier and Koler. Matured for two years in all-new oak barriques, it is bold, deeply coloured, mouthfilling and firm, in a 'masculine' style, with dense, ripe blackcurrant, plum and spice flavours. It should flourish for a decade. The 2013 vintage (★★★★★) is also highly impressive. Matured for 16 months in new French oak barriques, it has dark, youthful colour. A lovely rich and supple red, it is muscular, with generous, ripe blackcurrant/spice flavours, showing excellent complexity, real power through the palate and obvious potential; best drinking 2020+.

Gillman   ★★★★★

This rare Matakana red is blended from Cabernet Franc, Merlot and Malbec, French oak-aged. Tasted in 2016, the 2010 vintage (★★★★★) is a powerful, sweet-fruited, complex blend of Cabernet Franc (65 per cent), Merlot (31 per cent) and Malbec (4 per cent), matured for two years in French oak barrels (50 per cent new). Deeply coloured, with a fragrant, spicy, complex bouquet, it is sturdy, with generous, ripe plum, spice and nut flavours, in a savoury, very Bordeaux-like style, rich and rounded. The slightly lighter 2011 (★★★★) is medium to full-bodied, with a fragrant, spicy bouquet and strong, vibrant blackcurrant, plum and spice flavours; it's drinking well now. The 2012 vintage (★★★★★) is very elegant, with a cedary bouquet, deep, ripe blackcurrant, plum, spice and nut flavours, fine-grained tannins, and a lengthy, silky-smooth finish. These are classy wines, worth discovering.

Vintage	12	11	10	09	08	07	06
WR	6	6	7	6	7	7	6
Drink	17-24	16-23	16-30	16-22	16-24	16-20	16-18

DRY $70 AV

Gladstone Auld Alliance
★★★☆

The 'premier Bordeaux-style' red from this Wairarapa winery struggles to match those from Hawke's Bay – I prefer the Pinot Noir. The 2011 vintage (★★★☆) is a blend of Merlot (87 per cent) and Cabernet Franc (13 per cent), hand-picked from vines cultivated in stony soils in Dakins Road. Matured for over a year in French (90 per cent) and American oak casks (30 per cent new), it is full-coloured and mouthfilling, with fresh, firmly structured blackcurrant, herb and nut flavours, a herbal thread and very good depth.

Vintage	11
WR	5
Drink	16-20

DRY $45 –V

Heron's Flight Amphora
(★★★★★)

The classy and distinctive, strikingly packaged 2015 vintage (★★★★★) was made from Sangiovese, estate-grown at Matakana. Made in a 500-litre clay amphora, it spent six months on its skins and a further six months in the amphora before bottling (Heron's Flight reports that terracotta, being porous, allows the wine to develop, without – unlike oak – imparting a direct flavour impact). Deep and bright in colour, it is powerful and sweet-fruited, with highly concentrated blackcurrant and plum flavours, buried tannins, and lovely ripeness, drive and harmony. Already delicious, it also should be long-lived.

DRY $120 AV

Hunter's The Chase
★★☆

The 2013 vintage (★★☆) of this Marlborough red was made from Merlot and matured for 18 months in seasoned French oak casks. Medium-bodied, with lightish, slightly developed colour, it's an easy-drinking wine with berryish, slightly herbal flavours, a hint of oak, and a rounded finish. Ready.

DRY $18 –V

Kaimira Estate Brightwater Hui Whero
(★★★☆)

Certified organic, the 2014 vintage (★★★☆) is a Nelson 'blend of classic varieties', matured in seasoned oak casks. Full and bright in colour, it is mouthfilling, fresh and supple, with youthful plum, spice and slight liquorice flavours, showing some savoury complexity. Best drinking mid-2017+.

DRY $28 –V

Karikari Estate Hell Hole (★★★)

Estate-grown in Northland, the 2014 vintage (★★★) is a blend of Syrah, Pinotage and Merlot. Fullish in colour, it is medium-bodied, with satisfying depth of ripe, berryish, spicy, slightly earthy flavours, and a firm finish. A good, honest red, it's drinking well now.

DRY $22 –V

Linden Estate Dam Block ★★★★

The 2014 vintage (★★★☆), estate-grown and hand-picked in the Esk Valley, is a blend of Merlot (67 per cent), Cabernet Sauvignon (23 per cent) and Cabernet Franc (10 per cent), matured for 10 months in French oak barriques. Full and slightly developed in colour, it's drinking well now, with generous plum, spice and nut flavours, showing good complexity, a slightly leafy streak, and a smooth finish.

DRY $35 –V

Man O' War Ironclad ★★★★☆

Launched from 2008, this powerful red, grown at the eastern end of Waiheke Island, is typically a blend of Cabernet Franc and Merlot, with minor portions of Cabernet Sauvignon, Petit Verdot and Malbec. From a very cool, late-ripening season, the 2012 vintage (★★★★☆), matured in French oak casks (40 per cent new), is deeply coloured, powerful, generous and sweet-fruited, with blackcurrant, herb and nut flavours, showing excellent concentration and potential. The 2011 (★★★★), from a wet growing season, is slightly leaner, but tight and elegant, with excellent depth.

Vintage	12	11
WR	5	4
Drink	16-25	16-23

DRY $50 –V

Man O' War Warspite ★★★★☆

The 2013 vintage (★★★★☆) is a classy, generous blend of Cabernet Franc (60 per cent), Merlot (30 per cent) and Malbec (10 per cent), grown on Ponui Island, near Waiheke Island. Hand-harvested at 24.1–26.5 brix and matured for two years in French oak casks (42 per cent new), it is a deeply coloured, robust red (15 per cent alcohol), fragrant, sweet-fruited and supple, with generous red-berry, plum, herb and nut flavours, good complexity and gentle tannins. Highly enjoyable now, it should be at its best 2018+. The 2014 vintage (★★★★) is also a Ponui Island blend of Cabernet Franc, Merlot and Malbec, matured in French oak casks (45 per cent new). Deeply c oloured, with slightly herbal aromas, it is a powerful, sturdy (15 per cent alcohol) red, with generous plum, spice and herb flavours, seasoned with nutty oak, good complexity and a well-rounded finish. Drink now or cellar.

Vintage	14
WR	5
Drink	16-20

DRY $46 –V

Marsden Bay of Islands Cavalli ★★★

The easy-drinking 2014 vintage (★★★) is a Northland blend of Pinotage, Chambourcin and Merlot. Matured for nine months in French oak casks (20 per cent new), it is full-coloured, mouthfilling and smooth, with ripe, berryish, plummy, gently spicy flavours, a touch of complexity and good depth.

Vintage	14
WR	6
Drink	P

DRY $25 –V

Messenger ★★★★★

After the lovely debut 2008 (★★★★★), Messenger is established as one of Auckland's greatest reds. It is estate-grown at Stillwater, north of the city. French oak-matured for two years, the 2013 vintage (★★★★☆) is a blend of Merlot, Cabernet Franc and Malbec. Dense and inky in colour, it's a robust (14.8 per cent alcohol), almost super-charged red, very sweet-fruited, with highly concentrated plum, spice and slight liquorice flavours. Notable for its power and richness, rather than finesse, it is full of personality.

DRY $85 AV

Mission Jewelstone Gimblett Gravels Antoine ★★★★☆

Named after pioneer winemaker Father Antoine Gavin, the 2014 vintage (★★★★★) is a dark, powerful blend of Merlot (70 per cent), Cabernet Sauvignon (25 per cent) and Cabernet Franc (5 per cent), grown in the Gimblett Gravels, Hawke's Bay, and matured for 20 months in French oak casks (55 per cent new). Still very youthful, it is a fresh, firmly structured red, with concentrated, ripe blackcurrant, plum and spice flavours, complex and savoury, and buried tannins. Best drinking 2020+.

Vintage	14	13
WR	7	6
Drink	17-30	16-25

DRY $50 –V

Mokoroa (★★★☆)

From Puriri Hills, the 2011 vintage (★★★☆) was matured for three years in French oak barrels. Estate-grown at Clevedon, in South Auckland, it is a blend of Merlot (65 per cent), Cabernet Sauvignon (23 per cent), Malbec (8 per cent) and Carménère (4 per cent). Fullish and slightly developed in colour, it is mouthfilling, fleshy and ripe, with moderately concentrated plum, spice and herb flavours, savoury and supple. Drink now onwards.

Vintage	11
WR	6
Drink	16-18

DRY $30 –V

Monk Road Red ★★☆

From Kaipara Estate, in Auckland, the 2013 vintage (★★☆) is a slightly rustic red with lightish, moderately developed colour. It has plummy, spicy, herbal flavours, fresh acidity, and a slight lack of ripeness and richness. The 2014 vintage (★★★) is pleasantly fruity, with mouthfilling body and plummy, spicy, smooth flavours. Drink now.

DRY $15 AV

Mudbrick Vineyard Velvet ★★★★★

The 2013 vintage (★★★★★) is a secret blend, for when 'it is important to make a good impression'. Estate-grown on Waiheke Island (in the Mudbrick and Shepherds Point vineyards), and matured in French oak casks (40 per cent new), it is deep and youthful in colour, with very ripe, blackcurrant-like aromas. Finely poised and highly concentrated, it has cassis, plum, spice and nut flavours, a hint of dark chocolate, impressive density and complexity, and firm but not grippy tannins. It should flourish for a decade.

Vintage	13
WR	7
Drink	16-25

DRY $140 –V

Newton Forrest Estate Cornerstone ★★★★★

Grown in the Cornerstone Vineyard, on the corner of Gimblett Road and State Highway 50 – where the first vines were planted in 1989 – this is a distinguished Hawke's Bay blend, matured in French (principally) and American oak barriques. The 2013 vintage (★★★★★) is a blend of Cabernet Sauvignon, Merlot and Malbec. Deep and youthful in colour, it has dense blackcurrant, plum, spice and nutty oak flavours, showing excellent ripeness and complexity, and fine-grained tannins. Already approachable, it should be at its best 2018+.

DRY $60 AV

Obsidian Reserve The Obsidian ★★★★★

The Obsidian Vineyard at Onetangi produces one of the most stylish Waiheke Island reds. Blended from classic Bordeaux red varieties – Cabernet Franc, Merlot, Cabernet Sauvignon, Petit Verdot and Malbec – it is matured in French oak barriques. The 2013 vintage (★★★★★) has deep, moderately youthful colour. Fleshy and generous, it has dense blackcurrant, herb, spice and nut flavours, savoury notes adding complexity, and good tannin backbone. Still unfolding, it's full of potential; open 2018+.

Vintage	13	12	11	10	09	08	07	06	05
WR	7	6	6	7	6	7	5	NM	7
Drink	16-23	16-20	16-18	16-20	16-18	16-20	16-19	NM	P

DRY $68 AV

Obsidian Waiheke Island Reserve The Mayor ★★★★☆

Delicious now, the 2012 vintage (★★★★☆) is a blend dominated by Cabernet Franc (36 per cent), Petit Verdot (32 per cent) and Malbec (24 per cent), with a splash of Merlot. Still youthful, it is a graceful, concentrated, supple red, with strong blackcurrant, plum and herb flavours, seasoned with nutty French oak, and gentle tannins. Drink now or cellar.

Vintage	12	11
WR	5	6
Drink	16-20	16-18

DRY $45 –V

Ohinemuri Kaipaki Reserve Taniwha (★★★)

The youthful 2014 vintage (★★★) was grown at Kaipaki, between Hamilton and Cambridge, in the Waikato. A blend of Cabernet Franc (55 per cent), Pinotage (27 per cent) and Merlot (18 per cent), oak-aged for a year, it is full-coloured, with a slightly leafy bouquet, mouthfilling body and strong red-berry, plum and herb flavours, fresh and firm.

Vintage	14
WR	6
Drink	16-20

DRY $30 –V

Paritua 21:12 ★★★★☆

The 2010 vintage (★★★★) is a blend of Cabernet Sauvignon, Merlot, Cabernet Franc and Malbec, estate-grown in Hawke's Bay and matured for 18 months in French oak casks (50 per cent new). Deep and fairly mature in colour, it has a slightly minty bouquet, leading into a full-bodied palate with generous blackcurrant, plum, spice and nut flavours, now softening. The 2013 vintage (★★★★★) is a very powerful (15 per cent alcohol) red, matured for 18 months in oak casks (60 per cent new). Densely coloured, it is purple-flushed, with fresh, concentrated, very ripe blackcurrant, plum, spice and coffee flavours, and fine-grained tannins. Still youthful, it should be at its best 2018+.

Vintage	13
WR	7
Drink	16-25

DRY $100 –V

Paritua Hawke's Bay Red ★★★★☆

The 2013 vintage (★★★★☆) is a blend of Merlot, Cabernet Sauvignon, Cabernet Franc and Malbec, matured for 14 months in French oak casks (50 per cent new). Dark and youthful in colour, it is powerful (14.5 per cent alcohol), with dense blackcurrant, plum and spice flavours, a hint of coffee, integrated oak, and finely balanced tannins. It should be long-lived; open 2017+.

Vintage	13
WR	7
Drink	16-25

DRY $40 –V

Paroa Bay Bay of Islands CMC ★★★★

The 2014 vintage (★★★☆) is a full-bodied, slightly earthy Northland blend of Cabernet Franc (72 per cent), Cabernet Sauvignon (23 per cent) and Malbec (5 per cent). It has generous red-berry, spice and oak flavours, showing some complexity and aging potential.

 DRY $45 –V

Pask Small Batch Gimblett Gravels Trilliant (★★★★)

The debut 2014 vintage (★★★★) is a Merlot-based blend, with smaller amounts of Cabernet Sauvignon and Malbec, matured for 20 months in French and American oak casks (55 per cent new). Deeply coloured, with a fragrant, spicy bouquet, it is mouthfilling, with generous, ripe, plummy, spicy flavours, showing good complexity, finely balanced tannins and lots of drink-young appeal. Best drinking 2018+.

Vintage	14
WR	6
Drink	17-22

 DRY $35 –V

Passage Rock Waiheke Island Magnus ★★★★★

The delicious 2013 vintage (★★★★★) is a blend of Syrah, Cabernet Sauvignon, Merlot, Malbec and Petit Verdot, grown on Waiheke Island. Deeply coloured, it is sturdy (14.5 per cent alcohol) and still youthful, with concentrated, vibrant plum, blackcurrant and spice flavours, fine-grained tannins, and excellent ripeness, complexity and harmony. Drink now or cellar.

 DRY $70 AV

Passage Rock Waiheke Island Sisters ★★★☆

The 2012 vintage (★★★☆) is a blend of Merlot (41 per cent), Cabernet Sauvignon (34 per cent), Syrah (19 per cent) and Malbec (6 per cent). Deeply coloured, it has strong blackcurrant, spice and herb flavours, and nutty oak adding complexity. It's drinking well now.

 DRY $25 –V

Peacock Sky Le Côté de la Colline ★★★

The 2013 vintage (★★★☆) is a firmly structured Waiheke Island blend of Cabernet Sauvignon (63 per cent), Cabernet Franc (26 per cent) and Malbec (11 per cent). It has strong, ripe blackcurrant, plum and spice flavours, with hints of herbs, and good cellaring potential.

 DRY $42 –V

Pukeora Estate Ruahine Range The Benches Red ★★★☆

Grown at altitude in Central Hawke's Bay, the 2010 vintage (★★★☆) is maturing well. A blend of Merlot (45 per cent), Malbec (34 per cent), Cabernet Sauvignon (16 per cent) and Syrah (5 per cent), matured for 20 months in French and American oak barriques (22 per cent new), it is still fairly youthful in colour, with lively blackcurrant, plum and spice flavours and a perfumed, sweet oak influence. It reminded me of a decent Rioja.

Vintage	10	09
WR	5	6
Drink	16-20	P

DRY $25 –V

Puriri Hills Estate   ★★★★☆

Estate-grown at Clevedon, in South Auckland, this is a stylish, Merlot-based blend. The 2008 vintage (★★★★☆), made from Merlot (53 per cent), Cabernet Sauvignon (25 per cent), Malbec (16 per cent) and Carménère (6 per cent), was matured for two years in French oak barriques (40 per cent new). Deeply coloured, it is full-bodied, with a spicy bouquet and an array of blackcurrant, plum, herb, spice and nut flavours, showing excellent depth and complexity. The 2009 vintage (★★★★) is drinking well now – fragrant, nutty and savoury. The 2010 vintage (★★★★★) is a beauty – dark, fleshy and silky, with lovely ripeness and mouthfeel. (Opened in July 2016, the 2006 vintage was still offering a lot of pleasure; it's a generous, complex, harmonious red, probably at its peak.)

Vintage	10	09	08	07	06	05
WR	7	6	7	6	4	7
Drink	16-27	16-22	16-25	16-20	P	16-20

DRY $40 –V

Puriri Hills Pope   (★★★★★)

Named after Ivan Pope, who planted and tended the vines at this Clevedon, South Auckland vineyard. The 2008 vintage (★★★★★), made from Cabernet Franc (52 per cent), Merlot (32 per cent) and Carménère (16 per cent), was matured for two years in French oak barriques (80 per cent new). Deeply coloured, it is mouthfilling and supple, with substantial body and deep, lush blackcurrant, herb, spice and nut flavours, framed by fine, silky tannins. Showing lovely richness and texture, it's a drink-now or cellaring proposition. The 2010 vintage (★★★★★), a blend of Merlot (54 per cent), Cabernet Franc (25 per cent), Carménère (17 per cent) and Malbec (4 per cent), was matured for nearly two years in French oak casks (75 per cent new). Outstandingly lush and complex, with ripe, supple tannins and very deep plum, spice, herb and slight liquorice flavours, it shows great potential. (Retasted in 2015, it is still unfolding and not likely to peak until around 2020.)

DRY $120 –V

Puriri Hills Reserve   ★★★★★

A regional classic. Grown at Clevedon, in South Auckland, the 2008 vintage (★★★★★) is a deeply coloured blend of Merlot (51 per cent), Cabernet Franc (20 per cent), Carménère (13 per cent), Cabernet Sauvignon (9 per cent) and Malbec (7 per cent), matured for two years in French oak barriques (60 per cent new). Invitingly fragrant, with strong, beautifully ripe blackcurrant, plum, herb and spice flavours, seasoned with nutty oak, it is a complex wine with a seductively silky texture, flourishing with bottle-age. The 2009 (★★★★☆) is a relatively forward vintage, generous, savoury and harmonious. The 2010 (★★★★★) is outstanding – richly fragrant, ripe, densely packed, supple and very 'complete'.

Vintage	10	09	08	07	06	05	04
WR	7	6	7	NM	6	7	7
Drink	16-27	16-23	16-25	NM	16-20	16-20	16-20

DRY $70 AV

Ransom Dark Summit   ★★★★

The 2011 vintage (★★★★), grown at Mahurangi, north of Auckland, is a blend of Cabernet Sauvignon (47 per cent), Cabernet Franc and Malbec. Deep and still youthful in colour, it has a fragrant, spicy, slightly toasty bouquet. Mouthfilling, it is savoury and firmly structured, with plum, herb and nut flavours, showing very good complexity and depth. Drink now or cellar.

 DRY $35 –V

Ransom Mahurangi   ★★★☆

The full-coloured 2013 vintage (★★★☆), estate-grown north of Auckland, was blended mostly from Syrah, with smaller portions of Cabernet Sauvignon and Cabernet Franc. Barrel-aged for 20 months, it is medium-bodied, with fresh, spicy aromas and flavours, hints of plums and herbs, some savoury complexity, gentle tannins and good harmony. Drink now or cellar.

 DRY $27 –V

Runner Duck Black Velvet   (★★★★)

The 2010 vintage (★★★★), grown at Matakana, was blended mostly from Cabernet Franc, with smaller amounts of Merlot, Malbec and Petit Verdot. Full and still youthful in colour, it is medium to full-bodied, with plummy, berryish, savoury, slightly earthy flavours, showing good complexity, and a firm finish.

 DRY $40 –V

Runner Duck Passion   (★★★★)

The 2013 vintage (★★★★), grown at Matakana, was made solely from Syrah. Full and bright in colour, it is floral and supple, with vibrant plum and spice flavours, showing excellent depth, savoury notes adding complexity, and good potential. Best drinking 2017+.

 DRY $40 –V

Runner Duck The Knight   (★★★☆)

The 2011 vintage (★★★☆), grown at Matakana, is a blend of Cabernet Franc (principally), Merlot and Malbec. Drinking well now, it is fullish in colour, with moderately concentrated, berryish, spicy flavours, showing some savoury complexity, and supple tannins.

 DRY $32 –V

Sacred Hill Brokenstone   ★★★★★

Merlot-based, this is a typically outstanding Hawke's Bay red from the Gimblett Gravels (principally the company's Deerstalkers Vineyard). The powerful 2014 vintage (★★★★★), matured for 16 months in French oak casks (33 per cent new), is Merlot-dominant (83 per cent), with smaller portions of Malbec (8 per cent), Syrah (5 per cent), Cabernet Sauvignon (3 per cent) and Cabernet Franc (1 per cent). Boldly coloured, it is very generous, with rich, ripe plum and blackcurrant flavours, a hint of dark chocolate, good complexity, and the underlying structure to mature well. Still youthful, it's well worth cellaring to 2020+.

Vintage	14	13	12	11	10	09	08	07
WR	7	7	NM	6	7	7	6	7
Drink	17-26	16-23	NM	16-18	16-20	16-18	P	P

 DRY $50 AV

Sacred Hill Helmsman ★★★★★

This is a classy, single-vineyard Gimblett Gravels red from Hawke's Bay. The 2014 vintage (★★★★☆), blended from Cabernet Sauvignon (54 per cent), Merlot (42 per cent) and Cabernet Franc (4 per cent), was hand-picked and matured for 18 months in French oak barriques (50 per cent new). Deep and youthful in colour, it is fragrant and supple, with concentrated plum, spice and herb flavours, in a very elegant style, finely poised and persistent.

Vintage	14	13	12	11	10	09
WR	7	7	NM	6	7	7
Drink	18-29	16-28	NM	16-24	16-25	16-20

DRY $85 AV

🍷🍷

Sculptureum The Rodin Blend (★★★★☆)

The 2013 vintage (★★★★☆) is a classy Matakana red, blended from Cabernet Franc (60 per cent), Merlot (35 per cent) and Carménère (5 per cent), matured in French oak casks (50 per cent new). Full-coloured, it is savoury and earthy, with distinct overtones of Bordeaux. Sweet-fruited, with excellent concentration and complexity, it's already delicious.

DRY $30 AV

Sileni Estate Selection Hawke's Bay Ruber (★★★★☆)

The debut 2014 vintage (★★★★☆) is a classy blend of Cabernet Franc, Merlot and Syrah, grown in the Bridge Pa Triangle. It was matured for 14 months in French oak barriques (40 per cent new), then aged for a further five months in one-year-old barrels. Full-coloured, it has fragrant red-berry and spice aromas, leading into a mouthfilling, still very youthful wine, with generous berry, plum and spice flavours, complex, savoury and finely structured. Best drinking 2018+.

Vintage	14
WR	7
Drink	16-24

DRY $33 AV

Soho Blue Blood Zabeel Reserve (★★★★☆)

The debut 2013 vintage (★★★★☆) is a Waiheke Island blend of Merlot, Syrah and Malbec, estate-grown at Onetangi and matured in French oak casks (80 per cent new). Deep and youthful in colour, it is full-bodied and vibrantly fruity, with concentrated plum, red-berry and spice flavours, showing excellent vigour and complexity. Best drinking 2017+.

Vintage	13
WR	5
Drink	16-26

DRY $138 –V

Soho Revolver ★★★★☆

Estate-grown at Onetangi, on Waiheke Island, the 2014 vintage (★★★★) is a blend of Merlot, Cabernet Franc and Malbec, barrel-aged in new and one-year-old French oak. Deep and youthful in colour, it is mouthfilling and supple, with rich plum, herb and spice flavours, showing good complexity, and a smooth, finely textured finish. Drink now or cellar.

Vintage	14	13	12	11	10	09
WR	5	7	6	NM	7	7
Drink	16-22	16-20	16-18	NM	16-18	P

DRY $37 AV

St Nesbit   ★★★★☆

This South Auckland red is estate-grown at Karaka, on a southern arm of the Manukau Harbour. It enjoyed a high profile for its Bordeaux-style reds from 1984 to 1991, but following replanting, production ceased for a decade. I tasted the 2007, 2008 and 2009 vintages in mid-2015. The 2009 (★★★★) is a blend of Merlot (70 per cent), Cabernet Franc (20 per cent) and Petit Verdot (10 per cent), matured in French and American oak casks. An elegant rather than powerful red, it has considerable maturity, with a savoury, leathery, nutty complexity, a hint of herbs, and lots of current-drinking appeal. Still unfolding, the powerful 2008 (★★★★★) is dark, sturdy, fleshy and rich, with concentrated plum, blackcurrant, spice and nut flavours, a hint of dark chocolate, and obvious potential. My pick is the seductive 2007 (★★★★★), a very fragrant, complex red with rich blackcurrant, plum, spice and herb flavours, supple, generous and lingering. Savoury and silky, it's lovely now. (I tasted the debut 1984 and 1987 vintages in 2015. Medium-bodied, with slightly leafy, nutty, complex flavours, both were very mellow, but still alive and offering pleasure.)

 DRY $75 –V

Stone Paddock Hawke's Bay Scarlet   ★★★★

From Paritua, the 2013 vintage (★★★★) is a blend of Merlot, Cabernet Franc and Cabernet Sauvignon, matured for a year in seasoned oak barrels. Deep and youthful in colour, it is an age-worthy, full-bodied, generous red, with strong, ripe plum, spice and blackcurrant flavours, showing some nutty complexity. Drink now or cellar.

Vintage	13
WR	7
Drink	16-20

 DRY $25 AV

Stonyridge Larose   ★★★★★

Typically a stunning Waiheke Island wine. Dark and seductively perfumed, with smashing fruit flavours, at its best it is a magnificently concentrated red that matures superbly for a decade or longer, acquiring great complexity. The vines – Cabernet Sauvignon, Merlot, Cabernet Franc, Malbec and Petit Verdot – are grown in free-draining clay soils on a north-facing slope, a kilometre from the sea at Onetangi, and are very low-yielding (4 tonnes/hectare). The wine is matured for a year in French (80–90 per cent) and American oak barriques (half new, half one-year-old), and is sold largely on an 'en primeur' basis, whereby the customers, in return for paying for their wine about nine months in advance of its delivery, secure a substantial price reduction. The 2015 vintage (★★★★★) is a classic young claret-style red, dense but not tough, with power through the palate and obvious potential. Dark and purple-flushed, it is sturdy, rich and supple, with very ripe blackcurrant, plum and spice flavours, showing lovely freshness, harmony and length. Needing five years to unfold, it should mature gracefully for decades.

Vintage	13	12	11	10	09	08	07	06	05
WR	7	6	5	7	6	7	5	7	7
Drink	23-33	18-25	16-23	20-30	18-25	18-28	16-20	16-17	16-22

DRY $280 –V

Tantalus Waiheke Island Ecluse Reserve   (★★★)

The 2014 vintage (★★★), blended from Cabernet Sauvignon, Merlot, Cabernet Franc and Malbec, was grown at Onetangi and matured for 11 months in French oak barriques. Full and moderately youthful in colour, with an earthy bouquet, it is a mouthfilling red, revealing a slight lack of delicacy and finesse, but also good depth of blackcurrant and spice flavours, showing considerable complexity.

Vintage	14
WR	6
Drink	16-26

DRY $65 –V

Tantalus Waiheke Island Evoque Reserve   (★★★★☆)

The youthful 2014 vintage (★★★★☆), grown at Onetangi, is a blend of Merlot, Malbec, Cabernet Sauvignon and Cabernet Franc, matured for 11 months in French oak barriques. Deeply coloured, it is mouthfilling and sweet-fruited, with generous, plummy, gently spicy flavours, finely integrated oak, slightly earthy and savoury notes adding complexity, and a well-structured finish. Showing good potential, it should be at its best 2018+.

Vintage	14
WR	6
Drink	16-26

DRY $60 –V

Taraire Block Northland Summer   (★★)

'Produced in a Beaujolais style', the 2015 vintage (★★) is a Northland red, made from French hybrid Seibel grapes. Light ruby, it is a simple, berryish, slightly spicy red, light-bodied, offering fresh, easy drinking. (From Ivana Estate.)

DRY $21 –V

Te Mata Coleraine   ★★★★★

Breed, rather than brute power, is the hallmark of Coleraine (correctly pronounced Cole-raine rather than Coler-aine), which since its first vintage in 1982 has carved out an illustrious reputation among New Zealand's claret-style reds. In all vintages since 2007, Cabernet Sauvignon has been the predominant variety. At its best, it is a magical Hawke's Bay wine, with a depth, complexity and subtlety on the level of a top-class Bordeaux. The grapes are grown in the Havelock North hills, in the company's warm, north-facing Buck and 1892 vineyards, and the wine is matured for 17 to 20 months in French oak barriques, predominantly new. From a notably warm, early-ripening season, the striking 2014 vintage (★★★★★) is a blend of Cabernet Sauvignon (60 per cent), Merlot (28 per cent) and Cabernet Franc (12 per cent). (Malbec is definitely not in the recipe.) Dark and powerful, but not heavy (13.5 per cent alcohol), it has dense, ripe flavours of blackcurrants, plums, spices and dark chocolate, great complexity, and a firm foundation of tannin. Already highly expressive, it should flourish for at least a decade; best drinking 2020+. (Note: between the 2009 and 2014 vintages, the price has climbed from $75 to $110.)

Vintage	14	13	12	11	10	09	08	07	06	05
WR	7	7	NM	7	7	7	7	7	7	7
Drink	18-28	16-33	NM	17-23	16-22	16-21	16-20	16-27	16-26	16-25

DRY $110 AV

Te Motu ★★★★☆

This Waiheke Island red is grown at Onetangi, over the fence from Stonyridge. Compared to its neighbour, it has typically been less opulent than Larose, in a more earthy, slightly leafy style. Cabernet Sauvignon-predominant, the 2008 vintage (★★★★☆) has dark, mature colour. Rich and savoury, it has blackcurrant, herb and nut flavours, showing excellent depth and complexity. Ready.

 DRY $90 –V

Te Motu Kokoro ★★★★☆

Launched from 2012 (★★★★☆), this red is a major change in style for the long-established Waiheke Island producer – it's a lot more vibrant and youthful than past releases. Grown at Onetangi, the 2013 vintage (★★★★☆) was blended from Merlot (principally), with smaller amounts of Cabernet Sauvignon, Cabernet Franc, Malbec and Syrah. Dark and mouthfilling, it has fresh blackcurrant/plum flavours, ripe and generous, savoury notes adding complexity, good tannin backbone, and obvious potential.

 DRY $75 –V

Te Motu Tipua ★★★★★

'Within any vintage, there is always a varietal that transcends', according to the back label on this Waiheke Island red. The 2008 (★★★★★) was a powerful Syrah, but the 2013 vintage (★★★★★) is one of New Zealand's best-yet Cabernet Francs. Grown at Onetangi and matured for 20 months in French oak casks (30 per cent new), it has fragrant red-berry and spice aromas. A lovely, mouthfilling, silky-textured red, it is sweet-fruited, with youthful, ripe berry, spice and nut flavours, oak complexity, and excellent depth and harmony. Best drinking 2018+.

 DRY $115 AV

Te Whau The Point ★★★★★

This classy Waiheke Island red flows from a steeply sloping vineyard at Putiki Bay. The outstanding 2014 vintage (★★★★★) was blended from Cabernet Sauvignon (50 per cent), Merlot (31 per cent), Cabernet Franc (12 per cent), Malbec (5 per cent) and Petit Verdot (2 per cent), matured in French oak casks for 18 months. Deeply coloured and ripely fragrant, it is a powerful, weighty red, dense and savoury, with concentrated blackcurrant, plum and spice flavours, seasoned with nutty oak, and good tannin backbone. A top vintage that reminded me of a fine Pauillac, it should be long-lived, but is already a delicious mouthful.

Vintage	14	13	12	11	10	09	08	07	06	05	DRY $75 AV
WR	7	7	6	NM	7	7	7	7	6	7	
Drink	18-26	17-25	16-20	NM	16-25	16-18	16-22	16-24	P	16-20	

TerraVin J ★★★★☆

Can Marlborough produce a classy, Bordeaux-style red? The 2011 vintage (★★★★☆) was blended from Merlot, Malbec and Cabernet Sauvignon, matured in French oak barriques (50 per cent new), and bottled unfined and unfiltered. Sturdy and concentrated, with deep colour, it has strong blackcurrant, plum, spice and nut flavours, ripe and savoury, with good cellaring potential.

Vintage	11
WR	6
Drink	16-18

 DRY $60 –V

Trinity Hill Gimblett Gravels The Gimblett ★★★★★

Still very youthful, the 2014 vintage (★★★★★) is a concentrated, deliciously ripe and supple Hawke's Bay blend of Cabernet Franc (49 per cent), Cabernet Sauvignon (39 per cent), Merlot (9 per cent) and Malbec (3 per cent), matured for 16 months in French oak casks (35 per cent new). Dark and fragrant, it is full-bodied, with strong, vibrant blackcurrant/plum flavours, hints of dark chocolate and herbs, well-integrated oak and gentle tannins. Best drinking 2018+.

Vintage	14	13	12	11	10	09	08	07	06	05
WR	6	7	4	5	6	7	5	6	6	6
Drink	17-25	16-25	16-25	16-25	16-20	16-30	16-20	16-22	16-18	P

 DRY $35 V+

Trinity Hill Hawke's Bay The Trinity ★★★☆

The 2014 vintage (★★★☆) is a blend of Merlot (55 per cent), Tempranillo (17 per cent), 'Cabernets' (13 per cent), Malbec (8 per cent), and Syrah (7 per cent). Designed for early consumption, it is full-coloured, with generous, ripe berry and plum flavours, fresh and smooth, in a very fruit-driven style.

Vintage	14	13	12
WR	6	6	4
Drink	16-18	16-18	P

DRY $22 AV

Villa Maria Ngakirikiri The Gravels (★★★★★)

The debut 2013 vintage (★★★★★) is promoted as the company's 'icon' Bordeaux-style red. From vines planted in the Gimblett Gravels between 1998 and 2000, it is Cabernet Sauvignon-based (97 per cent), with a splash of Merlot (3 per cent). Matured for 18 months in French oak barrels (52 per cent new), it is densely coloured, with substantial body (14 per cent alcohol) and bold, still extremely youthful, blackcurrant and plum-evoking flavours, showing lovely richness, purity and complexity. It should flourish for decades; open 2020 onwards.

DRY $130 AV

Waitapu Estate Reef View La Dolce Vita (★★☆)

Made to be served 'well chilled, as you would a beer', the 2014 vintage (★★☆) is an estate-grown Northland blend of Pinotage and Tempranillo. Full-coloured, with a fresh, ripe, spicy bouquet, it is buoyantly fruity, with strong, plummy, spicy flavours, hints of prunes and liquorice, and a sweetish finish. For fans of sweet reds.

MED $25 –V

Cabernet Franc

New Zealand's sixth most widely planted red-wine variety, Cabernet Franc is probably a mutation of Cabernet Sauvignon, the much higher-profile variety with which it is so often blended. Jancis Robinson's phrase, 'a sort of claret Beaujolais', aptly sums up the nature of this versatile and underrated red-wine grape.

As a minority ingredient in the recipe of many of New Zealand's top reds, Cabernet Franc lends a delicious softness and concentrated fruitiness to its blends with Cabernet Sauvignon and Merlot. However, admirers of Château Cheval Blanc, the illustrious St Émilion (which is two-thirds planted in Cabernet Franc), have long appreciated that Cabernet Franc need not always be Cabernet Sauvignon's bridesmaid, but can yield fine red wines in its own right. The supple, fruity wines of Chinon and Bourgueil, in the Loire Valley, have also proved Cabernet Franc's ability to produce highly attractive, soft light reds.

According to the latest national vineyard survey, the bearing area of Cabernet Franc will be 108 hectares in 2017 – well below the 213 hectares in 2004. Over 70 per cent of the vines are clustered in Hawke's Bay and most of the rest are in Auckland. As a varietal red, Cabernet Franc is lower in tannin and acid than Cabernet Sauvignon; or as Michael Brajkovich, of Kumeu River, has put it: 'more approachable and easy'.

Boneline, The, Waipara Cabernet Franc (★★★☆)

From 'some of the oldest and most southerly Cabernet Franc vines in New Zealand', the graceful 2014 vintage (★★★☆) was harvested in early May at 24.5 brix and barrel-matured. Bright ruby, it is fresh, sweet-fruited and supple, with a hint of herbs, slightly nutty notes adding complexity, and drink-young appeal.

DRY $30 –V

Clearview Reserve Hawke's Bay Cabernet Franc ★★★★★

From vines nearly 30 years old, the 2013 vintage (★★★★☆) was estate-grown at Te Awanga, blended with a touch of Malbec, and barrel-aged for a year. It is dark and full-bodied, with rich blackcurrant, plum, spice and herb flavours, fresh acidity, toasty oak adding complexity and a good backbone of tannin. Best drinking 2017+.

DRY $49 AV

Crossroads Winemakers Collection Hawke's Bay Cabernet Franc ★★★★

The full-coloured 2013 vintage (★★★★) was estate-grown in Mere Road, in the Gimblett Gravels, and matured for 18 months in French oak barriques (42 per cent new). Fleshy, floral and supple, it's a mouthfilling red with vibrant, ripe blackcurrant, plum, spice and herb flavours, showing very good depth, and a finely textured, smooth finish. Retasted in early 2016, it's developing well. Drink now or cellar.

Vintage	13	12
WR	7	5
Drink	16-23	16-23

DRY $40 –V

Hawks Nest Back Paddock Cabernet Franc   (★★★)

Grown at Matakana, the 2013 vintage (★★★) was matured in French oak casks (partly new). Fullish in colour, it is mouthfilling, with good depth of berryish, spicy, slightly herbal flavours, showing some savoury complexity.

Vintage	13	DRY $20 –V
WR	6	
Drink	16-20	

Kaipara Estate Cabernet Franc/Malbec   (★★★☆)

The 2013 vintage (★★★☆) is an age-worthy Auckland red. Full and youthful in colour, it is mouthfilling, with very good depth of plum, spice and slight tamarillo flavours, showing considerable complexity, and firm tannins.

DRY $25 –V

Mills Reef Elspeth Gimblett Gravels Hawke's Bay Cabernet Franc   (★★★★)

Well worth cellaring, the 2013 vintage (★★★★) is a powerful, fragrant red with fresh, strong plum, red-berry and spice flavours, finely structured and youthful. Open 2017+.

DRY $49 –V

Mission Hawke's Bay Reserve Cabernet Franc   (★★★★)

The elegant, youthful, savoury 2013 vintage (★★★★) was grown in the Bridge Pa Triangle and matured for 15 months in French oak barrels (30 per cent new). It has full but not dense colour, with substantial body (14.5 per cent alcohol), ripe plum and spice flavours, showing good complexity, and a persistent, well-structured finish.

Vintage	13	DRY $25 AV
WR	6	
Drink	16-25	

Omaha Bay Vineyard Matakana Cabernet Franc/Malbec/Petit Verdot   (★★★★☆)

The 2010 vintage (★★★★☆) is a blend of Cabernet Franc (65 per cent), Malbec (25 per cent) and Petit Verdot (10 per cent), matured for 15 months in French oak casks (40 per cent new). Deeply coloured, it is sturdy, with concentrated, ripe plum and spice flavours, a hint of liquorice, and very good complexity. A generous, savoury red, it's probably at its peak now.

DRY $45 –V

Peacock Sky Waiheke Island Pure Franc   (★★★☆)

Fullish in colour, the 2014 vintage (★★★☆) is a fresh, smooth wine, like a very light Bordeaux, with youthful berry, plum, spice and herb flavours, savoury notes adding complexity, and some elegance.

DRY $40 –V

Pyramid Valley Vineyards Growers Collection
Howell Family Vineyard Hawke's Bay Cabernet Franc   ★★★★

The 2013 vintage (★★★★) was hand-picked in the Bridge Pa Triangle and matured for 15 months in seasoned French oak barrels. Deep and fairly youthful in colour, it is mouthfilling and sweet-fruited, with good concentration of fresh, vibrant blackcurrant, plum and spice flavours. Best drinking 2017+.

DRY $52 –V

Sileni Cellar Selection Hawke's Bay Cabernet Franc   ★★★

The clearly varietal 2014 vintage (★★★☆) was matured for nine months in French and American oak casks (20 per cent new). Full and youthful in colour, with fresh spice and herb aromas, it is mouthfilling (14.5 per cent alcohol), with vibrant plum, herb and spice flavours, gentle tannins and a very smooth finish. Good drinking now to 2017.

Vintage	14	13
WR	7	6
Drink	16-22	16-19

DRY $24 AV

Sileni Estate Selection Pacemaker Hawke's Bay Cabernet Franc   ★★★★

Grown in the Bridge Pa Triangle, the 2014 vintage (★★★★) was matured for 14 months in a 2:1 mix of French and American oak barriques (30 per cent new). Full-coloured, it is mouthfilling (14.5 per cent alcohol) and smooth, with fresh, generous red-berry, plum and slight herb flavours, oak-derived complexity and a finely balanced finish. Drink now or cellar.

Vintage	14
WR	7
Drink	16-24

DRY $37 –V

Thomas Cabernet Franc/Merlot   (★★★★☆)

The stylish 2013 vintage (★★★★☆) is a blend of Cabernet Franc (52 per cent), Merlot (34 per cent) and Cabernet Sauvignon (14 per cent), hand-picked at Onetangi, on Waiheke Island. Fermented with indigenous yeasts, it was matured for 18 months in French oak barriques (17 per cent new), and bottled unfined and unfiltered. Full-coloured and fragrant, it is a savoury, very elegant rather than powerful red, with fresh, ripe plum and spice flavours, gentle tannins, and excellent depth and complexity. Drinking well now, it should be at its best 2018+. (From Batch Winery.)

DRY $45 –V

Cabernet Sauvignon and Cabernet-predominant blends

Cabernet Sauvignon has proved a tough nut to crack in New Zealand. Mid-priced models were – until recently – usually of lower quality than a comparable offering from Australia, where the relative warmth suits the late-ripening Cabernet Sauvignon variety. Yet a top New Zealand Cabernet-based red from a favourable vintage can hold its own in illustrious company and the overall standard of today's middle-tier, $20 bottlings is far higher than many wine lovers realise – which makes for some great bargains.

Cabernet Sauvignon was widely planted here in the nineteenth century. The modern resurgence of interest in the great Bordeaux variety was led by Tom McDonald, the legendary Hawke's Bay winemaker, whose string of elegant (though, by today's standards, light) Cabernet Sauvignons under the McWilliam's label, from the much-acclaimed 1965 vintage to the gold medal-winning 1975, proved beyond all doubt that fine-quality red wines could be produced in New Zealand.

During the 1970s and 1980s, Cabernet Sauvignon ruled the red-wine roost in New Zealand. Since then, as winemakers – especially in the South Island, but also Hawke's Bay – searched for red-wine varieties that would ripen more fully and consistently in our relatively cool grape-growing climate than Cabernet Sauvignon, it has been pushed out of the limelight by Merlot, Pinot Noir and Syrah. Between 2003 and 2017, the country's total area of bearing Cabernet Sauvignon vines will contract from 741 to 280 hectares. Growers with suitably warm sites have often retained faith in Cabernet Sauvignon, but others have moved on to less challenging varieties.

Over 85 per cent of the country's Cabernet Sauvignon vines are clustered in Hawke's Bay, and Auckland also has significant plantings. In the South Island, Cabernet-based reds have typically lacked warmth and richness. This magnificent but late-ripening variety's future in New Zealand clearly lies in the warmer vineyard sites of the north.

What is the flavour of Cabernet Sauvignon? When newly fermented a herbal character is common, intertwined with blackcurrant-like fruit aromas. New oak flavours, firm acidity and taut tannins are other hallmarks of young, fine Cabernet Sauvignon. With maturity the flavour loses its aggression and the wine develops roundness and complexity, with assorted cigar-box, minty and floral scents emerging. It is unwise to broach a Cabernet Sauvignon-based red with any pretensions to quality at less than three years old; at about five years old the rewards of cellaring really start to flow.

Awaroa Cabernet/Merlot/Malbec ★★★★

Already drinking well, but also worth cellaring, the 2014 vintage (★★★★) was hand-picked on Waiheke Island and matured for a year in seasoned French oak barriques. The bouquet is fresh and fragrant; the palate is mouthfilling, with generous, ripe, plummy, spicy flavours, showing good density and complexity.

Vintage	14
WR	6
Drink	18-25

DRY $38 –V

Awaroa Requiem Waiheke Island Cabernet/Merlot/Malbec ★★★★

The fragrant, dark, youthful 2014 vintage (★★★★★) is a classy blend of Cabernet Sauvignon (70 per cent), Merlot (20 per cent) and Malbec (10 per cent), estate-grown, hand-picked and matured in French oak barriques (50 per cent new). Fragrant and sweet-fruited, it has generous, ripe blackcurrant, plum and spice flavours, supple tannins and obvious potential. Rich and finely textured, it's instantly appealing.

Vintage	14
WR	7
Drink	20-25

DRY $65 –V

Babich Irongate Gimblett Gravels Hawke's Bay Cabernet/Merlot/Franc ★★★★★

Grown in the Irongate Vineyard and matured in French oak barriques (typically 35 per cent new), this elegant, complex, firmly structured red is designed for cellaring and is typically a very stylish wine in the classic Bordeaux mould. The 2014 vintage (★★★★☆) is a blend of Cabernet Sauvignon (58 per cent), Merlot (29 per cent) and Cabernet Franc (13 per cent). Full-bodied, it is generous, firm and concentrated, with youthful blackcurrant, plum and spice flavours, savoury and complex, finely integrated oak and obvious potential; best drinking 2018+.

Vintage	14	13	12	11	10	09	08
WR	7	7	5	4	7	7	5
Drink	16-25	16-25	16-22	16-20	16-22	16-21	16-17

DRY $37 V+

Babich The Patriarch – see the Branded and Other Red Wines section

Beach House Hawke's Bay Gimblett Gravels Cabernet/Malbec (★★★★)

The 2013 vintage (★★★★) is a single-vineyard red, blended from Cabernet Sauvignon (60 per cent), Malbec (35 per cent) and Cabernet Franc (5 per cent). The colour is deep and purple-flushed; the palate is mouthfilling, with fresh, bold blackcurrant, plum and spice flavours, gently seasoned with oak, and a smooth finish.

DRY $25 AV

Brookfields Ohiti Estate Cabernet Sauvignon ★★★☆

Hawke's Bay winemaker Peter Robertson believes the warm, shingly Ohiti Estate, inland from Fernhill, produces 'sound Cabernet Sauvignon year after year – which is a major challenge to any vineyard'. The easy-drinking 2015 vintage (★★★☆) was matured in seasoned French and American oak casks. Full-coloured, it is mouthfilling, with generous berry, plum and spice flavours, tinged with sweet oak, and a smooth finish. Best drinking mid-2017+.

Vintage	15
WR	7
Drink	18-22

DRY $20 AV

Brookfields Reserve Vintage Cabernet/Merlot ★★★★★

Brookfields' top red is one of the most powerful, long-lived reds in Hawke's Bay. At its best, it is a thrilling wine – robust, tannin-laden and overflowing with very rich cassis, plum and mint flavours. The grapes are sourced from the Lyons family's sloping, north-facing vineyard at Bridge

Pa, and the wine is matured a year in new French oak barriques. The 2014 vintage (★★★★★) is dark, powerful and sturdy (14.5 per cent alcohol), with deep blackcurrant, plum, spice and nut flavours, and firm but not grippy tannins. Still a baby, it's built to last and should flourish for a decade. The 2015 vintage (★★★★☆) is deeply coloured, fragrant and rich, with mouthfilling body, concentrated blackcurrant, plum, spice and nut flavours, oak complexity and fine-grained tannins. Still very youthful, it should be at its best 2019+.

Vintage	15	14	13	12	11	10	09	08	07	06
WR	7	7	7	NM	NM	NM	7	NM	7	7
Drink	20-26	19-25	18-25	NM	NM	NM	16-20	NM	16-19	P

DRY $60 AV

Church Road Cabernet/Merlot – see Church Road Merlot/Cabernet/Malbec

Church Road Grand Reserve Hawke's Bay Cabernet Sauvignon/Merlot   (★★★★★)

Still very youthful, the 2013 vintage (★★★★★) is a powerful, concentrated blend of Cabernet Sauvignon (56 per cent) and Merlot (44 per cent), estate-grown in Redstone Vineyard, in the Bridge Pa Triangle, French oak-aged for 18 months, and bottled unfined and unfiltered. Bold and youthful in colour, it is sturdy (14.5 per cent alcohol), with dense, ripe blackcurrant, plum and spice flavours, a hint of minty, oak complexity and firm tannins. A very age-worthy wine, it should be at its best 2018+.

DRY $45 AV

Church Road McDonald Series Hawke's Bay Cabernet Sauvignon   ★★★★★

This consistently impressive red is grown principally in the company's Redstone Vineyard, in the Bridge Pa Triangle, and matured in French and Hungarian oak barrels (30–35 per cent new). Lovely young, the deeply coloured 2014 vintage (★★★★★) was bottled unfined and unfiltered. It is sturdy (14.5 per cent alcohol), with vibrant, pure blackcurrant, plum and spice flavours, showing excellent ripeness and concentration, a seasoning of nutty oak, fine-grained tannins and obvious potential. A top buy.

DRY $27 V+

Church Road Tom Cabernet Sauvignon/Merlot   ★★★★★

Pernod Ricard NZ's top Hawke's Bay claret-style red honours pioneer winemaker Tom McDonald, the driving force behind New Zealand's first prestige red, McWilliam's Cabernet Sauvignon. The early vintages in the mid-1990s were Cabernet Sauvignon-predominant, but since 1998 Merlot has emerged as an equally crucial part of the recipe. Made at the Church Road winery, it is typically not a blockbuster but a wine of great finesse; it is savoury, complex and more akin to a quality Bordeaux than other New World reds. Released in 2016, the 2013 vintage (★★★★★) is a densely coloured, 2:1 blend of Cabernet Sauvignon (estate-grown in the Redstone Vineyard, in the Bridge Pa Triangle) and Merlot (grown in the Gimblett Gravels). Harvested at over 24 brix and matured for 22 months in French oak barriques (92 per cent new), it conveys a sense of subtle power. Dark and weighty, it is graceful, with lovely depth of rich, youthful blackcurrant, plum and spice flavours, and a silky-textured, lasting finish. Already delicious, it's well worth cellaring to 2020+. (The 2014 vintage will be Merlot-predominant.)

Vintage	13	12	11	10	09	08	07	06	05
WR	7	NM	NM	NM	7	NM	7	NM	7
Drink	20-29	NM	NM	NM	16-25	NM	16-22	NM	16-20

DRY $200 –V

Collaboration Argent Cabernet Sauvignon   ★★★★☆

The distinctive, skilfully crafted 2013 vintage (★★★★★) is the finest yet. Hand-harvested at 'select vineyard sites' in Hawke's Bay and matured in French oak barrels (25 per cent new), it is deeply coloured, with a ripely fragrant bouquet. A refined, mouthfilling, generous red, it is a pure expression of Cabernet Sauvignon, with strong, vibrant blackcurrant, plum and spice flavours, fine-grained tannins, and excellent length. Best drinking now to 2020.

DRY $40 –V

Coopers Creek Reserve Hawke's Bay Cabernet Sauvignon   (★★★★★)

The outstanding 2013 vintage (★★★★★) has bold, dense colour. A powerful red, it was grown in the Gimblett Gravels and matured for a year in French oak casks (33 per cent new). Silky-textured, with concentrated blackcurrant, plum and spice flavours, showing beautiful ripeness and richness, it's a very harmonious wine, likely to be long-lived. It should be at its best 2018+.

DRY $57 AV

Coopers Creek SV Gimblett Gravels Hawke's Bay Cabernet Sauvignon/Merlot   ★★★★

The 2013 vintage (★★★★) is a full-coloured blend of Cabernet Sauvignon (73 per cent), Merlot (25 per cent) and Malbec (2 per cent), barrel-aged for a year. It shows very good concentration of plum, spice and slight coffee flavours, with a finely textured, lingering finish.

Vintage	13
WR	7
Drink	16-20

DRY $29 AV

Cornerstone Cabernet/Merlot/Malbec – see Newton Forrest Estate Cornerstone in the Branded and Other Red Wines section

Crossroads Winemakers Collection Hawke's Bay Cabernet/Merlot   ★★★★☆

The 2013 vintage (★★★★★) was grown at two sites and barrel-aged. Deep and youthful in colour, it's a powerful young red with concentrated blackcurrant, plum and spice flavours, a hint of herbs, oak complexity, good tannin backbone, and excellent vigour and depth. Still youthful, it shows obvious potential; open 2017+.

Vintage	13	12
WR	7	5
Drink	16-23	16-23

DRY $40 –V

Doubtless Bay Reserve Cabernets   (★★☆)

Currently on sale, the 2010 vintage (★★☆) is a Northland blend, based on Cabernet Sauvignon (73 per cent), with small portions of Cabernet Franc, Petit Verdot, Merlot and Syrah. Deep and still moderately youthful in colour, it lacks fragrance, but has good depth of blackcurrant, plum, herb and nut flavours. It's a sturdy, honest red, but slightly rustic.

DRY $26 –V

Dunleavy, The Strip Waiheke Island Cabernet/Merlot   ★★★★☆

Although made in a 'forward, fruit-driven style', the 2013 vintage (★★★★☆) was barrel-matured for 10 months. Deeply coloured, it is mouthfilling and smooth-flowing, with excellent depth of fresh blackcurrant, plum, herb and spice flavours. Enjoyable young, with savoury, earthy notes adding real complexity, it's a very harmonious wine; drink now or cellar.

DRY $45 –V

Johner Estate Lyndor Wairarapa Cabernet & Merlot   ★★★★

The 2011 vintage (★★★★) was grown in the northern Wairarapa and matured in French oak barrels (100 per cent new). Full-coloured, with a fragrant, slightly herbaceous bouquet, it is mouthfilling, with concentrated blackcurrant, plum and herb flavours, seasoned with nutty oak, and good complexity and harmony. It's drinking well now.

Vintage	11
WR	5
Drink	16-25

DRY $50 –V

Johner Estate Wairarapa Cabernet/Merlot/Malbec   ★★★☆

The 2013 vintage (★★★★), matured in French oak barrels (25 per cent new), has full, purple-flushed colour. Rich, youthful and vibrantly fruity, it has strong plum and spice flavours, a gentle seasoning of oak, and gentle tannins. Drink now or cellar.

Vintage	13
WR	6
Drink	16-20

DRY $40 –V

Kaipara Estate Cabernet Sauvignon/Malbec/Cabernet Franc   (★★☆)

Fullish in colour, the 2014 vintage (★★☆) of this Auckland red has a slightly rustic, earthy bouquet. It's a solid, medium-bodied wine, with red-berry, spice and tamarillo flavours, but shows a slight lack of ripeness and richness.

DRY $34 –V

Mahurangi River Cabernet Sauvignon/Merlot/Malbec   (★★★★)

The full-coloured 2014 vintage (★★★★) is a savoury Matakana red, Cabernet Sauvignon-based (67 per cent), with equal parts of Merlot and Malbec, matured for over a year in French and American oak casks (30 per cent new). It has fresh, concentrated blackcurrant, plum, herb and spice flavours, showing good complexity.

DRY $29 AV

Mahurangi River Winery Reserve Cabernet Sauvignon   (★★★★☆)

The stylish 2013 vintage (★★★★☆) was grown at Matakana and matured for a year in French oak casks (85 per cent new). Boldly coloured, it is mouthfilling, fresh and supple, with deep, ripe blackcurrant, plum and spice flavours, showing excellent varietal definition and potential.

Vintage	13
WR	6
Drink	16-22

 DRY $60 –V

Mills Reef Elspeth Gimblett Gravels Hawke's Bay Cabernet Sauvignon   ★★★★★

The lovely 2013 vintage (★★★★★) was hand-picked from mature, estate-grown vines and matured in a 4:1 mix of French and American oak barrels (43 per cent new). Densely coloured, it shows pure Cabernet Sauvignon characters, with dense blackcurrant, plum, spice and herb flavours, fine-grained tannins, and impressive power and elegance. It should be a 10-year wine.

Vintage	14	13	12	11	10	09	08	07	06	05
WR	7	7	NM	7	7	7	NM	7	7	7
Drink	16-24	16-25	NM	16-18	16-18	16-18	NM	16-18	16-17	P

 DRY $49 AV

Mills Reef Elspeth Gimblett Gravels Hawke's Bay Cabernet/Merlot   ★★★★★

Grown and hand-picked at the company's close-planted Mere Road site, this is a consistently impressive red. The 2013 vintage (★★★★☆) is a blend of Cabernet Sauvignon (79 per cent), Merlot (14.5 per cent) and Cabernet Franc (6.5 per cent), matured for 16 months in French (principally) and American oak barrels (40 per cent new). Deep and youthful in colour, it is mouthfilling and very age-worthy, with concentrated, ripe plum, spice and blackcurrant flavours, seasoned with slightly sweet oak, and a firmly structured finish. Best drinking 2018+.

Vintage	13	12	11	10	09	08	07	06	05
WR	7	NM	7	7	7	NM	7	7	7
Drink	16-25	NM	16-18	16-20	16-18	NM	16-17	P	P

 DRY $49 AV

Mills Reef Elspeth Trust Vineyard Gimblett Gravels
Hawke's Bay Cabernet Sauvignon   ★★★★☆

The 2013 vintage (★★★★☆), the first release of this label since 2010, was estate-grown in the Trust Vineyard, in Mere Road, and matured for 15 months in French (80 per cent) and American (20 per cent) oak casks (33 per cent new). Deeply coloured, it is generous and smooth, with gentle tannins and fresh, concentrated, plummy, spicy flavours, seasoned with sweet oak. Already highly approachable, it should be at its best 2017+.

Vintage	13	12	11	10	09	08	07	06
WR	7	NM	NM	7	7	NM	7	6
Drink	16-25	NM	NM	16-18	16-18	NM	16-17	P

 DRY $50 –V

Mills Reef Reserve Gimblett Gravels Hawke's Bay Cabernet/Merlot   ★★★★

The 2014 vintage (★★★★) was grown in the Gimblett Gravels and matured for a year in French (56 per cent) and American oak hogsheads (30 per cent new). Deeply coloured, it is mouthfilling, with blackcurrant, plum and spice flavours, generous, vibrant, youthful and smooth. Best drinking 2017+. Retasted in 2016 (and currently available), the 2013 vintage (★★★★) is a blend of Cabernet Sauvignon (62 per cent), Merlot (33 per cent and Cabernet Franc (5 per cent), matured for a year in barrels (mostly French, 27 per cent new.) Drinking well now, it's a skilfully crafted red, rich and smooth, with excellent body and depth of ripe berry and spice flavours.

Vintage	14	13	12
WR	6	7	6
Drink	16-20	16-19	P

 DRY $25 AV

Mission Hawke's Bay Cabernet Sauvignon   ★★★

The 2014 vintage (★★★) is a 'lightly oaked' red, full-coloured, fresh and vibrantly fruity, with satisfying depth of blackcurrant and spice flavours, ripe and smooth. Enjoyable young.

DRY $18 AV

Mission Reserve Gimblett Gravels Hawke's Bay Cabernet/Merlot   ★★★★

The 2013 vintage (★★★★) is a deeply coloured blend of Cabernet Sauvignon (49 per cent), Merlot (45 per cent) and Cabernet Franc (6 per cent), matured for 15 months in French oak casks (20 per cent new). Sweet-fruited, with firm, berryish flavours, it has hints of thyme and leather, and good density.

Vintage	13
WR	7
Drink	17-25

 DRY $25 AV

Mission Reserve Hawke's Bay Cabernet Sauvignon   ★★★★

The 2014 vintage (★★★★) was matured for a year in French oak barrels. Likely to be long-lived, it is deeply coloured and mouthfilling, with strong blackcurrant, herb and spice flavours, oak complexity and good tannin backbone. Best drinking 2018+.

Vintage	14	13
WR	5	7
Drink	17-22	16-25

DRY $29 AV

Obsidian Waiheke Island Cabernet/Merlot   ★★★★

The 2010 vintage (★★★★) is a blend of Cabernet Sauvignon and Merlot, with splashes of Petit Verdot, Cabernet Franc and Malbec. Matured in French oak barriques, it has full, slightly developed colour and generous blackcurrant, herb, spice and nut flavours, with a hint of liquorice, and supple tannins. Drink now.

Vintage	10	09
WR	7	6
Drink	16-20	P

 DRY $27 AV

Osawa Prestige Collection Hawke's Bay Cabernet Sauvignon/Merlot   (★★★★)

The 2013 vintage (★★★★) is a concentrated, ripe, slightly earthy, 50:50 blend of Cabernet Sauvignon and Merlot, grown at Maraekakaho. It has some slightly herby, gamey notes, in a fleshy, rich and complex style.

 DRY $60 –V

Pask Declaration Gimblett Gravels Hawke's Bay Cabernet/Merlot/Malbec   ★★★★☆

The 2014 vintage (★★★★☆) was matured for two years in French and American oak puncheons (100 per cent new). Full-coloured, it shows good concentration, with fresh, ripe blackcurrant, plum and spice flavours, complex and savoury, and fine-grained tannins. Well worth cellaring, it should be at its best 2019 onwards.

Vintage	14	13	12	11	10	09	08	07	06
WR	7	7	NM	NM	6	6	NM	7	6
Drink	16-25	16-25	NM	NM	16-20	16-19	NM	16-18	P

 DRY $50 –V

Pask Gimblett Road Cabernet/Merlot/Malbec   ★★★★

The attractive 2013 vintage (★★★★) was estate-grown in the Gimblett Gravels and matured for 14 months in French and American oak casks (20 per cent new). A blend of Cabernet Sauvignon (76 per cent), Merlot (14 per cent) and Malbec (10 per cent), it has full, youthful colour. Mouthfilling and supple, it offers ripe blackcurrant, herb, plum and spice flavours, gently seasoned with oak, in a finely balanced, vibrantly fruity style, for drinking now or cellaring.

Vintage	13
WR	7
Drink	16-20

 DRY $22 V+

Pask Small Batch Cabernet Sauvignon   ★★★★

The 2013 vintage (★★★☆) was estate-grown in the Gimblett Gravels, Hawke's Bay, and matured for 16 months in American oak casks (50 per cent new). Full-coloured, it is fresh and vibrant, with blackcurrant, plum, herb and spice flavours, tinged with sweet oak, and gentle tannins. The 2014 vintage (★★★★) was matured for 17 months in French and American oak casks (20 per cent new). Full-coloured, it is ripe and savoury, with concentrated blackcurrant, plum and spice flavours, a hint of herbs, good complexity and a finely poised finish. Drink 2017 onwards.

Vintage	14	13
WR	6	7
Drink	17-20	16-20

DRY $29 AV

Passage Rock Reserve Waiheke Island Cabernet Sauvignon/Merlot   ★★★★☆

The 2013 vintage (★★★★☆) is a blend of Cabernet Sauvignon (85 per cent), Merlot (10 per cent) and Malbec (5 per cent), matured in oak barriques for 15 months. Deep and youthful in colour, it is sturdy, fragrant and supple, with rich, ripe blackcurrant, plum, herb and spice flavours. Already highly enjoyable, it should be at its best 2018+. The 2014 vintage (★★★★) is dark, mouthfilling, generous and savoury, with a slightly green thread, but also good concentration and complexity.

 DRY $45 –V

Peacock Sky Waiheke Island Cabernet Sauvignon   ★★★☆

Medium to full-bodied, the 2014 vintage (★★★☆) is a blend of Cabernet Sauvignon (85 per cent), Cabernet Franc (10 per cent) and Malbec (5 per cent), French oak-aged for over a year. Deeply coloured, it is fresh, with plummy, spicy, slightly herbal flavours, in a clearly varietal style with good but not great depth.

DRY $40 –V

Saint Clair James Sinclair Gimblett Gravels Hawke's Bay Cabernet/Merlot   (★★★★)

The generous 2014 vintage (★★★★) is a boldly coloured blend of Cabernet Sauvignon (84 per cent) and Merlot (16 per cent), estate-grown in the Plateau Vineyard and partly American oak-aged. Fresh and youthful, it has concentrated blackcurrant, plum, herb and spice flavours, with a moderately firm finish.

DRY $25 AV

Saint Clair Pioneer Block 17 Plateau Gimblett Gravels Cabernet/Merlot   (★★★★)

The 2014 vintage (★★★★) was estate-grown in the Gimblett Gravels. A dark, vibrantly fruity blend of Cabernet Sauvignon (72 per cent) and Merlot (28 per cent), American oak-aged (half new), it is slightly green-edged, but weighty, ripe and rich, with impressive density and length.

DRY $38 –V

Squawking Magpie SQM Gimblett Gravels Cabernets/Merlot   ★★★★★

The 2013 vintage (★★★★★), French oak-matured, is deeply coloured and fleshy, with rich, youthful blackcurrant, plum, herb and spice flavours, supple tannins, and excellent texture and harmony. The 2014 vintage (★★★★★) is dark and refined, in a Bordeaux-like style, with concentrated, ripe blackcurrant, plum, spice and nut flavours. Still very youthful, it's crying out for cellaring; best drinking 2020+.

Vintage	13
WR	7
Drink	16-35

DRY $79 AV

Stonecroft Gimblett Gravels Hawke's Bay Cabernet Sauvignon   (★★★★☆)

The impressive 2014 vintage (★★★★☆) was matured for 18 months in French oak barriques (10 per cent new). It has bold, purple-flushed colour, mouthfilling body (14 per cent alcohol), ripe, concentrated flavours of blackcurrants, plums and spices, and gentle tannins. Best drinking 2018+.

Vintage	14
WR	7
Drink	19-26

DRY $47 –V

Te Mata Awatea Cabernets/Merlot ★★★★★

Positioned below its Coleraine stablemate in Te Mata's hierarchy of Hawke's Bay, claret-style reds, since 1995 Awatea has been grown at Havelock North and in the Bullnose Vineyard, inland from Hastings. A blend of Cabernet Sauvignon, Merlot and Cabernet Franc – with a splash of Petit Verdot in most years since 2001 – it is hand-harvested and matured for 15 to 18 months in French oak barriques (partly new). Compared to Coleraine, in its youth Awatea is more seductive, more perfumed, and tastes more of sweet, ripe fruit, but it is more forward and slightly less concentrated. The wine can mature gracefully for many years, but is also typically delicious in its youth. The 2014 vintage (★★★★☆) is a blend of Cabernet Sauvignon (45 per cent), Merlot (33 per cent), Cabernet Franc (14 per cent) and Petit Verdot (8 per cent). Dark, fresh and mouthfilling, it is ripe, berryish, savoury and supple, with a hint of dark chocolate, a gentle seasoning of oak, and fine-grained tannins. An elegant, youthful red, it should be at its best 2018+.

Vintage	14	13	12	11	10	09	08	07	06	05	DRY $35 V+
WR	6	7	6	7	7	7	7	7	7	7	
Drink	17-25	16-23	16-19	16-19	16-18	16-17	P	16-20	P	P	

Te Mata Coleraine – see the Branded and Other Red Wines section

Unison Selection Gimblett Gravels Cabernet Sauvignon/Merlot ★★★★☆

The 2012 (★★★★★) is one of the best reds from a cool, wet growing season in Hawke's Bay. A blend of Cabernet Sauvignon (86 per cent) and Merlot (14 per cent), it was estate-grown and matured for 20 months in French oak barrels (33 per cent new). Full-coloured, it is mouthfilling, with youthful, ripe blackcurrant, plum and nutty oak flavours, in a sturdy and savoury, slightly earthy, firmly structured style that reminded me of a good St Estèphe. It's built to last; open 2017+.

DRY $60 –V

Vidal Legacy Gimblett Gravels Hawke's Bay Cabernet Sauvignon (★★★★★)

The highly impressive 2014 vintage (★★★★★) is an unblended Cabernet Sauvignon, estate-grown in the Omahu Gravels Vineyard and matured for 20 months in French oak barriques (50 per cent new). Invitingly dark and fragrant, it is fleshy and concentrated, with dense, ripe blackcurrant, plum, spice and nut flavours, hints of dark chocolate and herbs, well-integrated oak adding complexity, and fine-grained tannins. A classic – and classy – young Cabernet Sauvignon, it should flourish for decades.

Vintage	14	DRY $70 AV
WR	7	
Drink	18-28	

Vidal Legacy Gimblett Gravels Hawke's Bay Cabernet Sauvignon/Merlot   ★★★★★

The youthful 2013 vintage (★★★★☆) is a blend of Cabernet Sauvignon (80 per cent) and Merlot (20 per cent), matured for 19 months in French oak casks (50 per cent new). Deeply coloured, it's a softly mouthfilling red with very vibrant blackcurrant, plum, spice and nut flavours, showing good complexity and richness, and supple tannins. It needs time; best drinking 2018+.

Vintage	13	12	11	10	09
WR	7	NM	NM	7	7
Drink	18-30	NM	NM	16-19	16-20

Villa Maria Reserve Gimblett Gravels Hawke's Bay
Cabernet Sauvignon/Merlot   ★★★★★

The 2014 vintage (★★★★★) is a dark, dense blend of Cabernet Sauvignon (75 per cent) and Merlot (25 per cent), matured for 18 months in French oak barriques (40 per cent new). Highly concentrated, with pure blackcurrant, plum and spice flavours, showing lovely weight, ripeness and structure, it's full of cellaring potential.

Vintage	14	13	12	10	09	08	07	06	05
WR	7	7	6	7	6	6	7	7	6
Drink	18-25	18-25	16-22	16-25	16-22	16-18	16-22	16-19	16-20

Villa Maria Reserve Library Release Gimblett Gravels
Hawke's Bay Cabernet Sauvignon/Merlot   (★★★★)

Released in 2014, the 2009 vintage (★★★★) is a blend of Cabernet Sauvignon (55 per cent) and Merlot (45 per cent). Deeply coloured, with strong blackcurrant, plum and spice flavours, and hints of herbs and olives, it is savoury, complex and firm.

DRY $70 –V

Carménère

Ransom, at Matakana, in 2007 released New Zealand's first Carménère. Now virtually extinct in France, Carménère was once widely grown in Bordeaux and still is in Chile, where, until the 1990s, it was often mistaken for Merlot. In Italy it was long thought to be Cabernet Franc.

In 1988, viticulturist Alan Clarke imported Cabernet Franc cuttings here from Italy. Planted by Robin Ransom in 1997, the grapes ripened about the same time as the rest of his Cabernet Franc, but the look of the fruit and the taste of the wine were 'totally different'. So Ransom arranged DNA testing at the University of Adelaide. The result? His Cabernet Franc vines are in fact Carménère.

Only 1 hectare of Carménère has been recorded in New Zealand, and the variety is not listed separately in New Zealand Winegrowers' *Vineyard Register Report 2015–2018*.

Ransom Carménère ★★★☆

Estate-grown at Mahurangi, north of Auckland, the 2013 vintage (★★★☆) is deeply coloured, with a fresh, slightly herbal bouquet. Mouthfilling, it shows good density, with vibrant plum and herb flavours, a hint of nuts, and fine-grained tannins. Drink now or cellar.

DRY $29 –V

Chambourcin

Chambourcin is one of the more highly rated French hybrids, well known in Muscadet for its good disease-resistance and bold, crimson hue. Rare in New Zealand (with 3 hectares of bearing vines in 2017), it is most often found as a varietal red in Northland.

Ake Ake Northland Chambourcin ★★★☆

Estate-grown near Kerikeri, in the Bay of Islands, the 2014 vintage (★★★☆) was matured for 10 months in seasoned American and French oak casks. Full and bright in colour, it is mouthfilling and smooth, with vibrant, plummy flavours, showing very good freshness and depth.

Vintage	14
WR	5
Drink	16-18

DRY $25 –V

Byrne Northland Chambourcin ★★★★☆

The 2014 vintage (★★★★☆), grown at Kerikeri and matured for eight months in a single seasoned oak puncheon, is one of this country's best-ever Chambourcins – and the 2015 vintage (★★★★★) is even more impressive. It has bold, purple-flushed colour and a fragrant, spicy bouquet. A wine that many producers of Syrah and Pinot Noir would enjoy, it is mouthfilling (14 per cent alcohol), with fresh, strong plum/spice flavours and a hint of dark chocolate. An exuberantly fruity red, it's delicious young.

DRY $20 V+

Mahinepua Bay Chambourcin (★★★★)

Estate-grown in Northland at a coastal site well north of the Bay of Islands, the 2014 vintage (★★★★) is a sturdy, boldly coloured red, fresh and fruit-packed, with generous plum and spice flavours, showing good vigour and concentration.

DRY $25 AV

Marsden Bay of Islands Chambourcin ★★★★

Top vintages of this Northland red are generous, deeply coloured and crammed with flavour. The 2014 vintage (★★★★) was matured for 16 months in American oak casks (20 per cent new). Densely coloured and perfumed, it is weighty, with rich plum/spice flavours, fresh acidity, gentle tannins and a seductively smooth finish.

Vintage	14	13	12	11	10
WR	6	6	4	5	7
Drink	16-20	P	P	P	P

DRY $28 –V

Okahu Chambourcin ★★★☆

The easy-drinking 2014 vintage (★★★☆) is a Northland red, grown at Kaitaia. Full-coloured, it is weighty and vibrantly fruity, with youthful, ripe, berryish, plummy flavours, showing good freshness, harmony and depth.

DRY $49 –V

Dolcetto

Grown in the north of Italy, where it produces purple-flushed, fruity, supple reds, usually enjoyed young, Dolcetto is extremely rare in New Zealand. Only 2 hectares of bearing vines have been recorded in New Zealand, mostly in Auckland, and the variety is not listed separately in New Zealand Winegrowers' *Vineyard Register Report 2015–2018*.

Hitchen Road Dolcetto ★★★☆

Grown at Pokeno, in North Waikato, the 2014 vintage (★★★★) was barrel-matured for 10 months. The colour is full and bright; the palate is mouthfilling, with ripe berry and spice flavours, earthy, savoury notes adding complexity, fine-grained tannins, and a persistent finish. Enjoyable young, but also worth cellaring, it offers outstanding value at its case price of under $12 per bottle.

 DRY $18 V+

Gamay Noir

Gamay Noir is single-handedly responsible for the seductively scented and soft red wines of Beaujolais. The grape is still very rare in New Zealand, with 7 hectares of bearing vines in 2017, almost all in Hawke's Bay. In the Omaka Springs Vineyard in Marlborough, Gamay ripened later than Cabernet Sauvignon (itself an end-of-season ripener), with higher levels of acidity than in Beaujolais, but at Te Mata's Woodthorpe Terraces Vineyard in Hawke's Bay, the crop is harvested as early as mid-March.

Te Mata Estate Vineyards Hawke's Bay Gamay Noir ★★★★

The summery 2016 vintage (★★★★) was matured for two months in seasoned French oak barrels. Bright ruby, it is floral, berryish and supple, with fresh, vibrant, plummy, spicy flavours and very gentle tannins. Very much in the Beaujolais mould, it's delicious young.

Vintage	16
WR	6
Drink	16-19

DRY $20 V+

Grenache

Grenache, one of the world's most extensively planted grape varieties, thrives in the hot, dry vineyards of Spain and southern France. It is also yielding exciting wines in Australia, especially from old, unirrigated, bush-pruned vines, but is exceedingly rare in New Zealand, with a total producing area in 2017 of 1 hectare, all in Hawke's Bay.

Villa Maria Cellar Selection Gimblett Gravels Hawke's Bay Grenache ★★★★

The instantly attractive 2014 vintage (★★★★) is the fourth of what will be a regular release of this very late-ripening variety. From 16-year-old vines in the company's Ngakirikiri Vineyard, it was hand-picked and matured for 11 months in French oak barrels of varying sizes (30 per cent new). Full-coloured and mouthfilling (14.5 per cent alcohol), with strong, vibrant plum/spice flavours, showing some smoky, savoury complexity, and a tight, finely textured finish, it's worth cellaring.

DRY $25 AV

Vintage	14	13	12	11	10
WR	7	6	NM	6	7
Drink	16-22	16-19	NM	16-17	16-17

Lagrein

Cultivated traditionally in the vineyards of Trentino-Alto Adige, in north-east Italy, Lagrein yields deeply coloured, slightly astringent reds with fresh acidity and plum/cherry flavours, firm and strong. The area of bearing vines in New Zealand will leap from 2 hectares in 2015 to 9 hectares in 2017, mostly in Hawke's Bay (6 hectares), but also Nelson and Marlborough.

Stanley Estates Awatere Valley Marlborough Lagrein (★★★☆)

The 2014 vintage (★★★☆) was estate-grown and hand-picked. Bright ruby, it is an easy-drinking, medium to full-bodied red, vibrantly fruity, berryish and slightly spicy, with a hint of cherries and a smooth finish. Enjoyable young, it's worth discovering.

DRY $25 –V

Malbec

With a rise from 25 hectares of bearing vines in 1998 to 132 hectares in 2017, this old Bordeaux variety is starting to make its presence felt in New Zealand, where over 75 per cent of all plantings are clustered in Hawke's Bay (most of the rest are in Auckland). It is often used as a blending variety, adding brilliant colour and rich, sweet-fruit flavours to its blends with Merlot, Cabernet Sauvignon and Cabernet Franc. Numerous unblended Malbecs have also been released recently, possessing loads of flavour and often the slight rusticity typical of the variety (or at least some of the clones established here).

Ash Ridge Premium Estate Hawke's Bay Malbec (★★★★)

Grown in the Bridge Pa Triangle and barrel-aged, the 2014 vintage (★★★★) is delicious young. A fruit-driven style with a gentle seasoning of oak, it is full-coloured, with gentle tannins and fresh, concentrated plum and spice flavours that avoid the rusticity often found in New Zealand Malbec. Drink now or cellar.

DRY $26 AV

Brookfields Hawke's Bay Sun Dried Malbec ★★★★☆

Labelled as 'Malbec on steroids', the 2015 vintage (★★★★☆) was made from grapes sun-dried to concentrate their sugars and flavours, then matured in one-year-old French and American oak casks. Deeply coloured, it is mouthfilling (14 per cent alcohol), with concentrated, ripe plum/spice flavours, a hint of liquorice, savoury notes adding complexity, and firm underlying tannins. Drink now or cellar.

Vintage	15	14	13
WR	7	7	7
Drink	19-24	18-25	17-23

DRY $25 V+

Coopers Creek SV Saint John Hawke's Bay Malbec ★★★★

The 2013 vintage (★★★★) was matured for a year in seasoned oak barrels. It's a dark, fragrant red with sweet, 'coconut' aromas and very good depth of vibrant plum/spice flavours.

Vintage	13
WR	7
Drink	16-20

DRY $29 AV

Fromm Malbec Fromm Vineyard ★★★★☆

Estate-grown in Marlborough and matured for 18 months in French oak casks, this wine is recommended by winemaker Hätsch Kalberer for drinking with 'a large piece of wild venison'. The 2013 vintage (★★★★☆) is rare – just three barrels were made. The colour is dense; the palate is sturdy and highly concentrated, with strong, plummy, spicy flavours, well-integrated oak, and a fresh, firm finish. It's a very age-worthy red; open 2017+.

Vintage	13	12	11	10	09	08	07	06	05
WR	7	7	6	7	6	6	7	6	6
Drink	16-28	16-28	16-26	16-27	16-23	16-22	16-24	16-21	16-20

DRY $54 –V

Kaipara Estate Malbec   (★★★)

The 2014 vintage (★★★), estate-grown in Auckland, is deeply coloured, sturdy and smooth, with a vague suggestion of sweetness amid its strong berry, spice and liquorice flavours.

DRY $30 –V

Man O' War Death Valley Malbec   (★★★★★)

The delicious 2014 vintage (★★★★★) was estate-grown on Waiheke Island. It was almost entirely (95 per cent) matured for 22 months in French oak (15 per cent new); the rest was handled in seasoned American oak. Deeply coloured, it is fragrant and mouthfilling, with dense, ripe blackcurrant, plum and spice flavours, hints of coffee and liquorice, and a finely textured, smooth finish. A classy young red, it should be long-lived, but is already hard to resist.

Vintage	14
WR	6
Drink	16-21

DRY $34 V+

Matua Single Vineyard Hawke's Bay Malbec   (★★★★★)

The youthful, fruit-drenched 2013 vintage (★★★★★) is a densely coloured, single-vineyard red, hand-picked in the Matheson Vineyard, in the Bridge Pa Triangle, and French oak-aged. Purple/black, it is powerful, with highly concentrated blackcurrant, plum and spice flavours, gentle tannins and a finely textured, very smooth finish. Best drinking 2018+.

DRY $58 AV

Mission Reserve Hawke's Bay Malbec   ★★★★★

The 2013 vintage (★★★★★), grown in the Bridge Pa Triangle and matured in French oak barrels (10 per cent new), has deep, purple-flushed colour. An elegant, very age-worthy wine, it is full-bodied (14 per cent alcohol), with youthful, concentrated blackcurrant, plum and spice flavours, finely textured, harmonious and long. Best drinking 2017+.

Vintage	13
WR	5
Drink	16-22

DRY $29 V+

One Off Hawke's Bay Malbec   (★★★★)

Enjoyable young, the partly barrel-matured 2014 vintage (★★★★) is deeply coloured, rich and smooth. Full-bodied, with fresh, strong plum/spice flavours and finely balanced tannins, it should be at its best 2017+. (From Rod McDonald.)

DRY $30 –V

Peacock Sky Waiheke Island Pure Malbec   ★★★☆

Matured for over a year in French oak barrels, the 2014 vintage (★★★★) is a deeply coloured, fruity red, medium to full-bodied, with strong, lively plum and spice flavours, slightly earthy notes adding complexity, and a fairly firm finish. Best mid-2017+.

DRY $40 –V

Ransom Matakana Malbec (★★★★)

The 2013 vintage (★★★★) has dark, still purple-flushed colour. Estate-grown and barrel-aged for 20 months, it's a mouthfilling, fleshy, very generous red, with concentrated, ripe berry, plum and spice flavours, a gentle seasoning of oak, and good tannin support. Well worth cellaring.

DRY $27 AV

Reserve Road Hawke's Bay Malbec/Merlot/Cabernet (★★★☆)

The 2015 vintage (★★★☆) is a full-coloured, mouthfilling red, vibrantly fruity, with a touch of complexity and fresh, generous, plummy, slightly herbal flavours. (From Otuwhero.)

DRY $37 –V

Saint Clair Hawke's Bay Malbec ★★★★

The generous 2014 vintage (★★★★) is a single-vineyard red from the Gimblett Gravels, handled in seasoned oak. Deeply coloured, fragrant and sweet-fruited, it has strong, ripe plum and spice flavours, delicious young.

DRY $25 AV

Saint Clair James Sinclair Gimblett Gravels Hawke's Bay Malbec (★★★★)

The dark, purple-flushed 2014 vintage (★★★★) was estate-grown in the Plateau Vineyard and French oak-aged. Mouthfilling, it has strong, plummy flavours, showing some savoury complexity, and gentle tannins, in a seductively rich, smooth style. Enjoyable now.

DRY $25 AV

Saint Clair Pioneer Block 17 Plateau Gimblett Gravels
Hawke's Bay Malbec (★★★★☆)

Instantly attractive, the 2014 vintage (★★★★☆) is a deeply coloured red, matured in French oak casks (30 per cent new). Fragrant, rich and supple, it is sweet-fruited and vibrant, with gentle tannins and concentrated, ripe, plummy flavours.

DRY $38 AV

Stonyridge Luna Negra Waiheke Island Hillside Malbec ★★★★★

Promoted as 'like going on an energetic dance with a Cuban beauty queen', this bold, classy red is estate-grown in the Vina del Mar Vineyard at Onetangi and matured in American oak barriques. The 2015 vintage (★★★★★) has dense, inky, purple-flushed colour. A powerful, sturdy wine, it has concentrated, well-ripened blackcurrant and plum flavours, in a structured, age-worthy style, already delicious, but likely to be at its best 2020+.

DRY $95 –V

Tironui Estate Hawke's Bay Malbec/Merlot/Cabernet   ★★★★☆

From an elevated site at Taradale, this single-vineyard red has strong personality. The 2014 vintage (★★★★☆) is a blend of Malbec (66 per cent), Merlot (25 per cent) and 'Cabernet' (9 per cent). Matured for a year in French oak barrels (20 per cent new), it is densely coloured, with a youthful, plummy, spicy bouquet. Full-bodied and fruit-packed, it is concentrated and finely textured, with fresh, ripe flavours, well-integrated oak, fine-grained tannins, and excellent balance, richness and flow. Drink now or cellar.

DRY $35 AV

Villa Maria Reserve Gimblett Gravels Hawke's Bay Malbec   ★★★★★

The dark, rich, youthful 2013 vintage (★★★★★) was matured for 18 months in French oak barriques (60 per cent new). Retasted in mid-2016, it is concentrated, with beautifully ripe plum, dark chocolate and liquorice flavours, fairly firm tannins and a lasting finish. Very age-worthy.

Vintage	13
WR	7
Drink	18-25

DRY $60 AV

Marzemino

Once famous, but today rare, Marzemino is cultivated in northern Italy, where it typically yields light, plummy reds. Established in New Zealand in 1995, Marzemino has been made commercially by Pernod Ricard NZ under the Church Road brand since 2005, but is not listed separately in New Zealand Winegrowers' *Vineyard Register Report 2015–2018*.

Church Road McDonald Series Hawke's Bay Marzemino ★★★★

Grown in the company's Redstone Vineyard, in the Bridge Pa Triangle, this wine is matured in French oak barriques. The 2012 vintage (★★★★) is dark, with an attractive bouquet of liquorice and peppermint. Fresh and sweet-fruited, it has generous, plummy flavours and a lingering, smooth finish.

DRY $27 AV

Merlot

Pinot Noir is New Zealand's red-wine calling card on the world stage, but our Merlots are also proving competitive. Interest in this most extensively cultivated red-wine grape in Bordeaux is especially strong in Hawke's Bay. Everywhere in Bordeaux – the world's greatest red-wine region – except in the Médoc and Graves districts, the internationally higher-profile Cabernet Sauvignon variety plays second fiddle to Merlot. The elegant, fleshy wines of Pomerol and St Émilion bear delicious testimony to Merlot's capacity to produce great, yet relatively early-maturing, reds.

In New Zealand, after initial preoccupation with the more austere and slowly evolving Cabernet Sauvignon, the rich, rounded flavours and (more practically) earlier-ripening ability of Merlot are now fully appreciated. Poor set can be a major drawback with the older clones, reducing yields, but Merlot ripens ahead of Cabernet Sauvignon, a major asset in cooler wine regions, especially in vineyards with colder clay soils. Merlot grapes are typically lower in tannin and higher in sugar than Cabernet Sauvignon's; its wines are thus silkier and a shade stronger in alcohol.

Hawke's Bay has over 85 per cent of New Zealand's bearing Merlot vines in 2017; the rest are clustered in Gisborne, Auckland and Marlborough. The country's fifth most widely planted variety, Merlot covers over four times the area of Cabernet Sauvignon. Between 2003 and 2017, the total area of bearing Merlot vines barely changed, from 1249 to 1327 hectares, but in top vintages, such as 2010, 2013 and 2014, the wines offer terrific value.

Merlot's key role in New Zealand was traditionally that of a minority blending variety, bringing a soft, mouthfilling richness and floral, plummy fruitiness to its marriages with the predominant Cabernet Sauvignon. Now, with a host of straight Merlots and Merlot-predominant blends on the market, this aristocratic grape is fully recognised as a top-flight wine in its own right.

Allan Scott Hawke's Bay Merlot (★★★☆)

The 2015 vintage (★★★☆) from this Marlborough-based producer is deeply coloured and mouthfilling, with generous, plummy, spicy, slightly herbal flavours. Gently oaked, with good tannin support, it's an age-worthy wine, likely to be at its best mid-2017+.

DRY $26 –V

Alluviale Hawke's Bay Merlot/Cabernet Sauvignon (★★★★☆)

The instantly appealing 2015 vintage (★★★★☆) is a blend of Merlot (76 per cent), Cabernet Sauvignon (14 per cent) and Cabernet Franc (10 per cent), matured for 15 months in French oak barrels (25 per cent new), and bottled unfined and unfiltered. The colour is deep and purple-flushed; the palate is mouthfilling and fruit-packed, with generous plum/spice flavours, a subtle seasoning of oak, and fine-grained tannins. Best drinking mid-2017+.

DRY $32 AV

Alpha Domus The Foxmoth Hawke's Bay Merlot (★★★☆)

Partly barrel-aged, the 2014 vintage (★★★☆) has full, slightly mature colour. Mouthfilling and smooth, it has very good depth of plummy, slightly nutty flavours, in an attractive, drink-young style.

DRY $24 AV

Alpha Domus The Pilot Merlot/Cabernet   ★★★☆

The 2013 vintage (★★★☆) is a blend of Merlot (91 per cent) and Cabernet Sauvignon (9 per cent), matured in seasoned French (mostly) oak barrels. Fullish and slightly developed in colour, it is mouthfilling, with generous, moderately firm blackcurrant, plum and spice flavours, showing some savoury complexity. It's drinking well now.

DRY $22 AV

Ash Ridge Estate Hawke's Bay Merlot   ★★★★

A consistently good buy. The 2015 vintage (★★★★) was grown in the Bridge Pa Triangle and matured in French and American oak casks (mostly seasoned). Deep ruby, it is mouthfilling, with strong, plummy, slightly spicy flavours, savoury notes adding interest, finely balanced tannins and good complexity. Best drinking mid-2017+.

DRY $20 V+

Askerne Hawke's Bay Merlot/Cabernet Franc/Cabernet Sauvignon/Malbec   ★★★

The 2015 vintage (★★★☆) is a deeply coloured, supple, drink-young blend of Merlot (65 per cent) with Cabernet Franc, Cabernet Sauvignon, Malbec and Petit Verdot, barrel-aged for 10 months. It has strong plum and spice flavours, showing some savoury complexity.

DRY $22 –V

Askerne Reserve Merlot/Cabernet Sauvignon/Cabernet Franc/Malbec   (★★★☆)

The 2013 vintage (★★★☆) of this Hawke's Bay blend is full-coloured, with very good depth of fresh plum, spice, herb and olive flavours, and a firm finish.

DRY $30 –V

Ataahua Waipara Merlot   ★★★☆

Delicious young, the 2014 vintage (★★★★) of this estate-grown red was matured for a year in seasoned French oak casks. Fragrant and full-coloured, it is mouthfilling, with fine-grained tannins and a strong surge of fresh plum/blackcurrant flavours. Best drinking mid-2017+.

DRY $30 –V

Babich Hawke's Bay Merlot/Cabernet   ★★★

Grown in the Gimblett Gravels and the Bridge Pa Triangle, the 2015 vintage (★★★) is a medium-bodied, ruby-hued blend with good depth of plum, spice and herb flavours, and lots of early-drinking appeal.

DRY $22 –V

Babich Winemakers Reserve Hawke's Bay Merlot ★★★★

Estate-grown in Gimblett Road, in the heart of the Gimblett Gravels, and matured for 14 months in French oak casks (25 per cent new), the youthful 2014 vintage (★★★★☆) is clearly from a top season. Deeply coloured and mouthfilling, it has strong blackcurrant, plum and spice flavours, hints of dark chocolate and nuts, and excellent ripeness, concentration and complexity. Showing obvious potential, it should be at its best 2018+.

Vintage	14	13	12	11	10
WR	7	7	5	5	6
Drink	16-22	16-22	16-20	16-19	P

DRY $30 –V

Bell Bird Bay Reserve Hawke's Bay Merlot/Cabernets (★★★☆)

Drinking well now, the 2011 vintage (★★★☆) still on sale is a blend of Merlot (58 per cent), Cabernet Franc (17 per cent), Malbec (15 per cent) and Cabernet Sauvignon (10 per cent), grown in the Bridge Pa Triangle. It has fullish, moderately youthful colour, mouthfilling body and moderately concentrated, ripe plum and slight herb flavours, showing some complexity. (From Alpha Domus.)

DRY $23 AV

Black Barn Vineyards Hawke's Bay Merlot/Cabernet Franc ★★★☆

The 2014 vintage (★★★★) is densely coloured, with an earthy bouquet. A full-bodied, powerful red with concentrated, youthful blackcurrant and plum flavours, hints of nutty oak, and ripe, supple tannins, it should be at its best 2017+.

DRY $33 –V

Brancott Estate Hawke's Bay Merlot ★★★☆

Fragrant, mouthfilling and supple, the deeply coloured 2014 vintage (★★★☆) is sweet-fruited, with generous plum and spice flavours, ripe and smooth. The 2015 vintage (★★★☆) is full-coloured, with very good body and depth of ripe, plummy, spicy flavours, a hint of dark chocolate, a touch of complexity and a smooth finish. Fine value.

DRY $17 V+

Bridge Estate Merlot/Cabernet (★★★★☆)

The delicious 2013 vintage (★★★★☆) is a fragrant, concentrated Gisborne blend – Merlot (40 per cent), Cabernet Franc (30 per cent), Cabernet Sauvignon (25 per cent) and Malbec (5 per cent) – from vines planted in 1985, oak-matured for 18 months. Deeply coloured, with rich, ripe blackcurrant, plum and spice flavours, a hint of dark chocolate, and fine-grained tannins, it's a stylish, harmonious wine, well worth cellaring.

DRY $42 –V

Brookfields Burnfoot Hawke's Bay Merlot ★★★★

Typically great value. The 2013 vintage (★★★★), grown in the Tuki Tuki Valley, was matured in seasoned French and American oak casks. Deep in colour, it is very full-bodied (14.5 per cent alcohol), with generous, ripe blackcurrant and plum flavours, a hint of dark chocolate, and a well-rounded finish. Delicious young, it should also age well.

Vintage	13
WR	7
Drink	16-20

 DRY $20 V+

Brookfields Highland Hawke's Bay Merlot/Cabernet ★★★★☆

The very youthful 2015 vintage (★★★★☆) is a blend of Merlot and Cabernet Sauvignon, matured for a year in new and one-year-old French and American oak casks. Deeply coloured, with plenty of personality, it has mouthfilling body and rich, vibrant plum, cassis and spice flavours, with a hint of coffee. Complex and savoury, it's still a baby; open 2019+.

Vintage	15	14
WR	7	7
Drink	20-26	18-25

 DRY $45 –V

Church Road Hawke's Bay Merlot/Cabernet/Malbec ★★★☆

This full-flavoured, Bordeaux-like red from Pernod Ricard NZ can offer wonderful value. Blended from Merlot (principally), with lesser amounts of Cabernet Sauvignon, Malbec and Cabernet Franc, it is matured in French and Hungarian oak barriques. The 2013 vintage (★★★★), estate-grown in the Redstone Vineyard, in the Bridge Pa Triangle, is a powerful, youthful blend of Merlot (86 per cent), Cabernet Sauvignon (9 per cent) and Malbec (5 per cent), oak-aged for a year. Deep and bright in colour, with substantial body (14.5 per cent alcohol) and bold, ripe blackcurrant, plum and spice flavours, it shows excellent depth and complexity. The tightly structured 2014 vintage (★★★) is deeply coloured and full-flavoured, with some herbal notes, oak complexity and firm tannins.

 DRY $20 AV

Church Road McDonald Series Hawke's Bay Merlot ★★★★★

Grown in the Gimblett Gravels and the Bridge Pa Triangle, and matured in French oak barriques, the 2013 vintage (★★★★★) is a dark, powerful, fragrant wine with dense, ripe, plummy, spicy flavours, a hint of coffee, and lovely softness and richness. It's a five-star wine at a four-star price.

 DRY $27 V+

Clearview Cape Kidnappers Hawke's Bay Merlot/Malbec ★★★★

The 2015 vintage (★★★★) is a finely textured, age-worthy, Merlot-based red, with 10 per cent Malbec. Weighty, it has strong, ripe plum and spice flavours, a hint of fruit cake, cedary oak in evidence, and good richness and roundness.

DRY $19 V+

Cliff Edge Awhitu Merlot/Cabernet Franc   ★★★★

The 2012 vintage (★★★★) of this single-vineyard red is a blend of Merlot (70 per cent) and Cabernet Franc (30 per cent), grown on the Awhitu Peninsula, in South Auckland, and matured for a year in French and American oak barrels. Fullish and fairly youthful in colour, it is medium to full-bodied, in an elegant style with fine-grained tannins, good complexity, and very satisfying depth of fresh plum, spice, herb and nut flavours. It's still developing; drink now to 2018.

DRY $33 –V

Collaboration Ceresia Merlot/Cabernet Franc   (★★★★★)

The very elegant, Bordeaux-like 2013 vintage (★★★★★) was hand-picked in Hawke's Bay at 'ideal sites', matured for 22 months in French oak barrels, and bottled unfined and unfiltered. Full and youthful in colour, it's a notably savoury and supple, full-bodied wine with concentrated, well-ripened blackcurrant, plum and spice flavours, oak complexity, and fine-grained tannins. Already delicious, it should be at its best from 2017 onwards.

DRY $40 AV

Coopers Creek Hawke's Bay Merlot   ★★★☆

This is Coopers Creek's most popular red. The 2013 vintage (★★★★), matured for a year in seasoned oak barrels, is an elegant, medium-bodied style, with plenty of fresh, ripe berry, plum, spice and nut flavours, supple tannins, and a finely balanced, lingering finish.

Vintage	13	12	11	10	09
WR	7	5	NM	6	7
Drink	16-18	P	NM	P	P

 DRY $20 AV

Coopers Creek SV Gravels and Metals Hawke's Bay Merlot/Malbec   ★★★★

The 2014 vintage (★★★★) is a youthful, purple-black blend of Merlot (77 per cent) and Malbec (23 per cent). A 'full-on' style, it is sweetly oaked, with concentrated plum, spice and slight liquorice flavours, and a soft, lengthy finish.

DRY $25 AV

Couper's Shed Hawke's Bay Merlot/Cabernet   ★★★★☆

The very classy 2013 vintage (★★★★★) is a great buy. Densely coloured, it is sturdy (14.5 per cent alcohol), with a powerful surge of fresh blackcurrant, plum, dark chocolate and nut flavours, showing impressive density, ripeness and complexity, and a finely textured, seductively smooth finish. Drink now or cellar. (From Pernod Ricard NZ.)

 DRY $27 V+

Craggy Range Gimblett Gravels Hawke's Bay Merlot   ★★★★☆

Still very youthful, the 2014 vintage (★★★★☆) is a marriage of Merlot (88 per cent) and Cabernet Franc (12 per cent), harvested (30 per cent by hand) at 23.5 brix and matured for 17 months in oak barriques (27 per cent new). Full-coloured, it is mouthfilling, with ripe, plummy, spicy flavours, gentle tannins, and excellent complexity and concentration. A generous, well-structured red with obvious potential, it should be at its best 2018+.

 DRY $32 AV

Crossroads Winemakers Collection Hawke's Bay Merlot   (★★★☆)

The 2013 vintage (★★★☆) was hand-picked and barrique-matured. Mouthfilling, with full, slightly developed colour and a slightly leafy bouquet, it offers very good depth of blackcurrant, plum, spice and herb flavours, generous and smooth.

Vintage	13
WR	7
Drink	16-23

 DRY $40 –V

Delegat Crownthorpe Terraces Merlot   ★★★★

The 2014 vintage (★★★★☆) was estate-grown in the company's elevated, inland vineyard at Crownthorpe, in Hawke's Bay. Deeply coloured, it is mouthfilling, generous and supple, with good density of ripe, plummy, slightly spicy and chocolatey flavours, harmonious and well-rounded. Fine value.

 DRY $22 V+

Doubtless Merlot   (★★★★)

Currently on sale, the 2010 vintage (★★★★) is maturing well and offers good value. Estate-grown at Doubtless Bay, in Northland, and matured in seasoned oak casks, it has deep, still fairly youthful colour. Fragrant, with hints of sweet oak, it is sturdy, with ripe berry/plum flavours, firm and concentrated. Drink now to 2020.

Vintage	10
WR	7
Drink	16-25

DRY $22 V+

Doubtless Merlot/Syrah/Cabernet   (★★★☆)

The 2010 vintage (★★★☆) was estate-grown at Doubtless Bay, in Northland, and matured in seasoned oak casks. Mouthfilling, with generous, ripe blackcurrant, plum, spice and herb flavours, it's drinking well now.

Vintage	10
WR	7
Drink	17-28

DRY $22 AV

Eaton Marlborough Merlot/Malbec/Cabernet   (★★★★☆)

The 2014 vintage (★★★★☆) is rare – only 540 bottles were produced. Grown in the Eaton Family Vineyard, in the Omaka Valley, it is a blend of Merlot (85 per cent), Malbec (10 per cent) and Cabernet Sauvignon (5 per cent), fermented with indigenous yeasts, matured for a year in French oak barrels, and bottled unfined and unfiltered. Dark and youthful in colour, it is a powerful red with concentrated, ripe plum, blackcurrant, spice and nut flavours, fine-grained tannins, and strong personality. Well worth cellaring, it should be at its best 2020+.

Vintage	14
WR	5
Drink	17-24

 DRY $48 –V

Elephant Hill Hawke's Bay Merlot/Malbec   ★★★★☆

The 2014 vintage (★★★★☆) is a dark, still purple-flushed blend of Merlot and Malbec, estate-grown and hand-picked in the Gimblett Gravels and the Bridge Pa Triangle. Matured for 14 months in French oak casks (30 per cent new), it is mouthfilling and vibrantly fruity, with concentrated, youthful plum/spice flavours, finely integrated oak, buried tannins and good harmony. Best drinking 2018+.

Elephant Hill Reserve Hawke's Bay Merlot/Malbec/Cabernet Sauvignon   ★★★★★

The powerful, finely textured, harmonious 2014 vintage (★★★★★) was hand-picked in the company's vineyards in the Gimblett Gravels and Bridge Pa Triangle, and matured for 19 months in French oak casks (40 per cent new). The colour is dark and youthful; the palate is sturdy and sweet-fruited, with dense plum, spice and nut flavours, hints of blackcurrants and dark chocolate, and a long, supple finish. A generous red, it's already enjoyable, but likely to be at its best 2018+.

Esk Valley Gimblett Gravels Merlot/Cabernet Sauvignon/Malbec   ★★★★

The 2015 vintage (★★★☆) is an easy-drinking blend of Merlot (44 per cent), Cabernet Sauvignon (30 per cent), Malbec (22 per cent) and Cabernet Franc (4 per cent), matured for a year in French oak barriques (15 per cent new). Full-coloured and vibrantly fruity, it has fresh, ripe, plummy, slightly herbal flavours, a gentle seasoning of biscuity oak, and very good balance and depth.

Vintage	15	14	13	12	11
WR	6	7	7	6	5
Drink	17-21	16-21	16-20	P	P

Esk Valley Winemakers Reserve Merlot/Malbec/Cabernet Franc   ★★★★★

This powerful, classy wine is typically one of Hawke's Bay's greatest reds (it is always Merlot-based, but the proportions of minor varieties vary). Grown in the company's Ngakirikiri Vineyard and the Cornerstone Vineyard, both in the Gimblett Gravels, it is matured for up to 20 months in French oak barriques (40 per cent new in 2014). The 2014 vintage (★★★★☆) is a concentrated blend of Merlot (54 per cent) with Malbec (31 per cent), Cabernet Franc (10 per cent) and Cabernet Sauvignon (5 per cent). Very full-bodied, with a strong surge of ripe dark berry and plum flavours, it has savoury notes adding complexity, supple tannins, and a rich, rounded finish.

Vintage	14	13	12	11	10	09	08	07	06
WR	7	7	NM	7	7	7	NM	7	7
Drink	16-30	16-30	NM	16-25	16-25	16-25	NM	16-25	16-20

Falconhead Hawke's Bay Merlot/Cabernet ★★★☆

Priced sharply, the 2014 vintage (★★★☆) is a smooth, full-coloured red, made in a fresh, fruit-driven style. It has generous, ripe, red-berry and spice flavours, with hints of herbs and dark chocolate. Showing very good depth, it should be at its best 2017+.

Vintage	14	13
WR	7	7
Drink	16-20	16-20

DRY $17 V+

Giesen Hawke's Bay Merlot (★★★☆)

Drinking well in its youth, the 2015 vintage (★★★☆) is full-coloured, fresh, vibrantly fruity and smooth, with ripe plum and spice flavours, gently seasoned with oak, fine-grained tannins, and very good balance and depth.

Vintage	15
WR	4
Drink	16-18

DRY $17 V+

Giesen The Brothers Hawke's Bay Merlot (★★★★)

Already enjoyable, the 2014 vintage (★★★★) is a single-vineyard red, grown in the Bridge Pa Triangle and matured for 13 months in French oak barrels (new and one-year-old). Deeply coloured, with spicy oak aromas, it is medium to full-bodied, with gentle tannins and strong, ripe plum and spice flavours. A youthful, age-worthy wine, it should be at its best 2017+.

Vintage	14
WR	6
Drink	16-19

DRY $33 –V

Gold Star Merlot/Malbec X (★★☆)

From Pukeora Estate, in Central Hawke's Bay, the 2010 vintage (★★☆) has lightish, moderately youthful colour and decent depth of slightly leafy flavour.

DRY $20 –V

Goldie Esslin Waiheke Island Merlot ★★★★★

The 2012 vintage (★★★★★) is from Goldie Wines, owned by the University of Auckland. Hand-harvested and matured in French oak casks (40 per cent new), it is a classy, distinctly Bordeaux-like red, rich and elegant. Full-coloured, it is very savoury and complex, with deep, ripe blackcurrant, plum and spice flavours, slightly nutty and leathery, and a silky-textured finish. Well worth cellaring.

DRY $60 AV

Greyrock Hawke's Bay Merlot (★★☆)

From Sileni, the very easy-drinking 2014 vintage (★★☆) is a 'lightly oaked' style. Full and youthful in colour, it is a very fruit-driven style, with mouthfilling body and plummy, slightly herbal flavours, fresh and smooth.

DRY $17 –V

Gunn Estate Reserve Hawke's Bay Merlot/Cabernet   ★★★☆

The 2015 vintage (★★★☆) is a fruit-driven style, blended from Merlot (83 per cent), Cabernet Sauvignon (11 per cent) and Malbec (6 per cent), French oak-aged for a year. Full-coloured, with generous, vibrant, plummy, slightly spicy flavours, ripe and smooth, it's enjoyable young.

Vintage 15
WR 6
Drink 16-20

DRY $20 AV

Haha Hawke's Bay Merlot   ★★★☆

Offering fine value, the 2015 vintage (★★★☆) is a full-coloured, vibrantly fruity red, predominantly (90 per cent) matured for six months in French oak barrels. It has very good depth of ripe, plummy, slightly herbal and nutty flavours, gentle tannins and some savoury complexity. Best drinking mid-2017+.

DRY $17 V+

Hans Herzog Spirit of Marlborough Merlot/Cabernet   ★★★★★

Who says you can't make outstanding claret-style reds in the South Island? Estate-grown on the banks of the Wairau River, matured for at least two years in new and one-year-old French oak barriques, and then bottle-aged for several years, this is typically a densely coloured wine with a classy fragrance, substantial body and notably concentrated blackcurrant, plum, herb and spice flavours. On sale now, the powerful 2007 vintage (★★★★★) has deep, moderately mature colour. A highly concentrated, still fairly youthful red, it has dense plum, blackcurrant and dried-herb flavours, showing excellent complexity, richness and harmony. Set for a very long life, it's a drink-now or cellaring proposition.

Vintage 08   07
WR 6   7
Drink 16-21   16-22

DRY $69 AV

Hunter's Marlborough Merlot   ★★★

Grown in the Wairau Valley, the 2013 vintage (★★★) is a single-vineyard red, hand-picked from 20-year-old vines, fermented with indigenous yeasts, and matured for 18 months in French oak barrels (30 per cent new). Lightish in colour, it is medium-bodied, with blackcurrant, plum and herb flavours, vibrant and smooth. Offering fresh, easy drinking, it's enjoyable now.

DRY $25 –V

Karikari Estate Calypso Merlot   (★★★☆)

Estate-grown in Northland, the 2014 vintage (★★★☆) is fullish in colour, mouthfilling and smooth, with good depth of ripe, berryish, plummy, spicy, nutty flavours, showing a touch of complexity, and gentle tannins. It's already drinking well.

DRY $29 –V

Kim Crawford Reserve Hawke's Bay Merlot ★★★

The generous, mouthfilling 2014 vintage (★★★☆) was partly barrel-aged. Full-coloured, it has strong, plummy flavours to the fore, with hints of spices and dried herbs, a gentle seasoning of oak, and good harmony. Drink now or cellar.

DRY $17 AV

Kumeu River Melba's Vineyard Merlot ★★★★

Estate-grown at Kumeu, in West Auckland, and barrel-aged for a year, the 2013 vintage (★★★★) is deeply coloured. An elegant rather than powerful red, it is sweet-fruited, with youthful, vibrant, plummy flavours, showing some savoury complexity, and a finely poised finish. Best drinking 2018+. (Bottled under screwcap and opened in 2016, the 2000 vintage, a Merlot/Malbec, was impressive – highly concentrated, spicy and leathery.)

DRY $30 –V

Kumeu Village Merlot ★★☆

Priced sharply, the 2014 vintage (★★☆) has fullish colour. Fresh and vibrantly fruity, with plummy flavours, it's an easy-drinking quaffer, enjoyable young. ($11 in six-bottle packs ex-winery.)

DRY $14 V+

Lake Chalice Vineyard Selection Merlot ★★★

The 2013 vintage (★★★) is a regional blend of Marlborough (95 per cent) and Hawke's Bay (5 per cent) grapes, grown mostly in the company's Falcon Vineyard and adjoining Quarry Block, and partly barrel-aged. Ruby-hued, it has good depth of berry, plum and spice flavours, a hint of toasty oak, gentle tannins, and drink-young appeal.

DRY $21 –V

Left Field Hawke's Bay Merlot ★★★★

Drinking well now, the 2014 vintage (★★★★) is a Gimblett Gravels blend of Merlot (85 per cent), Cabernet Sauvignon (10 per cent) and Cabernet Franc (5 per cent), matured for a year in French oak casks (10 per cent new). Full and bright in colour, it is fragrant and fleshy, with rich plum/spice flavours, savoury, nutty notes adding complexity, and a very smooth, harmonious finish. (From Te Awa.)

Vintage	14
WR	5
Drink	16-20

DRY $25 AV

Leveret Estate Hawke's Bay Merlot/Cabernet ★★★☆

Still unfolding, the 2014 vintage (★★★★) is a rich, deeply coloured blend, with generous plum, spice and nut flavours. Showing good concentration, with ripe, supple tannins and a well-rounded finish, it's a drink-now or cellaring proposition.

Vintage	14	13
WR	7	7
Drink	16-20	16-20

DRY $22 AV

Leveret Estate Reserve Hawke's Bay Merlot/Cabernet ★★★★

The 2013 vintage (★★★★) was grown in the Bridge Pa Triangle and matured for 15 months in French oak casks (new and one-year-old). A powerful red (14.5 per cent alcohol), it is deeply coloured, with blackcurrant, plum and spice flavours, ripe and concentrated. Firmly structured, it is very age-worthy and likely to be at its best 2017+. The 2009 vintage (★★★☆), released in 2015, is a mature, flavoursome blend of Merlot (65 per cent) and Cabernet Sauvignon (29 per cent), with a dollop of Syrah (6 per cent). Mouthfilling, leathery and spicy, with hints of herbs and plums, it shows considerable complexity, with a firm finish.

Vintage	13
WR	7
Drink	18-25

DRY $30 –V

Lime Rock Central Hawke's Bay Merlot (★★★☆)

The 2013 vintage (★★★☆), grown in Central Hawke's Bay, is an attractive red, full-coloured, with very good depth of ripe, plummy, spicy flavours, nutty and leathery notes adding complexity, and supple tannins. Drink now or cellar.

DRY $23 AV

Linden Estate Esk Valley Hawke's Bay Merlot (★★★★)

The 2013 vintage (★★★★) was grown in the Esk Valley and matured for 18 months in French oak casks. Full and bright in colour, it is generous, with fresh blackcurrant, plum and spice flavours, balanced tannins, and good concentration and complexity.

DRY $30 –V

Linden Estate Reserve Hawke's Bay Merlot ★★★★

Estate-grown and hand-harvested in the Esk Valley, the age-worthy 2014 vintage (★★★★☆) was matured for 14 months in French oak casks. Deeply coloured, it is fleshy and supple, with strong, ripe blackcurrant and plum flavours, integrated oak, good tannin support, and a finely textured finish. A youthful wine with obvious potential, it's well worth cellaring to mid-2017+.

DRY $48 –V

Mahurangi River Winery Merlot/Cabernet Sauvignon/Malbec ★★★★

The 2014 vintage (★★★★), grown at Matakana, is a blend of Merlot (54 per cent), Cabernet Sauvignon (31 per cent) and Malbec (15 per cent), matured for 14 months in French and American oak barrels (50 per cent new). Deeply coloured, with fresh plum/spice aromas, it is weighty and generous, with ripe blackcurrant, plum, herb and spice flavours, savoury notes adding complexity, finely integrated oak and obvious cellaring potential.

DRY $29 AV

Main Divide Waipara Valley Merlot/Cabernet ★★★☆

The 2014 vintage (★★★☆) from Pegasus Bay was fermented with indigenous yeasts and matured for a year in French oak barriques. Fullish in colour, it is mouthfilling and supple, with blackcurrant, plum and nut flavours, showing very good depth, ripeness and harmony. Drinking well now, it's priced right.

DRY $21 AV

Man O' War Merlot/Cabernet/Malbec/Petit Verdot ★★★★

The attractive 2014 vintage (★★★★) is a blend of Merlot (50 per cent), Cabernet Franc (20 per cent), Malbec (15 per cent), Petit Verdot (10 per cent) and Cabernet Sauvignon (5 per cent), matured in seasoned French oak casks. Deeply coloured, it's a youthful, fruit-driven wine with fresh, generous red-berry, plum, herb and spice flavours, showing a touch of complexity, and smooth, ripe tannins. Best drinking mid-2017+.

Vintage	14
WR	7
Drink	16-20

 DRY $29 AV

Marsden Bay of Islands The Winemaker's Daughter Merlot ★★★☆

The deeply coloured 2014 vintage (★★★☆) was grown at Kerikeri, matured for a year in French oak casks (30 per cent new), and bottled without fining or filtering. Fragrant and supple, it is fresh and vibrantly fruity, in a moderately complex style, with plum/spice flavours, ripe and generous. Best drinking 2017+.

Vintage	14	13
WR	6	5
Drink	16-20	16-19

 DRY $40 –V

Matawhero Gisborne Merlot ★★★☆

The 2013 vintage (★★★☆) was briefly barrel-aged. Deeply coloured, it is mouthfilling and fruit-packed, with vibrant, plummy, spicy flavours, in a gutsy style with gentle tannins and a smooth finish.

Vintage	13
WR	6
Drink	P

DRY $25 –V

Matua Single Vineyard Hawke's Bay Merlot (★★★★★)

Estate-grown in the Matheson Vineyard, the powerful, deeply coloured 2013 vintage (★★★★★) is a classy red that should unfold well for many years. It has concentrated plum, blackcurrant and spice flavours, with finely integrated, nutty oak and good tannin backbone. Dense, but not tough, with impressive depth, ripeness and structure, it should be at its best 2017+.

 DRY $60 AV

Matua Single Vineyard Hawke's Bay Merlot/Malbec ★★★★☆

The dark, purple-flushed 2014 vintage (★★★★★) is a classy, fruit-packed blend from the Matheson Vineyard, in the Bridge Pa Triangle. Hand-picked and matured in French (mostly) and American oak barrels, it is powerful, with concentrated, very ripe plum/spice flavours, a hint of dark chocolate, gentle tannins and a rich, finely textured finish.

DRY $58 –V

Milcrest Estate Nelson Merlot   (★★★☆)

The 2014 vintage (★★★☆) is a single-vineyard red, matured for 10 months in French oak barrels. Medium to full-bodied, with good colour depth, it is vibrantly fruity, with strong plum/spice flavours, a hint of herbs, fresh acidity and considerable complexity.

DRY $34 –V

Mills Reef Elspeth Gimblett Gravels Hawke's Bay Merlot   ★★★★☆

The 2013 vintage (★★★★☆) was grown in the company's Mere Road Vineyard and matured for 17 months in French oak barrels (28 per cent new). Deep and youthful in colour, it is floral, rich and smooth, with a smoky oak influence and concentrated, ripe plum/spice flavours, savoury and finely textured. Best drinking 2017+.

Vintage	13	12	11	10	09	08	07	06
WR	7	NM	NM	7	7	NM	7	7
Drink	16-25	NM	NM	16-18	16-18	NM	16-18	16-17

DRY $49 –V

Mills Reef Estate Hawke's Bay Merlot/Cabernet   ★★★

The 2014 vintage (★★★) was matured for nine months in French and American oak casks. Full-coloured, it is mouthfilling and smooth (5 grams/litre of residual sugar), with plum, blackcurrant and spice flavours, showing some complexity. It's drinking well now.

Vintage	15	14	13
WR	7	6	7
Drink	16-20	16-18	16-19

MED/DRY $19 AV

Mills Reef Reserve Gimblett Gravels Hawke's Bay Merlot   ★★★☆

The 2014 vintage (★★★☆) was matured for over a year in French and American oak casks (24 per cent new). Full-coloured, mouthfilling and supple, it is vibrantly fruity, with ripe, plummy, spicy flavours, seasoned with sweet oak, gentle tannins, and lots of drink-young appeal.

Vintage	15	14	13	12
WR	7	6	7	6
Drink	16-21	16-20	16-19	P

DRY $25 –V

Mills Reef Reserve Gimblett Gravels Hawke's Bay Merlot/Malbec   ★★★☆

The 2014 vintage (★★★☆) is full-coloured and sweet-fruited, with strong, ripe, plummy, spicy flavours, some oak complexity and a smooth finish. It's enjoyable young.

Vintage	15	14	13	12	11	10
WR	7	7	7	6	7	7
Drink	16-21	16-20	16-19	P	P	P

DRY $25 –V

Mission Hawke's Bay Merlot ★★★

The 'lightly oaked' 2014 vintage (★★★☆) offers fine value. Full-coloured and mouthfilling, it has generous, ripe blackcurrant and plum flavours, gentle tannins and a seductively smooth finish. Drink now onwards.

 DRY $18 AV

Mission Hawke's Bay Merlot/Cabernet Sauvignon ★★★

The 2014 vintage (★★★) is full-coloured, with a fresh, slightly herbaceous bouquet. Made in a 'lightly oaked' style, it is mouthfilling and vibrantly fruity, with plum and herb flavours, gentle tannins and a smooth finish. Drink now to 2018.

 DRY $18 AV

Mission Reserve Hawke's Bay Merlot ★★★★

The 2014 vintage (★★★★) is a generous red from the Gimblett Gravels, matured for 14 months in French oak casks (25 per cent new). Weighty, ripe and rich, it has plum, spice and nutty oak flavours, showing good complexity and harmony.

Vintage	14	13	12	11	10	09	08
WR	7	7	5	5	6	6	5
Drink	16-25	16-25	16-18	16-18	16-18	16-17	P

 DRY $25 AV

Mission Vineyard Selection Hawke's Bay Merlot ★★★☆

The 2014 vintage (★★★☆) was matured in French oak casks (18 per cent new). Deeply coloured, it has strong plum and spice flavours, braced by firm tannins. Worth cellaring.

 DRY $20 AV

Moana Park Hawke's Bay Merlot/Malbec ★★★☆

The 2014 vintage (★★★★) is a powerful, bold Gimblett Gravels blend of Merlot (80 per cent), Malbec (15 per cent) and Cabernet Franc (5 per cent), matured for a year in French oak barriques (30 per cent new). It has concentrated plum, spice and herb flavours, with smooth tannins. Sharply priced.

Vintage	14	13
WR	6	5
Drink	16-21	16-20

 DRY $20 AV

Moana Park Single Vineyard Reserve Merlot/Cabernet (★★★)

The 2013 vintage (★★★) is full-coloured, with a slightly leafy bouquet and good flavour depth. It's a generous, green-edged wine with a firm finish.

DRY $40 –V

Monarch Estate Vineyard Matakana Merlot (★★★☆)

The 2014 vintage (★★★☆) was matured in French and American oak barrels (45 per cent new). Full-coloured, it is mouthfilling and vibrant, with fresh, ripe, moderately concentrated, plummy flavours, an earthy streak, and drink-young appeal.

DRY $28 –V

Montana Winemakers' Series Hawke's Bay Merlot ★★★

From Pernod Ricard NZ, the 2015 vintage (★★★☆) is deeply coloured and mouthfilling, with generous plum and spice flavours. Priced sharply.

DRY $15 V+

Mount Riley Marlborough Merlot/Malbec ★★★

The 2013 vintage (★★★☆) is a sturdy, full-flavoured blend of Merlot (95 per cent) and Malbec (5 per cent), barrique-aged for 10 months. Deep and bright in colour, it is full-bodied and fleshy, with fresh, strong plum and spice flavours, a restrained oak influence and a smooth finish. A good, gutsy quaffer, it's priced right.

DRY $17 AV

Mudbrick Vineyard Reserve Merlot/Cabernet Sauvignon ★★★★☆

Estate-grown and hand-harvested at two sites on Waiheke Island, the 2013 vintage (★★★★☆) was matured for nine months in French oak barriques (30 per cent new). A blend of Merlot (60 per cent), Cabernet Sauvignon (35 per cent) and Malbec (5 per cent), it is deep and youthful in colour. Powerful (14.5 per cent alcohol), it has bold plum and spice flavours, hints of dark chocolate and herbs, impressive concentration and a firm backbone of tannin. Open 2017+.

Vintage	13	12
WR	7	6
Drink	16-25	16-25

DRY $55 –V

Ngatarawa Proprietors' Reserve Hawke's Bay Merlot/Cabernet (★★★★★)

This is my pick of the outstanding new Proprietors' Reserve selection. Grown in the Bridge Pa Triangle and the Gimblett Gravels, the 2013 vintage (★★★★★) is a memorable wine, in the classic Bordeaux style. Dark, with a fragrant, spicy, complex bouquet, it is rich and sweet-fruited, with highly concentrated blackcurrant, plum and spice flavours, a hint of dark chocolate, fine-grained tannins and obvious cellaring potential. It should flourish for a decade.

DRY $40 AV

Ngatarawa Stables Reserve Hawke's Bay Merlot ★★★

The 2015 vintage (★★★) is a full-coloured, berryish, slightly herbal red with plenty of flavour and a moderately firm finish.

DRY $19 AV

Obsidian Estate Waiheke Island Merlot/Cabernets/Petit Verdot (★★★☆)

The 2014 vintage (★★★☆) is fresh, vibrantly fruity and flavoursome, with a herbal thread. Full-coloured, with a slightly leafy bouquet, it is plummy and spicy, with some nutty, savoury complexity, very good depth, and moderate tannins. Enjoyable young.

DRY $29 –V

Old Coach Road Nelson New Zealand Merlot (★★)

Priced right, the 2013 vintage (★★) was matured for 10 months in French and American oak. Lightish in colour, it is a solid quaffer, with fresh plum and herb flavours. (From Seifried.)

Vintage	13
WR	5
Drink	16-18

DRY $13 AV

Old Coach Road Nelson New Zealand Merlot/Malbec/Cabernet Franc (★★)

Ready to roll, the French oak-aged 2014 vintage (★★) is lightish in colour, with fresh plum, spice and herb flavours. A pleasant quaffer, it's best drunk young.

Vintage	14
WR	5
Drink	16-18

DRY $13 AV

Omata Estate Russell Merlot (★★★★)

The 2013 vintage (★★★★) is a full-coloured Northland red, matured in all-new oak casks. Mouthfilling, it has strong, youthful berry, plum and spice flavours, seasoned with quality oak, good complexity and a lingering finish.

DRY $52 –V

Oyster Bay Hawke's Bay Merlot ★★★☆

From Delegat, this red accounts for a huge slice of New Zealand's exports of 'Bordeaux-style' wines (Merlot and/or Cabernet Sauvignon). Winemaker Michael Ivicevich aims for a wine with 'sweet fruit and silky tannins. The trick is – not too much oak.' It is typically fragrant and mouthfilling, with strong blackcurrant, herb and dark chocolate flavours, supple tannins, and plenty of drink-young appeal. The 2014 vintage (★★★★) was grown in the Gimblett Gravels (which provides 'structure') and at Crownthorpe ('fleshiness'), and 50 per cent of the blend was matured for 11 months in French oak barriques. It's a mouthfilling, rich wine with good concentration of plummy flavours, a hint of dark chocolate, and a deliciously smooth finish. Fine value.

DRY $20 AV

Paritua Hawke's Bay Merlot (★★★★☆)

The 2013 vintage (★★★★☆) is a powerful, youthful red, matured for over a year in barrels (50 per cent new). Densely coloured, with a fragrant, richly spiced bouquet, it's a strapping wine (15 per cent alcohol), with concentrated, ripe blackcurrant, plum and spice flavours, hints of dark chocolate and liquorice, and fine-grained tannins. Best drinking 2017+.

Vintage	13
WR	7
Drink	16-25

DRY $40 –V

Pask Declaration Hawke's Bay Merlot   ★★★★☆

Estate-grown in the Gimblett Gravels and matured for 21 months in French oak barrels (90 per cent new), the 2014 vintage (★★★★☆) is deeply coloured, mouthfilling, rich and smooth. Finely poised, with good varietal character, it has strong, youthful plum and spice flavours, showing very good complexity, and a finely balanced finish. Best drinking 2018+.

Vintage	14	13
WR	6	7
Drink	18-25	16-25

 DRY $50 –V

Pask Gimblett Gravels Merlot   ★★★☆

The 2014 vintage (★★★☆) was matured for over a year in French and American oak barrels (8 per cent new). Deep ruby, it is mouthfilling and vibrantly fruity, with ripe, plummy, slightly spicy flavours, a gentle seasoning of oak, and drink-young appeal.

Vintage	14	13
WR	6	7
Drink	16-22	16-20

 DRY $22 AV

Paulownia Estate Merlot   (★★★☆)

Grown in the northern Wairarapa, the 2013 vintage (★★★☆) has very good depth of plum, spice and slight herb flavours, showing some savoury complexity.

 DRY $25 –V

Peacock Sky Waiheke Island Merlot/Malbec   ★★★★

Showing good potential, the 2014 vintage (★★★★) is a youthful, 3:1 blend of Merlot and Malbec, French oak-aged for over a year. Deeply coloured, it has fresh, smooth, ripe blackcurrant, plum and spice flavours, gently seasoned with oak, and firm tannins.

 DRY $40 –V

Peacock Sky Waiheke Island Pure Merlot   ★★★☆

The sturdy 2014 vintage (★★★☆) was matured for over a year in French oak barrels. Full-coloured, it has strong, ripe, plummy, slightly spicy and nutty flavours, and a firm backbone of tannin.

 DRY $40 –V

Pegasus Bay Waipara Valley Merlot/Cabernet   ★★★★

The 2013 vintage (★★★★☆) is the best since 2010 (★★★★☆). Blended principally from Merlot, Cabernet Sauvignon and Cabernet Franc, with a splash of Malbec, it was matured for two years in French oak barriques. Deeply coloured, it is still youthful, with strong, vibrant blackcurrant, plum and spice flavours, finely integrated oak, ripe, supple tannins, and excellent depth, complexity and harmony. Best drinking 2018+.

Vintage	13	12	11	10
WR	7	6	6	7
Drink	16-24	16-22	16-21	16-21

DRY $31 –V

Peter Yealands Hawke's Bay Merlot (★★★☆)

Full-coloured and mouthfilling, the 2013 vintage (★★★☆) has lots of ripe, plummy, slightly spicy flavour and a hint of dark chocolate. A fruit-driven style, it's finely balanced for good, early drinking.

Vintage	13
WR	7
Drink	P

 DRY $19 V+

Poverty Bay Merlot/Cabernet (★★★★)

The 2013 vintage (★★★★) is a fleshy, ripe Gisborne red, based on vines planted in 1985 at Bridge Estate. Barrel-matured for 18 months, it is a blend of Merlot (46 per cent), Cabernet Sauvignon (24 per cent), Cabernet Franc (22 per cent), and a splash of Malbec. Fresh and vibrantly fruity, it has ripe blackcurrant and plum flavours, an earthy streak, a gentle oak influence, and excellent depth.

 DRY $30 –V

Quarter Acre Hawke's Bay Merlot/Malbec ★★★☆

The 2013 vintage (★★★★), a blend of Merlot, Malbec and Cabernet Franc, was hand-picked at Havelock North and matured for 16 months in French oak barriques (30 per cent new). Full-coloured, it has strong, youthful blackcurrant, plum and spice flavours, showing good complexity, and obvious cellaring potential; best drinking 2017+.

 DRY $35 –V

Redmetal Vineyards Basket Press Merlot/Cabernet Franc ★★★★

Grown in the Bridge Pa Triangle, Hawke's Bay, the 2013 vintage (★★★★☆) was made almost entirely from Merlot (only 2 per cent Cabernet Franc), and barrel-aged for over a year. Deep and bright in colour, it is mouthfilling and rich, with ripe blackcurrant, plum and spice flavours, hints of dark chocolate and nuts, and the concentration and structure to age well.

Vintage	13
WR	6
Drink	16-23

DRY $28 AV

Redmetal Vineyards Hawke's Bay Merlot/Cabernet Franc ★★★☆

The 2014 vintage (★★★★) is a good buy. Grown in the Bridge Pa Triangle, it was matured in a 50:50 split of tanks and barrels. Deeply coloured, it is mouthfilling, with generous, ripe plum, spice and dark chocolate flavours, savoury notes adding complexity, and a finely textured finish. Delicious from the start.

 DRY $18 V+

Redmetal Vineyards Resolution Hawke's Bay Merlot   (★★★★☆)

The powerful 2013 vintage (★★★★☆) was grown in the Bridge Pa Triangle and matured for 14 months in French (85 per cent) and American (15 per cent) oak barrels (30 per cent new). Dark and purple-flushed, it is mouthfilling, rich, fruit-packed and supple, with strong berry, plum and spice flavours. Fleshy, sweet-fruited and generous, it should be at its best 2017+.

Vintage	13
WR	6
Drink	17-25

DRY $60 –V

Regent of Tantallon Hawke's Bay Merlot Cabernet Limited Edition   (★★★★)

From The Wine Portfolio (formerly owner of Morton Estate), the 2009 vintage (★★★★), currently on the market, has full, slightly developed colour. It is a blend of Merlot (77 per cent), with minor amounts of Cabernet Sauvignon, Malbec, Cabernet Franc and Syrah. Mouthfilling, it has strong berry, plum, spice and slight herb flavours, savoury notes adding complexity, and a firm finish. Drink now.

DRY $40 –V

Renato Estate Nelson Merlot   ★★★

Estate-grown at Kina, on the coast, the 2013 vintage (★★★) was matured for a year in French oak barrels (15 per cent new). Deep ruby, it is ripely fragrant, with strong plum and spice flavours, showing some savoury complexity.

Vintage	13	12
WR	5	6
Drink	16-18	16-17

DRY $25 –V

Rongopai Hawke's Bay Merlot/Cabernet   (★★)

The 2014 vintage (★★) is lightish in colour, with green-edged aromas and moderate depth of slightly leafy flavour. (From Babich.)

DRY $20 –V

Sacred Hill Brokenstone Merlot – see Sacred Hill Brokenstone in the Branded and Other Red Wines section

Sacred Hill Halo Hawke's Bay Merlot/Cabernet Sauvignon   ★★★★

The 2014 vintage (★★★★), blended from Merlot (88 per cent) and Cabernet Sauvignon (12 per cent), was hand-picked in the Gimblett Gravels and matured for 18 months in French oak barrels (10 per cent new). Showing good potential, it is deeply coloured and mouthfilling, with fresh, strong, very youthful plum, blackcurrant and spice flavours, a subtle seasoning of oak and ripe, supple tannins. Best drinking 2018+.

Vintage	14	13	12	11
WR	6	7	6	6
Drink	16-20	16-18	P	P

DRY $28 AV

Sacred Hill Hawke's Bay Merlot/Cabernet Sauvignon ★★★★

Already delicious, the 2015 vintage (★★★★), partly barrel-aged, is a top buy. A full-coloured blend of Merlot (80 per cent), Cabernet Sauvignon (14 per cent) and splashes of Malbec and Cabernet Franc, it is mouthfilling, with strong, ripe blackcurrant, plum and spice flavours, hints of herbs and dark chocolate, and gentle tannins.

Vintage	15
WR	6
Drink	16-20

 DRY $20 V+

Sacred Hill Reserve Hawke's Bay Merlot/Cabernet Sauvignon ★★★☆

A fruit-driven style, the 2014 vintage (★★★☆) is a blend of Merlot (79 per cent) and Cabernet Sauvignon (21 per cent), aged for a year in French oak barrels. Full-coloured, it is mouthfilling, with some savoury complexity and very good depth of fresh plum, blackcurrant and spice flavours.

Vintage	14
WR	6
Drink	16-19

 DRY $25 –V

Saint Clair Hawke's Bay Merlot ★★★★

The 2014 vintage (★★★★) is a floral, deeply coloured, single-vineyard Gimblett Gravels red, American oak-matured. Mouthfilling, it has ripe blackcurrant, plum and spice flavours, showing some savoury complexity, and soft tannins.

 DRY $25 AV

Saint Clair Pioneer Block 17 Plateau Block Hawke's Bay Merlot ★★★★

The powerful 2014 vintage (★★★★☆) was estate-grown in the Gimblett Gravels and matured for 10 months in American oak casks (43 per cent new). Fragrant and youthful, it is deeply coloured, with red-berry, plum, spice, liquorice and nut flavours, gentle tannins, and excellent weight, ripeness and richness.

 DRY $38 –V

Saint Clair Vicar's Choice Marlborough Merlot ★★★

The 2014 vintage (★★★) is enjoyable young. A vibrant, 'fruit-driven' style of red, it was grown in the Wairau Valley and seasoned with American oak. Purple-flushed, it has fresh, berryish flavours to the fore, with hints of plums and spices, gentle tannins and a smooth finish.

DRY $19 AV

Satyr Three Roads Hawke's Bay Merlot (★★★★)

From Sileni, the 2013 vintage (★★★★) was grown in the Bridge Pa Triangle and barrel-matured (20 per cent new). Deep and still fairly youthful in colour, it is powerful and fleshy, with ripe, blackcurrant-like flavours, hints of liquorice and nuts, and good concentration. Drink now to 2018.

 DRY $34 –V

Selaks Founders Limited Edition Gimblett Gravels Hawke's Bay Merlot   (★★★★)

The 2013 vintage (★★★★) was matured in a mix of French and American oak barrels (25 per cent new). Deeply coloured, it is mouthfilling and rich, with concentrated, ripe blackcurrant, plum, herb and spice flavours, a hint of sweet oak, and fine-grained tannins.

DRY $40 –V

Selaks Reserve Hawke's Bay Merlot/Cabernet   (★★★☆)

Grown mostly in the company's Corner 50 Vineyard, in the Bridge Pa Triangle, the debut 2013 vintage (★★★☆) is a blend of Merlot (90 per cent) and Cabernet Sauvignon (10 per cent), matured in tanks and barrels (French and American). Full-coloured, it is mouthfilling, with fresh, strong, plummy, spicy flavours, hints of herbs and dark chocolate, and gentle tannins. A fruit-driven style, it's very skilfully crafted for early enjoyment and priced sharply.

DRY $19 V+

Sileni Cellar Selection Hawke's Bay Merlot   ·   ★★★☆

The generous, youthful 2015 vintage (★★★☆) is a lightly oaked red, full-coloured, with fresh plum, spice and herb flavours, and finely balanced tannins. An attractive, moderately complex wine, it's worth cellaring.

Vintage	15	14	13
WR	7	7	6
Drink	16-23	16-22	16-19

DRY $20 AV

Sileni Estate Selection Cut Cane Hawke's Bay Merlot   ★★★★★

The 2014 vintage (★★★★★) is a very powerful red, matured for 15 months in a 3:1 mix of French and American oak barriques (40 per cent new). Grown in the Bridge Pa Triangle, it is a single-vineyard wine. The crops were thinned to one bunch per shoot, before 'at optimal ripeness, the canes were cut, allowing the fruit on the vine to shrivel, concentrating the juice within'. Deeply coloured, with a fragrant, complex bouquet, it is robust (15.5 per cent alcohol) but not tough, with a strong surge of ripe plum/spice flavours, showing notable fruit sweetness and concentration, and the structure to mature well. A memorable mouthful.

Vintage	14	13
WR	7	7
Drink	16-26	16-23

DRY $40 AV

Sileni Estate Selection Triangle Hawke's Bay Merlot   ★★★★

The classy 2014 vintage (★★★★★) was matured for 16 months in French oak casks (30 per cent new). Deeply coloured and fragrant, it is sturdy (14.5 per cent alcohol) and sweet-fruited, with beautifully ripe, plummy flavours, hints of spices and dark chocolate, and fine-grained tannins. Lovely in its youth, it's the best vintage yet.

Vintage	14	13	12	11	10	09	08
WR	7	7	5	6	6	7	6
Drink	16-24	16-23	16-18	16-17	P	16-17	P

DRY $33 –V

Sileni Exceptional Vintage Hawke's Bay Merlot   ★★★★☆

The 2013 vintage (★★★★★) was matured for 15 months in French oak casks (40 per cent new). Boldly coloured, it's a powerful, strapping red (15 per cent alcohol), with vibrant, very deep blackcurrant, plum, spice and nut flavours, balanced tannins, and a long future ahead. Best drinking 2017+.

Vintage	13	
WR	7	
Drink	16-25	

 DRY $70 –V

Snapper Rock Hawke's Bay Merlot/Cabernet   (★★★☆)

Offering excellent value, the 2013 vintage (★★★☆) has deep, fairly youthful colour. Mouthfilling, it has fresh, ripe plum/spice flavours, showing very good depth, finely balanced tannins, and some cellaring potential. Drink now to 2018.

 DRY $17 V+

Soljans Tribute Hawke's Bay Merlot/Malbec   ★★★☆

The 2013 vintage (★★★☆), French oak-matured, is full and bright in colour. Mouthfilling and vibrantly fruity, it has very good depth of berry, plum, spice and nut flavours, showing some savoury complexity. Drink now or cellar.

Vintage	13	
WR	6	
Drink	16-18	

DRY $40 –V

Spy Valley Single Vineyard Marlborough Merlot/Malbec   ★★★★

The 2014 vintage (★★★★) is a full-coloured blend of Merlot and Malbec, matured for 18 months in French oak barrels (29 per cent new). Deeply coloured, with a fresh, plummy, spicy bouquet, it is mouthfilling and vibrantly fruity, with good density of ripe plum, berry and spice flavours, fine-grained tannins, and good aging potential.

Vintage	14	13	12	11	10
WR	6	5	6	7	7
Drink	16-21	16-18	16-18	16-18	P

DRY $23 V+

Stonecroft Ruhanui Gimblett Gravels Hawke's Bay
Merlot/Cabernet Sauvignon   ★★★★☆

Certified organic, the 2014 vintage (★★★★☆) is a blend of Merlot (60 per cent) and Cabernet Sauvignon (40 per cent), grown at Roys Hill and matured for 18 months in French oak barrels (10 per cent new). Deep and bright in colour, it is fragrant and supple, with generous, ripe blackcurrant, plum, spice and nut flavours, finely integrated oak, and good complexity. It's already delicious; drink now or cellar.

Vintage	14	13
WR	7	7
Drink	19-26	18-25

 DRY $37 AV

Stoneleigh Latitude Marlborough Merlot   (★★★☆)

The debut 2014 vintage (★★★☆) was grown in the relatively warm Rapaura district, on the north side of the Wairau Valley, and matured for nine months in French and Hungarian oak barrels. Full-coloured, it is mouthfilling, with very good depth of fresh blackcurrant, plum, dried-herb and spice flavours, finely balanced tannins, moderate complexity and lots of drink-young charm.

 DRY $23 AV

Stoneleigh Marlborough Merlot   ★★★☆

The 2015 vintage (★★★☆) from Pernod Ricard NZ is deeply coloured, with mouthfilling body, good depth of plummy, spicy flavours, showing some savoury complexity, and a finely balanced, smooth finish. Fine value.

 DRY $17 V+

Takatu Matakana Merlot/Franc/Malbec   ★★★★☆

The 2013 vintage (★★★★) is an elegant, full-coloured red with youthful, plummy, slightly earthy flavours, showing good complexity, and a lingering finish. Best drinking 2017+.

 DRY $39 AV

Tantalus Estate Waiheke Island Merlot/Cabernet Franc   (★★★★)

Grown at Onetangi, the 2014 vintage (★★★★) was matured for nine months in French and American oak casks. Full and fairly youthful in colour, it is mouthfilling, with generous, ripe, spicy, slightly earthy flavours, showing good freshness and complexity, underlying tannins, and lots of current-drinking appeal. Open now to 2018.

Vintage	14
WR	6
Drink	16-20

DRY $38 –V

Te Awa Single Estate Hawke's Bay Merlot/Cabernet Sauvignon   ★★★★☆

The fine-value 2014 vintage (★★★★★) is a dark, elegant blend of Merlot and Cabernet Sauvignon, matured for 20 months in French oak casks (45 per cent new). Well worth cellaring, it has rich blackcurrant, plum and spice flavours, with savoury, earthy notes adding complexity, and ripe, supple tannins.

Vintage	14	13
WR	7	7
Drink	17-24	16-23

DRY $30 AV

Te Awanga Estate Hawke's Bay Merlot/Cabernet Franc   (★★★★☆)

The 2013 vintage (★★★★☆) was harvested from 17-year-old Merlot and 12-year-old Cabernet Franc vines, and matured for 18 months in French oak casks (20 per cent new). Full-coloured, it is mouthfilling and sweet-fruited, with vibrant, plummy, spicy flavours, nutty, savoury elements adding complexity, and finely balanced tannins. An elegant, youthful, supple wine, it's well worth cellaring.

 DRY $28 V+

Te Mata Estate Vineyards Merlot/Cabernets   ★★★☆

The highly attractive 2015 vintage (★★★★) is a blend of Merlot, Cabernet Sauvignon and Cabernet Franc, oak-aged for a year. Deep and youthful in colour, it is concentrated, with generous, vibrant plum, berry and spice flavours, in a fruit-driven style, delicious young.

Vintage	15
WR	6
Drink	17-23

DRY $20 AV

Thornbury Hawke's Bay Merlot   ★★★☆

The 2015 vintage (★★★☆) is a floral, fruit-packed, youthful red, matured for 10 months with French and American oak staves. It offers plenty of plummy, spicy flavour, with a touch of complexity, and moderately firm tannins. Fine value. (From Villa Maria.)

Vintage	15	14	13	12	11	10
WR	5	6	7	4	5	6
Drink	16-20	16-19	16-18	P	P	P

DRY $16 V+

Tohu Hawke's Bay Merlot   (★★★☆)

The easy-drinking but not simple 2014 vintage (★★★☆) was hand-picked and matured in old French oak barriques. Full-coloured, it is mouthfilling, with moderately concentrated, ripe plum/spice flavours, showing some savoury complexity, finely balanced tannins, and lots of current-drinking appeal.

DRY $22 AV

Toi Toi Gisborne Merlot   ★★★

Enjoyable young, the 2014 vintage (★★★) has fullish colour. Mouthfilling, it has fresh, plummy, spicy flavours, in a fruit-driven style with good depth.

DRY $18 AV

Trinity Hill Hawke's Bay Merlot   ★★★★

This delicious, drink-young red is grown in the Gimblett Gravels and Bridge Pa Triangle. The 2015 vintage (★★★★) is full-coloured and mouthfilling, with strong, youthful plum/spice flavours, hints of liquorice and dark chocolate, some savoury complexity, and fine-grained tannins. Showing good ripeness, texture and density, it's a finely crafted red, likely to be at its best mid-2017+.

DRY $22 V+

Two Gates Hawke's Bay Merlot/Cabernet Franc/Cabernet Sauvignon   (★★★☆)

Currently on sale, the 2010 vintage (★★★☆) was grown at Maraekakaho, hand-picked and matured in French oak barriques (30 per cent new). The colour is dark and slightly developed; the palate is mouthfilling, with very good depth of plummy, nutty, spicy flavour, showing some complexity.

DRY $32 –V

Vidal Hawke's Bay Merlot/Cabernet Sauvignon ★★★

The good-value 2014 vintage (★★★☆) is a fresh, vibrant blend of Merlot (83 per cent), Cabernet Sauvignon (12 per cent) and Malbec (5 per cent), partly barrel-matured. Medium-bodied, it has plummy flavours, with hints of cassis and coffee, and a smooth finish.

DRY $16 V+

Vidal Reserve Gimblett Gravels Merlot/Cabernet Sauvignon ★★★★

The great-value 2014 vintage (★★★★☆) is a blend of Merlot (64 per cent), Cabernet Sauvignon (25 per cent), Malbec (10 per cent) and Cabernet Franc (1 per cent), matured for 20 months in French oak casks (25 per cent new). Fragrant, full-bodied and savoury, it is deep and youthful in colour, with rich, ripe plum and blackcurrant flavours, a hint of dark chocolate, a subtle seasoning of spicy oak, and good tannin backbone. Enjoyable now, it should age gracefully for several years.

Vintage	14	13	12	11	10
WR	7	7	5	6	7
Drink	16-23	16-22	16-18	P	16-17

DRY $20 V+

Villa Maria Cellar Selection Hawke's Bay Merlot/Cabernet Sauvignon ★★★★

Sharply priced, the 2014 vintage (★★★★) is a fragrant blend of Merlot (60 per cent), Cabernet Sauvignon (32 per cent) and Cabernet Franc (8 per cent), matured for 20 months in French, American and Hungarian oak barriques (15 per cent new). Deeply coloured, it is rich and supple, with strong, ripe plum, spice and slight herb flavours, a gentle seasoning of nutty oak, and finely balanced tannins. Best drinking 2018+.

Vintage	14	13	12	11	10	09
WR	7	7	6	6	7	7
Drink	16-22	16-22	16-19	16-17	16-17	P

DRY $20 V+

Villa Maria Cellar Selection Hawke's Bay Organic Merlot ★★★★

The full-coloured 2014 vintage (★★★☆) is a blend of Merlot (95 per cent) and Malbec (5 per cent), matured for 18 months in French, American and Hungarian oak casks (20 per cent new). Grown in the Gimblett Gravels, it is youthful, fresh and vibrantly fruity, with strong, plummy flavours, showing some savoury complexity, and a distinctly spicy finish. Best drinking mid-2017+.

Vintage	14	13
WR	6	7
Drink	16-20	16-20

DRY $20 V+

Villa Maria Library Release Gimblett Gravels Merlot/Cabernet Sauvignon   (★★★★★)

The 2010 vintage (★★★★★) is a classy, very refined blend of Merlot (62 per cent) and Cabernet Sauvignon (38 per cent), matured in French oak barriques (60 per cent new) for 18 months. It has deep, still youthful colour. Still unfolding, it has concentrated, ripe blackcurrant and spice flavours, showing good, savoury complexity, and fine-grained tannins. Built to last, it should be at its best 2017+.

Vintage	10
WR	7
Drink	16-22

DRY $70 AV

Villa Maria Private Bin Hawke's Bay Merlot   ★★★☆

The great-value 2015 vintage (★★★★) was matured in tanks and barrels. Rich, with a subtle oak influence and soft tannins, it is a deeply coloured, youthful red, with strong, ripe plum/spice flavours.

Vintage	15	14	13
WR	7	7	6
Drink	16-20	16-19	16-18

DRY $17 V+

Villa Maria Private Bin Hawke's Bay Merlot/Cabernet Sauvignon   ★★★☆

The 2014 vintage (★★★☆) is full-coloured and mouthfilling, with fresh, strong plum, spice and slight herb flavours, gently seasoned with oak. A generous, vibrantly fruity red, it should be at its best 2017+.

Vintage	14	13	12	11
WR	7	7	5	6
Drink	16-18	16-18	P	P

DRY $17 V+

Villa Maria Reserve Gimblett Gravels Hawke's Bay Merlot   ★★★★★

This consistently outstanding wine is grown at company-owned vineyards in the Gimblett Gravels and matured for 17 to 20 months in French oak barriques (35 per cent new in 2014). The 2014 vintage (★★★★★) is built for cellaring. A classy, dark, very youthful red, it is concentrated and firmly structured, with rich, beautifully ripe, red and black-berry fruit flavours, seasoned with spicy oak. Weighty, dense and complex, it has obvious potential.

Vintage	14	13
WR	7	7
Drink	19-26	17-23

DRY $50 AV

🍇🍇🍇

Villa Maria Single Vineyard Braided Gravels Hawke's Bay Merlot   (★★★★★)

Certified organic, the outstanding 2013 vintage (★★★★★) was grown in the Gimblett Gravels and matured for 17 months in French oak barriques (35 per cent new). Bold, bright and youthful in colour, it has rich, ripe plum/spice flavours, with fine-grained tannins. A powerful, dense red, it is sweet-fruited, soft and long.

Vintage	13	DRY $60 AV
WR	7	
Drink	16-23	

Wairau River Marlborough Merlot   (★★★)

The 2014 vintage (★★★) was matured in French and American oak casks (30 per cent new). Fullish in colour, it is mouthfilling, with fresh plum and spice flavours, showing a touch of complexity, gentle tannins and drink-young appeal.

Vintage	14	DRY $20 –V
WR	6	
Drink	16-20	

Montepulciano

Montepulciano is widely planted across central Italy, yielding deeply coloured, ripe wines with good levels of alcohol, extract and flavour. In the Abruzzi, it is the foundation of the often superb-value Montepulciano d'Abruzzo, and in the Marches it is the key ingredient in the noble Rosso Conero.

In New Zealand, Montepulciano is a rarity and there has been confusion between the Montepulciano and Sangiovese varieties. Some wines may have been incorrectly labelled. According to the latest national vineyard survey, between 2005 and 2017, New Zealand's area of bearing Montepulciano vines will expand slightly from 6 to 9 hectares (mostly in Auckland, Hawke's Bay, Nelson and Marlborough).

Blackenbrook Nelson Montepulciano ★★★☆

The 2014 vintage (★★★☆) was matured for a year in seasoned French oak barriques. It has full, bright colour, with a slightly herbal bouquet, and strong plum, berry and spice flavours, showing some savoury complexity. A youthful, finely balanced wine, it should be at its best 2017+.

Vintage	14
WR	7
Drink	16-20

 DRY $33 –V

Coopers Creek SV Guido In Velvet Pants Huapai Montepulciano ★★★★

Estate-grown at Huapai, in West Auckland, the 2014 vintage (★★★★) was matured for a year in seasoned oak barrels. Deep and youthful in colour, it is mouthfilling and vibrantly fruity, with concentrated blackcurrant, plum and spice flavours, showing good complexity, and fine-grained tannins. Best drinking 2017+.

Vintage	14	13
WR	6	6
Drink	16-19	16-18

 DRY $29 AV

De La Terre Hawke's Bay Montepulciano ★★★★★

The impressive 2014 vintage (★★★★★) is rare, but well worth tracking down. Hand-picked at Havelock North and matured for 14 months in French oak barriques (33 per cent new), it's a worthy follow-up to the similarly delicious 2013 vintage (★★★★★). Deeply coloured, it is mouthfilling, but not heavy, with rich berry, plum and spice flavours, showing good complexity, ripe, supple tannins and a long, harmonious finish. Already drinking well, it's a concentrated, finely structured red with good cellaring potential; open mid-2017 onwards.

Vintage	14	13
WR	7	6
Drink	16-25	16-28

DRY $40 AV

Framingham Marlborough Montepulciano   ★★★☆

The 2011 vintage (★★★), matured for 18 months in French oak casks (30 per cent new), has fairly full, slightly developed colour. Medium-bodied, with berry, plum and spice flavours, it shows some nutty complexity. Drinking well now, the superior 2010 vintage (★★★★) is full and bright in colour, with plum, chocolate and nut flavours, showing very good depth, texture and complexity.

Vintage	11
WR	5
Drink	16-20

DRY $30 –V

Hans Herzog Marlborough Montepulciano   ★★★★★

This powerful, classy, estate-grown red is typically overflowing with ripe, sweet-fruit flavours. The 2013 vintage (★★★★★) was hand-picked on the north side of the Wairau Valley, fermented with indigenous yeasts, matured for two and a half years in French oak barriques (partly new), and bottled unfined and unfiltered. Dark and purple-flushed, it is still very youthful, with inviting red-berry and spice aromas. Mouthfilling, it is a rich, complex, age-worthy wine, with an array of ripe plum, berry, spice, nut and dark chocolate flavours, and good tannin backbone. It should flourish for a decade; open 2018+. Certified organic.

Vintage	13
WR	7
Drink	16-23

DRY $64 AV

Hitchen Road Montepulciano   ★★★☆

The 2014 vintage (★★★) was estate-grown at Pokeno, in North Waikato, and barrel-matured for 10 months. Bold and purple-flushed in colour, it is medium to full-bodied, with fresh acidity and a herbal streak running through its strong, vibrant plum, cherry and spice flavours. It's a good wine, but slightly less attractive than the vineyard's 2014 Dolcetto.

DRY $18 V+

Milcrest Estate Nelson Montepulciano   ★★★

The 2014 vintage (★★★) is a single-vineyard red, grown at Hope. Handled without oak, it is full and youthful in colour, in a fruit-driven style, with strong, vibrant, plummy, spicy flavours, fresh acidity and gentle tannins. Enjoyable young.

DRY $32 –V

Obsidian Estate Waiheke Island Montepulciano   (★★★★)

The 2015 vintage (★★★★) is the first to be labelled as 'Estate'. Full-coloured, it is sturdy (14.5 per cent alcohol) and vibrantly fruity, with strong, ripe plum, blackcurrant and spice flavours, slightly earthy notes adding complexity, and gentle tannins. Delicious young, it's a drink-now or cellaring proposition.

DRY $38 –V

Obsidian Waiheke Island Montepulciano ★★★★★

The 2013 vintage (★★★★★), matured in French oak casks (20 per cent new), is one of New Zealand's best-yet examples of Montepulciano – densely coloured, ripely scented and fruit-packed. Already delicious, it has lovely depth of fresh blackcurrant and plum flavours, a subtle oak influence and a finely textured, spicy, sustained finish. Drink now or cellar.

Vintage	13	12
WR	7	6
Drink	16-22	16-20

 DRY $38 AV

Omaha Bay Vineyard Matakana Montepulciano ★★★★

The 2012 vintage (★★★★) was estate-grown at Matakana and matured for two years in oak casks (25 per cent new). Deep in colour, it is mouthfilling and supple, with blackcurrant, spice, herb and nut flavours, showing very good depth and complexity.

Vintage	12
WR	6
Drink	16-17

DRY $40 –V

Trinity Hill Gimblett Gravels Hawke's Bay Montepulciano (★★★★☆)

The 2014 vintage (★★★★☆) is impressive. Deep and very youthful in colour, it is mouthfilling and supple, with deep, ripe blackcurrant, plum and spice flavours, showing excellent texture and richness. A generous, sweet-fruited wine, partly barrel-aged, it's a drink-now or cellaring proposition.

DRY $35 AV

Nebbiolo

Nebbiolo is the foundation of Piedmont's most majestic red wines – Barolo, Barbaresco and Gattinara – renowned for their complex, leather and tar flavours, powerful tannins and great longevity. In New Zealand, only 1 hectare of vines will be bearing in 2016, mostly in Central Otago, Marlborough and Auckland.

Hans Herzog Marlborough Nebbiolo ★★★★☆

Estate-grown on the north side of the Wairau Valley, the very rare 2011 vintage (★★★★☆) was matured for two years in French oak barriques (100 per cent new). Full-coloured, it is youthful, with vibrant, deep plum, spice and blackcurrant flavours, hints of tar and liquorice, savoury notes adding complexity, and a sustained finish. Certified organic.

Vintage	11	
WR	7	
Drink	16-26	

DRY $115 –V

Petit Verdot

This traditional Bordeaux variety lost popularity in the region, due to its habit of ripening very late in the season, or not ripening at all in cool vintages. Petit Verdot means 'Small Green' – a reference to the grape's little berries and often unripe, 'green' flavours. However, this thick-skinned variety has good disease resistance and high levels of tannin. Petit Verdot is today slowly gaining ground in Spain, Italy, Australia and North and South America. In New Zealand, there will be 8 hectares of bearing vines in 2017, concentrated in Auckland and Hawke's Bay. Stonyridge, on Waiheke Island, describes Petit Verdot as 'like a supercharged Cabernet ... very high in tannin, colour, alcohol and acidity.'

Omaha Bay Vineyard Matakana Petit Verdot (★★★★☆)

Deeply coloured, the 2010 vintage (★★★★☆) was matured for over a year in barrels (50 per cent new). Fleshy, generous and supple, it has strong blackcurrant, plum and spice flavours, with hints of dark chocolate and nuts, in a tightly structured style, developing good complexity. It's maturing very gracefully.

Vintage	10
WR	6
Drink	16-20

DRY $50 -V

Pinot Noir

New Zealand Pinot Noir enjoys strong overseas demand and there are now countless Pinot Noir labels, as producers launch second and even third-tier labels, as well as single-vineyard bottlings (and others under 'buyer's own' and export-only brands you and I have never heard of). The wines are enjoying notable success in international competitions, but you need to be aware that most of the world's elite Pinot Noir producers, especially in Burgundy, do not enter. Between 2000 and 2017, New Zealand's area of bearing Pinot Noir vines is expanding from 1126 hectares to 5719 hectares, makng it the country's most widely planted red-wine variety (far ahead of Merlot, with 1327 hectares.)

Pinot Noir is the princely grape variety of red Burgundy. Cheaper wines typically display light, raspberry-evoking flavours, but great Pinot Noir has substance, suppleness and a gorgeous spread of flavours: cherries, fruit cake, spice and plums.

Pinot Noir is now New Zealand's most internationally acclaimed red-wine style. Well over 45 per cent of the country's total Pinot Noir plantings are in Marlborough, and the variety is also well established in Otago (27 per cent), Wairarapa (9 per cent), Canterbury (7 per cent), Hawke's Bay and Nelson.

Yet Pinot Noir is a frustrating variety to grow. Because it buds early, it is vulnerable to spring frosts; its compact bunches are also very prone to rot. One crucial advantage is that it ripens early, well ahead of Cabernet Sauvignon. Low cropping and the selection of superior clones are essential aspects of the production of fine wine.

Martinborough (initially) and Central Otago have enjoyed the highest profile for Pinot Noir over the past 30 years. As their output of Pinot Noir has expanded, average prices have fallen, reflecting the arrival of a tidal wave of 'entry-level' (drink-young) wines.

Of the other small regions, Nelson and Canterbury (especially Waipara) are also enjoying success. Marlborough's potential for the production of outstanding – but still widely underrated – Pinot Noir, in sufficient volumes to supply the burgeoning international demand, has also been tapped.

8 Ranges Barrel Selection Central Otago Pinot Noir ★★★☆

Estate-grown near Alexandra, the 2013 vintage (★★★☆) is ruby-hued and moderately youthful, with a slightly earthy bouquet. Matured in French oak barrels (42 per cent new), it is spicy and savoury, with hints of herbs and nuts, considerable complexity, fresh acidity and a fairly firm finish.

DRY $42 –V

8 Ranges Tussock Ridge Central Otago Pinot Noir ★★★☆

Estate-grown at Alexandra, the elegant 2014 vintage (★★★★) was matured for 10 months in French oak casks (30 per cent new). Deep ruby, it is fresh, ripe, plummy, spicy and youthful, with savoury, earthy notes adding complexity. Best drinking mid-2017+.

DRY $36 –V

36 Bottles Central Otago Pinot Noir ★★★☆

The 2013 vintage (★★★☆) is a charming, single-vineyard wine, hand-picked at Bendigo and matured for nearly a year in French oak (36 per cent new). Floral and supple, it is vibrantly fruity, with moderately concentrated cherry and plum flavours. Enjoyable young.

Vintage	13	12
WR	6	6
Drink	16-19	16-18

DRY $32 –V

12,000 Miles Pinot Noir   ★★★☆

From the Gladstone winery, in the northern Wairarapa, the deep ruby 2014 vintage (★★★☆) is drinking well in its youth. Floral, fresh and soft, it has generous, well-ripened plum/spice flavours, savoury notes adding a touch of complexity, gentle acidity, and fine-grained tannins. Verging on four stars.

DRY $25 AV

Aitken's Folly Riverbank Road Central Otago Pinot Noir   (★★★★☆)

Estate-grown at Wanaka, the impressive 2013 vintage (★★★★☆) was fermented with indigenous yeasts and matured in French oak barriques (30 per cent new). Deeply coloured, it is weighty, with deep, youthful, well-ripened plum, cherry and spice flavours, finely integrated oak, and a rich, finely balanced finish. A stylish wine with good potential, it should be at its best 2018+.

DRY $35 V+

Akarua Bannockburn Central Otago Pinot Noir   ★★★★★

Estate-grown, harvested from mature vines and matured in French oak barriques, the 2014 vintage (★★★★★) is deep ruby, with an encitingly fragrant bouquet. Generous, vibrantly fruity and supple, it has concentrated, well-ripened cherry, plum, spice and dried-herb flavours, showing excellent complexity, and a finely poised, lasting finish. Already delicious, it should be at its best 2018+.

Vintage	14	13	12	11	10	09
WR	7	7	7	7	7	7
Drink	16-24	16-23	16-22	16-20	16-18	16-18

DRY $42 V+

Akarua Rua Central Otago Pinot Noir   ★★★★

For a third-tier label, this regional blend can be remarkably good. Matured for six months in French oak barriques (10 per cent new), the highly attractive 2015 vintage (★★★★) was grown at three company-owned sites, two at Bannockburn. Delicious in its youth, it is floral, sweet-fruited and supple, with strong, plummy, cherryish, slightly nutty flavours, showing good complexity. More subtle and savoury than you'd expect at this price, it offers fine value.

DRY $28 V+

Akarua The Siren Bannockburn Central Otago Pinot Noir   ★★★★★

The second 2013 vintage (★★★★★) of Akarua's top Pinot Noir was estate-grown and selected from 13 barrels out of 650. Deeply coloured, it has a highly perfumed, savoury bouquet. Powerful and densely packed, it is very sweet-fruited and finely textured, with concentrated, vibrant cherry, plum and spice flavours, fresh acidity and silky tannins. Already delicious, it should be long-lived; best drinking 2018+.

Vintage	13	12
WR	7	7
Drink	20-24	19-23

DRY $100 –V

Akitu A1 Central Otago Pinot Noir ★★★★☆

Estate-grown by Hawkesbury Estates at Mt Barker, in the Wanaka sub-region, the 2015 vintage (★★★★☆) is a youthful, bright ruby-hued red, matured for 10 months in French oak barrels (25 per cent new). Fresh and finely textured, it is savoury and supple, with concentrated, ripe cherry, plum and spice flavours, showing good complexity. Well worth cellaring, it should break into full stride 2018+.

DRY $59 –V

Akitu A2 Central Otago Pinot Noir ★★★★

Grown at Mt Barker, in the Wanaka sub-region, the skilfully crafted 2015 vintage (★★★★) is enjoyable from the start. Matured for 10 months in French oak barrels (13 per cent new), it has a scented, savoury bouquet, leading into an elegant wine with ripe cherry, plum and spice flavours, showing very good delicacy, complexity and depth. Drink mid-2017+. (From Hawkesbury Estates).

DRY $40 –V

Alex K Big Backyard Central Otago Pinot Noir (★★★)

The 2015 vintage (★★★) is a fresh, medium-bodied, distinctly spicy blend of Alexandra and Bendigo fruit, bottled unfined and unfiltered. Bright ruby, it has red-berry, spice and dried-herb flavours, showing some savoury, smoky complexity, gentle acidity and a moderately firm finish.

DRY $28 –V

Alex Ridgeback Central Otago Pinot Noir (★★★☆)

The 2014 vintage (★★★☆) is a ruby-hued, full-bodied Alexandra red with very good depth of vibrant, ripe, plummy, spicy flavours and a smooth finish. A gently oaked style, it shows some complexity. (From Greylands Ridge.)

DRY $25 AV

Alexander Dusty Road Martinborough Pinot Noir ★★★★

Designed for early drinking, the 2013 vintage (★★★★) is a single-vineyard red, hand-picked and matured for 15 months in French oak barriques. Full ruby, it is mouthfilling and sweet-fruited, with ripe cherry, plum, spice and nut flavours, balanced tannins, and good complexity. Fine value.

DRY $25 V+

Alexandra Wine Company Alex Gold Central Otago Pinot Noir ★★★★

Delicious young, the 2014 vintage (★★★★) was matured in French oak casks (31 per cent new). Bright ruby, it is finely scented, in an elegant, supple style with cherry, plum and spice flavours, fresh and strong. Instantly likeable.

DRY $30 AV

Alexandra Wine Company Davishon Central Otago Pinot Noir ★★★★

The 2015 vintage (★★★☆) is a full ruby, mouthfilling red with fresh plum and spice flavours, showing a gentle oak influence, good tannin support, and some savoury complexity. Best drinking mid-2017+.

DRY $36 AV

Allan Scott Generations Marlborough Pinot Noir   (★★★☆)

Enjoyable young, the 2015 vintage (★★★☆) is a single-vineyard red, hand-picked and matured for 16 months in new French oak puncheons. Bright ruby, it is floral and supple, with attractive, berryish, slightly nutty flavours, showing some complexity. Best drinking mid-2017+.

DRY $36 –V

Allan Scott Marlborough Pinot Noir   (★★★☆)

Still youthful, the 2014 vintage (★★★☆) was matured in French oak casks (20 per cent new). Bright ruby, it is a medium to full-bodied, sweet-fruited wine with cherry, plum and spice flavours, a hint of herbs, considerable complexity and a fairly firm finish. Best drinking mid-2017+.

DRY $26 AV

Amisfield Central Otago Pinot Noir   ★★★★★

Estate-grown at Lowburn, in the Cromwell Basin, the 2014 vintage (★★★★☆) is from vines planted from 1999 to 2007. Hand-picked at 23–25 brix, fermented with indigenous yeasts and matured for 10 months in French oak barriques (23 per cent new), it is deep ruby and floral, mouthfilling and sweet-fruited, with generous, cherryish, plummy flavours, savoury notes adding compexity, good harmony and a rounded finish. Already delicious.

DRY $50 AV

Amisfield RKV Reserve Central Otago Pinot Noir   ★★★★★

Estate-grown at Pisa, in the Cromwell Basin, the youthful 2013 vintage (★★★★★) was harvested at 24–25 brix from 14-year-old vines in the Rocky Knoll block, fermented with indigenous yeasts, and matured for 18 months in French oak casks (35 per cent new). Deep ruby, with a fragrant, very savoury bouquet, it is ripe and supple, with highly complex plum, cherry, spice and nut flavours, fine-grained tannins, and obvious potential; open 2018+.

DRY $120 –V

Anchorage Family Estate Nelson Pinot Noir   ★★☆

The 2014 vintage (★★★) is a light ruby, medium-bodied, fruity style with plum and spice flavours, fresh and lively, and a tight finish.

DRY $21 –V

Ant Moore Signature Series Marlborough Pinot Noir   (★★★☆)

Certified organic, the 2014 vintage (★★★☆) was grown in the Wairau Valley. Ruby-hued, it is mouthfilling, with satisfying depth of plum, cherry and spice flavours, a hint of herbs, balanced tannins and good complexity.

DRY $27 AV

Ara Pathway Marlborough Pinot Noir   ★★★

Still on sale, the 2013 vintage (★★★☆) is drinking well now. Mouthfilling and smooth, with lightish, slightly developed colour, it has ripe, moderately concentrated cherry, plum and spice flavours.

Vintage	13
WR	5
Drink	16-17

DRY $22 –V

Ara Resolute Marlborough Pinot Noir   ★★★★☆

Still on sale, the 2012 vintage (★★★★☆) was estate-grown in the lower Waihopai Valley, hand-picked and matured in French oak casks (partly new). Deep in colour, it is graceful and finely poised, with strong cherry, plum, spice and nut flavours, silky-textured and long. Well worth cellaring.

Vintage	12
WR	7
Drink	16-20

DRY $60 –V

Ara Select Blocks Marlborough Pinot Noir   ★★★★

Estate-grown in the Waihopai Valley, the 2013 vintage (★★★☆) is mouthfilling, fresh and lively, with strong, ripe plum and cherry flavours, showing a touch of savoury complexity, gentle tannins, and lots of drink-young appeal. Still on sale, the 2012 vintage (★★★★) is concentrated, ripe, earthy and savoury, with good complexity.

DRY $30 AV

Ara Single Estate Marlborough Pinot Noir   ★★★★

The good-value 2014 vintage (★★★★) was estate-grown in the Waihopai Valley. Bright ruby, it is mouthfilling, sweet-fruited and supple, with youthful cherry, plum and spice flavours, showing very good depth, complexity and harmony. Best drinking mid-2017+.

Vintage	14
WR	5
Drink	16-18

DRY $25 V+

Aravin Central Otago Pinot Noir   ★★★★

Grown at Alexandra and barrel-aged, the 2014 vintage (★★★★) is bright ruby, floral and supple, with very good depth of ripe plum/spice flavours, finely integrated oak and gentle tannins. An elegant rather than powerful wine, it's a drink-now or cellaring proposition.

DRY $32 AV

Archangel Central Otago Pinot Noir   ★★★★

This single-vineyard red is grown at Queensberry, half-way between Cromwell and Wanaka, and matured for 10 months in French oak barriques (partly new). The 2013 vintage (★★★★) is full-coloured and fruit-packed, with strong, vibrant plum and spice flavours, gently seasoned with oak, youthful vigour, and obvious potential; open 2017+.

Vintage	13	12
WR	7	7
Drink	16-20	16-20

 DRY $32 AV

Aronui Adam's Block Nelson Pinot Noir   (★★★☆)

Enjoyable now, the 2013 vintage (★★★☆) is an estate-grown, Upper Moutere wine, mouthfilling, ruby-hued, vibrantly fruity and supple, with good depth of fresh plum/spice flavours, a hint of herbs, and some barrel-aged complexity.

 DRY $28 AV

Aronui Single Vineyard Nelson Pinot Noir   ★★★☆

From Kono (which also owns the Tohu brand), the 2014 vintage (★★★☆) was estate-grown at Upper Moutere, hand-picked and French oak-aged. Deep ruby, it is mouthfilling, sweet-fruited and supple, with cherry, plum and spice flavours, in a moderately complex style, enjoyable young.

 DRY $28 AV

Ashwell Martinborough Pinot Noir   ★★★☆

Still on sale, the 2010 vintage (★★★☆) was matured in French oak casks (50 per cent new). Mature in colour, it is mellow, slightly herbal, very nutty and savoury. Ready.

Vintage	10
WR	6
Drink	16-20

DRY $40 –V

Ashwell The Quails Martinborough Pinot Noir   ★★★

Still on sale, the 2010 vintage (★★★) was matured in French oak casks (30 per cent new). Lightish and mature in colour, it is herbal and nutty, with lively acidity, some savoury complexity and good flavour depth. Ready.

Vintage	10
WR	5
Drink	16-20

 DRY $30 –V

Askerne Hawke's Bay Pinot Noir   (★★☆)

The 2015 vintage (★★☆) was matured for 10 months in barrels (25 per cent new). Light ruby, it has slightly herbal flavours, showing moderate depth.

 DRY $22 –V

Astrolabe Province Marlborough Pinot Noir ★★★★

The 2014 vintage (★★★★) was grown in the Wairau Valley and at Kekerengu, fermented with indigenous yeasts and matured in French oak casks (25 per cent new). Full-coloured, it is mouthfilling and supple, with strong, vibrant plum and spice flavours, generous, finely textured and harmonious.

 DRY $30 AV

Ata Mara Central Otago Pinot Noir (★★★★)

Offering very good value, the 2014 vintage (★★★★) was estate-grown in the Cromwell Basin and matured for 10 months in French oak barrels (25 per cent new). Ruby-hued, with a slightly spicy bouquet, it is mouthfilling and sweet-fruited, with fresh plum/spice flavours, finely integated oak adding complexity, ripe, supple tannins and good harmony.

 DRY $25 V+

Ata Rangi Crimson Pinot Noir ★★★★☆

This second-tier label is 'a vibrant expression of younger' vines and made for relatively early drinking – but the majority of the vines are still 10 to 20 years old. Hand-harvested at Martinborough, fermented with indigenous yeasts and matured in French oak casks, the 2014 (★★★★★) is a top vintage. Deep and youthful in colour, mouthfilling and concentrated, it has lovely fruit sweetness and richness, with strong plum and spice flavours, finely structured and long. Best drinking 2017+.

Vintage	14	13
WR	7	7
Drink	16-18	16-17

DRY $38 V+

Ata Rangi Pinot Noir ★★★★★

One of the greatest of all New Zealand wines, this Martinborough red is powerfully built and concentrated, yet seductively fragrant and supple. 'Intense, opulent fruit with power beneath' is founder Clive Paton's goal. 'Complexity comes with time.' The grapes are drawn from numerous sites, including the estate vineyard, planted in 1980, and the vines, up to 36 years old, have a very low average yield of 4.5 tonnes of grapes per hectare. The wine is fermented with indigenous yeasts and maturation is for 11 months in French oak barriques (35 per cent new in 2014). From an early-ripening season, the 2014 vintage (★★★★★) is deeply coloured and mouthfilling, with very generous, youthful cherry, plum and spice flavours. Concentrated, vibrant and savoury, with notable complexity and the structure to mature well, it's a very harmonious red, already highly approachable, but likely to be at its best 2020+.

Vintage	14	13	12	11	10	09	08
WR	7	7	7	7	7	7	7
Drink	16-26	16-25	16-24	16-23	16-22	16-21	16-20

DRY $75 AV

Ataahua Waipara Pinot Noir ★★★★

The 2013 vintage (★★★★) is an elegant, ruby-hued wine, hand-picked, fermented with indigenous yeasts and matured for a year in seasoned French oak barrels. Mouthfilling and supple, with ripe cherry, plum and spice flavours, a gentle seasoning of nutty oak, and a finely poised, lingering finish, it is vibrantly fruity, with good harmony. Drink now or cellar.

Vintage	13	12	11	10
WR	7	6	7	6
Drink	16-20	16-18	16-20	P

DRY $37 AV

Auntsfield Hawk Hill Southern Valleys Pinot Noir (★★★★)

Currently on sale, the 2011 vintage (★★★★) is a single-block red, estate-grown on the south side of the Wairau Valley and matured for 14 months in French oak casks (38 per cent new). Full and fairly mature in colour, it is sturdy (14.5 per cent alcohol), with a nutty, herbal bouquet. Spicy and savoury, with fresh acidity and hints of liquorice and leather, it shows a slight lack of ripeness and harmony, but also excellent complexity and concentration.

Vintage	11
WR	6
Drink	16-25

DRY $59 –V

Auntsfield Heritage Marlborough Pinot Noir ★★★★★

From 'the very best seven barrels of the vintage', the 2010 (★★★★★) was estate-grown on the south side of the Wairau Valley and matured in French oak casks (43 per cent new). Deeply coloured, it's an authoritative red, with a beautifully fragrant, spicy, nutty, complex bouquet. Mouthfilling, with notably concentrated and vibrant flavours of cherries, plums, spices and nuts, and a moderately firm finish, it's delicious now, but should also flourish for a decade.

Vintage	10	09	08	07	06	05
WR	5	6	NM	6	NM	7
Drink	16-25	16-25	NM	16-21	NM	16-20

DRY $95 AV

Auntsfield Road Ridge Southern Valleys Marlborough Pinot Noir ★★★★

The 2012 vintage (★★★★) of this single-block, estate-grown red was matured for 10 months in French oak casks (33 per cent new). Sturdy, with fullish, slightly developed colour, it's a firm, concentrated style of Pinot Noir, with strong, slightly earthy, spicy flavours, a hint of herbs, and good, savoury complexity.

Vintage	12
WR	5
Drink	16-22

DRY $59 –V

Auntsfield Single Vineyard Southern Valleys Marlborough Pinot Noir ★★★★★

Grown on north-facing slopes at Auntsfield, on the south side of the Wairau Valley, the 2013 vintage (★★★★★) is fleshy and complex. Deep and youthful in colour, it is powerful (14.5 per cent alcohol), mouthfilling and sweet-fruited, with vibrant cherry, plum and spice flavours, good tannin support, and lovely depth and harmony. The 2014 vintage (★★★★★) is also impressive. Matured for 10 months in French oak casks (31 per cent new), it is deeply coloured, mouthfilling, warm and concentrated, with very ripe plum, cherry and spice flavours, nutty and savoury, good tannin backbone and strong personality. Best drinking 2018+.

Vintage	14	13	12	11	10	09	08
WR	7	7	7	6	7	6	5
Drink	16-23	16-23	16-22	16-20	16-17	P	P

DRY $40 V+

Aurum Central Otago Pinot Noir ★★★★

Estate-grown at Lowburn, in the Cromwell Basin, and matured for 12 months in French oak casks (18 per cent new), the 2014 vintage (★★★★☆) is still youthful. Deeply coloured, mouthfilling and supple, it has concentrated, ripe plum, cherry and spice flavours, with finely integrated oak adding complexity, and obvious cellaring potential. Certified organic.

Vintage	14	13	12	11	10	09
WR	5	5	6	6	6	6
Drink	16-18	16-19	16-18	16-19	16-18	P

DRY $35 AV

Aurum Madeleine Central Otago Pinot Noir ★★★★☆

Named after the winemaker's daughter, the 2013 vintage (★★★★☆) is a rare wine – only 75 cases were made. Estate-grown at Lowburn and matured for a year in French oak casks (30 per cent new), it is a distinctive wine – savoury and earthy, rather than fruit-packed. Full-bodied, it is an age-worthy style with rich, ripe cherry, plum and spice flavours, good tannin support and excellent complexity.

Vintage	13	12	11	10	09
WR	6	6	NM	NM	7
Drink	16-20	16-22	NM	NM	16-20

DRY $85 –V

Aurum Mathilde Central Otago Pinot Noir ★★★★

Estate-grown at Lowburn, in the Cromwell Basin, the full, bright ruby 2013 vintage (★★★★☆) was matured for a year in French oak casks (18 per cent new). Sturdy and built to last, it is mouthfilling and savoury, with strong, ripe cherry, plum, spice and nut flavours, showing excellent complexity, and the structure to mature gracefully. Drink now or cellar.

Vintage	13	12
WR	5	6
Drink	16-20	16-20

DRY $55 –V

Awatere River by Louis Vavasour Marlborough Pinot Noir ★★★☆

The 2014 vintage (★★★☆) is a floral, supple red, grown at three sites in the Awatere Valley and matured for nine months in French oak barriques (30 per cent new). Light ruby, it's an elegant style with moderately concentrated berry, plum, spice and dried-herb flavours, showing some savoury complexity.

DRY $31 –V

Babich Black Label Marlborough Pinot Noir ★★★☆

Ruby-hued, the 2014 vintage (★★★☆) was grown in the Waihopai and Wairau valleys, and aged for 10 months in oak casks (20 per cent new). A mouthfilling, supple red, it has good weight and depth of ripe cherry, plum, herb and spice flavours, youthful and harmonious. The 2015 vintage (★★★★) is instantly attractive. Deep ruby, it is fragrant and supple, with strong, ripe cherry, plum and spice flavours, showing some savoury complexity. Best drinking mid-2017+.

 DRY $25 AV

Babich Family Estates Headwaters Organic Pinot Noir ★★★★

Certified organic, the deep ruby 2014 vintage (★★★★) is a single-vineyard Marlborough red, oak-aged for seven months and bottled unfiltered. Generous, savoury and supple, it has concentrated plum/spice flavours, showing good ripeness and complexity, and the structure to age well. Fine value.

 DRY $27 V+

Babich Marlborough Pinot Noir ★★★

Ruby-hued, the 2015 vintage (★★★) is mouthfilling, with fresh, plummy, spicy flavours, showing a touch of complexity from five to eight months of oak aging. Youthful, with decent depth and gentle tannins, it's finely balanced for attractive, early drinking.

 DRY $25 –V

Babich Winemakers' Reserve Marlborough Pinot Noir ★★★★

The 2014 vintage (★★★★☆) is the best yet. Estate-grown in the Waihopai Valley, it was matured for 10 months in barrels (35 per cent new). Deeply coloured and fleshy, it is generous, with substantial body, concentrated, ripe, plummy, spicy flavours, nutty, savoury, earthy notes adding complexity, and good tannin backbone. A wine of strong personality, it's a drink-now or cellaring proposition.

Vintage	14	13	12	11	10
WR	7	7	7	7	7
Drink	16-20	16-19	16-18	16-17	P

 DRY $35 AV

Bald Hills Bannockburn Single Vineyard Central Otago Pinot Noir ★★★★★

The 2014 vintage (★★★★☆) is one of the finest yet. Matured in French oak barriques (30 per cent new), it is a stylish, deeply coloured red, mouthfilling and youthful, with strong cherry, plum and spice flavours, integrated oak, and fine-grained tannins. Vibrantly fruity and concentrated, with good harmony, it has excellent cellaring potential.

Vintage	14	13
WR	5	4
Drink	16-20	16-19

DRY $45 AV

Ballasalla Central Otago Pinot Noir ★★★★

From Folding Hill, at Bendigo, the 2014 vintage (★★★★☆) is a fruit-packed, single-vineyard red, matured for 10 months in French oak barriques (20 per cent new), and bottled unfined and unfiltered. Deep ruby, it has strong, vibrant plum/spice flavours to the fore, a subtle seasoning of oak adding complexity, gentle tannins and loads of drink-young appeal. Good value.

 DRY $32 AV

Bannock Brae Central Otago Pinot Noir ★★★★★

Top vintages of this single-vineyard Bannockburn red are outstanding. The classy 2014 vintage (★★★★★) was matured for 10 months in French oak casks (35 per cent new), and bottled unfined and unfiltered. Deep ruby, with an encitingly fragrant bouquet, it is full-bodied, with a sense of youthful vigour and concentrated, vibrant cherry, plum and spice flavours, showing excellent complexity and harmony. Best drinking mid-2017+.

Vintage	14	13	12	11	10	09	08
WR	7	7	NM	7	6	7	5
Drink	16-25	16-25	NM	16-25	16-24	16-17	P

 DRY $60 AV

Bannock Brae Goldfields Central Otago Pinot Noir ★★★★

This is typically a 'feminine', very graceful, supple wine. Offering excellent value, the 2014 vintage (★★★★☆), grown at Bannockburn, was matured for a year in French oak barriques (12 per cent new). Deep ruby, it is fragrant and mouthfilling, with concentrated, ripe plum, cherry and spice flavours, showing good complexity. A youthful, age-worthy wine, it should be at its best from 2017 onwards.

Vintage	14	13	12	11	10	09	08
WR	7	6	7	6	7	7	5
Drink	16-23	16-22	16-22	16-19	16-20	16-17	P

 DRY $30 AV

Bel Echo by Clos Henri Marlborough Pinot Noir ★★★★

The 2014 vintage (★★★★) was estate-grown on the stonier, less clay-bound soils at Clos Henri, in the Wairau Valley, and matured in large oak vats (40 per cent) and old French barrels (60 per cent). Full-coloured and mouthfilling, it is generous, savoury and supple, with strong, ripe plum, spice and nut flavours, showing good complexity. Enjoyable from the start, it's also well worth cellaring. Certified organic.

Vintage	14	13	12
WR	6	6	6
Drink	16-20	16-19	16-18

 DRY $31 AV

Bellbird Spring Block Eight Waipara Pinot Noir ★★★☆

The 2012 vintage (★★★☆) has lightish, developed colour. Mouthfilling and supple, with cherry, plum, herb and nut flavours, it is savoury and finely textured. Ready.

 DRY $40 –V

Bellbird Spring River Terrace Waipara Pinot Noir   ★★★☆

The 2012 vintage (★★★☆), matured for a year in French oak casks (15 per cent new), is a 'forward' vintage, with full, slightly developed colour, mouthfilling body, and very good depth of cherry and plum flavours, soft and harmonious. Ready.

Vintage	12	11
WR	6	6
Drink	16-19	16-18

 DRY $38 –V

Bird Big Barrel Marlborough Pinot Noir   ★★★☆

The floral, supple 2014 vintage (★★★☆) is a single-vineyard wine, grown at Rapaura and fermented and matured for 10 months in large, 900-litre barrels. Ruby-hued, it is mouthfilling, with fresh, ripe, plummy, slightly nutty flavours, showing considerable complexity and good harmony.

 DRY $35 –V

Black Cottage Marlborough Pinot Noir   ★★★

The 2014 vintage (★★★☆) is a sharply priced red, ruby-hued, fresh and finely textured, with cherry/plum flavours, showing good delicacy and harmony. Skilfully crafted, with a touch of complexity, it's drinking well now.

 DRY $20 AV

Black Cottage Reserve Central Otago Pinot Noir   ★★★☆

Enjoyable young, the partly barrel-aged 2015 vintage (★★★☆) is bright ruby, mouthfilling and smooth, with ripe cherry, plum and spice flavours, showing some savoury complexity. Drink now or cellar.

DRY $25 AV

Black Estate Damsteep Waipara Valley Pinot Noir   ★★★★☆

The 2014 vintage (★★★★☆) was grown at Omihi in the Damsteep Vineyard, planted in 1999. Fermented with indigenous yeasts, it was matured for a year in seasoned French oak barrels, and bottled unfined and unfiltered. Bright ruby, with a fragrant, savoury bouquet, it is a youthful, elegant, finely poised wine with concentrated, ripe plum, cherry and spice flavours, showing good complexity, and a lingering finish. Best drinking 2018+.

 DRY $42 AV

Black Estate Home Waipara Valley Pinot Noir   ★★★★

The 2014 vintage (★★★★) was grown in the home vineyard, planted in 1994, hand-picked, fermented with indigenous yeasts, matured for a year in seasoned French oak barriques, and bottled unfined and unfiltered. Light ruby, it is savoury and nutty, with moderately rich cherry, plum and spice flavours, showing good ripeness and complexity. Best drinking 2018+.

 DRY $42 –V

Black Estate Netherwood Pinot Noir

From the first hill-grown vineyard in North Canterbury, the 2014 vintage (★★★★) is from ungrafted, unirrigated vines, planted in 1986. Hand-picked, fermented with indigenous yeasts, matured for a year in seasoned oak barrels, and bottled unfined and unfiltered, it has lightish, youthful colour. Medium-bodied, it is a subtle, almost fragile red, with gentle cherry, plum, spice and nut flavours, showing very good complexity.

DRY $65 –V

Black Estate Waipara Valley Pinot Noir

This single-vineyard, estate-grown red is from vines planted at Omihi in 1994. The 2012 vintage (★★★★☆) was hand-picked, matured for a year in seasoned French oak barrels, and bottled unfined and unfiltered. Full of personality, it is ruby-hued and very harmonious, with ripe cherry and nut flavours, finely textured, complex, savoury and silky. Delicious drinking now onwards.

DRY $42 AV

Black Quail Estate Central Otago Pinot Noir

Grown at Bannockburn, the 2013 vintage (★★★★) is a youthful, single-vineyard red, floral, deeply coloured and mouthfilling, with fresh, ripe cherry, plum and dried-herb flavours, seasoned with toasty oak, and very good concentration and complexity.

DRY $39 AV

Black Stilt Waitaki Valley Pinot Noir

Barrel-matured (30 per cent new oak), the 2013 vintage (★★★☆) is mouthfilling, with good depth of ripe plum, spice and herb flavours, a touch of complexity, and a fairly firm finish.

DRY $36 –V

Blackenbrook Family Reserve Nelson Pinot Noir

The 2015 vintage (★★★★) was estate-grown, hand-picked and matured for a year in French oak barriques (23 per cent new). Deeply coloured, it is mouthfilling and supple, with generous, very ripe plum, spice and slight liquorice flavours. Fruit-packed, with some savoury complexity, it's an unabashedly bold style of Pinot Noir, already enjoyable but well worth cellaring.

Vintage	15	14
WR	6	7
Drink	16-26	16-25

DRY $38 V+

Bladen Marlborough Pinot Noir   ★★★

The 2013 vintage (★★★) is a single-vineyard, Wairau Valley red, hand-picked and matured for over a year in French oak barriques. Light ruby, with a hint of development, it is mouthfilling, with gentle, ripe cherry, plum and spice flavours, a slightly nutty oak influence, and a smooth finish. Ready.

DRY $33 –V

Blind River Awatere Valley Marlborough Pinot Noir ★★★☆

Estate-grown in the Awatere Valley, the 2013 vintage (★★★☆) was matured in French oak casks (25 per cent new). Full ruby, it is floral and supple, with a vibrantly fruity palate, showing cherry, plum and spice flavours, a hint of nutty oak, and gentle tannins.

Vintage	13
WR	7
Drink	16-20

DRY $36 –V

Bone Hill Kaituna Valley Banks Peninsula Pinot Noir (★★★★)

'Sourced from New Zealand's oldest commercial Pinot Noir vineyard', the 2013 vintage (★★★★) was grown at the head of the Kaituna Valley and matured in seasoned oak casks. Ruby-hued, it is scented and savoury, in a medium-bodied style with lively plum and spice flavours, hints of cherries and herbs, fresh acidity and good complexity. Drink now onwards.

Vintage	13
WR	5
Drink	16-20

DRY $30 AV

Boneline (The) Waipara Pinot Noir ★★★★☆

From 'venerable, old vines', the classy 2014 vintage (★★★★★) was hand-picked and matured for a year in French oak casks. A beautiful young wine, it is deep ruby, rich and poised, with fresh acidity, concentrated plum/spice flavours and ripe, silky tannins. Best drinking 2017+.

 DRY $40 AV

Boundary Vineyards Kings Road Waipara Pinot Noir ★★★

Offering great value, the 2015 vintage (★★★☆) from Pernod Ricard NZ is bright ruby, mouthfilling and supple, with very good depth of plummy, spicy flavour, showing a touch of complexity. Enjoyable young.

 DRY $20 AV

Brancott Estate Letter Series 'T' Marlborough Pinot Noir ★★★★

The 2015 vintage (★★★★☆), still very youthful, is a classy, vibrantly fruity red, well worth cellaring to 2018+. Bright ruby, with a fragrant, ripe, cherryish bouquet, it is full-bodied and supple, with strong, ripe cherry and plum flavours, savoury notes adding complexity, and a persistent finish.

 DRY $33 AV

Brancott Estate Living Land Series Marlborough Pinot Noir ★★★

The 2014 vintage (★★★☆) is ruby-hued, mouthfilling and supple. Already drinking well, it has moderately concentrated red-berry, strawberry and spice flavours, gentle tannins and good harmony. Certified organic.

 DRY $20 AV

Brancott Estate South Island Pinot Noir   ★★★

The pleasant 2014 vintage (★★☆) is a ruby-hued, easy-drinking style with cherry, plum and spice flavours, light and smooth. Ready.

DRY $17 V+

Brancott Estate Special Reserve Waipara Pinot Noir   ★★★☆

The 2013 vintage (★★★☆) is a ruby-hued, sweet-fruited red, fleshy, mouthfilling and supple. Enjoyable young, it has fresh plum and cherry flavours, showing good depth, and a gentle seasoning of toasty oak. Fine value.

DRY $20 V+

Brancott Estate Terroir Series Awatere Valley Marlborough Pinot Noir   ★★★

The 2015 vintage (★★★) is an attractive, light style. Ruby-hued, scented and supple, it has gentle, ripe cherry/plum flavours, showing a touch of complexity, good harmony and a smooth finish.

DRY $20 AV

Brennan B2 Central Otago Pinot Noir   ★★★☆

Estate-grown at Gibbston, the deep ruby 2014 vintage (★★★★) has a fragrant bouquet of plums and dried herbs. It is full-bodied and supple, with generous, ripe fruit flavours, a gentle seasoning of French oak (27 per cent new) adding complexity, and a well-rounded finish. Drink now or cellar.

DRY $31 –V

Brennan Gibbston Central Otago Pinot Noir   ★★★★☆

The impressively rich, complex 2012 vintage (★★★★☆) was estate-grown at Gibbston and matured in French oak casks (44 per cent new). Full, bright ruby, it is mouthfilling and savoury, with cherry, plum, spice and dried-herb flavours, showing excellent concentration and harmony. Drink now to 2018.

DRY $55 –V

Brightside Organic New Zealand Pinot Noir   (★★★)

Certified organic, the 2015 vintage (★★★) is not labelled by region, but was made by Nelson-based Kaimira Estate. Matured in French oak barrels (22 per cent new), it is deep ruby and full-bodied, with good depth of spicy, plummy flavours, showing a touch of complexity, and a fairly firm finish. Best drinking mid-2017+.

DRY $20 AV

Brightwater Vineyards Lord Rutherford Nelson Pinot Noir   ★★★★

The 2014 vintage (★★★★☆) was estate-grown, fermented with indigenous yeasts, and matured for 16 months in French oak barriques (25 per cent new). Bright ruby, it is fragrant, vibrant, savoury and supple, with strong, ripe cherry, plum and nutty oak flavours, showing good complexity, fine-grained tannins, and obvious potential. Best drinking 2018+.

DRY $40 –V

Brightwater Vineyards Nelson Pinot Noir ★★★★☆

Delicious young, the 2014 vintage (★★★★☆) was grown at Hope and matured for 11 months in French oak casks (25 per cent new). Bright ruby, it is floral and vibrantly fruity, with concentrated, ripe cherry, plum and spice flavours, gently seasoned with nutty oak, good drive through the palate, and lots of drink-young appeal. Best drinking mid-2017+.

Vintage	14	13	12	11	10
WR	7	6	6	7	6
Drink	16-19	16-18	16-17	16-17	P

DRY $35 V+

Brodie Estate Pinot Noir ★★★☆

The youthful 2013 vintage (★★★☆) was estate-grown in Martinborough, hand-picked and matured in French oak barrels (30 per cent new). Ruby-hued, it is mouthfilling, with fresh cherry, plum and spice flavours, vibrant and persistent. Best drinking 2017+.

Vintage	13	12	11	10	09
WR	5	5	6	7	6
Drink	16-20	16-20	P	16-17	P

DRY $48 –V

Bronte Nelson Pinot Noir ★★★☆

From Rimu Grove, the 2015 vintage (★★★★) was estate-grown and matured for 11 months in French oak casks. Deeply coloured, it is fragrant and full-bodied, with gentle tannins, fresh plum, cherry and spice flavours, showing very good ripeness and depth, and some savoury complexity. Delicious young.

Vintage	15
WR	7
Drink	16-26

DRY $24 V+

Brookby Road Single Vineyard Selection Marlborough Pinot Noir (★★★★)

From Giesen, the 2012 vintage (★★★★) has full, fairly mature colour. Showing good richness, it is full-bodied (14.5 per cent alcohol), with generous plum, spice and nut flavours, hints of herbs and tamarillos, good complexity and a fairly firm finish.

DRY $95 –V

Burn Cottage Central Otago Pinot Noir ★★★★★

Estate-grown in the Cromwell Basin, the 2014 vintage (★★★★★) was hand-harvested and matured in French oak barriques (29 per cent new). Full-coloured, it is scented, savoury and silky-textured, with ripe cherry, plum, spice and nut flavours that build to a long, well-rounded, very harmonious finish. A complex, age-worthy red, it's already delicious, but likely to be at its best 2018+.

Vintage	14	13	12	11	10	09
WR	7	7	7	6	6	6
Drink	16-25	16-25	16-21	16-19	16-19	16-19

DRY $63 AV

Burn Cottage Moonlight Race Central Otago Pinot Noir   (★★★★★)

The lovely 2014 vintage (★★★★★) is a highly auspicious debut. Grown at several sites (mostly the estate vineyard and Northburn Vineyard, both located in the Cromwell Basin, but also a third vineyard at Gibbston), it was fermented with indigenous yeasts, matured for a year in French oak casks (19 per cent new), and bottled unfiltered. Deeply coloured, it is mouthfilling and sweet-fruited, in a rich, very savoury style, complex, finely textured and long. Instantly appealing, it's also well worth cellaring.

DRY $45 AV

Burn Cottage Valli Vineyard Gibbston Central Otago Pinot Noir   (★★★★★)

For the 2014 vintage (★★★★★), Burn Cottage, based in the Cromwell Basin, drew grapes from the more elevated Valli Vineyard, at Gibbston (for their reverse swap, see Valli Burn Cottage Vineyard Central Otago Pinot Noir). Matured in French oak barriques (25 per cent new), it's a deep ruby, savoury, earthy, supple wine, with ripe cherry, plum, spice and dried-herb flavours, a hint of liquorice, gentle acidity, and lovely texture and harmony. Already delicious, it's a drink-now or cellaring proposition.

DRY $63 AV

Cable Bay Awatere Valley Marlborough Pinot Noir   (★★★)

The pale ruby 2014 vintage (★★★) is an estate-grown red, matured in tanks and barrels. A light style, it has ripe, cherryish, savoury, slightly nutty flavours, showing a touch of complexity, and good tannin support. Enjoyable now.

Vintage	14
WR	5
Drink	16-20

DRY $28 –V

Cable Bay Central Otago Pinot Noir   ★★★★

Grown and hand-picked in the Cromwell Basin, then vinified on Waiheke Island, the 2013 vintage (★★★★) was matured in French oak barrels (partly new). Bright ruby, it is weighty and generous, with vibrant cherry, plum and spice flavours, supple tannins, oak complexity and good cellaring potential.

Vintage	13
WR	6
Drink	16-18

DRY $44 –V

Cambridge Road Martinborough Pinot Noir   ★★★★

Deeply coloured, the 2013 vintage (★★★★) is fragrant, with strong, fresh cherry and plum flavours, lively and finely textured. Still youthful, it's well worth cellaring.

DRY $60 –V

Camshorn Waipara Pinot Noir ★★★☆

From Pernod Ricard NZ, the 2015 vintage (★★★☆) is deep ruby, mouthfilling and rounded, with moderately rich strawberry and spice flavours, showing some savoury complexity. Delicious young.

 DRY $23 V+

Carrick Bannockburn Central Otago Pinot Noir ★★★★★

A regional classic. The 2013 vintage (★★★★★) was matured for 14 months in French oak casks (25 per cent new). Deep and bright in colour, it is a lovely wine – rich, savoury, complex and supple, with layers of ripe plum and spice flavours, deep and harmonious. Drink now or cellar. Certified organic.

Vintage	13	12	11	10	09
WR	7	7	6	7	7
Drink	16-20	16-20	16-18	16-17	P

 DRY $45 AV

Carrick Excelsior Central Otago Pinot Noir ★★★★★

From mature, estate-grown vines at Bannockburn, the outstanding 2013 vintage (★★★★★) was matured for 18 months in French oak barriques (40 per cent new). Deep and youthful in colour, it is very fragrant, rich and silky, with highly concentrated flavours, showing lovely texture and complexity. A wine of great finesse, it's already very approachable.

DRY $95 AV

Carrick Unravelled Central Otago Pinot Noir ★★★★

Designed to be 'easy-drinking, laidback', the 2014 vintage (★★★★) doesn't claim to have been estate-grown at Bannockburn. Matured in French oak barriques (15 per cent new), it is deeply coloured, generous and harmonious, with ripe plum/spice flavours, slightly earthy, savoury, complex and smooth. Certified organic.

 DRY $28 V+

Catalina Sounds Marlborough Pinot Noir ★★★☆

Already delicious, the 2014 vintage (★★★★) is a generous, supple red, from sites in the Omaka Valley and Waihopai Valley. Deep ruby, with fresh, strong, berryish aromas, it is sweet-fruited, with good concentration, finely integrated oak and a well-rounded, rich finish.

 DRY $29 AV

Ceres Composition Central Otago Pinot Noir ★★★★

Grown at two sites at Bannockburn, in the Cromwell Basin, and matured in French oak casks (20 per cent new), the 2013 vintage (★★★★) is an attractive, sweet-fruited red, full-coloured, with mouthfilling body and strong cherry, plum and spice flavours, braced by firm tannins. Well worth cellaring.

 DRY $38 AV

Charcoal Gully Sally's Pinch Central Otago Pinot Noir ★★★☆

The full-coloured, savoury 2013 vintage (★★★☆) is a single-vineyard red, grown at Pisa, in the Cromwell Basin, and matured in French oak casks (32 per cent new). Floral, with very good depth of plum, spice and slight tamarillo flavours, and a fairly firm finish, it's still unfolding.

Vintage	13
WR	5
Drink	16-24

 DRY $32 –V

Chard Farm Mata-Au Central Otago Pinot Noir ★★★★

Pronounced 'Martar-O', Chard Farm's 'signature' red is estate-grown at Lowburn, in the Cromwell Basin. Bright ruby, the 2014 vintage (★★★★) is sweet-fruited and supple, with vibrant, delicate strawberry, plum, spice and nut flavours, in a 'feminine', finely balanced style, well worth cellaring.

 DRY $47 –V

Chard Farm Mk II Parkburn Central Otago Pinot Noir ★★★☆

The 2013 vintage (★★★★) is a single-vineyard red, grown at Parkburn, in the Cromwell Basin. Ruby-hued, floral and supple, it is an elegant, vibrantly fruity wine, with plum, dried-herb and nut flavours, showing good vigour and complexity.

 DRY $74 –V

Chard Farm River Run Central Otago Pinot Noir ★★★☆

This is a 'fruit-driven', gently oaked style that typically slides down very easily. The 2014 vintage (★★★☆) was hand-picked in two sub-regions: the Cromwell Basin and Gibbston. Ruby-hued, it is mouthfilling, sweet-fruited and supple, with fresh, moderately rich plum, cherry and spice flavours, showing a touch of complexity. Best drinking 2017–18.

 DRY $35 –V

Chard Farm The Tiger Lowburn Central Otago Pinot Noir ★★★★

The 2013 vintage (★★★★) is a single-vineyard red, estate-grown in the Cromwell Basin. Ruby-hued, it is floral and supple, in a graceful style, with plummy, spicy flavours, hints of dried herbs and nuts, and good complexity and harmony.

 DRY $78 –V

Chard Farm The Viper Parkburn Central Otago Pinot Noir ★★★★

A single-vineyard red, grown in the Cromwell Basin, the 2013 vintage (★★★★) is a graceful, elegant rather than powerful wine. Ruby-hued, it is sweet-fruited, savoury and supple, with moderately concentrated cherry, plum, dried-herb and spice flavours and gentle tannins. Drink now or cellar.

DRY $74 –V

China Girl by Crown Range Cellar Central Otago Pinot Noir   ★★★★☆

The powerful 2015 vintage (★★★★☆) was grown and hand-picked at Bendigo, in the Cromwell Basin. Deeply coloured and full-bodied, it is generous and sweet-fruited, with concentrated plum/spice flavours, a hint of liquorice, savoury notes adding complexity, and a rich, smooth finish. Forward in its appeal, it's already drinking well, but likely to be at its best 2018+.

 DRY $65 –V

Churton Marlborough Pinot Noir   ★★★★☆

Estate-grown at an elevated (200 metres above sea level) site in the Waihopai Valley, hand-picked, fermented with indigenous yeasts and matured in French oak barriquess (10 per cent new in 2013), this is 'a delicate, refined' Pinot Noir, according to winemaker Sam Weaver. The 2013 vintage (★★★★☆) is deeply coloured, complex and youthful. Savoury and concentrated, with strong plum, cherry and spice flavours, firm, ripe tannins and a long finish, it's an elegant, age-worthy red, likely to be at its best 2017+.

Vintage	13	12	11	10	09	08
WR	7	5	6	7	5	6
Drink	16-26	16-22	16-28	16-24	16-20	16-22

 DRY $45 –V

Churton The Abyss Marlborough Pinot Noir   ★★★★★

The 2013 vintage (★★★★★) was estate-grown on an elevated site in the Waihopai Valley, on a north-east-facing clay slope which catches the early morning sun. Hand-picked from vines planted in 1999, fermented with indigenous yeasts and matured for 18 months in French oak casks (30 per cent new), it is deeply coloured and highly fragrant, with rich plum/spice flavours, earthy notes adding complexity, firm tannins and obvious potential. Best drinking 2018+. Certified organic.

Vintage	13	12	11	10	09	08
WR	7	NM	NM	7	NM	6
Drink	20-30	NM	NM	16-22	NM	16-20

 DRY $75 AV

Circuit North Canterbury Pinot Noir   (★★★★)

From three sites at Waipara, including Black Estate, the debut 2014 vintage (★★★★) was hand-picked from 15 to 27-year-old vines, matured for a year in seasoned French oak barrels, and bottled without fining or filtration. Full ruby, it is mouthfilling and supple, with ripe plum/spice flavours and earthy, savoury notes adding considerable complexity. A very distinctive, youthful wine, it should be at its best 2017+. (From Black Estate.)

DRY $28 V+

Clark Estate Marlborough Pinot Noir   (★★★☆)

The 2014 vintage (★★★☆) is a single-vineyard, Awatere Valley red, matured in seasoned oak casks. Ruby-hued, it is mouthfilling, fresh and supple, with youthful, ripe, vibrantly fruity flavours of cherries and plums, gently seasoned with oak.

Vintage	14
WR	6
Drink	16-19

DRY $24 V+

Clevedon Hills Pinot Noir   ★★★★

Estate-grown at Clevedon, in South Auckland, this wine has plenty of personality and is of superior quality to most Pinot Noirs from the upper North Island. The impressive 2013 vintage (★★★★☆) is very skilfully crafted. Deeply coloured, it is mouthfilling, fleshy and sweet-fruited, with concentrated, vibrant plum/spice flavours, finely textured, well-rounded and rich. The 2014 vintage (★★★☆) is ruby-hued, with ripe, moderately concentrated, cherryish, slightly nutty flavours, showing some savoury complexity. A very harmonious and finely textured red, it's enjoyable now, but well worth cellaring.

DRY $40 –V

Clifford Bay Marlborough Pinot Noir   ★★★

Attractive young, the 2015 vintage (★★★☆) has full, bright ruby colour. Vibrantly fruity, it has good depth of youthful, plummy, spicy flavours, with slightly toasty and savoury notes adding complexity, and a well-rounded finish. Drink now or cellar.

Vintage	15	14
WR	7	7
Drink	16-19	16-18

DRY $20 AV

Clos de Ste Anne Naboth's Vineyard Pinot Noir   ★★★★

This Gisborne red from Millton is one of this country's northernmost quality Pinot Noirs. Grown at the hillside Clos de Ste Anne site at Manutuke, it is hand-harvested from vines up to 25 years old, fermented with indigenous yeasts, barrique-aged, and bottled without fining or filtering. Certified biodynamic, the 2014 vintage (★★★★) is ruby-hued, with a fragrant bouquet. It shows excellent complexity, with mouthfilling body (14 per cent alcohol), strong, ripe, plummy, spicy, slightly nutty flavours, and good tannin support. Drink now or cellar.

DRY $60 –V

Clos Henri Marlborough Pinot Noir   ★★★★☆

From Henri Bourgeois, a top Loire Valley producer with a site near Renwick, the 2013 vintage (★★★★☆) was hand-picked from eight to 13-year-old vines, fermented in large oak vats, and matured for a year in French oak casks (25 per cent new). Full ruby, it is a complex style, firm and savoury, with good concentration of ripe plum, cherry and spice flavours, and the backbone to age well. Best drinking 2017+. Certified organic.

Vintage	13	12	11	10	09	08	07
WR	6	6	6	7	6	6	6
Drink	16-22	16-21	16-20	16-18	16-17	P	P

DRY $43 AV

Cloudy Bay Pinot Noir   ★★★★☆

Consistently classy. Grown at sites on the cooler, more clay-influenced south side of the Wairau Valley – including the company's Mustang and Barracks vineyards – the 2014 vintage (★★★★☆), from a warm, early-ripening season, was matured for a year in French oak barriques (35 per cent new). A youthful, tightly structured, age-worthy red, it is deep ruby, with substantial body (14 per cent alcohol) and strong, ripe plum, cherry, dried-herb and spice flavours, seasoned with nutty oak. Best drinking 2018+.

Vintage	14	13	12	11	10	09
WR	7	7	7	6	7	6
Drink	16-21	16-20	16-18	16-17	P	P

DRY $45 –V

Cloudy Bay Te Wahi Central Otago Pinot Noir   ★★★★★

The debut 2010 vintage (★★★★★) marked Cloudy Bay's first foray beyond the Marlborough region. The 2014 vintage (★★★★★) of Te Wahi ('The Place') was estate-grown in the Calvert Vineyard at Bannockburn and Northburn Vineyard, on the east bank of Lake Dunstan. Fermented with indigenous yeasts, it was matured for 14 months in French oak barriques (30 per cent new). Deeply coloured, it is fleshy and dense, with poised, beautifully ripe plum/spice flavours, nutty and savoury, buried tannins, and excellent concentration and harmony. Already delicious, it should be at its best 2018+.

Vintage	14
WR	7
Drink	16-24

DRY $105 –V

Coal Pit Tiwha Central Otago Pinot Noir   ★★★★☆

The 2014 vintage (★★★★☆) is an elegant red, grown and hand-picked in the Gibbston (principally) and Bannockburn sub-regions. Full, bright ruby, it is fragrant and supple, with strong, ripe cherry and plum flavours, a hint of dried herbs, good complexity, and a finely textured finish.

Vintage	14	13	12	11	10	09
WR	7	7	6	5	7	7
Drink	16-22	16-21	16-20	16-18	16-18	16-17

DRY $42 AV

Coopers Creek Hawke's Bay Pinot Noir   ★★★☆

The generous, supple 2015 vintage (★★★☆) is deep ruby, with very satisfying depth of vibrant, plummy, slightly herbal flavours.

DRY $18 V+

Coopers Creek Marlborough Pinot Noir   ★★★

Offering good value, the 2014 vintage (★★★☆) is fresh and finely balanced, with vibrant, ripe red-fruit and spice flavours, showing a touch of complexity.

DRY $20 AV

Coopers Creek SV Gibsons Run Marlborough Pinot Noir   ★★★☆

Deep ruby, the 2014 vintage (★★★☆) has a fragrant, plummy, spicy bouquet, strong cherry, plum, dried-herb and spice flavours, and good texture and harmony.

Vintage	14	13
WR	6	6
Drink	16-19	16-18

DRY $25 AV

Cottier Estate Pinot Noir   (★★★☆)

Grown in the northern Wairarapa, the moderately mature 2012 vintage (★★★☆), on sale in 2016, is ruby-hued, with good depth of ripe cherry, plum, dried-herb and nut flavours. Ready.

DRY $26 AV

Crab Farm Winery Reserve Hawke's Bay Pinot Noir   (★★★☆)

The 2014 vintage (★★★☆) was matured for a year in French oak casks. Full-coloured, it's a slightly gutsy, very ripe style with strong plum, spice and slight liquorice flavours, and a firm tannin backbone.

DRY $40 –V

Craggy Range Te Muna Road Vineyard Martinborough Pinot Noir   ★★★★★

The 2013 vintage (★★★★☆) was estate-grown, hand-picked at 24.3 brix, fermented with indigenous yeasts and matured for 10 months in French oak barriques (25 per cent new). Bright ruby, it is floral, sweet-fruited, savoury and supple, with strong cherry, plum and spice flavours, showing good complexity, fine-grained tannins and a well-rounded finish. It's already delicious, but worth cellaring.

Vintage	13	12	11	10	09	08
WR	7	6	6	7	6	7
Drink	16-21	16-19	16-18	16-18	P	P

DRY $43 V+

Crossings, The, Marlborough Pinot Noir   ★★★☆

The 2014 vintage (★★★☆) is a ruby-hued, finely balanced Awatere Valley red, matured for seven months in French oak barriques (20 per cent new). Mouthfilling and supple, with very good depth of plum, cherry and spice flavours, showing some savoury complexity, it's drinking well now.

Vintage	14
WR	7
Drink	16-19

DRY $20 V+

Crossroads Milestone Series Marlborough Pinot Noir   ★★★☆

Drinking well from the start, the 2014 vintage (★★★☆) is bright ruby, full-bodied and smooth, with very good depth of ripe berry and plum flavours, gentle tannins and a touch of complexity.

Vintage	14
WR	6
Drink	16-23

DRY $22 V+

Crowded House Marlborough Pinot Noir ★★★☆

The 2014 vintage (★★★☆) is an attractive, drink-young style, ruby-hued, vibrant and supple, with moderately concentrated, ripe plum and dried-herb flavours, showing good freshness, delicacy and harmony.

 DRY $23 V+

Crown Range Cellar Signature Selection Central Otago Pinot Noir ★★★★☆

The 2015 vintage (★★★★☆) is rare – only 100 cases were produced. Grown in the Gibbston sub-region (although not labelled as such), it was crafted by pioneer Central Otago winemaker Grant Taylor (owner of the Valli brand). Full, bright ruby, with a floral, invitingly scented bouquet, it is mouthfilling, with vibrant, well-ripened cherry, plum, spice and dried-herb flavours, showing excellent concentration, supple tannins, and a strong sense of youthful drive and potential. Best drinking 2018+.

 DRY $179 -V

Darling, The, Marlborough Pinot Noir (★★★★)

Certified organic, the 2014 vintage (★★★★) is a ruby-hued, mouthfilling, supple red, with moderately rich, well-ripened cherry, plum, spice and nut flavours. Savoury and finely textured, with good complexity, it's a drink-now or cellaring proposition.

DRY $33 AV

Dashwood Marlborough Pinot Noir ★★★

Enjoyable young, the 2014 vintage (★★★) is a blend of Awatere Valley and Wairau Valley grapes. Ruby-hued, it is mouthfilling, with cherry, plum, spice and herb flavours, showing a touch of complexity, and a smooth finish.

Vintage	14	13	12
WR	7	6	6
Drink	16-18	16-17	16-17

 DRY $20 AV

Davishon Central Otago Pinot Noir ★★★

The bright ruby 2015 vintage (★★★) was grown at Alexandra and matured in French oak barriques (25 per cent new). It has good depth of fresh plum, herb and spice flavours, oak complexity and a fairly firm finish.

 DRY $35 -V

Delegat Awatere Valley Pinot Noir ★★★★

The great-value 2014 vintage (★★★★) is full-coloured, with rich plum, cherry and spice flavours, showing good complexity. Savoury and supple, it's already delicious, but also worth cellaring.

 DRY $25 V+

Delta Marlborough Pinot Noir   ★★★★

The 2014 vintage (★★★★) is mostly from Delta Farm Vineyard, on the south side of the Wairau Valley. Matured for eight months in seasoned French oak casks, it is bright ruby and mouthfilling, with good weight and depth of cherryish, plummy flavours, ripe, savoury and supple. Best drinking 2017+.

DRY $24 V+

Devil's Staircase Central Otago Pinot Noir   ★★★

From Rockburn, this is a drink-young style, handled without barrel aging. The 2014 vintage (★★★) is ruby-hued, mouthfilling, vibrantly fruity and smooth, with fresh, strong plum/spice flavours, gentle tannins, and good ripeness and depth. Enjoyable from the start, it has a Beaujolais-like charm.

DRY $23 AV

Devotus Reserve Single Vineyard Pinot Noir   ★★★★★

The refined, debut 2014 vintage (★★★★★), grown on the Martinborough Terrace, was harvested from 28-year-old vines, established by Dry River. Matured for 11 months in French oak barriques (25 per cent new), it is deep and youthful in colour, scented, rich and supple. A lovely young red, with plum, cherry and spice flavours, integrated oak, and a flowing, finely textured finish, it's already delicious, but well worth cellaring. The 2015 vintage (★★★★★) is a very powerful, bold style of Pinot Noir, deeply coloured and sweet-fruited, with highly concentrated plum and spice flavours, a hint of liquorice, and obvious potential; best drinking 2020+.

DRY $62 AV

Devotus Single Vineyard Pinot Noir   ★★★★☆

From vines planted at Martinborough in 1986, the 2014 vintage (★★★★☆) was matured for 11 months in French oak barriques, and bottled unfined and unfiltered. Richly coloured, it is mouthfilling, sturdy and sweet-fruited, with generous plum/spice flavours, gentle tannins and good, savoury complexity. Already drinking well, it should be at its best 2017+. The generous 2015 vintage (★★★★☆) is a deep ruby, fleshy wine with concentrated plum, spice and slight herb flavours, gentle acidity and good, savoury complexity. Best drinking 2018+.

Vintage	14	DRY $38 V+
WR	4	
Drink	16-20	

Discovery Point Martinborough Pinot Noir   (★★★★)

From wine distributor Steve Bennett, the 2014 vintage (★★★★) is from 'mature' vines and was aged for nine months in French oak barriques (one to two years old). Ruby-hued, with a hint of development, it is fragrant and mouthfilling, with ripe plum/spice flavours, nutty and savoury, and fairly firm tannins. Showing good personality, it offers fine value. Drink now to 2018.

Vintage	14	DRY $25 V+
WR	6	
Drink	17-20	

Distant Land Central Otago Pinot Noir   (★★☆)

Grown at Alexandra and Gibbston, the 2014 vintage (★★☆) was matured in French oak barriques (25 per cent new). Ruby-hued, it is a light style, with youthful, berryish flavours, hints of herbs, spices and nuts, and fresh acidity.

DRY $25 –V

Distant Land Reserve Central Otago Pinot Noir   (★★★)

The 2014 vintage (★★★) is a moderately concentrated blend of Alexandra and Gibbston fruit, matured for a year in French oak barrels (50 per cent new). Fullish in colour, it has plum, spice and herb flavours, showing a touch of complexity, and soft tannins.

DRY $38 –V

Doctors Flat Central Otago Pinot Noir   ★★★★★

The classy 2014 vintage (★★★★★) is a single-vineyard red, grown at Bannockburn, matured for a year in French oak barrels (25 per cent new), and bottled without fining or filtering. Deep ruby, it is mouthfilling, rich and savoury, with deep, ripe plum/spice flavours, showing excellent complexity, and fine-grained tannins. Very generous and savoury, it's approachable now, but likely to be at its best 2018+.

Vintage	14	13
WR	7	6
Drink	17-22	16-21

DRY $47 AV

Dog Point Vineyard Marlborough Pinot Noir   ★★★★★

This classy, finely structured red is estate-grown on the south side of the Wairau Valley and matured for 18 months in French oak barriques (40 per cent new in 2014). The delicious 2014 vintage (★★★★★) has deep, youthful colour. The bouquet is fragrant, plummy and spicy; the palate is mouthfilling, with well-ripened plum/spice flavours, showing excellent complexity and richness, in a very savoury style with gentle acidity and impressive harmony. Best drinking 2018+.

Vintage	14	13	12	11	10	09	08
WR	7	7	7	5	7	6	6
Drink	16-25	16-25	16-24	16-19	16-22	16-18	16-20

DRY $47 AV

Domain Road Vineyard Central Otago Pinot Noir   ★★★★☆

The 2013 vintage (★★★★☆) of this single-vineyard, Bannockburn red was matured for nine months in French oak barriques. Built to last, it's a tightly structured wine with full, youthful colour and a fragrant bouquet, suggestive of spices and dried herbs. Concentrated, it has plummy, nutty flavours, complex and savoury, and a persistent finish.

Vintage	13	12	11	10	09	08
WR	7	5	6	7	7	6
Drink	16-20	16-19	16-18	16-18	16-17	P

DRY $40 V+

Domaine Rewa Central Otago Pinot Noir ★★★★

The 2013 vintage (★★★★☆) is a youthful, single-vineyard red from Lowburn, in the Cromwell Basin. Matured for eight months in French oak barriques (31 per cent new), it is ruby-hued and mouthfilling, with deep, vibrant cherry, plum and spice flavours, fine-grained tannins, and a long, tight finish.

 DRY $38 AV

Dry River Martinborough Pinot Noir ★★★★★

Dark and densely flavoured, this Martinborough red ranks among New Zealand's greatest Pinot Noirs. It is grown in three company-owned vineyards – Dry River Estate, Craighall and Lovat – on the Martinborough Terrace, and most of the vines are over 20 years old. Matured for a year in French oak hogsheads (20–30 per cent new), it is a slower-developing wine than other New Zealand Pinot Noirs, but matures superbly. From the earliest harvest ever, the beautiful 2014 vintage (★★★★★) is deeply coloured, powerful and highly concentrated, with rich, ripe cherry, plum and spice flavours, scented, seamless and long. Graceful, with obvious potential, it should be at its best 2019+.

Vintage	14	13	12	11	10	09
WR	7	7	6	7	7	7
Drink	16-27	16-27	16-25	16-25	16-24	16-23

 DRY $87 AV

Dunnolly Single Vineyard Family Estate Waipara Valley Pinot Noir ★★★★

The 2013 vintage (★★★☆) is a bright ruby, sturdy North Canterbury red with fresh, ripe, moderately rich plum/spice flavours, a hint of dried herbs, and some savoury complexity. Worth cellaring.

 DRY $35 AV

Dunstan Road Central Otago Pinot Noir ★★★★

The 2013 vintage (★★★☆) is a single-vineyard red, hand-picked at Alexandra and matured for over a year in French oak barrels. Ruby-hued, it is mouthfilling, sweet-fruited and supple, with plummy, slightly cherryish and spicy flavours, showing some complexity, and good harmony. Drink now onwards.

Vintage	13
WR	6
Drink	16-18

 DRY $30 AV

Earth's End Central Otago Pinot Noir (★★★★)

From Mount Edward, the 2014 vintage (★★★★) is an excellent drink-young style – deep ruby, with generous, ripe, plummy, spicy flavours, slightly earthy notes adding complexity, gentle tannnins and good harmony.

 DRY $29 V+

Elder, The, Martinborough Pinot Noir ★★★★☆

Fragrant and supple, the 2014 vintage (★★★★★) was grown in the Hanson Vineyard, at Te Muna, and matured in French oak casks (13 per cent new). Deep ruby, it is mouthfilling and savoury, with a strong surge of well-ripened plum, cherry and spice flavours, showing good complexity, and a rich, finely textured finish. Already delicious.

 DRY $65 –V

Elephant Hill Central Otago Pinot Noir ★★★★

The 2014 vintage (★★★★) from this Hawke's Bay-based winery was matured for 10 months in French oak casks (25 per cent new). It is mouthfilling and vibrantly fruity, with bright, deep ruby colour and strong, youthful, plummy, slightly spicy flavours, finely textured and harmonious. Best drinking 2017+.

 DRY $34 AV

Ellero Pisa Terrace Central Otago Pinot Noir ★★★★

Certified organic, the 2014 vintage (★★★★) is one of the finest yet. Estate-grown and matured in French oak casks (20 per cent new), it is a rich, silky-smooth red, with deep plum and spice flavours, an earthy streak and good complexity. Highly approachable, it's a drink-now or cellaring proposition.

 DRY $40 –V

Eradus Awatere Valley Single Vineyard Marlborough Pinot Noir ★★★

Ruby-hued, fresh and smooth, the 2014 vintage (★★★) is a lightly oaked style, with gentle tannins and good depth of cherry, plum, spice and dried-herb flavours. A drink-young charmer.

 DRY $22 AV

Escarpment Kiwa by Escarpment Martinborough Pinot Noir ★★★★★

From vines planted in 1989, the 2012 vintage (★★★★★) was grown in the Cleland Vineyard, in Cambridge Road, and matured for a year in French oak barriques (30 per cent new). Escarpment's most arresting red of the vintage, superior to Kupe, it is very floral and generous, with deep, youthful colour, sweet-fruit characters, and an array of cherry, plum, olive and spice flavours, notably complex, savoury and harmonious. Full of personality, it's a drink-now or cellaring proposition.

DRY $65 AV

Escarpment Kupe by Escarpment Pinot Noir ★★★★★

This flagship, estate-grown red is based on vines closely planted at Te Muna, near Martinborough, in 1999, and matured in French oak barriques (typically 50 per cent new). The 2012 vintage (★★★★), from a cool growing season, is lower in alcohol than usual (12.5 per cent by volume, compared to the customary 13.5 per cent). It's a generous, supple wine with a savoury, spicy, earthy complexity, and hints of herbs and tamarillos, but less powerful, dense, ripe-tasting and lush than top vintages.

 DRY $85 AV

Escarpment Martinborough Pinot Noir ★★★★★

This 'district' blend is the third-tier label, after the single-vineyard wines and Kupe. The 2012 vintage (★★★★), from an 'uncharacteristically cool summer', is ruby-hued, savoury and supple, in a moderately concentrated style with cherry, plum and spice flavours and a slightly herbal twist. It's quite forward in its appeal; drink now.

Vintage	12	11	10	09	08	05
WR	6	7	7	7	7	6
Drink	16-20	16-20	16-19	16-18	P	P

 DRY $45 AV

Escarpment Pahi by Escarpment Martinborough Pinot Noir ★★★★☆

Based on mature vines (mostly of the 10/5 clone) in the McCreanor Vineyard, the 2012 vintage (★★★★☆) was matured in French oak barriques (30 per cent new). It is a fragrant, generous, vibrantly fruity red, medium to full-bodied, with cherry, plum, spice and herb flavours, very savoury and complex, and good tannin backbone. Drink now or cellar.

 DRY $65 –V

Escarpment Te Rehua by Escarpment Martinborough Pinot Noir ★★★★★

Grown in the warm, sheltered Barton Vineyard, where the Pinot Noir vines (of many clones) are well over 20 years old, the 2012 vintage (★★★★★) was matured for a year in French oak barriques (30 per cent new). A powerful, sweet-fruited red, it has generous, youthful cherry, plum and spice flavours, showing lovely poise and depth. Delicious drinking now onwards.

  DRY $65 AV

Esk Valley Marlborough Pinot Noir ★★★★

The 2015 vintage (★★★★) was hand-harvested in the Awatere Valley and Southern Valleys, and matured for 11 months in French oak barriques (13 per cent new). Delicious from the start, it is mouthfilling and savoury, with gentle tannins and strong cherry, plum and spice flavours, showing good complexity.

Vintage	15	14	13	12	11	10
WR	7	6	6	7	7	7
Drink	17-19	16-18	16-17	16-17	P	P

 DRY $27 V+

Explorer Central Otago Pinot Noir ★★★☆

The 2015 vintage (★★★☆) from Domaine Thomson was estate-grown at Lowburn, in the Cromwell Basin. Ruby-hued, it has moderately concentrated, plummy, spicy flavours, a hint of dried herbs, gentle tannins and some savoury complexity.

DRY $29 AV

Falconhead Hawke's Bay Pinot Noir   (★★☆)

A drink-young style, the 2013 vintage (★★☆) is ruby-hued, fresh and full-bodied, with plum, spice and slight herb flavours, and gentle tannins.

Vintage	13	DRY $17 AV
WR	7	
Drink	16-18	

Falconhead Marlborough Pinot Noir   ★★★

Drinking well in 2016, the 2014 vintage (★★★) is a light ruby red, mouthfilling (14.5 per cent alcohol), sweet-fruited and smooth, with ripe plum and spice flavours, showing a touch of complexity, and a well-rounded finish.

Vintage	14	13	DRY $18 V+
WR	6	6	
Drink	16-19	16-18	

Fancrest Estate Waipara Valley Pinot Noir   ★★★☆

Still on sale and from 'a dream season', the 2011 vintage (★★★★☆) is the best yet. Certified organic and bottled without fining or filtering, it has full, still youthful colour. Fragrant, ripe and rounded, it has generous, plummy, spicy, nutty flavours, showing excellent complexity, with a lingering finish. Delicious now, but still developing, it should be at its best around 2018. The 2012 vintage (★★★☆) has deep, slightly developed colour and a herbal bouquet. Full-flavoured, savoury and supple, it shows a slight lack of full ripeness, but also good personality; drink now.

DRY $45 –V

Felton Road Bannockburn Central Otago Pinot Noir   ★★★★★

The Bannockburn winery's 'standard' Pinot Noir is a distinguished wine, blended from its four sites in the district. Matured in French oak casks (30 per cent new in 2015), it is fermented with indigenous yeasts and bottled without fining or filtering. The 2015 vintage (★★★★☆) is already delicious. Ruby-hued, it is sweet-fruited and savoury, with strong cherry, plum, spice and nut flavours, showing good complexity, gentle tannins, and a silky-smooth finish. Impressing with its finesse, rather than power, it should be at its best for drinking 2018+.

Vintage	15	14	13	12	11	10	09	08	07	06	DRY $60 AV
WR	7	7	7	7	7	7	7	7	7	6	
Drink	16-26	16-25	16-24	16-26	16-23	16-22	16-21	16-20	16-18	16-17	

Felton Road Block 3 Central Otago Pinot Noir   ★★★★★

Grown at Bannockburn, on a north-facing slope 270 metres above sea level, this is a majestic Central Otago wine, among the finest Pinot Noirs in the country. The mature vines are cultivated in front of the winery, in a section of the vineyard where the clay content is relatively high, giving 'dried herbs and ripe fruit characters'. The wine is matured for about a year in Burgundy oak barrels (38 per cent new in 2015), and bottled without fining or filtration. The deeply coloured, generous 2015 vintage (★★★★★) is drinking well from the start. Fragrant, rich and rounded, it has concentrated cherry, plum, spice and nut flavours, showing excellent complexity and harmony. Very expressive and highly approachable in its youth, with strong, ripe, sweet-fruit characters and gentle tannins, it's a drink-now or cellaring proposition.

Vintage	15	14	13	12	11	10	09	08	07	06
WR	7	7	7	7	7	7	7	7	7	6
Drink	16-31	16-30	16-24	16-26	16-23	16-22	16-21	16-20	16-18	16-17

DRY $98 AV

Felton Road Block 5 Pinot Noir   ★★★★★

This is winemaker Blair Walter's favourite Felton Road red. Grown in a 'special' block of The Elms Vineyard at Bannockburn, in Central Otago, it is matured for a year in French oak barriques (33 per cent new in 2015), and bottled unfined and unfiltered. The 2015 vintage (★★★★★) is a deep ruby, powerful, generous wine, full-bodied and savoury, with concentrated, finely structured cherry, spice and nut flavours, good tannin backbone, and excellent complexity and harmony.

Vintage	15	14	13	12	11	10	09	08	07	06
WR	7	7	7	7	7	7	7	7	7	6
Drink	16-31	16-30	16-27	16-26	16-23	16-22	16-21	16-20	16-18	16-17

DRY $98 AV

Felton Road Calvert Pinot Noir   ★★★★★

Grown in the Calvert Vineyard at Bannockburn, matured in French oak barriques (30 per cent new in 2015), and bottled unfined and unfiltered, the 2015 vintage (★★★★★) is a deep ruby, very elegant, rich but not heavy wine. A lovely young red, it has fresh, concentrated berry and spice flavours, very complex, savoury, harmonious and long. Best drinking 2018+.

Vintage	15	14	13	12	11	10	09	08	07	06
WR	7	7	7	7	7	7	7	7	7	6
Drink	16-31	16-28	16-24	16-26	16-23	16-22	16-21	16-20	16-18	16-17

DRY $72 AV

Felton Road Cornish Point Pinot Noir   ★★★★★

From the company-owned Cornish Point Vineyard at the eastern end of Bannockburn, 6 kilometres from the winery, this is always one of my favourite Felton Road reds. The 2015 vintage (★★★★★) was matured for 13 months in French oak barriques (30 per cent new), and bottled without fining or filtering. Full ruby, it is generous, sweet-fruited, savoury and supple, with concentrated, ripe cherry, plum and spice flavours, showing lovely complexity, texture and harmony.

Vintage	15	14	13	12	11	10
WR	7	7	7	7	7	7
Drink	16-29	16-28	16-24	16-26	16-23	16-22

DRY $72 AV

Fickle Mistress Marlborough Pinot Noir   (★★★☆)

The 2014 vintage (★★★☆) from Treasury Wine Estates (Matua) is bright ruby, mouthfilling, fresh and supple, with ripe berry, plum and spice flavours, showing some savoury complexity, and lots of drink-young appeal.

DRY $21 V+

Fifth Bridge Central Otago Pinot Noir ★★★★

Already delicious, the floral, supple 2014 vintage (★★★★☆) was French oak-aged for nine months. Deep ruby, it is full-bodied, savoury and generous, with strong, ripe cherry, plum and spice flavours, fine-grained tannins and good complexity. Great value. (From Ceres Wines.)

DRY $28 V+

Fifth Innings, The, Marlborough Pinot Noir (★★★★)

The sturdy 2014 vintage (★★★★) was estate-grown at Rapaura, fermented with indigenous yeasts and matured for over a year in French oak puncheons. Deep ruby, it is fleshy, with strong, ripe, plummy, spicy, nutty flavours, a hint of coffee, and good tannin backbone. Still youthful, it should be at its best 2017+. (From Misty Cove.)

DRY $70 –V

Flying Sheep Hawke's Bay Pinot Noir ★★★

The 2013 vintage (★★★) is a single-vineyard red, estate-grown at Mangatahi and French oak-aged. Ruby-hued, it is a medium-bodied red with satisfying depth of vibrant, plummy flavours, a hint of dried herbs, fresh acidity and a smooth finish. Good, easy drinking. (From Osawa.)

DRY $30 –V

Folding Hill Bendigo Central Otago Pinot Noir ★★★★☆

The 2014 vintage (★★★★★) is a lovely, sweet-fruited and finely textured red, matured for 10 months in French oak barriques (25 per cent new), and bottled unfined and unfiltered. Deep ruby, it has generous cherry, plum and spice flavours, integrated oak, gentle acidity and tannins, and a long, very harmonious finish. Drink now or cellar.

DRY $45 –V

Folding Hill Orchard Block Bendigo Central Otago Pinot Noir ★★★★

The 2013 vintage (★★★★) is a mouthfilling, generous Bendigo red, hand-picked, fermented with indigenous yeasts, barrel-aged for 20 months, and bottled unfined and unfiltered. Deeply coloured, with a fragrant, complex bouquet, it is sweet-fruited, with concentrated, ripe cherry, plum, spice and nut flavours, and good tannin backbone. Best drinking mid-2017+.

DRY $55 –V

Folium Marlborough Pinot Noir ★★★★☆

The 2014 vintage (★★★★☆) is a good buy. Grown in the Brancott Valley and matured in French oak casks (15 per cent new), it is mouthfilling, savoury and complex, with ripe plum/spice flavours, fine-grained tannins, and good density. Best drinking 2017+.

Vintage	14
WR	6
Drink	16-25

DRY $30 V+

Folium Reserve Marlborough Pinot Noir ★★★★★

The classy 2013 vintage (★★★★★) of this Brancott Valley red was hand-picked from the oldest vines and matured in French oak casks (25 per cent new). Full-coloured, it is savoury, with strong, ripe plum/spice flavours, slightly earthy notes adding complexity, fine-grained tannins, and excellent density and harmony.

Vintage	13
WR	6
Drink	16-30

 DRY $40 V+

Foxes Island Belsham Awatere Estate Marlborough Pinot Noir (★★★★☆)

Released in late 2015, the 2010 vintage (★★★★☆) is full and bright in colour. Maturing well, it's an elegant red with rich plum, dried-herb and spice flavours, a hint of dark chocolate, fresh acidity, silky tannins and good, savoury complexity.

DRY $45 –V

Framingham F-Series Marlborough Pinot Noir ★★★★☆

The youthful 2014 vintage (★★★★☆) is 'from a vineyard with more clay content than those we have been using for Framingham', and was matured for over a year in French oak casks (33 per cent new). Deep ruby, it is mouthfilling, savoury and very finely textured, with strong, ripe cherry, plum, spice and nut flavours, smooth and long.

Vintage	14
WR	6
Drink	16-22

DRY $40 AV

Framingham Marlborough Pinot Noir ★★★★

This wine is 'feminine', says winemaker Andrew Hedley, meaning it is elegant, rather than powerful. The 2014 vintage (★★★★), matured for 10 months in French oak casks (20 per cent new), is ruby-hued, mouthfilling and savoury, with ripe plum, cherry and spice flavours, a subtle seasoning of oak, and gentle tannins. A very harmonious wine, showing good complexity, it's already delicious.

Vintage	14
WR	6
Drink	16-20

 DRY $30 AV

Fromm Clayvin Vineyard Pinot Noir ★★★★★

This acclaimed Marlborough red is grown and hand-picked at the hillside Clayvin Vineyard in the Brancott Valley, fermented with indigenous yeasts, matured for 18 months in French oak barriques (10–15 per cent new in 2013), and bottled without fining or filtering. In its youth, it is more floral and charming than its Fromm Vineyard stablemate. Certified organic, the youthful 2014 vintage (★★★★☆) is rare – only seven barrels were produced. Full ruby, it is mouthfilling and supple, with strong, vibrant cherry, plum and spice flavours, good tannin support, and excellent vigour and potential.

Vintage	14	13	12	11	10	09	08	07	06	05
WR	6	7	7	7	7	7	6	7	7	7
Drink	16-25	16-25	16-26	16-23	16-24	16-24	16-18	16-19	P	P

DRY $80 AV

Fromm Fromm Vineyard Pinot Noir ★★★★★

Winemaker Hätsch Kalberer describes this Marlborough red as 'not a typical New World style, but the truest expression of terroir you could find'. In the Fromm Vineyard near Renwick, in the heart of the Wairau Valley, many clones of Pinot Noir are close-planted on a flat site with alluvial topsoils overlying layers of clay and free-draining gravels. The wine is fermented with indigenous yeasts, matured for 18 months in Burgundy oak barrels, and bottled unfined and unfiltered. Certified organic, the savoury 2014 vintage (★★★★) is lightish in colour, with mouthfilling body, fairly firm tannins, and strong, ripe cherry, plum and nut flavours, showing good complexity.

Vintage	14	13	12	11	10	09	08	07	06	05	DRY $80 –V
WR	6	7	7	6	7	7	NM	7	6	7	
Drink	16-26	16-26	16-25	16-22	16-23	16-22	NM	16-21	P	P	

Fromm La Strada Marlborough Pinot Noir ★★★★

This wine is made to be ready for drinking upon release, by 'steering the fermentation towards more fruit expression and moderate tannins and structure'. Certified organic, the youthful 2014 vintage (★★★★) is a multi-site blend. Bright ruby, it is a graceful wine, fragrant and supple, with moderately rich, well-ripened plum, cherry and spice flavours, fine-grained tannins, and excellent complexity and harmony. Best drinking 2017+.

Vintage	14	13	12	11	10	09	08	DRY $40 –V
WR	6	7	7	6	7	7	7	
Drink	16-21	16-20	16-19	16-18	16-18	16-17	P	

Georges Road Williams Hill Waipara Pinot Noir ★★★★

The deeply coloured 2014 vintage (★★★★☆) is a single-vineyard red, hand-picked on the eastern slopes of the Waipara Valley and matured for over a year in French oak casks (20 per cent new). Still very youthful, it is mouthfilling and fruit-packed, with concentrated, ripe, plummy, spicy flavours, a hint of dried herbs, fine-grained tannins and obvious potential. Best drinking 2018+.

DRY $34 AV

Georgetown Vineyard Central Otago Pinot Noir ★★★★☆

Grown at the Cromwell end of the Kawarau Gorge, the 2012 vintage (★★★☆), bottled unfined and unfiltered, is from a cool growing season. Ruby-hued, it is flavoursome and savoury, berryish and nutty, but green-edged.

DRY $43 AV

Gibbston Highgate Soultaker Central Otago Pinot Noir ★★★

Estate-grown at Gibbston, the 2013 vintage (★★☆) was hand-picked and barrel-aged. A drink-young style, it is light ruby, with gentle berry and spice flavours.

DRY $30 –V

Gibbston Valley Central Otago Pinot Noir ★★★★☆

The powerful 2014 vintage (★★★★☆), blended from Bendigo (90 per cent) and Gibbston (10 per cent) grapes, was matured in French oak casks (20 per cent new). Boldly coloured, it is floral, fresh, mouthfilling (14 per cent alcohol) and supple, with youthful plum, spice, dried-herb and cherry flavours, showing excellent ripeness and depth, finely integrated oak and good complexity. Approachable from the start, it should reward cellaring for several years. (This label has been replaced from the 2015 vintage by the GV Collection Pinot Noir.)

Vintage	14	13	12	11	10	09
WR	7	7	7	7	7	7
Drink	16-21	16-20	16-20	P	16-18	16-17

DRY $45 –V

Gibbston Valley China Terrace Bendigo Central Otago Pinot Noir ★★★★★

Estate-grown at altitude (320 metres above sea level) in the China Terrace Vineyard, at Bendigo, the 2015 vintage (★★★★★) was hand-picked and matured for 11 months in French oak casks (30 per cent new). Deep and youthful in colour, it is a powerful, mouthfilling wine, finely balanced and supple, with densely packed, ripe cherry, plum and spice flavours. Still a baby, it has obvious potential for cellaring; best drinking 2019+.

Vintage	15	14	13	12	11	10	09
WR	7	7	7	7	7	7	6
Drink	16-27	16-26	16-25	16-23	16-22	16-20	16-17

DRY $65 AV

Gibbston Valley Glenlee Gibbston Central Otago Pinot Noir ★★★★☆

A single-vineyard red, grown at Gibbston, the 2014 vintage (★★★★☆) is a deeply coloured wine, matured in French oak barriques (30 per cent new). The bouquet is complex, with hints of dried herbs and earth; the palate is rich and supple, with generous, ripe plum and dried-herb flavours, gentle tannins and a finely balanced, long finish. Best drinking 2017+. (There is no 2015, due to frost.)

Vintage	15	14	13	12	11
WR	NM	7	7	7	7
Drink	NM	16-24	16-20	16-23	16-22

DRY $65 –V

Gibbston Valley Gold River Central Otago Pinot Noir ★★★☆

This is the Central Otago winery's 'lighter' red, for 'immediate enjoyment'. The 2015 vintage (★★★☆) is a blend of Gibbston (60 per cent) and Bendigo (40 per cent) fruit, matured for nine months in seasoned French oak casks. Full ruby, it is mouthfilling and buoyantly fruity, with generous plum and dried-herb flavours, fresh and smooth.

DRY $23 V+

Gibbston Valley GV Collection Central Otago Pinot Noir ★★★★★

This replaces the former 'Gibbston Valley Central Otago Pinot Noir' label. The classy, debut 2015 vintage (★★★★★) was mostly grown at Bendigo (95 per cent); the rest came from Gibbston. Hand-picked and matured for 10 months in French oak casks (20 per cent new), it is full-coloured, mouthfilling, savoury and supple, with lovely poise, texture and depth. Already delicious, it has ripe cherry, plum, dried-herb and spice flavours, showing excellent complexity and harmony. Drink now or cellar.

 DRY $46 AV

Gibbston Valley Le Maitre Gibbston Central Otago Pinot Noir ★★★★★

Grown in the Home Block at Gibbston, where most of the vines were planted in 1984, the 2015 vintage (★★★★★), certified organic, was matured for 11 months in French oak casks (30 per cent new). Full-coloured, it is mouthfilling, supple and very savoury, with deep plum, spice, dried-herb and nut flavours. The bouquet is highly fragrant, with a herbal thread; the palate is youthful, concentrated and beautifully poised, with notable complexity and a finely textured, long finish. A classy wine that impresses with its subtlety and finesse, rather than sheer power, it's already offering a lot of pleasure, but well worth cellaring to 2018+.

Vintage	15	14	13	12	11
WR	7	7	7	7	7
Drink	16-26	16-25	16-20	16-23	16-22

 DRY $100 AV

Gibbston Valley Reserve Central Otago Pinot Noir ★★★★★

At its best, this Central Otago red is mouthfilling and savoury, with superb concentration of sweet-tasting, plummy fruit and lovely harmony. The grapes have been drawn from various sub-regions and vineyards over the years and yields have been very low (under 5 tonnes/hectare). The 2015 vintage (★★★★★) was grown at Bendigo and matured for 11 months in French oak barriques (33 per cent new). Deep and youthful in colour, it is powerful, ripe and concentrated, with dense, vibrant plum, spice and nut flavours, earthy notes adding complexity, and obvious potential. Best drinking 2020+.

Vintage	15
WR	7
Drink	18-25

 DRY $120 –V

Gibbston Valley School House Central Otago Pinot Noir ★★★★★

This consistently classy red is estate-grown in the late-ripening School House Vineyard, at Bendigo, an extremely elevated site (up to 420 metres above sea level). Still a baby, the 2015 vintage (★★★★★) was matured for 11 months in French oak casks (33 per cent new). Bold and youthful in colour, it is powerful and fruit-packed, with dense, vibrant plum and spice flavours. Sweet-fruited, ripe and savoury, with fine-grained tannins, it's a very generous wine, full of potential; open 2018+.

Vintage	15	14	13	12	11	10	09
WR	7	7	7	7	7	7	7
Drink	16-37	16-26	16-25	16-23	16-22	16-20	16-17

 DRY $65 AV

Giesen Marlborough Pinot Noir   ★★★☆

The 2014 vintage (★★★☆), grown at multiple sites and oak-aged, is a deep ruby, fairly firm red, with a touch of complexity and cherry, plum and spice flavours, showing very good depth.

Vintage	14	DRY $26 AV
WR	5	
Drink	16-17	

Giesen Single Vineyard Selection Clayvin Marlborough Pinot Noir   ★★★★★

Deep ruby, the beautiful 2013 vintage (★★★★★) is sweet-fruited and concentrated, with impressive structure and harmony. Powerful, dense and silky, it has lovely flow across the palate, with a lingering finish.

Vintage	13	DRY $60 AV
WR	6	
Drink	16-22	

Giesen Single Vineyard Selection Ridge Block Marlborough Pinot Noir   ★★★★☆

Certified organic, the 2013 vintage (★★★★) was matured in French oak barrels (29 per cent new). Full-coloured, it is savoury, with concentrated, ripe flavours, showing good complexity.

Vintage	13	DRY $60 –V
WR	6	
Drink	16-19	

Giesen Single Vineyard Selection Waihopai Marlborough Pinot Noir   (★★★☆)

Harvested from 19-year-old vines, the 2012 vintage (★★★☆) was harvested at over 26 brix and matured in French oak casks (66 per cent new). Mouthfilling, it has very good depth of well-structured cherry, plum, spice and herb flavours, showing some complexity, and a strong oak influence.

Vintage	12	DRY $60 –V
WR	5	
Drink	16-17	

Giesen The Brothers Marlborough Pinot Noir   ★★★★

The 2013 vintage (★★★☆), oak-aged, is drinking well now. It has full, slightly developed colour, with generous, savoury, nutty flavours, showing good complexity.

Vintage	13	DRY $33 AV
WR	6	
Drink	16-18	

Giesen Winemaker's Selection Single Vineyard
Selection Marlborough Pinot Noir   (★★★)

Still on sale, the 2011 vintage (★★★) is mouthfilling and fairly firm, with spicy, nutty, slightly herbal flavours, strongly seasoned with oak, and some savoury complexity. Ready.

Vintage	11
WR	4
Drink	P

 DRY $40 –V

Gladstone Vineyard Pinot Noir   ★★★★☆

Estate-grown and hand-picked in the northern Wairarapa, and matured in French oak casks, the 2014 vintage (★★★★☆) has a fragrant, complex, inviting bouquet. Richly varietal, it is sweet-fruited and supple, with vibrant cherry, plum and spice flavours, gentle tannins and excellent harmony. Already approachable, it should be at its best 2018+.

Vintage	14	13	12	11	10
WR	7	6	NM	5	6
Drink	16-23	16-22	NM	16-20	16-20

 DRY $39 V+

Glasnevin Le Notaire Waipara Valley Pinot Noir   (★★★★★)

A powerful wine, deliciously savoury, complex and harmonious, the debut 2012 vintage (★★★★★) is from Barry Johns, formerly owner of Fiddler's Green, who wanted to make a rare, 'small batch' red (only 275 bottles were produced). From vines planted in 1998, the grapes were harvested by hand in early May at 23.6 brix, the juice was fermented with indigenous yeasts, and the wine was matured for nine months in a single, seasoned French oak barrique. Deep ruby in hue, it is a seductively sweet-fruited, generous and silky-textured red, with mouthfilling body, gentle acidity, concentrated cherry, strawberry, plum and spice flavours and a well-rounded finish. Already delicious, it's still youthful and should be at its best 2017+.

 DRY $95 AV

Glasnevin Limited Release Waipara Valley Pinot Noir   (★★★★☆)

Full of youthful vigour, the 2014 vintage (★★★★☆) is a richly varietal red, hand-picked, fermented with indigenous yeasts and matured for nine months in French oak barriques (33 per cent new). Deep ruby, it is mouthfilling, vibrant and supple, with very good concentration of fresh cherry, plum and spice flavours, finely integrated oak, and obvious cellaring potential. Best drinking 2017+.

DRY $35 V+

Goldwater Marlborough Pinot Noir   ★★★☆

The 2014 vintage (★★★☆) was matured in French oak casks (25 per cent new). It's a deep ruby, mouthfilling red with very good depth of ripe plum and spice flavours, showing some nutty complexity, and finely balanced tannins. The 2015 vintage (★★★☆) is a boldly fruity, sweet-fruited red with strong red-berry and plum flavours, showing a touch of complexity, and a smooth finish. Enjoyable young.

 DRY $23 V+

Grasshopper Rock Earnscleugh Vineyard Central Otago Pinot Noir   ★★★★★

Estate-grown in Alexandra, this is typically a wonderful buy. The powerful, concentrated 2014 vintage (★★★★★) was matured for 10 months in French oak barriques (26 per cent new). Deeply coloured, it is a savoury wine with deep, ripe plum, spice and dried-herb flavours, moderately firm tannins, and obvious potential; open 2017+. The graceful 2015 vintage (★★★★☆) is already delicious, but well worth cellaring. Matured in French oak barriques (28 per cent new), it is deep ruby, with rich, vibrant, plummy flavours, gentle tannins, savoury notes adding complexity, and an invitingly scented bouquet.

Vintage	15	14	13
WR	7	7	6
Drink	17-25	17-24	17-23

DRY $35 V+

Grava Martinborough Pinot Noir   (★★★☆)

The 2015 vintage (★★★☆) was grown at a site south of Martinborough township, formerly Hudson Vineyard. Matured for 10 months in oak barrels (10 per cent new), it was bottled unfined and unfiltered. Light ruby, it is a supple, medium-bodied red with fresh, moderately concentrated cherry/plum flavours. Showing some savoury complexity, it's still youthful; best drinking mid-2017+.

DRY $45 –V

Greenhough Hope Vineyard Nelson Pinot Noir   ★★★★★

One of Nelson's greatest reds, at its best powerful, rich and long-lived. It is estate-grown on an elevated terrace of the south-eastern Waimea Plains, where the vines, planted in gravelly loam clays, range up to 30 years old. Yields are very low – 4 to 5 tonnes of grapes per hectare – and the wine is matured for at least a year in French oak barrels (21 per cent new in 2014). Certified organic, the 2014 vintage (★★★★☆) is a ruby-hued, elegant, concentrated and savoury red, with ripe cherry, plum and spice flavours, showing excellent complexity, and a firm, sustained finish. Best drinking 2018+.

Vintage	14	13	12	11	10	09	08
WR	7	NM	NM	6	7	6	6
Drink	16-22	NM	NM	16-18	16-20	P	P

DRY $45 AV

Greenhough Nelson Pinot Noir   ★★★☆

This wine is handled in a similar way to its Hope Vineyard stablemate (above), but without the contribution of as much new oak or fruit from the oldest vines. Hand-picked from two sites at Hope, it is matured for a year in French oak casks (19 per cent new in 2014). The 2014 vintage (★★★★) is a deep ruby, full-bodied, sweet-fruited red, with generous cherry, plum and spice flavours, nutty and savoury, and a fairly firm finish. Best drinking mid-2017+.

Vintage	14	13	12	11	10	09
WR	7	6	6	6	6	6
Drink	16-20	16-19	16-18	16-17	P	P

DRY $26 AV

Greylands Ridge Central Otago Pinot Noir ★★★★

Grown at Alexandra, this single-vineyard red is matured in seasoned French oak casks. The 2014 vintage (★★★★) is a very youthful, mouthfilling, full-coloured red with strong, ripe cherry, plum and spice flavours, integrated oak and supple tannins. A stylish, generous wine, it's well worth cellaring.

Vintage	14	13
WR	6	7
Drink	16-19	16-20

 DRY $35 AV

Greyrock Hawke's Bay Pinot Noir (★★☆)

From Sileni, the 2015 vintage (★★☆) is ruby-hued, with a hint of development. Mouthfilling, fruity and smooth, it's a 'lightly oaked' style, with plum/spice flavours and gentle tannins. Easy, early drinking.

 DRY $17 AV

Greystone Thomas Brothers' Waipara Valley Pinot Noir ★★★★★

The 2013 vintage (★★★★★), grown in the steep Brothers Block, was hand-picked at over 24 brix, fermented with indigenous yeasts, matured for 15 months in French oak barriques (70 per cent new), and bottled without fining or filtering. A highly seductive red, it is deep and youthful in colour, with a welcoming fragrance, mouthfilling body, and rich, very ripe plum and spice flavours, with a hint of liquorice. Sweet-fruited and finely textured, with lovely harmony, it's a drink-now or cellaring proposition.

DRY $100 AV

Greystone Waipara Valley Pinot Noir ★★★★★

Deep ruby, mouthfilling and supple, the 2014 vintage (★★★★☆) is a classy young red, hand-picked, fermented with indigenous yeasts and matured for 11 months in French oak barriques (28 per cent new). Silky-textured, it has strong, ripe plum and spice flavours, with a hint of dried herbs, oak complexity and good potential; open 2017+. The delicious 2015 vintage (★★★★★) was matured in French oak barriques (25 per cent new). Deep and youthful in colour, it is highly fragrant, mouthfilling and supple, with rich, ripe cherry, plum and spice flavours, finely structured and long. A classy, age-worthy wine, it should be at its best 2018+.

Vintage	15
WR	7
Drink	16-30

DRY $42 V+

Greywacke Marlborough Pinot Noir ★★★★☆

Grown at elevated sites in the Southern Valleys, hand-harvested and matured for 18 months in French oak barriques (40 per cent new), the 2014 vintage (★★★★★) is deep ruby and richly fragrant, with mouthfilling body and strong, plummy, spicy flavours. Still very youthful, it is concentrated, very sweet-fruited and savoury, with buried tannins and impressive richness, complexity and harmony. Best drinking 2018+.

Vintage	14	13	12	11	10	09
WR	6	6	5	6	6	5
Drink	17-21	17-20	17-10	17-19	17-18	17-18

 DRY $47 –V

Grove Mill Marlborough Pinot Noir ★★★☆

The 2014 vintage (★★★☆) was grown in the Wairau Valley and matured in French oak casks (25 per cent new). Bright ruby, it is mouthfilling, fresh and smooth, with plum, spice and herb flavours, showing a touch of complexity.

Vintage	14	13
WR	7	7
Drink	16-20	16-19

DRY $25 AV

Gunn Estate Reserve Marlborough Pinot Noir ★★★☆

The 2015 vintage (★★★☆) from Sacred Hill offers fine value. More savoury and complex than most wines in its price category, it is ruby-hued, mouthfilling and supple, with satisfying depth of ripe, plummy, slightly spicy flavours, gentle acidity, good harmony and lots of drink-young appeal.

Vintage	15
WR	6
Drink	16-18

DRY $18 V+

Haha Marlborough Pinot Noir ★★★

From Fern Ridge, the 2014 vintage (★★★) was grown in the Awatere and upper Wairau valleys and matured in tanks (55 per cent) and French oak barrels (45 per cent). Ruby-hued, it is floral, lively and supple, with fresh, ripe, plummy flavours, in a slightly savoury style with lots of drink-young charm.

DRY $20 AV

Haha Reserve Marlborough Pinot Noir ★★★☆

The 2014 vintage (★★★★) was hand-harvested in the Awatere Valley and matured for a year in French oak barrels. Full-coloured, mouthfilling and fleshy, it has strong plum and spice flavours, showing good complexity, balanced tannins, and good aging potential.

DRY $28 AV

Hans Herzog Marlborough Pinot Noir ★★★★★

Still on sale, the 2011 vintage (★★★★) was estate-grown on the north side of the Wairau Valley, fermented with indigenous yeasts, matured for 18 months in French oak barriques, and bottled unfined and unfiltered. Ruby-hued, with moderately youthful colour, it is mouthfilling, with concentrated, ripe plum/spice flavours, slightly earthy notes adding complexity, gentle tannins, and a rounded finish. Drinking well now, it's certified organic.

Vintage	11	10	09	08
WR	7	7	7	7
Drink	16-21	16-20	16-19	16-20

DRY $49 AV

Harakeke Farm Nelson Pinot Noir ★★★☆

Estate-grown at Upper Moutere, the barrel-aged 2013 vintage (★★★☆) is a ruby-hued, moderately youthful wine, full-bodied, with strong, ripe, plummy, spicy flavours, hints of earth, herbs and nuts, and a savoury, fairly smooth finish.

 DRY $28 AV

Harwood Hall Marlborough Pinot Noir (★★★)

The 2013 vintage (★★★) has light, slightly developed colour. It has cherry, spice and nut flavours, with a hint of stalkiness, and some savoury complexity.

DRY $25 –V

Hawkshead Bannockburn Central Otago Pinot Noir ★★★★

Already drinking well but still youthful, the 2014 vintage (★★★★☆) is a single-vineyard red, matured in French oak casks (30 per cent new). Full, bright ruby, it is mouthfilling, ripe and savoury, with good concentration of plummy, spicy, slightly nutty flavours, gentle tannins and obvious potential. A very harmonious wine, it's a drink-now or cellaring proposition.

 DRY $49 –V

Hawkshead Central Otago Pinot Noir ★★★☆

The 2014 vintage (★★★★) of this regional blend was matured in French oak barriques (20 per cent new). Bright ruby, it is a youthful, generous, savoury red with strong, ripe, plummy, spicy flavours, showing good complexity. Best drinking 2017+.

 DRY $40 –V

Hawkshead First Vines Central Otago Pinot Noir ★★★☆

Estate-grown at Gibbston, this wine is hand-picked from the oldest vines and matured in French oak casks. The 2014 vintage (★★★☆) is ruby-hued, smooth and savoury, with gentle tannins and good depth of plum, spice, dried-herb and nut flavours, showing considerable complexity.

 DRY $49 –V

Highfield Marlborough Pinot Noir ★★★☆

The distinctive 2013 vintage (★★★☆), certified organic, was French oak-matured for a year. It has lightish, slightly developed colour, with very good depth of flavour, ripe, subtle and savoury. Ready.

Vintage	13	12	11	10	09
WR	6	6	7	7	6
Drink	16-18	16-18	16-17	P	P

DRY $38 –V

Hoppers Crossing Reserve Central Otago Pinot Noir ★★★

The buoyantly fruity 2013 vintage (★★★☆) is deep ruby, with mouthfilling body, strong cherry, plum and spice flavours and a fresh, smooth finish. Offering fine value, it's enjoyable now, but should offer good drinking over the next couple of years.

 DRY $20 V+

Huia Marlborough Pinot Noir   ★★★★

The 2012 vintage (★★★★) was barrel-matured for 11 months. Deep ruby, it is mouthfilling, with strong, vibrant plum and cherry flavours, a subtle seasoning of oak, good complexity, fine-grained tannins and excellent harmony. Certified organic.

DRY $39 AV

Humming Wire Pinot Noir   (★★★)

The 2013 vintage (★★★), grown in the Wairarapa, is a fruit-driven style, ruby-hued, with good depth of fresh, vibrant, plummy flavours and a smooth finish. (From Johner Estate.)

DRY $24 –V

Hunky Dory Marlborough Pinot Noir   ★★★☆

From Huia, the 2014 vintage (★★★☆) is deeply coloured, with mouthfilling body and strong, ripe plum/spice flavours, slightly earthy and firm. Certified organic.

DRY $25 AV

Hunter's Marlborough Pinot Noir   ★★★

Typically a supple, charming red. The 2013 vintage (★★★), matured for 10 months in French oak casks (20 per cent new), is ruby-hued, with mouthfilling body and moderately concentrated plum/spice flavours, showing a touch of complexity.

DRY $29 –V

Impromptu by Misha's Vineyard Central Otago Pinot Noir   ★★★☆

This wine is made principally for sale by the glass in restaurants and bars. Estate-grown at Bendigo, the 2013 vintage (★★★★) was matured in French oak hogsheads (18 per cent new). Bright ruby, it is elegant, sweet-fruited and savoury, with good weight, gentle tannins, and youthful, plummy, spicy flavours, showing good complexity.

Vintage	13	12	11	10
WR	6	7	5	7
Drink	16-21	16-20	16-18	16-17

DRY $29 AV

Invivo Central Otago Pinot Noir   ★★★☆

The 2014 vintage (★★★★) was grown at several sites, in the Cromwell Basin and Gibbston, and oak-aged. Full-coloured, it is mouthfilling, with concentrated cherry, plum and spice flavours. Sweet-fruited, with finely balanced tannins and considerable complexity, it's drinking well now. Good value.

Vintage	14	13	12
WR	7	7	6
Drink	16-25	16-25	16-24

DRY $29 AV

Invivo Michelle's Central Otago Pinot Noir   ★★★★☆

Seductive in its youth, the impressive 2015 vintage (★★★★★) is rare – only five barrels were produced. Grown at Bannockburn, it is full-coloured, fleshy, rich and rounded. Sweet-fruited, with substantial body (14.5 per cent alcohol) and deep plum/spice flavours, it is a powerful but not heavy wine, with gentle tannins, excellent complexity, and a lasting, very harmonious finish.

Vintage	15	14
WR	7	7
Drink	16-24	16-23

 DRY $45 –V

Jackson Estate Gum Emperor Single Vineyard
Waihopai Valley Marlborough Pinot Noir   ★★★★

Hand-picked in the Waihopai Valley and matured for over a year in old French oak casks, the 2011 vintage (★★★★☆) is a graceful, perfumed red with moderately youthful, ruby colour and lovely flow across the palate. Delicious now, it has sweet-fruit delights and vibrant cherry/plum flavours, savoury and supple. The 2013 vintage (★★★☆) is a ruby-hued, medium-bodied wine with fresh acidity and vibrant cherry, plum, spice and nut flavours, showing considerable complexity. Best drinking mid-2017+.

 DRY $49 –V

Jackson Estate Homestead Marlborough Pinot Noir   ★★★☆

Partly barrel-aged, the 2014 vintage (★★★☆) was estate-grown in the Gum Emperor Vineyard in the Waihopai Valley. Bright ruby, it is full-bodied, vibrantly fruity and smooth, with plummy, slightly spicy flavours, showing a touch of complexity, and lots of drink-young charm. Priced right.

Vintage	14	13
WR	6	6
Drink	16-18	16-17

 DRY $24 V+

Jackson Estate Somerset Single Vineyard
Waihopai Valley Marlborough Pinot Noir   ★★★☆

Hand-picked in the Waihopai Valley and matured in French oak casks, the 2013 vintage (★★★☆) is ruby-hued, with a hint of development. Medium to full-bodied, with a slightly herbal bouquet, it has cherryish, slightly nutty and herbal flavours, gentle tannins and some complexity. Drink now onwards.

DRY $49 –V

Jackson Estate Vintage Widow Marlborough Pinot Noir   ★★★★

The finely balanced 2014 vintage (★★★★) was estate-grown in the Waihopai Valley, hand-picked and matured for 10 months in French oak casks. Full ruby, it is mouthfilling, with good concentration of ripe cherry, plum and spice flavours, and nutty, savoury notes adding complexity. Drinking well now, it's also worth cellaring.

Vintage	14	13	12
WR	6	6	6
Drink	16-21	16-20	16-19

 DRY $36 AV

Johanneshof Maybern Single Vineyard Reserve Marlborough Pinot Noir ★★★☆

Estate-grown on a steep (30 degrees), north-facing slope at Koromiko, between Picton and Blenheim, the 2013 vintage (★★★★) of this distinctive wine is the best yet. Hand-harvested, fermented with indigenous yeasts and barrel-aged, it is ruby-hued, attractively scented and savoury, with strong, cherryish, nutty flavours, a hint of herbs, good complexity and plenty of personality. Drink now or cellar.

Johner Estate Gladstone Pinot Noir ★★★★

Estate-grown in the northern Wairarapa, matured for a year in French oak barrels (25 per cent new), and bottled unfined and unfiltered, the 2014 vintage (★★★★☆) is a powerful, deeply coloured red. It is sturdy (14.5 per cent alcohol) and sweet-fruited, with concentrated plum, spice and dried-herb flavours, and fine-grained tannins. It's still youthful but already highly approachable; drink now or cellar. Good value.

Vintage	14	DRY $36 AV
WR	7	
Drink	16-22	

Johner Estate Gladstone Reserve Pinot Noir ★★★★☆

The powerful, full-bodied 2014 vintage (★★★★★) is a single-vineyard, estate-grown Wairarapa red, hand-picked from the oldest vines and matured for a year in French oak casks (75 per cent new). Bold and youthful in colour, it is very rich, ripe and supple, with dense plum, spice and dried-herb flavours, showing excellent complexity and harmony, and a deliciously smooth finish. A classy young red, it should be long-lived.

Vintage	14	DRY $60 –V
WR	7	
Drink	16-25	

Johner Estate Moonlight Wairarapa Pinot Noir ★★★☆

Offering good value, the 2014 vintage (★★★) was matured for a year in seasoned oak barrels. Deep ruby, it is mouthfilling and savoury, with generous, ripe plum, spice and dried-herb flavours, showing good complexity, and a fairly firm finish. Drink now or cellar.

Vintage	14	13	DRY $26 AV
WR	6	7	
Drink	16-20	16-18	

Joss Bay Central Otago Pinot Noir ★★★

Grown at Alexandra and partly barrel-aged, the 2014 vintage (★★☆) is ruby-hued, with an earthy bouquet. Firmly structured, it has plenty of plummy, spicy flavour, in a slightly rustic style. (From Tarras Wines.)

Judge Rock Alexandra Central Otago Pinot Noir ★★★★☆

This single-vineyard red is estate-grown at Alexandra and French oak-matured. The graceful 2014 vintage (★★★★) is a bright ruby, medium to full-bodied, savoury wine with ripe cherry, spice and dried-herb flavours, gentle tannins and excellent harmony. The 2015 vintage (★★★★☆), to be released in 2017, is ruby-hued, with mouthfilling body, fresh acidity, generous cherry, plum, dried-herb and spice flavours, and fine-grained tannins. Still unfolding, it's an age-worthy wine, likely to be at its best 2018+.

 DRY $40 AV

Judge Rock Venus Central Otago Pinot Noir (★★★★)

Made 'to be cherished between friends, family and lovers', the 2013 vintage (★★★★) was estate-grown at Alexandra. Bright ruby, savoury and supple, it has ripe, cherryish, slightly spicy flavours, a gentle seasoning of nutty oak, good complexity and a smooth finish. Drink now to 2018.

 DRY $30 AV

Jules Taylor Marlborough Pinot Noir ★★★★☆

The 2015 vintage (★★★★☆) was grown in the Awatere Valley and Southern Valleys, and matured in French oak barrels (partly new). Deep ruby, with a fragrant, spicy bouquet, it is mouthfilling, youthful and vibrant, with concentrated, ripe cherry, plum and spice flavours, finely poised, supple and very harmonious. Best drinking 2017+.

Vintage	15	14
WR	6	6
Drink	16-20	16-20

 DRY $33 V+

Jules Taylor OTQ Single Vineyard Marlborough Pinot Noir ★★★★☆

The powerful 2015 vintage (★★★★☆), made 'On The Quiet', was hand-picked at Ballochdale Estate, in the upper Awatere Valley, fermented with indigenous yeasts, and matured for 10 months in French oak barrels. Deep ruby, it is full-bodied, with a fragrant bouquet, suggestive of plums and dried herbs. Still very youthful, it is concentrated, ripe and finely textured, in a fruit-packed style with integrated oak, supple tannins and obvious potential. Best drinking 2018+.

Vintage	15
WR	6
Drink	16-20

 DRY $43 AV

Julicher 99 Rows Martinborough Pinot Noir ★★★★

Estate-grown at Te Muna, the 2013 vintage (★★★★) was matured for 10 months in French oak casks (5 per cent new). Enjoyable now, it is mouthfilling and savoury, with very satisfying depth of ripe plum, cherry and spice flavours, hints of herbs and nuts, good complexity, and a well-rounded finish. Drink now to 2018.

Vintage	13	12	11	10	09	08
WR	7	5	5	6	7	7
Drink	16-20	16-18	16-17	16-17	P	P

DRY $32 AV

Julicher Martinborough Pinot Noir   ★★★★★

Estate-grown at Te Muna, the 2013 vintage (★★★★☆) was hand-harvested and matured for 11 months in French oak casks (15 per cent new). Bright ruby, it's a very harmonious wine, with mouthfilling body, low acidity and generous, ripe cherry, plum, spice and nut flavours, complex, savoury and smooth. Drink now onwards.

Vintage	13
WR	7
Drink	16-23

DRY $42 V+

Junction Possession Central Hawke's Bay Pinot Noir   (★★★)

Grown on the Takapau Plains, the 2014 vintage (★★★) was hand-picked and matured for 18 months in French oak casks (30 per cent new). Ruby-hued, with distinctly spicy, slightly herbal aromas and flavours, it is moderately concentrated, with some complexity. Still youthful, it should be at its best mid-2017+.

DRY $27 –V

Kaimira Estate Brightwater Vintner's Selection Pinot Noir   ★★★

Certified organic, the 2014 vintage (★★★) was estate-grown in Nelson and matured for a year in French oak barrels (20 per cent new). Full ruby, with a hint of development, it is vibrantly fruity, with hints of dried herbs and nuts, a touch of complexity, and current-drinking appeal. The 2015 vintage (★★★) was matured for a year in French oak casks (30 per cent new). Ruby-hued, it has generous, plummy flavours, a hint of liquorice, and drink-young charm. Certified organic.

Vintage	15	14
WR	7	6
Drink	16-21	16-19

DRY $30 –V

Kalex Central Otago Pinot Noir   ★★★★

The highly attractive 2014 vintage (★★★★☆) was hand-harvested, French oak-matured, and bottled unfined and unfiltered. Deep ruby, it is savoury and supple, sweet-fruited and silky, with concentrated cherry, plum and spice flavours, good complexity, and a finely textured, long finish. Drink now or cellar.

DRY $40 –V

Kim Crawford Reserve Marlborough/Central Otago Pinot Noir   (★★★☆)

The ruby-hued 2014 vintage (★★★☆) is a blend of Marlborough and Central Otago grapes, partly barrel-aged. Full-bodied, it has good depth of cherry, plum and spice flavours, gently seasoned with toasty oak, moderate tannins and some savoury complexity. Drink now or cellar. (Note: the word 'Reserve' is only on the capsule.)

DRY $25 AV

Kina Cliffs Nelson Pinot Noir ★★★☆

Estate-grown, hand-picked and matured for 10 months in French oak barrels, the 2013 vintage (★★★☆) is ruby-hued, mouthfilling and smooth, with ripe plum, cherry and spice flavours, showing some savoury complexity.

DRY $30 –V

Kina Cliffs Reserve Nelson Pinot Noir (★★★★)

Currently on sale and maturing well, the 2012 vintage (★★★★) was made from very ripe (over 25 brix) grapes and matured in French oak casks (50 per cent new). A powerful, savoury red, it has generous plum and dried-herb flavours, showing good complexity, and a finely textured, lingering finish.

DRY $45 –V

Kingsmill Tippet's Dam Bannockburn Central Otago Pinot Noir ★★★★☆

A single-vineyard Bannockburn red, the 2013 vintage (★★★★★) offers great value. Fragrant and full-coloured, it is mouthfilling, with concentrated, youthful plum, cherry and spice flavours, showing lovely ripeness, freshness and density. A rich, harmonious wine with finely integrated oak and good tannin backbone, it should be at its best 2017+.

DRY $35 V+

Konrad Marlborough Pinot Noir ★★★☆

The 2013 vintage (★★★☆) was estate-grown in the Waihopai Valley and matured for 10 months in seasoned French oak barriques. Bright ruby, it is mouthfilling, with very good depth of plum/spice flavours, ripe and smooth. It's drinking well now.

DRY $29 AV

Kumeu River Hunting Hill Pinot Noir ★★★★

Grown on the slopes above Mate's Vineyard, directly over the road from the winery at Kumeu, the 2014 vintage (★★★★) is a top example of Pinot Noir from the Auckland region. Deep ruby, it is fresh, vibrant and sweet-fruited, with mouthfilling body and concentrated cherry, plum and spice flavours. An elegant, savoury, finely structured wine, it should be at its best 2017+.

DRY $50 –V

Kumeu Village Pinot Noir ★★☆

Estate-grown by Kumeu River, in West Auckland, the 2015 vintage (★★☆) was hand-picked and fermented with indigenous yeasts. Ruby-hued, it's a light, supple, easy-drinking red, with gentle tannins and fresh berry/plum flavours. Priced right.

DRY $18 AV

Kuru Kuru Central Otago Pinot Noir ★★★★

The 2013 vintage (★★★★) is a youthful, regional blend, full-bodied, with strong, ripe plum, cherry and spice flavours, showing impressive depth and complexity. (From Tarras Wines.)

DRY $38 AV

Lake Chalice Marlborough Pinot Noir   ★★★

The 2013 vintage (★★★) was estate-grown, mostly in the lower Waihopai Valley, and matured for seven months in French oak barrels. Ruby-hued, it is sweet-fruited and vibrantly fruity, with fresh, plummy, berryish flavours to the fore, gentle tannins, and lots of drink-young charm.

DRY $20 AV

Lake Hayes Central Otago Pinot Noir   ★★★☆

From Amisfield, the 2014 vintage (★★★★) is a drink-young style, estate-grown at Pisa and partly barrel-aged. Deep and bright in colour, it is mouthfilling and vibrantly fruity, with plum/spice flavours showing excellent ripeness and depth. A generous, savoury wine, it's already drinking well, but also worth cellaring.

DRY $30 –V

Last Shepherd, The, Central Otago Pinot Noir   ★★★☆

The 2014 vintage (★★★☆) is ruby-hued and mouthfilling, with good depth of ripe plum, spice and dried-herb flavours, showing some savoury complexity. Best drinking 2017+. The 2015 vintage (★★★☆) is moderately concentrated, with ripe cherry, plum and dried-herb flavours, supple, savoury and balanced for easy drinking. (From Pernod Ricard NZ.)

DRY $25 AV

Latitude 41 Nelson Pinot Noir   (★★★☆)

From Spencer Hill, the attractive 2013 vintage (★★★☆) was grown at seven sites and matured 'on' French oak for 10 months (meaning it was not barrel-aged). Ruby-hued, it is mouthfilling and supple, with good depth of ripe cherry and plum flavours, showing some spicy, earthy, nutty complexity.

DRY $22 V+

Lauregan Single Vineyard Central Hawke's Bay Pinot Noir   (★★★★)

The 2013 vintage (★★★★) is a very ripe expression of Pinot Noir – no surprise, given its northern origins. Grown in Central Hawke's Bay, it was hand-picked and matured for nine months in French oak barrels (one-third new). Boldly coloured, it is mouthfilling, fresh and fruit-packed, with strong, plummy, spicy flavours, ripe, smooth and generous. It shows considerable complexity and plenty of personality.

DRY $40 –V

Lawson's Dry Hills Marlborough Pinot Noir   ★★★☆

A fruit-driven style, the 2014 vintage (★★★☆) was grown in the Southern Valleys and matured in tanks (40 per cent) and French oak barrels (60 per cent). Bright ruby, it is mouthfilling, with fresh berry, plum and spice flavours and some savoury notes, in a moderately complex style, still fresh and youthful. Best drinking mid-2017+.

Vintage	14
WR	6
Drink	16-20

DRY $24 V+

Lawson's Dry Hills Reserve Marlborough Pinot Noir ★★★★☆

Offering fine value, the deeply coloured 2014 vintage (★★★★☆) was grown in the Waihopai Valley and matured in French oak barriques (25 per cent new). Mouthfilling, savoury and supple, it is sweet-fruited, with cherry, plum and spice flavours, finely integrated oak, and excellent ripeness and richness. It should be long-lived. Open 2018+.

Vintage	14	13	12
WR	6	7	7
Drink	16-20	16-19	16-18

 DRY $30 V+

Lawson's Dry Hills The Pioneer Marlborough Pinot Noir ★★★★☆

The 2013 vintage (★★★★☆) was grown at the adjacent Barnsley and Lawson's Dry Hills sites, in the Waihopai Valley, and French oak-matured. Deep ruby, it is mouthfilling, sweet-fruited, savoury and supple, with excellent complexity. Very harmonious and smooth-flowing, it's probably at its peak now. Drink to 2017.

Vintage	13	12
WR	7	7
Drink	16-25	16-20

 DRY $35 V+

Left Field Nelson Pinot Noir ★★★☆

The 2015 vintage (★★★☆) is from Nelson – previous releases were grown in Marlborough. Matured in French oak barrels (75 per cent) and tanks (25 per cent), it is deep ruby, with good depth of ripe cherry, plum and spice flavours, showing some savoury complexity. Fine value. (From Te Awa.)

Vintage	15
WR	5
Drink	16-19

 DRY $18 V+

Leveret Estate Marlborough Pinot Noir ★★★

Bright ruby, the 2014 vintage (★★★) is sturdy, with generous, ripe plum/spice flavours and a fairly firm finish. Priced right, it's enjoyable young.

Vintage	14	13
WR	7	6
Drink	16-19	16-18

DRY $21 AV

Leveret Estate Reserve Hawke's Bay Pinot Noir ★★★☆

Deeply coloured, the 2014 vintage (★★★☆) is a fleshy, youthful red with strong, plummy, spicy, slightly cherryish flavours, nutty oak and balanced tannins.

Vintage	14	13
WR	7	7
Drink	16-19	16-18

 DRY $31 –V

Leveret Estate Reserve Marlborough Pinot Noir (★★☆)

The 2013 vintage (★★☆) was grown in the Awatere Valley and barrel-aged for over a year. It has bright, light ruby colour. Showing some development, it is slightly herbal and nutty, with some savoury complexity and a green-edged finish.

Vintage	13
WR	6
Drink	16-20

DRY $31 –V

Lime Rock Central Hawke's Bay Pinot Noir ★★★☆

Light ruby, the 2013 vintage (★★★★) is vibrantly fruity and supple, with generous, ripe plum and spice flavours, showing very good depth, vigour and harmony. Drink now or cellar.

DRY $42 –V

Lime Rock White Knuckle Hill Central Hawke's Bay Pinot Noir ★★★★☆

The 2013 vintage (★★★★☆) is ruby-hued, very savoury and supple, with mouthfilling body and excellent density of ripe cherry, plum and spice flavours. Well worth cellaring.

DRY $60 –V

Little Black Shag Nelson Pinot Noir (★★☆)

Low-priced, the 2014 vintage (★★☆) has light, fairly mature colour. Light-bodied, it has fresh acidity and spicy, slightly herbal and nutty flavours. Ready.

DRY $14 V+

Locharburn Central Otago Pinot Noir ★★★☆

Hand-picked in the Cromwell Basin, the 2013 vintage (★★★☆) is a buoyantly fruity red, deep ruby, with strong plum, cherry and spice flavours, a gentle seasoning of oak (French, 20 per cent new) and gentle tannins. It's a moderately complex style; drink now or cellar.

DRY $35 –V

Loveblock Central Otago Pinot Noir ★★★★

The 2013 vintage (★★★★) is a bright ruby, single-vineyard red with a fresh, youthful bouquet, showing good complexity. Sweet-fruited, it has vibrant cherry, plum and spice flavours, showing good vigour and potential. Best drinking 2017+.

DRY $40 –V

Lowburn Ferry Home Block Central Otago Pinot Noir ★★★★☆

The 2014 vintage (★★★★★) is a single-vineyard red, hand-harvested at 24 brix at Lowburn, and matured for 10 months in French oak casks (31 per cent new). Deeply coloured, it is fragrant, sweet-fruited and concentrated, with deep, ripe plum, cherry and spice flavours, showing excellent complexity, and fine-grained tannins. Still youthful, it's an age-worthy, very harmonious wine; open 2017+.

Vintage	14	13	12
WR	7	7	7
Drink	16-21	16-20	16-20

DRY $55 –V

Lowburn Ferry Skeleton Creek Central Otago Pinot Noir ★★★★

The 2014 vintage (★★★★) was grown at two nearby sites in the Cromwell Basin, including the estate vineyard at Lowburn (55 per cent). Hand-picked and matured for 10 months in French oak barriques (26 per cent new), it is deeply coloured, mouthfilling and supple, with fresh plum/spice flavours, integrated oak and good concentration. Approachable young, it should be at its best 2017+.

Vintage	14	13
WR	7	7
Drink	16-19	16-18

 DRY $45 –V

Lowburn Ferry The Ferryman Reserve Pinot Noir ★★★★★

Estate-grown in the Home Block at Lowburn, in Central Otago, this is the producer's flagship red, made only in top vintages. Hand-harvested at over 24 brix and matured for over a year in French oak barriques (33 per cent new), the 2014 vintage (★★★★★) is deeply coloured and mouthfilling, with dense, ripe, plummy, spicy, nutty flavours, very savoury and complex. It should flourish with cellaring; open 2017+.

 DRY $85 AV

Luminary, The, Martinborough Pinot Noir ★★★☆

From Palliser Estate, the 2013 vintage (★★★★) is a great buy (especially on special in supermarkets). Matured for 11 months in French oak casks (25 per cent new), it is full-coloured, mouthfilling and sweet-fruited, with generous, ripe plum, spice and nut flavours, smooth and savoury. Instantly appealing.

 DRY $22 V+

Lynfer Estate Wairarapa Pinot Noir ★★★

Grown at Gladstone, the 2013 vintage (★★★☆) is ruby-hued, mouthfilling and supple, with cherry, plum and spice flavours, showing some savoury complexity. Enjoyable young.

 DRY $28 –V

Ma Maison by Leung Estate Phoenix Cuveé Pinot Noir (★★★★☆)

The very graceful, supple 2013 vintage (★★★★☆) is rare – only 900 bottles were produced. Bottled unfined and unfiltered, it is a distinctive, silky-textured wine with ripe, cherryish, plummy flavours, fresh acidity, and youthful poise and charm. Likely to be long-lived, it should be at its best 2017+.

DRY $90 –V

Ma Maison by Leung Estate Pinot Noir ★★★★☆

Estate-grown at Martinborough, barrel-matured, and bottled without fining or filtering, the 2014 vintage (★★★★☆) is already drinking well, but also well worth cellaring. Full ruby, it is mouthfilling (14.5 per cent alcohol), sweet-fruited, savoury and generous, with fine-grained tannins and strong plum, cherry, spice, herb and nut flavours, showing good complexity. Best drinking 2018+.

 DRY $49 –V

Mahi Byrne Marlborough Pinot Noir   (★★★★)

The 2013 vintage (★★★★) is a single-vineyard red, hand-picked at Conders Bend, in the Wairau Valley, and matured for 11 months in French oak barriques. Ruby-hued, with a hint of development, it is ripe and savoury, with cherry and spice flavours, showing good complexity. Drink now to 2018.

Vintage	13
WR	7
Drink	16-22

 DRY $45 –V

Mahi Marlborough Pinot Noir   ★★★★

The 2014 vintage (★★★☆) was hand-picked at three sites in the Wairau and Awatere valleys, fermented with indigenous yeasts and matured for 11 months in French oak barriques. Light ruby, it is savoury and supple, with moderately rich cherry/spice flavours, showing good complexity. Drink now or cellar.

Vintage	14	13	12
WR	6	6	6
Drink	16-20	16-20	16-18

 DRY $30 AV

Main Divide Tehau Reserve Waipara Valley Pinot Noir   ★★★★

The 2014 vintage (★★★★) was fermented with indigenous yeasts and matured for 18 months in new barriques. Deep ruby, it is mouthfilling, with generous, plummy, spicy flavours. Youthful and concentrated, with ripe, supple tannins, it's already drinking well. (From Pegasus Bay.)

 DRY $33 AV

Main Divide Waipara Valley Pinot Noir   ★★★★

A consistently rewarding, drink-young style from Pegasus Bay. From a 'perfect' growing season, the 2013 vintage (★★★★) was matured for 18 months in French oak barriques (15 per cent new). Ripely scented, it is ruby-hued, mouthfilling and smooth, with good concentration of cherry, plum and spice flavours, savoury notes adding complexity, gentle tannins and some aging potential. Fine value.

Vintage	13	12	11	10	09
WR	7	7	5	7	7
Drink	16-23	16-20	16-18	16-20	16-18

DRY $25 V+

Maori Point Central Otago Pinot Noir   ★★★★

The generous 2014 vintage (★★★★☆) of this single-vineyard wine, grown at Tarras, in the Cromwell Basin, was matured in French oak barrels (20 per cent new), and bottled unfined and unfiltered. Deep ruby, it is mouthfilling, savoury and supple, with youthful, ripe, cherryish, slightly nutty flavours, gentle tannins, and very good depth and complexity. Drink now or cellar.

 DRY $36 AV

Map Maker Marlborough Pinot Noir ★★★☆

From Staete Landt, the 2014 vintage (★★★☆) was estate-grown and hand-picked at Rapaura, and matured in French oak barriques. A deep ruby, floral red with ripe cherry and plum flavours, generous and smooth, and a gentle seasoning of oak, it's enjoyable young, but also worth cellaring.

DRY $26 AV

Marble Point Hanmer Springs Pinot Noir ★★★☆

Estate-grown in North Canterbury, the 2013 vintage (★★★) was matured in French oak casks (25 per cent new). Drinking well now, it is light ruby, with fresh, moderately concentrated, plummy flavours, showing a touch of complexity, and gentle tannins.

Vintage	13
WR	6
Drink	16-20

DRY $28 AV

Margrain Home Block Martinborough Pinot Noir ★★★★

The 2013 vintage (★★★★) was harvested from 22-year-old vines and matured for over a year in French oak casks (20 per cent new). Ruby-hued, it is youthful, with mouthfilling body, ripe cherry, plum and spice flavours, a nutty, savoury complexity, and good texture.

Vintage	13
WR	7
Drink	16-25

DRY $42 –V

Margrain Reserve Martinborough Pinot Noir (★★★★☆)

The refined 2013 vintage (★★★★☆) was matured for a year in French oak casks (40 per cent new). Bright ruby, it is very graceful and silky-textured, with plum, cherry and spice flavours, youthful, finely poised and lingering.

Vintage	13
WR	7
Drink	16-25

DRY $55 –V

Margrain River's Edge Martinborough Pinot Noir ★★★☆

Designed for early drinking, this wine is 'barrel selected for its smoothness and charm'. The 2014 vintage (★★★☆), matured for a year in seasoned oak casks, then six months in tanks before bottling, is light ruby, mouthfilling, savoury and supple, with ripe cherry, plum and spice flavours, a touch of tannin, and considerable complexity. Best drinking now to 2017.

Vintage	14	13
WR	6	6
Drink	16-22	16-20

DRY $24 V+

Martinborough Vineyard Home Block Pinot Noir   ★★★★☆

The 2013 vintage (★★★★☆) is an elegant, ruby-hued, still fairly youthful red. Tightly structured and savoury, it has strong, ripe cherry, plum and spice flavours, woven with fresh acidity, and very good complexity. Best drinking mid-2017+. The 2014 vintage (★★★★☆) is deep ruby, with generous cherry, plum and spice flavours, vibrant and youthful. Savoury and slightly nutty, with good complexity, it's well worth cellaring; open 2018+.

DRY $68 –V

Martinborough Vineyard Marie Zelie Reserve Pinot Noir   ★★★★★

The intriguing 2013 vintage (★★★★★) is the first since 2010. Hand-picked from the oldest vines and matured in French oak barriques, it is all about refinement, rather than sheer power. Light ruby in hue, it is very finely perfumed, with cherry, red-berry and nut flavours, highly complex, very savoury and harmonious. Still a baby, it's a gentle, persuasive, persistent wine, likely to be at its best 2018+.

DRY $225 –V

Martinborough Vineyard Te Tera Pinot Noir   ★★★★

Te Tera ('The Other') is made for early drinking, compared to its stablemates. The 2014 vintage (★★★★) offers good value. Mouthfilling, savoury and supple, it was matured for 10 months in French oak barriques (10 per cent new). Bright ruby, it has ripe, plummy, spicy flavours, showing good freshness, vigour and complexity.

DRY $29 V+

Matahiwi Estate Holly Wairarapa Pinot Noir   ★★★☆

The 2013 vintage (★★★), estate-grown in the northern Wairarapa, represents 'the best that the Matahiwi home vineyard can achieve'. Retasted in 2016, it is youthful, but only moderately complex, with fresh acidity and vibrant, fruity, slightly nutty flavours.

Vintage	13
WR	6
Drink	16-18

DRY $39 –V

Matahiwi Estate Wairarapa Pinot Noir   ★★★☆

The finely poised 2015 vintage (★★★★) is already highly enjoyable, but worth cellaring to mid-2017 onwards. Deep ruby, it is mouthfilling and smooth, with fresh acidity, a subtle seasoning of oak, and strong, ripe plum and spice flavours. Priced right.

DRY $29 AV

Matawhero Gisborne Pinot Noir   ★★★

The 2013 vintage (★★★) is ruby-hued and vibrantly fruity, with ripe cherry/plum flavours, showing good depth and moderate complexity, and plenty of drink-young appeal.

Vintage	13
WR	7
Drink	P

DRY $25 –V

Matua Lands & Legends Central Otago Pinot Noir   ★★★☆

The 2013 vintage (★★★☆) is full-coloured, mouthfilling, fleshy and supple, with generous, ripe, plummy, slightly spicy and nutty flavours, showing some complexity. Enjoyable young, it offers good value.

DRY $23 V+

Matua Marlborough Pinot Noir   ★★☆

The good-value 2014 vintage (★★★) was sourced mostly from Marlborough, 'with a little from Central Otago'. Bright ruby, it is sweet-fruited and smooth, with vibrant cherry/plum flavours in a 'fruit-driven' (lightly oaked) style with a Beaujolais-like freshness and charm. Drink young.

DRY $15 AV

Matua Single Vineyard Bannockburn Pinot Noir   (★★★★☆)

The 2013 vintage (★★★★☆) was matured in French oak barriques (28 per cent new). Rich, silky and harmonious, it is full-coloured, mouthfilling and supple, with ripe cherry and plum flavours, earthy and nutty notes adding complexity, gentle tannins, and obvious potential.

DRY $60 –V

Matua Single Vineyard Central Otago Pinot Noir   (★★★★★)

More expressive in its youth than its 'Single Vineyard Bannockburn' stablemate (above), the 2013 vintage (★★★★★) was also grown at Bannockburn and matured in French oak barriques (35 per cent new). Deeply coloured, it is fragrant, mouthfilling (14.5 per cent alcohol) and supple, with strong, vibrant plum, cherry and spice flavours, showing lovely poise and harmony. A very elegant and tightly structured wine, it should mature well.

DRY $60 AV

Maude Central Otago Pinot Noir   ★★★★☆

The 2015 vintage (★★★★☆) is a floral, finely textured wine, harvested from sites including the home vineyard at Wanaka, and matured for a year in French oak barriques (30 per cent new). Instantly appealing, it is sweet-fruited, with concentrated cherry, plum and spice flavours, well-integrated oak, supple tannins and a long, harmonious finish. Fine value.

Vintage	15	14	13	12	11	10	09	08
WR	6	7	6	6	5	6	5	4
Drink	16-22	16-22	16-22	16-22	16-18	16-20	16-18	P

DRY $32 V+

Maude Mt Maude Vineyard Wanaka Reserve Central Otago Pinot Noir   ★★★★★

Estate-grown at Wanaka, this wine is hand-picked from vines planted in 1994. The 2014 vintage (★★★★☆) was barrel-aged for 16 months (40 per cent new). Deep and bright in colour, it is mouthfilling, savoury and complex, with concentrated, ripe cherry, plum and spice flavours and a well-structured finish. Showing strong personality, it's still youthful. The 2015 vintage (★★★★☆) was matured for 16 months in French oak casks (40 per cent new). Ruby-hued, it is floral, savoury and complex, with strawberry and spice flavours, hints of dried herbs and nuts, and a fairly firm finish. A distinctive, very age-worthy red, with some ethereal notes, it should be at its best 2019+.

Vintage	15	14	13	12	11	10	09
WR	6	7	6	6	5	6	6
Drink	16-22	16-24	16-22	16-20	16-18	16-20	16-20

DRY $62 AV

Milcrest Estate Nelson Pinot Noir ★★★

The 2014 vintage (★★) was French oak-aged for 10 months. Light and slightly developed in colour, it is sturdy (14.5 per cent alcohol), with moderate depth of plum/spice flavours, showing a slight lack of freshness. Drink young.

DRY $29 –V

Mills Reef Reserve Marlborough Pinot Noir ★★★

The 2015 vintage (★★★☆) was grown in the Wairau Valley and French oak-aged. Ruby-hued, it is a fruit-driven style, plummy, ripe and smooth, with good flavour depth, a touch of complexity, and lots of drink-young appeal. Best mid-2017+.

Vintage	15	14	13	12
WR	7	6	7	6
Drink	16-20	16-18	16-17	P

DRY $25 –V

Millton Clos de Ste Anne Naboth's Vineyard Pinot Noir – see Clos de Ste Anne Naboth's Vineyard Pinot Noir

Millton La Cote Gisborne Pinot Noir ★★★★

Certified organic, the 2014 vintage (★★★★) was hill-grown, hand-picked, fermented in small wooden French cuves, and bottled unfiltered. Finely crafted, it is a graceful red, sweet-fruited, with ripe cherry/spice flavours, savoury and harmonious, and good complexity. The thought-provoking 2015 vintage (★★★★☆) is even better. Mouthfilling and savoury, with ripe cherry, plum and spice flavours, it is youthful and complex, with excellent harmony and potential; open 2018+. Certified organic.

Vintage	15	14
WR	6	6
Drink	16-20	16-19

DRY $30 AV

Miner's Daughter, The, Reserve McAndrews Reach North Canterbury Pinot Noir ★★★

The 2014 vintage (★★★) is bright ruby, with mouthfilling body, ripe plum and spice flavours, showing a touch of complexity, and a very smooth finish.

Vintage	14
WR	5
Drink	16-18

DRY $17 V+

Misha's Vineyard The High Note Central Otago Pinot Noir ★★★★☆

Maturing well, the 2010 vintage (★★★★★), estate-grown in the Cromwell Basin, was harvested from very low-yielding vines (4.5 tonnes/hectare), fermented with indigenous yeasts and matured in French oak hogsheads (38 per cent new). Deep and still fairly youthful in colour, it's a powerful, savoury red with dense, plummy, spicy flavours, showing excellent complexity, and a finely textured finish. Delicious drinking now onwards.

Vintage	10	09	08	07
WR	7	6	6	7
Drink	16-20	16-19	16-18	P

 DRY $45 –V

Misha's Vineyard Verismo Central Otago Pinot Noir ★★★★☆

This 'reserve style' is oak-aged longer, with greater exposure to new oak, than its High Note stablemate. The refined 2011 vintage (★★★★☆) was matured in French oak hogsheads (43 per cent new) and not bottled until December 2012. A generous, silky red, it has lightish colour, with plum, spice and nut flavours, showing excellent complexity and harmony.

Vintage	11	10	09	08
WR	6	7	6	6
Drink	16-22	16-22	16-19	16-20

 DRY $63 –V

Mission Martinborough Barrique Reserve Pinot Noir ★★★★

The 2015 vintage (★★★★☆) is a single-vineyard red, matured for a year in French oak barriques. Full-coloured, it is mouthfilling, with generous, ripe cherry, plum and spice flavours, complex and savoury, and a firm, lingering finish. Still youthful, it's well worth cellaring to 2018+. The 2014 vintage (★★★★) is a very ripe style, with substantial body (15 per cent alcohol). It has full, moderately youthful colour, concentrated cherry and spice flavours, a hint of liquorice, and a fairly firm finish.

Vintage	15	14
WR	7	6
Drink	18-27	16-27

 DRY $29 V+

Mission Martinborough Pinot Noir ★★★☆

The 2013 vintage (★★★☆), 'lightly oaked', is ruby-hued, mouthfilling and supple, with ripe plum/spice flavours, showing very good depth, and lots of upfront appeal. Drink now.

Vintage	13
WR	6
Drink	16-20

 DRY $20 V+

Mission Reserve Central Otago Pinot Noir ★★★☆

The 2013 vintage (★★★★) was grown at Pisa, in the Cromwell Basin, and matured in French oak barrels (18 per cent new). Deeply coloured, it is fleshy and supple, with ripe, concentrated cherry, plum and spice flavours, seasoned with toasty oak, good aging potential, and a perfumed bouquet.

DRY $30 –V

Mission Reserve Martinborough Pinot Noir ★★★☆

The 2013 vintage (★★★★) is a single-vineyard red, hand-picked and lightly oak-influenced. Ruby-hued, it is scented and sweet-fruited, with cherry, strawberry, spice and nut flavours, gentle tannins, and a silky-textured, lingering finish. Impressing with charm and elegance, rather than power, it offers delicious drinking now.

Vintage	13
WR	5
Drink	16-25

DRY $29 AV

Mission Vineyard Selection Marlborough Pinot Noir   (★★★☆)

Like a good Beaujolais, the charming 2013 vintage (★★★☆) is bright and youthful in colour, with vibrant, ripe cherry/plum flavours, gentle tannins, and little sign of oak (it was barrel-aged for three months). A delicious drink-young style.

DRY $20 V+

Mission Vineyard Selection Martinborough Pinot Noir   (★★★)

Grown at two sites, in Te Muna and Lake Ferry Road, the 2014 vintage (★★★) was gently oak-aged. Enjoyable young, it is full-bodied (14.5 per cent alcohol), with fresh cherry, plum and spice flavours, a hint of herbs, and good depth.

DRY $20 AV

Misty Cove Signature Marlborough Pinot Noir   ★★★☆

The 2013 vintage (★★★☆) was estate-grown and hand-picked at Rapaura, in the Wairau Valley, and matured for nine months in two and three-year-old barrels. Full-coloured, it is mouthfilling, with very good depth of plum and spice flavours, showing considerable complexity, and a moderately firm finish. A 'serious' rather than 'sensuous' red, it's well worth cellaring. The 2014 vintage (★★★☆) only has the word 'Signature' on the back label. Light ruby, it is a savoury, oak-influenced style with ripe cherry, plum and spice flavours, showing some nutty complexity, balanced tannins, and drink-young appeal.

DRY $30 –V

Momo Marlborough Organic Pinot Noir   ★★★☆

Certified organic, the 2014 vintage (★★★☆) from Seresin was estate-grown in the Raupo Creek Vineyard, hand-picked, fermented with indigenous yeasts and matured for a year in mostly seasoned French oak barriques (4 per cent new). Light ruby, it is savoury, with good depth of ripe, plummy, spicy, slightly nutty flavours, showing considerable complexity, and a fairly firm finish. Drink now or cellar.

DRY $25 AV

Mondillo Bella Central Otago Pinot Noir   (★★★★★)

The 2013 vintage (★★★★★) is not to be missed . . . but it will be by the vast majority of Pinot Noir fans, since there are just 840 bottles. A selection of three 'exceptional' barrels out of 65, it was estate-grown at Bendigo and matured for 22 months in one-year-old French oak casks. Deeply coloured, with a seductively perfumed, complex bouquet, it is generous, sweet-fruited and finely textured, with deep, vibrant cherry, plum and spice flavours, deliciously savoury, silky and 'complete'. A memorable debut.

Vintage	13
WR	7
Drink	16-22

 DRY $85 AV

Mondillo Central Otago Pinot Noir   ★★★★★

Estate-grown at Bendigo, in the Cromwell Basin, the 2015 vintage (★★★★☆) was matured for a year in French oak casks (30 per cent new). Deep ruby, it is sturdy (14.5 per cent alcohol), vibrant and supple, with fresh, concentrated, plummy, spicy flavours, slightly earthy and nutty notes adding complexity, and a well-rounded, harmonious finish. Still very youthful, it should be at its best 2018+.

Vintage	15	14	13	12	11	10
WR	7	7	7	7	6	7
Drink	17-22	16-22	16-22	16-20	16-18	16-18

 DRY $45 AV

Motueka Vineyards Nelson Pinot Noir   (★★☆)

Floral and ruby-hued, the 2014 vintage (★★☆) is fresh and light, with berryish, slightly herbal and spicy flavours, balanced for easy drinking. Priced right. (From Anchorage.)

DRY $18 AV

Mount Brown Grand Reserve Waipara Valley Pinot Noir   (★★★★)

The 2014 vintage (★★★★), a ruby-hued, moderately youthful red, was fermented with indigenous yeasts and matured for 18 months in oak barriques (25 per cent new). Fragrant and savoury, it has strong, ripe plum, spice and nut flavours, with good underlying tannins, and considerable cellaring potential; open mid-2017+.

Vintage	14
WR	7
Drink	16-20

 DRY $40 –V

Mount Brown Waipara Valley Pinot Noir   ★★☆

The 2013 vintage (★★★), matured in French oak barrels, is a deep ruby, vibrant red with cherryish flavours to the fore, a sweet oak influence, fresh acidity, and a touch of earthy complexity. The 2014 vintage (★★☆) was matured for 18 months in French oak barrels (25 per cent new). Light ruby, it is slightly herbal and rustic, but also shows some savoury complexity.

 DRY $19 –V

Mount Edward Central Otago Pinot Noir

The 2013 vintage (★★★★★) is a regional blend, bottled without fining or filtration. Full and bright in colour, it is mouthfilling and savoury, with excellent concentration and complexity. Clearly from a top season, it is a 'serious' rather than 'sexy' red, with deep, ripe plum/spice flavours, a hint of dried herbs, nutty, savoury notes adding complexity, and good tannin support. Drinking well now, it's a generous, age-worthy wine, worth cellaring to 2017+.

DRY $45 –V

Mount Riley Marlborough Pinot Noir
★★★☆

The 2014 vintage (★★★) was grown in the Wairau Valley and matured for nine months in French oak barriques. Ruby-hued, it is mouthfilling and smooth, with fresh, ripe, plummy, berryish flavours to the fore, hints of dried herbs and spices, and gentle tannins. A drink-young charmer.

Vintage	14	13
WR	6	6
Drink	16-19	16-18

DRY $20 V+

Mount Riley Seventeen Valley Marlborough Pinot Noir
★★★★

The savoury 2014 vintage (★★★☆) was matured for 10 months in French oak barrels (partly new). Deep ruby, it is fresh and youthful, with generous cherry/plum flavours, an earthy streak, and a tight finish. It needs time; open 2017+.

Vintage	14	13
WR	6	6
Drink	16-23	16-22

DRY $39 AV

Mountain Road Taranaki Pinot Noir
★★★

From vines planted south of Waitara in 2004, the 2013 (★★★☆) is a top vintage. Hand-picked and matured for a year in French oak barriques, it is sturdy (14.4 per cent alcohol), fleshy and full-coloured, with generous, ripe, plummy, berryish, slightly spicy and nutty flavours and a smooth finish. Retasted in mid-2016, it's probably in full stride.

DRY $30 –V

Moutere Hills Nelson Pinot Noir
★★★★

The 2013 vintage (★★★★) is a single-vineyard red, matured for 11 months in French oak barrels. Floral, berry and spice aromas lead into a ruby-hued, full-bodied, savoury red with generous, well-ripened cherry, plum, spice and nut flavours, showing good complexity.

DRY $32 AV

Moutere Hills Sarau Reserve Nelson Pinot Noir
(★★★★☆)

Delicious now, the 2013 vintage (★★★★☆) was hand-picked, matured for 23 months in French oak barriques, and bottled unfined and unfiltered. Full-coloured, with a fragrant, savoury bouquet, it is mouthfilling and sweet-fruited, with deep, plummy, spicy flavours, showing good complexity, and a finely textured, well-rounded finish.

DRY $53 –V

Mt Beautiful North Canterbury Pinot Noir   ★★★☆

The easy-drinking 2015 vintage (★★★☆) was grown at Cheviot, north of Waipara, and matured for a year in French oak barriques. Full-coloured, it is mouthfilling, with youthful plum, spice and dried-herb flavours, showing good depth, a touch of complexity, gentle tannins and a smooth finish. Best drinking mid-2017+.

Vintage	15
WR	6
Drink	16-22

DRY $33 –V

Mt Difficulty Bannockburn Central Otago Pinot Noir   ★★★★☆

This popular red is grown at Bannockburn, in the Cromwell Basin. Matured for a year in French oak casks (30 per cent new), the 2014 vintage (★★★★☆) is deep ruby, mouthfilling and supple, with concentrated cherry, plum and spice flavours, gentle tannins, and excellent complexity and harmony. Delicious drinking now onwards.

Vintage	14	13
WR	6	6
Drink	16-26	16-25

DRY $47 –V

Mt Difficulty Growers Series Packspur Vineyard Pinot Noir   ★★★★

The 2013 vintage (★★★★) is a single-vineyard Central Otago wine, grown at Lowburn. Matured for 16 months in French oak casks (30 per cent new), it is ruby-hued, with generous plum, spice and dried-herb flavours, earthy, nutty and complex. It's quite forward; drink now onwards.

Vintage	13
WR	6
Drink	16-25

DRY $75 –V

Mt Difficulty Limited Edition Inspiration Cuveé Bannockburn Pinot Noir   (★★★★★)

An official wine of the New Zealand Olympic team in 2016, the classy, concentrated 2013 vintage (★★★★★) was grown at four sites at Bannockburn, in Central Otago. Deep and youthful in colour, it is mouthfilling, sweet-fruited and graceful, with an array of cherry, plum, spice, dried-herb and nut flavours that build to a powerful, very harmonious finish. Still youthful, it should be long-lived; best drinking 2018+.

DRY $95 AV

Mt Difficulty Single Vineyard Long Gully Bannockburn Pinot Noir   ★★★★★

From a site that supplies core fruit for the Mt Difficulty Central Otago Pinot Noir label, this is promoted as a more 'feminine' style than its Pipeclay Terrace stablemate. The powerful 2013 vintage (★★★★☆) was matured for 16 months in French oak casks (30 per cent new). Deep and bright in colour, it is very fresh and vibrant, with strong plum/spice flavours, a hint of dried herbs, and good complexity. Still very youthful, it should be at its best 2018+.

Vintage	13
WR	7
Drink	16-30

DRY $90 –V

Mt Difficulty Single Vineyard Mansons Farm Bannockburn Pinot Noir   (★★★★★)

The strapping 2013 vintage (★★★★★) was matured for 16 months in French oak casks (30 per cent new). Bold and youthful in colour, it is powerful and sweet-fruited, with plum and spice flavours, very ripe and dense, good tannin support, and obvious potential. It should be long-lived; best drinking 2018+.

Vintage	13
WR	7
Drink	16-30

 DRY $90 AV

Mt Difficulty Single Vineyard Pipeclay Terrace Bannockburn Pinot Noir   ★★★★★

This powerful Central Otago red is grown on a steep, relatively hot slope, with gravelly soils. The 2013 vintage (★★★★★) was matured for 16 months in French oak casks (30 per cent new). Deeply coloured, it is powerful, ripe, savoury and concentrated, with deep plum/spice flavours, an earthy streak, and excellent harmony and potential. Open 2017+.

Vintage	13
WR	7
Drink	16-30

 DRY $90 –V

Mt Difficulty Single Vineyard Target Gully Pinot Noir   ★★★★★

From an elevated, late-ripening block at Bannockburn, in Central Otago, the very classy 2013 vintage (★★★★★) was matured for 16 months in French oak casks (30 per cent new). Deep ruby, it is finely perfumed and sweet-fruited, with lovely power, depth and poise. A notably graceful red, with dense plum/spice flavours, a hint of dried herbs, and finely integated oak, it should be at its best 2017+.

Vintage	13
WR	7
Drink	16-30

 DRY $90 AV

Mt Hector Wairarapa Pinot Noir   ★★☆

From Matahiwi, the 2013 vintage (★★☆) is full-coloured, with vibrant flavours of berries, plums, herbs and spices to the fore. It's not a complex style, but enjoyable young.

DRY $18 AV

Mud House Central Otago Pinot Noir   ★★★★

Estate-grown at Bendigo, in the Claim 431 Vineyard, and matured in tanks and barrels, the 2013 vintage (★★★★) is a delicious drink-young style. Full and bright in colour, it is weighty and fruit-packed, with generous plum/spice flavours, a gentle seasoning of oak, and ripe, supple tannins. The 2014 vintage (★★★★) is a fragrant, full-coloured red, mouthfilling and sweet-fruited, with rich plum and spice flavours and supple tannins. Delicious drinking 2016+.

 DRY $25 V+

Mud House Estate Claim 431 Vineyard Central Otago Pinot Noir   ★★★★☆

The 2013 vintage (★★★★☆) was estate-grown at Bendigo, hand-picked, fermented with indigenous yeasts and matured in French oak barriques (20 per cent new). Deep ruby, it is floral, vibrant and supple, in a fruit-driven style with strong, lively cherry, plum, spice and herb flavours, woven with fresh acidity.

Vintage	13	
WR	6	
Drink	16-20	

 DRY $34 V+

Mud House Single Vineyard Dambuster Marlborough Pinot Noir   (★★★★)

The debut 2014 vintage (★★★★) is the first single-vineyard red from the company's Woolshed Vineyard, in the upper Wairau Valley. Matured for a year in French oak barrels (25 per cent new), it is ruby-hued, full-bodied and silky-textured, with fresh cherry/plum fruit flavours to the fore, a gentle seasoning of oak adding complexity, and good vigour and harmony. Best drinking 2017+.

 DRY $40 –V

Muddy Water Hare's Breath Waipara Pinot Noir   ★★★★☆

From 'a block on limestone slopes at the back of the property', the 2012 vintage (★★★★☆) was hand-picked, fermented with indigenous yeasts, matured for 16 months in French oak barrels (40 per cent new), and bottled unfined and unfiltered. Certified organic, it is full-coloured, mouthfilling and youthful, in a refined, very graceful and distinctly savoury style. Finely textured, it has deep cherry and plum flavours, showing excellent complexity and harmony.

 DRY $61 –V

Muddy Water Slowhand Waipara Pinot Noir   ★★★★★

This is the Waipara winery's top red. Based on the oldest, ungrafted vines (clone 10/5), planted in 1993, and 'tended by slow hands', it reveals outstanding personality. Harvested at 24.6 brix, matured for 16 months in French oak barrels (40 per cent new), and bottled unfined and unfiltered, the 2012 vintage (★★★★★) is certified organic. Full-coloured and ripely scented, it is mouthfilling (14.5 per cent alcohol), sweet-fruited and supple, with deep cherry, plum, spice and nut flavours, notably complex and savoury. A thought-provoking wine, very graceful and harmonious, it should be at its best 2017+.

Vintage	12	
WR	6	
Drink	16-28	

 DRY $74 AV

Muddy Water Waipara Pinot Noir   ★★★★☆

Delicious now, the 2013 vintage (★★★★☆) is a ruby-hued, estate-grown red, hand-harvested at over 24 brix, matured in French oak barrels (30 per cent new) for 15 months, and bottled unfined and unfiltered. Certified organic, it is mouthfilling, very savoury and supple, with ripe cherry, plum and spice flavours, showing excellent complexity and harmony. The promising

2015 vintage (★★★★☆) was matured in French oak casks (25 per cent new). Still extremely youthful, it is deeply coloured, sweet-fruited and supple, with mouthfilling body, a rich surge of cherry, spice and nut flavours, fine-grained tannins, and obvious potential. Open 2018 onwards.

Vintage	15	DRY $42 AV
WR	7	
Drink	16-30	

Murdoch James Blue Rock Martinborough Pinot Noir   ★★★★

Estate-grown south of the township, the 2014 vintage (★★★★) was hand-picked and matured in French oak barrels. Delicious young, but also worth cellaring, it is bright ruby, floral and supple, with ripe cherry, plum and spice flavours, gentle tannins, good complexity and a smooth, harmonious finish.

 DRY $50 –V

Murdoch James Estate Martinborough Pinot Noir   ★★★

The 2013 vintage (★★★☆) is a floral, fruit-driven style. Bright ruby, it is mouthfilling, with fresh, ripe cherry, plum and spice flavours, showing some complexity, finely balanced tannins and some aging potential.

 DRY $33 –V

Nanny Goat Vineyard Central Otago Pinot Noir   ★★★★☆

The attractive 2015 vintage (★★★★☆) is a generous, deep ruby red with vibrant, ripe plum, cherry and spice flavours, showing excellent depth and complexity. A refined wine, it is weighty and harmonious, with fine-grained tannins and good aging potential.

 DRY $36 V+

Nanny Goat Vineyard Super Nanny Central Otago Pinot Noir   (★★★★☆)

The 2013 vintage (★★★★☆) is a ripely scented, deeply coloured Bannockburn red, densely packed with vibrant plum, cherry and spice flavours. A concentrated wine with oak complexity and fine-grained tannins, it's a drink-now or cellaring proposition.

DRY $51 –V

Nautilus Awatere River Vineyard Marlborough Pinot Noir   (★★★★★)

Grown in the upper Awatere Valley, the debut 2014 vintage (★★★★★) is a single-vineyard red, matured in French oak casks (33 per cent new). Full ruby, it is very finely textured, with rich, vibrant plum, spice and dried-herb flavours, gentle tannins and a long finish. Already lovely, but also age-worthy, with a sense of youthful drive, it should be at its best 2018+.

 DRY $70 AV

Nautilus Clay Hills Vineyard Marlborough Pinot Noir   (★★★★☆)

The debut 2014 vintage (★★★★☆) is a sturdy, single-vineyard red, grown in the Southern Valleys and matured in French oak casks (33 per cent new). Ruby-hued, it is generous, savoury and complex, with ripe, slightly earthy flavours and a fairly firm finish. Best drinking 2017+.

 DRY $70 –V

Nautilus Four Barriques Marlborough Pinot Noir ★★★★★

The beautiful 2013 vintage (★★★★★) is rare – four out of over 120 barrels. Matured for 18 months in French oak barrels (50 per cent new), it has deep, fairly youthful colour. Very fragrant and sweet-fruited, it has rich cherry, plum, spice and dried-herb flavours, finely textured and seamless. Drink now or cellar.

Vintage	13	12	11	10	09
WR	7	7	NM	7	7
Drink	16-23	16-20	NM	16-20	16-18

 DRY $85 AV

Nautilus Marlborough Pinot Noir ★★★★☆

The 2013 vintage (★★★★☆), barrel-aged, is a very elegant wine. Full ruby, it is mouthfilling, sweet-fruited and savoury, with strong cherry, plum and spice flavours, showing excellent complexity, finely balanced tannins and good potential. (This label has recently been replaced by the Southern Valleys Pinot Noir – see below).

Vintage	13	12	11	10	09
WR	7	7	6	7	7
Drink	16-19	16-18	16-17	P	P

DRY $42 AV

Nautilus Southern Valleys Marlborough Pinot Noir ★★★★☆

(This label has replaced the former Nautilus Marlborough Pinot Noir.) The debut 2014 vintage (★★★★☆) was matured for a year in French oak casks (30 per cent new). Full ruby, it is scented, sweet-fruited, savoury and supple, with generous cherry, plum, spice, dried-herb and nut flavours. Finely textured, with good complexity, it's a drink-now or cellaring proposition.

Vintage	14
WR	7
Drink	16-22

DRY $42 AV

Neudorf Moutere Pinot Noir ★★★★★

Typically a very classy Nelson red. It is hand-picked from 'older vines' at Upper Moutere, fermented with indigenous yeasts, matured for 10 to 12 months in French oak barriques (25 per cent new in 2014), and usually bottled without fining or filtering. The 2014 vintage (★★★★☆) has fullish, slightly developed colour. Mouthfilling, savoury and slightly earthy, it has cherry, plum, spice and nut flavours, showing excellent complexity, and a finely textured finish.

Vintage	14	13	12	11	10	09	08
WR	6	6	7	6	7	6	6
Drink	16-21	16-20	16-23	16-18	16-18	16-17	16-17

 DRY $59 AV

Neudorf Tom's Block Nelson Pinot Noir   ★★★★

This regional blend can offer fine value. The 2014 vintage (★★★★) was hand-harvested at three Moutere sites (including the Home Block), matured for 10 months in French oak barriques (25 per cent new), and bottled without fining or filtration. Ruby-hued, it is fragrant, with generous, ripe cherry, plum, spice and nut flavours, showing good complexity and harmony. Drink now or cellar.

Vintage	14	13	12	11	10
WR	6	6	7	6	7
Drink	16-21	16-20	16-19	P	P

 DRY $33 AV

Nevis Bluff Central Otago Pinot Noir   ★★★

Still on sale, the 2011 vintage (★★★) was matured for 10 months in French oak casks (25 per cent new). It has lightish, fairly developed colour, with plum, spice, herb and nut flavours, showing some complexity.

Vintage	11	10
WR	5	6
Drink	16-18	16-18

 DRY $48 –V

Nevis Bluff Reserve Central Otago Pinot Noir   (★★★★)

Still on sale, the 2012 vintage (★★★★) is drinking well now. A ruby-hued, moderately mature red, it was grown at Pisa and matured for a year in French oak casks (50 per cent new). It has cherry, spice and nut flavours, with a hint of dried herbs, supple tannins and good complexity.

Vintage	12
WR	6
Drink	16-22

 DRY $85 –V

Nga Waka Martinborough Lease Block Pinot Noir   ★★★★☆

The 2014 vintage (★★★★★) is a single-vineyard red, from vines planted in 1999. Matured for a year in French oak casks (40 per cent new), it is deeply coloured, powerful and very finely structured, with concentrated, ripe plum, spice and nut flavours, showing good complexity, and lovely depth and harmony. Already delicious, it should be at its best 2017+.

Vintage	14	13
WR	7	7
Drink	16-23	16-18

DRY $50 –V

Nga Waka Martinborough Pinot Noir   ★★★★

The attractive 2015 vintage (★★★★) was matured for a year in French oak casks (35 per cent new). Ruby-hued, with a fragrant, savoury bouquet, it is mouthfilling, with ripe cherry, plum, spice and nut flavours that linger well. Best drinking mid-2017+.

Vintage	15	14	13
WR	6	7	7
Drink	17-24	16-23	P

 DRY $40 –V

Ngatarawa Stables Reserve Hawke's Bay Pinot Noir   ★★☆

A drink-young style. The 2014 vintage (★★☆) is light ruby, floral and supple, with cherry, plum and dried-herb flavours, gentle tannins and a smooth finish.

Vintage	14	13
WR	6	6
Drink	16-20	16-17

 DRY $20 –V

Odyssey Reserve Iliad Marlborough Pinot Noir   (★★★★☆)

The 2014 vintage (★★★★☆) is an impressive debut. Certified organic, it was estate-grown in the Brancott Valley, hand-picked and matured in French oak casks (27 per cent new). A powerful, sweet-fruited and generous wine, it has deep, youthful plum and spice flavours, good complexity and a finely textured, lasting finish. Already delicious, it should be at its best 2017+.

Vintage	14
WR	6
Drink	16-20

 DRY $42 AV

Okiwa Bay Marlborough Pinot Noir   (★★☆)

From Highfield, the 2013 vintage (★★☆) is ruby-hued, with moderate depth of strawberry/ spice flavours, slightly leafy notes, and a touch of complexity. Drink now.

 DRY $25 –V

Old Coach Road Nelson Pinot Noir   ★★☆

From Seifried, the 2014 vintage (★★☆) was matured for a year in French oak barriques (partly new). Light ruby, it is fresh and light, with strawberry and spice flavours, a hint of herbs, gentle tannins and drink-young appeal. Priced right.

 DRY $16 AV

Omeo Central Otago Five Barriques Pinot Noir   ★★★★

Offering good value, the 2012 vintage (★★★★) was grown at Alexandra and matured for 10 months in French oak casks. It's a generous wine, cherryish, plummy and spicy, with a hint of dried herbs, and a savoury, nutty complexity. The 2013 vintage (★★★★☆) is bright ruby, with mouthfilling body and concentrated, ripe cherry, plum and spice flavours. Showing good complexity, it is earthy and savoury, with obvious cellaring potential; open 2017+.

Vintage	13	12
WR	6	6
Drink	16-21	16-20

DRY $28 V+

Omihi Hills Limestone Ridge Pinot Noir   ★★★★

The great-value 2014 vintage (★★★★) was grown at Waipara and handled in seasoned oak. 'Made to be enjoyed in its youth', it is bright ruby, with mouthfilling body, strong, plummy, spicy flavours, balanced tannins and good complexity. Well worth cellaring, it's a great buy.

Vintage	14	13
WR	5	7
Drink	16-18	16-19

DRY $20 V+

Omihi Hills Omihi Reserve Pinot Noir   ★★★★☆

The deeply coloured 2013 vintage (★★★★☆) was harvested at Omihi, North Canterbury, from vines planted in 1999 and 2000, matured in seasoned French oak casks, and bottled unfined and unfiltered. Still youthful, it is mouthfilling, sweet-fruited, spicy and plummy, in a savoury, very age-worthy style with moderately firm tannins and very good complexity. Best drinking 2017+.

Vintage	13	12	11	10
WR	7	6	5	6
Drink	16-25	16-24	16-24	16-18

DRY $35 V+

Omihi Hills The Triangle Waipara Pinot Noir   ★★★★☆

From a block in the Omihi Hills home vineyard, the 2013 vintage (★★★★☆) is a deeply coloured, mouthfilling, graceful red, matured in seasoned French oak casks. A classy young wine, it has gentle tannins and cherry, plum, spice and nut flavours, strong, ripe, savoury and complex. Already delicious, it's also well worth cellaring; best drinking 2017+.

Vintage	13	12
WR	7	7
Drink	16-25	16-26

DRY $45 –V

Omihi Hills Waipara Selection Pinot Noir   ★★★★

The 2013 vintage (★★★★) was matured in seasoned French oak barrels. Ruby-hued, it is mouthfilling and supple, with fresh, ripe red-berry and spice flavours, a hint of dried herbs, and a nutty, savoury complexity. It's drinking well now.

Vintage	13	12	11	10
WR	7	6	6	6
Drink	16-20	16-18	16-20	16-20

DRY $29 V+

Opawa Marlborough Pinot Noir   ★★★☆

From Nautilus, the 2015 vintage (★★★☆) was harvested from mature vines grown on the Wairau Valley floor, fermented with indigenous yeasts and fully barrel-aged (10 per cent new). Deep ruby, it is fleshy and sweet-fruited, with vibrant, youthful cherry/plum flavours to the fore, a slightly earthy streak and very good depth.

DRY $28 AV

Osawa Prestige Collection Hawke's Bay Pinot Noir ★★★

Estate-grown at Mangatahi, hand-picked and matured in French oak casks, the 2013 vintage (★★★) is lively, with ripe plum, spice, herb and nut flavours, showing some complexity, and a fairly firm finish.

Vintage	13	12	11	10	09
WR	5	5	5	7	6
Drink	16-19	16-18	16-18	16-17	P

DRY $52 –V

Ostler Blue House Vines Waitaki Valley Pinot Noir ★★★★

Part of Ostler's 'grower selection' (it is not estate-grown), the 2013 vintage (★★★★) was matured in old French oak barriques. Ruby-hued, it is fragrant and savoury, with a spicy, nutty, slightly herbal bouquet. Strongly varietal, with cherry, plum, spice and dried-herb flavours, it shows good complexity and richness.

Vintage	13
WR	6
Drink	16-19

DRY $30 AV

Ostler Caroline's Waitaki Valley Pinot Noir ★★★☆

Grown in the Waitaki Valley of North Otago, the 2013 vintage (★★★☆) was matured for a year in French oak casks (20 per cent new). Ruby-hued, it is enjoyable now, with moderately concentrated plum, spice and herb flavours, savoury, nutty notes adding complexity, and a harmonious, well-rounded finish.

Vintage	13	12	11	10	09	08
WR	6	NM	6	7	6	6
Drink	16-20	NM	16-18	16-18	16-17	P

DRY $59 –V

Overstone Hawke's Bay Pinot Noir ★★★

From Sileni, the 2015 vintage (★★★) is light ruby, mouthfilling and sweet-fruited, with gentle tannins, slightly savoury notes and plenty of flavour. Fine value.

DRY $13 V+

Oyster Bay Marlborough Pinot Noir ★★★☆

From Delegat, the 2014 vintage (★★★★) offers great value. Grown in the Awatere and Wairau valleys and partly barrel-aged, it is mouthfilling and silky-textured, with vibrant, ripe plum/spice flavours, some savoury complexity, and impressive depth and harmony.

DRY $25 AV

Paddy Borthwick Falloon Block New Zealand Pinot Noir (★★★☆)

Mouthfilling and supple, the 2015 vintage (★★★☆) was grown in the Wairarapa. Deep ruby, it has youthful, plummy, spicy, slightly nutty flavours, showing a hint of tamarillo, and good complexity and depth. Best drinking mid-2017+.

DRY $26 AV

Paddy Borthwick New Zealand Pinot Noir ★★★★

Grown in the Wairarapa, the 2015 vintage (★★★★) is a deep ruby, full-bodied red, with plum, cherry and spice flavours, hints of herbs and nuts, finely balanced tannins, and good ripeness and concentration. Best drinking 2018+.

 DRY $34 AV

Palliser Estate Martinborough Pinot Noir ★★★★★

This is typically an enticingly perfumed, notably elegant, rich and harmonious red. Most but not all of the grapes come from the company's own vineyards – Palliser, Om Santi, Clouston, Pinnacles and East Base – where the vines range up to over 20 years old. Maturation is for a year in French oak barriques (partly new). The 2014 vintage (★★★★☆) is refined, with a fragrant, floral bouquet. Mouthfilling, it has vibrant, ripe cherry, plum and spice flavours, showing good, savoury complexity, and a harmonious, finely textured finish. Still youthful, it's well worth cellaring to 2017+.

DRY $54 AV

Palliser Pencarrow Martinborough Pinot Noir –
see Pencarrow Martinborough Pinot Noir

Paper Road Pinot Noir (★★☆)

A pleasant, drink-young style, the 2013 vintage (★★☆) is a single-vineyard red, grown in the northern Wairarapa. Lightish in colour, it has slightly herbal flavours, showing a touch of complexity.

 DRY $20 –V

Paua Marlborough Pinot Noir ★★★

From Highfield, the 2014 vintage (★★★) was French oak-aged for 10 months. Enjoyable young, it has lightish, moderately youthful colour, mouthfilling body and ripe cherry, plum, spice and herb flavours, showing a touch of complexity.

Vintage	14
WR	6
Drink	16-17

DRY $25 –V

Pearson Estate Mon Cheval Waipara Valley Pinot Noir ★★★★☆

Retasted in early 2016, the 2010 (★★★★☆) is drinking well now and probably at its peak. Grown at the entrance to the Weka Pass, matured in French oak barrels for 18 months, and bottled without fining or filtering, it has full, fairly mature colour. The bouquet is fragrant, with dried-herb and spice aromas; the palate is mouthfilling, very savoury and supple, with rich plum, herb, spice and nut flavours, showing good freshness and complexity, and strong personality. The 2009 vintage (★★★★), also retasted in early 2016, is very similar. Full-bodied and complex, with mature colour, it shows excellent depth of spice, dried-herb and nut flavours, savoury, rounded and ready.

 DRY $45 –V

Pegasus Bay Prima Donna Pinot Noir ★★★★★

For its top Waipara red, Pegasus Bay wants 'a heavenly voice, a shapely body and a velvety nose'. Based on the oldest vines, it is matured for 18 months in French oak barriques (50 per cent new). The 2012 vintage (★★★★★) is deep and youthful in colour. A powerful, silky-textured red, with concentrated cherry, plum, spice and nut flavours, possessing a strong sense of depth and potential, it is lovely now, but still youthful and likely to be long-lived.

Vintage	12	11	10	09	08	07	06
WR	7	6	7	7	NM	NM	7
Drink	16-28	16-23	16-25	16-17	NM	NM	16-18

DRY $90 AV

Pegasus Bay Waipara Valley Pinot Noir ★★★★★

This is one of North Canterbury's greatest Pinot Noirs, typically very rich in body and flavour. Many of the vines are over 25 years old and the wine is matured for 18 months in French oak barriques (about 40 per cent new). The 2013 vintage (★★★★☆) is a mouthfilling red with a core of ripe, cherryish, plummy flavours. Concentrated and savoury, it has a finely textured, rich finish.

Vintage	13	12	11	10	09	08
WR	7	7	6	6	6	6
Drink	16-29	16-28	16-23	16-20	16-18	P

DRY $49 AV

Pencarrow Martinborough Pinot Noir ★★★★

This is Palliser Estate's second-tier label, but in most years it is impressive and a good buy. Drinking well from the start, the 2013 (★★★★☆) is a top vintage. Deeply coloured, with a fragrant, ripe, savoury bouquet, it is sweet-fruited and supple, with cherry, plum and spice flavours, showing excellent complexity and harmony.

DRY $29 V+

People's, The, Central Otago Pinot Noir ★★★

From Constellation NZ, the 2014 vintage (★★★) has lightish, moderately youthful colour. A mouthfilling red, grown at Alexandra, it is enjoyable young, with satisfying depth of plummy, spicy flavour, showing some toasty, savoury complexity, and a smooth finish.

DRY $24 AV

Peregrine Central Otago Pinot Noir ★★★★★

Outstanding in top seasons, this classic red is grown mostly in the Cromwell Basin, but also at Gibbston. The 2013 vintage (★★★★☆) is an elegant, finely poised blend of Bendigo (52 per cent), Pisa (43 per cent) and Gibbston (5 per cent) grapes, matured for 10 months in French oak barriques. Deep ruby, with a fragrant bouquet, it has sweet-fruit characters, fresh acidity, supple tannins and strong plum and dried-herb flavours.

DRY $45 AV

Peter Yealands Marlborough Pinot Noir   ★★★

The 2014 vintage (★★★) was made for early consumption; 'a portion of the parcels spent some time in third-year French oak barrels'. Ruby-hued, it is fresh and vibrant, with lively plum and dried-herb flavours, showing good vigour and depth.

Vintage	14	13
WR	7	7
Drink	16-18	P

DRY $18 V+

Peter Yealands Reserve Marlborough Pinot Noir   ★★★☆

The 2014 vintage (★★★☆) is drinking well from the start. A bright ruby, very fresh and lively red, partly barrel-aged, it is mouthfilling and supple, with very good depth of plummy, spicy flavours, showing some savoury, toasty complexity.

Vintage	15	13
WR	7	7
Drink	16-18	16-17

DRY $22 V+

Petit Clos by Clos Henri Marlborough Pinot Noir   ★★★☆

Based on young vines, estate-grown and hand-harvested in the Wairau Valley, the 2014 vintage (★★★☆) was matured for 11 months in large (7500-litre) French oak vats. Bright ruby, it is mouthfilling, with generous, ripe cherry, plum and spice flavours, earthy and savoury notes adding complexity, and a very smooth finish. Certified organic.

Vintage	14	13	12	11	10
WR	6	5	6	6	6
Drink	16-18	P	P	P	P

DRY $26 AV

Pied Stilt Nelson Pinot Noir   ★★☆

The 2014 vintage (★★★) is a single-vineyard red. Ruby-hued, it is mouthfilling and supple, with cherry, plum, spice and herb flavours, showing a touch of complexity. Enjoyable young.

DRY $25 –V

Pirinoa Road Martinborough Reserve Pinot Noir   (★★★★)

Still youthful, the 2013 vintage (★★★★) is a single-vineyard red, matured for 13 months in French oak barriques (30 per cent new). Full-coloured, it is mouthfilling, sweet-fruited and supple, with fresh, generous fruit flavours, good complexity, finely balanced tannins and obvious cellaring potential. Best drinking mid-2017+.

DRY $60 –V

Pisa Range Estate Black Poplar Block Pinot Noir ★★★★★

Estate-grown at Pisa Flats, north of Cromwell, in Central Otago, this classy, enticingly scented wine is well worth discovering. The 2014 vintage (★★★★★) was picked from the oldest vines and matured for a year in French oak barriques (33 per cent new). Deeply coloured, it is weighty and highly concentrated, with deep, ripe, youthful plum and spice flavours, showing excellent complexity, good tannin backbone, and obvious cellaring potential; open 2018+.

Vintage	14	13	12	11	10	09	08
WR	6	7	6	NM	6	7	7
Drink	17-26	16-25	16-23	NM	16-23	16-18	16-17

 DRY $56 AV

Pisa Range Estate Run 245 Central Otago Pinot Noir ★★★★

The 2014 vintage (★★★★) was hand-harvested from 'younger' vines (averaging over 10 years old) and matured in French oak barriques. It's a mouthfilling, generous red, full-coloured, with rich, ripe, plummy, spicy, youthful flavours, showing some savoury complexity, finely balanced tannins and good harmony.

Vintage	14
WR	7
Drink	16-18

DRY $32 AV

Prophet's Rock Home Vineyard Central Otago Pinot Noir ★★★★☆

Labelled in the past as 'Prophet's Rock Central Otago Pinot Noir', this consistently rewarding red is estate-grown at a high-altitude site at Bendigo, in the Cromwell Basin. Barrel-aged for 17 months (35 per cent new oak) and bottled unfiltered, the 2013 vintage (★★★★☆) is the first to be labelled 'Home Vineyard'. Fragrant and deeply coloured, it is mouthfilling, vibrant and savoury, with concentrated, ripe plum, cherry and spice flavours, showing good complexity. Already delicious, it's a drink-now or cellaring proposition. Tasted in May 2016, the elegant, supple 2012 vintage (★★★★) – still on sale – and generous, savoury 2011 vintage (★★★★☆) are both drinking well now.

Vintage	13
WR	7
Drink	16-26

DRY $52 –V

Prophet's Rock Retrospect Central Otago Pinot Noir (★★★★★)

Released in 2016, the 2010 vintage (★★★★★) was estate-grown at Bendigo. A rare wine (only 708 bottles were produced), it was made from 'the best fruit', says winemaker Paul Pujol, given the same oak handling as the standard wine. Slowly evolving, deep and still youthful in colour, it's a powerful red with notably concentrated, ripe plum, cherry and spice flavours, very deep, savoury and complex. Still unfolding, it's full of potential.

DRY $125 –V

Pruner's Reward, The, Waipara Valley Pinot Noir   ★★☆

From Bellbird Spring, the 2013 vintage (★★★) was matured for a year in French oak casks (15 per cent new). It is mouthfilling, with good depth of cherry, plum, herb and spice flavours, showing a touch of complexity, and a rounded finish. Drink now.

DRY $27 –V

Pyramid Valley Vineyards Angel Flower Pinot Noir   ★★★★

From a north-facing slope at Waikari, in North Canterbury, the 2013 vintage (★★★★) was hand-picked from 13-year-old vines, matured in seasoned French oak barriques, and bottled unfined and unfiltered. Showing strong personality, it has mature, slightly cloudy colour, with a fragrant, herbal bouquet, gentle tannins and concentrated flavours, complex and savoury. Drink now.

DRY $120 –V

Pyramid Valley Vineyards Earth Smoke Pinot Noir   ★★★★☆

Estate-grown on an east-facing block at Waikari, in North Canterbury, the 2013 vintage (★★★★) was harvested from 13-year-old vines, matured in seasoned French oak barriques, and bottled unfined and unfiltered. Deep and fairly mature in colour, it is mouthfilling, with plum, herb and spice flavours, fresh acidity, a nutty, savoury complexity, and fine-grained tannins. Drink now to 2017.

DRY $120 –V

Quartz Reef Bendigo Estate Pinot Noir   ★★★★★

Designed for cellaring, this Central Otago red is estate-grown on a steep, north-facing, 'seriously warm' site at Bendigo. The 2014 vintage (★★★★★) was matured for 15 months in French oak barriques. Deeply coloured, it is a powerful, full-bodied wine, with concentrated, youthful cherry, plum and spice flavours, ripe, complex and savoury, excellent harmony and a sense of real potential; best drinking 2020 onwards. Certified biodynamic.

Vintage	14	13	12	11	10	09	08
WR	7	7	7	6	6	NM	7
Drink	16-22	16-20	16-19	16-18	16-17	NM	P

DRY $80 AV

Quartz Reef Central Otago Single Vineyard Pinot Noir   ★★★★★

Certified biodynamic, the classy 2015 vintage (★★★★★) was estate-grown at Bendigo, hand-picked and matured for a year in French oak barriques. Deep ruby, with an invitingly scented bouquet, it is mouthfilling and savoury, with rich, vibrant cherry, plum and spice flavours, showing excellent complexity, fine-grained tannins and lovely harmony. Still youthful, it's a top vintage, likely to be at its best 2018+.

Vintage	15	14	13	12	11	10
WR	6	7	7	7	6	6
Drink	16-22	16-20	16-19	16-18	P	P

DRY $45 AV

Quest Farm Grand Central Central Otago Pinot Noir   (★★★☆)

Estate-grown in the Cromwell Basin, the graceful 2013 vintage (★★★☆) is designed as a 'serious, entry-level wine'. Matured in seasoned French oak casks, it is full-coloured, mouthfilling and supple, with vibrant cherry and plum flavours, some savoury notes adding complexity, and lots of drink-young charm.

DRY $27 AV

Quest Farm Home Vineyard Central Otago Pinot Noir   ★★★★

Still on sale, the 2012 vintage (★★★☆) was estate-grown in the Cromwell Basin. Light ruby, it is mouthfilling, with good but not great depth of cherry, spice and herb flavours, showing considerable complexity. Ready.

DRY $40 –V

Ra Nui Marlborough Wairau Valley Pinot Noir   ★★★☆

The 2013 vintage (★★★☆) was hand-picked and matured in seasoned French oak casks. Deep ruby, it is mouthfilling, with moderately concentrated cherry and plum flavours, hints of herbs and nuts, and a smooth finish.

DRY $34 –V

Rapaura Springs Marlborough Pinot Noir   ★★★

The 2015 vintage (★★★) is ruby-hued and sweet-fruited, with plummy, spicy flavours, showing a touch of complexity, and a well-rounded finish. Enjoyable young.

Vintage	15	14	13	12
WR	6	6	6	5
Drink	16-21	16-20	16-19	16-17

DRY $25 –V

Rapaura Springs Reserve Central Otago Pinot Noir   ★★★☆

The 2015 vintage (★★★☆), barrel-aged, is a deep ruby, mouthfilling, supple red with moderately rich cherry, plum and spice flavours, oak complexity and a smooth finish. Drink now or cellar.

Vintage	15	14	13	12	11
WR	7	5	7	6	6
Drink	16-22	16-20	16-20	16-20	16-17

DRY $29 AV

Rapaura Springs Reserve Marlborough Pinot Noir   (★★★☆)

Showing very good depth, the 2015 vintage (★★★☆) is a bright ruby, mouthfilling red with vibrant, plummy, spicy flavours, considerable complexity and some cellaring potential. Open mid-2017+.

Vintage	15
WR	7
Drink	16-22

DRY $29 AV

RD Central Otago Pinot Noir   (★★★☆)

The 2014 vintage (★★★☆) is a bargain-priced, attractive Bannockburn red with good depth of plum, spice and dried-herb flavours in a floral, easy-drinking style.

DRY $22 V+

Renato Nelson Pinot Noir   ★★★☆

The 2014 vintage (★★★☆) was hand-picked at Kina and matured for 11 months in French oak barriques (25 per cent new). Bright ruby, it has good depth of cherry, plum, spice and dried-herb flavours, with savoury notes adding complexity, and a moderately firm finish.

Vintage	14	13	12	11	10
WR	7	5	7	6	5
Drink	16-21	16-18	16-19	16-17	P

DRY $25 AV

Resurgence Riwaka River Estate Nelson Pinot Noir   ★★★

The 2013 vintage (★★★☆), French oak-aged for a year, is a full-bodied red with generous plum and dried-herb flavours, a slightly earthy streak, some savoury complexity and a firm finish. Drink now or cellar.

DRY $35 –V

Ribbonwood Marlborough Pinot Noir   ★★★

The 2014 vintage (★★★) is light ruby, mouthfilling and supple, with satisfying depth of ripe plum, strawberry and spice flavours, showing a touch of complexity. Enjoyable young. (From Framingham.)

DRY $25 –V

Richmond Plains Nelson Pinot Noir   ★★★☆

Certified biodynamic, the 2015 vintage (★★★★) was matured in French oak casks (22 per cent new). Bright ruby, it is fresh and youthful, with concentrated, ripe plum and spice flavours, showing some oak complexity, and a lingering finish. Best drinking mid-2017+.

DRY $29 AV

Ridgeback Alex Central Otago Pinot Noir   (★★★)

A charming, drink-young style, the 2013 vintage (★★★) is a single-vineyard Alexandra red, from Greylands Ridge. Ruby-hued, it is floral and full-bodied, with gentle tannins and fresh cherry, plum and spice flavours, showing a touch of complexity.

Vintage	13
WR	6
Drink	16-19

DRY $25 –V

Rimu Grove Nelson Pinot Noir ★★★★☆

Estate-grown near Mapua, on the Nelson coast, this is typically a rich wine with plenty of personality. The 2014 vintage (★★★★), French oak-aged for 11 months, is deep ruby, fragrant and generous, with plum, cherry, spice and nut flavours, slightly leafy notes and good complexity. Drinking well now, it's also worth cellaring.

 DRY $39 V+

Vintage	14	13	12	11	10	09	08
WR	7	7	7	7	7	6	6
Drink	16-30	16-30	16-30	16-27	16-25	16-23	16-22

Rippon Emma's Block Mature Vine Pinot Noir ★★★★★

From an east-facing, lakefront block at Lake Wanaka, in Central Otago, this classy red is matured for a total of 17 months in French oak barrels (for the first year, 30 per cent new, subsequently all older barrels) and bottled unfined and unfiltered. The deep ruby 2012 vintage (★★★★★) has a highly fragrant, complex bouquet. Mouthfilling and supple, it has notably concentrated cherry, spice and nut flavours, with a hint of dried herbs, and lovely depth, texture and complexity.

 DRY $92 –V

Rippon Jeunesse Young Vine Pinot Noir ★★★★

Made from vines in their youth ('jeunesse'), defined as 'under 12 years old', at Lake Wanaka, in Central Otago, the impressive 2012 vintage (★★★★☆) was fermented with indigenous yeasts, matured for a year in seasoned French oak barrels, and bottled unfined and unfiltered. Deep ruby, with a spicy bouquet, it is mouthfilling, youthful and fruit-packed, with strong, ripe plum, herb and spice flavours, concentrated, savoury and age-worthy.

DRY $39 AV

Rippon 'Rippon' Mature Vine Central Otago Pinot Noir ★★★★★

This Lake Wanaka red has a long, proud history. Estate-grown but not a single-block wine – winemaker Nick Mills views it as 'the farm voice' – it is typically a very elegant, 'feminine' style, rather than a blockbuster. Hand-picked from ungrafted vines planted between 1985 and 1991, the outstanding 2012 vintage (★★★★★) was matured for 17 months in French oak barrels (30 per cent new), and bottled unfined and unfiltered. Full and youthful in colour, it has lovely fullness, complexity and harmony. A 'serious' but seductive wine, with strong, ripe cherry, plum and spice flavours, it is savoury, finely textured and already delicious.

 DRY $59 AV

Rippon Tinker's Bequest Central Otago Pinot Noir (★★★★★)

From mature, ungrafted vines at Wanaka, over 25 years old, the debut 2013 vintage (★★★★★) was made without any fining, filtration or sulphur addition. 'This wine is absolutely alive,' says winemaker Nick Mills, 'from fruit with such balance that it needed no adjustment or additions ...' Deep and youthful in colour, it is a powerful wine, fresh, vibrant and supple, with deep plum, cherry and spice flavours, finely poised and lasting. Still youthful, with a sense of unlocked power, it needs time; open 2017+.

 DRY $110 AV

Rippon Tinker's Field Mature Vine Pinot Noir   ★★★★★

Named after Rippon's co-founder, Rolfe Mills ('Tink' to his friends), this exceptional wine is based on 'the oldest vines on the property'. Grown on a north-facing slope at Lake Wanaka, in Central Otago, it is matured for 17 months in French oak barriques (30 per cent new), and bottled without fining or filtering. Deeply coloured, the 2012 vintage (★★★★★) is a majestic red, mouthfilling and very generous, with layers of blackcurrant, plum, spice and nut flavours, firm and complex. A powerful, concentrated wine, built to last, it should flourish for a decade.

 DRY $105 AV

Riverby Estate Marlborough Pinot Noir   ★★★☆

This single-vineyard wine is grown in the heart of the Wairau Valley and matured for a year in French oak casks (30 per cent new in 2013). The 2013 vintage (★★★☆) is bright ruby, mouthfilling, fresh and supple, with good depth of ripe cherry and plum flavours, and a subtle seasoning of oak. Finely balanced, it's drinking well now.

Vintage	13
WR	7
Drink	16-22

 DRY $27 AV

Riverby Estate Reserve Marlborough Pinot Noir   ★★★

The 2013 vintage (★★★) was barrel-aged for 15 months. Ruby-hued, it is mouthfilling and supple, with fresh cherry, plum, spice and herb flavours, finely balanced for current drinking.

 DRY $35 –V

Roaring Meg Central Otago Pinot Noir   ★★★☆

From Mt Difficulty, the 2014 vintage (★★★★) of this popular red was hand-picked and matured for nine months in French oak casks. Bright ruby, it is sweet-fruited, with strong, ripe, plummy, spicy flavours, nutty and savoury notes adding complexity, and drink-young appeal. Enjoyable now, it should be at its best mid-2017+.

DRY $30 –V

Rock Ferry 3rd Rock Central Otago Pinot Noir   ★★★★☆

(This label recently replaced the former 'Rock Ferry Central Otago Pinot Noir'.) Estate-grown at a high-altitude site at Bendigo, in the Cromwell Basin, the delicious 2013 vintage (★★★★☆) was matured for over a year in French oak barriques (30 per cent new). Bright ruby, it is floral, mouthfilling and supple, in a savoury style with an array of cherry, plum, dried-herb and nut flavours, gentle tannins, and excellent complexity and harmony. Drink now or cellar.

 DRY $45 –V

Rock Ferry Trig Hill Vineyard Pinot Noir ★★★★★

The lovely 2013 vintage (★★★★★) was estate-grown, 400 metres above sea level, at Bendigo, in Central Otago. Hand-picked, it was fermented with indigenous yeasts, matured for 20 months in French oak barriques and puncheons (30 per cent new), and bottled unfined and unfiltered. Deep and bright in colour, it is finely scented and supple, with deep, ripe plum/spice flavours, hints of dried herbs and nuts, excellent complexity, and a long, tightly structured finish. Drink now or cellar. Certified organic.

DRY $65 AV

Rockburn Central Otago Pinot Noir ★★★★★

This consistently stylish blend of Cromwell Basin (mostly) and Gibbston grapes typically has concentrated cherry, plum and dried-herb flavours, silky-textured and perfumed. The 2014 vintage (★★★★★) was grown at Parkburn (89 per cent) and Gibbston (11 per cent), and matured for 10 months in French oak casks (18 per cent new). A very elegant, deep ruby wine, it is floral and smooth, with deep, youthful, well-ripened cherry, plum and spice flavours, showing good complexity, gentle acidity, and a finely poised, lingering finish. The 2015 vintage (★★★★☆) is floral and finely textured. Mouthfilling, supple and fruit-packed, it is deep ruby, with strong cherry, plum and herb flavours. Harmonious, with plenty of drink-young appeal, it also has good potential. Best drinking 2018+.

Vintage	15	14	13	12	11	10	09
WR	6	7	7	6	6	7	7
Drink	17-24	16-24	16-23	16-22	16-20	16-20	16-18

DRY $50 AV

Rockburn Eleven Barrels Central Otago Pinot Noir ★★★★★

The 2013 vintage (★★★★★) is a powerful, fragrant, deliciously sweet-fruited red, estate-grown at Pisa and matured for 16 months in French oak casks (45 per cent new). Deeply coloured and sturdy (14.5 per cent alcohol), it has rich cherry/plum flavours, with a hint of liquorice, a strong seasoning of oak and ripe, supple tannins. Still youthful, it's likely to be long-lived.

DRY $96 –V

Rocky Point Central Otago Pinot Noir ★★★★

From Prophet's Rock, the 2015 vintage (★★★★) was hand-picked at Bendigo and matured in French oak casks. Deep ruby, it is fragrant and sweet-fruited, with good concentration of fresh plum and spice flavours, showing considerable complexity. Already delicious, it's well worth cellaring. Fine value.

DRY $28 V+

Rod McDonald One Off Martinborough Pinot Noir (★★★★)

The 2014 vintage (★★★★) was grown at Te Muna and matured in French oak barriques (10 per cent new). Deep ruby, it is fragrant, with good weight and depth of cherryish, plummy, spicy, slightly nutty flavours. Savoury and supple, with good complexity, it's drinking well now.

DRY $32 AV

Rossendale Canterbury Pinot Noir   (★★★)

Ruby-hued, the 2015 vintage (★★★) is a fresh, medium-bodied red, vibrantly fruity, with plummy, slightly spicy and toasty flavours and gentle tannins. An attractive drink-young style, it's priced sharply.

Ruru Central Otago Pinot Noir   ★★★☆

The 2014 vintage (★★★★) is a sharply priced, top-value red from Immigrant's Vineyard, at Alexandra. French oak-aged for six months, it is deep ruby, with generous, youthful berry and dried-herb flavours, showing good vigour, and some savoury complexity. The 2015 vintage (★★★☆) was French oak-aged for 10 months. Full ruby, it is mouthfilling, with very good depth of ripe plum and spice flavours, earthy, savoury notes and a moderately firm finish.

Russian Jack Martinborough Pinot Noir   ★★★☆

From Martinborough Vineyard, the 2014 vintage (★★★) was partly barrel-aged. Light ruby, it is moderately concentrated, with ripe plum and spice flavours, a hint of dried herbs, gentle tannins and a touch of complexity.

Sacred Hill Halo Marlborough Pinot Noir   ★★★★

The 2015 vintage (★★★★) is a deep ruby, generous, supple red, hand-picked in the Omaka Valley and matured for eight months in French oak barrels (25 per cent new). It has good concentration of plummy, cherryish flavours, a sense of youthful vigour, and fine-grained tannins. Best drinking 2018+.

Vintage	15	DRY $28 AV
WR	6	
Drink	16-18	

Sacred Hill Marlborough Pinot Noir   ★★★

The 2015 vintage (★★★☆), partly barrel-aged, offers good, early drinking. A more generous, savoury red than most modestly priced Pinot Noirs, it is mouthfilling and sweet-fruited, with plenty of ripe, plummy, strawberryish, spicy flavour, showing some savoury complexity, and a well-rounded finish.

Vintage	15	DRY $20 AV
WR	6	
Drink	16-18	

Sacred Hill Reserve Marlborough Pinot Noir   (★★★☆)

The 2014 vintage (★★★☆) was matured for six months in French oak barrels. Ruby-hued, it is mouthfilling and supple, with vibrant plum, cherry, spice and dried-herb flavours, showing good freshness, vigour and depth, and some complexity. Enjoyable young.

Saint Clair James Sinclair Marlborough Pinot Noir   (★★★☆)

Partly barrel-aged, the 2014 vintage (★★★☆) is a ruby-hued, moderately youthful red, grown in the Southern Valleys. Mouthfilling and smooth, it has ripe, plummy, slightly nutty flavours, gentle tannins and some savoury complexity. It's drinking well now.

DRY $28 AV

Saint Clair Marlborough Pinot Noir   ★★★☆

The 2014 vintage (★★★) is fresh, vibrantly fruity and supple. A medium-bodied style, it has good depth of fresh, ripe red-fruit flavours, gentle tannins and some oak-derived complexity.

DRY $26 AV

Saint Clair Omaka Reserve Marlborough Pinot Noir   ★★★★☆

This is Saint Clair's top Pinot Noir, but understanding where the grapes were grown can be a challenge. Despite the prominence of 'Omaka' (a prestigious district for Pinot Noir, on the south side of the Wairau Valley) on its front label, past vintages have been grown in the Ure Valley, the Waihopai Valley, and 'carefully selected vineyards'. The 2014 vintage (★★★☆) is a single-vineyard red from the Southern Valleys, barrel-aged for 10 months. Mouthfilling, with a spicy, savoury bouquet, it has very good depth of plummy, spicy flavours, with hints of tamarillo and dried herbs, gentle tannins and good complexity. Worth cellaring.

DRY $44 –V

Saint Clair Pioneer Block 4 Sawcut Marlborough Pinot Noir   (★★★★)

The deep ruby 2013 vintage (★★★★) is a fragrant, vibrantly fruity and supple red from the Ure Valley, midway between Blenheim and Kaikoura. Matured for 10 months in French oak barriques (45 per cent new), it has ripe cherry and plum flavours, with finely integrated oak, in a powerful but elegant style, focused and tightly structured.

DRY $38 AV

Saint Clair Pioneer Block 5 Bull Block Omaka Valley Marlborough Pinot Noir   ★★★★

Grown in clay soils on the south side of the Omaka Valley, the ruby-hued 2014 vintage (★★★★) was barrel-aged for 10 months. Floral and mouthfilling, it is sweet-fruited and finely textured, with cherryish, plummy flavours, a subtle seasoning of oak, and considerable complexity. Best drinking 2017+.

DRY $38 AV

Saint Clair Pioneer Block 10 Twin Hills Omaka Valley Marlborough Pinot Noir   ★★★★

The 2014 vintage (★★★★) is an Omaka Valley red, matured for 10 months in French oak barriques. A weighty, generous, finely textured wine, it is deeply coloured, with rich, ripe cherry/plum flavours, well-integrated oak and an invitingly fragrant bouquet.

DRY $38 AV

Saint Clair Pioneer Block 12 Lone Gum Marlborough Pinot Noir   ★★★★☆

Grown in the lower Omaka Valley and matured for 10 months in French oak barriques (30 per cent new), the 2013 vintage (★★★★) is a fresh, medium-bodied red with strong, ripe cherry, plum and spice flavours, showing good complexity, and fine-grained tannins.

DRY $38 V+

Saint Clair Pioneer Block 14 Doctor's Creek Marlborough Pinot Noir   ★★★★

Estate-grown in the lower Omaka Valley and matured for 10 months in French oak barriques (41 per cent new), the 2014 vintage (★★★★) is ruby-hued, sweet-fruited and softly textured, with ripe plum, cherry and spice flavours, and nutty notes adding complexity. Showing very good but not great depth, it's delicious young.

DRY $38 AV

Saint Clair Pioneer Block 15 Strip Block Marlborough Pinot Noir   ★★★★☆

Grown in the lower reaches of the Waihopai Valley, the 2015 vintage (★★★★☆) was matured in French oak barriques. Deep ruby, with a ripely scented bouquet, it is a powerful, concentrated wine, youthful and fruit-packed, with fresh, rich plum and spice flavours, a hint of liquorice, and obvious cellaring potential; open 2018+.

DRY $38 V+

Saint Clair Pioneer Block 16 Awatere Pinot Noir   ★★★★

Showing good personality, the 2014 vintage (★★★★) is a sweet-fruited red with a smoky, savoury, oak-influenced bouquet. Matured in French oak barriques (38 per cent new), it is mouthfilling and supple, with strong plum, spice and dried-herb flavours, and some 'funky' notes adding complexity.

DRY $38 AV

Saint Clair Vicar's Choice Marlborough Pinot Noir   ★★★

Designed as Saint Clair's 'entry-level' Pinot Noir, the 2014 vintage (★★★) is an easy-drinking style, ruby-hued, with plum, cherry and spice flavours, a hint of herbs, a gentle seasoning of oak and a well-rounded finish.

DRY $23 AV

Sanctuary Marlborough Pinot Noir   ★★★☆

Offering good value, the 2015 vintage (★★★☆) is ruby-hued, mouthfilling and supple, in a vibrantly fruity style with generous, ripe, plummy, spicy flavours. Delicious young.

DRY $20 V+

Satellite Marlborough Pinot Noir   ★★★

From Spy Valley, the 2014 vintage (★★★) was hand-picked and barrel-aged. An easy-drinking red, it is ruby-hued, mouthfilling, sweet-fruited and smooth, with ripe cherry and plum flavours, a touch of complexity and gentle tannins. Drink now to 2017.

DRY $23 AV

Satyr Foothills Hawke's Bay Pinot Noir   ★★★★

The 2015 vintage (★★★★) was grown at coastal and elevated, inland sites, and matured in French oak barrels (20 per cent new). Full ruby, it is very vibrant and supple, with a strong surge of fresh cherry, plum and spice flavours, and gentle tannins. A graceful red with youthful vigour, it should be at its best 2018+. (From Sileni.)

DRY $34 AV

Satyr Hawke's Bay Pinot Noir   ★★☆

Ruby-hued, the 2015 vintage (★★☆) is a fruit-driven style with vibrant, ripe cherry/plum flavours, a hint of herbs, fresh acidity and a smooth finish. (From Sileni.)

DRY $20 –V

Schubert Marion's Vineyard Pinot Noir   ★★★★☆

Estate-grown at Gladstone, in the northern Wairarapa, the 2013 vintage (★★★★) was matured for 18 months in French oak barriques (35 per cent new). Mouthfilling, savoury and supple, it is ruby-hued, with plum, cherry and spice flavours, showing excellent depth and complexity.

DRY $48 –V

Scott Base Central Otago Pinot Noir   (★★★)

Estate-grown in the Cromwell Basin, the powerful 2014 vintage (★★★) was matured in French oak casks (25 per cent new). Full-coloured, it is sturdy and sweet-fruited, with strong flavours and firm tannins, but lacks a bit of finesse and fragrance. (From Allan Scott.)

DRY $38 –V

Seifried Nelson Pinot Noir   ★★★

Matured for 15 months in French oak barriques (new to three years old), the 2015 vintage (★★★☆) is drinking well in its youth. Full ruby, it is mouthfilling and savoury, with plummy, spicy flavours, showing very good complexity and depth. Fine value.

Vintage	15	14	13	12	11
WR	7	5	6	6	6
Drink	16-21	16-22	16-21	16-20	P

DRY $20 AV

Selaks Founders Limited Edition Central Otago Pinot Noir   (★★★☆)

The full-coloured 2013 vintage (★★★☆) was mostly (82 per cent) grown at Bendigo, supplemented by fruit from Bannockburn (14 per cent) and Alexandra (4 per cent). Matured in French oak barrels (20 per cent new), it has very good depth of plum/spice flavours, strongly seasoned with oak, and gentle tannins.

DRY $40 –V

Seresin Leah Pinot Noir   ★★★★☆

Unlike the single-vineyard reds, this wine is estate-grown at three sites – mostly the Raupo Creek Vineyard, in the Omaka Valley – and is less new oak-influenced. The 2014 vintage (★★★★) was hand-picked, fermented with indigenous yeasts, matured for 11 months in

French oak barriques (10 per cent new), and bottled without filtering. Light ruby, it is savoury and firm, with youthful plum, spice and dried-herb flavours, showing good concentration and complexity. Best drinking 2018+. Certified organic.

DRY $35 V+

Seresin Marlborough Pinot Noir   (★★★★)

The 2014 vintage (★★★★) was estate-grown and hand-picked at three sites – mostly Raupo Creek Vineyard, in the Omaka Valley – fermented with indigenous yeasts, and matured for 11 months in seasoned French oak barriques. Ruby-hued and savoury, it is already drinking well, with ripe cherry and spice flavours, moderately firm tannins and very good complexity. Certified organic.

DRY $30 AV

Seresin OSIP Marlborough Pinot Noir   (★★★★)

The debut 2014 vintage (★★★★) was grown organically and biodynamically and made with no use of sulphur in the winery. Full-coloured, fragrant and fruity, it is mouthfilling, with generous, ripe plum, cherry and spice flavours, showing good freshness, and earthy, savoury notes adding complexity. (Tasted side by side with its OSIP Sauvignon Blanc 2015 stablemate, I preferred the more attractively scented red.) Drink now or cellar.

DRY $42 –V

Shelter Bay Marlborough Pinot Noir   (★★★★)

The 2014 vintage (★★★★) is a deeply coloured, generous red with concentrated, youthful, plummy flavours and a tight, firm finish. Great value from Jackson Estate.

DRY $20 V+

Sherwood Estate Stoney Range New Zealand Pinot Noir   (★★★☆)

Offering fine value, the 2015 vintage (★★★☆) is a blend of Waipara and Marlborough grapes, oak-matured for four months. Full-coloured, it is mouthfilling and supple, with generous, well-ripened dark berry, plum and spice flavours, gentle tannins, and loads of drink-young appeal.

DRY $19 V+

Sherwood Estate Waipara Collection Nor' Wester Pinot Noir   ★★★☆

The 2013 vintage (★★★☆) is ruby-hued, mouthfilling and smooth, with strong, plummy, spicy, slightly nutty and savoury flavours, showing good complexity. Drink now or cellar.

DRY $30 –V

Sherwood Estate Waipara Valley Pinot Noir   (★★★☆)

Barrel-aged for nine months, the 2014 vintage (★★★☆) is ruby-hued, with very good depth of fresh berry and spice flavours, gently seasoned with oak, gentle tannins, and a touch of complexity. It's drinking well now.

DRY $25 AV

Sileni Cellar Selection Hawke's Bay Pinot Noir ★★★

Top vintages offer lots of drink-young charm. The bright ruby 2015 vintage (★★★) is floral, with fresh, ripe, plummy, slightly spicy flavours, gentle acidity, and a touch of oak-derived complexity.

Vintage	15	14	13
WR	7	7	6
Drink	16-21	16-20	16-18

DRY $20 AV

Sileni Estate Selection Plateau Hawke's Bay Pinot Noir ★★★★

The graceful 2015 vintage (★★★★) was grown at two sites – mostly the elevated, inland Plateau Vineyard, at Mangatahi, but also at Parkhill, near the coast. Matured for nine months in French oak casks (25 per cent new), it is deep ruby and vibrantly fruity, with generous, youthful plum, cherry and spice flavours, a subtle seasoning of oak, gentle tannins, and lots of drink-young appeal. Best drinking mid-2017+.

Vintage	15	14	13	12	11	10
WR	7	7	7	5	4	NM
Drink	16-23	16-22	16-20	16-17	P	NM

DRY $33 AV

Sileni Estate Selection Springstone Hawke's Bay Pinot Noir NR

The highly promising 2015 vintage was tasted as a barrel sample (and so not rated) in May 2016. Grown in the inland, elevated Mangatahi district and matured in mostly seasoned French oak barrels (5 per cent new), it is full-bodied (14.5 per cent alcohol), with deep ruby colour. Full of personality, it has vibrant cherry, plum, herb and spice flavours, showing excellent complexity, and good tannin backbone. In a 'blind' tasting, you could easily pick it as a Pinot Noir from much further south.

Vintage	15
WR	7
Drink	16-25

DRY $33 AV

Sileni Exceptional Vintage Hawke's Bay Pinot Noir ★★★★☆

Is this the finest Pinot Noir in Hawke's Bay? The deeply coloured 2014 vintage (★★★★☆) was matured for nine months in French oak casks (20 per cent new). Fleshy and rich, it is full-bodied (14.5 per cent alcohol) and sweet-fruited, with very generous cherry, plum, spice and nut flavours, showing excellent complexity and harmony. The 2015 vintage (★★★★☆) was estate-grown at Mangatahi and matured for nine months in French oak barriques (20 per cent new). Bright ruby, it is very elegant and supple, with a savoury bouquet and powerful, ripe, concentrated, complex flavours. Crying out for cellaring, it should be at its best 2018+.

Vintage	15	14	13	11	10	09
WR	7	7	7	NM	NM	6
Drink	16-25	16-24	16-21	NM	NM	16-17

DRY $70 –V

Sileni Parkhill Hawke's Bay Pinot Noir ★★★★

Full ruby, the 2014 vintage (★★★★) was grown in Sileni's coolest vineyard, a coastal site at Haumoana. Matured for nine months in French oak casks (20 per cent new), it is mouthfilling and savoury, with fresh, generous, plummy, spicy flavours, fine-grained tannins, and good complexity.

Vintage	15	14	13
WR	NM	7	6
Drink	NM	16-21	16-19

 DRY $32 AV

Sisters, The, Marlborough Pinot Noir ★★★

The 2013 vintage (★★★☆) is ruby-hued, with mouthfilling body and vibrant cherry, plum and herb flavours. Gently seasoned with oak, it has fresh acidity, very good depth and lots of drink-young charm. (From Lawson's Dry Hills.)

 DRY $23 AV

Snapper Rock Marlborough Pinot Noir (★★☆)

The easy-drinking 2014 vintage (★★☆) is light ruby, with gentle, berryish, plummy flavours, showing a touch of complexity, and a well-rounded finish. Priced right.

 DRY $17 AV

Soderberg Home Block Single Vineyard Marlborough Pinot Noir ★★★★

This rare wine flows from a tiny, 1-hectare vineyard at the base of the Wither Hills that previously supplied the grapes for Koru. The 2014 vintage (★★★★) was matured in French oak casks (25 per cent new). Full ruby, it is mouthfilling, smooth and very ripe-tasting, with plum, spice and slight liquorice flavours, slightly earthy, youthful and complex. Drink now or cellar. Certified organic.

Vintage	14	13	12	11	10
WR	7	NM	7	6	7
Drink	17-20	NM	16-18	P	P

 DRY $34 AV

Soho Havana Marlborough Pinot Noir ★★★★☆

The 2015 vintage (★★★★☆) is a single-vineyard red, hand-harvested in the Southern Valleys and matured in French oak barrels (25 per cent new). An elegant, age-worthy wine, it is full-coloured, mouthfilling and generous, with ripe sweet-fruit characters. Tightly structured, it is finely balanced, with rich, youthful plum/spice flavours, a hint of dried herbs, and good complexity. Best drinking 2018+.

 DRY $38 V+

Soho Marlborough Pinot Noir ★★★☆

The 2014 vintage (★★★) is light ruby, with slightly herbal aromas. Mouthfilling and smooth, it has gentle tannins and berry, plum, spice and herb flavours, showing a touch of earthy, nutty complexity.

DRY $27 AV

Soho McQueen Central Otago Pinot Noir ★★★★☆

The youthful 2014 vintage (★★★★) was blended from grapes hand-picked at Bendigo (50 per cent), Gibbston (35 per cent) and Bannockburn (15 per cent). Matured for a year in French oak casks, it is a floral, full-coloured, mouthfilling wine with good tannin backbone and rich, vibrant plum and spice flavours. Best drinking 2018+.

Vintage	14	13	12	11	10
WR	7	6	7	6	7
Drink	16-23	16-22	16-22	16-20	16-20

DRY $50 –V

Soljans Barrique Reserve Marlborough Pinot Noir ★★★

The 2013 vintage (★★★☆) is bright ruby, with a fragrant, spicy bouquet. Mouthfilling, it is sweet-fruited, with ripe, plummy, spicy flavours, slightly smoky and toasty notes adding complexity, finely balanced tannins and good depth.

Vintage	13
WR	6
Drink	16-18

 DRY $29 –V

Spencer Hill Coastal Ridge Pinot Noir (★★★☆)

Estate-grown at Upper Moutere, the 2015 vintage (★★★☆) was harvested from 26-year-old vines. Deep ruby, it is ripely scented and sweet-fruited, with cherry, plum and spice flavours, showing moderate complexity, gentle tannins and very good depth.

DRY $35 –V

Spencer Hill The Wild One Pinot Noir (★★★★)

Grown at Upper Moutere, in Nelson, the 2015 vintage (★★★★) was harvested from 26-year-old vines and French and American oak-aged. Full ruby, with a slightly earthy bouquet, it is mouthfilling and sweet-fruited, with generous, fairly firm plum/spice flavours, showing good complexity. Still youthful, it should be at its best 2018+.

DRY $35 AV

Spinyback Nelson Pinot Noir ★★★

From Waimea Estates, the 2014 vintage (★★★) was grown on the Waimea Plains. Bright ruby, it is a full-bodied, fruit-driven style, with plenty of plummy, berryish flavour, fresh and smooth.

 DRY $17 V+

Springs, The, Waipara Pinot Noir ★★☆

From Waipara Springs, the 2013 vintage (★★☆) was matured in a 50:50 split of tanks and French oak (10 per cent new). Ruby-hued, it is berryish and herbal, in a light, smooth, easy-drinking style.

 DRY $16 AV

Spy Valley Envoy Johnson Vineyard Waihopai Valley
Marlborough Pinot Noir   ★★★★☆

The 2014 vintage (★★★★☆) is a mouthfilling, ripely flavoured, savoury red, estate-grown in the Waihopai Valley and French oak-aged for 16 months. A slightly 'masculine' style, with good tannin backbone and strong plum, nut and spice flavours, showing excellent complexity, it's built to last; best drinking 2018+.

Vintage	14	13	12	11	10	09	08
WR	6	NM	7	7	6	6	6
Drink	16-20	NM	16-18	16-17	P	P	P

DRY $55 –V

Spy Valley Envoy Outpost Vineyard Omaka Valley Marlborough Pinot Noir   ★★★★☆

From hill-grown vines in the Omaka Valley, the 2014 vintage (★★★★☆) is a youthful wine, hand-picked, fermented with indigenous yeasts and matured for 18 months in French oak casks. Showing excellent complexity, it is full-bodied, with ripe cherry, plum and nut flavours, complex and savoury, and a firmly structured finish.

Vintage	14	13	12	11	10
WR	6	6	7	6	6
Drink	16-20	16-19	16-18	16-18	P

DRY $55 –V

Spy Valley Marlborough Pinot Noir   ★★★★

The 2014 vintage (★★★★) is a refined, age-worthy red, grown in the Southern Valleys and oak-aged for nearly a year. Bright ruby, it is very finely balanced, with strong, ripe cherry, plum and spice flavours, a subtle seasoning of oak, and good complexity. Drink now or cellar.

Vintage	14	13	12	11	10
WR	6	6	6	6	6
Drink	16-20	16-17	P	P	P

DRY $32 AV

Squealing Pig Central Otago Pinot Noir   ★★★☆

The charming 2013 vintage (★★★★) was matured for 10 months in French oak barriques (30 per cent new). Deep ruby, it is mouthfilling and fruit-packed, with strong, ripe cherry, plum and spice flavours, well seasoned with nutty oak.

DRY $28 AV

Staete Landt Paladin Marlborough Pinot Noir   ★★★★

This single-vineyard red is typically very fragrant and supple. The 2013 vintage (★★★★) was grown at Rapaura, hand-picked and matured for 14 months in French oak casks. Fragrant and savoury, it is ruby-hued, with strawberry, plum and spice flavours, showing good complexity, and a finely textured, harmonious finish. Delicious drinking now onwards.

DRY $35 AV

Stanley Estates Block 8 Awatere Valley Marlborough Pinot Noir ★★★

The 2013 vintage (★★★) was estate-grown, hand-picked and matured in French oak barrels (20 per cent new). Ruby-hued, it is fresh, lively and smooth, in a fruit-driven style with ripe plum and dried-herb flavours. Enjoyable young.

DRY $27 –V

Starborough Family Estate Marlborough Pinot Noir ★★★

The 2013 vintage (★★★☆) was estate-grown in the heart of the Wairau Valley and matured for 11 months in French oak barrels (35 per cent new). Bright ruby, it is scented, savoury and supple, with vibrant cherry, plum and spice flavours, showing very good depth and complexity.

DRY $30 –V

Stoneburn Marlborough Pinot Noir ★★☆

From Hunter's, the 2014 vintage (★★☆) is ruby-hued, fresh, vibrantly fruity and supple, with berry/plum flavours and a smooth finish. Enjoyable young.

DRY $18 AV

Stoneleigh Latitude Marlborough Pinot Noir ★★★☆

Celebrating the 'Golden Mile' along Rapaura Road, on the stony north side of the Wairau Valley, the 2015 vintage (★★★☆) is deep ruby, mouthfilling and well-rounded, with generous, ripe plum and spice flavours, showing some savoury complexity.

DRY $23 V+

Stoneleigh Marlborough Pinot Noir ★★☆

From Pernod Ricard NZ, this red is grown on the relatively warm north side of the Wairau Valley. The 2014 vintage (★★☆) is light ruby, with moderate depth of strawberry and spice flavours, slightly earthy and leafy. An easy-drinking style, it's priced right.

DRY $17 AV

Stoneleigh Nature's Collection Marlborough Pinot Noir (★★★)

The 2014 vintage (★★★) was grown at Conders Bend, in the Wairau Valley. Ruby-hued, it is mouthfilling and supple, with good depth of fresh, ripe cherry/plum flavours, seasoned with toasty oak. Enjoyable young.

DRY $18 V+

Stoneleigh Rapaura Series Marlborough Pinot Noir ★★★★

The 2014 vintage (★★★★) is a deep ruby, sturdy, savoury wine, named after the Rapaura series of soils, rather than the district in the Wairau Valley. A single-vineyard red, it is full-bodied, with ripe plum and spice flavours, revealing good complexity, and a moderately firm finish. It's still youthful; open 2017+.

DRY $28 V+

Stoneleigh Wild Valley Marlborough Pinot Noir   (★★★)

The ruby-hued 2015 vintage (★★★) was grown at Rapaura, on the northern side of the Wairau Valley, and fermented with indigenous (wild) yeasts (hence the 'Wild' Valley). Buoyantly fruity, with a floral bouquet, it is a sweet-fruited wine with satisfying depth of berryish, plummy flavours, fresh and smooth. A drink-young charmer.

DRY $19 AV

Stonyridge Fallen Angel Central Otago Pinot Noir   (★★★★)

Well worth cellaring, the 2014 vintage (★★★★) is richly coloured and mouthfilling. Matured in French oak casks (30 per cent new), it is fruit-packed, with strong, ripe plum, cherry and spice flavours, very fresh and youthful. Open 2018+.

DRY $55 –V

Summerhouse Central Otago Pinot Noir   (★★★☆)

The 2015 vintage (★★★☆) is a bright ruby, vibrantly fruity and supple blend of grapes grown at Alexandra and in the Cromwell Basin. Matured in French and American oak barriques, it is medium to full-bodied, with fresh plum, herb and spice flavours, showing good depth, oak-derived complexity and a smooth finish.

Vintage	15
WR	7
Drink	16-21

DRY $29 AV

Summerhouse Marlborough Pinot Noir   ★★★★

Grown in the Southern Valleys, the 2015 vintage (★★★☆) was matured in new and seasoned oak barriques. Deep ruby, it is a mouthfilling, moderately complex wine, fruit-packed, with vibrant cherry and plum flavours.

Vintage	15	14
WR	7	7
Drink	16-21	16-22

DRY $29 V+

Super Nanny Central Otago Pinot Noir   ★★★★

The sturdy, full-flavoured 2015 vintage (★★★★) was grown at Bannockburn and Pisa, barrel-aged (40 per cent new) and bottled unfined and unfiltered. Still youthful, it is concentrated and savoury, with strong strawberry, spice and dried-herb flavours, oak complexity and the structure to age well.

DRY $49 –V

Supper Club Central Otago Pinot Noir   ★★★

The 2014 vintage (★★★) is enjoyable now. A regional blend, it was mostly grown in the Cromwell Basin, with smaller parcels from Gibbston and Alexandra. Hand-harvested and matured in French oak barriques (15 per cent new), it is ruby-hued, with mouthfilling body, satisfying depth of plummy flavours, a hint of dried herbs, and a moderately firm finish.

DRY $20 AV

Surveyor Thomson Single Vineyard Central Otago Pinot Noir ★★★★

From Domaine Thomson, at Lowburn, the 2013 vintage (★★★★) has fullish, slightly developed colour. Mouthfilling and savoury, with fresh acidity, it's an elegant wine, with fairly youthful cherry, plum, herb and nut flavours, showing good intensity and complexity. Best drinking 2018.

 DRY $44 –V

Tablelands Marlborough Pinot Noir (★★★)

Drinking well now, the 2013 vintage (★★★) was barrique-aged for 10 months. It has lightish, slightly developed colour, with cherry, plum and dried-herb flavours, showing a touch of savoury complexity.

Vintage	13
WR	7
Drink	16-19

DRY $22 AV

Tarras The Canyon Central Otago Pinot Noir ★★★★

The 2013 vintage (★★★★) of this single-vineyard, Bendigo red was matured for nine months in French oak casks (35 per cent new). Mouthfilling and savoury, with spice and dried-herb flavours, earthy notes, structured tannins, and good complexity and depth, it's well worth cellaring.

 DRY $60 –V

Tarras Vineyards Central Otago Pinot Noir ★★★★

The 2014 vintage (★★★★) is a deeply coloured, rich blend of grapes from Bendigo (The Canyon Vineyard), other parts of the Cromwell Basin and Alexandra. It has strong plum and spice flavours, with ripe, supple tannins, oak complexity and a persistent finish.

 DRY $39 AV

Tatty Bogler Otago Pinot Noir ★★★★★

This is sometimes blended from Bannockburn (Central Otago) and Waitaki Valley (North Otago) grapes, but the delicious 2013 vintage (★★★★★) was estate-grown at Bannockburn. Matured for over a year in French oak barriques, it is full-coloured, generous and silky, with mouthfilling body, deep, vibrant cherry/plum flavours, savoury, earthy notes adding complexity, gentle acidity and a finely poised finish. Already delicious. (From Forrest Estate.)

DRY $35 V+

Te Kairanga John Martin Martinborough Pinot Noir ★★★★★

The powerful 2014 vintage (★★★★★) is a classic regional style, based on the 'best vineyard parcels'. Matured for a year in French oak barriques, it's a very harmonious wine, deep ruby, mouthfilling, fleshy and savoury, with highly concentrated plum, cherry and spice flavours, showing lovely ripeness, texture and complexity. Well worth cellaring.

Vintage	14	13
WR	7	7
Drink	16-25	16-24

 DRY $49 AV

Te Kairanga Martinborough Pinot Noir ★★★★

The refined 2015 vintage (★★★★☆) is instantly appealing. Deep ruby, it is mouthfilling, ripe and supple, with generous plum/spice flavours, gentle tannins, and good complexity. Skilfully crafted, it is beautifully poised; drink now or cellar. Fine value.

Vintage	14	13
WR	7	7
Drink	16-20	16-19

DRY $28 V+

Te Kairanga Runholder Martinborough Pinot Noir ★★★★☆

This is the middle-tier label. The 2014 vintage (★★★★☆) is deep ruby, floral, rich and supple, with good density of cherry, spice, plum and dried-herb flavours and a finely textured, very harmonious finish. An elegant wine, with a sense of youthful vigour, it's well worth cellaring. Fine value.

Vintage	14	13
WR	7	7
Drink	16-22	16-22

DRY $34 V+

Te Mania Nelson Pinot Noir ★★★

The 2015 vintage (★★★☆) was mostly barrel-aged. Still very youthful, it is bright ruby, with mouthfilling body (14.5 per cent alcohol) and vibrant, plummy fruit flavours to the fore, fresh, ripe and generous. Best drinking mid-2017+.

DRY $25 –V

Te Mania Reserve Nelson Pinot Noir ★★★★

Certified organic, the age-worthy 2014 vintage (★★★★) was hand-picked and matured for 10 months in French oak barrels (20 per cent new). Full ruby, it is sturdy (14.5 per cent alcohol), with strong, youthful, plummy, spicy, slightly toasty flavours, oak complexity and a fairly firm finish. Best drinking mid-2017+.

DRY $36 AV

Ten Sisters Marlborough Pinot Noir (★★★)

The 2014 vintage (★★★), from distributor Sanz Global, is enjoyable now. Light ruby, mellow and moderately concentrated, it is mouthfilling, with raspberry, strawberry and spice flavours, showing some savoury complexity.

DRY $29 –V

Terra Sancta Estate Bannockburn Central Otago Pinot Noir ★★★★☆

The 2014 vintage (★★★★☆) was estate-grown at Bannockburn and matured in French oak barrels (10 per cent new). A savoury, full-coloured, age-worthy red, it is mouthfilling and concentrated, with ripe cherry, plum and spice flavours, oak-derived complexity, and a finely structured finish. Well worth cellaring, it offers excellent value.

Vintage	14	13
WR	7	6
Drink	16-22	16-20

DRY $35 V+

Terra Sancta Jackson's Block Bannockburn Central Otago Pinot Noir ★★★★★

The classy, finely textured 2015 vintage (★★★★★) was matured in French oak barriques (25 per cent new). Bright ruby, it is very fragrant, savoury and supple, with cherry, plum, spice, dried-herb and nut flavours, showing excellent delicacy, depth and complexity. Conveying a strong sense of youthful potential, it's well worth cellaring to 2018 onwards.

Vintage	15	14	13	12	11
WR	6	6	5	7	7
Drink	16-25	16-24	16-20	16-24	16-20

DRY $50 AV

Terra Sancta Mysterious Diggings Bannockburn Central Otago Pinot Noir ★★★★

Estate-grown, the 2015 vintage (★★★★) was matured in seasoned French oak barrels and bottled unfined and unfiltered. Floral, savoury and supple, it's a very harmonious, softly seductive wine, with gentle, ripe berry, spice and nut flavours, a silky texture and good complexity. Fine value.

Vintage	15	14	13	12
WR	6	6	6	7
Drink	16-19	16-18	16-17	16-17

DRY $27 V+

Terra Sancta Shingle Beach Bannockburn Central Otago Pinot Noir ★★★★☆

From a block of mature, close-planted vines, the impressive 2014 vintage (★★★★★) was matured in French oak barriques and puncheons (20 per cent new). Deeply coloured, it is very fragrant and savoury, in a highly complex style showing excellent density of ripe plum, spice and nut flavours. Already delicious, it's a drink-now or cellaring proposition.

Vintage	14	13	12
WR	6	7	7
Drink	16-24	16-23	16-22

DRY $49 –V

Terra Sancta Slapjack Block Bannockburn Pinot Noir ★★★★★

From the oldest vines in Bannockburn, planted in 1991, and matured in French oak barriques (25 per cent new), the beautiful 2014 vintage (★★★★★) is a deep ruby, deliciously fragrant and savoury wine, full-bodied, concentrated and harmonious. Still youthful, it has deep, ripe plum/spice flavours, showing excellent complexity, and a finely textured, lingering finish. Best drinking 2018+.

Vintage	14	13	12	11
WR	7	6	7	7
Drink	16-25	16-24	16-24	16-25

DRY $80 AV

Terrace Edge Waipara Valley Pinot Noir ★★★★

A consistently good buy. The attractive 2015 vintage (★★★★) was hand-harvested, fermented with indigenous yeasts and matured for a year in French oak casks (25 per cent new). Full ruby, it is mouthfilling and sweet-fruited, with fresh, generous cherry, plum and spice flavours, gentle tannins, savoury notes adding complexity, and very good depth and harmony. Best drinking mid-2017 onwards.

Vintage	15	DRY $28 V+
WR	7	
Drink	16-24	

TerraVin Calrossie Vineyard Marlborough Pinot Noir (★★★★)

The 2013 vintage (★★★★) has full, maturing colour. Matured in French oak casks (43 per cent new), it is savoury and mouthfilling, with strong, ripe cherry, plum, dried-herb and spice flavours, showing good complexity. It's drinking well now.

DRY $78 –V

TerraVin Eaton Family Vineyard Marlborough Pinot Noir ★★★★

The 2012 vintage (★★★★) was bottled unfined and unfiltered. Medium to full-bodied, with ripe plum and spice flavours, woven with fresh acidity, it has nutty, savoury notes adding complexity, and a tightly structured finish. Still unfolding, it's worth cellaring to 2018+.

DRY $82 –V

TerraVin Marlborough Pinot Noir ★★★★

I tasted the 2011–2013 vintages together in mid-2016. The 2013 (★★★★) is the finest. Grown in the Southern Valleys (70 per cent in the Calrossie Vineyard, in the southern Wither Hills), it was matured in French oak barriques for over a year, and bottled unfined and unfiltered. Mouthfilling and savoury, it has fresh, ripe cherry, plum and spice flavours, showing good complexity, and finely balanced tannins. Drink now or cellar. The 2012 (★★★☆) is probably at its peak, with good depth, delicacy and complexity, but slightly leafy notes detracting. The 2011 (★★★☆) has a mature ruby colour, with an earthy streak and good depth of moderately ripe cherry, spice and nut flavours.

Vintage	13	12	11	DRY $38 AV
WR	7	5	6	
Drink	16-20	16-18	16-18	

Thistle Ridge Waipara Block 2 Pinot Noir (★★★)

From Greystone, the 2013 vintage (★★★) was barrel-aged for 18 months. Ruby-hued, it is fragrant and full-bodied, with cherry, plum, spice and herb flavours, and some leafy, earthy notes adding a touch of complexity.

DRY $22 AV

Thistle Ridge Waipara Pinot Noir (★★★)

The 2014 vintage (★★★☆) from Greystone offers great value. Full-bodied, generous and smooth, it is bright ruby, with good depth of cherry, plum, dried-herb and spice flavours. Softly textured, with some complexity, it's enjoyable now.

Thornbury Central Otago Pinot Noir ★★★★

Offering fine value, the 2015 vintage (★★★★) was grown at Bannockburn and matured for 11 months in French oak barriques (24 per cent new). A mouthfilling, sweet-fruited and supple red, it has ripe cherry and spice flavours, showing a touch of complexity, gentle tannins and excellent harmony.

Three Paddles Martinborough Pinot Noir ★★★☆

From Nga Waka, this second-tier red is a rewarding drink-young style. The 2014 vintage (★★★★) was barrel-aged for a year. Deep ruby, it is mouthfilling and savoury, with generous, ripe cherry, plum and spice flavours, showing good complexity. Best drinking mid-2017+.

Vintage	14	13
WR	7	7
Drink	16-21	16-20

Tiki Estate Single Vineyard Marlborough Pinot Noir ★★★☆

Showing some development, the 2013 vintage (★★★☆) is a ruby-hued, fruity red, grown in the upper Wairau Valley and barrel-aged for a year. Drinking well now, it has good depth of cherry, plum and nutty oak flavours, showing considerable complexity, and a fairly firm finish.

Tiki Koro Central Otago Pinot Noir ★★★☆

Drinking well now, the 2014 vintage (★★★★) was grown at Wanaka and matured for 14 months in French oak casks. Rich and finely balanced, it is mouthfilling and full-coloured, with cherry, plum, dried-herb and spice flavours, well-integrated oak and a floral bouquet.

Tiki Marlborough Pinot Noir ★★★

The 2015 vintage (★★☆), lightly oaked, is a ruby-hued, vibrantly fruity red, with plummy, berryish flavours, offering pleasant, easy drinking.

Tinpot Hut Marlborough Pinot Noir ★★★

The 2014 vintage (★★★☆) is a blend of grapes estate-grown at Blind River, supplemented by fruit from the Wairau Valley. A mouthfilling, full-coloured red with very good depth of ripe plum/spice flavours, considerable complexity and fine-grained tannins, it's a skilfully crafted wine, enjoyable now.

DRY $25 –V

Tohu Awatere Valley Marlborough Pinot Noir ★★★☆

The 2015 vintage (★★★★), grown in the upper Awatere Valley and French oak-aged, is deeply coloured and mouthfilling, with strong plum and spice flavours in an exuberantly fruity style, showing good concentration and some complexity. Best drinking mid-2017+.

DRY $28 AV

Tohu Rore Reserve Marlborough Pinot Noir ★★★★

Estate-grown in the upper Awatere Valley and French oak-aged, the 2013 vintage (★★★★) is a graceful wine, mouthfilling, with strong cherry, plum, spice and dried-herb flavours, oak complexity and fine-grained tannins.

DRY $39 AV

Toi Toi Central Otago Reserve Pinot Noir ★★★☆

The 2014 vintage (★★★☆) is a single-vineyard, Lowburn (Cromwell Basin) red. Deep ruby, it is mouthfilling and sweet-fruited, with cherryish, plummy, moderately complex flavours, showing good vibrancy and vigour, and a smooth finish. Best drinking mid-2017+.

| Vintage | 14 | DRY $40 –V |
| Drink | 17-22 | |

WR 7

Toi Toi Clutha Central Otago Pinot Noir ★★★

The 2015 vintage (★★★) is a bright ruby, fresh, full-bodied wine with ripe plum/spice flavours, showing some complexity, and plenty of drink-young charm.

DRY $27 –V

Tongue in Groove Clavyin Vineyard Marlborough Pinot Noir (★★★★★)

The 2013 vintage (★★★★★) from this tiny, Waipara-based producer was grown in Marlborough's famous hillside vineyard, Clayvin. Hand-picked, fermented with indigenous yeasts, and matured for 16 months in French oak casks (20 per cent new), it has a scented, complex bouquet. Already drinking well, it is generous and age-worthy, with deep plum, cherry, spice and nut flavours, and a distinctly earthy streak, in a powerful style, well worth cellaring. Priced right.

DRY $45 AV

Tongue in Groove Waipara Valley Pinot Noir (★★★★★)

The 2013 vintage (★★★★★), grown in the Cabal Vineyard, was fermented with indigenous yeasts and matured for 16 months in French oak barrels (25 per cent new). Deep ruby, mouthfilling, rich and sweet-fruited, it has a caressing texture and concentrated, plummy, gently spicy flavours. Fleshy and supple, with good density and a savoury, earthy complexity, it's delicious now, but also well worth cellaring.

DRY $45 AV

Totara Marlborough Pinot Noir   ★★☆

The 2014 vintage (★★★) is a ruby-hued, fruit-driven style with vibrant, plummy, slightly spicy flavours to the fore, fresh acidity and gentle tannins.

DRY $26 –V

Trinity Hill Hawke's Bay Pinot Noir   ★★★

The 2015 vintage (★★★) is an easy-drinking, vibrantly fruity red with good depth of cherry, plum, spice and herb flavours, fresh and smooth.

DRY $22 AV

Triplebank Awatere Valley Marlborough Pinot Noir   ★★★☆

Offering very good value, the 2015 vintage (★★★☆) is full-bodied, with fresh, moderately concentrated strawberry, spice, dried-herb and nut flavours, showing a touch of complexity, and a smooth finish. (From Pernod Ricard NZ.)

DRY $20 AV

Tupari Awatere Valley Marlborough Pinot Noir   ★★★☆

The 2013 vintage (★★★☆) is a single-vineyard red. Ruby-hued, it is mouthfilling and supple, with vibrant, moderately concentrated cherry, plum, spice and herb flavours, some earthy notes, considerable complexity and a well-rounded finish.

DRY $35 –V

Two Degrees Central Otago Pinot Noir   ★★★★☆

Grown at Queensberry, in the Cromwell Basin, on a site with a 'gentle two degree slope', and matured in French oak casks, the 2014 vintage (★★★★☆) is a stylish wine, mouthfilling and savoury, with a fragrant bouquet, fresh, strong cherry, plum and spice flavours, revealing good complexity, and a finely poised finish. The highly attractive 2015 vintage (★★★★☆) is fragrant and supple, with youthful, ripe cherry, plum, spice and dried-herb flavours, gentle tannins, and savoury, nutty notes adding complexity. A graceful, finely textured wine, it should be at its best mid-2017+.

DRY $39 V+

Vintage	15	14	13
WR	7	6	6
Drink	17-23	16-20	16-22

Two Paddocks Central Otago Pinot Noir   ★★★★★

The 2014 vintage (★★★★★) is the best yet. Grown in the company's vineyards at Bannockburn (49 per cent), Alexandra (32 per cent) and Gibbston (19 per cent), and matured in French oak casks, it is deep ruby, very fragrant and supple. A generous, savoury, complex red, it is intensely varietal, with strong, ripe cherry, plum and dried-herb flavours, finely structured and age-worthy. Best drinking 2017+.

DRY $55 AV

Two Paddocks Picnic Central Otago Pinot Noir ★★★☆

Promoted as 'the people's Pinot', the 2014 vintage (★★★☆) of this drink-young red was hand-harvested and French oak-aged. Bright ruby, it is mouthfilling, with gentle tannins and good depth of cherry, plum, spice and herb flavours, fresh and smooth.

DRY $30 –V

Two Paddocks Proprietor's Reserve The First Paddock
Central Otago Pinot Noir ★★★★☆

The 2013 vintage (★★★★☆) was estate-grown at Gibbston and matured in French oak barrels. Ruby-hued, with moderately youthful colour, it has an invitingly fragrant bouquet of herbs and spices. A true expression of the Gibbston Valley sub-region, it has an array of plum, spice and herb flavours, seasoned with nutty oak, fine-grained tannins and good complexity. Drink now or cellar.

DRY $70 –V

Two Paddocks Proprietor's Reserve The Fusilier
Bannockburn Vineyard Pinot Noir (★★★★★)

The debut 2014 vintage (★★★★★) was estate-grown at Bannockburn, at the western end of Felton Road. Hand-picked, it was fermented with indigenous yeasts and matured for 11 months in French oak barriques (33 per cent new). Showing excellent density and complexity, it is mouthfilling and fleshy, with concentrated, ripe, plummy, spicy flavours, very gentle tannins, slightly fungal, earthy notes adding complexity, and obvious potential; open 2019+.

DRY $75 AV

Two Paddocks Proprietor's The Last Chance
Earnscleugh Vineyard Pinot Noir ★★★★★

From a vineyard 'perched above the Earnscleugh Valley' at Alexandra, the 2013 vintage (★★★★★) was released in 2016. Hand-harvested, it was fermented with indigenous yeasts and matured for 11 months in French oak barriques (one-third new). Floral, mouthfilling and supple, it is an elegant, youthful wine, very savoury, with an array of vibrant, ripe cherry, dried-herb and nut flavours, finely integrated oak, and excellent complexity, harmony and length. Delicious now, it should be at its best 2018+.

DRY $75 AV

Two Rivers Altitude Marlborough Pinot Noir ★★★★☆

Grown at two sites, in the Awatere Valley and upper Wairau Valley, the 2014 vintage (★★★★☆) was hand-picked, matured for 11 months in French oak barrels (40 per cent new), and bottled unfined and unfiltered. Deeply coloured, it is mouthfilling, very savoury and generous, with concentrated, ripe, plummy, spicy flavours, showing excellent complexity. Drink now onwards.

Vintage	14
WR	6
Drink	17-21

DRY $50 –V

Two Rivers of Marlborough Tributary Pinot Noir   ★★★★

The 2015 vintage (★★★★) is a regional blend, hand-picked and matured for 11 months in French oak barrels (25 per cent new). Full ruby, it is mouthfilling, savoury and fresh, with vibrant plum, cherry, herb and spice flavours, showing good complexity. Still very youthful, it's worth cellaring to 2018+.

Vintage	15
WR	6
Drink	16-20

 DRY $36 AV

Two Sisters Central Otago Pinot Noir   ★★★★

Released in 2016, the 2011 vintage (★★★★) is a single-vineyard wine from Lowburn, in the Cromwell Basin. Matured for 11 months in French oak casks (25 per cent new), it is a deep ruby, sturdy red with an array of cherry, plum, spice and dried-herb flavours, showing good complexity and harmony. It's drinking well now.

 DRY $45 –V

Two Tails Marlborough Pinot Noir   ★★★☆

The 2015 vintage (★★★☆) was grown in the Wairau Valley. Ruby-hued, it's attractive young, with gentle, ripe cherry and spice flavours, showing a touch of savoury, nutty complexity, and a finely balanced, smooth finish.

 DRY $23 V+

Urlar Gladstone Pinot Noir   ★★★★

This wine is estate-grown in the northern Wairarapa. The 2014 vintage (★★★★) is savoury, full-coloured and mouthfilling, with concentrated plum, spice and dried-herb flavours, fairly firm tannins, and good complexity. Still youthful, it should be at its best 2018+. Certified organic.

 DRY $38 AV

Urlar Select Parcels Gladstone Pinot Noir   (★★★★★)

The finely scented 2013 vintage (★★★★★) was hand-harvested at 24 brix and matured in French oak barriques (20 per cent new). Ruby-hued, it is mouthfilling and silky-textured, savoury and complex, with ripe plum, spice and nut flavours that build well across the palate to a long, well-rounded finish. A multi-faceted wine with lovely harmony, it's certified organic.

 DRY $60 AV

Valli Bannockburn Vineyard Central Otago Pinot Noir   ★★★★★

The 2014 vintage (★★★★☆) is still very youthful. Hand-picked at 24 brix from 14-year-old vines, it was matured for 11 months in French oak barriques (30 per cent new), and bottled unfined and unfiltered. Fragrant, generous and supple, it has excellent depth of vibrant, well-ripened cherry, plum and spice flavours. Refined, fresh and full of vigour, it's well worth cellaring. The impressive 2015 vintage (★★★★★) is deep ruby, mouthfilling and savoury, with concentrated plum, spice and nut flavours, very fine-grained tannins, excellent harmony and obvious potential; open 2018+.

Vintage	15	14	13	12	11	10
WR	6	7	7	7	6	6
Drink	17-27	16-26	16-26	16-25	16-24	16-23

DRY $65 AV

Valli Bendigo Vineyard Central Otago Pinot Noir   ★★★★★

The lovely 2014 vintage (★★★★★), harvested at 24.5 brix from eight-year-old vines on Chinaman's Terrace, was matured in French oak casks (34 per cent new), and bottled unfined and unfiltered. Deeply coloured, it is sturdy and rich, with a powerful surge of lush, ripe plum and spice flavours, oak complexity, fine-grained tannins, and a finely balanced, sustained finish. A youthful, age-worthy wine, it's already delicious, but likely to be at its best 2018+. The 2015 vintage (★★★★★) is deeply coloured, sweet-fruited and bold, with mouthfilling body and rich, plummy, spicy flavours. Still very youthful, it's a complex, well-structured wine, best opened 2019+.

Vintage	15	14	13	12	11	10
WR	6	7	7	7	5	6
Drink	17-25	16-25	16-25	16-24	16-23	16-23

DRY $65 AV

Valli Burn Cottage Vineyard Central Otago Pinot Noir   (★★★★★)

The 2014 vintage (★★★★★) is part of a collaboration between Valli and Burn Cottage, involving access to each other's grapes to explore key aspects of terroir. From vines planted in 2008 near Lowburn, it was harvested at 23.6 brix (a higher grape sugar level than Burn Cottage's own 2014 Pinot Noir), matured in French oak barriques (35 per cent new), and bottled unfined and unfiltered. Deep ruby, it is a powerful wine, with rich, lush cherry, plum and spice flavours and ripe, supple tannins. Savoury and complex, it's a very 'complete' wine, likely to be at its best 2018+.

DRY $65 AV

Valli Gibbston Vineyard Otago Pinot Noir   ★★★★★

The deeply coloured, purple-flushed, highly concentrated 2014 vintage (★★★★★) is the greatest of Valli's 2014 reds. Fragrant, generous, mouthfilling and supple, it has dense, ripe plum, cherry, dried-herb and spice flavours, showing lovely harmony and length. A very classy young wine, it should be in full stride from 2018 onwards. The 2015 vintage (★★★★★) is deep ruby, mouthfilling and supple, with rich, vibrant cherry, plum and spice flavours, woven with fresh acidity, gentle tannins and a savoury, nutty complexity. A graceful, 'brooding' young red, it's well worth cellaring to 2018+.

Vintage	15	14	13	12	11	10	09
WR	7	7	7	6	7	7	7
Drink	16-24	16-25	16-25	16-23	16-24	16-23	16-18

DRY $65 AV

🍇

Valli Waitaki Vineyard Otago Pinot Noir   ★★★★☆

The impressive 2014 vintage (★★★★☆) was hand-picked at 22.7 brix from 13-year-old vines in North Otago, matured for 11 months in French oak barriques (35 per cent new), and bottled unfined and unfiltered. Deep ruby, it is fragrant, mouthfilling and supple, with very generous plum/spice flavours, hints of dried herbs and nuts, fine-grained tannins, and excellent texture and complexity. Still youthful, it's a top wine, likely to be at its best 2018+. The 2015 vintage (★★★★☆) is a finely scented, ruby-hued wine, very elegant and approachable. Mouthfilling, it is finely poised, with strong cherry, spice and dried-herb flavours, smooth and persistent. Best drinking 2018+.

Vintage	15	14	13	12	11	10
WR	6	7	7	7	5	6
Drink	17-25	16-25	16-25	16-25	16-23	16-23

DRY $65 –V

Vavasour Awatere Valley Marlborough Pinot Noir   ★★★★

The 2013 vintage (★★★★) was matured in French oak barriques (30 per cent new). A powerful red, it is full-coloured and sweet-fruited, with strong, plummy, spicy flavours and finely balanced tannins. Full-bodied and concentrated, it's well worth cellaring.

Vintage	13	12	11
WR	7	7	6
Drink	16-20	16-20	16-18

DRY $31 AV

Vicar's Mistress, The, Waipara Valley Pinot Noir   ★★★☆

The 2013 vintage (★★★★) was matured in French oak casks (25 per cent new). It's a substantial, generous red with deep colour and concentrated, ripe plum and spice flavours, showing good complexity.

Vintage	13
WR	6
Drink	16-18

DRY $35 –V

Vidal Reserve Marlborough Pinot Noir   ★★★★

The 2014 vintage (★★★★), grown in the Wairau (52 per cent) and Awatere (48 per cent) valleys, was matured for 10 months in French oak barriques (13 per cent new). Full-coloured and freshly scented, it is an excellent example of a 'fruit-driven' style, with strong, ripe plum, cherry and spice flavours, a gentle seasoning of oak, fine-grained tannins, and loads of drink-young charm. The 2015 vintage (★★★★) was grown in the Wairau Valley (60 per cent) and Awatere Valley (40 per cent), and matured for 10 months in French oak barriques (11 per cent new). Instantly attractive, it has fresh, strong cherry, plum and spice flavours, showing good ripeness and complexity, and a smooth, lingering finish. Fine value.

Vintage	15	14	13
WR	7	6	7
Drink	16-20	16-19	16-18

DRY $26 V+

Villa Maria Cellar Selection Marlborough Pinot Noir   ★★★★☆

Typically delightful, this is one of New Zealand's best-value Pinot Noirs. The 2013 vintage (★★★★) was grown in the Wairau (60 per cent) and Awatere (40 per cent) valleys, and matured for 10 months in French oak barriques (15 per cent new). Deep ruby, it is scented and supple, with strong cherry, plum and spice flavours, showing considerable complexity. A very elegant wine, it's a drink-now or cellaring proposition.

Vintage	14	13	12	11	10	09
WR	6	6	7	7	6	6
Drink	16-20	16-18	16-20	16-18	P	P

DRY $26 V+

Villa Maria Cellar Selection Organic Marlborough Pinot Noir ★★★★

The 2014 vintage (★★★★☆) was matured in French oak barriques (17 per cent new). Deep ruby, it is very finely textured, with fresh, concentrated plum and spice flavours, showing excellent varietal character and immediacy. The 2015 vintage (★★★★) was matured in French oak barriques (10 per cent new). Deep ruby, it is fresh and vibrantly fruity, with strong, plummy, gently spicy flavours, savoury notes adding complexity, and a smooth, harmonious finish.

Vintage	15	14
WR	6	6
Drink	16-20	16-20

DRY $26 V+

Villa Maria Private Bin Marlborough Pinot Noir ★★★☆

The 2015 vintage (★★★☆) was grown in the Wairau and Awatere valleys, and partly barrel-aged. Bright ruby, it is instantly appealing, with good depth of ripe, plummy, spicy flavours, showing a touch of complexity, and a well-rounded finish. Fine value.

Vintage	15	14	13	12	11	10
WR	5	6	6	6	6	6
Drink	16-20	16-20	16-18	16-18	P	P

DRY $21 V+

Villa Maria Reserve Marlborough Pinot Noir ★★★★★

Launched from the 2000 vintage, this label swiftly won recognition as one of the region's boldest, lushest reds. Grown in the Awatere Valley and Southern Valleys, it is hand-picked, matured in French oak barriques (22 per cent new in 2014), and bottled with minimal fining and filtration. The very refined, youthful 2013 vintage (★★★★★) is deeply coloured and powerful, with rich plum, cherry and spice flavours, finely textured, very savoury and concentrated. The 2014 vintage (★★★★★) is deep ruby, mouthfilling and sweet-fruited, with deep, plummy, spicy flavours, very complex and savoury, gentle tannins and excellent harmony. Best drinking 2018+.

Vintage	14	13	12	11	10	09
WR	7	7	7	7	7	7
Drink	16-22	16-20	16-22	16-19	16-19	16-18

DRY $50 AV

Villa Maria Single Vineyard Attorney Organic Marlborough Pinot Noir (★★★★★)

Grown in the Southern Valleys, the 2014 vintage (★★★★★) was hand-picked and matured in French oak barriques (11 per cent new). Bright ruby, it is very elegant and persistent, with strong, vibrant, beautifully ripe fruit flavours of cherries, plums and spices, gently seasoned with nutty oak, and a finely poised, long finish.

Vintage	14
WR	7
Drink	16-22

DRY $55 AV

Villa Maria Single Vineyard Seddon Marlborough Pinot Noir ★★★★★

From an Awatere Valley site even further inland and higher than its stablemate (below), the 2014 vintage (★★★★★) was hand-picked and matured for 14 months in French oak barriques (21 per cent new). Full, bright ruby, it is very fragrant and supple, with strong, ripe cherry, plum and spice flavours, showing excellent complexity and harmony.

Vintage	14	13	12	11	10	09	08
WR	7	7	7	7	7	7	NM
Drink	16-22	16-20	16-22	16-19	16-19	16-17	NM

DRY $55 AV

Villa Maria Single Vineyard Southern Clays Marlborough Pinot Noir ★★★★★

Hand-picked from north-facing slopes of the Rutherford Vineyard, on the south side of the Wairau Valley, the 2014 vintage (★★★★★) was matured for 14 months in French oak barriques (23 per cent new). Deeply coloured, it is rich and savoury, with mouthfilling body, generous, ripe cherry, plum, spice and nut flavours, and excellent complexity and harmony. Drink now or cellar.

Vintage	14	13	12	11	10	09
WR	7	7	7	7	7	7
Drink	16-22	16-20	16-22	16-19	16-19	16-18

DRY $55 AV

Villa Maria Single Vineyard Taylors Pass Marlborough Pinot Noir ★★★★★

Estate-grown in the upper Awatere Valley, the 2014 vintage (★★★★☆) was hand-harvested and matured for 14 months in French oak barriques (25 per cent new). Silky-textured, it is deep ruby, with vibrant, ripe plum and spice flavours, gentle tannins, and excellent depth and harmony. Still youthful, it's well worth cellaring to 2018+, but already very approachable.

Vintage	14	13	12	11	10
WR	7	7	7	7	7
Drink	16-22	16-20	16-22	16-18	16-17

DRY $55 AV

Vista Nelson Pinot Noir (★★★)

Grown at Kina, the 2014 vintage (★★★) was matured for 11 months in French oak casks (40 per cent new). It's an upfront style, with strong, ripe, spicy fruit flavours to the fore, and some smoky, savoury notes.

DRY $25 –V

Volcanic Hills Central Otago Pinot Noir ★★★☆

The 2013 vintage (★★★☆) was matured in French oak casks (20 per cent new). Ruby-hued, it is mouthfilling, with moderately concentrated cherry, plum and spice flavours, a hint of dried herbs, some savoury complexity and good harmony. Drink now or cellar.

DRY $36 –V

Volcanic Hills Martinborough Pinot Noir   (★★★☆)

The ruby-hued 2013 vintage (★★★☆) was matured in French oak casks (25 per cent new). Enjoyable young, it is a finely balanced red with satisfying depth of ripe plum, cherry and spice flavours, showing good complexity, and a smooth finish.

DRY $45 –V

Volcanic Hills SV Central Otago Pinot Noir   ★★★★

The 2013 vintage (★★★★) was hand-picked at Bannockburn and matured in French oak barrels (27 per cent new). Full-coloured, sturdy and supple, it is vibrantly fruity and savoury, with good concentration of cherry, plum, spice and nut flavours, oak complexity, and ripe, supple tannins.

DRY $70 –V

Waimea Nelson Pinot Noir   ★★★☆

The 2014 vintage (★★★☆), promoted as 'Pinot off the plains', was estate-grown at four sites on the Waimea Plains and barrel-aged for 10 months. Full ruby, it is fragrant and supple, with fresh, strong, plummy flavours and gentle tannins. A youthful, charming rather than complex wine, it's delicious young.

DRY $25 AV

Waipara Hills Waipara Valley Pinot Noir   ★★★☆

The 2013 vintage (★★★☆) is an easy-drinking, fruit-driven style, full-bodied and ruby-hued, with strong, plummy, slightly cherryish flavours, a hint of herbs and gentle tannins. Delicious young.

Vintage	13
WR	6
Drink	16-17

DRY $22 V+

Waipara Springs Waipara Pinot Noir   ★★★

The 2013 vintage (★★★☆), matured in a 50:50 split of tanks and French oak barrels (10 per cent new), is ruby-hued, mouthfilling and fragrant, with good depth of plum, spice, herb and nut flavours, considerable complexity and lots of drink-young appeal.

DRY $22 AV

Wairau River Marlborough Pinot Noir   ★★★☆

Estate-grown on the north side of the Wairau Valley, the 2015 vintage (★★★☆) was matured for 10 months in French oak barriques. Full ruby, it is mouthfilling and smooth, with vibrant plum and spice flavours, showing some savoury complexity, and very good depth. Best drinking mid-2017+.

Vintage	15	14
WR	6	6
Drink	16-20	16-20

DRY $25 AV

Wairau River Reserve Marlborough Pinot Noir ★★★★

Estate-grown at Rapaura, the 2015 vintage (★★★★) was matured in French oak casks and bottled unfined and unfiltered. Deeply coloured, it is mouthfilling, with concentrated, ripe plum and spice flavours, showing good complexity. A youthful, savoury, well-structured wine, it's worth cellaring; open 2018+.

Vintage	15	14
WR	6	7
Drink	16-22	16-23

 DRY $40 –V

Walnut Block Collectables Marlborough Pinot Noir ★★★

The 2013 vintage (★★★) is a ruby-hued, vibrantly fruity red with plum and red-berry flavours, showing a touch of oak complexity, in a forward, easy-drinking style. Certified organic.

DRY $25 –V

Walnut Block Nutcracker Marlborough Pinot Noir ★★★★

Certified organic, the ruby-hued 2014 vintage (★★★★) was hand-picked, fermented with indigenous yeasts, matured for 11 months in French oak casks (25 per cent new), and bottled unfiltered. Mouthfilling and savoury, it is youthful, with strong, ripe plum, spice and nut flavours, showing good complexity, and a fragrant bouquet. Best drinking 2017+.

Vintage	14	13
WR	7	6
Drink	16-25	16-24

 DRY $40 –V

Wanaka Road Central Otago Pinot Noir ★★★★

From Mount Edward, the 2014 vintage (★★★★) was grown at vineyards in the Cromwell Basin. Full-coloured, generous, ripe and supple, it's a very harmonious wine with strong plum, cherry and spice flavours, a subtle seasoning of oak, earthy, savoury notes adding complexity, and good drive and harmony. Fine value.

DRY $29 V+

Ward Valley Estate Mt Victoria Block Pinot Noir (★★★☆)

The 2014 vintage (★★★☆) was grown in Marlborough. Lightish in colour, with a hint of development, it is moderately concentrated, with strawberryish, nutty flavours, showing some savoury, mushroomy complexity, gentle tannins and good harmony. Drink now to 2017.

DRY $25 AV

Whitehaven Greg Marlborough Pinot Noir ★★★★☆

The 2013 vintage (★★★★☆) was grown in the Wairau Valley and Awatere Valley, and matured in French oak barriques. Bright ruby, it is mouthfilling and sweet-fruited, with vibrant cherry, plum and dried-herb flavours, oak complexity and gentle tannins. Delicious in its youth, it's well worth cellaring.

Vintage	13	12	11	10
WR	7	7	7	7
Drink	16-22	16-20	16-17	P

 DRY $45 –V

Whitehaven Marlborough Pinot Noir   ★★★★

The 2013 vintage (★★★★) was grown in the Wairau Valley, Awatere Valley and Southern Valleys, hand-picked and matured for 11 months in French oak barriques (partly new). Bright ruby, it is fragrant and supple, with vibrant, well-ripened, cherry/plum flavours, silky-textured and harmonious. Drink now onwards.

Vintage	13	12	11	10
WR	7	7	6	7
Drink	16-20	16-18	16-17	16-17

Wild Earth Vineyards Central Otago Pinot Noir   ★★★★

Still on sale, the 2012 vintage (★★★☆) was grown at Bannockburn (80 per cent) and Lowburn (20 per cent), hand-picked and matured for a year in French oak casks (34 per cent new). Enjoyable now, it is a ruby-hued, savoury red, medium to full-bodied, with satisfying depth of cherryish, spicy, slightly herbal and nutty flavours, balanced tannins and good complexity.

Wild Grace Central Otago Pinot Noir   (★★★☆)

Launched from the 2015 vintage (★★★☆), this is an easy-drinking red, full ruby, mouthfilling and supple, with generous, ripe cherry, plum, spice and nut flavours. Moderately complex, it's still youthful; open mid-2017+. (From Constellation NZ.)

Wild River Waipara Pinot Noir   ★★☆

The 2013 vintage (★★☆) is ruby-hued and fruity, in a fairly light style with fresh, pleasant berry, plum and herb flavours, offering smooth, easy drinking. (From Mount Brown.)

Wild South Marlborough Pinot Noir   ★★★

From Sacred Hill, the 2015 vintage (★★★) was partly barrel-aged. Ruby-hued, it is an attractive, drink-young charmer. Mouthfilling, it is vibrantly fruity, with cherryish, plummy, slightly spicy flavours and an ultra-smooth finish. Priced right.

Wither Hills Single Vineyard Taylor River Marlborough Pinot Noir   ★★★★

Offering fine value, the softly mouthfilling 2013 vintage (★★★★) was matured for 16–18 months in French oak barriques (about 25 per cent new). Bright ruby, it is a subtle, savoury wine with vibrant, ripe cherry, plum, spice and nut flavours, showing very good complexity, and a silky texture. Drinking well now, it's still youthful and likely to be at its best 2018+.

DRY $28 V+

Wooing Tree Beetle Juice Central Otago Pinot Noir ★★★★

This single-vineyard Cromwell red is hand-picked and matured for eight or nine months in French oak casks (partly new). The 2015 vintage (★★★★) has full, bright ruby colour. Fragrant and supple, it's a refined, highly drinkable wine, with ripe plum and spice flavours, finely integrated oak, good complexity, and lots of drink-young appeal. Drink now or cellar.

 DRY $28 V+

Wooing Tree Central Otago Pinot Noir ★★★★★

This single-vineyard Cromwell red is typically classy. The 2015 vintage (★★★★☆) was hand-picked and matured in French oak casks. Deep ruby, it is fragrant, full-bodied and sweet-fruited, with strong, vibrant, plummy, spicy flavours, showing very good complexity, and a backbone of ripe tannins. Still very youthful, it's well worth cellaring to 2018+.

 DRY $48 AV

Wooing Tree Sandstorm Reserve Single Vineyard Central Otago Pinot Noir ★★★★★

Estate-grown at Cromwell, this wine is hand-picked from especially low-yielding vines and given extended oak-aging. The 2014 vintage (★★★★★) is a powerful, youthful red, deep ruby, with concentrated, ripe cherry, plum, spice and nut flavours, very complex and savoury, balanced tannins and a long life ahead. Best drinking 2018+.

 DRY $85 –V

Yealands Estate Awatere Valley Marlborough Pinot Noir ★★★★

The 2013 vintage (★★★★) is a single-vineyard red, ruby-hued, mouthfilling and supple, with generous cherry, plum and spice flavours. Sweet-fruited and finely textured, it's a very harmonious wine, for drinking now onwards.

Vintage	13
WR	7
Drink	16-18

 DRY $30 AV

Yealands Estate Land Made Marlborough Pinot Noir ★★★

The 2014 vintage (★★★) is bright ruby, mouthfilling and smooth, with ripe plum and spice flavours, a touch of savoury complexity, and good depth. Drink now or cellar.

Vintage	14	13
WR	7	7
Drink	16-18	P

DRY $20 AV

Yealands Estate Single Vineyard Awatere Valley Marlborough Pinot Noir ★★★★

Estate-grown in the Seaview Vineyard and barrel-matured, the 2014 vintage (★★★★) has full, fairly youthful colour. Mouthfilling and smooth, with ripe cherry, plum and spice flavours, and fine-grained tannins, it shows good complexity. The 2015 vintage (★★★★) is enjoyable from the start. Full-coloured, it is mouthfilling and fruit-packed, with generous, plummy, spicy flavours, fresh, lively and smooth. Best drinking mid-2017+.

Vintage	15	14
WR	7	7
Drink	16-20	16-19

 DRY $27 V+

Yealands Estate Winemaker's Reserve
Awatere Valley Marlborough Pinot Noir ★★★★☆

The classy, powerful yet elegant 2014 vintage (★★★★★) was estate-grown on an elevated (180 metres above sea level), north-facing slope in the Willowflat Vineyard and matured for a year in French oak barriques (15 per cent new). Deep ruby, it is fleshy, concentrated and supple, with very generous plum/spice flavours, complex and savoury. A rich, harmonious and very 'complete' wine, it should be at its best 2017+.

Vintage	14	13
WR	7	7
Drink	16-23	16-22

DRY $40 AV

Yealands Estate Winemaker's Reserve Gibbston Central Otago Pinot Noir ★★★★☆

The classy young 2014 vintage (★★★★☆) was grown in the Holtzmann Vineyard, 320 metres above sea level at Gibbston, and matured for a year in French oak barriques (25 per cent new). Deep ruby, it is mouthfilling, with generous cherry, plum and dried-herb flavours, vibrant, supple, rich and flowing.

Vintage	14	13
WR	7	6
Drink	16-23	16-22

DRY $40 AV

Zephyr Marlborough Pinot Noir ★★★★

Still unfolding, the 2014 vintage (★★★★) is a sweet-fruited, savoury red, grown in the Southern Valleys and matured for 10 months in French oak casks (15 per cent new). Ruby-hued, it is floral and supple, with ripe cherry and spice flavours, showing good complexity, and a lingering finish.

DRY $32 AV

Pinotage

Popular in New Zealand in the 1960s and 1970s, Pinotage is today overshadowed by more glamorous varieties, with just 28 hectares of bearing vines in 2017. Pinotage now ranks as the country's seventh most extensively planted red-wine variety, well behind Cabernet Franc, ranked sixth, and fifth-placed Malbec.

Pinotage is a cross of the great Burgundian grape, Pinot Noir, and Cinsaut, a heavy-cropping variety popular in the south of France. Cinsaut's typically 'meaty, chunky sort of flavour' (in Jancis Robinson's words) is also characteristic of Pinotage. Valued for its reasonably early-ripening and disease-resistant qualities, and good yields, its plantings are mostly in Gisborne (32 per cent), Marlborough (21 per cent) and Auckland (21 per cent), with smaller pockets in Hawke's Bay and Northland.

A well-made Pinotage displays a slightly gamey bouquet and a smooth, berryish, peppery palate that can be reminiscent of a southern Rhône. It matures swiftly and usually peaks within two or three years of the vintage.

Hitchen Road Pinotage ★★★★

The bargain-priced 2014 vintage (★★★★) was estate-grown and hand-picked at Pokeno, in North Waikato. Oak-matured for 10 months, it is full-coloured, mouthfilling and supple, with strong, ripe plum and spice flavours, the slightly earthy notes typical of Pinotage, and strong drink-young appeal. A generous, instantly attractive wine, it offers good value (even better by the case at under $12 per bottle).

DRY $18 V+

Karikari Estate Pinotage ★★★★

Estate-grown on the Karikari Peninsula, in the Far North, the 2014 vintage (★★★★) is full-coloured and mouthfilling, with generous, ripe, plummy, spicy flavours and the earthy streak typical of Pinotage. Concentrated and firmly structured, it should be at its best 2017+.

DRY $48 –V

Marsden Bay of Islands Pinotage ★★★☆

Maturing gracefully, the 2014 vintage (★★★★) was harvested at over 25 brix and matured for a year in French oak casks (25 per cent new). You could easily mistake it for a red from the Rhône Valley. Full-coloured, it is weighty and warm, with strong, plummy, spicy flavours, ripe tannins and some savoury complexity. Drink now or cellar.

Vintage	14	13
WR	6	6
Drink	16-17	P

DRY $32 –V

NTN Jubilee Reserve Pinotage (★★★★☆)

'NTN' is Nick Nobilo, who in the 1970s was a key pioneer of Pinotage in New Zealand. Released in January 2016, the 2007 vintage (★★★★☆) is a 'once-only' wine, harvested in Gisborne at 24 brix and aged for two years in French and American oak barriques. Deep and mature in colour, with the gamey, 'wild' bouquet typical of Pinotage, it is powerful, fleshy, rich and smooth, with generous, savoury, spicy, earthy flavours. Full of personality, it's currently at the peak of its powers, and certainly proves Pinotage's ability to mature for a decade.

DRY $70 –V

Sangiovese

Sangiovese, Italy's most extensively planted red-wine variety, is a rarity in New Zealand. Cultivated as a workhorse grape throughout central Italy, in Tuscany it is the foundation of such famous reds as Chianti and Brunello di Montalcino. Here, Sangiovese has sometimes been confused with Montepulciano and its plantings are not expanding. Only 8 hectares of Sangiovese vines will be bearing in 2017, mostly in Auckland and Hawke's Bay.

Heron's Flight Matakana Sangiovese ★★★★☆

North of Auckland, David Hoskins and Mary Evans specialise in traditional Italian grape varieties. The 2013 vintage (★★★★☆), from vines averaging 15 years old, was matured for six months in French oak barriques (20 per cent new). The colour is bold, youthful and purple-flushed; the palate is powerful, with mouthfilling body, balanced acidity and rich, plummy, spicy flavours, showing good complexity.

DRY $60 –V

St Laurent

This Austrian variety is known for its deeply coloured, silky-smooth reds. It buds early, so is prone to frost damage, but ripens well ahead of Pinot Noir. Judge Rock imported the vine in 2001, but St Laurent is still extremely rare in New Zealand, with just 1.4 hectares of bearing vines in 2017, clustered in Waipara, Otago and Marlborough.

Hans Herzog Marlborough St Laurent ★★★★

Certified organic, the 2012 vintage (★★★★☆) was matured for 30 months in French oak barriques. Full and bright in colour, it is weighty and supple, with vibrant plum, spice, herb and dark chocolate flavours, showing excellent density and complexity. Drink now or cellar.

Vintage	12	11
WR	7	7
Drink	16-22	16-19

 DRY $64 –V

Judge Rock Central Otago St Laurent (★★★)

The 2012 vintage (★★★) is a fresh, brightly coloured, light to medium-bodied red (11.2 per cent alcohol). Still youthful, it is moderately ripe-tasting, with plenty of plummy, berryish flavour, threaded with lively acidity.

DRY $35 –V

Syrah

Hawke's Bay and the upper North Island (especially Waiheke Island) have a hot, new-ish red-wine variety, attracting growing international acclaim. The classic 'Syrah' of the Rhône Valley, in France, and Australian 'Shiraz' are in fact the same variety. On the rocky, baking slopes of the upper Rhône Valley, and in several Australian states, this noble grape yields red wines renowned for their outstanding depth of cassis, plum and black-pepper flavours.

Syrah was well known in New Zealand a century ago. Government viticulturist S.F. Anderson wrote in 1917 that Shiraz was being 'grown in nearly all our vineyards [but] the trouble with this variety has been an unevenness in ripening its fruit'. For today's winemakers, the problem has not changed: Syrah has never favoured a too-cool growing environment (wines that are not fully ripe show distinct tomato or tamarillo characters). It needs sites that are relatively hot during the day and retain the heat at night, achieving ripeness in Hawke's Bay late in the season, at about the same time as Cabernet Sauvignon. To curb its natural vigour, stony, dry, low-fertility sites or warm hillside sites are crucial.

Four hundred and forty-nine hectares of Syrah will be bearing in 2017 – a steep rise from 62 hectares in 2000. Syrah is now New Zealand's third most widely planted red-wine variety, behind Pinot Noir and Merlot, but well ahead of Cabernet Sauvignon, Malbec and Cabernet Franc. Over 75 per cent of the vines are in Hawke's Bay, with most of the rest in Auckland and Northland (although there are pockets as far south as Central Otago).

Syrah's potential in this country's warmer vineyard sites is finally being tapped. The top wines possess rich, vibrant blackcurrant, plum and black-pepper flavours, with an enticingly floral bouquet, and are winning growing international applause.

Could Syrah replace Bordeaux-style Merlot and Cabernet Sauvignon-based blends over the next decade or two as the principal red-wine style from Hawke's Bay and the upper North Island? Don't rule it out.

Ake Ake Northland Syrah ★★★

The 2014 vintage (★★★☆) was matured in tanks and seasoned American oak casks. The colour is dense and inky; the palate is mouthfilling and vibrantly fruity, with strong, plummy, spicy flavours, a restrained oak influence, fresh acidity and gentle tannins. Worth cellaring.

Vintage	14	DRY $25 –V
WR	5	
Drink	16-18	

Alpha Domus The Barnstormer Hawke's Bay Syrah ★★★★

The 2015 vintage (★★★★) is a fragrant, generous wine, estate-grown in the Bridge Pa Triangle and matured for over a year in mostly French oak barriques. Age-worthy, it is firmly structured, with strong, plummy, spicy, nutty, peppery flavours, showing good complexity and length.

Vintage	15	DRY $34 –V
WR	6	
Drink	17-21	

Anchorage Family Estate Nelson Syrah (★★★)

Enjoyable young, the 2015 vintage (★★★) has a Pinot Noir-ish charm. Wood-aged for six months, it is a full-coloured, medium-bodied red with good depth of fresh, ripe, plummy and spicy flavours, gentle tannins and a smooth, slightly peppery finish. Priced right.

DRY $18 AV

Ash Ridge Estate Hawke's Bay Syrah ★★★☆

The 2015 vintage (★★★☆), estate-grown in the Bridge Pa Triangle, is this fast-emerging producer's top-selling wine. Matured in French and American oak barrels (mostly seasoned), it is a deep ruby, medium to full-bodied red with vibrant, spicy, slightly earthy flavours, showing some complexity, and velvety tannins. Priced right.

Vintage	15	14	13	12	11	10	09
WR	6	7	7	6	6	7	7
Drink	16-20	16-21	16-20	16-18	16-18	16-17	P

DRY $20 AV

Ash Ridge Premium Estate Hawke's Bay Syrah (★★★★☆)

The debut 2014 vintage (★★★★☆) was matured in predominantly French oak casks (15 per cent new). Dark and mouthfilling, it is savoury and harmonious, with deep, ripe plum and black-pepper flavours, fine-grained tannins, and a long, spicy finish. Best drinking 2018+.

DRY $30 AV

Ash Ridge Vintners Reserve Hawke's Bay Syrah (★★★★☆)

The 2013 vintage (★★★★☆) was grown in the Bridge Pa Triangle, blended with a splash of Viognier (1 per cent), and matured for 15 months in French and American oak casks (20 per cent new). Deeply coloured, it is richly fragrant, with deep plum, spice and nut flavours, a hint of liquorice, and a moderately firm, lingering, spicy finish. A 'serious' wine, designed for cellaring, it should be at its best 2017+.

DRY $45 –V

Askerne Hawke's Bay Syrah ★★☆

The 2013 vintage (★★★) is a fresh, medium-bodied red, purple-flushed, blended from Gimblett Gravels Syrah and estate-grown Viognier (5 per cent). Matured for over a year in French oak casks (15 per cent new), it's a drink-young style with a peppery bouquet and plummy, spicy flavours, vibrant and smooth. The 2014 vintage (★★☆) is full-coloured, with slightly rustic, gamey, earthy notes.

DRY $22 –V

Awaroa Melba Peach Waiheke Island Syrah ★★★★★

Dark and dense, the powerful 2014 vintage (★★★★★) is still very youthful. Matured for a year in French oak barriques (50 per cent new), it has highly concentrated, ripe plum and black-pepper flavours, woven with fresh acidity, and a tightly structured, long, spicy finish. In a vertical tasting held in September 2016, the 2013 (★★★★★) and 2010 (★★★★★) vintages showed notable ripeness and density; the 2012 was slightly less ripe-tasting, but still maturing well.

Vintage	14	13	12	11	10
WR	7	7	5	NM	7
Drink	18-22	17-21	16-18	NM	16-24

DRY $65 AV

Awaroa The Dan Syrah/Cabernet/Malbec   (★★★★☆)

Deeply coloured, fragrant and very youthful, the 2014 vintage (★★★★☆) is Awaroa's first reserve blend of Syrah (65 per cent) and Cabernet Sauvignon (23 per cent), with a splash of Malbec (12 per cent). Matured in all-new French oak barriques, it is powerful, with concentrated, ripe plum, blackcurrant and spice flavours, good tannin backbone, and obvious cellaring potential.

Vintage	14
WR	7
Drink	19-23

 DRY $65 –V

Awaroa Waiheke Island Syrah   ★★★★

The very harmonious 2014 vintage (★★★★☆) was hand-picked and matured for a year in seasoned French oak barriques. Full-coloured, with a fragrant, clearly varietal bouquet, it is mouthfilling, ripe and smooth, with strong plum/spice flavours, a hint of dark chocolate, and a long, well-rounded finish. Best drinking 2018+.

Vintage	14
WR	6
Drink	16-20

 DRY $38 –V

Babich Hawke's Bay Syrah   ★★★

The 2015 vintage (★★★) was grown in the Gimblett Gravels and Bridge Pa Triangle. Deep ruby, with a fresh, peppery bouquet, it is a medium-bodied, fruit-driven style, with plum, spice and black-pepper flavours and gentle tannins. Enjoyable young.

 DRY $22 –V

Babich Winemakers Reserve Hawke's Bay Syrah   ★★★★☆

The 2015 vintage (★★★★) is a concentrated, firmly structured red, grown in the Bridge Pa Triangle and French oak-aged for a year. Dark, with a fragrant bouquet of violets, oak complexity and a strong surge of plum, spice and slight liquorice flavours, it's well worth cellaring.

DRY $30 AV

Bell Bird Bay Reserve Hawke's Bay Syrah   (★★★☆)

Grown in the Bridge Pa Triangle, the 2014 vintage (★★★☆) was matured in French oak barriques. Full-coloured, it is mouthfilling and savoury, with strong, spicy, slightly toasty flavours, woven with fresh acidity. Drink now to 2018. (From Alpha Domus.)

 DRY $28 –V

Bilancia Hawke's Bay Syrah ★★★★☆

The 2013 vintage (★★★★☆), matured in French oak casks (20 per cent new), has bold, purple-flushed colour. The bouquet is floral, fresh, strong and peppery; the palate is mouthfilling, with ripe, concentrated plum and spice flavours, a subtle seasoning of oak, savoury notes adding complexity, and a lingering finish. It's still youthful; open 2017+.

Vintage	13	12	11
WR	6	6	6
Drink	16-20	16-18	16-17

 DRY $35 AV

Bilancia La Collina Syrah ★★★★★

La Collina ('The Hill') is grown at the company's steep, early-ripening site on the northern slopes of Roys Hill, overlooking the Gimblett Gravels, Hawke's Bay, co-fermented with Viognier skins (but not their juice, giving a tiny Viognier component in the final blend), and matured for up to 22 months in 70 per cent new (but 'low-impact') French oak barriques. A majestic red, it ranks among the country's very finest Syrahs. The beautifully poised 2010 vintage (★★★★★) is densely coloured, powerful and very sweet-fruited, with exceptional concentration of plum, liquorice and spice flavours, and a well-rounded finish. Already approachable, it should be a 20-year wine. The 2013 vintage (★★★★★) is a memorable wine, arguably the country's greatest Syrah. Dense, inky and youthful in colour, it has a beautifully fragrant, ripe, plummy, spicy bouquet. Powerful but not tough, it has layers of plum, spice, nut and slight liquorice flavours, good tannin backbone, and striking concentration and complexity. A memorable mouthful, it should break into full stride 2018+.

Vintage	13	12	11	10
WR	7	NM	NM	7
Drink	16-30	NM	NM	16-28

DRY $120 AV

Boundary Vineyards Farm Lane Hawke's Bay Syrah ★★★★

From Pernod Ricard NZ, the 2015 vintage (★★★★) was estate-grown in the Bridge Pa Triangle. Delicious young, it is deeply coloured, with strong plum, spice and black-pepper flavours, savoury notes adding complexity, and good ripeness and harmony.

DRY $20 V+

Brookfields Back Block Hawke's Bay Syrah ★★★☆

Matured in seasoned oak casks, the 2015 vintage (★★★☆) is full-coloured, mouthfilling, vibrantly fruity and smooth, with ripe, plummy, spicy flavours, a gentle oak influence and very good depth. Drink now or cellar.

Vintage	15
WR	7
Drink	18-22

DRY $20 AV

Brookfields Hillside Syrah ★★★★★

This distinguished red is grown on a sheltered, north-facing slope between Maraekakaho and Bridge Pa, in Hawke's Bay (described by winemaker Peter Robertson as 'surreal – a chosen site'). The 2015 vintage (★★★★★), matured in new French (mostly) and American oak casks, is deeply coloured, fragrant and concentrated, with deep, ripe blackcurrant, spice, plum and black-pepper flavours, a hint of liquorice, and lovely density and smoothness. Best drinking 2018+.

Vintage	15	14	13
WR	7	7	7
Drink	20-26	18-25	18-23

Byrne Northland Syrah   (★★★★☆)

Grown in the Rushbrook Vineyard, at Kerikeri, the highly impressive 2013 vintage (★★★★☆) was blended with Viognier (3 per cent), matured in French oak barriques (a third new), and bottled unfined and unfiltered. Deeply coloured, it is poised, youthful and highly concentrated, with rich, ripe blackcurrant, plum and spice flavours, finely balanced and lingering. An elegant, tightly structured wine, it's built to last.

Vintage	13
WR	7
Drink	16-20

DRY $32 AV

Cable Bay Waiheke Island Syrah   ★★★☆

The 2014 vintage (★★★☆) is a single-vineyard red, hand-harvested and matured in French oak barrels (20 per cent new). Full-coloured, it is floral and supple, in a medium-bodied style with plum, spice and black-pepper flavours, a hint of tamarillo, fresh acidity, and gentle tannins. Best drinking 2017+.

Vintage	14	13	12	11	10	09
WR	5	6	6	5	7	7
Drink	16-22	16-23	16-20	16-18	16-20	P

DRY $48 –V

Church Road Grand Reserve Hawke's Bay Syrah   ★★★★★

Likely to be long-lived, the 2014 vintage (★★★★★) is a weighty, dark, purple-flushed red, estate-grown in the Gimblett Gravels, matured for 16 months in French (principally) and Hungarian oak barrels (34 per cent new), and bottled unfined and unfiltered. Perfumed and sturdy (14.5 per cent alcohol), it is sweet-fruited, with highly concentrated plum and black-pepper flavours, a hint of dark chocolate, gentle tannins, and excellent complexity and harmony. It's already very approachable.

DRY $44 AV

Church Road Hawke's Bay Syrah   ★★★★

The 2014 vintage (★★★★☆) is a great buy. Estate-grown in the Bridge Pa Triangle (77 per cent) and the Gimblett Gravels (23 per cent), it was matured in French and Hungarian oak barriques (25 per cent new). A powerful, sweet-fruited red, it is deeply coloured and floral, with concentrated, youthful, very ripe flavours of red fruits and spices, a hint of liquorice, and supple tannins. Drink now to 2020.

Church Road McDonald Series Hawke's Bay Syrah ★★★★★

The bargain-priced 2014 vintage (★★★★★) was estate-grown in the Gimblett Gravels (75 per cent) and the Bridge Pa Triangle (25 per cent). Matured for 20 months in French and Hungarian oak barriques (32 per cent new), it has bold, dense colour, with a fragrant bouquet of spices and liquorice. Highly concentrated, with good weight, it has rich, very ripe plum, spice and liquorice flavours, and a firm backbone of tannin. Best drinking 2017+. A great buy.

DRY $27 V+

Church Road Tom Syrah (★★★★★)

Syrah is the latest addition to Church Road's elite Tom selection. The debut 2013 vintage (★★★★★) was estate-grown in the Redstone Vineyard, in the Bridge Pa Triangle, Hawke's Bay. Harvested at over 25 brix, it was matured in French oak barriques (71 per cent new) for nearly two years. Delicious from the start, it has deep, youthful colour. Full-bodied (14.5 per cent alcohol) and rich, it is seductively smooth (winemaker Chris Scott aims to 'melt the tannins into the wine'), with concentrated, ripe blackcurrant and spice flavours, a hint of pepperiness, gentle tannins and acidity, and lovely fragrance, depth and harmony.

DRY $200 –V

Clayvin Single Vineyard Selection Marlborough Syrah (★★★★☆)

From Giesen, the elegant 2013 vintage (★★★★☆) is still unfolding. Grown in the elevated Clayvin Vineyard, on the south side of the Wairau Valley, it is a full-coloured, medium to full-bodied red with concentrated, ripe plum/spice flavours, vibrant and youthful, and very good complexity. Best drinking 2018+.

Vintage	13
WR	6
Drink	16-22

DRY $70 –V

Clearview Cape Kidnappers Hawke's Bay Syrah ★★★★

Delicious young, the 2015 vintage (★★★★) is a deeply coloured, purple-flushed red, grown at Te Awanga and matured in French oak casks (10 per cent new). Mouthfilling and supple, it is sweet-fruited, with strong, plummy, spicy flavours, in a generous, clearly varietal style, very finely balanced for early enjoyment.

DRY $27 AV

Clevedon Hills Syrah ★★★★☆

Estate-grown at Clevedon, in South Auckland, the 2014 vintage (★★★★) is youthful, with deep, bright colour. Mouthfilling, it is rich and supple, with vibrant plum, spice and black-pepper flavours, gently seasoned with oak, and a finely textured, harmonious finish. Well worth cellaring.

DRY $45 –V

Clos de Ste Anne The Crucible Syrah ★★★★★

The outstanding 2014 vintage (★★★★★) is one of the finest yet. Grown biodynamically in Millton's elevated Clos de Ste Anne vineyard in Gisborne, it was hand-harvested, co-fermented with Viognier (5 per cent), and matured in large, seasoned French oak casks. Deep and youthful in colour, it is ripely fragrant and sweet-fruited, with concentrated plum and spice flavours, nutty, savoury and complex, fine-grained tannins and a lasting finish. Full of personality, it is a very harmonious wine, already delicious but sure to reward cellaring.

 DRY $75 AV

Coopers Creek Hawke's Bay Syrah ★★★☆

The dark, medium-bodied 2013 vintage (★★★★), matured in seasoned oak casks, has strong, ripe, plummy, well-spiced flavours, gentle tannins and good length.

DRY $22 AV

Coopers Creek Reserve Hawke's Bay Syrah ★★★★★

The 2013 vintage (★★★★★) is a bold, rich red, dark and strongly varietal, with dense blackcurrant, plum and black-pepper flavours. A powerful, youthful wine with ripe tannins, it has impressive concentration and length.

Vintage	13
WR	7
Drink	16-20

DRY $57 AV

Coopers Creek SV Chalk Ridge Hawke's Bay Syrah ★★★★

Dark, with an invitingly fragrant, aromatic bouquet (1.5 per cent Viognier) of violets, boysenberry and liquorice, the 2014 vintage (★★★★★) is fresh, with intense, ripe plum and spice flavours, vibrant, silky-textured and long. Fine value.

Vintage	14	13
WR	7	7
Drink	16-21	16-20

DRY $28 AV

Coopers Creek SV Gimblett Gravels Hawke's Bay Syrah (★★★★★)

Highly expressive in its youth, but very age-worthy, the 2014 vintage (★★★★★) is a dark, fragrant blend (2 per cent Viognier), matured in French oak casks (20 per cent new). Concentrated, sweet-fruited and finely structured, it is rich, ripe and smooth, with hints of liquorice. Great value.

DRY $28 V+

Couper's Shed Hawke's Bay Syrah ★★★☆

Delicious young, the strongly varietal 2015 vintage (★★★★) is deeply coloured, mouthfilling and supple, with excellent depth of plum/spice flavours, showing some savoury complexity. Fine value. (From Pernod Ricard NZ.)

DRY $23 AV

Craft Farm Lyons Vineyard Hawke's Bay Syrah   (★★★★☆)

From an elevated site, overlooking Bridge Pa, the graceful 2014 vintage (★★★★☆) was hand-picked from young vines, matured for 14 months in French oak barrels (50 per cent new), and bottled unfined and unfiltered. Floral, deeply coloured, sweet-fruited and supple, it is still very youthful, with mouthfilling body, concentrated, ripe plum/spice flavours, and gentle tannins. It shows obvious cellaring potential; open 2018+.

Craggy Range Gimblett Gravels Vineyard Hawke's Bay Syrah   ★★★★★

This label is overshadowed by the reputation of its stablemate, Le Sol, but proves the power, structure and finesse that can be achieved with Syrah grown in the Gimblett Gravels of Hawke's Bay. The outstanding, age-worthy 2014 vintage (★★★★★) was hand-harvested at 23.7 brix and matured for 16 months in French oak barriques (26 per cent new). Dark and purple-flushed, it is mouthfilling, with concentrated, ripe plum and black-pepper flavours, a hint of dark chocolate, and a long, spicy finish. Densely packed and still very youthful, it should hit full stride 2019+.

Craggy Range Le Sol Syrah – see Craggy Range Le Sol in the Branded and Other Red Wines section

Crossroads Milestone Series Hawke's Bay Syrah   ★★★☆

The 2013 vintage (★★★☆) was grown in the Gimblett Gravels and oak-aged. Deeply coloured, it is fresh and youthful, with strong, ripe plum/spice flavours, a restrained oak influence, and gentle tannins. Best drinking 2017+.

Vintage	13	12	11	10
WR	7	5	5	5
Drink	16-23	16-19	16-18	16-18

DRY $22 AV

Crossroads Talisman Gimblett Gravels Syrah   ★★★★★

The floral, graceful, very finely textured 2014 vintage (★★★★★) was estate-grown in The Elms Vineyard and matured in French oak barriques. Deeply coloured, with rich, ripe blackcurrant and spice flavours, hints of dark chocolate and liquorice, and a long, slightly peppery finish, it's already delicous, but should be at its best 2019+.

Vintage	14	13
WR	7	7
Drink	16-23	16-23

DRY $45 AV

Crossroads Winemakers Collection Gimblett Gravels Hawke's Bay Syrah ★★★★☆

The sturdy, youthful, clearly varietal 2014 vintage (★★★★☆) was estate-grown and hand-harvested in The Elms Vineyard, and matured for 14 months in French oak barriques (20 per cent new). It has concentrated plum and spice flavours, seasoned with nutty oak, earthy notes adding complexity, and good tannin backbone. Best drinking 2018+.

Cypress Hawke's Bay Syrah ★★★☆

Estate-grown at the base of Roys Hill, hand-picked and matured for eight months in seasoned oak barrels, the 2014 vintage (★★★★) is sweet-fruited, with strong plum/spice flavours, showing very good depth, complexity and harmony.

Cypress Terraces Hawke's Bay Syrah ★★★★

Estate-grown at an elevated, terraced site on Roys Hill, in the Gimblett Gravels, the 2013 vintage (★★★★☆) was matured for 20 months in French oak casks. It's a very savoury, complex wine with strong plum and spice flavours, a hint of liquorice, and fine-grained tannins. Best drinking 2017+.

De La Terre Hawke's Bay Syrah ★★★★

Enjoyable already, the 2014 vintage (★★★★) was estate-grown at Havelock North and matured for over a year in French oak barriques (20 per cent new). Floral, with a slightly peppery fragrance, it is mouthfilling, with generous, vibrant, plummy, spicy flavours, oak complexity, and deep, youthful colour. Drink now or cellar.

Vintage	14	13
WR	6	6
Drink	16-20	16-20

De La Terre Reserve Hawke's Bay Syrah ★★★★☆

The impressive 2014 vintage (★★★★★) was estate-grown at Havelock North and matured for 18 months in French oak barriques (33 per cent new). Full-coloured, it is fragrant and concentrated, with dense, ripe plum, spice and black-pepper flavours, a hint of liquorice, good complexity and fine-grained tannins. Sweet-fruited and finely textured, it's already approachable, but well worth cellaring.

Vintage	14	13
WR	7	6
Drink	16-25	16-25

DRY $40 –V

Doubtless Reserve Syrah   (★★★)

Still on sale, the 2010 vintage (★★★) is a Northland blend of Syrah (88 per cent), Viognier (6 per cent) and 'other reds' (6 per cent). It has full, moderately developed colour. Mouthfilling, with generous blackcurrant, plum and spice flavours, braced by firm tannins, it's drinking well now.

Vintage	10
WR	7
Drink	17-28

DRY $26 –V

Dry River Lovat Vineyard Martinborough Syrah   ★★★★☆

The 2013 vintage (★★★★☆) is labelled 'Amaranth', meaning it is recommended for long-term cellaring. Deep and youthful in colour, it is medium-bodied (12 per cent alcohol), floral and supple, with rich plum, spice and pepper flavours, tightly structured and smooth-flowing. Still very youthful, it should be at its best 2018+.

Vintage	13	12	11	10	09	08	07	06	05
WR	7	NM	6	6	7	7	6	7	7
Drink	17-29	NM	16-26	16-20	16-23	16-22	16-21	16-20	P

DRY $64 –V

Easthope Moteo Hawke's Bay Syrah   (★★★★☆)

The 2014 vintage (★★★★☆) was matured in thick concrete, egg-shaped tanks, and bottled without fining or filtration. Deeply coloured, it is mouthfilling and savoury, with concentrated, ripe plum/spice flavours, fine-grained tannins and good harmony. Drink now or cellar.

DRY $45 –V

Elephant Hill Airavata Hawke's Bay Syrah   (★★★★★)

Promoted as 'our flagship Syrah', the lovely 2013 vintage (★★★★★) was estate-grown in the Gimblett Gravels and at Te Awanga, and matured for 17 months in French oak casks (60 per cent new). Rich and youthful in colour, it is deliciously rich, supple and harmonious, with deep plum, spice and black-pepper flavours, complex, savoury and smooth-flowing. Combining power and elegance, it's a notably 'complete' wine, likely to be at its best 2020+.

DRY $105 AV

Elephant Hill Gimblett Vineyard Hawke's Bay Syrah   (★★★★★)

The classy, debut 2013 vintage (★★★★★) is a single-vineyard red, grown in the heart of the Gimblett Gravels and matured for 16 months in French oak casks (35 per cent new). It is fragrant, dense but supple, with tight-knit, vibrant plum/spice flavours and a long, well-spiced finish. Still very youthful, it should reward several years' cellaring.

DRY $80 AV

Elephant Hill Hawke's Bay Syrah   ★★★★☆

The youthful, dense 2014 vintage (★★★★☆) was grown in the Gimblett Gravels, at Te Awanga and in the Bridge Pa Triangle, and matured for a year in French oak barriques (30 per cent new). Retasted in August 2016, it is boldly coloured, firm and concentrated, with strong, tight-knit, plummy, spicy flavours, an earthy streak adding complexity, and ripe, balanced tannins. Approachable now, but still unfolding, it should be at its best 2018+.

Elephant Hill Reserve Hawke's Bay Syrah   ★★★★★

The stylish, finely poised 2014 vintage (★★★★★) was hand-picked in the Gimblett Gravels, at Te Awanga and in the Bridge Pa Triangle, and matured for 19 months in French oak casks (35 per cent new). Dark and purple-flushed, it is densely packed, with ripe, youthful plum and spice flavours, a hint of liquorice, good tannin backbone, excellent complexity, and a long future ahead. Best drinking 2019+.

Esk Valley Hawke's Bay Syrah   ★★★★

Grown in the Gimblett Gravels, the 2014 vintage (★★★★) was matured for 17 months in French oak casks (15 per cent new). A youthful, deeply coloured red, mouthfilling and smooth, it has strong, ripe plum/spice flavours, with hints of dark chocolate and toasty oak, gentle tannins, and a well-spiced finish.

Vintage	14	13	12	11	10	09
WR	7	7	6	5	6	6
Drink	16-21	16-21	16-19	P	16-18	P

Esk Valley Winemakers Reserve Gimblett Gravels Hawke's Bay Syrah   ★★★★★

Densely coloured, the youthful 2014 vintage (★★★★★) was grown in the Cornerstone Vineyard and matured for 16 months in French oak barriques (55 per cent new). A richly varietal, youthful, vibrantly fruity red, it is sturdy (14.5 per cent alcohol), with highly concentrated, ripe plum, blackcurrant and spice flavours and a tightly structured, firm, lasting finish.

Vintage	14	13	12	11	10	09	08	07
WR	7	7	NM	NM	7	7	NM	7
Drink	16-30	16-25	NM	NM	16-20	16-20	NM	16-18

Expatrius Waiheke Island Syrah   ★★★★★

Grown on an 'elevated coastal headland', the 2013 vintage (★★★★★) was matured in new French oak barrels for 15 months. Deep and bright in colour, it is sturdy (14 per cent alcohol), youthful and very finely textured, with generous, ripe, plummy, gently spicy flavours, fine-grained tannins and obvious potential. Showing great harmony, it's already delicious, but should be at its best 2018 onwards.

Falconhead Hawke's Bay Syrah ★★★☆

Offering great value, the 2014 vintage (★★★☆) is a finely balanced Syrah that includes a splash of Viognier (4.5 per cent). Full and bright in colour, it is mouthfilling and smooth, with youthful plum/spice flavours, a hint of dark chocolate, gentle tannins, and some savoury complexity. Drink now to 2017.

Vintage	14	13
WR	7	7
Drink	16-20	16-20

DRY $16 V+

Frenchmans Hill Estate Waiheke Island Rock Earth Syrah (★★★★★)

Set for a long life, the powerful, concentrated 2010 vintage (★★★★★) is still youthful. Grown in The 8 Vineyard and matured for 16 months in all-new oak barriques, it is deeply coloured and muscular (15 per cent alcohol), but not heavy, with dense blackcurrant, black-pepper and spice flavours, complex, savoury and firm. Best 2018+.

DRY $75 AV

Fromm La Strada Marlborough Syrah ★★★★

A cool-climate, 'fruit-driven' style – with style. The 2014 vintage (★★★☆), which includes a splash of Viognier, is certified organic. Deeply coloured, it is a fragrant, medium-bodied red (12 per cent alcohol), fresh, vibrantly fruity and supple, with lively acidity, a Pinot Noir-ish texture and good immediacy. Enjoyable young.

Vintage	14	13	12	11	10
WR	7	7	7	7	7
Drink	16-21	16-21	16-20	16-20	16-19

DRY $40 –V

Fromm Syrah Fromm Vineyard ★★★★☆

Estate-grown in the Wairau Valley, Marlborough and blended with Viognier (3 per cent), the elegant 2014 vintage (★★★★☆) is a very rare red (only four barrels were produced). Certified organic, it is a deep ruby, intensely varietal wine, medium to full-bodied, with vibrant, plummy, distinctly peppery aromas and flavours. Concentrated, lively and finely textured, with a long finish, it's still very youthful; open 2018+.

DRY $63 –V

Georges Road Block One Waipara Syrah ★★★☆

The 2013 vintage (★★★☆) was estate-grown, hand-harvested and matured in French oak barriques (20 per cent new). Ruby-hued, it is floral and supple, with good depth of ripe, plummy, spicy, slightly nutty and peppery flavours, gentle tannins, and lots of drink-young charm.

DRY $29 –V

Giesen Single Vineyard Selection Clayvin Marlborough Syrah   ★★★★☆

From mature vines in the Brancott Valley, the 2012 vintage (★★★★) is dark, with a fragrant, peppery, spicy, earthy, savoury bouquet. It has rich, ripe plum, spice and dried-herb flavours, strongly seasoned with oak, and good texture and complexity.

DRY $70 –V

Giesen The Brothers Marlborough Syrah   (★★★★☆)

Still on sale, the 2011 vintage (★★★★☆) is a cool-climate, vibrantly fruity style, hand-picked from mature vines in the upper Brancott Valley. Deeply coloured and weighty, it has impressive concentration of plum and black-pepper flavours, seasoned with toasty oak, savoury notes adding complexity, and a long, firmly structured finish.

Vintage	11
WR	6
Drink	16-20

DRY $50 –V

Glazebrook Hawke's Bay Syrah   ★★★

The 2013 vintage (★★★) is a strongly varietal red with deep colour. Mouthfilling and vibrantly fruity, it has good depth of fresh plum and black-pepper flavours, and gentle tannins.

DRY $20 –V

Goldie Reserve Waiheke Island Syrah   (★★★★☆)

Well worth cellaring, the 2013 vintage (★★★★☆) was matured for 14 months in French oak barriques (30 per cent new). It is powerful (14.8 per cent alcohol), rich and vibrant, with good weight, strong, fresh plum and spice flavours and supple tannins.

DRY $60 –V

Goldie Waiheke Island Syrah   ★★★★☆

Delicious from the start, the 2013 vintage (★★★★☆) is a dark, softly mouthfilling red (14.8 per cent alcohol), with rich, beautifully ripe plum and black-pepper flavours. A big wine, in terms of body and flavour, it is intensely varietal and very harmonious, with finely integrated oak (French, 20 per cent new) and gentle tannins.

DRY $42 –V

Harwood Hall Marlborough Syrah   ★★☆

Matured for a year in French oak barriques, the easy-drinking 2013 vintage (★★☆) is a ruby-hued, medium-bodied wine with plum, spice and slight herb flavours, showing a touch of complexity, and a smooth finish. Drink now.

DRY $24 –V

Hopesgrove Estate Silver Lining Hawke's Bay Syrah   (★★★★☆)

Currently on sale, the 2010 vintage (★★★★☆) is a rare wine (only 70 cases were produced), hand-harvested and matured in French oak casks (50 per cent new). Deep and still fairly youthful in colour, it has a fragrant bouquet of spices and olives. A powerful, sturdy wine (14.5 per cent alcohol), it is concentrated, firmly structured and likely to be long-lived; best drinking 2017+.

Vintage	10	
WR	5	
Drink	16-25	

 DRY $65 –V

Hopesgrove Estate Single Vineyard Hawke's Bay Syrah   ★★★★☆

Estate-grown and hand-picked, the 2011 vintage (★★★★) is deeply coloured, mouthfilling and generous, with concentrated, plummy, spicy flavours and a fairly firm finish. The 2013 vintage (★★★★☆) was matured in French oak casks (40 per cent new). Dark and youthful, it is mouthfilling and strongly varietal, with rich, plummy, peppery flavours, showing good complexity, and a finely textured, harmonious finish. Best drinking 2017+.

Vintage	13	12	11
WR	6	NM	4
Drink	17-25	NM	16-19

 DRY $45 –V

Johner Gladstone Syrah   ★★★☆

Dark and youthful in colour, the mouthfilling, supple 2013 vintage (★★★★) was matured in French oak casks (30 per cent new). Finely textured, it is rich and smooth, with strong, ripe plum/spice flavours, showing good complexity. Drink now or cellar.

Vintage	13	
WR	6	
Drink	16-25	

 DRY $50 –V

Kaimira Estate Brightwater Syrah   ★★★

The 2012 vintage (★★★) was grown in Nelson and matured for over a year in French and American oak casks (25 per cent new). Deep and bright in colour, it is a medium-bodied wine, with vibrant plum and red-berry flavours, woven with fresh acidity, and a smooth finish.

Vintage	12	
WR	5	
Drink	16-21	

 DRY $35 –V

Kainui Road Bay of Islands Syrah   (★★★☆)

The 2013 vintage (★★★☆) is a deeply coloured, mouthfilling red, French oak-aged. Floral and fresh, it has strong plum and black-pepper flavours, with a finely textured, smooth finish.

DRY $35 –V

Karikari Estate Syrah ★★★★

Showing what can be achieved with Syrah in the warmth of the Far North, the powerful 2013 vintage (★★★★☆) was estate-grown on the Karikari Peninsula. The colour is deep and youthful; the palate is sturdy and well-rounded, with very generous, plummy, spicy, nutty flavours, ripe tannins and a fragrant, slightly peppery bouquet. Concentrated, with earthy notes adding complexity, it's a very age-worthy red, but already drinking well.

Landing [The] Bay of Islands Syrah ★★★★

The stylish, fine-value 2013 vintage (★★★★☆) was grown at the Mountain Landing Vineyard, in Northland, and matured for 18 months in French oak barriques (30 per cent new). The colour is deep and purple-flushed; the palate is powerful, sweet-fruited and concentrated, with dense, ripe, plummy, spicy flavours, showing good structure and complexity. Already approachable, it's likely to be at its best 2018+.

Vintage	13
WR	5
Drink	16-19

Left Field Hawke's Bay Syrah ★★★☆

The 2014 vintage (★★★☆) was estate-grown in the Gimblett Gravels and matured for a year in French oak casks (5 per cent new). It's a mouthfilling red with very good depth of plummy, spicy flavours, showing some savoury complexity, and a moderately firm finish. The 2015 vintage (★★★★) is delicious young. It's a generous, mouthfilling wine, with ripe plum, spice and black-pepper flavours, gentle tannins, good complexity and a well-rounded finish. (From Te Awa.)

Vintage	15	14
WR	5	5
Drink	17-21	16-20

Leveret Estate Hawke's Bay Syrah ★★★☆

The 2014 vintage (★★★☆) is a fruit-driven style, blended from Syrah (95 per cent) and Viognier (5 per cent). Full-coloured and supple, with vibrant plum and black-pepper flavours, fresh and generous, it's delicious young.

Vintage	14	13
WR	7	7
Drink	16-21	16-20

DRY $20 AV

Leveret Estate Reserve Hawke's Bay Syrah ★★★★

The 2014 vintage (★★★★), blended with Viognier (5 per cent), is full-coloured, sturdy and generous, with ripe plum/spice flavours, savoury notes adding complexity, good backbone and excellent depth. Best drinking 2017+.

Vintage	14	13
WR	7	7
Drink	18-25	18-25

Linden Estate Esk Valley Reserve Syrah (★★★☆)

The 2013 vintage (★★★☆) was matured for 19 months in French oak casks. Full and bright in colour, it is mouthfilling, with strong plum/spice flavours, a hint of tamarillo, balanced tannins and considerable complexity. Drink now onwards.

DRY $50 –V

Linden Estate Hawke's Bay Syrah ★★★☆

Worth cellaring, the 2014 vintage (★★★☆) was hand-picked in the Esk Valley and Bridge Pa Triangle sub-regions, and French oak-matured for a year. Full-coloured, it is mouthfilling, with very good depth of youthful plum, spice and tamarillo flavours, nutty, savoury notes adding complexity, and a fairly firm finish. Best drinking mid-2017+.

DRY $30 –V

Mad Dog Vineyard Bay of Islands Syrah (★★★)

Grown in Northland and matured for a year in new American oak casks, the 2013 vintage (★★★) is a full-coloured, medium-bodied red, with fresh, plummy, peppery flavours, a smooth finish, and an easy-drinking charm.

Vintage	13
WR	6
Drink	P

DRY $22 –V

Mahinepua Bay Shiraz (★★★☆)

From a coastal site in Northland – well north of the Bay of Islands – the deeply coloured 2014 vintage (★★★☆) is labelled Shiraz (a synonym for Syrah, used far more frequently in Australia). Mouthfilling and sweet-fruited, it has good depth of fresh plum/spice flavours and a fairly firm finish.

DRY $35 –V

Mahurangi River Winery Reserve Syrah (★★★★☆)

Grown at Matakana, the classy 2013 vintage (★★★★☆) was matured for a year in French oak casks (65 per cent new). Full-coloured, it is a graceful, savoury, concentrated red with vibrant, well-ripened plum, spice and black-pepper flavours, showing excellent complexity and depth, and a finely textured, long finish.

Vintage	13
WR	6
Drink	16-22

DRY $60 –V

Maimai Hawke's Bay Syrah ★★★

The 2013 vintage (★★★★) – clearly the best yet – is intensely floral, with bold colour. Full-bodied, vibrant and supple, it offers ripe plum and black-pepper flavours, fresh and concentrated, in an intensely varietal, 'fruit bomb' style with gentle tannins and loads of drink-young charm.

DRY $25 –V

Man O' War Waiheke Island Bellerophon Syrah/Viognier   ★★★★☆

Designed as an alternative to Man O' War's more 'robust' Dreadnought Syrah, this is intended to be 'more feminine, savoury, funky', with 3 per cent Viognier included in the blend and limited use of new oak (25 per cent in 2014). The 2014 vintage (★★★★☆) is full-coloured, fragrant and supple, with strong, vibrant, plummy, spicy flavours, showing excellent complexity. Best drinking 2018+.

Vintage	14
WR	7
Drink	16-21

 DRY $59 –V

Man O' War Waiheke Island Dreadnought Syrah   ★★★★★

Estate-grown at the eastern end of the island, the classy 2013 vintage (★★★★★) was harvested at 24.7–26.6 brix and matured for two years in French oak puncheons (50 per cent new). Dark and deep, it is sturdy (14.5 per cent alcohol), with an inviting, peppery fragrance. Already delicious, but also well worth cellaring, it is finely textured, with gentle tannins and highly concentrated, ripe blackcurrant, plum, spice and nut flavours. Best drinking 2018+. The 2014 vintage (★★★★★) was matured in French oak casks (30 per cent new). Bold and youthful in colour, it is a classy, highly concentrated, well-structured red, with dense, ripe blackcurrant, plum and spice flavours, a hint of liquorice and fine-grained tannins. It should be long-lived; open 2019+.

Vintage	14
WR	6
Drink	16-21

 DRY $52 AV

Marsden Bay of Islands Vigot Syrah   ★★★★

The 2014 vintage (★★★★☆) is a deeply coloured Northland red, matured for a year in French oak casks (30 per cent new). Mouthfilling and firmly structured, it is concentrated, with ripe plum and spice flavours, seasoned with nutty oak, and excellent complexity and density. Well worth cellaring.

Vintage	14	13
WR	6	6
Drink	16-20	16-19

 DRY $40 –V

Martinborough Vineyard Limited Edition Martinborough Syrah/Viognier   ★★★☆

The floral 2014 vintage (★★★☆) includes a splash of Viognier. The colour is full and youthful; the palate is supple and graceful, with plum, spice and black-pepper flavours, showing some savoury complexity, and a Pinot Noir-ish texture. A graceful rather than powerful style, it should be at its best mid-2017+.

DRY $48 –V

Matua Single Vineyard Hawke's Bay Syrah ★★★★★

The instantly attractive 2014 vintage (★★★★★) was estate-grown in the Matheson Vineyard, in the Bridge Pa Triangle, hand-picked and matured in French (mostly) and American oak barrels. Deeply coloured, it is mouthfilling, with fresh, concentrated, plummy, peppery flavours, ripe and generous, savoury notes adding complexity, and a very finely textured, smooth finish. Best drinking 2017+.

Mills Reef Elspeth Gimblett Gravels Hawke's Bay Syrah ★★★★★

In top vintages, this is one of Hawke's Bay's greatest Syrahs. The 2013 (★★★★★), hand-picked in the company's Mere Road and Trust Block vineyards, was matured for 17 months in French oak hogsheads (46 per cent new). Deeply coloured, it is deliciously fragrant and supple, with fresh, concentrated plum and black-pepper flavours and a sustained, spicy finish. Rich, finely textured and very harmonious, it's already drinking well, but should be at its best 2017+.

Vintage	13	12	11	10	09
WR	7	NM	7	7	7
Drink	16-25	NM	16-18	16-18	16-18

Mills Reef Elspeth Trust Vineyard Gimblett Gravels Hawke's Bay Syrah ★★★★

The 2013 vintage (★★★★☆) was grown principally (87 per cent) in the company's Trust Vineyard and matured for 15 months in French (80 per cent) and American (20 per cent) oak hogsheads (41 per cent new). Full-coloured, it is floral, vibrantly fruity and supple, with strong, ripe plum and black-pepper flavours and a softly textured finish. A refined rather than powerful red, it's delicious young. (Note: the name 'Trust Vineyard' appears only on the back label.)

Vintage	13	12	11	10	09
WR	7	NM	7	7	7
Drink	16-25	NM	16-17	16-18	16-18

Mills Reef Estate Hawke's Bay Syrah (★★★)

The 2014 vintage (★★★), estate-grown in Mere Road, in the Gimblett Gravels, was matured for nine months in a 50:50 split of French and American oak barrels. Full-coloured, it is mouthfilling, plummy and spicy, in a clearly varietal, vibrantly fruity style, showing a touch of complexity.

Vintage	14
WR	7
Drink	16-18

DRY $18 AV

Mills Reef Reserve Gimblett Gravels Hawke's Bay Syrah ★★★★

The easy-drinking 2015 vintage (★★★☆) was grown at two sites and matured for eight months in French oak casks (72 per cent), American oak casks (8 per cent) and tanks (20 per cent). Full-coloured, it is fresh and vibrantly fruity, with very good depth of plum and spice flavours, showing moderate complexity, and a smooth, well-rounded finish. Best drinking mid-2017+.

Vintage	15	14	13	12	11	10
WR	7	7	7	6	7	7
Drink	16-21	16-20	16-19	P	P	P

DRY $25 AV

Mission Hawke's Bay Syrah ★★★

A highly enjoyable, drink-young red, the 2015 vintage (★★★) is 'lightly oaked'. Fresh and smooth, it's a fruit-driven style, strongly varietal, with plenty of vibrant, plummy, peppery flavour.

DRY $18 AV

Mission Huchet Gimblett Gravels Syrah ★★★★★

Named in honour of nineteenth-century winemaker Cyprian Huchet, the 2013 vintage (★★★★★) is a powerful red with a fragrant, spicy bouquet. Estate-grown in Mere Road, in the Gimblett Gravels, and French oak-matured for 18 months (33 per cent new), it is deeply coloured, with a fragrant, spicy bouquet. Still a baby, it is mouthfilling, with richly varietal, concentrated blackcurrant, plum and spice flavours, fine-grained tannins, and a very harmonious finish. An elegant, youthful red, it should be at its best 2018+.

Vintage	13	12	11	10	09	08	07
WR	7	NM	NM	6	NM	NM	6
Drink	16-25	NM	NM	16-23	NM	NM	16-20

DRY $130 –V

Mission Jewelstone Hawke's Bay Syrah ★★★★★

The 2013 vintage (★★★★★) was grown in the Gimblett Gravels and matured in French oak casks (33 per cent new). Dark and purple-flushed, it is powerful and concentrated, yet supple, with lovely plum and spice flavours that build to a savoury, lasting finish. Classy, youthful, elegant and tight-knit, it's a top year. The 2014 vintage (★★★★) is a dark, concentrated red, matured for a year in French oak casks (23 per cent new). It has rich, well-ripened flavours of blackcurrants, plums and spices, with a finely textured finish.

Vintage	14	13
WR	7	7
Drink	17-30	16-30

DRY $45 AV

Mission Reserve Gimblett Gravels Hawke's Bay Syrah   ★★★★

The 2015 vintage (★★★★) was hand-picked and matured in French oak casks (15 per cent new). Dark and purple-flushed, with strong plum/spice flavours and some earthy, gamey notes adding complexity, it is firm, peppery and savoury, with very good depth, structure and potential.

Vintage	15
WR	5
Drink	17-22

 DRY $25 AV

Mission Vineyard Selection Hawke's Bay Syrah   ★★★☆

The deeply coloured 2015 vintage (★★★☆) was partly grown in the Gimblett Gravels and mostly barrel-aged. It has a fresh, strong, peppery bouquet, mouthfilling body, and generous, plummy, peppery, distinctly spicy flavours, gently seasoned with oak. Best drinking mid-2017+.

 DRY $20 AV

Moana Park Gimblett Road Syrah   ★★★

The 2013 vintage (★★★), barrel-aged for a year and bottled unfiltered, is full-coloured, with fresh, strong plum and spice flavours.

Vintage	13
WR	6
Drink	16-20

 DRY $23 –V

Mount Riley Marlborough Syrah   ★★★

Estate-grown in the 17 Valley Vineyard, hand-picked and oak-aged, the 2013 vintage (★★★☆) is ruby-hued, fruity and supple, with good depth of fresh, ripe cherry, plum and spice flavours, gentle tannins, and drink-young appeal.

Vintage	13
WR	5
Drink	16-18

 DRY $22 –V

Mudbrick Vineyard Reserve Syrah   ★★★★★

From Waiheke Island, the 2013 vintage (★★★★★) was hand-picked and matured for nine months in French oak barriques (35 per cent new). Deep and youthful in colour, it is a refined, mouthfilling, supple wine with concentrated plum and black-pepper flavours, integrated oak, fine-grained tannins, and a long, spicy finish. Very stylish and age-worthy, it's already delicious.

Vintage	13	12
WR	7	6
Drink	16-25	16-23

 DRY $55 AV

Murdoch James Martinborough Blue Rock Syrah   ★★★☆

Worth cellaring, the 2014 vintage (★★★☆) is a medium-bodied style, bright ruby, fruity and supple. Estate-grown in the Blue Rock Vineyard, it is a tightly structured, distinctly cool-climate red, with very good depth of fresh, plummy, spicy, peppery flavours.

DRY $50 –V

Nanny Goat Vineyard Central Otago Syrah   ★★★☆

The 2015 vintage (★★★☆) is full-coloured, with an attractively scented bouquet. It has gentle tannins and ripe, plummy, spicy, slightly peppery flavours, showing very good balance and depth. Best drinking 2018+.

DRY $36 –V

Ngatarawa Proprietors' Reserve Hawke's Bay Syrah   (★★★★★)

The debut 2013 vintage (★★★★★) is a refined wine, grown in the Bridge Pa Triangle. Dark, with youthful, purple-flushed colour, it is mouthfilling, with rich, vibrant plum and black-pepper flavours, good density, a nutty oak complexity, and a long, firm, spicy finish. A strongly varietal red, it's likely to be at its best from 2018 owwards.

DRY $40 AV

Ngatarawa Stables Reserve Hawke's Bay Syrah   ★★★

The 2014 vintage (★★★☆) is full-coloured, with very good depth of plum, spice and black-pepper flavours, ripe and smooth. The 2015 vintage (★★★) is deep ruby, with plummy, spicy flavours, showing some earthy, gamey notes.

Vintage	15	14	13
WR	6	5	7
Drink	16-20	16-20	16-17

DRY $20 –V

Obsidian Reserve Waiheke Island Syrah   ★★★★★

Already delicious, the impressive 2013 vintage (★★★★★) was matured for a year in French oak casks (40 per cent new). Deeply coloured, it is mouthfilling, sweet-fruited and dense, with rich, ripe blackcurrant, plum and black-pepper flavours, good tannin backbone, and a long, spicy finish. Still youthful, it shows obvious potential; best drinking 2018+.

Vintage	13	12
WR	7	6
Drink	16-23	16-20

DRY $63 AV

Obsidian Waiheke Island Syrah   ★★★★☆

The 2014 vintage (★★★★☆), matured in French oak casks (20 per cent new), is a dark, youthful, mouthfilling red, with concentrated, well-ripened plum, spice and black-pepper flavours. Vibrant, with good density and supple, fine-grained tannins, it's well worth cellaring.

Vintage	13	12
WR	7	6
Drink	16-20	16-18

DRY $35 AV

Okahu Estate Syrah ★★★★

The 2014 vintage (★★★★) of this Northland red is generous and savoury, with fine-grained tannins, good weight and strong, ripe plum/spice flavours.

DRY $59 –V

Omata Estate Old Vines Russell Syrah (★★★★★)

The outstanding 2013 vintage (★★★★★) of this Northland red is from vines planted in 1996. Deeply coloured, it is finely scented, with highly concentrated, ripe plum and spice flavours, a hint of dark chocolate, and fine-grained tannins. A poised, immaculate wine, it's already delicous, but likely to be at its best 2017+.

DRY $55 AV

Omata Estate Russell Syrah (★★★★)

From the estate's younger vines, the 2013 vintage (★★★★) is dark and rich, with mouthfilling body, strong, ripe plum and spice flavours, and gentle tannins. It's an excellent example of the recent wave of classy Northland reds.

DRY $39 –V

Paritua Hawke's Bay Syrah ★★★★

The dark, floral 2013 vintage (★★★★) was matured for over a year in oak barrels (50 per cent new). Full-bodied and supple, it is vibrantly fruity, with strong, youthful plum and black-pepper flavours, showing good complexity, and a well-rounded finish. It's already enjoyable, but well worth cellaring.

Vintage	13
WR	6
Drink	16-25

DRY $40 –V

Paroa Bay Bay of Islands Syrah ★★★☆

The 2014 vintage (★★★) is a deeply coloured Bay of Islands, Northland red with a perfumed, spicy bouquet. It has red-berry, spice and toasty oak flavours (French, new), with a firmly structured finish.

DRY $40 –V

Pask Declaration Hawke's Bay Syrah ★★★★

The 2013 vintage (★★★★) was estate-grown in Gimblett Road and matured for 16 months in French oak casks (70 per cent new). Deeply coloured, with a fragrant, spicy bouquet, it is mouthfilling and supple, with vibrant, ripe blackcurrant, plum and spice flavours, a hint of dark chocolate, fresh acidity and gentle tannins. The 2014 vintage (★★★★☆) is deeply coloured, mouthfilling, ripe and rounded, with generous plum/spice flavours, savoury and complex, and instant appeal. Best drinking 2018+.

Vintage	14	13
WR	6	6
Drink	19-22	17-21

DRY $50 –V

Pask Gimblett Road Hawke's Bay Syrah   ★★★☆

Estate-grown, the 2014 vintage (★★★☆) was matured for a year in old French oak casks. Full-coloured, it is mouthfilling and fairly firm, with strong, ripe plum/spice flavours, a hint of nuts, and a slightly chewy finish.

Vintage	14	13
WR	6	6
Drink	16-20	16-19

DRY $22 AV

Passage Rock Reserve Waiheke Island Syrah   ★★★★★

Waiheke's most awarded wine of the past decade is partly estate-grown at Te Matuku Bay, on the south side of the island, supplemented by fruit from Oneroa. Matured in American and French oak barriques, mostly new, it is typically a powerful, opulent red, rich and well-rounded. The 2014 vintage (★★★★★) is still very youthful. Dark, full-bodied and sweet-fruited, with vibrant blackcurrant, plum and spice flavours, it is notably concentrated, but also supple and fragrant. Best drinking 2018+.

DRY $55 AV

Passage Rock Waiheke Island Syrah   ★★★★★

This Waiheke Island red is consistently rewarding. Partly estate-grown and fully matured for a year in American (mostly) and French oak barriques (30 per cent new), the 2014 vintage (★★★★☆) is deeply coloured, mouthfilling, fresh and supple. A generous, strongly varietal red, it is sturdy, with ripe, plummy, spicy flavours, showing excellent concentration and complexity, and good cellaring potential.

DRY $35 V+

Peter Yealands Hawke's Bay Syrah   ★★★

Full-coloured, the 2013 vintage (★★★) is mouthfilling, vibrantly fruity and smooth, with satisfying depth of fresh plum, spice and black-pepper flavours, gentle tannins, and drink-young appeal.

Vintage	13	12
WR	7	7
Drink	16-18	P

DRY $19 AV

Peter Yealands Reserve Hawke's Bay Syrah   (★★★☆)

The generous 2013 vintage (★★★☆) is deeply coloured, with mouthfilling body and fresh, strong plum and black-pepper flavours. A vibrantly fruity style, with a gentle oak influence, it's a drink-now or cellaring proposition.

Vintage	13
WR	7
Drink	16-18

DRY $21 AV

Quarter Acre Hawke's Bay Syrah   (★★★★★)

The classy 2013 vintage (★★★★★) was hand-harvested at two sites and matured in French oak barriques (40 per cent new). Full and very youthful in colour, it is mouthfilling, concentrated and supple, with deep, ripe plum and black-pepper flavours and a well-rounded finish. A generous, finely textured red, it should be long-lived, but is already delicious. Fine value.

DRY $35 V+

Ransom K Matakana Syrah   ★★★★☆

The 2013 vintage (★★★★) is fragrant, rich and supple. Medium to full-bodied, it's a very approachable red with ripe plum and spice flavours, a gentle seasoning of nutty oak, and a finely textured, smooth finish.

DRY $33 AV

Redmetal Basket Press Hawke's Bay Syrah   ★★★★☆

Grown in the Bridge Pa Triangle and barrel-aged for over a year, the 2013 vintage (★★★★) is deeply coloured and fragrant, with fresh, ripe plum/spice flavours, slightly peppery and nutty, and good concentration and harmony. A youthful, vibrant and strongly varietal wine, it's well worth cellaring. The 2014 vintage (★★★★☆) was oak-aged for nine months. Deeply coloured, it is mouthfilling, with dense, very ripe blackcurrant and spice flavours, a hint of liquorice, and good complexity. A powerful, extroverted wine, it's already drinking well, but also age-worthy.

DRY $32 AV

Vintage	14	13
WR	5	5
Drink	16-23	16-20

Rochfort Rees Gimblett Gravels Hawke's Bay Syrah   (★★★★)

The full-coloured, youthful 2013 vintage (★★★★) is a mouthfilling red with good concentration of ripe plum and black-pepper flavours, nutty oak adding complexity, finely balanced tannins and a well-spiced finish. Well worth cellaring.

DRY $32 –V

Sacred Hill Deerstalkers Hawke's Bay Syrah   ★★★★★

Estate-grown and hand-picked in the Gimblett Gravels, fermented with indigenous yeasts and matured for 16 months in French oak barriques (30 per cent new), the 2014 vintage (★★★★★) is dark, with a slightly peppery, beautifully perfumed bouquet. Rich, ripe and supple, it's an elegant, finely textured wine with dense, but not tough, blackcurrant, plum and spice flavours, a hint of dark chocolate, and a long, harmonious finish. Still a baby, it should be at its best 2020+.

DRY $60 AV

Vintage	14	13	12	11	10	09	08
WR	7	7	6	NM	7	7	6
Drink	16-24	16-22	16-20	NM	16-19	16-18	P

Sacred Hill Halo Hawke's Bay Syrah   ★★★☆

The 2014 vintage (★★★★) was hand-picked and matured for a year in French oak barrels (20 per cent new). A mouthfilling, generous wine, it has concentrated plum, pepper and spice flavours, in a clearly varietal style, with gentle tannins and lots of drink-young appeal.

Vintage	14	13	12
WR	6	7	6
Drink	16-20	16-18	P

DRY $30 –V

Sacred Hill Reserve Hawke's Bay Syrah   ★★★☆

A 'fruit-driven' style, the debut 2014 vintage (★★★☆) was hand-harvested and matured 'on', rather than 'in', French oak (meaning not barrel-aged). Full-coloured, with a floral, spicy bouquet, it has fresh plum and black-pepper flavours, gentle tannins and very good depth. The 2015 vintage (★★★) was matured for eight months in seasoned French barrels. Ruby-hued, it is peppery and slightly herbal, in a smooth, vibrantly fruity style, offering easy, early drinking.

Vintage	15
WR	6
Drink	16-18

DRY $30 –V

Saint Clair Gimblett Gravels Hawke's Bay Syrah   ★★★☆

The 2014 vintage (★★★★) is finely balanced for early consumption, but also worth cellaring. An estate-grown, single-vineyard red, partly barrel-aged, it is full-coloured, with a perfumed bouquet, strong plum and black-pepper flavours, gentle tannins and excellent harmony.

DRY $27 –V

Saint Clair James Sinclair Gimblett Gravels Hawke's Bay Syrah   (★★★☆)

Partly oak-aged, the 2014 vintage (★★★☆) is a youthful, deeply coloured red, estate-grown in the Plateau Vineyard. Medium to full-bodied, it is strongly varietal, with plum, spice and black-pepper aromas and flavours, fresh, vibrant and smooth. Best drinking 2017+.

DRY $25 –V

Saint Clair Pioneer Block 17 Plateau Block
Gimblett Gravels Hawke's Bay Syrah   ★★★★

The 2015 vintage (★★★★) was matured for 11 months in French oak casks (30 per cent new). A fresh, rich, youthful red, it is deeply coloured and mouthfilling, with ripe plum, spice and liquorice flavours that linger well.

DRY $38 –V

Satyr Hawke's Bay Syrah   ★★★

From Sileni, the 2015 vintage (★★★) is a medium-bodied, smooth red with fullish colour and good depth of fresh, spicy flavours, showing a touch of complexity. Best drinking mid-2017+.

DRY $20 –V

Sculptureum Cezanne Syrah   (★★★★☆)

The 2013 vintage (★★★★☆) is a boldly coloured Matakana red, fresh and full-bodied. Strongly varietal, with concentrated plum and black-pepper flavours, slightly earthy notes adding complexity and balanced tannins, it's an age-worthy red. Priced right.

 DRY $30 AV

Seifried Nelson Syrah   ★★★

Grown at Brightwater, on the Waimea Plains, the attractive 2014 vintage (★★★☆) has a Pinot Noir-ish appeal. Light ruby, it is mouthfilling and supple, with lively, ripe plum/spice flavours, gentle tannins, and very good vigour and depth. It's delicious young. The 2015 vintage (★★☆) was matured for 15 months in new, one and two-year-old barriques. Lightish in colour, it is mouthfilling, with moderately ripe, spicy, slightly herbal and nutty flavours, showing a touch of complexity, and a smooth finish.

Vintage	15
WR	5
Drink	16-20

 DRY $20 –V

Selaks Reserve Hawke's Bay Syrah   (★★★☆)

The ruby-hued 2013 vintage (★★★☆) is a medium-bodied style with very good depth of ripe red-berry, plum and pepper flavours, showing some nutty oak complexity. Drink now or cellar.

 DRY $20 AV

Sileni Cellar Selection Hawke's Bay Syrah   ★★★☆

The 2015 vintage (★★★☆) is deeply coloured, with a fresh, peppery bouquet. Medium-bodied and supple, with strong, vibrant fruit flavours and a touch of complexity, it is a very good drink-young style, with an almost Pinot Noir-ish texture and charm. Best drinking mid-2017+.

Vintage	15	14	13
WR	7	6	6
Drink	16-21	16-20	16-19

 DRY $20 AV

Sileni Estate Selection Peak Hawke's Bay Syrah   ★★★★

Deeply coloured, the 2015 vintage (★★★★) was grown in the Bridge Pa Triangle and matured for nine months in French oak casks (12 per cent new). It has a fragrant, fresh, spicy bouquet, leading into a full-bodied, strongly varietal wine, with good complexity and excellent depth of plum, spice and black-pepper flavours. Best drinking 2018+.

Vintage	15	14	13
WR	7	6	7
Drink	16-23	16-22	16-23

DRY $33 –V

Sileni Exceptional Vintage Hawke's Bay Syrah   (★★★★★)

The delicious 2013 vintage (★★★★★) was matured for 10 months in French oak casks (60 per cent new). Dark and mouthfilling, with sweet-fruit characters and concentrated blackcurrant, plum, spice and liquorice flavours, it's an impressively weighty and complex red, finely textured and long.

Vintage	13
WR	7
Drink	16-23

DRY $70 –V

Soho Valentina Waiheke Island Syrah   ★★★★☆

Estate-grown at Onetangi, the 2014 vintage (★★★★☆) was matured for nine months in French and American oak barriques (14 per cent new). Richly coloured, with fresh, deep blackcurrant, plum and black-pepper flavours, it is mouthfilling, sweet-fruited and supple, with good concentration and fine-grained tannins. Already enjoyable, it should be at its best 2017+.

DRY $37 AV

Spade Oak Heart of Gold Gisborne Syrah/Tempranillo   ★★★☆

Estate-grown and barrel-aged, the 2013 vintage (★★★☆) is deeply coloured and fragrant, with good depth of fresh, ripe plum and spice flavours, gently seasoned with sweet oak, considerable complexity and a smooth finish. Drink now or cellar.

DRY $23 AV

Spade Oak Vineyard Voysey Gisborne Syrah   ★★★

The 2013 vintage (★★☆) is a blend of Syrah (90 per cent) and Viognier (10 per cent). Full-coloured, it's a slightly earthy red with plummy, berryish and spicy flavours, showing decent depth.

DRY $19 AV

Spy Valley Marlborough Syrah   ★★★☆

An elegant, cool-climate style, the 2013 vintage (★★★★) was hand-picked at up to 24.6 brix, fermented with indigenous yeasts and barrel-aged for over two years. Deep, bright ruby, it is mouthfilling and supple, with strong, vibrant plum, spice and nut flavours, showing good complexity, and a tightly structured finish. Best drinking 2018+.

Vintage	13	12	11	10	09
WR	5	7	6	6	5
Drink	16-18	16-18	16-17	P	P

DRY $32 –V

Squawking Magpie Gimblett Gravels Stoned Crow Syrah   ★★★★☆

The 2014 vintage (★★★★★) is an estate-grown, single-vineyard red, matured for 20 months in French oak casks (partly new). Dark and youthful in colour, it is fragrant and rich, with concentrated, ripe plum and spice flavours, seasoned with nutty oak, excellent complexity and a finely textured, long finish. A classy young red, it's already enjoyable, but should be at its best 2018+.

Vintage	14	13
WR	7	7
Drink	16-35	16-35

DRY $50 –V

Squawking Magpie The Chatterer Gimblett Gravels Hawke's Bay Syrah   ★★★★

Still very youthful, the 2014 vintage (★★★★) of this barrel-aged red is deeply coloured, with a fragrant, spicy bouquet. A strongly varietal wine, it is mouthfilling, with vibrant plum and black-pepper flavours, showing excellent ripeness, depth and harmony.

Vintage	14
WR	6
Drink	16-25

DRY $25 AV

Stone Paddock Hawke's Bay Syrah   (★★★☆)

From Paritua, the 2013 vintage (★★★☆) was matured for a year in seasoned oak casks. Deeply coloured, it is fragrant, with generous plum/spice flavours and a moderately firm finish. Drink now or cellar.

Vintage	13
WR	6
Drink	16-20

DRY $25 –V

Stonecroft Gimblett Gravels Hawke's Bay Reserve Syrah   ★★★★★

Certified organic, the very classy 2014 vintage (★★★★★) was harvested from estate-grown vines, including the region's first Syrah plantings in 1984. Matured for 18 months in French oak casks (40 per cent new), it has dark, youthful colour. Mouthfilling, very rich and flowing, it is vibrant and supple, with concentrated, beautifully ripe blackcurrant, plum and spice flavours, showing lovely texture, harmony and length.

Vintage	14	13	12	11	10	09
WR	7	7	6	NM	7	6
Drink	19-26	18-25	16-24	NM	16-23	16-22

DRY $65 AV

Stonecroft Gimblett Gravels Hawke's Bay Serine Syrah ★★★★

Certified organic, the 2014 vintage (★★★★) was estate-grown at Mere Road and Roys Hill, hand-harvested and matured for 18 months in French oak casks (35 per cent new). Fresh and elegant, rather than powerful, it is deeply coloured, with a floral, slightly earthy bouquet. Vibrantly fruity, it is a youthful, medium to full-bodied red, with strong plum/spice flavours, showing clear-cut varietal character, and very good density and complexity. Best drinking 2018+.

Vintage	14	13	12	11	10	09
WR	6	7	5	NM	7	7
Drink	16-21	16-21	16-20	NM	16-18	P

DRY $31 –V

Stonecroft The Original Gimblett Gravels Hawke's Bay Syrah   (★★★★★)

Still a baby, the 2014 vintage (★★★★★) is rare – fewer than 300 bottles were produced. Hand-harvested from the original vines, planted in Mere Road in 1984, it was matured for 18 months in a single, new French oak barrique. Deeply coloured, it is mouthfilling, with dense, vibrant blackcurrant, plum and black-pepper flavours, firm and savoury. Built for a long life, it's well worth cellaring to 2019+.

Vintage	14
WR	7
Drink	19-26

DRY $100 AV

Stonyridge Faithful Waiheke Island Syrah   (★★★★)

Designed for early consumption, the 2015 vintage (★★★★) was matured in French oak casks (20 per cent new). Deeply coloured, it has a spicy, slightly earthy bouquet, leading into a full-bodied, sturdy wine with good concentration of fresh, ripe, plummy, spicy flavours.

DRY $35 –V

Stonyridge Pilgrim Waiheke Island
Syrah/Mourvedre/Viognier/Grenache   ★★★★★

This distinguished Rhône-style blend is estate-grown at Onetangi and matured for a year in French oak barriques (30 per cent new in 2015). The 2015 vintage (★★★★★) is delicious in its youth, but also well worth cellaring. Deeply coloured, it is sturdy (14.5 per alcohol), vibrantly fruity and supple, with dense plum and spice flavours, complex and savoury, and ripe, supple tannins. Very finely textured and harmonious, it's already highly approachable, but should be at its best 2020+.

Vintage	15
WR	7
Drink	17-25

DRY $95 AV

Summerhouse Marlborough Syrah   ★★★☆

The easy-drinking, fruity 2015 vintage (★★★☆) was matured in French oak barriques. The colour is deep and youthful; the palate is mouthfilling, with fresh, generous plum, spice and black-pepper flavours, showing a touch of complexity, and gentle tannins. Enjoyable young.

Vintage	15
WR	7
Drink	16-26

DRY $29 –V

Tantalus Voilé Reserve Waiheke Island Syrah   (★★★★☆)

Showing plenty of personality, the 2014 vintage (★★★★☆) was estate-grown and hand-picked at Onetangi and matured for 11 months in French oak barriques. Deep and youthful in colour, it is mouthfilling, with strong, ripe, plummy, spicy flavours, good tannin backbone, and an earthy, savoury, nutty complexity. Already drinking well, but still youthful, it should be at its best 2018+.

Vintage	14
WR	6
Drink	16-26

 DRY $60 –V

Te Awa Single Estate Hawke's Bay Syrah   ★★★☆

The elegant 2014 vintage (★★★★) was matured in French oak casks (35 per cent new). Very youthful, it is floral and fruit-packed, with deep, bright colour and a strong surge of fresh, plummy, peppery flavours, smooth and long.

Vintage	14	13
WR	7	7
Drink	17-24	16-23

 DRY $30 –V

Te Awanga Estate Hawke's Bay Syrah   ★★★★

Grown inland from Hastings, the 2014 vintage (★★★☆) was matured for 16 months in French oak barrels. Full ruby, it is floral and supple, in a medium-bodied style, with vibrant, ripe, moderately concentrated plum/spice flavours, and lots of drink-young charm.

 DRY $28 AV

Te Mania Nelson Syrah   ★★★

Certified organic, the 2013 vintage (★★★) is a ruby-hued, medium-bodied, strongly varietal red, with fresh plum and black-pepper flavours, showing a touch of complexity.

DRY $22 –V

Te Mata Estate Bullnose Syrah   ★★★★★

Grown in the Bullnose Vineyard, in the Bridge Pa Triangle inland from Hastings, in Hawke's Bay, this classy red is based on mature vines, hand-picked and matured for 15 to 16 months in French oak barriques (about 35 per cent new). Unlike its Estate Vineyards stablemate (below), it is not blended with Viognier, and the vines for the Bullnose label are cropped lower. Fragrant and richly coloured, the 2014 vintage (★★★★★) is a very elegant, supple red with concentrated, well-ripened plum/spice flavours, hints of black pepper and dark chocolate, fine-grained tannins, and a long, harmonious finish. Already delicious, it should be at its best 2018+.

Vintage	14	13	12	11	10	09	08	07	06
WR	7	7	7	6	7	7	7	7	7
Drink	17-24	16-23	16-21	16-19	16-19	16-19	P	16-17	P

 DRY $49 AV

Te Mata Estate Vineyards Hawke's Bay Syrah ★★★★

The 2015 vintage (★★★★) is already delicious. Estate-grown in the Dartmoor Valley and Bridge Pa Triangle, it was blended with a splash of Viognier and French oak-matured for seven months. Full-coloured, it is freshly scented, with strong plum, spice and black-pepper flavours, gentle tannins, and savoury notes adding complexity. Drink now or cellar. Fine value.

Vintage	15
WR	6
Drink	17-23

 DRY $20 V+

Te Rere Motukaha Reserve Waiheke Island Syrah (★★★★★)

The distinguished 2010 vintage (★★★★★) was grown in Church Bay Road, near the western end of the island. A rare wine (only 98 cases were produced), it's a blend of Syrah (92 per cent) and Cabernet Sauvignon (8 per cent), matured for 16 months in an even split of French and American oak casks (100 per cent new). A very powerful (14.8 per cent alcohol), commanding but not heavy wine, it is deep and still youthful in colour. Generous, sweet-fruited and harmonious, it has concentrated plum/spice flavours, with a hint of black pepper, fine-grained tannins and a long finish. Drinking well now, it should flourish for many years.

DRY $65 AV

Te Whau Vineyard Waiheke Island Syrah ★★★★☆

This wine is hand-picked from hill-grown vines, fermented with indigenous yeasts and matured for over a year in French oak barrels (partly new). The distinctive 2014 vintage (★★★★★) is full-coloured, fragrant and very finely textured. The bouquet is fragrant, ripe and spicy; the palate possesses a strong sense of youthful vigour, with strong, ripe plum, blackcurrant and nut flavours, very harmonious and lasting. Drink now onwards.

Vintage	14	13	12	11	10	09	08	07
WR	7	7	7	NM	7	7	7	7
Drink	17-24	16-23	16-25	NM	P	P	P	P

 DRY $110 -V

Terrace Edge Waipara Valley Syrah ★★★☆

Grown on a '45-degree north facing "roasted slope"' and matured for over a year in French oak (25 per cent new), the 2015 vintage (★★★☆) is certified organic. Deeply coloured, it is full-bodied and generous, with strongly varietal, peppery aromas and flavours, spicy and earthy notes adding interest, and considerable cellaring potential.

Vintage	15
WR	7
Drink	16-25

 DRY $31 -V

Theory & Practice Hawke's Bay Syrah (★★★☆)

The 2013 vintage (★★★☆) was grown mostly in the Bridge Pa Triangle and partly barrel-aged. It's a fragrant, finely balanced wine with strong, lively plum and spice flavours, gently seasoned with oak, and drink-young appeal.

DRY $25 -V

Tinpot Hut Hawke's Bay Syrah   ★★★

The full-coloured 2013 vintage (★★★) is a medium-bodied, finely textured wine with good depth of plummy, slightly spicy flavours, ripe and smooth.

 DRY $28 –V

Tohu Hawke's Bay Syrah   ★★★

The ruby-hued, easy-drinking 2014 vintage (★★★) was matured for over a year in old French oak barriques. It shows good depth of plummy, spicy flavours, with savoury notes adding a touch of complexity and gentle tannins. Drink now to 2018.

 DRY $28 –V

Trademark Hawke's Bay Syrah   (★★★★☆)

The 2011 vintage (★★★★☆) has deep, still fairly youthful colour. A powerful, sturdy red (14.5 per cent alcohol), it has concentrated plum, spice and liquorice flavours, seasoned with nutty oak. Fleshy and lush, it's an age-worthy wine; drink now or cellar. (From Rod McDonald.)

DRY $75 –V

Trinity Hill Gimblett Gravels Syrah   ★★★★★

Estate-grown in the Gimblett Gravels and matured for 14 months in French oak barriques and 5000-litre ovals (new and old), the 2014 vintage (★★★★☆) is a blend of Syrah (97 per cent) and Viognier (3 per cent). A stylish, youthful red, it is dark and fragrant, in a medium to full-bodied, vibrantly fruity style. It has strong, ripe plum, spice and black-pepper flavours, savoury notes adding complexity, and good cellaring potential. Best drinking 2018+.

Vintage	14	13	12	11	10	09	08
WR	7	6	5	5	7	7	5
Drink	17-25	16-25	16-18	16-18	16-20	16-20	P

 DRY $35 V+

Trinity Hill Hawke's Bay Syrah   ★★★★

The 2015 vintage (★★★★) is a good buy. Full-coloured, it is mouthfilling, with youthful, ripe plum and spice flavours, showing good density, and some savoury complexity. Delicious young, it should be at its best mid-2017+.

 DRY $22 V+

Trinity Hill Homage Hawke's Bay Syrah   ★★★★★

One of the country's most distinguished – and expensive – reds. Harvested by hand, mostly from 19-year-old vines in the Gimblett Gravels, the outstanding 2014 vintage (★★★★★) was matured for 14 months in French oak barriques (mostly new) and 5000-litre oak ovals. Dark and youthful in colour, it is mouthfilling, dense and yet supple, with a floral bouquet and highly concentrated plum, blackcurrant, spice and nut flavours. Impressively rich, complex and savoury, with good tannin backbone, it should flourish with long-term cellaring.

Vintage	14	13	12	11	10	09
WR	7	7	NM	NM	7	7
Drink	16-25	16-25	NM	NM	16-25	16-25

 DRY $130 AV

Vidal Legacy Gimblett Gravels Hawke's Bay Syrah ★★★★★

The outstanding 2014 vintage (★★★★★) was estate-grown in the Omahu Gravels and Twyford Gravels vineyards, and matured for 18 months in French oak barriques (38 per cent new). Deeply coloured, it is concentrated and silky-textured, with vibrant, densely packed, well-ripened plum and spice flavours, finely integrated oak and supple tannins. A highly refined wine, it's already approachable, but should blossom with long-term cellaring. Best drinking 2020+.

Vintage	14	13	12	11	10	09
WR	7	7	NM	7	7	7
Drink	16-28	16-25	NM	16-20	16-20	16-20

DRY $80 AV

Vidal Reserve Gimblett Gravels Hawke's Bay Syrah ★★★★

Priced sharply, the 2014 vintage (★★★★☆) was estate-grown and matured for 15 months in French oak barriques (20 per cent new). Deeply coloured, it has a complex bouquet, leading into a rich, youthful, well-structured palate with fresh acidity and vibrant plum, spice, black-pepper and nut flavours, finely textured and lingering. An obvious candidate for cellaring, it should be at its best 2018+.

Vintage	14	13	12	11	10	09
WR	7	7	6	6	7	7
Drink	16-23	16-22	16-18	16-17	P	P

DRY $25 AV

Villa Maria Anniversary Selection Gimblett Gravels Hawke's Bay Syrah   (★★★★★)

Sold only at the cellar door in Mangere, Auckland, the 2011 vintage (★★★★★) is Villa Maria's 'finest red wine produced from the 2011 vintage'. Matured for 17 months in French oak barriques (50 per cent new), it is dense and still youthful in colour. A powerful, sweet-fruited wine, it is savoury and complex, with rich, plummy, nutty flavours, a hint of liquorice, good tannin backbone, and obvious potential; best drinking 2018+.

DRY $115 –V

Villa Maria Cellar Selection Hawke's Bay Syrah ★★★★★

The refined, bargain-priced 2014 vintage (★★★★★) is an instantly appealing, deliciously rich and smooth-flowing red. Grown in the Gimblett Gravels (two-thirds) and the Bridge Pa Triangle (one-third), it was matured for 17 months in French oak barriques (20 per cent new). Mouthfilling and boldly coloured, it has concentrated plum, spice, liquorice and dark chocolate flavours, excellent fruit/oak balance and a silky-textured, long finish.

Vintage	14	13	12	11	10	09
WR	7	7	6	6	7	7
Drink	17-24	16-22	16-20	P	P	P

DRY $26 V+

Villa Maria Private Bin Hawke's Bay Shiraz   ★★★☆

The 2014 vintage (★★★★) is labelled 'Shiraz', rather than 'Syrah', to attract supermarket shoppers long familiar with Australian Shiraz. Matured in barrels (80 per cent) and tanks (20 per cent), it offers fine value. Boldly coloured, with deep, ripe, well-rounded flavours of spices and liquorice, it has a slightly earthy streak, and good acidity and length.

Vintage	14	13	12
WR	7	6	5
Drink	16-20	16-19	16-17

 DRY $20 AV

Villa Maria Reserve Gimblett Gravels Hawke's Bay Syrah   ★★★★★

The 2014 vintage (★★★★★) is a dark, purple-flushed, densely packed red, matured for 17 months in French oak barriques (35 per cent new). Still extremely youthful, it offers highly concentrated plum, spice and black-pepper flavours, with lovely fruity sweetness, integrated oak, good tannin support and a long, finely textured finish. Best drinking 2019+.

Vintage	14	13	12
WR	7	7	6
Drink	19-26	18-25	16-22

 DRY $60 AV

Waiheke Road Syrah   (★★★★)

The 2013 vintage (★★★★) is dark and fleshy, with strong plum and spice flavours, hints of herbs, olives and liquorice, and ripe, chewy tannins. (From Awaroa.)

DRY $34 –V

Wairau River Reserve Marlborough Syrah   ★★★★

A single-vineyard red, grown on the banks of the Wairau River, the generous, youthful 2015 vintage (★★★★) was matured in French oak casks and bottled unfined and unfiltered. Deeply coloured, it is full-bodied, with fresh, concentrated plum/spice flavours, gentle tannins, good harmony and a lingering finish. Drink now or cellar.

Vintage	15	14
WR	6	7
Drink	16-22	16-23

 DRY $40 –V

Waitapu Estate Intrepid Syrah/Tempranillo   (★★★)

Estate-grown, the 2013 vintage (★★★) is a blend of Syrah (50 per cent) and Tempranillo (50 per cent). French oak-aged for a year, it is deeply coloured, with fresh, plummy, spicy, slightly earthy flavours and a smooth finish.

DRY $25 –V

Waitapu Estate Reef View Syrah Tempranillo   (★★★)

The deeply coloured 2013 vintage (★★★) is a moderately ripe Northland blend of Syrah and Tempranillo. It has blackcurrant-like flavours, with hints of herbs, and a smooth finish.

DRY $25 –V

William Murdoch Syrah   ★★★★

Certified organic, the 2014 vintage (★★★★☆) was grown in the Gimblett Gravels, Hawke's Bay, and matured for 15 months in French oak barriques (30 per cent new). Full-coloured, it is a medium to full-bodied style, with fresh, concentrated, distinctly spicy flavours, balanced tannins, good ripeness and density, and the structure to age well. Best drinking 2018+.

DRY $37 –V

Tannat

Although extremely rare in New Zealand, Tannat is well known in south-west France, especially as a key ingredient in the dark, firm, tannic reds of Madiran. Tannat is also a star variety in Uruguay, yielding firm, fragrant reds with rich blackberry flavours. According to New Zealand Winegrowers' *Vineyard Register Report 2015–2018*, only 2 hectares of Tannat vines will be bearing in 2017, mostly in Auckland, Hawke's Bay and Northland.

De La Terre Hawke's Bay Tannat   (★★★★)

The deeply coloured 2014 vintage (★★★★) was estate-grown at Havelock North and matured for over a year in French oak barriques (20 per cent new). Still very fresh, it is fruit-packed, with plum and spice flavours, a hint of liquorice, and excellent ripeness and depth. Best drinking mid-2017+.

Vintage	14
WR	6
Drink	16-22

DRY $34 –V

De La Terre Reserve Hawke's Bay Tannat   ★★★★☆

The impressive 2014 vintage (★★★★☆) was grown and hand-harvested at Havelock North, and matured for 18 months in French oak barriques (50 per cent new). Dark and still purple-flushed, it is sweet-fruited and smooth, with concentrated, plummy, spicy flavours, showing excellent density, and firm tannins beneath. Well worth cellaring.

Vintage	14	13
WR	7	7
Drink	17-28	16-30

DRY $65 –V

Kaipara Estate Tannat   (★★★)

The 2014 vintage (★★★) of this Auckland red has full, youthful colour, with a slightly rustic bouquet. It has good depth of fresh plum, spice and slight herb flavours, woven with lively acidity, and drink-young appeal.

DRY $48 –V

Tempranillo

The star grape of Rioja, Tempranillo is grown extensively across northern and central Spain, where it yields strawberry, spice and tobacco-flavoured reds, full of personality. Barrel-aged versions mature well, developing great complexity. The great Spanish variety is starting to spread into the New World, but is still rare in New Zealand, with 20 hectares of bearing vines in 2017, mostly in Hawke's Bay (12 hectares) and Marlborough (3 hectares).

Brennan B2 Central Otago Tempranillo (★★★)

The 2013 vintage (★★★) was grown at Gibbston and bottled unfined and unfiltered. Ruby-hued, it is medium-bodied, with good depth of spicy, slightly nutty flavour, showing some savoury complexity, and a firm finish. Drink now to 2017.

Catherine's Block Waipara Valley Tempranillo ★★☆

From Mount Brown, the 2013 vintage (★★★) was matured for 18 months in French oak barriques (30 per cent new). Full-coloured, it has good depth of vibrant red-berry, dried-herb and spice flavours, showing some complexity.

Church Road McDonald Series Hawke's Bay Tempranillo (★★★★★)

The 2013 vintage (★★★★★) is a top debut. A powerful, dark red, it was estate-grown in the Redstone Vineyard, in the Bridge Pa Triangle, harvested at over 24 brix, barrel-aged, and bottled unfined and unfiltered. Still youthful, it is sturdy (14.5 per cent alcohol), with generous blackcurrant, plum and spice flavours in a very concentrated but accessible style, with gentle acidity and tannins. Deliciously rich, savoury and soft, it should mature well.

Hans Herzog Marlborough Tempranillo ★★★★☆

The top-flight 2013 vintage (★★★★★), estate-grown on the north side of the Wairau Valley, was matured for two years in French oak barriques. Deeply coloured, with a hint of maturity, it is sturdy, savoury and firm, with concentrated blackcurrant, plum and spice flavours, slightly nutty and leathery notes adding complexity, and obvious potential. Best drinking 2018+.

Vintage	13	12	11	10	09
WR	7	7	7	7	7
Drink	16-23	16-22	16-21	16-22	16-21

DRY $64 –V

Kainui Road Bay of Islands Tempranillo ★★★☆

The 2014 vintage (★★★☆) was hand-picked at Kerikeri and matured in French oak casks. Full and bright in colour, it is medium-bodied, with good depth of ripe blackcurrant, plum and spice flavours, toasty oak in evidence, and a smooth finish.

Marsden Bay of Islands Tempranillo   ★★★☆

The very easy-drinking 2014 vintage (★★★☆) is a Northland red, matured for a year in French oak barriques. Full and youthful in colour, it is sweet-fruited, with ripe berry, plum and spice flavours, slightly nutty and leathery, gentle tannins, and very good body and depth.

Vintage	14	13
WR	5	6
Drink	16-18	16-17

DRY $32 –V

Mudbrick Vineyard Reserve Waiheke Island Tempranillo   (★★★★☆)

The impressive 2013 vintage (★★★★☆) is a single-vineyard red, hand-picked and matured for seven months in French oak barriques (10 per cent new). Full-coloured, it is rich and smooth, with concentrated, berryish, plummy, slightly earthy flavours, hints of blackcurrant and chocolate, savoury notes adding complexity, and strong personality. A very auspicious debut.

Vintage	13
WR	7
Drink	16-20

DRY $55 –V

Rock Ferry Trig Hill Vineyard Tempranillo   (★★★★☆)

Well worth discovering, the 2013 vintage (★★★★☆) was estate-grown at Bendigo, in Central Otago, fermented with indigenous yeasts, and matured for 20 months in French oak puncheons (30 per cent new). Full, bright ruby, it is full-bodied (14.5 per cent alcohol) and vibrantly fruity, with generous, well-ripened plum/spice flavours, youthful, savoury, complex and smooth. Certified organic.

 DRY $40 –V

Te Awa Single Estate Hawke's Bay Tempranillo   ★★★★☆

The 2014 vintage (★★★★★) is a classy, youthful Gimblett Gravels red, full-coloured, with strong berry and spice flavours, well-integrated oak adding complexity, and excellent ripeness and depth. A dense, savoury, 'serious' wine, it's well worth cellaring.

DRY $30 AV

Tono Hawke's Bay Tempranillo   (★★★★)

Showing good personality, the 2014 vintage (★★★★) from Salvare Estate was grown at Mangatahi and in the Bridge Pa Triangle. Made in a gently oaked style, it is full-coloured, mouthfilling and supple, with strong, plummy flavours, savoury notes adding complexity, and a finely textured finish. Drink now or cellar.

 DRY $25 AV

Trinity Hill Gimblett Gravels Tempranillo   ★★★★☆

This is a consistently attractive Hawke's Bay red, full of personality. The 2015 vintage (★★★★☆) was matured in tanks and French and American oak barriques. The colour is dark and youthful; the palate is mouthfilling, with strong, vibrant cassis, plum and spice flavours, gently seasoned with oak, and fine-grained tannins. A very elegant, age-worthy wine, still very youthful, it's well worth cellaring to 2018+.

Vintage	15
WR	7
Drink	17-22

DRY $35 AV

Yealands Estate Single Vineyard Awatere Valley
Marlborough Tempranillo   (★★★★)

Enjoyable young, the 2015 vintage (★★★★) is a rare example of South Island Tempranillo. Matured in French oak barriques (partly new), it is deep ruby, fresh and supple, with generous, ripe blackcurrant, dried-herb and spice flavours, gently seasoned with oak, and savoury notes adding complexity. Worth cellaring.

DRY $27 AV

Touriga Nacional

Touriga Nacional is the most prized blending variety in the traditional ports of the Douro Valley of Portugal, and is also used widely in the Dao region for table reds. The low-cropping vines produce small berries that yield sturdy, concentrated, structured wines with high tannin levels. However, Touriga Nacional is extremely rare here and is not listed separately in New Zealand Winegrowers' *Vineyard Register Report 2015–2018*.

Trinity Hill Gimblett Gravels Touriga (★★★★★)

The non-vintage wine (★★★★★) now on sale is a 'port style', blended from Touriga Nacional – the key variety in classic port – Touriga Francesca and Tinta Roriz. From base wines back to 2004, matured in oak barrels for two to nine years, it has dense, inky colour. Highly fragrant, it is robust (19 per cent alcohol), with notably concentrated, spicy, plummy flavours. Overflowing with fruit, it is not a mellow style, but still a lovely mouthful – sweet and delicious.

SW $45 (500ML) AV

Zinfandel

In California, where it is extensively planted, Zinfandel produces muscular, heady reds that can approach a dry port style. It is believed to be identical to the Primitivo variety, which yields highly characterful, warm, spicy reds in southern Italy. There will be only 4 hectares of bearing Zinfandel vines in New Zealand in 2017, clustered in Hawke's Bay, with no expansion projected. Alan Limmer, formerly of Stonecroft winery in Hawke's Bay, believes 'Zin' has potential here, 'if you can stand the stress of growing a grape that falls apart at the first sign of a dubious weather map!'

Stonecroft Gimblett Gravels Zinfandel

A top vintage of this extremely rare variety in New Zealand, the 2014 (★★★★) was estate-grown at Roys Hill, in the Gimblett Gravels of Hawke's Bay, hand-picked, and matured for 18 months in seasoned American oak casks. Fragrant, with deep, youthful colour, it is medium-bodied, with strong, fresh, ripe plum/spice flavours, seasoned with sweet oak, and gentle tannins. It's drinking well now, but worth cellaring.

DRY $31 –V

Zweigelt

Austria's most popular red-wine variety is a crossing of Blaufränkisch and St Laurent. It's a naturally high-yielding variety, but cropped lower can produce appealing, velvety reds, usually at their best when young. Zweigelt is extremely rare in New Zealand, with 3 hectares believed to be planted, mostly in Nelson and Marlborough (but the variety is not listed separately in New Zealand Winegrowers' *Vineyard Register Report 2015–2018*).

Hans Herzog Marlborough Zweigelt ★★★★☆

The outstanding 2014 vintage (★★★★★) was estate-grown on the north side of the Wairau Valley and matured for 18 months in French oak barriques. Dark and purple-flushed, with a fragrant bouquet of blackcurrants and spices, it is a powerful, very youthful wine. Fleshy, sweet-fruited and smooth, it is packed with cassis, plum and spice flavours, with savoury notes adding complexity, and obvious potential. Best drinking 2018+. Certified organic.

Vintage	14	13	12	11	10	09
WR	7	7	7	7	7	7
Drink	16-26	16-25	16-24	16-23	16-21	16-21

DRY $53 –V

Seifried Nelson Zweigelt ★★★

The excellent 2014 vintage (★★★★) was matured for a year in new and seasoned French oak barriques. Full-coloured, it is sturdy and firmly structured, with strong, ripe plum/spice flavours, showing a touch of complexity, and definite cellaring potential; open mid-2017+.

Vintage	14
WR	5
Drink	16-19

DRY $21 –V

Index of Wine Brands

This index should be especially useful when you are visiting wineries as a quick way to find the reviews of each company's range of wines. It also provides links between different wine brands made by the same producer (for example, Amisfield and Lake Hayes).

8 Ranges 152, 332, 427
36 Bottles 201, 332, 427
12,000 Miles 152, 234, 428
Abbey Cellars 201
Aitken's Folly 48, 332, 428
Akarua 48, 152, 201, 318, 319, 333, 428
Ake Ake 48, 153, 235, 305, 333, 385, 539
Akitu 429
Alex 429
Alexander 429
Alexandra Wine Company 48, 153, 429
Allan Scott 48, 153, 202, 235, 305, 333, 395, 430 (*see also* Scott Base)
Alluviale 235, 333, 350, 395
Alpha Domus 49, 298, 305, 333, 350, 395, 396, 539 (*see also* Bell Bird Bay)
Amisfield 124, 153, 202, 235, 333, 430 (*see also* Lake Hayes)
Anchorage 49, 130, 153, 202, 236, 333, 430, 539 (*see also* Motueka Vineyards, Okiwi Bay, Torrent Bay)
Ant Moore 49, 153, 334, 430
Aotea 236
Ara 153, 154, 236, 237, 305, 334, 431
Aravin 431
Archangel 49, 154, 432
Aronui 35, 50, 130, 145, 154, 203, 237, 334, 432
Ascension 298
Ash Ridge 50, 237, 298, 306, 350, 390, 396, 540 (*see also* Hills & Rivers)
Ashwell 50, 237, 334, 432
Ashwood 50, 154

Askerne 50, 51, 130, 154, 298, 396, 432, 540
Astrolabe 35, 51, 124, 154, 203, 237, 334, 433 (*see also* Durvillea)
Ata Mara 145, 155, 203, 433
Ata Rangi 51, 155, 238, 351, 433
Ataahua 51, 130, 203, 238, 306, 334, 396, 434
Auntsfield 52, 238, 434
Aurum 41, 52, 155, 203, 319, 334, 435
Awaroa 373, 374, 540, 541 (*see also* Waiheke Road)
Awatere River 52, 155, 306, 435

Babich 35, 52, 53, 131, 145, 155, 203, 238, 239, 298, 306, 335, 351, 374, 396, 397, 436, 541 (*see also* Rongopai)
Baby Doll 240
Bald Hills 156, 204, 436
Ballasalla 437
Bannock Brae 145, 204, 437
Beach House 53, 156, 204, 374
Bel Echo 240, 437
Bell Bird Bay 54, 397, 541
Bellbird Spring 41, 156, 240, 335, 437, 438 (*see also* Pruner's Reward)
Bent Duck 54
Bilancia 54, 156, 542 (*see also* La Collina)
Bird 156, 240, 438
Bishop's Head 54, 124, 240
Black Barn 54, 156, 319, 335, 397
Black Cottage 55, 157, 241, 335, 438
Black Estate 55, 124, 204, 335, 438, 439 (*see also* Circuit)

Black Peak 204
Black Quail 439
Black Stilt 204, 439
Blackenbrook 55, 56, 131, 149, 157, 241, 335, 422, 439
Bladen 131, 157, 241, 439
Blind River 440
Boatshed Bay 241
Bone Hill 440
Boneline, The 56, 370, 440
Boundary 56, 157, 241, 440, 542
Brancott 56, 131, 157, 158, 205, 242, 293, 306, 335, 397, 440, 441
Brennan 41, 441, 575
Brick Bay 158, 336
Bridge Estate 397 (see also Poverty Bay)
Brightside 57, 158, 205, 243, 441
Brightwater 57, 158, 243, 441, 442
Brodie 57, 336, 442
Bronte 57, 159, 442
Brookby Road 442
Brookfields 58, 159, 307, 374, 390, 398, 542
Burn Cottage 205, 442, 443
Bushhawk 128
Byrne 58, 243, 299, 336, 385, 543
  (see also Bent Duck)

C.J. Pask   See Pask
Cable Bay 58, 59, 159, 244, 299, 351, 443, 543
Cambridge Road 336, 443
Camshorn 205, 444
Carrick 59, 159, 206, 244, 336, 444
Catalina Sounds 159, 244, 444
Catherine's Block 575
Caythorpe Family 244
Ceres 159, 160, 206, 444
  (see also Fifth Bridge)

Charcoal Gully 131, 307, 445
Chard Farm 59, 160, 206, 445
Charles Wiffen 59
China Girl 446
Church Road 60, 160, 245, 336, 375, 394, 398, 543, 544, 575
Churton 245, 246, 299, 446
Cicada 132
Circuit 160, 446
Clark 160, 207, 246, 447
Clayvin 544
Clearview 61, 62, 132, 161, 246, 293, 294, 336, 351, 370, 398, 544
Clearwater Cove 352
Clevedon Hills 39, 447, 544
Cliff Edge 399
Clifford Bay 62, 161, 246, 447
Clos de Ste Anne 62, 125, 299, 447, 545
Clos Henri 247, 447 (see also Bel Echo, Petit Clos)
Clos Marguerite 247
Cloudy Bay 42, 62, 319, 448
Coal Pit 448
Collaboration 63, 376, 399
Coney 207
Coopers Creek 35, 39, 63, 64, 148, 161, 207, 247, 299, 300, 337, 352, 376, 390, 399, 422, 448, 449, 545
Cottier 64, 449
Couper's Shed 161, 248, 399, 545
Crab Farm 161, 352, 353, 449
Craft Farm 64, 132, 545
Craggy Range 42, 64, 161, 207, 248, 337, 353, 354, 399, 449, 545
Crazy By Nature 65, 125, 354
Crossings, The 162, 248, 449
Crossroads 65, 132, 162, 354, 370, 376, 400, 449, 545, 546

Crowded House 248, 450
Crown Range Cellar 450 (*see also* China
    Girl, Drowsy Fish)
Cypress 65, 162, 547
Cypress Terraces 66, 547

Daniel Le Brun 319, 320
Darling, The 66, 450
Dashwood 66, 162, 207, 248, 450
Davishon 450
De La Terre 66, 67, 300, 307, 349, 422,
    547, 574
De Vine 67, 162
Delegat 67, 248, 400, 450 (*see also* Oyster Bay)
Delta 248, 451
Destiny Bay 355
Deutz 320
Devil's Staircase 451
Devotus 451
Discovery Point 249, 451
Distant Land 452
Doctors', The 207
Doctors Flat 452
Dog Point 42, 67, 249, 452
Domain Road 162, 452
Domaine Rewa 67, 453
Doubtless 35, 297, 400, 548
Doubtless Bay 376 (*see also* True North)
Drowsy Fish 207, 249
Drumsara 163
Dry River 68, 132, 163, 208, 300, 453, 548
Dunleavy 377
Dunnolly 453
Dunstan Road 132, 163, 453
Durvillea 163, 249

Earth's End 453
Easthope 68, 163, 548

Eaton 400
Elder, The 164, 337, 454
Elephant Hill 68, 249, 355, 356, 401, 454,
    548, 549
Ellero 133, 454
Elstree 321
En Rose 321
Eradus 164, 249, 454
Escarpment 68, 454, 455
Esk Valley 69, 125, 164, 208, 250, 296,
    307, 337, 356, 401, 455, 549
Expatrius 42, 549
Explorer 455

Fairbourne 250 (*see also* Two Tails)
Fairhall Downs 250
Fairmont 164
Falcon Ridge 250
Falconhead 164, 208, 250, 300, 402,
    456, 550
Fancrest 456
Felton Road 69, 70, 208, 209, 308,
    456, 457
Fern Ridge 164
Fickle Mistress 457
Fifth Bridge 458
Fifth Innings 458
Flying Sheep 458
Folding Hill 458
Folium 251, 458, 459
Forrest 126, 133 (*see also* The Doctors',
    Newton Forrest, Tatty Bogler)
Foxes Island 459
Framingham 70, 133, 165, 209,
    251, 300, 308, 309, 423, 459
    (*see also* Ribbonwood)
French Peak 70, 165, 337
Frenchman's Hill 70, 356, 550

Fromm 71, 165, 252, 309, 337, 390, 459,
    460, 550
Fuder, The 71, 252

Georges Road 165, 460, 550
Georgetown 460
Gibbston Highgate 71, 460
Gibbston Valley 72, 150, 165, 166, 210,
    310, 321, 338, 461, 462
Gibson Bridge 133, 166
Giesen 72, 133, 166, 210, 252, 253, 310,
    321, 338, 402, 463, 464, 551 (see also
    Brookby Road, Clayvin, The Fuder)
Gillman 356
Gladstone 167, 253, 301, 338, 357, 464
    (see also 12,000 Miles)
Glasnevin 464
Glazebrook 72, 551
Gold Digger 321
Gold Star 167, 402
Goldie 72, 402, 551
Goldwater 73, 167, 254, 464
Graham Norton's Own 254
Grasshopper Rock 465
Grava 211, 254, 338, 465
Greenhough 73, 150, 211, 254, 465
Greylands Ridge 43, 466 (see also
    Ridgeback)
Greyrock 73, 167, 254, 338, 402, 466
Greystone 73, 74, 133, 167, 211, 255,
    310, 466 (see also Muddy Water,
    Thistle Ridge)
Greywacke 74, 168, 212, 255, 310, 466
Grove Mill 74, 134, 168, 212, 255, 467
Gunn 74, 168, 255, 403, 467

Haha 74, 168, 256, 322, 403, 467
Hans Herzog 39, 43, 75, 145, 168, 212,

256, 301, 322, 403, 423, 425, 467, 538,
    575, 580
Harakeke Farm 75, 468
Harwood Hall 169, 468, 551
Hawk's Nest 75, 371
Hawkshead 169, 212, 338, 468
Heron's Flight 357, 537
Highfield 75, 212, 256, 322, 468 (see also
    Elstree, Okiwa Bay, Paua)
Hihi 36
Hills & Rivers 169
Hitchen Road 76, 386, 423, 536
Hopesgrove 76, 301, 552
Hoppers Crossing 468
Huia 76, 134, 169, 213, 256, 322, 469
    (see also Hunky Dory)
Humming Wire 469
Hunky Dory 43, 257, 469
Hunter's 46, 76, 134, 169, 213, 257,
    310, 322, 323, 338, 357, 403, 469
    (see also Stoneburn)
Hyperion 76, 169

Impromptu 469
Invivo 77, 170, 213, 257, 258, 339, 469,
    470 (see also Graham Norton's Own)

Jackson 77, 213, 258, 311, 470 (see also
    Shelter Bay)
Johanneshof 134, 170, 213, 258, 323, 471
Johner 77, 170, 213, 259, 311, 323, 339,
    377, 471, 552 (see also Humming Wire)
Joiy 323
Joss Bay 471
Judge Rock 472, 538
Jules Taylor 78, 146, 170, 259, 311,
    339, 472
Julicher 214, 472, 473

Junction 78, 170, 214, 323, 473
June 324

Kaimira 43, 78, 134, 150, 170, 214,
    259, 301, 357, 473, 552 (see also
    Brightside, June)
Kaipara Estate 43, 371, 377, 391, 574 (see
    also Monk Road)
Kainui Road 171, 260, 301, 552, 575
Kakapo 78, 171
Kalex 79, 214, 473
Kapiro 171
Karikari Estate 79, 358, 403, 536, 553
Kate Radburnd 171
Kidnapper Cliffs 79
Kim Crawford 171, 260, 404, 473
Kina Cliffs 171, 260, 474
Kingsmill 474
Konrad 134, 260, 474
Kumeu River 79, 80, 135, 172, 404, 474
    (see also Kumeu Village)
Kumeu Village 81, 172, 474
Kuru Kuru 474

La Collina 301
La Michelle 324
Lake Chalice 172, 214, 404, 475
Lake Hayes 172, 260, 475
Landing, The 81, 553
Last Shepherd 475
Latitude 41 475
Lauregan 475
Lawson's Dry Hills 81, 135, 172, 215,
    260, 261, 339, 475, 476 (see also
    Mount Vernon)
Lazy Dog, The 126
Left Field 36, 82, 173, 261, 339, 404,
    476, 553

Leveret 82, 324, 404, 405, 476, 477, 553
Lime Rock 405, 477
Lindauer 325
Linden 82, 135, 173, 214, 302, 358,
    405, 554
Little Black Shag 173, 261, 477
Locharburn 340, 477
Lochiel 82
Longview 82
Loveblock 135, 173, 215, 261, 312,
    325, 477
Lowburn Ferry 477, 478
Luminary, The 261, 478
Luna 83
Lynfer 173, 478

Ma Maison 478
Mad Dog 83, 554
Mahi 83, 136, 173, 174, 262, 340, 479
Mahinepua Bay 385, 554
Mahurangi River 36, 84, 233, 340, 377,
    378, 405
Maimai 554
Main Divide 84, 136, 174, 215, 262,
    405, 479
Man O' War 44, 84, 174, 262, 294, 325,
    340, 358, 391, 406, 555
Maori Point 175, 340, 479 (see also
    Gold Digger)
Map Maker 85, 175, 480
Marble Point 85, 215, 480
Margrain 85, 126, 136, 146, 175, 216,
    263, 312, 340, 480 (see also En Rose,
    La Michelle)
Marsden 85, 136, 175, 263, 302, 359, 385,
    406, 536, 555, 576
Martinborough Vineyard 86, 175, 216, 263,
    481, 555 (see also Russian Jack)

Matahiwi 86, 175, 263, 326, 481
(see also Mt Hector)
Matakana Estate 86
Matawhero 36, 86, 87, 126, 137, 176, 341,
406, 481
Matua 36, 87, 264, 391, 406, 482, 556
Maude 87, 176, 216, 482
Maui 176, 264
Messenger 359
Milcrest 176, 407, 423, 483
Mills Reef 87, 88, 137, 176, 264, 371, 378,
379, 407, 483, 556, 557
Millton 88, 126, 137, 149, 216, 302, 312,
341, 483 (see also Clos de Ste Anne,
Crazy By Nature)
Miner's Daughter, The 483
Misha's Vineyard 137, 177, 217, 264, 312,
341, 484
Mission 88, 89, 137, 177, 217, 264, 265,
312, 341, 359, 371, 379, 391, 408, 484,
485, 557, 558
Misty Cove 89, 217, 265, 485 (see also
Fifth Innings)
Moana Park 90, 408, 558
Mokoroa 359
Momo 90, 177, 265, 485
Monarch 90, 409
Mondillo 217, 313, 486
Monk Road 360
Montana 177, 178, 218, 265, 409
Morepork 178
Motueka Vineyards 486
Mouku 266
Mount Brown 178, 266, 486 (see also
Catherine's Block)
Mount Edward 90, 218, 487 (see also Earth's
End, Wanaka Road)
Mount Riley 90, 91, 138, 178, 218, 266,
341, 409, 487, 558
Mount Vernon 178, 266
Mountain Road 267, 487
Moutere Hills 91, 179, 218, 267, 487
Mt Beautiful 91, 179, 218, 267, 488
Mt Difficulty 91, 138, 179, 218, 219, 267,
488, 489 (see also Roaring Meg)
Mt Hector 179, 489
Mud House 91, 179, 219, 267, 489, 490
Mudbrick 92, 360, 409, 558, 576
Muddy Water 92, 219, 490
Murdoch James 491, 559 (see also Luna)

Nanny Goat 92, 491, 559 (see also
Super Nanny)
Nautilus 36, 92, 146, 180, 268, 326, 491,
492 (see also Opawa, Twin Islands)
Neudorf 37, 92, 93, 180, 219, 220, 268,
341, 492, 493
Nevis Bluff 150, 180, 181, 313, 342, 493
Newton Forrest 360
Nga Waka 94, 220, 268, 342, 493 (see also
Three Paddles)
Ngatarawa 94, 181, 313, 409, 494, 559
(see also Glazebrook)
NTN 536

O:TU 313 (see also Reserve Road)
Obsidian 94, 95, 181, 302, 342, 360, 361,
379, 410, 423, 424, 559
Odyssey 95, 181, 494
Ohinemuri 95, 138, 181, 220, 361
Okahu 302, 385, 560
Okiwa Bay 494
Old Coach Road 95, 96, 138, 181, 220,
221, 268, 269, 410, 494
Omaha Bay 182, 312, 326, 371, 424, 426
Omata 182, 410, 560

Omeo 221, 494
Omihi Hills 96, 269, 495
One Off 391
Opawa 182, 269, 342, 495
Osawa 96, 313, 326, 380, 496 (*see also* Flying Sheep)
Ostler 182, 221, 496
Overstone 182, 269, 496
Oyster Bay 96, 183, 269, 327, 410, 496

Paddy Borthwick 96, 183, 221, 269, 496, 497
Palliser 97, 183, 221, 270, 327, 342, 497 (*see also* The Luminary, Pencarrow)
Paper Road 497
Paritua 97, 361, 410, 560 (*see also* Stone Paddock)
Paroa Bay 97, 270, 362, 560
Parr & Simpson 97
Pask 97, 98, 270, 362, 380, 411, 560, 561 (*see also* Kate Radburnd)
Pass, The 183
Passage Rock 362, 380, 561
Paua 497
Paulownia 183, 221, 411
Peacock Sky 98, 362, 371, 381, 391, 411
Pearson 497
Pegasus Bay 98, 99, 138, 222, 270, 314, 411, 498 (*see also* Main Divide)
Pencarrow 99, 498
People's, The 99, 183, 498
Peregrine 99, 183, 327, 498
Peter Yealands 44, 99, 184, 222, 270, 271, 327, 412, 499, 561
Petit Clos 271, 499
Pied Stilt 184, 499
Pirinoa Road 499
Pisa Range 222, 500

Poverty Bay 294, 342, 412
Prophet's Rock 184, 222, 500 (*see also* Rocky Point)
Pruner's Reward, The 271, 501
Pukeora 99, 100, 362 (*see also* Gold Star)
Puriri Hills 363 (*see also* Mokoroa)
Pyramid Valley 100, 151, 372, 501

Quarter Acre 100, 302, 412, 562
Quartz Reef 185, 328, 501
Queensbury 127
Quest Farm 44, 185, 502

Ra Nui 502
Ransom 37, 44, 185, 233, 342, 364, 384, 392, 562
Rapaura Springs 101, 185, 271, 272, 343, 502
RD 503
Redmetal 37, 343, 412, 413, 562
Regent of Tantallon 413
Renato 101, 186, 272, 413, 503
Reserve Road 392
Resurgence 503
Ribbonwood 186, 223, 503
Richmond Plains 44, 101, 186, 272, 503
Ridgeback 503
Rimu Grove 101, 139, 223, 504 (*see also* Bronte)
Rippon 139, 223, 504, 505
Riverby 102, 146, 186, 223, 224, 314, 505 (*see also* Cicada)
Roaring Meg 186, 272, 505
Rochfort Rees 562
Rock Ferry 102, 151, 186, 187, 224, 272, 273, 314, 328, 329, 505, 506, 576
Rockburn 187, 224, 273, 506 (*see also* Devil's Staircase)

Rocky Point 187, 343, 506

Rod McDonald 37, 187, 343, 506
  (*see also* One Off, Te Awanga Estate,
  Trademark, Two Gates)

Rongopai 102, 413

Rossendale 102, 187, 273, 507

Runner Duck 187, 364

Ruru 139, 187, 343, 507

Russian Jack 273, 507

Sacred Hill 103, 104, 188, 273, 274, 364,
  365, 413, 414, 507, 562, 563 (*see also*
  Gunn, Wild South, Ti Point)

Sailfish Cove 188, 224

Saint Clair 104, 105, 139, 146, 188, 224, 225,
  274, 275, 303, 314, 315, 329, 343, 344,
  381, 392, 414, 508, 509, 563

Sanctuary 105, 189, 225, 275, 509

Satellite 276, 509

Satyr 106, 189, 276, 329, 414, 510, 563

Schubert 510

Scott Base 510

Sculptureum 365, 564

Sea Level 106, 140, 189

Seifried 106, 140, 147, 189, 225, 276,
  315, 510, 564, 580 (*see also* Aotea,
  Old Coach Road)

Selaks 106, 189, 415, 510, 564

Seresin 44, 107, 190, 225, 276, 277, 329,
  510, 511 (*see also* Momo)

Shelter Bay 511

Sherwood 107, 140, 190, 277, 344, 511
  (*see also* Stoney Range)

Shipwreck Bay 129

Sileni 37, 45, 107, 108, 140, 141, 190, 277,
  278, 295, 303, 315, 330, 344, 365, 372,
  415, 416, 512, 513, 564, 565 (*see also*
  Greyrock, Overstone, Satyr)

Silver Fern 190

Sisters, The 513

Snapper Rock 278, 330, 416, 513

Soderberg 513

Soho 108, 190, 191, 226, 278, 344, 365,
  513, 514, 565

Soljans 191, 330, 416, 514

Spade Oak 37, 108, 191, 565

Spencer Hill 514

Spinyback 108, 191, 226, 278, 514

Springs, The 514

Spy Valley 108, 109, 141, 191, 192, 226,
  278, 279, 315, 330, 344, 416, 515, 565
  (*see also* Satellite)

Squawking Magpie 381, 566

Squealing Pig 515

St Nesbit 366

Staete Landt 109, 279, 303, 316, 515
  (*see also* Map Maker)

Stanley 109, 389, 516

Starborough 109, 192, 279, 516

Stone Paddock 110, 366, 566

Stoneburn 280, 516

Stonecroft 110, 141, 142, 280, 345, 381,
  416, 566, 567, 579

Stoneleigh 110, 111, 192, 227, 280, 281,
  345, 417, 516, 517

Stoney Range 227

Stonyridge 111, 227, 281, 366, 392,
  517, 567

Sugar Loaf 111, 345

Summerhouse 111, 193, 281, 296, 345,
  517, 567

Super Nanny 517

Supernatural, The 45

Supper Club 112, 281, 517

Surveyor Thomson 518 (*see also* Explorer)

Tablelands 518

Takatu 193, 417

Tantalus 112, 193, 367, 417, 568

Taraire 281, 331, 367

Tarras 193, 518 (*see also* Joss Bay)

Tatty Bogler 518

Te Awa 112, 281, 417, 568, 576 (*see also* Kidnapper Cliffs, Left Field)

Te Awanga 112, 142, 193, 417, 568

Te Kairanga 112, 113, 193, 227, 281, 518, 519

Te Mania 113, 142, 194, 227, 282, 345, 519, 568 (*see also* Richmond Plains)

Te Mata 113, 282, 303, 367, 382, 387, 418, 568, 569

Te Motu 368 (*see also* Dunleavy)

Te Rere 114, 569

Te Whau 114, 368, 569

Ten Sisters 282, 519

Terra Sancta 45, 114, 194, 227, 346, 519, 520

Terrace Edge 194, 227, 228, 521, 569

TerraVin 114, 282, 283, 316, 369, 521

Theory & Practice 114, 569

Thistle Ridge 521, 522

Thomas 115, 372

Thomas & Sons 129

Thornbury 115, 194, 228, 283, 346, 418, 522

Three Paddles 115, 228, 283, 522

Ti Point 115, 346

Tiki 115, 194, 283, 346, 522 (*see also* Maui)

Tinpot Hut 116, 195, 522, 570

Tironui 393

Tohu 116, 195, 228, 284, 303, 316, 331, 346, 418, 523, 570

Toi Toi 116, 195, 228, 284, 316, 331, 418, 523 (*see also* Marlborough Vines, Mouku)

Tongue in Groove 523

Tono 576

Tony Bish 116

Torea 195

Torrent Bay 195

Totara 524

Trademark 570

Trinity Hill 117, 148, 195, 285, 347, 369, 418, 424, 524, 570, 577, 578

Triplebank 196, 285, 524

True North 347

Tupari 196, 285, 316, 524

Twin Islands 285, 331

Two Degrees 524

Two Gates 117, 142, 418

Two Paddocks 229, 524, 525

Two Rivers 117, 196, 229, 285, 286, 347, 525, 526 (*see also* Black Cottage)

Two Sisters 196, 229, 526

Two Tails 286, 526

Unison 118, 382

Urlar 196, 286, 316, 526

Valli 197, 229, 316, 526, 527

Vavasour 118, 197, 229, 286, 528 (*see also* Dashwood, The Pass)

Vicar's Mistress, The 528

Vidal 118, 197, 230, 286, 287, 382, 383, 419, 528, 571

Villa Maria 38, 40, 119, 120, 121, 142, 143, 197, 198, 230, 287, 288, 289, 296, 303, 304, 317, 347, 369, 383, 388, 393, 419, 420, 421, 528, 529, 530, 571, 572 (*see also* Esk Valley, Te Awa, Thornbury, Vidal)

Vinoptima 143

Vista 198, 530

VNO 121, 198, 289, 348
Volcanic Hills 121, 530, 531

Waiheke Road 121, 122, 289, 572
Waimea 38, 122, 143, 147, 198, 230, 289, 293, 304, 531 (see also Spinyback)
Waipara Hills 122, 199, 230, 531
Waipara Springs 231, 531 (see also The Springs)
Wairau River 38, 122, 143, 147, 199, 231, 290, 304, 317, 348, 421, 531, 532, 572
Waitapu 369, 572, 573
Walnut Block 123, 290, 532
Wanaka Road 532
Ward Valley 532
Whitehaven 123, 144, 147, 199, 231, 290, 317, 348, 532, 533

Wild Earth 533
Wild Grace 291, 348, 533
Wild River 533
Wild South 291, 533
William Murdoch 573
Wither Hills 123, 199, 291, 533
Wooing Tree 45, 123, 199, 317, 348, 534

Yealands 45, 144, 147, 199, 200, 231, 232, 291, 292, 317, 348, 534, 535, 577 (see also Baby Doll, Clearwater Cove, Peter Yealands, Silver Fern)

Zephyr 123, 144, 232, 535

Visit Michael Cooper's

New Zealand

Wines

website

---

www.michaelcooper.co.nz

TRY OUR FREE FULL-ACCESS 7-DAY TRIAL

BECOME A MEMBER and have access to over 18,500 of Michael's tasting notes from his annually updated, best-selling *New Zealand Wines*, plus new reviews throughout the year (based on the finest quality and best-value wines tasted). Get detailed, region-by-region vintage reports, vintage charts, and regional maps from the prize-winning *Wine Atlas of New Zealand*. Enjoy the use of the My Wines function, where you can save, organize and make notes about your favourite wines.

GET FREE ACCESS to news about forthcoming wine events; a monthly 'Best Buy' and 'Treat Yourself'; notes on grape varieties and wine regions; cellaring guidelines; a list of Classic Wines of New Zealand; Best Buys of the Year; and vintage reports.